Growth, profits, and property

Growth, profits, and property

Essays in the revival of political economy

Edited by Edward J. Nell
New School for Social Research

Cambridge University Press
Cambridge
London New York New Rochelle
Melbourne Sydney

CAMBRIDGE UNIVERSITY PRESS
Cambridge, New York, Melbourne, Madrid, Cape Town, Singapore, São Paulo

Cambridge University Press
The Edinburgh Building, Cambridge CB2 8RU, UK

Published in the United States of America by Cambridge University Press, New York

www.cambridge.org
Information on this title: www.cambridge.org/9780521223966

First published 1980
First paperback edition 1984
Re-issued in this digitally printed version 2008

A catalogue record for this publication is available from the British Library

Library of Congress Cataloguing in Publication data

Main entry under title:

Growth, profits, and property.

1. Economics - Addresses, essays, lectures.
1. Nell, Edward J.
HB34.G76 330.1 76-47192

ISBN 978-0-521-22396-6 hardback
ISBN 978-0-521-31918-8 paperback

This book of essays was conceived at the 1971 convention of the American Economics Association, at a meeting called by Joan Robinson for those dissatisfied with orthodox economics. Hence in a very real sense, this book is a tribute to her, and to the influence she has exercised over the profession. Her influence in one form or another has been decisive in shaping a new and critical approach to economics. All of us would like to take this occasion to honor her contributions to the field.

Contents

Editorial preface

In the Introduction I have tried to show that neoclassicism cannot encompass a concept of capital rich enough to account for both capital as a fund and capital as specific equipment and goods; so that it cannot present both a theory of the firm and a theory of distribution, determined by supply and demand in product and factor markets, respectively. Yet it must present both if it is to be true to its contradictions. Defenders of the faith where factor endowments include fertile imaginary lands, have produced a plentiful supply of models whose lithe proportions may enable them to evade one or another of these objections. But the purpose of this book is not criticism. It is important to understand the shortcomings of neoclassicism, but it is more important to try to develop a more adequate account of the working and misworking of the capitalist system. That is the chief object of the essays collected here.

Two principal positions are set forth in Part I and run throughout the book. One, which could be dubbed a post-Keynesian position, represented by my essay, starts from the fact that neoclassicism misrepresents the nature of circulation and distribution. Correcting this requires the reconstruction of the theory of effective demand, and, in particular, developing a theoretical link between pricing and investment decisions.

The other, which could be called neo-Marxian, represented by Hymer's paper, begins from orthodoxy's failure to grasp the relations of dominance and subordination in production. Correcting this leads to a rethinking of the way theory represents both the relationships of production and the way markets operate. These positions are complementary, but they can also lead their proponents into conflict as the last section shows.

A third position is set forth in Section 8. Neoclassicism and neo-Keynesianism both have failed to deal with the questions of authority and institutional hierarchy, in particular with the nature and development of the firm. This view has close affinities with some concerns of Marxists, though it differs on others. What unites all these approaches is a common concern with the theoretical implications of the institutions of capitalism.

The essays in this book deal with the building of an economic theory based on the actual institutions of capitalism, and especially with the concept of capital and its institutional embodiment, the business firm or corporation. Once the neoclassical vision is abandoned, it becomes possible to develop a theory, of both circulation and of production, that takes account of the pervasive influence of social class. These two lines of development are the ones sketched, respectively, in the essays by myself and by Hymer. (Most of the essays collected here were written or rewritten especially for this volume, although owing to the long time lag in preparation, several have come out in other publications in the meantime.)

Part II surveys the criticism of the neoclassical approach to capital and growth. Harris provides a detailed and critical presentation of the neoclassical parable and sketches an alternative; Moss gives us a comprehensive account of the technical flaws in the standard version, in a simplified two-sector setting; and Shaikh explains why the empirical results of working with neoclassical models, though actually worthless, have seemed so good.

Parts III – VI then cover standard ground: micro, macro, trade, and welfare. Hymer and Shaikh are rooted in Marx; Harcourt and Davidson and Kregel in Keynes; Eatwell and Medio in Marx and Kalecki; but all the papers approach fairly traditional subject matter in a manner that brings out entirely new possibilities. In Part III, I try to show some of the ways economic power can play a significant role even in competitive markets, and Eichner explores the important connections between investment and pricing in large firms. In Part IV, Davidson and Kregel refer to Keynes to develop a theory of money, while Harcourt takes us through an unorthodox examination of a simplified Keynesian model, relating it to income distribution and cyclical fluctuations. Medio takes up the question of fluctuations in detail, and develops a classical–Marxian model of fluctuations in the wage and profit rates, stabilized, in an important but unusual sense, by the consequent variations in effective demand. Eatwell considers the effects of taxation in conditions of mark-up pricing, allowing for the impact of taxes on effective demand, and working through the problem in the context of a multisectoral model. Part V provides two different but highly original perspectives on international trade. Hymer develops the implications of the internationalizing of the institutions of wage – labor and capital, where these are understood as complementary, but standing in an antagonistic relationship of dominance and subordination. Shaikh shows that the harmonistic implications of the free trade doctrine rested on an invalid theory of money. When this is replaced along lines suggested by Marx, it can be seen that absolute, not comparative advantage rules, and that free trade in competitive conditions leads weaker nations into a trap of prolonged deficits and mounting debt.

Part VII is concerned with questions that both orthodox economists and their major critics have often ignored, questions about the nature, causes and justification of property and the hierarchical organization of work. Ellerman examines the nature of the firm, showing how economists have systematically misrepresented the property relations defining it, while Hunt presents a systematic exploration of the flaws in the orthodox teaching on welfare.

Finally, in Part VII, the two main streams of anti-neoclassical thinking, Cambridge post-Keynesianism, interpreted by Kregel, and Marxism, as presented by Roosevelt, confront one another.

Viewed in their entirety, these essays attempt to show that economics can and should be considered outside the confining and unrealistic framework of the neoclassical tradition.

As editor I would like to thank the contributors for their patience during the book's long gestation period. Anna Freeman helped enormously in preparing the manuscript, as did Lillian Salzman, and I am deeply grateful to both. Donna Walcavage prepared the diagrams, and Lillian managed a complex job of proofreading with great dispatch. At the very end of the project Jan Kregel took on the administrative responsibilities for the book, and together with Colin Day of Cambridge University Press, handled an exceptionally difficult job with great skill, for which I and the authors are grateful.

Edward J. Nell

Contributors

Davidson, Paul, Department of Economics, Rutgers, The State University of New Jersey, New Brunswick, NJ 08903 (Chap. 8)

Eatwell, John, Trinity College, Cambridge, England (Chap. 10)

Eichner, Alfred S., Department of Economics, State University of New York, Purchase, NY 12201 (Chap. 7)

Ellerman, David P., Department of Economics, University of Massachusetts, Harbor Campus, Boston, MA 02125 (Chap. 15)

Harcourt, G. C., Department of Economics, University of Adelaide, Adelaide, Australia 5001 (Chap. 9)

Harris, Donald J., Department of Economics, Stanford University, Stanford, CA 94305 (Chap. 3)

Hunt, E. K., Department of Economics, University of Utah, Salt Lake City, Utah 84112 (Chap. 14)

Hymer, Stephen (deceased), formerly of the Department of Economics, New School for Social Research, New York, NY 10011 (Chap. 2, Chap. 12)

Kregel, J. A., Department of Economics, Livingston College, Rutgers, The State University of New Jersey, New Brunswick, NJ 08903 (Chap. 8, Chap. 16)

Medio, Alfredo, United Nations Conference on Trade and Development, Palais des Nations, Geneva 10, Switzerland (Chap. 11)

Moss, Scott, Department of Economics, Manchester Polytechnic, Manchester, England (Chap. 4)

Nell, Edward J., Department of Economics, New School for Social Research, New York, NY 10011 (Intro., Chap. 1, Chap. 6)

Roosevelt, Frank, Department of Economics, Sarah Lawrence College, Bronxville, NY 10708 (Chap. 17)

Shaikh, Anwar, Department of Economics, New School for Social Research, New York, NY 10011 (Chap. 5, Chap. 13)

Vietorisz, Thomas, Department of Economics, New School for Social Research, New York, NY 10011 (Epilogue)

Introduction. Cracks in the neoclassical mirror: on the break-up of a vision

Edward J. Nell

By now, most economists are aware of the flaws in the aggregative neoclassical models of growth, productivity, and income distribution. Whether neoclassicism in its full generality is open to the same sorts of objections is still a matter of dispute. It is not the object of this book to enter that dispute. Instead, it will first chart some of the territory that neoclassicism has been forced to yield, and then stake out a claim and begin building new edifices there. This introduction will try to relate one of the central purposes of these constructions – understanding what capital is – to the critique of neoclassical theory.

For many economists neoclassicism *is* economic science, and attacks upon it simply create a sense of unease. Without theory, there is no science; economists will be left with nothing to say that could not be said as well by any intelligent observer who takes the trouble to study the facts. But the attacks on neoclassicism are not attacks on theory as such. They are attacks on a theory regarded as wrong and have been designed as a prelude to replacing that theory with a better one. As will become evident, there is more agreement on the defects of orthodox theory than there is on what theory is to replace it; but all are agreed that the point of the criticism is to clear the ground for construction.

The standard version of orthodox theory

The critique of neoclassicism grew out of a concern with the way orthodox economics treated capital and wage–labor, and has been principally directed against what may be called the standard version of orthodox theory. This latter is not necessarily a "one-sector" or an aggregate model, although the most favored presentation of the theory normally takes that form. What distinguishes it, rather, is the way the supply side is treated. All forms of neoclassicism postulate households where preferences are described by utility functions, as the basis for demand. The standard version treats supply symmetrically – postulating the existence of a definite number of firms each of whose technical production possibilities are described by a production function relating factor inputs and outputs. However, neoclassicism can also be developed using the methods of activity analysis, in which case no firms are represented at all.[1] Production functions in activity analysis show the inputs required for a *product,* rather than the inputs required by a *firm.* Only firms can make market decisions; the cost of a product, in the abstract, may be interesting, but it is the cost *to the firm,* not in the abstract, that will be relevant to the firm's strategy in the marketplace. The standard version is a theory of the marketplace, and tries to deal with and classify different market forms, according to the competitive environments firms face and create for one another.

It is because the standard version deals with the concrete activities of firms, rather than with the abstract technology of products, that it must employ what is misleadingly referred to as an "aggregative" concept of capital. The point is not so much that the various inputs under the firm's control are valued and aggregated. As participants on all sides of the capital controversy have observed, this in itself is of little interest. Everyone agrees that given the prices, it is easy to *aggregate* capital goods; *without* prices no proxy measure will do. The question is, why bother aggregating capital?

The answer is as basic as it is obvious. A firm's capital is what makes it what it is. The firm is the institutional form which a particular capital takes. Its permanent existence is not as a set of capital goods, but as a *fund* of capital. The fund will be embodied from time to time in capital goods, such as plant and equipment, and inventories. But capital remains while capital goods are used up, inventories are converted to output and sold off, all of which is another way of saying that the activity of a firm is to *turn over* its capital, making a profit in doing so. Marx captured the essence of this process in a simple formulation, encompassing what he called the three circuits of capital – the circuits of production, commodity, and money capital.

$$M—C\begin{array}{l}\nearrow L\\ \searrow MP\end{array}\;\cdots P$$

$$\cdots C'\left\{\begin{array}{r}C—\\ —M'\\ c—\end{array}\right.\left\{\begin{array}{l}M—C\begin{array}{l}\nearrow L\\ \searrow MP\end{array}\\ m—c\end{array}\right.$$

$$\cdots P\cdots C'$$

Money capital is used to buy means of production and labor which then produce an expanded set of commodities, C', sold again for money, M', which then exchanges for productive commodities, C, and for luxury consumption, c (Marx, 1967, Vol. II, Ch. 4).

Marx's way of representing the circuits of capital is valuable because it highlights the fact that in turning over, capital is regularly and repeatedly transformed from capital goods into inventories, then sales revenue, and finally, into capital goods again. At the point when it is in money form, the managers of capital must decide on the most advantageous selection of capital goods. The inherent – and sequential – connection between capital as a fund and capital as plant and equipment is made plain. Of course on any realistic account there are restrictions on the extent to which changes in the form of invested capital can be made at any given time. But this is no comfort to those who assume "malleable capital." To the extent that capital is malleable, and conditions competitive, there will be movements of capital towards the highest rate of return. J. B. Clark, who understood very well the dual modes of existence of capital as a fund and as instruments of production, gives the example of New England capital leaving whaling for textiles.[2] No ships were converted to mills. "As the vessels were worn out, the part of their earnings that might have been used to build more vessels was actually used to build mills. The nautical form of the capital perished; but the capital survived and, as it were, migrated from the one set of material bodies to the other" (Clark, 1893, p. 118). Such mobility has traditionally been taken to establish a tendency to form a uniform rate of profit. At the very least nonuniformity of the rate of profit on capital funds is inconsistent with equilibrium in competitive conditions.

An analogous point holds true for labor. Competitive workers are on short-term contracts – daily wages – that either side can abrogate costlessly. Hence workers will always seek employment at the highest wages, while employers will try to hire only those willing to work for the lowest wages. The only position consistent with equilibrium is one in which the wage is uniform, at a level which clears the labor market. (Of course wages will not be uniform as between noncompeting labor groups but within such groups they must be uniform, and must clear the market for each group.)

Such points are elementary, and are of course widely recognized in the standard version of neoclassical theory, which seeks to determine the rate of interest on capital, the wage rate of labor and the rent of land in the factor markets, "coordinating the laws of distribution" through the theory of marginal productivity. But, surprisingly, these elementary features of competition are not consistent with the activity analysis version of neoclassicism, at least as ordinarily presented.

Main features of neoclassicism

Activity analysis emphasizes different aspects of the market system, and in many ways marks a new departure in neoclassical thinking. It is analytically more powerful, and it permits a far more detailed representation of the economy. To understand the relation between activity analysis and the thinking that preceded it let us try to sum up the main features of neoclassicism in a few basic propositions. This will not be easy. Neoclassical writers had different interests, and frequently advanced different and competing theories. But there are certain common threads, and these can be woven into a fabric of ideas. Not all neoclassical writers would be content to wear the resulting garment, at least without alterations, and some might claim it was made up of whole cloth. Nevertheless the following ideas do constitute a complete, coherent and thoroughly familiar picture of a market economy, obviously recognizable as the common ground of most of the profession.

The point. The purpose of neoclassical economic theory is (a) to exhibit and explain the working of the market system, or the price system; thus to establish the forces determining prices and quantities exchanged, (b) to establish the circumstances under which and the extent to which the market system encourages efficiency in allocation of resources, (c) to determine the effects of market conditions on the economic welfare of the agents, as measured by their preferences.

The analysis may be carried out for an economy with given resources and endowments, or for an economy with expanding resources.

The method. Neoclassical thinking proceeds by means of the behavioral equilibrium method. Prices, rates of return (usually treated as prices, e.g., interest is the price of capital) and sometimes quantities are *signals*, to which behavior and decision making respond. Supply and demand functions thus have a stimulus – response form. Equilibrium is defined in two ways: (a) *Market clearing*, the model is solved for that set of signals and responses consistent with clearing, (b) *Pareto-optimal*, the model is solved for that set of signals and responses that leaves everyone in the most preferred position attainable without pushing others to a less preferred position.

The two notions of equilibrium are closely linked but not identical. The method is to solve the model for equilibrium, and then predict that actual behavior will tend to approximate equilibrium behavior, or that it will be understandable as a deviation from equilibrium caused by an identifiable special circumstance.

An assumption. The method of behavioral equilibrium implies that there must be some tendency to equilibrium in some sense. Otherwise there would be no reason to solve the model for equilibrium – if it is no more likely in reality than any other position, why bother with it? (Unfortunately for the method, in some very important models it can be shown that no such tendency exists in general. Worse, unstable equilibria are the least likely points to be found in reality. This either requires modification of the model, or it means that the model can only illuminate reality by contrast.)

The agents. The agents whose behavior is to be studied can be separated into two broad groups. Agents who demand final products and supply factor services are *households;* agents who supply final products and demand factor services are *firms*. The same agent, playing different roles can appear in both groups. Households, behaving as demanders, exhibit their preferences in the product markets; firms, behaving as suppliers, exhibit a desire for earnings constrained by technological possibilities. Households and firms reappear in the factor markets, as *suppliers* exhibiting preferences such as work/leisure time, and *demanders*, reflecting the technological conditions which determine costs. The behavior of the agents is described by carefully specified functions, showing how far the agent should carry a desired course of actions, and stating exactly the constraints binding him. Objective factors, like initial endowments, are clearly separated from subjective ones, like expectations and uncertainty.

The markets. Markets can be divided mutually exclusively, though not exhaustively into markets for final products and markets for factors of production. Intermediate goods can be neglected – they swim around in Pigou's lake (Hicks, 1946, p. 118; Pigou, 1932; Clark, 1893). Market analysis proceeds by building on the analysis of the behavior of the individual units, the firm, and households. The object is to determine the equilibria of these units, and then by aggregation, of a market as a whole. From this one proceeds to groups of related markets and finally to the general equilibrium of the whole system, product and factor markets both. Sometimes, as when pure exchange is considered, the analysis is confined to product markets. Clearly this is only an approximation. If a factor market is not in equilibrium, there will be shifts in the supply functions of any products employing that factor, as its market adjusts. For neoclassical theory production is a one way street running from factors, of which there are initial endowments, to final products. The markets for factors and for final products are markets in the same sense, and are to be analyzed in similar ways. However, the two groups of markets are interconnected. The demand for factors is derived from the demand for final products; the supply of factor services is the source of the income which makes product preferences effective.

Supply and demand. Equilibrium is arrived at through a balance of the forces of supply and demand, whether in one market or in many interrelated ones. Supply functions are based on choices from among given methods of production; demand functions are based on preferences for goods, and the whole is constrained by the initial endowments. The range of choice is assumed to be very wide so that systems with narrowly constrained choices are treated as special cases, which implies that *nothing essential to the working of markets depends on the constraints on choice*.[3] Supply and demand are both necessary to the determination of both prices and quantities. (Thus in traditional welfare economics giving rise to both consumer and producer surpluses.)

Roles and class. Nothing essential depends on who or how many are capitalists and workers. Social classes can be introduced, but do not appear in the most general models. Whether one is a capitalist or a worker is a matter of preference – labor can hire capital just as readily as capital can hire labor, in the absence of inflexibilities and imperfections in markets.

The preceding delineation of general neoclassical features is a broad enough approach to encompass both the standard version and the general equilibrium model of Walras and Cassel. The standard version incorporates the effect of competition in equalizing the wage on all substitutable grades and skills of labor, and in equalizing the rate of return across the entire field of capital goods within which capital funds can be invested. The Walras–Cassel activity analysis model treats each capital good and each type of labor separately, determining their efficient use and particular rental values.

Specifying the initial endowments

The distinction between the two senses of capital – funds versus factories – leads to a difficulty when we come to consider how neoclassical theory presents the social context within which economic activity is to take place. A universal property system is assumed, sometimes explicitly, more often implicitly; all means of production are owned, generally by private institutions, normally households or firms, where ownership implies alienability. Hence all products, including liabilities incurred in production are the property of the owner of the means of production, or of the contractual operator of those means, according to the terms of the contract. So far, so good; correct enough, though sparse in detail. The trouble comes in specifying the initial endowments, for neoclassical theory is not about to try to explain how property of various kinds came to be concentrated in certain hands. *Given* the initial distribution of ownership of factors, the theory determines equilibrium in produce and factor markets, and examines the conditions under which these equilibria define efficient allocations of resources and welfare – maximizing patterns of consumption. But how the initial distribution of ownership came about is none of its concern.

However, it still has to assume that such an initial distribution exists, and here is where a problem arises for the standard version. Households' initial endowments of land and labor are easily specified; the appropriate move would be to endow them with capital, also. But capital funds, or capital goods? If households are given specific machines, we are no longer operating with the broad concept of the factor. Households will trade their endowments of machines each trying to obtain the most profitable selection. More of this later; the point is that initial endowments of specific goods will be traded. So we have left the framework of the standard version. But if households are endowed with *funds*, we have to ask how such a value concept can be given meaning in advance of the determination of prices.

Even endowing households with funds, however, does not free the standard version from problems in its account of the factor market. There is a general difficulty concerned with the relationship between the concept of capital, as a factor supplied by households and demanded by firms, and the concept of the firm itself, the owner of the means of production and therefore of the product and the liabilities incurred in production. This difficulty suggests that capital may be more complex than capital theorists have realized. It is neither *funds*, as in the standard version, nor *goods*, as in activity analysis. Neither will it do to treat it as both together, goods *and* funds, at successive stages in circulation. There are other aspects to capital, not expressed by either goods or funds. Let us explore this further. To do this we must examine a problem that arises even in these very general accounts of neoclassicism.

A neoclassical problem

The expenditure of households is constrained by their incomes, which are obtained by selling the services of factors of production. But there is a curious difficulty here. In competitive conditions firms will not buy more of a factor than the last or marginal unit is worth to them (in terms of its productive contribution); nor on the other hand, being profit maximizers, will they fail to buy additional units if the productive contribution is worth more than the factor costs. Hence the value of the marginal product must equal the competitive factor price. This applies to all factors, all being governed by the laws of supply and demand, which operate the same way in factor markets as in markets for final products. (Of course the particular elasticities of supply and demand may vary widely.) However there is an important constraint here: The income paid out consists of claims in real terms, and these claims must exactly add up to the real product produced. Suppose the claims issued as factor payments were less than the product. Then the firm would necessarily be the owner of the residual, and could not be in equilibrium. Moreover, part of the product would then be distributed in accordance with a principle other than marginal productivity. Suppose the claims added up to more than the product. Then the claims – the income payments – *cannot* be made in *real* terms, even though each factor receives its *real* marginal product. At least one factor must end up with less than its marginal product. But which one and why?

We must explore this more carefully. For neoclassical competitive equilibrium to be possible two conditions must be met: factors must receive their marginal products in real terms, and these payments must exactly add up to the total product. These are *necessary* but of course not *sufficient* conditions. Both could be met, while factor supplies were out of equilibrium. But if they are *not* met, a stronger statement can be made: the system should not merely be described as being in *disequilibrium*. Rather it is a case where the *model* must be considered an *improper representation* of neoclassical ideas.

The distinction is subtle but important. A disequilibrium position is one from which, given suitable incentives, agents *could*, conceivably move towards the equilibrium. By contrast, an unstable position is one in which incentives are so structured that agents' choices will tend to move them away from equilibrium. A system may possess no equilibrium, meaning that no set of choices can simultaneously satisfy all agents. These are all to be distinguished from the case where the model improperly represents the underlying ideas.[4] In this case the problem arises from an inconsistency between the *functional relations* between variables postulated in the model, and the *meanings assigned* to the agents and the variables of the model. When competitive conditions prevail, so that factors receive their real marginal product, and yet the income paid out does not add up to the output produced, the resulting situation is not a disequilibrium, nor has the situation arisen because agents' motivations are mutually incompatible. The problem is that the output produced in a system of private property always and necessarily belongs to someone, so the assignment of the rights to it and claims over it, must be *exact* at all times, whether or not that assignment is compatible with the agents' plans, incentives and motivations. But if the system is supposed to determine earnings on market principles, that is, by supply and demand, then there can be no portion of output falling to a residual claimant, nor can real claims be distributed in excess of output, for that would imply a net liability on the part of the residual claimant, i.e., the firm. Income as a residual contradicts the basic idea that income results from the sale of factor services, that is, that it is a reward for a productive contribution. Note that *residual income* is not the same as disequilibrium factor reward. Out of equilibrium, we would expect to find factor services being sold in disequilibrium amounts at prices which failed to clear the markets. We would expect disequilibrium incomes to result, that is, incomes greater or less than the factors' marginal productivity. But that is no reason to expect to find a different *kind* of income appearing: positive or negative incomes which are not the result (either implicitly or explicitly) of a sale of factor services. Where could such incomes come from? Income in excess of costs will be a net surplus; are there surplus goods as well? Will such income be saved or spent, and what effects will result? Such questions are clearly disruptive; they portend a shift to a different framework of ideas, one which sees production, organized along class lines, characteristically resulting in a surplus appropriated by the dominant class, through the exchange and property system. The magic of neoclassicism lies precisely in its ability to make the surplus disappear; all income results from a sale; it is payment for productive services.

So the problem stems from the need to reconcile two ideas basic to neoclassicism, the concept of the firm as one of the basic agents in the market, and the doctrine that income payments represent a market sale of factor services. The firm as an agent supplying products in the market entails that the firm is the residual claimant – the owner of the total product, including all liabilities incurred in production. But the conception of income as the sale of factor services requires that any residual net claims to product, positive or negative, incurred by the firm, be represented as the proceeds of a sale of a factor service. Generally this has been held to be the service of entrepreneurship, which was, however, never specified in any concrete way. It was only, and could be only, the service of incurring the residual claims. This was seen to involve risk, so the service was "risk-bearing." But this is simply the service of being the residual claimant, that is, of being the firm.[5]

We can begin to see how interwoven neoclassical theory is. Its parts are interdependent; one doctrine or model cannot be revised, "other things being held constant" for the interdependence is logical. The doctrine that incomes are rewards for productive service, the theory of the firm and the marginal productivity theory of distribution all have implications for one another.[6] For example, the employer, conceived as the risk-bearing residual claimant, is clearly not supplying a factor of production. Hence any earnings received would not represent revenue from a sale of factor services. Wicksell and others therefore argued that the entrepreneurs' earnings had to be zero, in equilibrium. An alternative was to treat entrepreneurship as a factor entering production, which would be supplied as a function of earnings, and whose marginal product would decline.

But then Euler's theorem would apply; if, when all factors, including entrepreneurship, were increased, returns increased less than proportionately, there would be residual profits, while a *more* than proportional increase entails residual losses. Who would bear these gains and losses? The entrepreneurs were supposed to be the residual claimants. If entrepreneurship is now a factor entering into actual production, another residual claimant will have to be found who buys the service of entrepreneurship, and takes the ultimate gains or losses. Alternatively we can assume that the production function, including entrepreneurship, always shows constant returns to scale, in which case there are no ultimate gains or losses, and all factors always receive their marginal products.

Consider the first case, where increases in all factors lead first to increasing then to diminishing returns for the firm. The only point consistent with the proposition that income is the reward for the productive services of factors is the minimum point of the average cost curve.[7] This will be the competitive price, and the corresponding quantity will be the competitive output, both determined without reference to demand. Demand for the commodity as a whole will have a role to play in setting the size of the market only if all firms are identical. In that case the long-range marginal cost for the industry will reflect the entry or exit of firms producing at their minimum cost point. As such firms enter producing at their least–cost size, the price will fall, since more is thrown on the market. So long as price is above everyone's minimum average cost, entry will continue, until price is reduced to average equals marginal cost. Both the size of the market and the number of firms will be determined by demand and supply, though the equilibrium size of each firm is wholly independent of demand. But if there are economies of scale, external to firms but internal to the industry,[8] then as firms enter, not only do prices fall, but so does everyone's average costs. If average costs fall faster than demand price, then no equilibrium may exist. But even when one does there is still a problem in the long run. The long-run average cost curve is the envelope of the short-run curves (which in this case are the curves for the firms); hence when returns to scale for the industry are increasing, the long-run curve will always touch the short-run curves to the left of the lowest point. So, as firms set price equal to short-run marginal cost, which is also equal to minimum short-run average cost, there will always exist long-run profits, accruing as residual windfalls to the firms. But if there are initially economies of scale, external to the firm but internal to the industry, and then at a larger size, similar diseconomies of scale, the size of the industry will also be determined by the requirements of distribution, independent of demand. In *either* case, price is determined independent of demand, by the requirements of distribution.

Suppose, however, that competition is imperfect. Firms will hire factors up to the point where the marginal revenue product equals the marginal cost of the factor, in money, to the firm. Assume physical constant returns to scale, with perfect factor and imperfect product markets. Then there will be diminishing returns in value terms, since marginal revenue falls. (If the factor market is imperfect, but marginal factor cost rises more slowly than marginal revenue falls, this will remain true.) As a consequence there will be positive profits accruing to the firm as the residual claimant. These profits arise from the combination of constant costs and falling average revenue, and are in no sense a reward for factor services.

Finally, these difficulties reappear at the aggregate level of analysis. Marginal productivity theory began as a theory of the demand for factor services, at the level of the firm. But obviously factor services are sold economy-wide, and first-order efficiency conditions require that the marginal value products in all lines be equated, while the second-order conditions require for stability that these marginal value products be diminishing. Observation seems to indicate the presence of conditions broadly approximating those of competition: wage rates between large groups of similar laborers are both equalized and stable. Hence the inference can be drawn that the wage equals the marginal product of labor in aggregate output, and further, that this marginal product diminishes. A similar inference can be drawn for capital, and together with the doctrine that all income represents payments for factor services, this permits the postulate of an aggregate production function, from which the income shares of the factors can be derived. The same kind of difficulties, of course, arise. If the function is not linear and homogeneous, residual income, positive or negative, will exist. But who will get this residual? For the function deals with *aggregate* capital, and the aggregate capital includes the ultimate ownership of all the firms. Hence any residual is already assigned to capital. In the case of the aggregate production function, the difficulty reconciling the concepts of *the firm* and *factors of production* becomes a problem within the concept of *capital* itself, since capital is at once a factor of production and represents the ownership of all the firms in the economy.

Perhaps this discussion could be summed up by looking at it formally. The neoclassical approach requires that factor markets be analogous to product markets. Income results from the sale of factor services, and the markets are governed by supply and demand. Looking at the aggregate picture, we have five variables to determine: the real wage; the rate of interest; the amount of labor employed; the amount of capital used; and the total output. But there are six equations to determine them: demand for labor; demand for capital; supply of labor; supply of capital; the production function; and the distributional identity. It is this overdetermination which gives rise to the overpayment or underpayment of income, the positive or negative residual incomes. To eliminate this difficulty, neoclassical theory has adopted assumptions that make the distributional identity depend on the production function, reducing the number of independent equations to five. But this simply creates problems for the theory of the firm since the cost curves of suppliers in product markets reflect the same data that determine distribution.

The firm and factor rewards

How then is the concept of the firm to be reconciled with the notion of income as a reward for the productive contributions of factors? If supply curves are marginal cost curves, and if cost curves are derived from the firm's production function, then for the long-run supply curve to rise, returns to scale must diminish. This is consistent with Marshall's dictum that supply and demand are like two scissor blades – both equally involved in the cutting – and it permits the study of both equilibrium for the firm and for the market. But as we have just seen, diminishing returns to scale does not permit a coherent theory of distribution; less than the value of output will be distributed, the remainder remaining in the hands of the firm, leaving the account of the firm, as well as the theory of distribution, in an unsatisfactory state.

The simplest way around the problem has been to adopt Wicksteed's solution (Wicksteed, 1894), to assume that production functions were linear and homogeneous. This solves the problem of distribution without determining the size and equilibrium of both the firm and the market independently of demand, which is the unfortunate consequence of following the route suggested by Walras (1954) and Wicksell (1934). And it eliminates the necessity of explaining the existence of residual incomes, not paid for productive services. Moreover, only a linear and homogeneous production function makes sense in the aggregate case, where there cannot be a residual claimant, since aggregate capital includes the equity, and so the ownership, of all firms.

But there is, nevertheless, a heavy price to pay for this solution. Three points spring to mind. First, the assumption of constant returns requires that technical progress be treated as a *shift* in the production function. But for long-run problems this seems artificial. On what grounds could one distinguish between a shift and a movement along a function? Second, the scissors no longer cut with both blades. The long-run marginal cost curve is horizontal, so prices are fixed independent of demand. Third, under perfect competition the size of the firm and the distribution of output between firms is altogether indeterminate. All three of these, and particularly the third, cut deep into the standard version's ability to deal with the analysis of particular markets.

If making sense of marginal productivity theory requires one to assume that production functions are linear and homogeneous, there may be little gained by remaining within the format of the standard version. For one thing, that format is open to the Cambridge objections.[9] Yet if production functions are linear and homogeneous, the principal strength of the standard version, its detailed and precise analysis of markets, is largely lost. One might as well go all the way, and adopt the Walras-Cassel approach, leaving the position of the firm indeterminate, but gaining the advantages of mathematical power, coupled with a detailed representation of production.

Costs of abandoning the standard version

Let us examine this more closely. The Walras-Cassel approach is concerned with processes, irrespective of how the process is owned or operated. Yet it is the latter – the conditions the firm faces – which provides the starting point for the theory of market behavior. Most of the main propositions of orthodox economics, at least those normally put forward in textbooks and policy discussions, revolve around market analyses, and often depend on factor market analysis, where the factor is understood in an aggregate sense, for example, labor in general, or capital in general. The standard version is admirably suited for this sort of analytical task, but the activity analysis model is not. There is a cost to orthodox economics in abandoning the standard version in favor of activity analysis. To see just what this cost is, we must look at the doctrines and disputes of orthodox economics. Simply to illustrate this point, consider three groups of topics, by no means of equivalent theoretical significance, but on which a great deal has been written by leading economists in the last several decades. In the first group let us put those discussions that do not and cannot make sense apart from the conception of income as the reward to a factor's productive contribution, where each factor is defined broadly as consisting of all those elements that can substitute for one another in a certain production role. The second group comprises discussions that have made use of the broad concept of a factor, and of marginal productivity theory, but that could conceivably be restated on some other basis. The third group concerns the fundamental neoclassical concept of market efficiency and can be stated without reference to the broad conception of a factor. To abandon the standard version, then, is to dismiss the first group altogether, requires rethinking the second, and a shift in emphasis in the third. Let us consider each group of topics in turn.

First, those claims and results that could not conceivably be stated or established without drawing on aggregate marginal productivity theory – that is, that involve economy-wide factor markets, understood and analyzed according to neoclassical principles. Some examples include: the studies of the sources of growth; evaluating the respective contributions of capital, education, and technical progress; the very statement of the problem under study assumes marginal productivity theory. Similarly, the theory of human capital only makes sense if human productive capacities of different kinds can be measured and compared in terms of earning power. The assumption is that earning power measures productive contribution at the margin – not indeed for every individual, but for the average of groups of similar workers. On the basis of this assumption, it can be seen that investments in human capital can be calculated and used to help explain growth, the distribution of earned income, investment in education, and related matters (Thurow, 1970). But if earning power does not measure productive contribution, then the conception simply breaks down. Acquiring a skill may increase earning power, but it cannot be called human capital accumulation unless it enhances productivity. Two other related fields are the neoclassical theory of growth, both one- and two-sector models, an adaptation of which provides the basic framework for the modern approach to international trade – the Hecksher–Ohlin factor price equalization theory. Again it is difficult even to describe either neoclassical growth or trade theory apart from the concept of a broadly based, or aggregate factor of production, the return to the ownership of which measures the factor's productive contribution. Activity analysis retains the essential idea of a factor of production, but restricts the concept to limited physically identical commodity groups, making it impossible to examine the contributions of labor-in-general or capital-in-general, in situations where prices are variable.

To this first group we should add the studies of portfolio management, in particular the debate over the Modigliani–Miller proposition that the cost of capital to the firm is independent of the firm's debt-equity ratio, for this proposition is formulated in terms of homogeneous fund capital, and the interest rate, neither of which have a place in activity analysis.

It appears that this first group comprises matters, the discussion of which simply has to be dropped, if neoclassical theory abandons the standard version as unjustifiable. It is not so much that anything in particular is wrong; it is that the problems to be investigated have been defined in terms which have been admitted to lack any sense. If the aggregate production function is an unjustifiable construct, then the marginal products of labor and capital in general have no well-defined meaning, whether we mean the societywide marginal products or those for a particular industry, or specific firm. The point is that when the price changes and the composition and substitution effects entailed by competition have been taken into account, the resulting change in factor earnings bears no orderly relationship to any reasonable and unambiguous measure of productive contribution.

Let us look at the second group of discussions. These certainly depend, in common discourse, on the neoclassical theory of factor pricing, but they seem to depend less strongly on it. They might perhaps be analyzed on the basis of some modified version of the activity analysis model, though no such presentation has so far attained any wide currency. The debate over the Phillips curve is an example. In many, perhaps most discussions, the contention that a change in the level of unemployment will affect the rate of inflation of prices, as opposed to wages (where the effect may be supposed to be direct), depends on the theorem that the real wage is fixed at the level of the full capacity marginal product, so that, assuming competition, price equals marginal cost equals the money wage divided by the marginal product; hence a rise in wages – productivity constant – raises marginal cost. This presumably justifies the contention that the rate of price inflation equals the rate of wage inflation minus the rate of productivity growth.[10] Critics of the Phillips curve, however, rely no less heavily on marginal productivity theory. The argument that there exists a natural rate of unemployment is usually presented as a denial of workers' money illusions. An increase in exogenous demand initially raises prices, temporarily lowering real wages, thereby inducing employers to expand employment and production. But workers will revise their price expectations, and incorporate their new perception into their wage demands. Wage rate increases will eventually catch up to prices, raising real wages once again, so that employers will cut back to their original level of output and employment. The original level of unemployment will be restored, but the rate of inflation will be permanently higher.[11]

Both sides of the dispute, those who defend the negatively sloped Phillips curve, and those who maintain that it is a vertical line cutting the horizontal axis at the natural rate of unemployment, state their position in terms of the theory that factor incomes arise from their productive contributions at the margin. Labor's real wage cannot be permanently raised above nor lowered below its marginal product.

Much the same sort of argument accompanies the discussions of the Pigou effect, where the emergence of unemployment in competitive conditions will lead both wages and prices to fall together, raising the real value of cash balances, so leading to increased spending.[12] Again both wages and prices fall together because in competitive conditions the real wage cannot (except temporarily) deviate from the marginal product. In general, textbook discussions of the Keynesian system present the labor market in terms of a demand curve based on labor's marginal product.

But it is not clear in any of these cases how much depends on factor incomes being rewards for productive contributions. All that is necessary is that *for some reason* the real wage must be fixed, so that price and wage inflation have to move together. Marginal productivity theory provides a reason, but if that is disallowed, perhaps another theory could be found. Unlike the first group, where abandoning economy-wide factor markets based on marginal productivity undermined the rationale of the question at issue, in the second group of discussions, an alternative to marginal productivity could perhaps be found, as the "post-Keynesians," for example, have proposed. Indeed, it is not even necessary to maintain that all income constitutes a reward for productive contribution. So long as the real wage is fixed, while employment and demand vary, profit income could be a residual. (By contrast, if profits are a residual, they do not measure the productive contribution of a factor; if a person's salary reflects the status of his family or school, then it does not measure the productive capacity embodied in his human capital.) However, it might not be easy to adapt the activity analysis model to this case, for these discussions do concern the economy as a whole, hence require an analysis of labor on an economy-wide basis, just as the standard version provides. But activity analysis treats each job separately just as it treats each machine separately. It is difficult to see how this more detailed approach could help.

The third group consists of one proposition, expressed in many different ways. It is the claim that the price system brings about an efficient allocation of resources among competing ends. The efficiency of competitive markets is the centerpiece of neoclassical theory, and the activity analysis approach demonstrates this rigorously, and in vivid detail. Indeed the standard version relying on aggregates in the factor markets cannot do it well; activity analysis can exhibit the productive contributions at the margin of any and every kind of equipment or labor. However, for that reason precisely, activity analysis cannot represent the formation, through competition, of uniform factor prices – a uniform wage for labor of a common level of skill in a wide variety of occupations and industries, or a uniform rate of profit on capital. The standard version is superior, therefore, in this important respect – it represents competition in the factor market better.

Capital in the Walras-Cassel model

This situation has led some economists to view the two approaches as complementary. For some purposes one uses the standard version, for others activity analysis.[13] This is acceptable when the problem concerns a particular event on some definite occasion in a particular market. It is another matter when the issue concerns the nature of the whole economic system. Both approaches offer a general characterization of the competitive market *system,* and if they are both accepted as revealing different aspects of the truth, then they must be mutually compatible.

The standard version deals with factors in competitive conditions; laborers compete with one another for jobs, and capital funds flow to where they will receive the highest rate of return. The activity analysis model determines the earnings, for example, of particular machines, or workers. But these earnings are rents, and are subject to requirement that,

> [The] permanent fund of capital . . . is put into such forms that the rent secured by one concrete form or capital-good, is as large a fraction of its value as is that received by another . . . This equalizing force determines the number of capital-goods of each kind; and this, again governs the rents they severally earn. (Clark, 1893, p. 125)

The question confronting us is whether the modern activity analysis model is compatible with the capital theory of the standard version.

This can be answered by examining a simple Walras-Cassel general equilibrium model. Let there be a vector of resources, $r = r_1 \ . \ . \ . \ , rm$, representing nonproduced means of production. Let $x = x_1, \ . \ . \ . \ , xn$ represent the output of the n various goods. The input matrix, A is $m \times n$, shows the amount of resources per unit output of the goods. The price vector is p and the vector of rental values of the resources is v. The model can be formulated in programming fashion as follows:

$$\begin{aligned} &\max\ p'x \\ &\text{subject to } Ax \leq r \\ &\qquad x \geq 0 \\ &\qquad x = F(p, v) \end{aligned} \qquad\qquad \begin{aligned} &\min\ r'v \\ &\text{subject to } A'v \geq p \\ &\qquad v \geq 0 \end{aligned}$$

The function F gives the demands for the goods, x, as a function of prices and the incomes of households received from the rental of their resources.

A principal concern of those who have worked with this model has been to show that it possesses a solution – that a general equilibrium will exist under plausible conditions.[14] Let us assume that such an equilibrium exists, and interpret the model further. A crucial question concerns the meaning of the resource-vector, r. These resources enter into production but are not themselves produced, and evidently *need no renewal*. For if they were used up or worn out, the *equilibrium* determined would simply be a one-shot affair, or not even that. To be an equilibrium, an economic configuration must not only be capable of persisting, it must also account for all the market-related costs and benefits. But if using the sources uses them up or wears them down, then such *user cost* must be represented in the model.

Are there any resources capable of being appropriated and marketed which enter into production, but are not used up? Ricardo spoke of "the original and indestructible powers of the soil," but after the dust bowls of the 1930s we should know better (Ricardo, 1973). Space or location might be an example, but such things enter production more in a metaphorical than an engineering sense. In general, resources entering production are used up or worn out, and will eventually need replacement. Unless this is shown, the model simply lacks application, not because it is too abstract, or unrealistic, but because it *misrepresents the nature of production*. It is guilty of an error of commission, not merely, as the phrase unrealistic suggests, of omission.

Yet this is easily remedied. Let some of the commodities produced be the same goods as the resources. Resource holdings can represent the initial endowments, and the coefficients then represent the user cost, which must be made good by replacement.

The implications of admitting that some of the goods in the initial endowments may be produced means of production are dramatic. Consider a simple model, containing only corn and iron:

$$\begin{aligned} \max \quad & x_c p_c + x_I p_I \\ \text{subject to} \quad & a_c x_c + a_{cI} x_I \leq C \\ & a_{Ic} x_c + a_{II} x_I \leq I \\ & x_c, x_1 > 0 \end{aligned}$$

$$\begin{aligned} \min \quad & Cv_c + I_{vI} \\ \text{subject to} \quad & a_{cc} v_c + a_{Ic} v_I \geq p_c \\ & a_{cI} v_c + a_{II} v_I \geq p_I \\ & v_c, v_I > 0 \end{aligned}$$

Let the demand function $F(p,v)$ be such that prices satisfying it result in the production of both corn and iron, and further suppose that these quantities permit the necessary replacement to take place. No loss of generality is involved; this merely guarantees a solution compatible with replacement. Consider the diagram (Figure I.1) first of the maximizing, then of the minimizing problem. So long as the slope of the price ratio lies between the slopes of the two constraints, both goods will be produced. If both goods are produced both resources will be assigned positive values. The minimizing problem yields these shadow values, which represent the rentals that can be obtained from the commodities. The slope of the line joining the optimal value of v_I to the optimal value of v_c gives the ratio of the rental values. The slope of v_I/v_c need not equal p_I/p_c. If it did, p_I/p_c could be changed without changing v_I/v_c so long as the change stays within the limits prescribed by the slopes of the constraints.[15] But if $(v_I/v_c) \gtreqless (p_I/p_c)$, then $(v_I/p_I) \gtreqless (v_c/p_c)$, that is the ratio of rental earnings to supply price, for the two goods will be different. But capitalists will invest

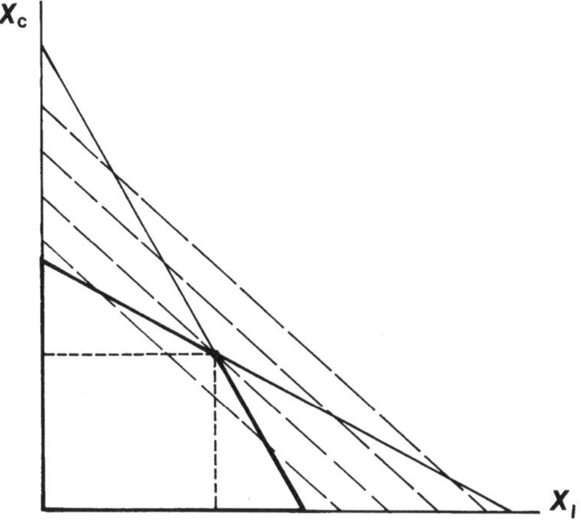

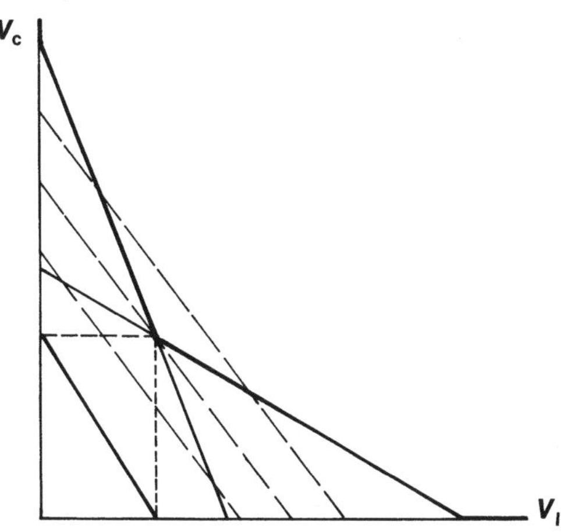

Figure I.1

their capital in (pay the supply price of) equipment whose earning power is the highest. Hence in equilibrium, as defined by the Walras-Cassel model, all capital funds will flow into the purchase of only one of the goods, the one whose rental value in relation to supply price is the greatest. Clearly this is inconsistent with equilibrium, and consequently, the Walras-Cassel model is, in general, incompatible with the notion of capital as a freely moving fund, responsive to competitive pressures and opportunities. It follows that the standard version and the activity analysis approaches are not mutually compatible either. The standard version, in its account of the behavior of the firm and for the structure of markets, (in either single or multi-market analysis) rests on a *broad* conception of a factor, allowing for a wide range of substitution among particular capital goods and workers or kind of worker. This is essential for the derivation of its cost curves and for its account of the equilibrium of the firm. But this leads straight to the internal difficulties just discussed, and, of course, more fundamentally to the Cambridge critique.

Activity analysis, since it has no theory of the firm, has no such internal difficulties, and since it employs a narrow conception of factors, is not subject to the Cambridge critique of factor pricing, either. But for precisely these reasons it stands directly opposed both to the standard version and to important strands of neoclassical tradition. Without a theory of the firm it is difficult to examine market structure or market adjustments. But a theory of the firm cannot be grafted on to the activity analysis model without providing an account of the firm's *cost and capital structure*. But this is exactly what the model cannot accommodate, for it would require consideration of factor markets broadly defined. It would require a concept of capital as a mobile fund. Hence these are mutually exclusive approaches, rather than alternative tools in the economist's famous kit. And neither can accommodate a full concept of capital.

In summary, then, each of the two principal versions of neoclassicism has its characteristic defect, namely the absence from it of the concept of capital that defines the other. Each is therefore fatally one-sided, and represents a failure to live up to Clark's original version. But the two versions share a further flaw: neither can offer an adequate theory of the firm, for neither is able to integrate the theory of the firm, where supply price is based on costs, with the theory of distribution, where costs reappear in the guise of factor incomes. But the doctrine of prices as signals of efficient allocation requires that costs represent relative scarcities; which means that no factor incomes can be pure residuals – all must be determined by supply and demand. This causes the theory of the firm to break down, since rising supply prices cannot be explained. Nor can an adequate account be given of the relation between capital funds and capital goods. The result is a complex, three-way incompatibility: neoclassical theory cannot simultaneously encompass a full-blooded concept of capital (funds *and* goods successively), a concept of the firm in which its position defines the nature of the market, and a theory of distribution determined by supply and demand in factor markets.

The retreat from neoclassical theory

In recent years, a major effort has been made to evade these problems while retaining the concept of efficiency pricing. A number of neoclassical writers have accepted the classical–Marxian representation of prices, wages and profits for a given technique in matrix notation: $(1 + r)\ Ap + wL = p$, where r is the rate of profits, w the real wage, p, the price vector, A the input – output matrix and L the labor vector. They have set out to graft the neoclassical ideas of utility, choice, and substitution onto this model in order to rescue the doctrine that prices, wages, and profits are market signals of efficient allocation.

This move marks a retreat from a number of traditionally important neoclassical positions. It abandons the theory of the firm and accepts the classical separation of supply and demand; supply conditions – cost and distribution – determine prices, while demand determines relative quantities. Perhaps most important in this scheme, wages and the rate of profits represent divisions of the surplus in exchange value terms; they are not analogous to prices and in no sense are they payments for the productive contributions of factors. This is even marked by a formal distinction; relative prices are given by the characteristic *vector* of the matrix, but the rate of profits is derived from the characteristic *root*.

Yet, the appeal of this program can be seen. Households' time preference sets the rate of interest, which in turn determines the choice of technique. In the process of "switching," the marginal product of capital can be found. Once technique is fixed the real wage and relative prices follow. The money wage, in turn, is set by some combination of bargaining and supply and demand, and the price level will have to adjust accordingly (since the real wage is already fixed). Clearly there is a basis here for an alternative account of the Phillips curve. Moreover, there are clear grounds for claiming "consumer sovereignty" – household time preferences fix the rate of profit, from which the rest follows.

But we are back to Ricardo; one of the forms of income, wages, in this case, is a residual. Incomes are no longer rewards for productive contributions and the symmetry of product and factor markets must be given up. The neoclassical program of coordinating the laws of returns has been thrown over.

Nor can it be otherwise. It might seem that drawing on utility theory to explain the supply of new capital would require an analogous account of the supply of labor, in terms of the choice between work and leisure. But if both capital and labor markets are supposed to work according to the principles of supply and demand, the system will be overdetermined, with six equations to determine five unknowns. If technique is variable, there will be six unknowns, but either an inefficient choice of technique will be possible, or the condition will have to be added that the final position must be on the frontier, in which case the result can easily be indeterminate.

In the hope of avoiding these problems, some theorists, following Irving Fisher, have interpreted wages as present consumption and profits, because they will be invested (where there are no problems of effective demand!) as "future consumption" (Fisher, 1930). There will then be only one price, the rate of interest, which will express the ratio of future gain in consumption to present sacrifice, so that neither income category will be a residual even though only one price is determined. But, the argument breaks down entirely as soon as an additional factor, such as land, is introduced. Rents cannot be identified exclusively with either present or future consumption; they effectively make the distribution of income indeterminate, which puts costs and supply prices in the same situation. In any case, the concept of the rate of interest as the ratio of consumption gained to consumption sacrificed contains serious ambiguities. The crucial step in the argument, that the Fisherian "rate of return" (defined as the gain in consumption divided by foregone consumption) equals the rate of profit at which two techniques switch, has been subjected to devastating criticisms (Nell and Eatwell, 1975, 1976; Pasinetti, 1969).

Let us take stock. If one factor's income is a pure residual, or if any part of any factor's income is residual, then no factor's earnings can represent a scarcity price, for the payments to any of the factors could be increased at the expense of the residual, without any inefficiency being generated. Further, if factor costs do not indicate relative scarcities, then neither do the supply prices of final products. It is therefore *essential* to the doctrine of the price mechanism that no factor obtain any part of its income in equilibrium as a residual.

This suggests that there is something fundamentally amiss not merely with these particular formulations of neoclassical theory, but with the essential ideas which these formulations express. And the Cambridge critics think they know what it is: net income is not in general a payment for a productive contribution; rather, net income is the distribution of a surplus in accordance with property rights and other claims, which mostly reflect class position. *Capital* is not a factor of production, nor is it to be identified with a set of means of production materials, instruments, or means of subsistence:

What is a Negro slave? A man of the black

race. The one explanation is as good as the other.

A Negro is a Negro. He only becomes a slave in certain relations. A cotton spinning jenny is a machine for spinning cotton. It becomes capital only in certain relations. Torn from these relationships, it is no more capital than gold in itself is money . . .

Capital . . . is a social relation of production. (Marx, 1933)

The central doctrine of neoclassicism, that competitive markets tend to bring about an "efficient allocation of scarce resources," is therefore fundamentally suspect, and the way is open to treat capital, not as a "scarce factor," but as a social relationship that is maintained and reproduced by economic activity. For many contemporary economists, this marks a welcome scientific advance, a triumph of reason over ideology.

Notes

1 Activity analysis is a method which is perfectly valid in what we term "programming" models in *Rational Economic Man,* or what Lowe (1976) calls "instrumental" analysis. But activity analysis has been used to develop the Walras-Cassel theory of general economic equilibrium, an approach which differs significantly from the standard version of neoclassicism. The problems we shall be discussing do not arise in activity analysis as such, but in its application to the Walras-Cassel scheme.

2 "[Capital itself is] . . . a fund, a sum of active and productive wealth that continues in industry, as successive instruments of production live, as it were, their productive lives and die" (p. 121). Or again, "We may think of capital as a sum of productive wealth, invested in material things which are perpetually shifting – which come and go continually – although the fund abides" (pp. 119 – 20). Clark is less detailed than Marx. He does not represent the circuits explicitly, nor does he distinguish commodity from productive capital, although the distinction is latent in his work. But the idea that capital must be understood as a process by which a fund of value expands through undergoing a succession of changes in form is clearly central to Clark's theory.

3 By contrast, Lowe argues that the process of growth cannot be understood without understanding the constraints industrial production puts on the possibilities of making transition from one growth path to another; Richardson (1960) argues that constraints on changes of technique, on amount of capacity, etc., are the *prime source of market information*. It is hard to find out what your competitors will do or want to do, but knowing their technology and capacity, you can determine what they *can* or *cannot* do.

4 I have argued elsewhere that neoclassical ideology *cannot* be adequately represented because the conditions for the continued existence, which, we contend, necessarily means regular *reproduction,* of the agents, not only are not shown, but cannot be shown, consistent with the image of production as a *one-way street* from factors to final products (Hollis and Nell, 1975).

5 "There is thus implicit in the view we are adopting, the notion that each individual can, as a formal matter, be regarded as owning two types of resources: 1) his resources . . . 2) A resource that reflects the difference between the productivity of his resources viewed solely as hired resources and their productivity when owned by his firm – we may call this *Mr. X's entrepreneurial capacity* . . . It should be emphasized that this distinction between two types of resources is purely formal. Giving names to our ignorance may be useful; it does not dispel the ignorance. A really satisfactory theory would do more than say there must be something other than hired resources; it would say what the essential characteristics of the *something other* are" (Friedman, 1962, p. 95). There is no end of problems here. For example, what would the supply function of this fictitious factor be based on? The real trouble is that "the essential characteristics of the something other" contradict the notion that all incomes are rewards for productive services. That is why these characteristics, which are perfectly obvious, must be concealed behind opaque names. Even the "risk" is peculiar. What kind of "risk" depends only on the technical conditions of production? (And does it really make sense to claim that employers make a profit under diminishing returns and a loss under increasing returns?) For in competition, in stationary conditions, the earnings of entrepreneurship depend wholly and only on the returns to scale among the factors directly entering production, that is, on the nature of the production function. With constant returns to scale, entrepreneurship earns nothing. If returns to the factors directly involved in production diminish then the total product is greater than payments to direct factors; and entrepreneurs, as residual claimants, obtain the difference. If returns are increasing, the total product is less than factor payments and entrepreneurs owe a net liability, i.e., take a loss. So either there is residual income or at least one factor does not receive its marginal product. Either way, the neoclassical theory fails to account for distribution; only constant returns are consistent with a stable position. But in that case the theory of the firm breaks down.

6 One of the strengths of the "partial equilibrium" approach was that it helped to conceal these internal difficulties. To analyze the behavior of the firm, one assumed the income and behavior of factors as given and derived the cost curves from the production function. The implications for the income received by factors need not be considered. Later, when considering distribution, the behavior of the firm and the product market would be taken as given, without considering the implications of distribution for the cost curve of the firm.

7 This needs to be set forth formally. The notation should be obvious. The unknowns are P, L, K, π, C.

(1) $P = P(L, K)$	The well-behaved production function
(2) $\pi_L = \dfrac{\partial P}{\partial L}$	Factors will each be employed up to the point where the value of their marginal product equals their price.
(3) $\pi_K = \dfrac{\partial P}{\partial K}$	
(4) $P = \dfrac{\partial P}{\partial L} L + \dfrac{\partial P}{\partial K} K$	The value of the total output must be distributed as wages to labor and interest to capital.
(5) $C = \pi_L L + \pi_K K$	Total cost of production equals total income paid out.

There are five equations and five unknowns. From the form assumed for the production function we know that $\lambda^N P = P(\lambda L, \lambda K)$ where λ is an arbitrary proportionality factor. N varies from greater than unity, to less than unity as P increases; hence $N = N(P)$ and $dN/dP < O$. When L and K are increased by the factor λ, C increases by λ also: $\lambda C = \pi_L \lambda L + \pi_K \lambda K$. Since P is increased by λ^N, $\Delta P = P_2 - P_1$, and since $P_1 = P(L,K)$, $\lambda^N P_1 = P_2 = P(\lambda L, \lambda K)$, $\Delta P = P(\lambda^N - 1)$, or $P/P = \Delta P/P = \lambda^N - 1$. By a similar argument, it is clear that $\Delta C/C = \lambda - 1$. Consequently the ratio of the proportionate change in P to the proportionate change in C will be:

$$\frac{\Delta P/P}{\Delta C/C} = \frac{\lambda^N - 1}{\lambda - 1}$$

Taking limits and rearranging:

$$\frac{dP}{P} = \frac{dC}{C}\frac{\lambda^N - 1}{\lambda - 1}$$

Suppose $N = 1$. Then, for that value of P, $dC/C = dP/P$ or $dC/dP = C/P$, which says that marginal cost equals average cost. When $N > 1$, $(\lambda^N - 1)/(\lambda - 1) > 1'$ and consequently $dC/dP > C/P$; marginal cost less than average cost. The usual diagram can be drawn, with the MC curve cutting the AC curve at the lowest point (Figure I.2). The equation for the marginal cost curve will be $dC = \pi_L dL + \pi_K dK = \pi(\partial P/\partial L)\ dL + \pi(\partial P/\partial K)dK$. Total cost C is the integral of marginal cost $\int dC = \pi_L \int dL + \pi_K \int dK$, and can be diagrammed as a function of P (Figure I.3). Equations 1 and 4 will only be satisfied together when $N = 1$. Under the above assumptions there is one and only one such point, where $dC/dP = C/P$. Both price and quantity are determined independent of demand.

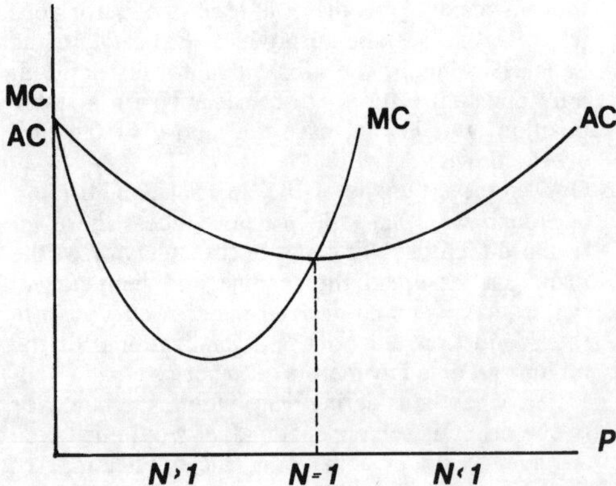

Figure I.2

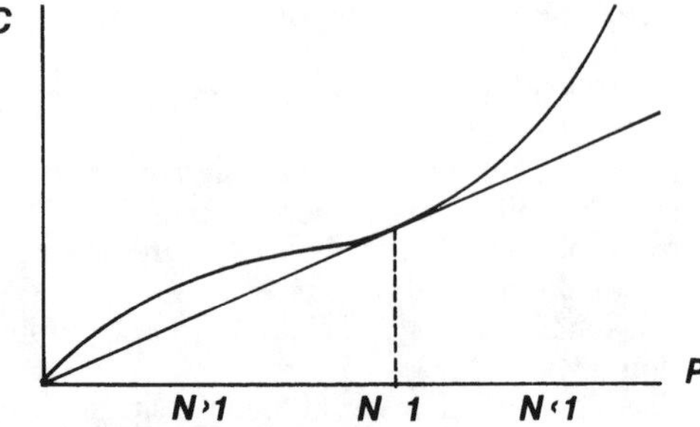

Figure I.3

8 There is a problem in interpreting economies of scale. Economies of scale internal to the firm are incompatible with competitive conditions, since marginal cost would decrease. But economies of scale arising from general growth are irrelevant to the analysis of a particular market. However, "those economies which are external from the point of view of the individual firm, but internal as regards the industry in its aggregate, constitute precisely the class which is most seldom to be met with" (Sraffa, 1926, p. 59).

9 The Cambridge criticisms focus on the concept of capital. Essentially the critics present neoclassicism with a dilemma: the problem is that neoclassicism cannot accommodate a concept of capital in which both capital funds and capital goods are represented, and in which the turnover relation between them is explicit. Hence, neoclassical theory must choose either to work with a homogeneous funds concept (as in aggregate production function models) or with an itemized list of capital goods, as in activity analysis. The standard version, especially as it was presented by some of its earliest developers, such as J. B. Clark, and, of course, in Samuelson's construction of the surrogate production function, tried to relate the two aspects of capital, but we now know that that cannot be done in the manner required.

However, the barbs of the Cambridge critics can be temporarily dodged, at the price of impaling neoclassicism on one horn or the other of the dilemma. A production function containing *leets*, or jelly, can simply be postulated in hope of some future justification. More commonly now the funds concept of capital, and sometimes the rate of return too, are simply dropped, and the efficiency properties of the price system are displayed in the determination of the rental values of a definite list of capital goods.

10 The argument is difficult to justify on Kalecki – Keynes grounds. Suppose there is an initial reduction in unemployment, due to an exogenous rise in spending, ΔG, which leads to a bidding up of money wages. The total increase in demand is $\Delta G + WL + (W + \Delta W)\ L$. In Kaleckian terms, the proposition doesn't hold. Workers spend what they get, capitalists get what they spend. If $I + G$ is fixed, then higher wages, leading to additional worker spending will not affect profits one way or the other, as can be seen from (Figure I.4).

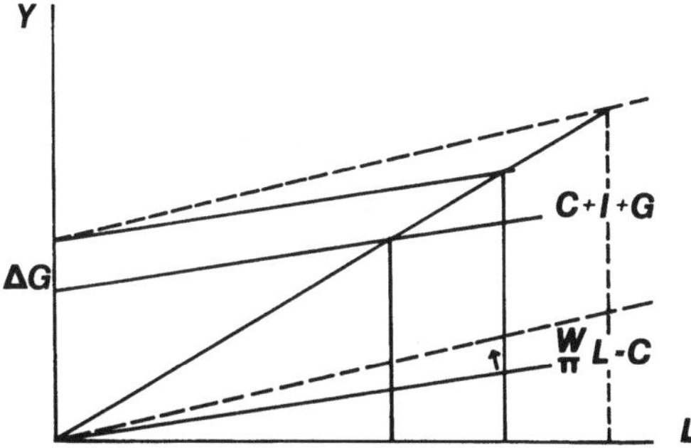

Figure I.4

11 In Kalecki – Keynes terms this argument makes no sense at all. Suppose an increase in exogenous demand raised prices in relation to money wage rates; then the wage line would swing down as the exogenous demand shifted up. Instead of Y_l, the new equilibrium level of income will be Y_l', as in Figure I.5. The level of realized profit will continue to be equal to the level of investment and exogenous demand. Changes in the real wage will alter the composition of demand, so will affect the allocation of total profit to sectors, but will not affect the overall level of profits.

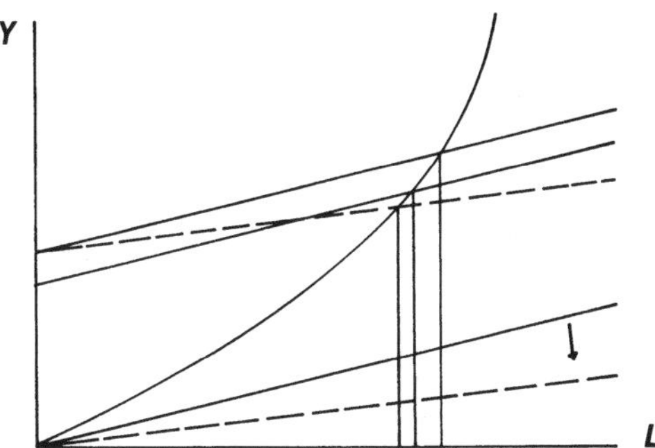

Figure I.5

12 Just as cash balances are held for transactions purposes, so are goods inventories. Lower wages and prices raise the real value of cash balances, but they reduce the value of inventory in terms of fixed obligations. The two effects will work in opposite directions and it is by no means clear which will predominate. In any case the *Pigou effect* amounts to a claim that a change in relative asset prices, will lead to a net change in the amount of assets, spending on consumption instead of a rearrangement of asset holdings, e.g., buying or selling bonds. Not only is there no justification for this, it runs counter to established neoclassical doctrine, which holds that the decision to save is a function solely of the rate of interest.

13 It might seem that the standard version is practical while the Walras – Cassel model has the virtue of mathematical elegance but limited use. The standard version is widely used, but it is not on that account useful. Business firms have never found any help in discussions of $MC = MR$; by contrast, activity analysis is of enormous help in solving scheduling, queueing, transportation, etc. problems. But this is activity analysis proper, not general equilibrium theory.

14 Unfortunately the equilibrium does not guarantee the survival of consumers (Koopmans, 1958, pp. 55, 59). Moreover, rather strong assumptions are required to ensure survival. This is therefore *equilibrium* in rather a weak sense – markets clear, but the system may not be able to survive.

15 Shift the intersection of the constraints in the Max problem to the origin. Then construct perpendiculars to the constraint lines at the origin. These normal lines span a cone and any line in this cone will be perpendicular to a line through the origin lying *between* the two constraints. The cone therefore defines the set of price vectors for which the optimal point remains unchanged.

References

Clark, J. B. 1893. *The Distribution of Wealth.* 1st ed. New York: Macmillan.

Dorfman, R., Samuelson, P., and Solow, R. 1956. *Linear Programming and Economic Analysis.* New York: McGraw-Hill.

Fisher, I. 1930. *The Theory of Interest.* New York: Macmillan.

Friedman, M. 1962. *Price Theory.* Chicago: Aldine.

Hicks, J. R. 1946. *Value and Capital.* 2nd ed. New York: Oxford University Press.

Hollis, M., and Nell, E. 1975. *Rational Economic Man.* Cambridge: Cambridge University Press.

Kalecki, M. 1971. *Selected Essays on the Dynamics of the Capitalist Economy.* Cambridge: Cambridge University Press.

Koopmans, R. 1958. *Three Essays on the State of Economic Science.* New York: McGraw-Hill.

Lowe, A. 1976. *The Path of Economic Growth.* Cambridge: Cambridge University Press.

Marx, K. 1967. *Capital.* Vol. II. New York: International Publishers.

1933. *Wage, Labor and Capital.* New York: International Publishers.

Nell, E. J., and Eatwell, J. 1976. "Rate of Return in Intertemporal Theory," in *Modern Capital*

Theory. M. Brown, K. Sato, and P. Zarembka, eds. Amsterdam: North Holland.

Nell, E. J. 1975. "Black Box Rate of Return." *Kyklos*, Vol. 28, no. 4, pp. 803 - 826.

1978. "The Simple Theory of Effective Demand." *Inter-Mountain Economic Review*, Vol. IV, No 2, pp. 1-32.

Pasinetti, L. 1969. "Switches of Technique, 'Rate of Return' in Capital Theory," *Economic Journal*, 79: 508 - 31.

Pigou, A. C. 1932. *The Economics of Welfare*. 4th ed. New York: Macmillan.

Ricardo, D. 1973. *The Principles of Political Economy and Taxation*. New York: Dutton.

Richardson, G. B. 1960. *Information and Investment*. New York: Oxford University Press.

Samuelson, P. 1962. "Parable in Realism in Capital Theory: The Surrogate Production Function," *Review of Economic Studies*. Vol. XXIX, pp. 193 - 206.

Solow, R. M. 1953. *Capital Theory and the Rate of Return*. Amsterdam: North Holland.

1967. "The Interest Rate and the Transition Between Techniques," in M. Dobb, *Socialism, Capitalism and Economic Growth*. C. H. Feinstein, ed. Cambridge: Cambridge University Press.

Sraffa, P. 1926. "The Laws of Return Under Competitive Conditions," *Economic Journal*, 36, pp. 535-50.

1960. *Production of Commodities by Means of Commodities*. Cambridge: Cambridge University Press.

Thurow, L. C. 1970. *Investment in Human Capital*. Belmont, Calif.: Wadsworth.

Walras, L. 1954. *Elements of Pure Economics*. Homewood, Ill.: Irwin.

Wicksell, K. 1934. *Lectures on Political Economy*. Vol. 1. New York: Macmillan.

Wicksteed, P. H. 1894. *An Essay on the Coordination of the Laws of Distribution*. London: Macmillan.

Part I

Class relations in circulation and production

1

The revival of political economy

Edward J. Nell

The theory of the market

Since the latter decades of the nineteenth century, orthodox economic theory has made its main business the demonstration that a well-oiled market mechanism will produce the most efficient allocation of scarce resources among competing ends. This preoccupation has in turn dictated a characteristic mode of analysis, in which the economy is conceived in terms of "agencies," or institutions, which, whatever their other differences, find their common denominators in terms of their market functions. Thus Rockefellers and sharecroppers are both "households," GM and the corner grocery are both "firms." Households, rich and poor, all demand "final goods" and supply labor and other "services" (meaning the use of capital and land); firms, big and small, demand labor and other factor services, and in turn supply final goods.

This way of subdividing the economy fits neatly into the framework of "rational choice." Factors supply services and demand goods in the amounts and proportions that will maximize their "utilities," given their "initial endowments," a polite way of referring to property holdings. It can be shown that the amounts finally chosen, the so-called equilibrium supplies and demands, will be simultaneously compatible solutions to all these different individual maximizing problems.

The task of high theory, then, is twofold: first, since the models are complex, *to show that there are, indeed, such simultaneous, mutually compatible solutions.* This is not obvious, and, in fact, not always true. Second, of equal mathematical and of greater ideological importance, are what might be called the *Invisible Hand Theorems,* which *show that the system of market incentives will direct the economy toward these equilibrium prices, supplies, and demands.* In other words, the invisible hand theorems demonstrate that the system is automatically self-adjusting and self-regulating.

This architecture of thought has many strengths. Market incentives often *do* direct the system in various predictable ways. Maximizing is, under some conditions, an indispensible part of rational behavior, and so must be spelled out. That it is all done at an exceptionally high level of abstraction is not only not an objection, but – it is claimed – may be a positive merit. The analysis is not cluttered with irrelevancies.

But when all is said, the theory of the efficiency of competitive markets has never provided much practical insight into historical reality. Since it presupposes effective market incentives and institutions devoted to maximizing behavior, it cannot easily be applied to the study either of premarket economics or of postmarket ones – i.e., ideal communist (or anarchist) societies. More important, traditional theory fails to provide a good model for studying the working and misworking of present day capitalism.

There is a simple reason for this very important failure. Basically, orthodox theory is a theory of markets and market interdependence. It is a theory of general equilibrium as applied to *exchange,* extended almost as an afterthought to cover production and distribution. But exchange is a limited aspect of economic, much less social, reality. Therefore, orthodox theory is not a theory of economic power and social class, much less of a social system in its entirety. As we have noted, the initial "endowments," wealth, skills, and property of the populations are taken as *given.* Moreover, since the object of the theory is to demonstrate the tendency

This article was originally published in *Social Research,* Vol. 39, No. 1, Spring 1972, pp. 32–52. Reprinted by permission of the Graduate Faculty, New School for Social Research, New York.

toward equilibrium, class and sectoral conflict tend to be ruled out almost by assumption.

As a result, the orthodox approach has comparatively little interesting to say about such important socioeconomic questions as the distribution of wealth and income. It cannot say how these came about originally; nor how different they might be under another kind of economic system. It does, however, have one major claim to social and historical relevance. It offers a definite though limited theory of the division of the value of net output between land, labor, and capital in a market system. This is known as "marginal productivity" theory. Briefly, it states that each agent in the system will tend to be rewarded in proportion to – and as a limiting case, in direct equivalence with – the contribution he makes to output. Thus a man earns what he (literally) makes; a landlord reaps what he (metaphorically) sows.

But with the revival of interest in recent years in the great problems of political economy, this central claim has come under increasingly heavy attack. This attack, which began as particular and limited objections to specific orthodox doctrines, has in the past few years developed into an alternative conception of the economic system as a whole. It is no longer simply a rival theory of market dispensations – a "non-neoclassical" theory; nor can it be regarded merely as a return to the approach of the Classical greats – Smith, Ricardo, and Marx. It is both of these, but it is considerably more. In currently fashionable terminology, it is the emergence of a new paradigm.

The new paradigm

To see this, let us contrast the view of income distribution given by the new paradigm with that of orthodox marginal productivity theory. At first glance, marginal productivity theory appears eminently sensible. Essentially, it states that factors – land, labor, and capital – will be hired as long as they produce more than they cost to hire. Expanding the employment of any one factor, the others held constant, will (the theory assumes) cause the returns on the extra units of that factor to decline, since it has proportionately less of the others to work with. Thus employment will cease when the declining returns to the factor in question just equal the cost of hiring more of the factor. Competition will cause each factor to be used up to the point where its marginal product equals that of the other factors. The total earnings of any factor will then be equal to the amount of it that is employed, times its marginal product, summed up over all the industries in which it is used. Clearly the relative shares of factors – land, labor, and capital – will then depend on their respective marginal products.

So far so good. To be sure, this story depends on the existence of markets, specifically on markets for land, labor, and capital, so that the theory won't be much use in examining the emergence or evolution of the market system. But note that, in a sleight of hand so deft as to have passed virtually unnoticed for an intellectual generation, the theory attributes responsibility for the distribution of income (under market competition) wholly and solely to the impersonal agency of *technology*. It is technology, not man, nor God, least of all politics, that has decreed what the shares of labor and capital are to be in the total product. *For it is technology that determines how rapidly returns diminish.* Thus only through technological changes, inventions that alter the engineering possibilities, can relative shares be changed. For if income shares are to change, marginal products must change faster or slower than they will change simply by the slow changes in the relative supplies of factors, e.g., population growth. Thus everything depends on how rapidly marginal returns to the different factors diminish, relative to one another, and this is a matter that depends only on technology.[1]

From this perspective the class struggle is an illusion, and unions are valuable only as mother substitutes – providers of security and a sense of identification. Minimum-wage legislation may or may not raise wages, but in all cases the effect will depend entirely on what the technology permits. Only moves that change the relative marginal products of labor and capital can affect income distribution (though even they might not change if, for example, the movement in the relative amounts of labor and capital employed just offsets the changes in their marginal products). The influence of factor supplies is felt only through marginal productivity. Hence technology is what finally determines income distribution. Aggregate demand, monetary policy, inflation, unions, politics, even revolutions, are, in the end, all alike, irrelevant insofar as who gets what.

Socialist and left-wing economists, indeed social critics generally, have always gagged on this.[2] Property and power, they maintain, are the essential elements in class struggles and sectional conflicts; it is ridiculous to say they don't matter – that the outcome, given the competitive market, is predetermined by the accidents of technological inventiveness. From their vantage point, income distribution – the division of society's annual product among the members of society – is *the* central question. For if we put income distribution at the center of the stage, the concern of the orthodox theorists with how factors spend their incomes seems relatively minor. The framework of rational choice looks flimsier and more makeshift; essentially a consumer-oriented theory, it has come to resemble so many consumer products: ingenious, brilliant, but unsuited to human needs.

This is not to say that the political economist rejects the theory of rational choice outright: he rejects it merely as an appropriate framework for the analysis of production and distribution *in the aggregate*. The framework he erects in its place is one that reveals the *links* between sectors and classes; shows how the products of one industry or set of industries are used as inputs by other industries (whose products, in turn, are used by still others); and makes clear how the earnings of one class are spent supporting production in some sector or industry. These interindustry and intersectoral relations are crucial to understanding how changes in demand or in technology transmute themselves into prosperity for some, disaster for others. Links between revenue from sales, social classes, and spending are crucial for understanding how the distribution of income is established and maintained in the face of considerable changes in the composition of output and in government policy.

The difference may seem one more of emphasis than of substance, but putting income distribution at the center and relating it to different patterns of linkages, of payment streams, and of technological dependencies between industries, sectors, and classes, leads to an altogether different vision of how the economy works.

Contrasts between the new and the old

The new vision can be called a "general equilibrium" approach, if one likes. But it immediately departs from the orthodox meaning of that phrase by emphasizing the interdependence of *production*, rather than of markets; technical and institutional "interlocks" – or their absence – rather than purely market relationships.

A second difference between the new approach and the old lies in the treatment of "substitution." In the old picture, substitution is the law of life on both the supply and demand sides. In response to price changes, different patterns of goods and/or factors will be chosen; when prices change, cheaper things will be substituted for more expensive ones in household budgets and industrial processes. The problem is that this conventional picture assumes that households and firms have *given* ends – the maximization of "utility" or output respectively. Hence, it does not deal with the more important questions of introducing altogether new products and processes, changes that often alter the parameters of the system or perhaps even the consciousness of society. Even within the narrow focus of the neoclassical lens, however, many alleged cases of "substitution" involve something quite different – technological progress, changes in the nature of the product, external effects on parameters of the system, and so on. Indeed, in this wider sense, neoclassical substitution is only a *special* case, and that is how the matter is treated in the new vision.

Third, the old vision treats the consumer as sovereign, and the effects of his choices enter into the determination of all major variables. This, of course, does not render the old vision incapable of discussing market power, producer sovereignty, or the "new industrial state." But, inevitably, such phenomena appear as special cases, limitations on the *general* principle of consumer sovereignty. In the new vision the consumer is cut down to size from the start. His preferences have little or no effect on prices or income distribution.

As a consequence, markets and the "price mechanism" are not seen in the new vision as a stable method of bringing about social optimality. On the contrary, prices are seen as determined largely from the supply side, and so depend on income distribution, which in turn may be influenced by many nonmarket and even noneconomic considerations. Ideologically, this means that the "market" should not be seen as some sort of alternative to bureaucracy, or as a method of allocating resources. Allocation depends on distribution, which depends at least in part on property and class.[3]

A further fundamental difference can be seen when we consider the *purposes* of the two visions. The basic constituents of the old vision are consumers and firms, agents whose optimizing behavior, individually or in the aggregate, the equations of the models describe. In particular, maximizing behavior is what the theory is all about, and the *object of the theory, by and large, is to predict the consequences of such behavior*. But the circumstances in which this behavior takes place are taken for granted.

By contrast – and oversimplifying – the new vision is primarily interested in structure, in the patterns of dependency between established institutions, in how the system hangs together, and how it works or fails to work. The job of economic theory is to delineate the *blueprint* of the economic system, of the environment in which economic behavior takes place. The basic constituents of theory are industries, sectors, processes, or activities, defined in technological terms; so defined, the new vision's basic constituents normally will not coincide with decision-making "agencies." Neither the word "household" nor the word "firm," nor any synonym for either, appears in Sraffa's *Production of Commodities by Means of Commodities* (1960), the basic work laying the foundation of the new paradigm. For decision-making, the prediction of behavior or of what *will* happen, is not the goal. The new vision is concerned with seeing how an economy keeps going, what is *supposed* to happen; from that to discover what makes it break down and what makes it develop into an economy of a different kind. These are seen as questions addressed primarily to the analysis of the system of production, and of the social relations surrounding production.

The central distinction between the two visions, then, lies in the treatment of production and distribution. For the traditional neoclassical economist, production is a one-way street, running from primary "factors" to "final products." Among the primary factors are land, labor, and, above all, *capital,* each receiving in competition a reward proportional, in some sense (depending on market circumstances), to its "contribution."

But not so in the new paradigm. The notion that the three traditional factors are on the same footing is discarded altogether. The great achievement of the marginalist revolution, as seen by its nineteenth-century proponents – namely, the development of a unified theory applying to all three factors – is dismissed. This can be seen nowhere so clearly as in the new conception of "capital," in reality a revival of a point well understood before the marginalists confused things. "Capital" has two meanings. On the one hand, it is property in the means of production, enabling owners of equal amounts of claim in these means to receive equal returns (given competitive conditions). In this sense it is a homogeneous fund of value, capable of being embodied in different forms. On the other hand, "capital" also means produced means of production – that is, specific materials, tools, instruments, machines, plant, and equipment, on which, with which, and by means of which labor works. In this sense it is a set of heterogeneous, disparate products. *Capital goods are not the same thing as capital.* "Capital" is relevant to the analysis of the division of income among the members of society, but a nonspecific fund has no bearing on production. "Capital goods" are relevant to the study of production, but have no bearing on the distribution of income, since profit is earned and interest is paid on the *fund* (value) of capital invested, regardless of its specific form. "Capital goods," specific instruments, can only be converted into a fund of "capital" on the basis of a given set of prices for those instruments; but to know these prices we must already know the general rate of profit (in a reasonably competitive capitalist economy).[4] Hence the amount of "capital" cannot be among the factors that set the level of the rate of profit. But in the orthodox, or neoclassical, theory the "contribution" of "capital" to *production* supposedly determines the demand for capital, which together with the supply determines the rate of profit. This must be rejected. No sense can be given to the "contribution" to production of a *fund* of capital.

This is not to say that *saving and investment,* and their long-run consequences, are irrelevant to determining the rate of profits and relative shares. Quite the reverse; by eliminating the alleged "contribution of capital" in production as an influence or determinant of distribution, we open the way for a theory of distribution based on the relation between the growth of spending, of capacity, and of the labor force, on the one hand; and on the market power available to the various parties, on the other. Unequal rates of inflation of money wages and prices necessarily imply changes in the relative shares going to capital and labor, as Keynes pointed out in the *Treatise on Money,* his early major, and now neglected, work. Inflation is partly a consequence of the ratio of demand to supply, but it also reflects relative market power. And here is where the rules of the game – the rules of property – come in. For property confers advantages, though not absolute ones, in the setting of prices and in bargaining for money wages. Exactly what these advantages are, how they work, and by what kinds of forces, are among the questions that a theory of distribution should be able to answer.

In short, the new vision adopts a picture of the relation between production and distribution altogether distinct from that which has ruled the economist's roost since the marginalist revolution. This, in turn, entails rejecting some widely used techniques of empirical analysis, in favor with both radical and orthodox economists. In particular, "production function" studies, e.g., of technical progress, the contribution of education, the effects of discrimination, and of shares during growth, all involve a fatal flaw. For insofar as they proceed by assuming that a factor's *income share* indicates in any way its *productive power* at the margin, they are based on precisely the relationship that the new vision rejects.[5]

It thus seems that conventional theory, although it contains much of value and impor-

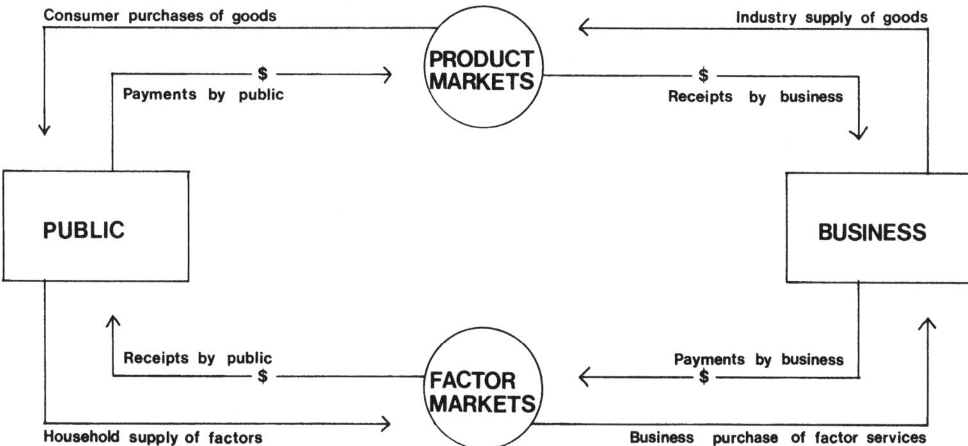

Figure 1.1

tance, contains serious deficiencies.[6] The neoclassical theory of the general equilibrium of production, distribution, and exchange holds that the payments in the *factor markets* are *exchanges* in the same sense as payments in the *product markets*. "Distribution is the species of exchange," wrote Edgeworth, "by which produce is divided between the parties who have contributed to its production" (Edgeworth, 1970). Distribution, say the proponents of the new vision, is *not* a species of exchange; and capital *goods,* rather than capital, contribute to production. The ideological teeth begin to bite; an exchange, in equilibrium, means that *value equivalent is traded for value equivalent.* No exploitation there. But if distribution is *not* a form of exchange, then we must ask Who and Whom?

This catalogue of differences, and especially the last point, can be nicely illustrated by comparing two simple diagrams that visually summarize the two paradigms. The first, adapted from Samuelson and echoed in all major textbooks, presents what might be called a same-level division of society: business and the public (producers and consumers) confront each other more or less as equals in the markets for both products and factors. (The equality is an overall one; there are some large or allied firms, some collective consumers.) Households demand final goods and services and supply the services of productive factors, in both cases in accord with what economists rather pompously call "their given relative preference schedules," meaning, what they like best. Businesses supply final goods and services according to their cost schedules in relation to the prices that consumers are prepared to pay, and demand the services of productive factors according to their technical opportunities and needs in relation to consumer demand for products.

So goods and services flow counterclockwise, while money flows clockwise (Figure 1.1). In each set of markets, *equivalents are traded for equivalents,* the value of goods and services flowing in one direction being just matched by the stream of revenue in the other. No exploitation is possible in competitive equilibrium. The value of household factor supplies just matches aggregate household demand, and the output of goods and services matches business demands. This may seem to ignore the fact that households save and businesses invest, meaning that some final demand flows not from the public but from business. But that is easily allowed for. To finance this demand, business must borrow household savings, by supplying bonds that the public demands. Bonds are treated as a kind of good, flowing counterclockwise. These points enable the microflow picture to be summed up as a macroflow picture, illustrating in the simplest way how macro rest on microfoundations.

Obvious objections to this economic schema can easily be raised. For instance, not all "households" are on a par, since some *own* all the firms between them, while the rest merely *work* for the firms. Also the distribution of profit and similar income is not an exchange, since the only "service" that the owner of a business (in his capacity as owner) need supply in return for its profits is that of permitting it to be owned by him. He does bear risks, of course, but so do the employees who will be out of their jobs in the event of failure. Other objections were mentioned earlier in the charge that orthodox neoclassicism ignores technological interdependences and institutional relationships, as the circular flow picture makes evident. Nowhere in it

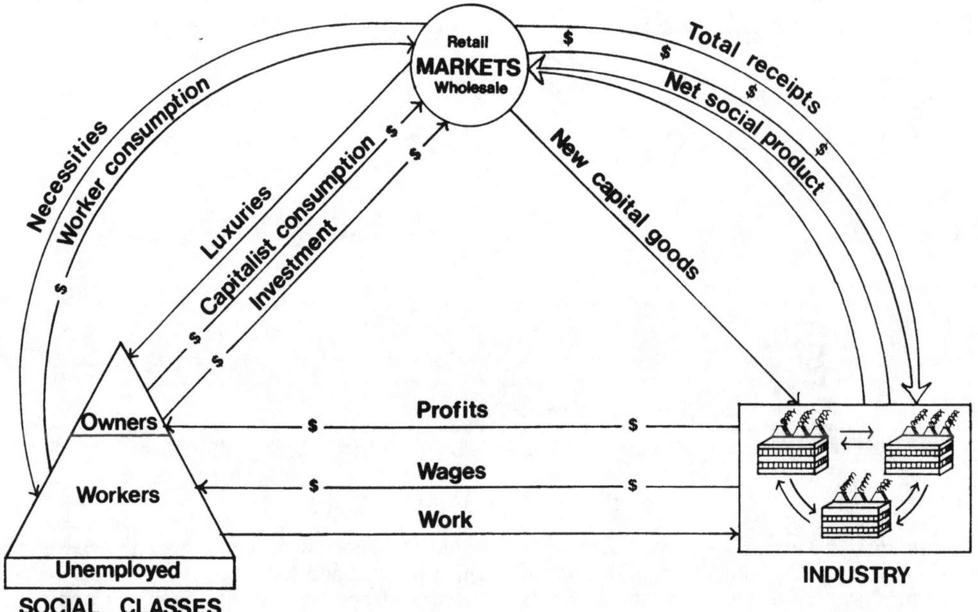

Figure 1.2

can one find social classes or any specific information about patterns of technical interdependence.

All these objections look at first like strong empirical problems that neoclassicists should meet head on. In fact, however, the customary orthodox defense is oblique and of dubious validity. To the charge that their model rests on unrealistic assumptions, they reply that the *only* test of a model is the success of its predictions. So there is no a priori error in making unrealistic assumptions. Moreover, "simplifying assumptions" and "theoretical constructs" are bound to be, in some sense, "unrealistic," and there is no predicting without them. Unrealistic assumptions may therefore be warranted and the warrant is philosophical, positivism itself.

We will return to these defenses. But first consider quite a different picture of capitalist society. The following diagram epitomizes the new approach, which, if the old is "neoclassical," could be dubbed "classical-Marxian." It cannot be claimed that this is the only, or necessarily the best, distillation of an alternative picture from that tradition, but it will serve to illustrate the contrasts.

To keep the diagram comparable to the first, we retain the circle for the final goods market and the box standing for industry, though we shall interpret both quite differently. "Households" and the "factor market" disappear altogether. Instead we have a pyramid, representing the social hierarchy, divided into two parts: a small upper class of owners and a large lower class of workers. Owners own industry and receive profits; workers work for industry and receive wages. Workers consume, but do not, in this simplified model, save; owners both consume and save, in order to invest. See Figure 1.2.

Now consider the flows of services and money payments. Labor is the only "factor input"; other inputs are produced by industry itself, which is assumed to have access to land, mines, etc. (We are lumping landlords and capitalists together.) Hence we might expect to be able to value the total product in terms of labor, and though the mathematics is complicated, this can indeed be done, though not in all cases. The arrows running back and forth between factories represent interindustry transactions, the exchanges between industries necessary to replace used-up means of production. The net social product is sold for total receipts, and consists of all goods over and above those needed for replacement. These can be divided (for convenience) into necessities, luxuries, and new capital goods.[7] Necessities go for worker consumption, luxuries for capitalist consumption, and new capital goods are installed in the factories in return for investment payments. Hence, the national accounts work out:

Total receipts = net social product = wages + profits = wage consumption + capitalist consumption + investment demand = necessities + luxuries + new capital goods.

From the point of view of political economy, however, the most important fact is that while wages are paid for work, and one can (and in some circumstances should) think of the wage bill, equal here to worker consumption, as reproducing the power to work, *profits are not paid for anything at all.* The flow of profit income is not an exchange in any sense. The Samuelson diagram is fundamentally misleading; there is no "flow" from "household supply" to the factor market for capital. The *only* flow is the flow of profit income in the other direction. And this, of course, leads straight to that hoary but substantial claim that the payment of wages is not an exchange either, or at any rate, not a fair one. For wages plus profits adds up to the net income product; yet profits are not paid for anything, while wages are paid for work. Hence the work of labor (using the tools, equipment, etc., replacement and depreciation of which is already counted in) has produced the entire product. Is labor not therefore exploited? Does it not deserve the whole product?

Profits

The latter question opens Pandora's box; as for the former, it all depends on what you mean. What does certainly follow, however, is that distribution is *not* an exchange, profits are not paid *for* anything and serve no function which cannot be met in other ways. This may not be exploitation but it shows clearly that the traditional economic justification – the "reward" for services – cannot be applied to profits, interest, dividends, and the like.[8] Moreover, since the payment of profit is no exchange, there can be no equilibrium in the usual sense. A century-old school of thought, holding that our troubles come from the *excessive* profits sucked in by giant monopolies, and idolizing small competitive enterprise earning "normal profits," is thereby undercut. There is no merit in "normal profit"; indeed there is no such thing. The issue for political economy is the profit system itself, not its alleged abuse.

But surely, under both capitalism and market socialism, do not profits serve the essential function of indicating where investment can most advantageously be directed? Does not the *rate* of profit, similarly, serve to allocate productive resources between producing for current consumption and expansion for the future?

There are two things wrong with this common claim. First (as sophisticated neoclassical economists will quickly admit), the function of profits and the rate of profit as indicators require merely that they be *calculated, not that they be actually paid out.* Calculated profit indicators are compatible with many different incentive schemes (e.g., salary bonuses to managers of state-owned enterprises, moral incentives, etc.). Second, profit-based indicators are only one set among several. In a stationary economy, for example, the correct indicators to achieve maximum output would be based not on profits but on *labor values!*[9] Indeed, profit indicators alone are likely to be misleading; the rate and pattern of growth must also be considered in trying to identify the best investment plans. Thus, from the strict economic point of view, forgetting social complications, the best choices for maximizing consumption may differ from the best choices for maximizing growth. Once we allow for quality, the effect on the environment, and so on, the variety of possible indicators becomes considerable.

To return to the diagram: the new model helps us to understand how the division of income comes about. Remember that the orthodox doctrines held that the distribution of income was determined in the factor market, by the marginal "contribution" of factors in conjunction with their relative scarcity. The diagram makes it clear that income distribution interacts with all aspects of the economy, not just with the "factor market." This point can be made quite simply, though its consequences are far-reaching. Labor's share is given by the real wage times the amount of work. But the *real* wage is the *money* wage divided by an index of consumer goods prices. The money wage is set in the labor market, but prices are set in the final goods market. Labor's share, then, depends on *both* markets. Thus the system is interdependent in ways no hint of which can be found in orthodox teaching.[10]

This puts inflation in a new and clearer light. The standard approach is to distinguish "demand-pull" inflation (originating in the final goods market) from "cost-push" inflation (originating in the factor market). Very few actual cases seem to fit either category. On the new approach this should come as no surprise, for the question has been wrongly posed. This issue is not where inflation originates, but how fast it proceeds in different markets. In the orthodox diagram it is natural to suppose that a price increase in the product market will be transmitted directly to the factor market, and vice versa. Unless costs and prices rise together the circular flow cannot continue unimpeded. In the new diagram it is evident that this is not so – costs and prices rising in the same proportion will be the special, limiting case. In all other cases the effect will be to raise or lower profits. When wages rise faster than prices, there will be profit deflation; when prices rise faster than wages, profit inflation, to use the terminology suggested by Keynes in the *Treatise on Money*. In all cases except the limiting one, then, inflation will affect income distribution and so aggregate demand and employment.[11]

What determines the relative rate of price and wage increases? The first answer, of course, must be "supply and demand," and this is surely right. For example, large numbers of unemployed will tend to act as a drag on money wages. But the same balance of supply and demand may have a very different total impact on price in different circumstances, depending on market power; on the financial position of companies and unions; on the ability to make use of the law, or state agencies, to manipulate the press and the media; and so on. These considerations are preeminently ones of Political Economy, but they play an essential role in theory, for they determine the relative responsiveness of markets, and hence the relative speed of wage and price inflation.

Summary

We have now presented and contrasted the two paradigms. The neoclassical one is far better known, and most contemporary work is conceived in its terms. But if the preceding argument is sound, it is significantly misleading. The new paradigm, by contrast, is clearly more realistic sociologically, and is capable of handling questions, such as those concerning property income and social class, that the other tends to submerge.

These two claims, that the old paradigm is misleading and the new more realistic, suggest that there is a strong *prima facie* case for adopting the new. This conclusion, however, is widely resisted, and the reasons, already mentioned, are interesting. Those who defend the old approach often contend that a paradigm cannot be "misleading" in its representation of institutions *if it leads to models that predict well*. "Realism" is not important; abstraction must take place, and a model can abstract from anything, so long as it performs well.

Such a defense must be seen for what it is. It is a methodological claim, and one based on a particular, and today rather questionable, philosophy of science. One straightforward retort might be that neoclassical models have not done very well on their chosen ground (Schoeffler, 1957). Predicting has not been the greatest success of modern economics. But a more fundamental response would be to challenge the methodology itself. There is no time to argue the case now, but there is an intuitive appeal to the idea that a model of social institutions must be a good representation of things as they are at a given moment of time, regardless of how they work out over time. To demand of economics that it predict what will happen may be asking too much (Lowe, 1965). In modern industrial societies the economic system is too closely interlocked with other aspects of society; it cannot be isolated enough for effective tests to be run. But to add a long string of *ceteri paribus* clauses simply tends to reduce predictions to vacuity. Instead, we must examine the definitions and assumptions of our models for their realism, and for the extent to which they incorporate the essentials. If they are realistic, then the working of the model should mirror the working of the economic system in relatively simple and abstract form. To argue this further would take us far afield (Hollis and Nell, 1975). It should be clear, though that the case we have presented can be defended from the methodological objections of the positivists.

In short, the new approach presents a coherent picture of the economy, perfectly adapted to modern empirical methods and capable of providing technical analysis of a sophisticated nature.[12] But it has not been developed for its own sake, or simply because it presents a better, more accurate picture of capitalism. The new picture is intended precisely as *political* economics, as a guide to the criticism of the capitalist socioeconomic system. Its basic challenge to orthodox thinking is that, in treating the distribution of income as a form of exchange, it misrepresents the way the system works. But if it is not an exchange then someone is getting something for which he is not giving a value-equivalent. The step to social criticism is then short.

Orthodox economics tries to show that the markets allocate scarce resources according to relative efficiency; political economics tries to show that markets distribute income according to relative power. It is good to know about efficiency, but in the world we live in, it tends to be subservient to power.[13] By failing to appreciate this, and consequently failing also to accord the distribution of income between labor and capital a properly central role, orthodox economics has become cut off from the central economic issues of our time, drifting further into ever more abstract and mathematically sophisticated reformulations of essentially the same propositions. The heart of the matter is the concept of "capital" and its relation to social class and economic power. When this is put right, as in the new paradigm, economic theory can once again speak to the critical issues of the day.

Notes

1 The point can be put more accurately in technical language: relative shares will change with factor supplies according to the elasticity of substitution, which, in turn, depends only on technology. If the elasticity of substitution is unity, then proportional changes in factor ratios will just be offset by proportional changes in marginal products, so that relative shares will be unaltered. In other cases, changes in the relative amounts of factors employed will alter relative shares, but both by how much and in what direction will depend solely on the technology.

2 Of course, the available technical possibilities do influence income distribution. Clearly, if it is known that a machine can do a certain job now being performed manually, the laborer doing the job would be most unwise to ask more than the annual cost of installing and running the machine. But this point can be made without accepting the strait jacket of marginal productivity theory. This is important because the technical possibilities of substitution are only one of several sets of influences that bear upon the division of the national income. Differential rates of inflation, both between wages and prices and between sectors, aggregate the level of employment and monopoly power, and are at least equally important, for example. Marginal productivity theory tends to blind us to these influences, or to treat them as "market imperfections," exceptions rather than the normal working of the system.

3 There is also an interesting technical point. In the neoclassical vision macroeconomic relationships are supposed to be based on markets and the price mechanism, which are seen as fundamental. But in the new vision, prices depend on income distribution, and that, insofar as it is determined by economic forces, depends largely on macroeconomic factors. The direction of causal influence is reversed.

4 This is perhaps the central issue in the recent dispute over capital theory between the "two Cambridges," Cambridge, England, maintaining the view presented here, against Cambridge, Massachusetts, which argued that the essential neoclassical story could be developed in a "heterogeneous – capital" model. Unfortunately, to do this, Cambridge, Mass., found it had to assume conditions in which a simple Labor Theory of Value held! It is now widely agreed that neoclassical capital theory is defective (Harcourt, 1972).

5 Put this baldly, of course, it seems an extraordinary assumption for anyone to make seriously. Given what we know about how our society works, if we read the newspapers we would never in our ordinary thinking expect to explain a change in the income of a group primarily by reference to a change in its marginal productivity. We would certainly think of demand and supply, and of income elasticity; these would provide the framework within which bargaining, power plays, and politics would settle the final (or temporary) outcome. Marginal productivity might or might not come into it; just as it might or might not be measurable, but it would hardly be decisive. Is the shift in the income going to the top few per cent since 1960 to be taken seriously as reflecting an increase in their marginal productivity? Is the relative rise in professional income from 1900 – 1970 evidence of a long-term upward drift in their productivity at the margin? Yet, in spite of common sense and advanced theory, the production-function studies, aggregate and individual, continue.

6 This should be distinguished from the commonplace (though correct) criticisms that opportunities for substitution are not legion, that changes in techniques of production and consumption are time consuming and costly, that information is hard to come by (and perhaps should be treated as itself a product!), that mobility is sluggish, foresight myopic, and expectations an irregular compound of habit and hope. These points will be readily admitted, for they merely indicate how far the actual world falls short of its own ideal type. The point of the present criticism is that the neoclassical ideal market economy is *not* a picture of how the economic system would work under ideal conditions, for it fundamentally misrepresents the relationship of distribution to exchange, whether conditions are "ideal" or not.

7 The traditional interest in classifying goods along lines such as these, largely abandoned in the face of positivist criticism – "these are just value judgements" – has been revived in the light of Sraffa's important and far-reaching distinction between basics (goods that enter directly or indirectly into the means of production of all goods) and non-basics.

8 Marxists traditionally relate exploitation to relations of *production*, whereas the present discussion is concerned with the problems of developing an adequate model of circulation.

9 The point follows directly from the golden rule of accumulation, which states that consumption per head is maximized when the rate of growth equals the rate of profit. When the rate of growth is zero, then in the stationary state, for optimality – maximum consumption per head, or in this case, maximum national income per head – the rate of profit must be zero. But the prices which obtain when the rate of profit is zero can easily be shown to be equal to the amounts of direct and indirect labor embodied, i.e., the labor theory of value holds (Goodwin, 1970).

10 This diagram also illustrates a proposition first discovered in the 1930s by the great Polish Marxist economist, Michel Kalecki, who independently and at the same time set forth the main propositions of the *General Theory*.

Investment, I, is the change in the capital stock, written ΔK where Δ means "change in," and comes entirely from savings out of profits. Let sp stand for the fraction of profits saved. So $\Delta K = sp\ P$, where P is profits. Divide both sides by K, the capital stock. We have $\Delta K/K = sp(P/K)$. But $\Delta K/K = g$, the rate of growth, and $P/K = r$, the rate of profits. Hence $g = sp\ r$, a simple formula connecting the growth rate and the profit rate. Remembering that $\Delta K = I$, we also have $I/sp = P = rK$. So, for a given technology, *profits are higher and the growth rate lower the greater is the average propensity of the capitalist class to consume out of profits*. The extreme simplicity and great generality of this proposition, even now not widely known in the profession, are typical of the results obtained by the new approach.

11 A parallel point should be made about the relative prosperity of different sectors during inflation. The relative rates of price and wage inflation will determine the relative changes in profits, which (on the assumption that most investment is financed by retained earnings) will set the relative growth rates. Thus inflation, except in the limiting case, will over the course of time bring about changes in the composition of the aggregate economy.

12 The picture can be very much improved as a representation of the modern economy by channeling profits, not directly to owners but to Wall Street, where banks, boards of directors, and financial institutions decide how much to retain, how much to invest, and how much to pay out in dividends. Then capitalist consumption will come out of distributed profits and realized capital gains, and savings will flow back to Wall Street in the form of bond and share purchases. This properly separates ownership and control, and shows the separation of financial and production decisions, the former dominating the latter. The model can also be modified to take account of worker savings, which, however, are empirically inconsequential.

13 Power, of course, is usually enhanced by efficiency, but the two are nevertheless quite distinct. Economic power ultimately rests on the ability to inflict a loss – the stick. A subsidiary form is the ability to bribe – the carrot. If economists paid as much attention to bribery and extortion as they do to marginal utility, we would be able to develop rough quantitive indices, by means of which one could sensibly discuss (and plan strategy to alter) the distribution of economic power in society.

References

Edgeworth, F. Y. 1970. "Theory of Distribution." *Papers Relating to Political Economy*. New York: Burt Franklin.

Goodwin, R. M. 1970. *Elementary Economics From the Higher Standpoint*. Cambridge: Cambridge University Press.

Harcourt, G. C. 1972. *Some Cambridge Controversies in the Theory of Capital*. Cambridge: Cambridge University Press.

Hollis, M., and Nell, E. 1975. *Rational Economic Man*. Cambridge: Cambridge University Press.

Lowe, A. 1965. *On Economic Knowledge*. New York: Harper & Row.

Schoeffler, S. 1957. *The Failures of Economics: A Diagnostic Study*. Cambridge, Mass.: Harvard University Press.

Sraffa, P. 1960. *Production of Commodities by Means of Commodities*. Cambridge: Cambridge University Press.

2

Robinson Crusoe and the secret of primitive accumulation

Stephen Hymer

Every living being is a sort of imperialist, seeking to transform as much as possible of the environment into itself and its seed. Bertrand Russell

This primitive accumulation plays in political economy about the same part as original sin in theology. Adam bit the apple, and thereupon sin fell on the human race. Its origin is supposed to be explained when it is told as an anecdote of the past. In times long gone by there were two sorts of people: one, the diligent, intelligent, and above all, frugal elite; the other, lazy rascals, spending their substance, and more, in riotous living. The legend of theological original sin tells us certainly how man came to be condemned to eat his bread in the sweat of his brow; but the history of economic original sin reveals to us that there are people to whom this is by no means essential. Never mind! Thus it came to pass that the former sort accumulated wealth, and the latter sort had at last nothing to sell except their skins. And from this original sin dates the poverty of the great majority that, despite its labor, has up to now nothing to sell but itself, and the wealth of the few that increases constantly although they have long ceased to work. Such insipid childishness is everyday preached to us in the defense of property . . . In actual history it is notorious that conquest, enslavement, robbery, murder, briefly force, play the great part. In the tender annals of political economy, the idyllic reigns from time immemorial . . . As a matter of fact, the methods of primitive accumulation are anything but idyllic. Karl Marx, *Capital* (1967), Vol. 1, Part 8, Chapter 26, "The Secret of Primitive Accumulation."

The solitary and isolated figure of Robinson Crusoe is often taken as a starting point by economists, especially in their analysis of international trade. He is pictured as a rugged individual – diligent, intelligent, and above all frugal – who masters nature through reason. But the actual story of Robinson Crusoe, as told by Defoe, is also one of conquest, slavery, robbery, murder, and force (Defoe, 1948). That this side of the story should be ignored is not at all surprising, "for in the tender annals of political economy the idyllic reigns from time immemorial." The contrast between the economist's Robinson Crusoe and the genuine one mirrors the contrast between the mythical description of international trade found in economics textbooks and the actual facts of what happens in the international economy.

The paradigm of non-Marxist international trade theory is the model of a hunter and fisher-

---

Stephen Hymer was Professor of Economics at the New School for Social Research until his death on February 2, 1974, in an automobile accident. Before his death he wrote, "I would like to thank Heidi Hartmann, Harry Magdoff, and Frank Roosevelt for their help. I have not seen the Buñuel movie of Robinson Crusoe but have been influenced by a secondhand account of it."

Note on primitive accumulation: The word *primitive* is here used in the sense of "belonging to the first age, period, or stage," i.e., of being "original rather than derivative," and not in the sense of "simple, rude, or rough." Marx's original term was "ursprüngliche akkumulation," and as Paul Sweezy suggests, it would have been better translated as "original" or "primary" accumulation. But it is too late to change current usage, and the word *primitive* should be interpreted in a technical sense, as in mathematics, where a *primitive* line or figure is a line or figure "from which some construction or reckoning begins." In economics primitive accumulation refers to the period from which capitalist accumulation springs. It was not simple, though it was rude and rough.

This article was first published in *Monthly Review*, 1971.

man who trade to their mutual benefit under conditions of equality, reciprocity, and freedom. But international trade (or, for that matter, interregional trade) is often based on a division between superior and subordinate rather than a division between equals; and it is anything but peaceful. It is trade between the center and the hinterland, the colonizers and the colonized, the masters and the servants. Like the relation of capital to labor, it is based on a division between higher and lower functions: one party does the thinking, planning, organizing; the other does the work. Because it is unequal in structure and reward it has to be established and maintained by force, whether it be the structural violence of poverty, the symbolic violence of socialization, or the physical violence of war and pacification.

I would like to go over the details of Crusoe's story – how, starting as a slave trader, he uses the surplus of others to acquire a fortune – in order to illustrate Marx's analysis of the capitalist economy, especially the period of primitive accumulation which was its starting point.

For capitalist accumulation to work, two different kinds of people must meet in the market (and later in the production process); on the one hand, owners of money eager to increase their capital by buying other people's labor power; on the other hand, free laborers unencumbered by precapitalist obligations or personal property. Once capitalism is on its legs, it maintains this separation and reproduces it on a continuously expanding scale. But a prior stage is needed to clear the way for the capitalist system and get it started – a period of primitive accumulation.

In the last part of Volume I of *Capital,* Marx sketched the historical process by which means of production were concentrated in the hands of the capitalist, leaving the worker no alternative but to work for him. He showed how a wage labor force was created through the expropriation of the agricultural population and he traced the genesis of the industrial capitalist to, among other things, the looting of Africa, Asia, and America "in the rosy dawn of the era of capitalist production." In the story of Robinson Crusoe, Defoe describes how a seventeenth-century Englishman amassed capital and organized a labor force to work for him in Brazil and in the Caribbean. Of course what Crusoe established was not a market economy such as emerged in England but a plantation and settler economy such as was used by capitalism in the non-European world. It might therefore be called the story of primitive underdevelopment.

Defoe (1659–1731) was particularly well placed to observe and understand the essence of the rising bourgeoisie and the secrets of its origins. The son of a London butcher, he was engaged in the business of a hosiery factor and a commission merchant until he went bankrupt. During his life he wrote many essays and pamphlets on economics, discussing among other things, banks, road management, friendly and insurance societies, idiot asylums, bankruptcy, academies, military colleges, women's education, social welfare programs, and national workshops. He was one of the first writers to rely on the growing market of the middle class to earn his living (Robertson, 1933; Fitzgerald, 1954; Van Ghent, 1961; Novak, 1962; Watt, 1963; Macherey, 1966; Richetti, 1969).

Merchants' capital

Robinson Crusoe's story can be told in terms of a series of cycles, some running simultaneously, through which he accumulates capital. In the early days these take the form M-C-M, i.e., he starts off with money, exchanges it for commodities, and ends up with more money. In the later phases when he is outside the money economy, they take the form C-L-C, as he uses his stock of commodities to gain control over other people's labor and to produce more commodities, ending up with a small empire.

Robinson Crusoe was born in 1632. The son of a merchant, he could have chosen to follow the middle station of life and raise his fortune "by application and industry, with a life of ease and pleasure." Instead he chose to go to sea – partly for adventure, partly because of greed.

In his first voyage he starts off with £40 in "toys and trifles," goes to the Guinea coast (as mess-mate and companion of the captain whom he befriended in London), and comes back with five pounds nine ounces of gold worth £300. This is the first circuit of his capital. He leaves £200 of this sum in England with the captain's widow (the captain died soon after their return) and, using the remaining £100 as fresh capital, sets off on a second voyage as a Guinea trader in order to make more capital. Instead he meets with disaster. The ship is captured by Moors and he becomes a slave in North Africa. He escapes slavery in a boat taken from his master, accompanied by a fellow slave Xury, a black man, to whom he promises, "Xury, if you will be faithful to me, I'll make you a great man." Together they sail a thousand miles along the coast of Africa, until they are met and rescued by a Portuguese captain.

Fortunately for Robinson, there is honor among capitalists. The captain, who is on his way to Brazil, feels it would be unfair to take everything from Robinson and bring him to Brazil penniless. "I have saved your life on no other terms than I would be glad to be saved myself. . . When I carry you to Brazil, so great a way from your own country, if I should take from you what you have, you will be starved there, and then I only take away that life I have given."

Robinson of course does not tell the captain that he still has £200 in England. Instead, he sells the captain his boat (i.e., the boat he took when he escaped) and everything in it, *including Xury*. An African is an African, and only under certain conditions does he become a slave. Robinson has some pangs of guilt about selling "the poor boy's liberty who had assisted me so faithfully in procuring my own." However the captain offers to set Xury free in ten years if he turns Christian. "Upon this, and Xury saying he was willing to go to him, I let the captain have him" (for sixty pieces of eight). Commodities are things and cannot go to market by themselves. They have to be taken. If they are unwilling, they can be forced.

Robinson arrives in Brazil where he purchases "as much land that was uncured as my money would reach, and formed a plan for my plantation and settlement, and such a one as might be suitable to the stock which I proposed to myself to receive from England." He soon finds "more than before, I had done wrong in parting with my boy Xury," for he needed help and found there was "no work to be done, but by the labor of my hands."

He sends a letter to the widow in England through his Portuguese captain friend instructing that half of his £200 be sent to him in the form of merchandise. The captain takes the letter to Lisbon where he gives it to some London merchants who relay it to London. The widow gives the money to a London merchant who, "vesting this hundred pounds in English goods, such as the captain had writ for, sent them directly to him at Lisbon, and he brought them all safe to me to Brazil; among which, without my direction (for I was too young in my business to think of them), he had taken care to have all sorts of tools, ironwork, and utensils necessary for my plantation, and which were of great use to me."

The cargo arrives, bringing great fortune to Robinson. The Portuguese captain had used the £5 the widow had given him for a present to purchase and bring to Robinson, "a servant under bond for six years service, and would not accept of any consideration, except a little tobacco which I would have him accept, being of my own produce." Moreover, he is able to sell the English goods in Brazil "to a very great advantage" and the first thing he does is to buy a Negro slave and a second indentured servant.

This series of transactions presupposes an elaborate social network of capitalist intercommunications. The mythical Robinson is pictured as a self-sufficient individual, but much of the actual story, even after he is shipwrecked, shows him as a dependent man belonging to a larger whole and always relying on help and cooperation from others. The social nature of production turns out to be the real message of his story as we shall see again and again. There is no real paradox in this. To capitalism belong both the production of the most highly developed social relations in history and the production of the solitary individual.

Robinson now integrates himself into the community as a successful planter and accumulates steadily. But he cannot be content and soon leaves "the happy view I had of being a rich and thriving man in my new plantation, only to pursue a rash and immoderate desire of rising faster than the nature of the thing admitted."

The plantations in Brazil were short of labor, for "few Negroes were brought, and those excessive dear" since the slave trade at that time was not far developed and was controlled by royal monopolies of the kings of Spain and Portugal. Robinson had told some friends about his two voyages to the Guinea Coast and the ease of purchasing there "for trifles not only gold dust but Negroes in great numbers." (N.B. that the trifles listed are beads, toys, knives, scissors, hatchets, bits of glass, and the like – all but the first two are by no means trifles, as Robinson would soon find out.) These friends approached him in secrecy with a plan for outfitting a ship to get slaves from the Guinea Coast who would then be smuggled into Brazil privately and distributed among their own plantations. They asked Robinson to go as "supercargo in the ship to manage the trading part and offered [him] an equal share of the Negroes without providing any part of the stock."

Robinson accepts, and it is on this voyage that his famous shipwreck occurs. Years later, in the depths of isolation, he had cause to regret this decision which he views in terms of his original sin of "not being satisfied with the station wherein God and nature hath placed [him] . . ."

> What business had I to leave a settled fortune, a well-stocked plantation, improving and increasing, to turn supercargo to Guinea, to fetch Negroes, when patience and time would have so increased our stock at home that we could have bought them from those whose business it was to fetch them? And though it

had cost us something more, yet the difference of that price was by no means worth saving at so great a hazard.

In fact he comes out ahead for by the end of the story Robinson has succeeded in accumulating much faster than if he had remained content, for he adds a new fortune from his island economy to the growth of his plantation. True, he must suffer a long period of isolation, but in many ways his solitary sojourn represents the alienation suffered by all under capitalism – those who work and receive little as well as those like Robinson who accumulate and always must go on, go on.

Island economy: the pretrade situation

The key factors in Robinson Crusoe's survival and prosperity on his island in the sun are not his ingenuity and resourcefulness but the pleasant climate and the large store of embodied labor he starts out with. In thirteen trips to his wrecked ship he was able to furnish himself with many things, taking a vast array of materials and tools he never made but were still his to enjoy. These he uses to gain command over nature and over other men. Of chief importance in his initial stock of means of production is a plentiful supply of guns and ammunition, which give him decisive advantage in setting the terms of trade when his island economy is finally opened up to trade.

Table 1. *Items taken by Robinson Crusoe from the shipwreck*

Defense: ammunition, arms, powder, 2 barrels musket bullets, 5–7 muskets, large bag full of small shot
Food: biscuits, rum, bread, rice, cheese, goat flesh, corn, liquor, flour, cordials, sweetmeats, poultry feed, wheat and rice seed
Clothing: men's clothes, handkerchiefs, colored neckties, 2 pairs of shoes
Furniture and miscellaneous: hammock, bedding, pens, ink, paper, 3 or 4 compasses, some mathematical instruments, dials, perspectives, charts, books on navigation, 3 Bibles
Tools: carpenter's chest, 203 bags full of nails & spikes, a great screwjack, 1 or 2 dozen hatchets, grindstone, 2 saws, axe, hammer, 2 or 3 iron crows, 2 or 3 razors, 1 large scissors, fire shovel and tongs, 2 brass kettles, copper pots, gridiron
Raw materials: rigging, sails for canvas, small ropes, ropes and wire, ironwork, timber, boards, planks, 2–3 hundredweight of iron, 1 hundredweight of sheet lead
Animals: dog, 2 cats
Things he misses badly: ink, spade, shovel, needles, pins, thread, smoking pipe

Robinson himself is fully aware of the importance of his heritage (see Table 1). "What should I have done without a gun, without ammunition, without any tools to make anything or work with, without clothes, bedding, a tent, or any manner of coverings?" he asks. And "by making the most rational judgment of things every man may be in time master of every mechanic art. I had never handled a tool in my life, and yet in time, by labor, application, and contrivance, I wanted nothing but I could have made it, *especially if I had had the tools*" (emphasis added). A European is a European and it is only under certain conditions that he becomes a master. It was not their personal attributes that gave Robinson and other European adventurers their strength vis-à-vis non-Europeans but the equipment they brought with them, the power of knowledge made into objects. This material base was the result of a complicated social division of labor of which they were the beneficiaries not the creators.

His island is a rich one, again thanks in part to the activities of other people. He surveys it with little understanding since most of the plants were unfamiliar to him. He makes no independent discovery but finds certain familiar items – goats, turtles, fruits, lemons, oranges, tobacco, grapes – many of which I imagine could not have gotten there except if transplanted by previous visitors from other islands. His own discovery of agriculture is accidental. Among the things he rescued from the ship was a little bag which had once been filled with corn. Robinson seeing nothing in the bag but husks and dust, and needing it for some other purpose, shook the husks out on the ground. A month or so later, not even remembering he had thrown them there, he was "perfectly astonished" to find barley growing.

Conditioned by capitalist tradition, Crusoe tries to keep account of his activities and "while my ink lasted, I kept things very exact; but after that was gone, I could not, for I could not make any ink by any means I could devise." He draws up a cost-benefit analysis of his position, stating in it "very impartially like debtor and creditor, the comforts I enjoyed, against the miseries I suffered." He finds his day divided into three. It took him only about three hours going out with his gun, to get his food. Another portion of his day was spent in ordering, curing, preserving, and cooking. A third portion was spent on capital formation, planting barley and rice, curing raisins, building furniture and a canoe, and so forth.

This passion for accounting might seem to confirm the economist's picture of Robinson as the rational man par excellence, allocating his time efficiently among various activities in order to maximize utility. But then comes this astonishing observation, "But my time or labor was little worth, and so it was as well employed one way as another"! Contrary to the usual models of economic theory, Robinson Crusoe, producing only for use and not for exchange, finds that there is no scarcity and that labor has no value. The driving force of capitalism, the passion for accumulation vanished when he was alone. "All I could make use of was all that was valuable . . . The most covetous, griping miser in the world would have been cured of the vice of covetousness, if he had been in my case."

Robinson's own explanation of this phenomenon is mainly in terms of demand. Because he is alone, his wants are limited and satiated before he exhausts his available labor time:

> I was removed from all the wickedness of the world here. I had neither the lust of the flesh, the lust of the eye or the pride of life. I had nothing to covet; for I had all that I was now capable of enjoying. I was lord of the whole manor; or if I pleased, I might call myself king, or emperor over the whole country which I had possession of. There were no rivals. I had no competitor.

This is true as far as it goes, but it is one-sided. Robinson's greed went away because there were no people to organize and master. Marx's proposition was that surplus labor was the sole measure and source of capitalist wealth. Without someone else's labor to control, the capitalist's value system vanished; no boundless thirst for surplus labor arose from the nature of production itself; the goals of efficiency, maximization, and accumulation faded into a wider system of values.

Later, when Robinson's island becomes populated, the passion to organize and accumulate returns. It is only when he has no labor but his own to control that labor is not scarce and he ceases to measure things in terms of labor time. As Robinson's reference to the miser shows, it is not merely a question of the demand for consumption goods. The miser accumulates not for consumption but for accumulation, just as the purposeful man in the capitalist era, as Keynes noted, "does not love his cat, but his cat's kittens; nor, in truth, the kittens, but only the kittens' kittens, and so on forward forever to the end of cat-dom. For him jam is not jam unless it is a case of jam tomorrow and never jam today" (Keynes, 1963, p. 370). Money and capital are social relations representing social power over others. Regardless of what goes on in the minds of misers and capitalists when they look at their stock, it is power over people that they are accounting and accumulating, as they would soon find out if they, like Robinson, were left alone.

Robinson is partially aware of this when he meditates on the uselessness of gold on his island:

> I smiled to myself at the sight of this money. "O drug!" said I aloud, "what art thou good for? Thou art not worth to me, no not the taking off of the ground, one of those knives is worth all this heap; I have no manner of use for thee; e'en remain where thou art, and go to the bottom as a creature whose life is not worth saving." However, upon second thoughts, I took it away.

He thus negates the Mercantilist system which made a fetish out of gold, but does not fully pierce the veil of money to uncover the underlying basis of surplus labor – does not in his theories, that is; in his daily practice he is fully aware of the real basis of the economy. This shows up when he discusses the concept of Greed. In Robinson's eyes, his original sin is the crime of wanting to rise above his station instead of following the calling chosen for him by his father. Isolation and estrangement are his punishment, and he feels that his story should teach content to those "who cannot enjoy comfortably what God has given them." He feels guilty for violating the feudal institutions of status, patriarchy, and God. He does not consider that when he accumulates, he violates those whom he exploits – Xury, the Africans he sold into slavery, his indentured servants, and soon Friday and others. From the ideological point of view, Robinson is a transitional man looking backward and upward instead of forward and downward. This is why he learns nothing (morally speaking) from his loneliness. The miser is not in fact cured, the vice of covetousness easily returns.

Since the relationship of trade, accumulation, and exploitation is so crucial to understanding economics, we might dwell on it a little longer. The argument can be traced back to Aristotle, who felt that a self-sufficient community would not be driven by scarcity and accumulation, since natural wants were limited and could easily be satisfied with plenty of time left over for leisure. Such a community would practice the art of householding which has use value as its end. But Aristotle, an eyewitness to the growth of the market at its very first appearance, noted that there was another art of wealth getting – commercial trade – which had no limit, since its end was the accumulation of exchange value for its own sake. Aristotle was more interested in the effects of the rise of commerce than in its base and did not make the connection between exchange value and surplus labor. But it was there for all to see. The emergence of the market in ancient Athens was a by-product of its imperial expansion, the looting of territories liberated from the Persians, the collection of tribute and taxes from other Greek states for protection, and the forced diversion of the area's trade to Athens' port (French, 1964; Polyani, 1957).

Keynes, though analytically imprecise, glimpsed the same point in his article on "National Self-Sufficiency" (Keynes, 1934), where he instinctively saw that some withdrawal from international trade was necessary to make the life made possible by science pleasant and worthwhile. He wanted to minimize rather than maximize economic entanglements among nations so that we can be "our own masters" and "make our favorite experiments toward the ideal social republic of the future." He was all for a free exchange of ideas, knowledge, science, hospitality, and travel, "but let goods be home-spun whenever it is reasonably and commercially possible, and, above all let finance be primarily national." He knew that it was not invidious consumption that was the problem, but the desire to extend oneself by penetrating foreign markets with exports and investment, which in the end comes down to an attempt to transform as much as possible of the world into oneself and one's seed, i.e., imperialism.

To return to Robinson Crusoe. It is important to note that his isolation was accompanied not so much by loneliness as by fear. The first thing he did when he arrived on his beautiful Caribbean paradise was to build himself a fortress. It was only when he was completely "fenced and fortified" from all the world that he "slept secure in the night." His precautions during the first eleven years when he is completely alone are astonishing. Yet during these years he is in no danger from wild animals or any living thing. His chief problem comes from birds who steal his seeds. He deals with them with dispatch, shooting a few and then "I took them up and served them as we serve notorious thieves in England, viz., hanged them in chains for a terror to others." And, as we shall see in the next section, when signs of other human beings come to him, he does not run out with joy, ready to risk everything to hear a human voice after so many years in solitary confinement. Instead his fears and anxieties rise to a frenzied pitch, and he fences and fortifies himself more and more, withdrawing further and further into isolation.

Perhaps this is what one should expect from a man isolated for so long a period. But at times it seems to me that Defoe, in describing Robinson Crusoe, was not only talking about a man who by accident becomes isolated, but is presenting an allegory about the life of all men in capitalist society – solitary, poor, uncertain, afraid. The isolation is more intense in Robinson's mind than in his actual situation. For what comes out clearly, in encounter after encounter, is that whenever Robinson has to face another person he reacts with fear and suspicion. His isolation, in short, is no more nor less than the alienation of possessive individualism, repeated a million times in capitalist society, and in our days symbolized by the private civil-defense shelter protected from neighbors by a machine gun.

Opening up of trade: forming an imperial strategy

The opening up of his economy to the outside world does not come to Robinson Crusoe in the form of abstract prices generated in anonymous markets but in the form of real people with whom he must come to terms. After fifteen years on the island, he comes upon the print of a naked man's foot on the shore. His first reaction is fear. He was "terrified to the last degree, looking behind me at every two or three steps, mistaking every bush and tree, and fancying every stump at a distance to be a man." He goes to his retreat. "Never frightened hare fled to cover, or fox to earth, with more terror of mind, than I." From then on he lived "in the constant snare of the fear of man . . . a life of anxiety, fear and care."

He thinks of destroying his cattle enclosure, cornfield, and dwelling, "that they might not find such a grain there . . . and still be prompted to look further, in order to find out the persons inhabiting." He builds a second wall of fortifications, armed with seven muskets planted like a cannon and fitted "into frames that held them like a carriage, so that I could fire all the seven guns in two minutes' time. This wall I was many a weary month a-finishing and yet never thought myself safe till it was done." He pierces all the ground outside his wall with stakes or sticks so that in five or six years' time he had "a wood before my dwelling growing so monstrous thick and strong that it was indeed perfectly impassable; and no men of what kind soever would ever imagine that there was anything beyond it."

Three years after he sees the footprint, he comes across bones and other remains of cannibalism. (We leave aside the historical question of whether or not cannibalism was practiced by the Caribbeans. It is enough that Robinson thought so. European readiness to believe other people were cannibals, regardless of fact, plays the same role in determining trade patterns as the inter-European solidarity exhibited, for example, between the Portuguese captain and Robinson.) He withdrew further and "kept close within my circle for almost two years."

Gradually fear wears off, and he begins to come out more. But he proceeds cautiously. He does not fire his gun, for fear it would be heard, and he is always armed with a gun, two pistols, and a cutlass. At times he even thinks of attack, and builds a place from which he can "destroy some of these monsters in their cruel bloody entertainment and, if possible, save the victim they should bring hither to destroy." But then he thinks, "These people had done me no injury . . . and therefore it could not be just for me to fall upon them." He chastises the Spaniards for their barbarities in America "where they destroyed millions of these people . . . a mere butchery, a bloody and unnatural piece of cruelty, unjustifiable either to God or man; as for which the very name of a Spaniard is reckoned to be frightful and terrible to all people of humanity or of Christian compassion." He decides it is "not my business to meddle with them unless they first attacked me."

During the next few years he keeps himself "more retired than ever," seldom going from his cell. Fear "put an end to all invention and to all the contrivances I had laid for my future accommodations." He was afraid to drive a nail, or chop a stick of wood, or fire a gun, or light a fire for fear it would be heard or seen. He wants "nothing so much as a safe retreat," and finds it in a hidden grotto. "I fancied myself now like one of the ancient giants which were said to live in caves and holes in the rocks, where none could come at them." Yet even in this deep isolation, it is only people that he feared. With some parrots, cats, kids, and tame seafowl as pets, "I began to be very well contented with the life I led, if it might but have been secured from the dread of the savages."

In his twenty-third year he finally sights some of the Caribbeans who periodically visit the island. He first retreats to his fortifications; but, no longer "able to bear sitting in ignorance," he sets himself up in a safe place from which to observe "nine naked savages sitting round a small fire." Thoughts of "contriving how to circumvent and fall upon them the very next time" come once more to his mind and soon he is dreaming "often of killing the savages." His loneliness intensifies when one night he hears a shot fired from a distressed ship and next day finds a shipwreck. He longs for contact with Europeans. "O that there had been one or two, nay, or but one soul saved out of this ship, to have escaped to me, that I might have one companion, one fellow creature to have spoken to me and to have conversed with!"

His thoughts move from defense to offense. His moral misgivings about Spanish colonization recede into the background, and he begins to form an imperial strategy. The plan comes to him in a dream in which a captured savage escapes, runs to him, and becomes his servant. Awaking, "I made this conclusion, that my only way to go about an attempt for an escape was, if possible, to get a savage into my possession; and if possible it should be one of the prisoners." He has some fears about whether he can do this and some moral qualms about whether he should; but though "the thoughts of shedding human blood for my deliverance were terrible to me," he at length resolved "to get one of those savages into my hands, cost what it would."

About a year and a half later a group of about twenty or thirty Caribbeans come ashore. Luck is with him. One prisoner escapes, followed by only two men. "It came now very warmly upon my thoughts and indeed irresistibly, that now was my time to get me a servant, and perhaps a companion or assistant."

Robinson knocks down one of the pursuers and shoots a second. The rescued prisoner, cautious and afraid, approaches. "He came nearer and nearer, kneeling down every ten or twelve steps . . . At length he came close to me, and then he kneeled down again, kissed the ground, and laid his head upon the ground, and taking me by the foot, set my foot upon his head; this, it seems, was in token of swearing to be my slave forever." Robinson has his servant. An economy is born.

Colonization

Friday, tired from his ordeal, sleeps. Robinson evaluates his prize. The relationship they are about to enter into is an unequal and violent one. ("Violence," writes R. D. Laing in *The Politics of Experience,* "attempts to constrain the other's freedom, to force him to act in the way we desire, but with ultimate lack of concern, with indifference to the other's own existence or destiny.") It requires an ideological superstructure to sustain it and make it tolerable. Friday is an independent person with his own mind and will. But Robinson's rule depends upon the extent to which his head controls Friday's hand. To help himself in his daily struggle with Friday, Robinson begins to think of Friday not as a person but as a sort of pet, a mindless body that is obedient and beautiful. ("The use made of slaves and of tame animals is not very different; for both with their bodies minister to the needs of life." Aristotle, *The Politics.) The following* is a verbatim quote of his description of Friday, except for the substitution of "she" for "he," "her" for "him." This is not done to suggest homosexuality but to emphasize how rulers conceive of the ruled only as bodies to minister to their needs. (To quote Aristotle again, "the male is by nature superior, and the female inferior; and the one rules, and the other is ruled.")

> She was a comely, hansome woman, perfectly well made, with straight strong limbs, not too large, tall and well-shaped, and, as I reckon, about twenty-six years of age. She had a very good countenance, not a fierce and surly aspect, but seemed to have something very manly in her face and yet she had all the sweetness and softness of a European in her countenance too, especially when she smiled. Her hair was long and black, not curled like wool; her forehead very high and large; and a great vivacity and sparkling sharpness in her eyes. The color of her skin was not quite black, but very tawny; and yet not of an ugly yellow, nauseous tawny, as the Brazilians and Virginians, and other natives of America are; but of a bright kind of a dun olive color that had in it something very agreeable, though not very easy to describe. Her face was round and plump; her nose small, not flat like the Negroes', a very good mouth, thin lips, and her fine teeth well set, and white as ivory.

Robinson has a gun, but he cannot rule by force alone if he wants Friday to be productive. He must socialize his servant to accept his subordinate position. Robinson is at a great advantage for he has saved the man's life, but a careful program is still necessary, going through several stages of development, before the servant internalizes the authoritarian relationship and is able to act "independently" in a "dependent" fashion. The parallels between Robinson's education of Friday, and the actual procedures of colonization used in the last two hundred years are striking.

Step 1. The first thing Robinson does is set the stage for discourse by giving himself and Friday names that are humiliating to Friday and symbolic of his indebtedness. "First I made him know his name should be Friday, which was the day I saved his life; I called him so for the memory of the time; I likewise taught him to say Master, and then let him know that was to be my name."

Step 2. Robinson further establishes relative status by covering Friday's nakedness with a pair of linen drawers (taken from the shipwreck) and a jerkin of goat's skin and a cap of hareskin he had made himself. He "was mighty well pleased to see himself almost as well clothed as his master."

Step 3. Robinson gives Friday a place to sleep between the two fortifications, i.e., a middle position, partly protected but outside the master's preserves. He sets up a burglar alarm so that "Friday could in no way come at me in the inside of my innermost wall without making so much noise in getting over that it must needs waken me," and takes other precautions such as taking all weapons into his side every night. Yet as Robinson says, these precautions were not really needed, "for never man had a more faithful, loving, sincere servant than Friday was to me; without passions, sullenness, or designs, perfectly obliged and engaged; his very affections were tied to me like those of a child to a father; and I dare say he would have sacrificed his life for the saving of mine upon any occasion whatsoever." The allocation of space helps remind Friday of his position and keep him subordinate.

Step 4. Friday is then given the skills necessary for his station and his duties, i.e., the ability to understand orders and satisfy Robinson's needs. "I . . . made it my business to teach him everything that was proper to make him useful, handy, and helpful; but especially to make him speak and understand me when I spoke."

Step 5. Next comes a crucial moment in which Robinson, through a cruel show of force, terrifies poor Friday into complete submission. Robinson takes Friday out and shoots a kid with his gun. (He is no longer afraid of being heard.)

> The poor creature, who had at a distance indeed seen me kill the savage, his enemy, but did not know or could imagine how it was done, was sensibly surprised . . . He did not see the kid I had shot at or perceive I had killed it, but ripped up his waistcoat to feel if he was not wounded, and as I found presently, thought I was resolved to kill him, for he came and kneeled down to me, and, embracing my knees, said a great many things I did not understand; but I could easily see the meaning was to pray me not to kill him.

In this ritual death and rebirth, Friday learns the full extent of Robinson's power over him. Robinson then kills various animals, and teaches Friday "to run and fetch them" like a dog. But he takes care that Friday never sees him load the gun, so that he remains ignorant of the fact that you have to put in ammunition.

Step 6. The first stage of initiation is completed, Robinson can move on to establishing the social division of labor on a more subtle base. He teaches Friday to cook and bake, and "in a little time Friday was able to do all the work for me, as well as I could do it for myself." Then Robinson marks out a piece of land "in which Friday not only worked very willingly and very hard, but did it cheerfully." Robinson explains that it was for corn to make more bread since there were now two of them. Friday, by himself, discovers the laws of property and capitalist distribution of income in fully mystified form. "He appeared very sensible of that part, and let me know that he thought I had much more labor upon me on his account than I had for myself, and that he would work the harder for me, if I would tell him what to do."

Step 7: Graduation. Robinson now instructs Friday in the knowledge of the true God. This takes three years, during which Friday raises such difficult questions that Robinson for a time withdraws, realizing that one cannot win by logical argument alone, and only divine revelation can convince people of Christianity. Finally, success. "The savage was now a good Christian." The two become more intimate, Robinson tells Friday his story and at long last "let him into the mystery, for such it was to him, of gunpowder and bullet and taught him how to shoot." Robinson gives Friday a knife and a hatchet and shows him the boat he was planning to use to escape.

Step 8: Eternal Policeman. Even after granting independence, Robinson cannot trust Friday. The master can never rest secure. One day, while watching the mainland from the top of a hill on the island, Robinson observes

> an extraordinary sense of pleasure appeared on Friday's face . . . and a strange eagerness, as if he had a mind to be in his own country again; and this observation of mine put a great many thoughts into me, which made me at first not so easy about my new man Friday as I was before; and I made no doubt but that if Friday could get back to his own nation again, he would not only forget all his religion, but all his obligation to me; and would be forward enough to give his countrymen an account of me, and come back, perhaps with a hundred or two of them, and make a feast upon me, at which he might be as merry as he used to be with those of his enemies, when they were taken in war.

Robinson continuously pumps Friday to see if he could uncover any cracks; then he feels guilty over his suspicion. Imperialism knows no peace.

Partnership and expanded reproduction

For roughly ten years, between the time he first saw the print of a foot in the sand until he met Friday, Robinson Crusoe led a life of fear, anxiety, and care during which time his productive activities were reduced to a minimum and he scarcely dared to venture outside the narrow confines of his strongholds. When Friday comes, he becomes expansive again, teaching, building, accumulating. Though no mention is made of accounting, one can deduce that labor again became valuable, for Robinson is once more purposeful, and interested in allocation and efficiency, as he orders, causes, gives Friday to do one thing or another, instructs him, shows him, gives him directions, makes things familiar to him, makes him understand, teaches him, lets him see, calls him, heartens him, beckons him to run and fetch, sets him to work, makes him build something, etc., etc. Through his social relation with Friday, he becomes an economic man. Friday becomes labor and he becomes capital – innovating, organizing, and building an empire.

About three years after Friday arrives, Robinson's twenty-seventh year on the island, an opportunity for enlargement comes. Twenty-one savages and three prisoners come ashore. Robinson divides the arms with Friday and they set out to attack. On the way, Robinson again has doubts as to whether it was right "to go and dip my hands in blood, to attack people who had neither done or intended me any wrong." "Friday," he observes, "might justify it, because he was a declared enemy, and in a state of war with those very particular people; and it was lawful for him to attack them," but, as he could not say the same for himself, he resolves unilaterally for both of them not to act unless "something offered that was more a call to me than yet I knew of."

The call comes when he discovers one of the victims is a white man and he becomes "enraged to the highest degree." As it turns out, the prisoner is a Spaniard; given what Robinson had previously said about Spanish colonial policy, one might have thought he would have some doubts about what was lawful. But he does not, and along with Friday, attacks – killing seventeen and routing four. (Friday does most of the killing, in part because he "took his aim so much better" than Robinson, in part because Robinson was directing and Friday doing.) The Spaniard is rescued and they find another victim in a boat who turns out to be Friday's father, his life luckily saved because his fellow captive was white.

Now they were four. Robinson has an empire which he rules firmly and justly with a certain degree of permissiveness and tolerance.

> My island was now peopled, and I thought myself very rich in subjects; and it was a merry reflection, which I frequently made, how like a king I looked. First of all, the whole country was my own property, so that I had an undoubted right of dominion. Second, my

people were perfectly subjected. I was absolute lord and lawgiver; they all owed their lives to me, and were ready to lay down their lives, if there had been occasion of it for me. It was remarkable, too, we had but three subjects, and they were of three different religions. My man Friday was a Protestant, his father was a pagan and a cannibal, and the Spaniard was a Papist. However I allowed liberty of conscience throughout my dominions.

The period of primitive accumulation is over. Robinson now has property. It is not based on his previous labor, but on his fortunate possession of arms. Though his capital comes into the world dripping blood from every pore, his ownership is undisputed. Friday was not a lazy rascal spending his subsistence and more in riotous living, yet in the end he still has nothing but himself, while the wealth of Robinson Crusoe increases constantly although he has long ceased to work.

With time, more people arrive on his island. Robinson shrewdly uses his monopoly of the means of production to make them submit to his rule. As the empire grows, its problems become more complex. But Robinson is ever resourceful in using terror, religion, frontier law, and the principle of delegated authority to consolidate his position and produce a self-reproducing order.

Robinson learns that there are fourteen more Spaniards and Portuguese staying with the Caribbeans, "who lived there at peace indeed with the savages." They had arms but no powder and no hope of escape, for they had "neither vessel, or tools to build one, or provisions of any kind." Robinson of course has the missing ingredients for their rescue, but how can he be sure he will be paid back? "I feared mostly their treachery and ill usage of me, if I put my life in their hands, for that gratitude was no inherent virtue in the nature of man; nor did men always square their dealings by the obligations they had received so much as they did by the advantages they expected."

Robinson cannot depend on the law to guard his property. Instead he uses religion. Europeans do not require so elaborate a socialization procedure as Friday because they have come by education, tradition, and habit to look upon private property as a self-evident law of nature. The Spaniard and Friday's father are to go to where the other Europeans are staying. They would then sign a contract, "that they should be absolutely under my leading, as their commander and captain; and that they should swear upon the Holy Sacraments and the Gospel to be true to me and to go to such Christian country as that I should agree to, and no other; and to be directed wholly and absolutely by my orders." Robinson converts their debt to him into an obligation towards God. Thus men are ruled by the products of their mind.

The trip is postponed for a year, while Robinson's capital stock is expanded so that there will be enough food for the new recruits. The work process is now more complicated because of the increase in numbers. A vertical structure separating operations, coordination, and strategy is established on the basis of nationality – a sort of multinational corporation in miniature. "I marked out several trees which I thought fit for our work, and I set Friday and his father to cutting them down; and then I caused the Spaniard, to whom I had imparted my thought on that affair, to oversee and direct their work."

When the harvest is in, the Spaniard and Friday's father are sent out to negotiate. While they are away, an English ship arrives at the island. Robinson is filled with indescribable joy at seeing a ship "manned by [his] own countrymen, and consequently friends." Yet at the same time, "some secret doubts hung about [him]," for perhaps they were thieves and murderers. This we have seen is a typical reaction of Robinson Crusoe to other people; it is a prudent attribute in a society of possessive individuals where all are the enemy of each. *Caveat emptor.*

Some of the crew come ashore with three prisoners. When the prisoners are left unguarded, Robinson approaches them: "I am a man, an Englishman, and disposed to assist you, you see; I have one servant only; we have arms and ammunition; tell us freely, can we serve you?" The three prisoners turn out to be the captain of the ship, his mate, and one passenger. The others are mutineers, of whom the captain says, "There were two desperate villains among them that it was scarce safe to show any mercy to"; but if they were secured, he believed "all the rest would return to their duty."

The charges being laid, a quick decision and verdict is reached. Robinson sides with authority. The captain offers a generous contract to Robinson: "Both he and the ship, if recovered, should be wholly directed and commanded by me in everything; and if the ship was not recovered, he would live and die with me in what part of the world soever I would send him; and the other two men the same." Robinson asks for much less: recognition of his undisputed authority while they are on the island, free passage to England for himself and Friday if the ship is recovered.

The men who brought the captain ashore are attacked. The two villains are summarily executed in the first round, the rest are made prisoners or allowed to join the captain and Robinson. More men are sent to shore from the ship, and are soon captured. One is made prisoner, the others are told Robinson is governor of the island and that he would engage for their pardon if they helped capture the ship. The ship is seized with only one life lost, that of the new captain. Robinson, still posing as governor, interviews the five prisoners and hearing the "full account of their villainous behavior to the captain, and how they had run away with the ship and were preparing to commit further robberies," offers them the choice of being left on the island or being taken to England in chains to be hanged. They choose the island and Robinson is so much the richer. Laws make criminals and criminals make settlers. In a repeat of his lesson to the birds, Robinson orders the captain "to cause the new captain who was killed to be hanged at the yardarm, that these men might see him."

On the 19th of December, 1686, twenty-eight years and two months after his arrival, Robinson goes on board the ship, taking with him his great goatskin cap, his umbrella, one of his parrots, and the money he had taken off the ship. He also takes Friday but does not wait for the return of Friday's father and the Spaniards. Instead he leaves a letter for them with the prisoners being left behind, after making them "promise to treat them in common with themselves."

He returns to civilization and discovers capital's power for self-sustaining growth. His trustees

> had given in the account of the produce of my part of the plantation to the procurator fiscal, who had appropriated it, in case I never came to claim it, one third to the king, and two thirds to the monastery of St. Augustine, to be expended for the benefit of the poor and for the conversion of Indians to the Catholic faith; but for that if I appeared, or anyone for me, to claim the inheritance, it should be restored: only that the improvements, or annual production, being distributed to charitable uses, could not be restored.

He was thus a rich man, "master all on a sudden of about £5,000 sterling in money, and had an estate, as I might well call it, in Brazil, of about a thousand pounds a year, as sure as an estate of lands in England."

He also had his island to which he returns in 1694. He learns how the Spaniards had trouble with the villains when they first returned but eventually subjected them, of their battles with the Caribbeans, "of the improvement they made upon the island itself and of how five of them made an attempt upon the mainland, and brought away eleven men and five women prisoners, by which, at my coming, I found about twenty young children on the island." Robinson brings them supplies, a carpenter, and a smith and later sent seven women "such as I found proper for service or for wives to such as would take them."

Before he leaves the island, he reorganizes it on a sound basis. Dividing it into parts, he reserves to himself the property of the whole, and gives others such parts respectively as they agreed upon. As to the Englishmen, he promised to send them some women from England, "and the fellows proved very honest and diligent after they were mastered and had their properties set apart for them." With property and the family firmly established, the ground is clear for steady growth.

Moral

We may stop at this point and consider the very high rate of return earned by Robinson on his original capital of 40. It cannot be said that he worked very hard for his money, but he was certainly a great organizer and entrepreneur, showing extraordinary capacity to take advantage of situations and manage other people. He suffered the pains of solitude and the vices of greed, distrust, and ruthlessness, but he ended up with "wealth all around me" and Friday – "ever proving a most faithful servant upon all occasions."

The allegory of Robinson Crusoe gives us better economic history and better economic theory than many of the tales told by modern economics about the national and international division of labor. Economics tends to stay in the market place and worry about prices. It has more to say about how Robinson's sugar relates to his clothing than how he relates to Friday. To understand how capital produces and is produced, we must leave the noisy sphere of the market where everything takes place on the surface and enter into the hidden recesses of the factory and corporation, where there is usually no admittance except on business.

Defoe's capitalist is transported to a desert island outside the market system, and his relations to other people are direct and visible. Their secret of capital is revealed, namely, that it is based on other people's labor and is obtained through force and illusion. The birth certificate of Robinson's capital is not as bloody as that of many other fortunes, but its coercive nature is clear.

The international economy of Robinson's time, like that of today, is not composed of equal partners but is ordered along class lines. Robinson occupies one of the upper-middle levels of the pyramid. (The highest levels are in the capitals of Europe.) Captains, merchants, and planters are his peer group. With them he exchanges on the basis of fraternal collaboration. (Arab captains excepted.) They teach him, rescue him, do business for him, and keep him from falling beneath his class. He in turn generally regards them as honest and plain-dealing men, sides with them against their rebellious subordinates, and is easy with them in his bargaining. Towards whites of lower rank he is more demanding. If they disobey, he is severe; but if they are loyal, he is willing to share some booty and delegate some authority. Africans and Caribbeans are sold, killed, trained, or used as wives by his men, as the case may be. About the white indentured servants, artisans, etc., little is said by Defoe in this story.

The contradictions between Robinson and other members of the hierarchy give the story its dynamics. He is forever wrestling with the problem of subordinating lower levels and trying to rise above his own. The fact that he does not see it this way but prefers to make up stories about himself makes no difference. He denies the conflict between himself and Friday by accepting Friday's mask of willing obedience. And he conceives of his greed as a crime against God instead of against man. But his daily life shows that his social relations are antagonistic and that he knows it.

In the last analysis, however, the story is only partly dialectical. We hear only of how Robinson perceives the contradictions and how he resolves them. In this work of fiction he is always able to fuse two into one. In actual life one divides into two, and the system develops beyond the capitalist's fantasy of proper law and order. Economic science also needs the story of Friday's grandchildren.

References

Defoe, D. 1948. *Robinson Crusoe*. New York: Modern Library.

Fitzgerald, B. 1954. *Daniel Defoe*. London: Decker and Warburg.

French, A. 1964. *The Growth of the Athenian Economy*. London: Routledge & Kegan Paul.

Keynes, J. M. 1963. "Economic Possibilities for our Grandchildren," in *Essays in Persuasion*. New York: W. W. Norton.

1934. "National Self-Sufficiency," *Yale Review*.

Laing, R. D. 1967. *The Politics of Experience*. New York: Pantheon Books.

Macherey, P. 1966. *Pour une Théorie de la Production litteraire*. Paris: François Maspero.

Marx, K. 1967. *Capital*. 3 vols. New York: International Publishers.

Novak, E. M. 1962. *Economics and the Fiction of Daniel Defoe*. Berkeley, Calif.: University of California Press.

Polyani, K., et al. 1957. *Trade and Markets in the Early Empires*. New York: Free Press.

Richetti, J. 1969. *Popular Fiction Between Defoe and Richardson*. Oxford: Clarendon Press.

Robertson, H. M. 1933. *Aspects of the Rise of Economic Individualism*. Cambridge: Cambridge University Press.

Van Ghent, D. 1961. *The English Novel*. New York: Harper Torchbook.

Watt, I. 1963. *The Rise of the Novel*. New York: Peregrin Books.

Part II

The Cambridge criticisms

3

A postmortem on the neoclassical "parable"

Donald J. Harris

Introduction

Recent controversies in capital theory have centered around a number of related issues concerning, for instance, the meaning and measurement of *capital,* the problem of *reswitching* of techniques of production and *capital reversal,* the significance, if any, to be attached to the neoclassical propositions that the equilibrium rate of profits in a capitalist economy is equal to the social rate of return to saving or equal to the "marginal product of capital" (Bhaduri, 1969; Dobb, 1970; Robinson, 1970; Harcourt, 1972). Some of those standing on the sidelines tend to dismiss this whole debate as a matter of meaningless formalism. Indeed, the terms on which the debate is conducted sometimes appear to be rather like those of medieval scholastic discussions concerning the number of angels that could stand on the head of a pin. But to dismiss the substance of the recent debate as a meaningless matter would be a serious mistake. Underlying it are deep and far-reaching issues in economic theory going back in time to the classical economists and which have reappeared from time to time in different forms.[1]

The central theoretical problem which lies at the root of these debates has two sides, one qualitative, the other quantitative. On the *qualitative* side is the question of what is the nature and origin of profits in a capitalist economy. On the *quantitative* side is the question of what determines the relative shares of profits and wages (or of capitalists and workers) in the net product and hence the magnitude of the overall rate of profits.[2] These two sides are quite clearly interlinked, though in any particular set of answers to the quantitative question the links with the qualitative side may not be made explicit nor be sharply drawn. There is nevertheless within any theory of distribution, *qua* theory, a fairly well defined set of answers to both of these questions, those answers being quite different as between one theory and another.

In the history of economic thought there have been two major and opposing sets of answers to these questions. One conceives of profits (as well as interest and rent) as a surplus originating in production, that is, as a difference between the output produced and the "necessary costs" of maintaining the laborers during the production period and replacing the worn out means of production. This difference accrues to the owners of property on account of their monopoly of ownership of the means of production and control over the use of labor in production. The other conceives of profits as the return to a factor of production, imputed to the services of that factor in accordance with the *relative scarcity* of the factor and the technology governing its use. The former conception is found in the work of the classical economists (chiefly Ricardo) and in Marxian theory. An earlier version, as applied specifically to agricultural production, is found also in the work of the physiocrats. The latter conception is found in neoclassical theory as developed by Jevons, Walras, Wicksell, J. B. Clark, among others. The debate regarding these two conceptions and the opposing elements involved in them emerge rather sharply in the work of Bohm-Bawerk.

Associated with these different conceptions are various views on the nature and meaning of *capital* as a category in the analysis of capitalist production. In the neoclassical view, the con-

This chapter was originally distributed as Memorandum No. 165, Research Memoranda Series, Center for Research in Economic Growth, Stanford University, November 1973. The last section is reprinted from Harris, D. J. (1975), "The Theory of Economic Growth: A Critique and Reformulation," *American Economic Review*, Papers and Proceedings, May, 65: 329–37.

cept of capital is tied to the use of *round-about methods of production* and the associated passage of time between application of physically specified inputs (*capital goods* and labor) and the subsequent flow of output. Since such methods of production enhance the productivity of a given quantity of labor (otherwise those methods would never be adopted) it is possible to seek to attribute the extra output to the quantity of the extra inputs (which may be only the extra time spent in using the round-about method). This difference in output, in this view, constitutes the return to capital as a factor of production or, in a related view, the reward of waiting.

The classical and Marxian theories assume that there are round-about methods which enhance the productivity of labor. The existence of such methods is regarded as part of the description of the technical conditions of production in any society. Beyond this, and as an essential condition of *capitalist* society, capital is conceived to be *a property relation,* a sum of exchangeable value tied up in means of production, the ownership of which enables the capitalist to employ propertyless laborers in production and reap the difference between the net product and the amount paid out as wages. The clearest case of this conception is that of the simplest type of agricultural production, say, corn growing, where the capitalist farmer advances the corn requirements of the laborer for subsistence (the *wages fund*), the laborer being unable in his propertyless state to provide this for himself, and reaps the difference (excluding rent, which the capitalist pays to the landlord, and interest on *borrowed* finance) at the end of the harvest.

The recurrence of the debate on these questions at this time reflects the fact that the internal contradictions in the neoclassical theory have never been effectively resolved, despite its considerable elaboration in the interim into a complex formal system. In other words, it reflects the fact that there continue to be inherent logical weaknesses in certain aspects of the neoclassical approach to the problem. One of these aspects, the one which has been seized upon in the recent debate, involves the application of the marginal productivity theory of pricing of factors (or of the services of such factors) to the quantitative problem of explaining aggregate income distribution (so-called factor-shares) in a capitalist economy.[3] It is in the specific form of the marginal productivity theory that the conception of different factor returns as reflecting relative factor scarcities and technical conditions of production is embodied. It was thought that this conception would carry over to an interpretation of capital as a factor of production, on the same footing as labor, and of profits as a return to such a factor. Indeed it was felt that this transition could be made logically and without hitch from one situation to the other and back again, because the interpretation of capital as a factor of production was presumed to be merely a special and convenient instance of a more general case involving production with many different *capital goods,* or many factors of production, as many as one wished to assume.[4]

The aggregate production function was the particular construction developed for conveying the neoclassical conception of profits as reflecting the relative scarcity and technical productivity of the factor capital. In recent times it has been reconstituted by Samuelson in the form of a "parable" utilizing the concept of a "surrogate production function" (Samuelson, 1962).[5] It is this construction with which I am dealing here. The outcome of the recent debate has been to show that this construction is based on very weak foundations. Indeed, some go so far as to suggest that the whole analytical structure of marginal productivity theory, insofar as it purports to provide a theory of relative shares and of the rate of profits in a capitalist economy, has come crashing down (Garegnani, 1970). This outcome, however one views its actual dimensions, is perhaps the best that could have happened under the circumstances. It clears the air and makes it possible now to return to the basic questions and issues and to the Classical and Marxian manner of treating them.[6]

In what follows, I examine first the internal structure and meaning of the neoclassical parable taken by itself. To appreciate the full meaning of this construction, however, one must situate it in its broader theoretical context. Accordingly, I go on to show how the parable fits into the framework of a specifically neoclassical theory of growth and distribution. The main elements of the recent theoretical critique of this construction are then presented. Some broad conclusions are drawn in the last section, and an alternative approach to analysis of the substantive problem is sketched.

It must be emphasized that I am concerned throughout with *theoretical* considerations, specifically with the theoretical structure and foundations of the neoclassical parable, and *not* with problems of empirical application and testing.[7] Suffice it to say that the analytical structure of the neoclassical conception as presented here has been applied to the study of a wide range of problems at both a theoretical and empirical level. These studies relate to problems of the labor market, the demand for capital and investment, the optimal rate of saving, economic stagnation in underdeveloped economies, the sources of economic growth, the economic effects and requirements of government policy regarding all of these matters, international comparisons of income distribution and factor prices, and the economic history of capitalist economies. Many such studies exist and are easily accessible to the interested observer. It should be clear that any assessment of the neoclassical conception at the level of its analytical structure must have direct consequences for accepting or rejecting its application at the level of such studies.

The production function and distribution

The neoclassical parable is set out in terms of an economy which produces a single commodity, say, corn, using labor and stocks of corn as capital good. At the center of the parable is the production function for corn or the surrogate production function:

$$Y = F(K, L) \tag{1}$$

which relates output of corn Y to inputs of corn-as-capital-good K and labor L.[8] Production is assumed to be subject to constant returns to scale (F is linear homogeneous). Because of this we can rewrite (1) per unit of labor as

$$y = f(k);\ y = Y/L,\ k = K/L \tag{2}$$

The function $f(\cdot)$ is continuously differentiable with positive and diminishing marginal products of the factors. In particular, a well-behaved production function satisfies the conditions (Inada, 1965):

$$\begin{aligned} &f(0) = 0; && f(\infty) = \infty \\ &f'(k) > 0; && f''(k) < 0 \\ &\lim_{k\to 0} f'(k) = \infty; && \lim_{k\to\infty} f'(k) = 0 \end{aligned} \tag{3}$$

The full significance of these conditions will appear subsequently. For the moment their meaning should be clear: it is always possible to find techniques for producing more (or less) output of corn per man by adding to (or reducing) the stock of corn relative to labor (the corn–labor ratio) no matter what the size of that stock is, short of infinity.

The preceding describes the available technology. Given this technology and facing competitive markets with given price of output, wage rate of labor w, and rental rate of the capital good r (which, in this context, is the same as the rate of profit), firms choose that technique of production (a corn–labor ratio corresponding to a point on the production function) which maximizes profits for the firm (minimizes costs). This requires that in equilibrium that technique is chosen at which the marginal product of each input equals its price. We therefore have the equilibrium conditions

$$r = \partial Y/\partial K = f'(k) \tag{4}$$

$$w = \partial Y/\partial L = f(k) - f'(k)k \tag{5}$$

By combining Equations (2), (4), and (5), we get

$$y = f(k) = w + rk \tag{6}$$

Thus, payment of the factors according to their marginal products automatically exhausts the total product, which is in keeping with Euler's theorem.

The marginal product conditions (4) and (5) express in this context the profit maximizing (or cost minimizing) criterion for choice of technique that would be observed by each and every producer operating in competitive markets. Of course, under competitive conditions, the prices w and r are *given* to the producers. But, from the point of view of the economy as a whole, there is still a question of how these variables are determined. We may express this point another way by saying that Equations (4) and (5) by themselves are sufficient to determine only two of the three variables, w, r, k. One of these variables (or a ratio of two of them, say, the wage–rental ratio w/r) must be given independently in terms of additional equation(s).

Note that it is at this point that certain analytical complications are being suppressed due to the assumption that there is only one capital good which is the same commodity as the output. In a model of production with many capital goods, if we continue to maintain the neoclassical assumption of a well-behaved production function with the different capital goods as inputs, then there is a marginal product for each of the capital goods taken separately in each line of production. The competitive equilibrium condition expressing the profit-maximizing choice of technique is that the money value of the marginal product (which is the marginal product times the price of output) of each type of capital good is equal to the money rental of the capital good (which is the price of the capital good times the rate of profit) and is the same in all lines. Thus the connection between the marginal product of the individual capital goods and the rate of profit is indirect: it goes by way of the prices which themselves depend on the rate of profit. When there is only one produced commodity which serves as capital good the situation becomes quite different. For then the relative price of this commodity is unity (it exchanges one to one against itself). Prices, therefore, drop out of the marginal product condition and, there being only one capital good, only one such condition correspondingly exists. A direct relation is thereby established between the marginal product of the capital good, which is a purely technological datum, and the rate of profit.[9] The marginal product of the capital good is in turn uniquely related to the stock of the capital good per man due to the assumptions concerning the production function. It follows that there is a one-to-one correspondence between the stock of the capital good and the rate of profit.

At a given rate of profit, one technique is chosen. At a different rate of profit, corresponding to a different equilibrium position for the economy as a whole, the technique chosen, and hence the corn–labor ratio, would be different. We can derive from the production function and the marginal-product conditions the exact relations that would prevail among the wage rate, profit rate and quantity of the capital good per man in different equilibria. Specifically, by differentiating Equations (4) and (5) we get

$$dr/dk = f''(k) < 0 \tag{7}$$

$$dw/dk = -f''(k)k > 0 \tag{8}$$

which give the slopes of the equilibrium relations, the signs of which reflect the assumptions governing the production function. These relations are graphed in Figures 3.1 and 3.2. Associated with any corn–labor ratio is a unique set of factor prices and vice versa. An increase (decrease) in the quantity of one factor relative to the other is associated with a lower (higher) relative price of that factor.

We can combine the two relations (4) and (5) to get a relation between the wage and profit rates that would prevail in different equilibria. By virtue of the Inada conditions (3), $r = f'(k)$ is a single valued function and therefore has an inverse such that

$$k = k(r);\ k' < 0 \tag{9}$$

Substituting (9) and (4) into (5) gives

$$w = f[k(r)] - rk(r) \tag{10}$$

This is the *wage–profit frontier* corresponding to the given technical conditions. A frontier such as this, giving the wage and profit rates consistent with the given technology under competitive conditions, could be computed from any technology in which any number of commodities (not just one) are produced by themselves and labor (Sraffa, 1960).[10] Because of the special conditions underlying this particular frontier, however, certain special results follow. Specifically, from differentiation of Equation (10) (or from dividing Equation (8) by (7)) it follows that

$$-(dw/dr) = k, \tag{11}$$

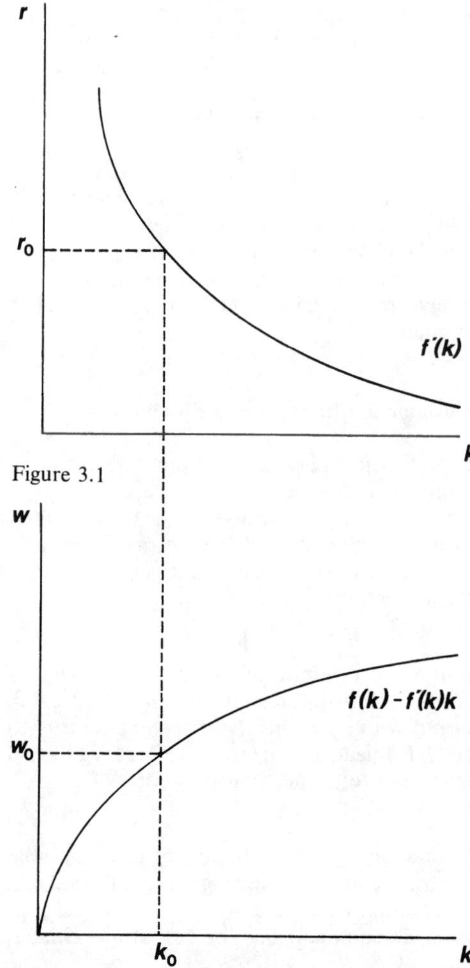

Figure 3.1

Figure 3.2

so that the absolute value of the slope of the frontier at any point on that frontier is equal to the quantity of the capital good per man. Furthermore, after multiplying Equation (11) by r/w we get

$$-\frac{r}{w}\frac{dw}{dr} = \frac{rk}{w} = \pi \tag{12}$$

which says that the elasticity of the frontier at any point is equal to the ratio of total profits per man and wages per man or the relative share π of profits and wages in the net product.[11]

Thus the parable tells us that, knowing only the quantity of the capital good per man and the technology, we can find from the frontier the corresponding wage and profit rates that would rule under competitive conditions. The elasticity of the frontier at that point gives the relative share of profits and wages. The distribution of income is therefore completely determined by technology and relative factor endowments. An increase (decrease) in the quantity of one factor relative to the other lowers (raises) its price. The distribution of income varies accordingly, depending on the particular form of the technology, that is, depending on the "elasticity of substitution" (Allen, 1967, Chapt. 3; Hicks, 1936).[12] In this way, the analysis incorporates the argument that relative factor prices reflect relative scarcity of the different factors and the amount which each factor gets from the national product is determined by technology and relative factor endowments.[13]

All of this story is true, meaning logically consistent, for a one-commodity world, that is, a world in which only one commodity is produced. Beyond this, it is claimed that this story can be used as a parable, or a stand-in, for a more complex world in which many commodities are produced and there are many different capital goods. The production function, it is argued, can serve as a *surrogate* for the relations which prevail in this sort of world.[14]

On the face of it, given the very special assumptions on which the parable is constructed – the one-commodity assumption is especially severe – one might be tempted to dismiss the parable as simply uninteresting, if not irrelevant. As Joan Robinson has suggested in this connection, it is like putting the rabbit into the hat in full view of the audience and then pulling it out again. Suppose, however, that we agree to treat it seriously as a theoretical construct. We might then examine to what extent, if at all, the relations which hold in the parable world can be said to represent the relations in a more complex world. One need not thereby accept the conception of theory as "parable" or "fairy tale."[15] Instead, it is possible to view the preceding formulation as a first approximation based on simplifying assumptions. Further *theoretical* analysis then needs to be carried out through introducing the relevant complications and checking to see whether the essential propositions of the parable continue to hold. The implications of introducing some of these complications form the chief basis of the recent critique of the neoclassical parable. The main elements of this critique are presented in later sections. Before going on to that, we consider in the next section how the parable fits into the broader context of the neoclassical theory of growth and distribution.

The neoclassical theory of growth

Is it possible to have steady growth with full employment in a capitalist economy? This is the question, posed in recent times by Harrod (1948), to which the neoclassical theory of growth was designed to provide an answer.[16] Harrod's answer to this question, it will be recalled, was that there existed only one "warranted" rate of growth at which the economy could expand consistent with equilibrium of saving and investment. Therefore, only by accident could this rate equal the "natural" rate made possible by growth of the labor force and technical change. If the actual rate happened to differ from the warranted rate the system was unlikely ever to achieve equilibrium. Instead it might proceed by a series of investment booms interrupted by slumps or relapse into a state of complete stagnation.

In the neoclassical theory, by contrast, the warranted growth rate can always be made equal to the natural rate whatever the latter might be. Furthermore the system tends to approach an equilibrium of steady growth starting from any position different from that which is required for steady growth. The essential core of this theory, starting with the contribution of Solow (1956), was set out utilizing the concept of an aggregate production function as described in the previous section. Its contents can be sketched as follows.

Let there be given quantities of corn-as-capital-good K_0 and of labor L_0 available for employment. At any moment the available supply of factors is thrown inelastically upon the market. Factor markets can clear if factor prices settle at a level such that firms are willing to choose, in accordance with the profit maximizing criterion expressed in Equations (4) and (5), the particular combination of factors consistent with the available supply (K_0, L_0). In this sense there can always be full employment of available labor and capital provided that wage and rental rates in real terms (that is, in terms of corn as numeraire) are free to settle at the appropriate level. Unemployment can occur only if, for some unexplained reason, the wage rate (or rental rate) is too high. In formal terms, what this means is that the procedure described in the previous section for obtaining the profit maximizing choice of technique is now reversed. Instead of finding the corn–labor ratio appropriate to a given wage or profit rate we now find the wage and profit rates appropriate to given quantities of the factors. The assumed properties of the production function ensure the existence of a unique solution at positive levels of w and r for any arbitrary quantities K_0, L_0.

It is required for equilibrium in the flow of income and expenditure that saving equals investment. Of course, in the parable world, whatever is not consumed (saved) from the total output of corn must be invested. This is because corn is the only form in which wealth can be accumulated and its investment in production always yields the going rate of profit. Thus, there can never be any discrepancy between saving and investment decisions. The Keynesian problem of unemployment due to shortage of effective demand and the Marxian problem of realization of surplus value are, therefore, ruled out.

With full employment assured the equilibrium level of income is obtained from the production function. Assume now that saving is a fixed proportion s of total income. For saving–investment equilibrium we have

$$I = sY \tag{13}$$

and the warranted rate of growth of capital is then

$$g = \frac{I}{K} = \frac{sf(k)}{k} \tag{14}$$

Suppose that available labor grows over time at a constant rate n which is exogenously determined

$$L = L_0 e^{nt} \tag{15}$$

For steady full-employment growth at a constant corn–labor ratio it is required that the stock of corn grow at the same rate as labor, or

$$g = n \tag{16}$$

From (16) and (14) we see that what is required is that

$$\frac{f(k)}{k} = \frac{n}{s} \tag{17}$$

The assumptions concerning the production function ensure that there always exists a unique value of the corn–labor ratio which provides a solution to this equation. The solution is illustrated in Figure 3.3. Given the labor-force growth rate n, the saving proportion s (or their ratio n/s) and the technology represented by $f(k)$, we find a value of $k = k^*$ such that $n/s = f(k^*)/k^*$ and it is unique.

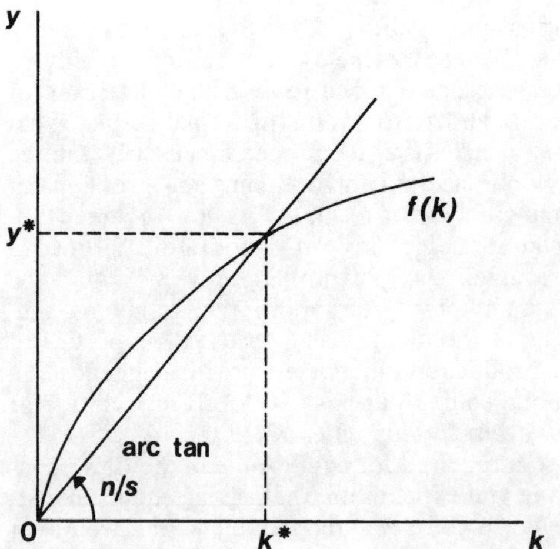

Figure 3.3

It is easy to go on to show in this framework that, starting from any position which is different from that required for steady growth (implying that $k_0 \neq k^*$), the economy will undergo an adjustment process leading eventually to attainment of steady growth. Suppose that, by historical accident as it were, the economy starts out in a position where saving out of full-employment income exceeds the investment required at the existing corn–labor ratio to provide employment for the increment in the labor force. The existing corn–labor ratio is, so to speak, too low. In Harrod's terms we have a situation where the warranted growth rate exceeds the natural rate. Since the available saving is automatically invested, the total stock of corn per man rises by the amount of this saving. Once the investment has been made, it turns out that there is too much corn to employ the available labor with the existing production technique. Competition among firms for the available labor drives up the wage rate and, correspondingly, the rate of profit falls. At a higher wage rate (lower profit rate) firms find it now profitable to adopt a technique with a higher corn–labor ratio. The wage rate rises to the point where that corn–labor ratio is selected at which all the available stock of corn is fully utilized and the excess demand for labor disappears.

If the warranted growth rate continues to exceed the natural rate in subsequent periods, these adjustments are repeated. As the process continues, the total stock of corn per man is rising all the time, the rate of profit is falling and the technique of production is being continually adjusted, a higher corn–labor ratio for a lower profit rate, so as to maintain full utilization of capital and labor. But, as the corn–labor ratio rises in this way, the same amount of saving provides less and less employment. Eventually, a point is reached where the corn–labor ratio is such that the available saving is just sufficient to employ the increment in the labor force. The gap between warranted and natural growth rates is then eliminated and the situation becomes consistent with a steady state.

When the warranted rate is less than the natural rate, a similar process operates in the opposite direction. In this case, the amount of saving is not enough to employ the increment in the labor force. The wage rate falls (the profit rate rises), and correspondingly the corn–labor ratio falls until a steady state is reached. All of this

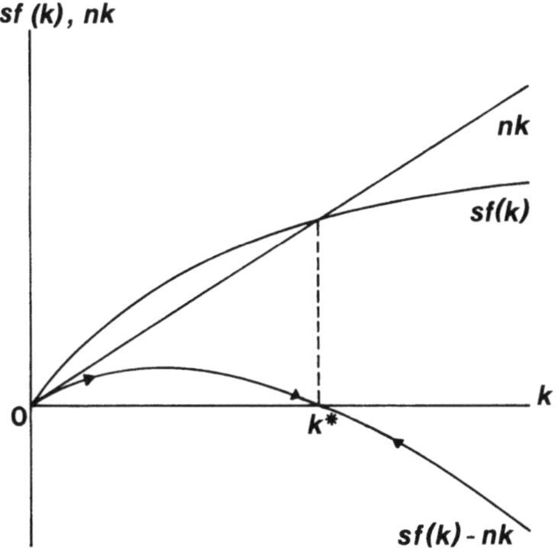

Figure 3.4

shows that the system is *stable* in the sense that any departure from the steady state will bring into operation an adjustment process such as to induce a return to it.

The argument is illustrated in Figure 3.4 for the case of a uniform saving proportion. The curve $sf(k)$ represents the amount of saving at full employment for each level of the corn–labor ratio k. The curve nk represents the investment required to maintain full employment at each corn–labor ratio when the labor force grows at the rate n. If $sf(k)$ is above nk then k is rising; if below, then k is falling. The arrows indicate the direction of movement in each case. The appropriate steady-state value of k is k^*.

It may be noted that the argument is conducted throughout in terms of a process of movement "up" (or "down") the production function. Specifically, the economy is assumed to undergo a process of accumulation involving a continuous increase (decrease) in the stock of corn per man while the rate of profit falls (rises) and the technique of production is continually adjusted to each successive level of the profit rate. Here we see the significance of the assumptions concerning technology and production. In particular, accumulation consists of adding part of the output of corn to the stock of corn already in existence. A change in production technique for the entire stock of preexisting and new corn can be implemented instantaneously and without cost in response to a change in factor prices simply by varying the quantity of corn per man employed. In this sense, there is direct *substitution* of capital for labor. Because of the assumptions concerning the production function, such substitution can be carried out indefinitely while continuing to yield positive wage and profit rates. Therefore, full employment of available labor and capital is always guaranteed whatever might be the size of the labor force and stock of capital. Furthermore such substitution can always go on until the steady state is reached.

A striking feature of this analysis is that there is no need to distinguish between the comparison of different steady states and a process of change through which an economy moves. Every point on the production function corresponds to a particular steady state, each with a given set of conditions, as well as to a point on the path of movement of an economy towards a steady state. All of this is made possible by the assumption of a one-commodity economy. In such an economy, there is no such thing as a given stock of *capital goods* specific to particular uses. The stock of capital can at any moment be adapted to employ any quantity of labor and produce any quantity of output without requiring a process of transformation of the preexisting stock. Accordingly there is no problem of the degree of utilization of a given stock of capital equipment varying with the level of demand in the short run. Indeed, there can be no problem of demand at all since whatever is produced is either consumed or invested. Say's law holds without exception. It is assumed, moreover, that factor prices are free to respond appropriately in any given situation. In particular, the *real* wage rate moves up or down to the appropriate extent in response to any excess demand or supply of labor. The profit rate falls or rises as soon as there is any oversaving or undersaving.

There is an obvious question as to whether and, if so, how the process of adjustment would work itself out in an economy in which stocks of equipment are specific to different uses and there is a (changing) structure of relative prices of the different commodities, in which firms make investment decisions in the light of expectations of future profits, wealth is held in the form of money and the wage rate is set in terms of money by bargaining between workers and employers. The preceding analysis is incapable of dealing with these matters by virtue of the assumptions on which it is based. In this connection, it may be noted that the process by which a capitalist economy is supposed to adjust from any arbitrary initial position to a steady state raises a number of serious analytical problems for the neoclassical theory, once allowance is made for the existence of more than one capital good (Hahn, 1968). These problems are effectively suppressed within the framework of assumptions of a one-commodity model. What is involved, quite apart from the other matters discussed here, is the failure of the neoclassical theory to provide an account of the *process of change* ("disequilibrium dynamics") in a capitalist economy, except through the artificial device of a "sequence of momentary equilibria." [17]

Neoclassical theory of growth and distribution

We can now bring together the basic elements of the scheme so as to exhibit the nature of the interdependencies and causal links that are involved. These relations are depicted in Figure 3.5. The production function is drawn in quadrant I. Quadrant II gives the equilibrium profit rate consistent with each corn–labor ratio, Quadrant III describes the wage–profit frontier corresponding to the given technology.

From the point of view of the problem of distribution, it can be seen that the basic idea here is that of a one-to-one correspondence between the relative size of factor endowments (the corn–labor ratio) and the price of those factors and hence the distribution of income. Once we know the factor endowment k and the technology corresponding to the production function $f(k)$, we can find from the frontier the corresponding distribution of income. When this notion is imbedded in a theory of growth, a further explanation is provided concerning the determination of relative factor endowments. Corresponding to a given saving proportion and growth rate of labor there is a unique corn–labor ratio consistent with steady growth, as in quadrant I. A higher saving rate is associated with a higher corn–labor ratio; a higher growth rate of labor with a

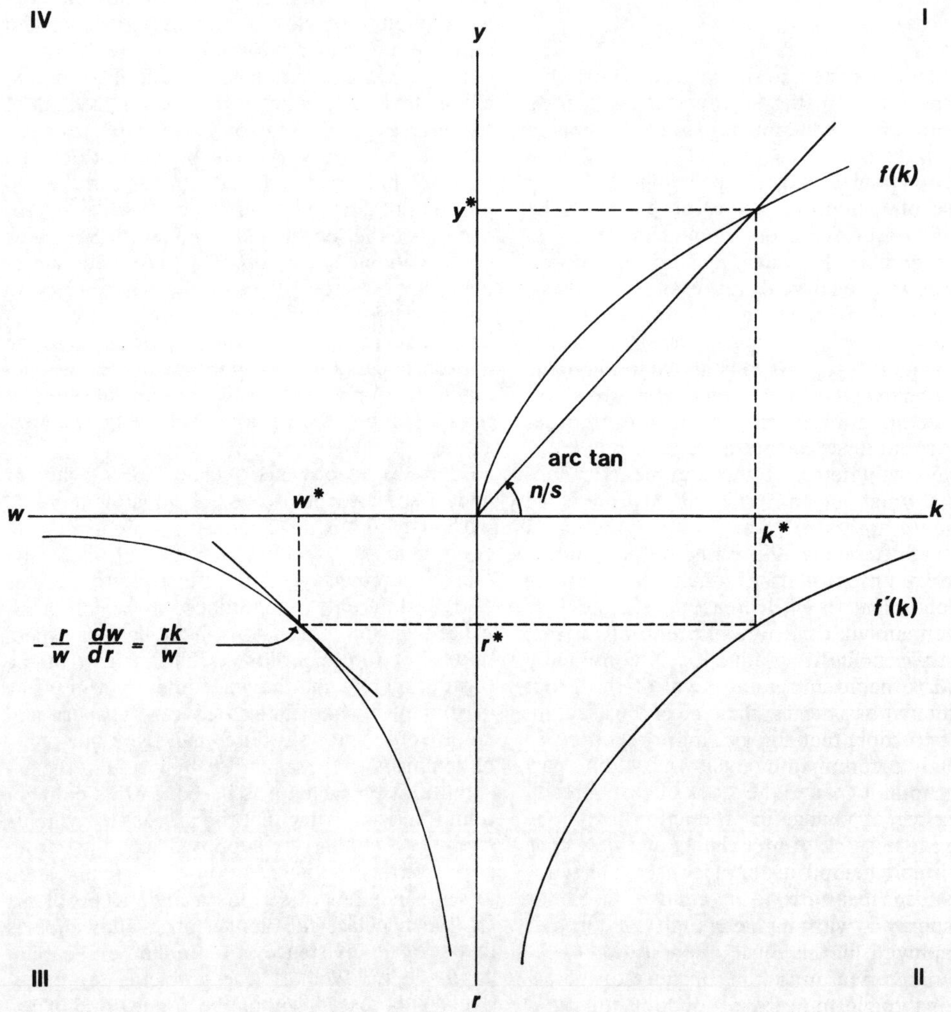

Figure 3.5

lower corn–labor ratio. From quadrants II and III we see that the distribution of income varies according to the level of the corn–labor ratio. We conclude from this that the distribution of income depends on factor endowments and on technology. Factor endowments are in turn the result of the habits of thrift of the population represented by the uniform saving proportion s and the forces underlying expansion of the labor force at the rate n.[18]

It is also evident that what pulls the economy forward in this scheme is the expansion of the labor force, the rate of such expansion being an unexplained datum. Given this growth rate and the saving habits represented by s, the rate of accumulation adjusts so as to provide the capital required to maintain full employment of the available labor force at the corn–labor ratio appropriate to a steady-state. Steady growth at full employment is guaranteed by the assumptions that: (1) firms are willing to carry out investment corresponding to whatever saving is going on; (2) a technology exists that always allows for choice of the appropriate technique of production, and (3) markets exist for labor and capital, ensuring wage and profit rates consistent with that technique.

It is important to see that, insofar as the saving proportion s and the labor force growth-rate n are merely taken as *given* (that is, their status in the theory is that of *parameters*), then this formulation is consistent with *any* theory of saving and *any* theory of labor force growth which determines the quantities s and n in terms of exogenous conditions.[19] Of course, the assumption that these quantities can be considered as exogenously determined is already quite special. But what is specific to the neoclassical theory *as a theory of growth* is the attempt to argue that there always exists in a capitalist economy a unique state of steady growth with full employment to which the economy will adjust given enough time. What is even more specific to the neoclassical theory *as a theory of distribution* is the attempt to argue (on the basis of the particular assumptions about technology and saving behavior) that the distribution of income is uniquely determined by technology and factor endowments.

A number of theoretical elaborations of this scheme are possible, all hinging on the specified properties of the production function. For instance, it can be shown that lower profit rates are associated with higher corn–labor ratios and these with higher levels of output and consumption per man up to a maximum. This association is thought to be consistent with the neoclassical idea that lower profit rates give rise to investment in "more mechanized" techniques of production which yield greater output and consumption per man as a return to the "sacrifice" of current consumption involved in investing in the more mechanized technique.[20] The golden rule of accumulation can be shown to hold so that consumption per man is maximized when the rate of profit is set equal to the rate of growth (Phelps, 1966; Koopmans, 1965). By a slight reconstruction, the analysis has also been made to apply to the problem of stagnation in underdeveloped economies (Buttrick, 1958, 1960; Nelson, 1956; Solow, 1956, p. 90).

A theoretical critique

So far as the formal structure of this scheme is concerned, it might appear, on the surface of it, to be a charming edifice. For, in one stroke, two sets of problems appear to be solved. First, the analysis shows that steady growth with full employment is always possible in a capitalist economy and will tend to be established starting from any position. Second, the distribution of income on the steady-state path is explained as a function of technology and prevailing factor endowments, those endowments being related to saving behavior and population growth. But it is necessary to examine further the substance of this construction and the propositions derived from it.

There are a number of directions in which it is possible to go. One could point to the existence of periods of chronic unemployment of labor and excess capacity in the advanced capitalist economies and note that there is no room in this scheme for introduction of such considerations. There is no room also for introduction of any distinction between saving and investment decisions and therefore for assigning any autonomous role to investment plans of firms in the accumulation process. For, in the one-commodity world, saving represents a decision not to consume part of the current output of corn and this amount of corn automatically corresponds to an investment in corn as capital good. Beyond this, one could go on further to confront this scheme with alternatives which allow for the introduction of such elements and which offer answers to the relevant questions (Harris, 1978).

A more limited task is undertaken here – I consider some reasons for the failure of the neoclassical conception related to the internal logic of that conception itself.[21] One may note in this connection that a central element of the parable is the idea of an inverse monotonic relation between the quantity of capital per man and the rate of profit. On this relation rests the conception that profits are the return to a factor of production, the *rate* of profits varying according to the scarcity of that factor relative to labor. On this relation rests also the notion that technical substitution between capital and labor as factor prices change can be relied upon to bring about a state of steady growth with full employment. For this relation to hold in a world of heterogeneous capital goods the parable strictly requires that there exist some measure of the quantity of capital, representing all of the different capital goods, which, when it is put into a production function of the form

$$y = f(k) \qquad f'(k) > 0, f''(k) < 0 \tag{18}$$

would satisfy the marginal product condition

$$r = f'(k) \tag{19}$$

and satisfy, in addition, the product-exhaustion condition

$$y = w + rk \tag{20}$$

The relation in Equation (19) provides the linchpin of this whole approach. More generally, it posits a single-valued relation between the quantity of capital per man and the rate of profit such that

$$r = \phi(k) \qquad \phi' < 0$$

and

$$k = k(r) = \phi^{-1}(k)$$

If such a relation existed, it is argued, the parable would provide a good representation of the world of heterogeneous capital goods. With the production function, we could predict the unique value of r corresponding to any given value of k. In this sense we could say that technical conditions and relative factor endowments explain the rate of profit.

Outside of the conditions under which the parable itself is constructed, however, there is no *theoretical* justification for assuming in general that the overall quantity of capital per man should be inversely related to the profit rate, let alone that it should go from zero to infinity (with output per man increasing accordingly) through technical substitution of capital for labor and that the relation should be continuously differentiable. In general, the *capital goods* which enter into production consist of heterogeneous commodities. They can be expressed as a single quantity by valuing them at their respective prices, or exchange values, in terms of a chosen numeraire. There is a different set of prices for each level of the profit rate, the exact pattern of differences depending on the technical conditions of production of the different commodities.[22] The physical quantity of the capital goods and the methods by which they are produced may also be different from one equilibrium profit rate to another. The variation of the overall *exchange-value of capital per man* between different steady states can be viewed in terms of a price effect, a composition effect and a substitution effect (Harris, 1973). But, conceived in this way, the ratio of *capital* to labor cannot be regarded as necessarily an inverse function of the profit rate.

The quantity of *capital* in this sense, that is, as a sum of exchange value obtained by valuing the different capital goods at the ruling prices, *depends on* the rate of profit.[23] Therefore, one cannot argue that the quantity of this *capital* (or its *marginal product,* whatever that means in this context) *determines* the rate of profit without reasoning in a circle. For there is in general no one-way connection going from the quantity of *capital* in this sense to the rate of profit.

To express the different capital goods in terms of a single number one could have recourse instead to a number such as their physical weight. But then there would be, in general, no unique inverse relation between that number and the rate of profit. And, whether unique or not, it would be an economically uninteresting relation except to the extent that all commodities embody some quantity of a particular commodity, say, steel. By contrast, the number representing the exchange value of the stock of capital goods *does* have economic interest, though from a different point of view. Namely, it represents the market value of the *property* which the capitalists own and, in terms of which, each receives a share in the total profits generated in the economy (and in terms of which, also, his social position is presumably measured).

Heterogeneous capital goods, as the products of labor, can of course be reduced to the quantity of labor directly and indirectly embodied in them, that is to say, to their *labor value*. This particular quantity provides as good a measure as any other of the quantity of "capital" in homogeneous units. It would not, however, be an appropriate measure from the point of view of the neoclassical conception. This is for the reason that, measured in this way, capital is then simply a quantity of labor, embodied or stored up in means of production. Therefore the quantity of capital in this sense could be assigned no independent existence *as a factor of production,* separate and distinct from labor, which receives a share in the product in accordance with its technical productivity. By contrast, from the point of view of Marxian theory, the labor value measure would be the theoretically correct one for analysis of distribution and carries a special qualitative significance within the framework of that theory. Specifically, its significance is that, among other things, it expresses the social–historical character of capital as the productive power of labor materialized and transformed into objects that become instruments for domination of the laborer through his employment to the capitalist. Marx points out that "his [the capitalist's] domination is only that of materialised labor over living labor, of the laborer's product over the laborer himself" (Marx, 1963).

In moving from the parable world of one commodity to a more complex world of production with heterogeneous capital goods we find also that the neoclassical argument runs up against another difficulty which is related to, but analytically distinct from, the previous one. This takes the form of the *reswitching of techniques of production,* that is, the recurrence of the same technique at different levels of the profit rate even though that technique is dominated by others at intermediate levels of the profit rate (Sraffa, 1960, Chapt. 12). It follows from this result that, in general, techniques cannot be uniquely ordered according to the rate of profit. The neoclassical production function is based on the assumption that such a unique ordering exists. It is on this basis, as we have seen, that an attempt is made to draw a direct and unique connection between technology and distribution. But this assumption is contradicted as soon as allowance is made for such a small complication as that the method of production of the capital good differs from one technique to another (Bruno, et al., 1966). The presumed connection between technology and distribution is thereby effectively destroyed.

As a formal matter, the essential point in all this is that the neoclassical parable assumes that capital is a homogeneous substance measurable independently of distribution, the quantity of which can therefore be made to explain distribution. In this form, capital is a direct input into the production process and can thus be put on the same footing as labor (considered as a homogeneous unit). But capital can be so regarded on one assumption only, that is, that there is a given price system for measuring the various commodity inputs and that this price system is invariant with respect to the rate of profit. This in turn presupposes that only one commodity is produced or that different commodities are perfect technical substitutes in production so that the price ratio between them is fixed.[24] This is the special construction on which the neoclassical parable is initially based. When the scaffolding is removed, various assumptions have to be introduced if the initial structure is to be maintained. These assumptions are essentially of an ad hoc character.[25] They, therefore, provide weak foundations on which to base a theory of distribution and growth.

Consumption and the rate of profit

Another element of the neoclassical conception is the notion that capital is productive in the sense that investment in more capital–intensive, more mechanized, or more roundabout, methods of production yields greater consumption per man (up to a maximum). As Samuelson (1973, p. 598) expresses it, "It is taken to be a technological fact of life that you can get more future consumption product by using indirect or roundabout methods." The increment in consumption is regarded as the return to the "sacrifice" of current consumption involved in investing in the more mechanized technique. The profit (interest) rate is supposed to reflect, on the one hand, the trade-off between the return of future consumption and the sacrifice of current consumption consistent with the prevailing preference of society. On the other, it is supposed to reflect the "net productivity of capital" viewed as a technical characteristic of the roundabout methods.

It is not evident, at this level of analysis, what meaning is to be given to the concept of society conceived independently of the social classes which compose it in a capitalist economy and the distribution of income and property among those classes and to the concept of sacrifice related to saving which the argument presupposes. For this purpose, an appeal must be made to the presumed preference for present over future consumption or the "marginal rate of time preference" of the *rentiers* who lend finance to the capitalist firms to carry out accumulation. But as to why there should necessarily be a positive rate of time preference in this sense for society as a whole has never been satisfactorily explained.[26]

Whatever might be thought of the presumption concerning time preference (or "abstinence," or "waiting"), it can be seen that the logic of the argument requires, first, that the profit rate falls as the degree of capital intensity or roundaboutness increases in consequence of the sacrifice of present consumption. Here we have reliance being placed again on the presumption of an inverse relation between the rate of profit and the capital-intensity of production as measured, for instance, by the quantity of capital per man. Now, however, it is required in addition that consumption per man rises as the profit rate falls and capital per man increases. On this basis, we should therefore expect to find in any production system that there exists an inverse relation between consumption per man and the profit rate (up to a maximum of consumption) within the range of available techniques. This is a relation which is required to hold *at the level of production.*

It turns out, however, when we examine a given production system, that the very opposite relation may be found. In particular, as between different steady states, a lower rate of profit may be associated with either the same or a lower level of consumption per man (Morishima, 1964, p. 126). This possibility is clearly demonstrated by the existence of reswitching of techniques of production. Specifically, reswitching means that the same technique is adopted at both a high and a low rate of profit though not at profit rates in between. With the same growth rate prevailing in the two situations, consumption per man would be the same. Thus it is possible for the profit rate to be lower without any alteration in technical conditions and in the associated stocks of capital goods and without any difference in consumption per man. It would thus seem, in this case, that the profit rate is divorced from any connection with the net productivity of capital and from anything to do with the sacrifice of consumption for future return. The situation described could, of course, be explained within the framework of a theory of exploitation by noting that, at the lower profit rate, the wage rate is higher. Therefore the rate of exploitation is correspondingly lower.

The possibility of reswitching of techniques of production cannot be ruled out in general. Moreover, even in production systems where reswitching does not occur, it could happen that consumption per man is lower when the profit rate is lower (Bruno, et al., 1966, pp. 548–50). All of this makes for the untenability of the neoclassical conception insofar as this particular element of it is concerned. Samuelson (1966), in his "summing up" of the reswitching debate, acknowledges this. He seems also to suggest (p. 582) that there is some way in which it may be possible to discover that situations which are incompatible with the neoclassical requirement are "empirically rare." But it is not at all clear what sort of empirical evidence, if any, could be brought to bear on the matter at this level of analysis. The issue is a *theoretical* rather than an *empirical* one. The conclusion one can draw is that there is no reason, at the level of abstractness and generality at which this analysis is situated, to assume the validity of the neoclassical conception *except by arbitrarily ruling out the situations in which it is invalid.*

Neoclassical theory in general

Going beyond the failure of the neoclassical parable, however, it needs to be recognized that the parable, as a theoretical construct, does not stand by itself in complete isolation. Rather, it stands in a very definite relation to the whole corpus of neoclassical theory. Samuelson (1962, p. 193) grants as much when he indicates that "such simple models or parables do, I think, have considerable heuristic value in giving insights into the fundamentals of interest theory in all its complexities." We come here to the real meaning and significance of the neoclassical parable. What the neoclassical parable reveals is the *basic conceptual structure,* the fundamentals, of a theory that, in all its complexities, was designed to explain distribution (and growth) in a capitalist economy. The parable serves to give an identifiable shape to that structure, to reveal its essential links, to expose its internal logic. It follows that, if some of the links in that structure have now become unhinged at the level of the parable, this can only reflect back upon the base from which it derives its theoretical validity and in relation to which it has its heuristic value (Garegnani, 1970). What is called into question also is the application of that structure, whether in the form of the parable or otherwise, to the study and analysis of any "real" capitalist economy (Abramovitz and David, 1973).

In general terms, the conceptual structure here referred to is one which conceives of the distribution of income in a capitalist economy as emerging from the pricing of goods and factors of production in a general equilibrium of competitive markets, the outcome being determined by the quantity of available factor endowments, the technology of production and the preferences of individuals.[27] Using Euler's theorem it can be shown, under well-known conditions, that the value of the output produced with those factors and estimated at the prevailing market prices is exhausted by distribution back to the factors in accordance with their marginal productivities. The owners of the factors receive an amount of income corresponding to specified amounts of the factors which each owns times their productivities.[28]

The basic feature of this conception is that the process of determination of distribution is conceived to occur *at the level of the market* for goods and factors, that is, in the sphere of circulation and exchange. No reference is made to the *social relations of production* and their role in determining the outcome, nor to the *reproduction* requirements of the system in terms of its material and social conditions.

The set of formal relations characterizing this theory emerges in a particularly simple and straightforward way in the one-commodity model with two factors. Upon this set of formal relations, however simple or complex, neoclassical economists have sought to build a conception of factors of production, other than labor, or specific capital goods, as independently productive of value. Consistent with this pattern, they conceive of accumulation as a matter of the addition of new capital goods from the flow of current output to the preexisting stock of capital goods, and, hence, as a matter of the time path of evolution of the stock of factors (Burmeister and Dobell, 1970). The capitalist firm is seen merely as an intermediary between the individuals as suppliers of factors from their predetermined endowments of those factors, and the individuals as *rentiers* engaged in arranging the pattern of their consumption over time by exchanging consumption today for consumption tomorrow. The interest rate (or profit rate) is supposed to emerge from all this as a reflection, on the one hand, of the productivity of the capital goods and, on the other, of the presumed intertemporal preferences (sacrifice) of the rentiers involved in refraining from consuming the current output of goods (or the existing stock).

A central conception here, one which the parable brings directly to the fore, is that of capital goods as independently productive of value. This conception constitutes one blade of the scissors with which it had been thought possible to cut the connection Marx had drawn between the existence of profits, the exploitation of labor, and the accumulation of capital as exchange value.[29] It is this conception which has now been shown to be meaningless and which must, therefore, be abandoned.[30] There is in general no analytical connection which can be drawn between the technical productivity of factors (capital goods) and the income which capitalists receive from the total product, which would be consistent with the requirements of the neoclassical theory. That particular point having been made, attention can now again be turned to those forces in capitalist society, operating at the level of the *social* relations of production, which account for the exploitation of labor and determine the share of income which capitalists receive. Consistent with this, the problem of accumulation and the role of capitalist firms can also be reformulated. It should then be possible to dispense with the other blade of the scissors represented by the conception of rentiers' intertemporal preferences as a determinant of the profit rate.[31,32] The next section outlines such an approach.

An alternative approach to the theory of growth

Speaking broadly and briefly, a theory of economic growth is to be conceived as an explanation of the causes of the contradictory development of the capitalist mode of production, based on the observable historical reality of an immense expansion of productive forces and revolution in methods of production under capitalism combined with the persistence of unevenly developed sectors over large areas of the capitalist world and with periodically recurring crises affecting all or most of the major branches of industry. What is to be explained is this specific form of capitalist development: the nature of the forces which propel the system forward in this way and which account for the particular (contradictory) form of its forward movement. A theory of growth is, in this view, *a theory of the expanded reproduction of the capitalist mode of production on a world scale*. There are three central and interrelated elements involved in the construction of such a theory. These are: (1) the process of production of value and surplus value, at the heart of which is the conflicting *social* relation of capital to labor beginning in production and extending to other spheres; (2) the process of capital accumulation involving a continual drive for expansion of capital accompanied by changes in methods of production; and (3) the role of the state as dictated by the requirements of reproduction of capital and the contradictions associated therewith.[33] It is impossible to go into the details here (see Harris, 1978). Instead, in the following section I sketch some limited features of the general approach as applied to analysis of the problem which gave impetus to development of the modern theory of economic growth beginning with Harrod, that is, the problem of capitalist crises.

Surplus value, accumulation, and capitalist crises

The purpose of this analysis is to constitute on an abstract and simple level the process of reproduction of the aggregate social capital in an expanding capitalist economy. Crises emerge as a result of the failure or inability of the system to satisfy completely the requirements of continued reproduction. This failure is shown to derive from one or another of several *proximate* causes.[34]

The starting point of the analysis is the process of production of value and surplus value under conditions of capitalism. Production consists of the production of commodities through employment of labor and means of production which are themselves the product of labor.[35]

From the value produced in a day's labor, a proportion, say ω, goes to sustain and reproduce the labor power of the worker. The rest constitutes surplus value or unpaid labor. ω is a socially determined magnitude. It is the labor value of the "necessaries" required to maintain the worker at a given standard of life as determined by historical and social conditions, including in those conditions the organized struggle of the workers vis-à-vis the capitalists, i.e., the conditions of the class struggle.[36] The rate of surplus value (or rate of exploitation), ϵ, is related to the value of labor power as

$$\epsilon = (1 - \omega)/\omega \qquad (21)$$

and it is the same in all sectors as long as ω is uniform.

Capitalists appropriate surplus value at the rate ϵ and competition dictates that the total amount of surplus value is redistributed among them at a uniform rate in proportion to the total price of their respective capitals. The rate of (net) profit, r, is thus the outcome of a market process of free exchange in which competition reigns because capital is freely mobile and prices of commodities are equated to their costs of production consisting of wages, plus profits, plus depreciation. In the equilibrium conditions of the price system, there exists a well-defined relationship between the rate of profit, the value of labor power, and the embodied-labor ratios corresponding to the given technique of production.[37] In the simple case where there are only two sectors of production, this relationship takes the form:

$$r = \rho(m_1, m_2, \omega) \qquad (22)$$

Given the value of labor power ω and the embodied-labor ratios (m_1, m_2), the rate of profit consistent with the conditions of production and reproduction is uniquely determined from (22). The associated rate of exploitation is given by (21).

Consider now the requirement for overall balance of production and demand. In the aggregate, capitalists save a proportion s of their total profits.[38] Workers' saving is for consumption and their net saving as a class is zero. Investment is divided between increments to capital in each sector. For balance in the flow of output and expenditure it is required that savings equal investment. Thus,

$$sr = g = t_1 g_1 + t_2 g_2 \qquad t_1 + t_2 = 1 \qquad (23)$$

where g is the overall rate of accumulation, g_1, g_2 are the rates of accumulation in each sector and t_1, t_2 are appropriate weights. For the sake of simplicity we confine attention to the case of *balanced* growth where it is assumed that $g_1 = g_2 = g$.[39]

Next consider the investment plans of the capitalists. These may be represented as an increasing function of the expected rate of profit, r^e, and it is assumed for simplicity that the expected rate of profit is equal to the realized rate. Assume also that there is a minimum rate of profit, r_0, below which capitalists do not invest. Thus,

$$g = g(r^e), \qquad r^e = r, \; g(r_0) = 0 \qquad (24)$$

This formulation is readily recognized to be a short-hand though fully adequate expression for a complex process.[40] It leaves aside the specific concrete conditions which may at one time or another govern the state of investment activity. For present purposes these may be regarded as causing shifts in the function $g(\cdot)$.

The only remaining condition to be introduced is that concerning the availability of labor for production. Accumulation at any positive rate with the given technique of production sets up an increasing demand for labor. The requirement of an increasing labor force to match this demand is an independent condition of the problem.[41] Where the labor force grows at the rate ℓ this condition is

$$g = \ell \qquad (25)$$

These formal relationships constitute the basic structural conditions governing the expanded reproduction of capital. Consistency among them, taken together, is required for the process of reproduction and circulation to be smoothly carried out. Inconsistency among them accounts for a rupture or a crisis in the process. There are different possible types of crises and underlying causes, depending on the particular pattern of such inconsistency. These are illustrated with the aid of a diagram.

The left-hand quadrant of Figure 3.6 describes the relationship between the rate of profit and value of labor power for given technical conditions. At a given value of labor power, $\omega = \omega^*$, and associated rate of exploitation, the equilibrium rate of profit which allows competitive redistribution of the surplus among capitalists is $r = r^*$. In the right-hand quadrant the ray OG defines the relationship between the growth rate and profit rate which is consistent with overall

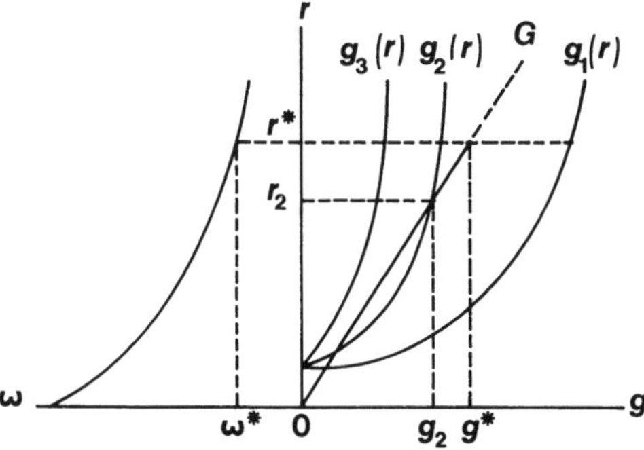

Figure 3.6

balance of production and demand when capitalists save at the rate s. Call this the *profit realization curve*. It represents the profit rate that would be realized from sales of the product at a given rate of accumulation. It has a maximum at (r^*, g^*) corresponding to the existing rate of exploitation. The curves $g(r)$ represent the planned rate of accumulation as a function of the (expected) rate of profit. Three such curves are drawn, each representing a different state of investment plans corresponding to a particular set of historical conditions. Consider the meaning of each case.

Case 1. When investment plans are at the level corresponding to $g_1(r)$, accumulation at any positive rate above some minimum enables the capitalists to realize a rate of profit which induces them to expand at a higher rate. The capitalists are seeking then to increase the rate of accumulation. With a higher rate of accumulation, a higher rate of profit would be realized and the capitalists would plan to grow at a still higher rate. There is, however, an upper limit to the rate of profit and rate of accumulation given by (r^*, g^*). At this limit the capitalists are, so to speak, straining at the bits to expand the size of their capital, $g_1(r^*) > g^*$. They are held in check by the rate of exploitation corresponding to the existing conditions. Under these conditions the planned rate of accumulation cannot be sustained. We may say that there exists a crisis. It is due in this case to excessive accumulation in relation to the pool of available surplus. It may be manifested, for instance, in the form of an inflationary spiral (compare Robinson's concept of an inflation barrier).

The actual rate of accumulation could be higher if the value of labor power were lower, thereby permitting a higher rate of profit. This would require a readjustment of existing class relations as related to the costs of reproduction of labor. Alteration of the technique of production, such as to lower the embodied-labor ratios and the labor embodied in wage goods, would have the same effect.[42] The actual rate of accumulation could also be higher if capitalists were to save at a higher rate. Otherwise, the only possible basis for resolving the crisis is through an adjustment in the rate of accumulation itself.

Case 2. This is the case of investment plans corresponding to $g_2(r)$. Under such conditions, there exists a point (r_2, g_2) such that, when capitalists accumulate at the rate g_2, the realized rate of profit is just sufficient to induce them to continue to accumulate at the same rate. There exists an equilibrium, in this sense, with respect to the overall balance between production and demand. At the same time, however, the realized rate of profit is less than that which is allowed to them at the existing rate of exploitation, but the latter cannot be realized. Thus there exists a crisis. Call this a *realization crisis*. It may manifest itself, for instance, in a deflationary tendency (under competition) as prices fall below values and the rate of utilization of productive capacity declines below normal.

The realized rate of profit could be higher if the level of investment plans were higher than $g_2(r)$, or if the capitalists were to consume at a higher rate. In this sense, a realization crisis is due either to underinvestment or underconsumption on the part of capitalists, or to both. It is a matter of interpretation to which the analysis at this level is indifferent. Whatever the case, it is evident that there is no connection between the realized rate of profit and consumption on the part of workers. A higher level of workers' consumption leaves the realized rate of profit at the same level but *reduces* the rate at which capitalists as a whole can appropriate surplus value. In any event, this cannot come about without an adjustment in the prevailing class relations.

Case 3. With investment plans at the level corresponding to $g_3(r)$, the system is in a process of decelerating to a condition of zero growth with the realized rate of profit at its minimum level. There exists what we may call a *stagnation crisis*. It may be viewed as a degenerate case of a realization crisis.

Case 4. What if the state of investment plans were such as to correspond to a curve which passed through the point (r^*, g^*) from below? Then, at g^*, the realized rate of profit equals that which is appropriate to the existing rate of exploitation and is exactly what is required to maintain accumulation at the rate g^*. The situation need not, however, be fully consistent with equilibrium. This is because the requirement of a labor force to match the expanding demand for labor may not be fulfilled. The system may be in the course of exhausting the available reserve army of labor, being unable to replenish it sufficiently through internal or external means. Alternatively, the reserve army may be expanding because the rate of accumulation is too low to absorb the labor which is becoming available. Whatever the case, it is to be expected that each of these possibilities would, in turn, have effects on the rest of the system. These effects are likely to operate through variations in the bargaining power of workers and therefore on the rate of exploitation, with consequent feedback effects on the rate of accumulation. In this way the mechanism of operation of the reserve army of labor turns out to be crucial for the system as a whole, perhaps dominating every other form of crisis (Sweezy, 1956, p. 150).

Apart from the foregoing, there is more that can be said with this simple scheme. For instance, it is easy to recognize crises due to disproportionality between production of means of production and means of consumption. The role of monopoly, associated with different sectoral rates of profit, can be considered. To complicate the analysis, we have to introduce the conditions of technical change, the role of money, and so on. Further analysis would also require explicit recognition of the fact that the wage bargain is conducted in terms of *money wages*. The analytical difficulties are compounded when the problem of the state (an underdeveloped area of theory) is introduced. The objective of the analysis throughout is to provide historically based explanations as to why one or another set of crisis conditions comes to dominate the process of expansion of capital, to account for the mechanisms through which the crisis is resolved, and to explain the associated structural changes which occur in the system as it moves from one crisis to another.

Enough has been said here to indicate some broad features of the theoretical analysis. Meanwhile, yet another economic crisis is occurring in the capitalist world.

Appendix A

Let there be two produced commodities, each produced with one of them (number 1) and labor. The other (number 2) is consumed. There is a single, uniform period of production and stocks are used up in the period. For their maintenance and reproduction, workers consume a given quantity b per unit of labor. Labor values embodied in production of commodity i and labor power are

$$\lambda_i = a_{0i} + a_{1i}\lambda_1 = a_{0i} + A_{0i}, \quad i = 1,2$$

$$\omega = b\lambda_2$$

where a_{0i} are direct labor coefficients, a_{1i} are stocks and A_{0i} indirect labor. The rate of surplus value is

$$\epsilon = (\lambda_i - a_{0i}\omega - A_{0i})/a_{0i}\omega = (1 - \omega)/\omega$$

In the price system:

$$p_i\lambda_i = (p_1A_{0i} + p_2a_{0i}\omega)(1 + r), \quad i = 1,2$$

where wages are paid out of capital and p_i are prices per unit of value. Setting $p_2 = 1$ and solving for r gives a quadratic from which, taking $r > 0$,

$$r = \rho(m_1, m_2, \omega), \quad m_i = A_{0i}/a_{0i}$$

Notes

1 As examples of these different forms reference might be made to the Hayek – Knight debate during the 1930s, Wicksell's struggle with the concept of an "average period of production," the nineteenth-century controversies on the problem of "maintaining capital intact," and Bohm-Bawerk's attack on what he called the "naive" and "motivated" productivity theories of interest. A relevant example from the work of the classical economists is Ricardo's problem of an "invariable standard of value" and from Marxian economics the so-called transformation problem. In the light of this long record of intense debate, it can be seen that the recent controversy is not at all new in substance. The practice of referring to it as a "Cambridge controversy" appears to reduce the substance of the debate to a matter of geography and personality.

2 For present purposes, the rate of profits and rate of interest are regarded as synonymous. It refers to the income which accrues to the owners of capital, no distinction being made between the different categories of capitalists' income. In the context of investment decisions, the rate of profit or "rate of discount" is a measure of *expected* capitalist income.

3 There is another side of the neoclassical conception which is not dealt with in the recent debates. This is the notion that profits are explained also by the presumed preference of individuals for present over future consumption or their "marginal rate of time preference."

4 The confusion involved in this transition was pointed out very early by Bohm-Bawerk. At a later date, Schumpeter again called attention to it when he wrote: "For the votaries of the triad scheme and of the theory that incomes are essentially prices (times quantities) of productive services, the natural thing to do was to interpret the yield of capital goods . . . as a price for the productive services of those capital goods. This again may be done in several ways, though, unfortunately, all of them meet with this fatal objection: nothing is easier than

to show that capital goods or their services, being both requisite and scarce, will have value and fetch prices; nor is it difficult to show that their ownership will often yield temporary net returns; but all the more difficult is it to show that – and, if so, why – these values and prices are *normally* higher than is necessary in order to enable their owners to replace them, in other words, why there should be a permanent net return attached to their ownership. This point was not fully brought home to the profession at large until the publication of Bohm-Bawerk's history of interest theories . . . Until that time (perhaps in some cases even now) people thought (or think) that the easy proof of the proposition that capital goods must yield a return establishes *ipso facto* that they must yield an income to their owners. This confusion of two different things vitiates all the pure productivity theories of interest . . . both the primitive ones . . . and the more elaborate ones . . ." (Schumpeter, 1954, pp. 655–56).

5 Recognizing that there are "major troubles" with the neoclassical production function, Hicks has proposed the alternative concept of a "sophisticated production function." The arguments considered here apply also to this conception (Hicks, 1965, chapt. 24).

6 There is no intention here of equating the classical (or Ricardian) system of thought with the Marxian theoretical system. For purposes of the present discussion, the basic distinctions which exist between them regarding these and other issues may be ignored.

7 Some of these latter questions are taken up by A. Shaikh in a later chapter (editor's note).

8 All that is said here applies with equal force to the neoclassical notion of a production function which shifts over time in accordance with technical change.

9 Ricardo dealt with a similar case in constructing his analysis of distribution. With an eye to the importance of agriculture in the conditions of his time, he chose corn as the relevant commodity. Corn could be both an input into its own production and an output which serves as wage-good for the workers. With the wage rate fixed in terms of corn, the rate of profit in corn production is determined as the ratio of net output of corn per man on marginal land minus the wage to the stock of corn per man. In this sense the rate of profit is uniquely determined by technical conditions in the production of corn and by the conditions accounting for the subsistence wage rate in terms of corn. Competition ensures that the same rate of profit enters into the price of all other commodities that are produced with indirect labor. But as soon as it is recognized that the wage consists of other commodities besides corn, the rate of profit can no longer be determined in this way. For the money value of the wage then depends on the prices of the commodities constituting the wage and these prices incorporate the rate of profit. Attention then has to be directed to explaining the rate of profit in terms of the production system as a whole and, for this, the assumption that corn in agriculture is both capital good and output is of no relevance. Even then, there is still a sense in which the rate of profit is uniquely determined by technical conditions and a wage rate specified in terms of physical quantities of the commodities. This is so, for instance, in the case of von Neumann's "classical" model (see the interpretation of this model by Champernowne, 1945). On the other hand, for the neoclassical parable to hold, it is required not only that there exists a commodity such as corn but that it is the only produced commodity.

10 This relation was named the "factor–price frontier" by Samuelson. The importance of this particular name is that it expresses the neoclassical conception of profits as the *price* or *reward* of a "factor." But this is to attach a *particular view* of the nature and origin of profits arising out of a *particular theory* of profits to a relation which is equally consistent with *any* relevant theory of profits (Samuelson, 1962).

11 Were it not for the special conditions underlying it, this might be thought to be a remarkable result. Samuelson, who was the first to derive it, evidently thought so. He remarked in this connection, "The frontier can . . . give us more information than merely what the wage and profit rates will be at any point. Improbable as it may first seem to be, it is a fact that the behavior of stationary equilibria *in the neighborhood* of a particular equilibrium point will completely determine the possible level(s) of relative factor shares in total output *at* that point itself. It is as if going from New York to its suburbs were necessary and sufficient to tell us the unseen properties of New York City itself."

12 When the elasticity of substitution is unity, as in the case of the well-known Cobb–Douglas production function, the distribution of income is independent of the capital–labor ratio and depends only on the technology.

13 As J. B. Clark earlier expressed it: "What a social class gets is, under natural law, what it contributes to the general output of industry" (Clark, 1891, p. 313).

14 ". . . we can sometimes predict exactly how certain quite complicated heterogeneous capital models will behave by treating them *as if* they had come from a simple generating production function (even when we know they did not really come from such a function). ". . . simple neoclassical models in a rigorous and specifiable sense can be regarded as the stylized version of a certain quasi-realistic . . . model of diverse heterogeneous capital goods processes" (Samuelson, 1962, pp. 194, 201).

15 Neoclassical writers in the recent tradition have been noticeably reluctant to state explicitly their own methodology. It is therefore difficult to grasp what exactly is intended to be the scientific status of the notion of "parable" or "fairy tale" (these terms are due to Samuelson). This is especially so in view of the innumerable attempts that have been made to obtain direct estimates of the production function, recognized as a relation located in a "parable" world, from empirical data generated in the "real" world.

16 Consideration of this question did not, of course, *begin* with Harrod's formulation of it, contrary to the impression conveyed by subsequent discussions. Indeed, it needs to be emphasized that the problem of accumulation and expansion in the capitalist economy was a central concern of the classical economists and of Marx. Marx, in particular, had succeeded in formulating a clear-cut and consistent theory providing answers to the relevant questions, including the one which Harrod posed (Harris, 1972; Marx, 1967, Vol. 1, Chapt. 25).

17 Joan Robinson refers to the neoclassical conception of a process of accumulation with changing technique and falling rate of profit as a "Wicksell process," noting that "Wicksell himself gave it up in despair." She points out that "The difficulty of the problem arises . . . from attempting to rig up assumptions to make it seem plausible that a private-enterprise economy would continuously accumulate, under long-period equilibrium conditions, with continuous full employment . . . , without any cyclical disturbances, in face of a continuously falling rate of profit" (Robinson, 1959, p. 433).

18 Note, however, that this interpretation hinges critically upon the assumption of a uniform saving proportion for all categories of income and all classes. When the overall rate of saving depends upon the distribution of income between profits and wages, the profit rate and corn – labor ratio are simultaneously determined. There is then no room for a one-way relationship between factor endowments, technology and income distribution. Furthermore, if it is assumed that saving out of wages is zero, the profit rate is determined by the growth rate and the saving proportion for profits and is *independent of technology and factor endowments*. Similarly, under the conditions of Pasinetti's theorem (Pasinetti, 1962), the profit rate is completely determined by the growth rate and saving propensity of a class of "pure capitalists."

19 This means specifically that there is no necessity, *except for the purposes of a particular theory*, to appeal to the presumed "intertemporal preferences" of individuals as the determinant of savings and the presumed "work-leisure preferences" of individuals as the determinant of the labor supply. This is an appeal which is usually made on the basis of a full-blown neoclassical theory, the *neoclassical theory of general equilibrium*. But what should be clear from the present discussion is that *any other theory* would do just as well.

20 This element of the neoclassical conception is discussed in the following section entitled, *Consumption and the rate of profit*.

21 The argument is based on analytical results established in the work of various participants in the recent debate.

22 The reason for this is clear. In competitive equilibrium, prices equal money costs of production consisting of wages plus profits calculated at the ruling rate on the exchange value of the stock of capital goods employed. At a higher (lower) rate of profit the wage rate is lower (higher). The difference in total costs and price depends on the exact pattern of employment of labor and means of production throughout the whole interdependent production system (Sraffa, 1960).

23 So far as the *prices* are concerned it can be shown that, under fairly general conditions, these are uniquely determined in terms of technical conditions and the rate of profit and are independent of the composition of demand. This is the full significance of the well known nonsubstitution theorem. For this result to hold, the rate of profit has to be, so to speak, given in advance.

24 Champernowne has constructed a "chain index of capital" which, under some quite restrictive conditions, permits a unique ordering of techniques in relation to the profit rate and satisfies the marginal product condition for any two consecutive techniques in that ordering. For such a "chain" to be constructed, however, the rate of profit must be treated as an independent variable which cannot therefore be explained by the quantity of "capital" in this sense. Recently, in seeking to get away from the problem of an aggregate measure of "capital" that would be consistent with the neoclassical parable, Solow has defined a new concept, the "social rate of return," and shown that it is equal to the rate of profits. Pasinetti shows that this concept is a purely definitional relation and cannot in any meaningful sense be said to determine the level of the rate of profits (Pasinetti, 1969; Solow, 1963; Champernowne, 1953).

25 Hahn grants that they are all "terrible" assumptions (Hahn, 1965).

26 Ultimately, the presumption is based on Bohm-Bawerk's "Reasons" for the existence of interest (Bohm-Bawerk, 1959). The weaknesses of the conception have long been known (Bukharin, 1972).

27 As Solow puts it, "The theory of capital is after all just a part of the fundamentally microeconomic theory of the allocation of resources, necessary to allow for the fact that commodities can be transformed into other commodities over time" (Solow, 1963, p. 14). Bliss restates this view in the light of the reswitching debate (Bliss, 1972).

28 These conditions apply only to the market for factors. The formal statement of the theory is completed by addition of markets, in the present and in the future, for the flow of goods which are produced with those factors, some or all of which goods may themselves constitute the stock of factors, viewed as produced capital goods.

29 "The marginal theories of distribution were developed after Marx; their bearing on the doctrines of Marxian socialism is so striking as to suggest that the challenge of Marxism acted as a stimulus to the search for more satisfactory explanations. They undermine the basis of Marxian surplus value doctrine by basing value on utility instead of on labour cost and furnish a substitute for all forms of exploitation doctrine, Marxian or other, in the theory that all factors of production are not only productive but receive rewards based on their assignable contribution to the joint product" (Clark, 1931, pp. 64–65).

30 Lying behind this failure is a failure to conceive of the existence of *social classes* with a specific loca-

tion in the production system. In neoclassical theory, society is conceived rather as an aggregation of particular individuals each with a particular vector of endowments and particular preferences.

31 Of course, in the formal statement of the equilibrium conditions of the neoclassical system, there still remains a condition of equality of the relative rentals of different factors and their relative marginal productivities or "marginal rates of transformation." As a condition for minimizing money costs of production in competitive factor markets, these marginal equalities must hold and hold rigourously. Differentiability of the production functions describing the relation between inputs (factors) and output is not a necessary requirement for this condition to hold. With discreteness in the technology it can be reformulated in terms of marginal inequalities. All that is necessary is that the technology set be linear and convex in the neighborhood of an equilibrium point. The condition can be shown to hold, in particular, either in a model of production with discrete production processes (the "linear model of production") or in a model with smooth substitutability. Whether this condition contains an accurate description of the rules actually observed by capitalist firms faced with the problem of choice of technical methods of production can be debated. But that is a different matter. The point is that this condition expresses, within the framework of this theory, only the criterion for cost-minimizing choice of technique subject to *given* prices of goods, *given* rentals of the factors and *given* technology. It cannot by itself provide any explanation of the determination of those rentals and prices.

32 Another matter for debate concerns the assumption of linearity in the technology (or constant returns to scale) *under conditions of technical change*. Little attention has been paid to this assumption in the recent debates. But in the context of a larger critique of the basic structure of neoclassical theory it is another damaging issue that was raised quite early (Young, 1928; Sraffa, 1926). Recently Kaldor raised the issue again (Kaldor, 1972).

33 There is no room in this view for conceiving of a separate and distinct theory of underdevelopment, as commonly understood, except as a theory of the transition from noncapitalist production to capitalism. Some glimpses of the latter are beginning to emerge, mostly through the work of anthropologists (Terray, 1972; Hilton et al., 1976). There is room, however, for a theory of uneven development under capitalism, encompassing international trade and imperialism. Some steps are being taken in this direction (Amin, 1974; Emmanuel, 1972).

34 This analysis does not deal with the mechanism of the business cycle, which represents the practical working out of the crisis, but with the broad conjunctures which may at one time or another underlie the existence of a crisis.

35 The problem of fixed nonproduced resources (such as land) arises at a lower level of abstraction and, for purposes of a theory of accumulation, has to be dealt with in the context of an analysis of technical change which is being left out of account in this discussion.

36 This is obviously not all there is to be said about the role of class struggle in the operation of the capitalist economy. The determination of the real consumption of workers is simply one point, and a significant one, at which it enters the system. Other relevant points in production are, for instance, the length of the working day and the technical conditions of the labor process. Further analysis would require introduction of these complications and recognition of the fact that, in practice, the wage bargain is conducted in terms of money wages while being tied to a cost of living index. When the workers' struggle is assumed to center around the share of wages in national income rather than around the real wage, the analysis would turn out rather differently (Harris, 1972). It could be argued that the former is the case which is appropriate to the conditions of modern capitalism (Robinson, 1973). What all of this points to is the need not only for abstract theoretical analysis but also for more concrete historical study of the labor-capital relation in modern capitalism.

37 In the light of the work of Sraffa, this proposition can now be readily understood as one which holds in the *general* case of production of many commodities with or without joint production (in the form of fixed capital) and with one or many alternative techniques of production.

38 This assumption is consistent with a more concrete formulation of the behavioral conditions in terms of corporations which retain a proportion α of total profits and distribute the rest to a rentier class who save at the rate s_r out of distributed profits. The saving rate of the whole capitalist class is then, $s = \alpha + s_r(1 - \alpha)$.

39 There is, of course, no *empirical* basis for the assumption of balanced growth. Use of this assumption requires justification on other and quite different grounds. The rationale is strictly a *theoretical* one and is to be found in the specific focus of the analysis at this stage. In particular, the analysis is concerned with the reproduction and expansion of capital *as a whole*. For this purpose, the assumption of balanced growth is a convenient one. It leaves aside the problem of relative expansion of different sectors of capital, this being the purview of a theory of *uneven* development. For an equilibrium of balanced growth to exist, initial conditions must be appropriate. This requires a specific allocation of labor and means of production between the different sectors.

40 On a social and historical plane, this process encompasses not only the inducement mechanisms of the market operating through obsolescence and technical change in methods of production, as well as the accelerator-multiplier effect of investment itself and the effect of wars, but also the social mechanisms determining entry and mobility within the capitalist class and various methods of "primitive" accumulation. While all of this is not capable of being captured in the simple formula of an investment function, it does require further articulation and analysis in theoretical terms. There is already a

substantial basis for such an analysis in the works of Kalecki, Steindl, Sylos-Labini, and Baran and Sweezy, among others. Nevertheless, these more specific considerations are not strictly necessary at this stage of the analysis. This is again because of the particular level of abstraction at which the analysis is situated, that is, at the level of the reproduction and circulation of capital as a whole. At this level it is fully adequate to recognize that the drive for profits is the basic motive force underlying the expansion of capital. In this respect investment activity springs from the most fundamental characteristic of capitalist production and not from any arbitrary subjective or psychological motives (e.g., time preference) on the part of individuals.

41 Expansion of the available labor force may take place in a variety of ways which are *internal* to the system of production as, for instance, through increase in the number of hours worked per worker or through absorption of the existing reserve army of labor viewed on a world scale (by means of immigration and capital export). It may take place also *on the margins* of the system of capitalist production as, for instance, through erosion of household work and other noncapitalist forms of production. In these and other ways accumulation creates the labor supply required for its own continuation. The connection is, however, neither fully automatic nor perfectly synchronized.

42 It is the possibility of such an adjustment in production coefficients, viewed singularly as a matter of substitution along a given production function, which constitutes the central idea of the neoclassical parable. While it would be foolish to deny the technical feasibility of such adjustments, it is quite another matter to raise this to the level of a sufficient or even necessary condition for the resolution of a crisis. Because means of production are technically specific and particular patterns of organization of work and hierarchical relations of production are built around them in the factory, changes in methods of production are neither costless nor instantaneous. Neither are such changes a purely technical matter; they run up against the organized resistance of the workers.

References

Abramovitz, M., and David, P. A. 1973. "Reinterpreting Economic Growth: Parables and Realities," *American Economic Review*, Papers and Proceedings, 63:428–39.

Allen, R. G. D. 1967. *Macro-Economic Theory*. New York: St. Martin's Press.

Amin, S. 1974. *Accumulation on a World Scale*. New York: Monthly Review Press.

Bhaduri, A. 1969. "On the Significance of Recent Controversies on Capital Theory: A Marxian View," *Economic Journal*, 79:532–39.

Bliss, C. J. 1972. "Rates of Return in a Linear Model," Discussion Paper No. 44. Essex, Eng.: University of Essex, Department of Economics.

Bohm-Bawerk, E. von. 1959. *Capital and Interest*. Vols. I, II, III. South Holland, Ill.: Libertarian Press.

Bruno, M., Burmeister, E., and Sheshinski, E. 1966. "Nature and Implications of the Reswitching of Techniques," *Quarterly Journal of Economics*, 80:526–53.

Bukharin, N. 1972. *Economic Theory of the Leisure Class*. New York: Monthly Review Press.

Burmeister, E., and Dobell, A. R. 1970. *Mathematical Theories of Economic Growth*. New York: Macmillan.

Buttrick, J. 1958. "A Note on Professor Solow's Growth Model," *Quarterly Journal of Economics*, 72:633–36.

1960. "A Note on Growth Theory," *Economic Development and Cultural Change*, 8:75–82.

Champernowne, D. G. 1945. "A Note on J. von Neumann's Article on 'A Model of Economic Equilibrium,'" *Review of Economic Studies*, 13:10–18.

1953. "The Production Function and the Theory of Capital: A Comment," *Review of Economic Studies*, 21:112–35.

Clark, J. B. 1891. "Distribution as Determined by a Law of Rent," *Quarterly Journal of Economics*, 5:289–318.

Clark, J. M. 1931. "Distribution." *Encyclopaedia of the Social Sciences*, 1931. Reprinted in *Readings in the Theory of Income Distribution*. American Economic Association. Homewood, Ill.: Irwin.

Dobb, M. 1970. "The Sraffa System and Critique of the Neoclassical Theory of Distribution," *De Economist*. Reprinted in *A Critique of Economic Theory*. E. K. Hunt and J. G. Schwartz, eds. New York: Penguin, 1972.

Emmanuel, A. 1972. *Unequal Exchange*. New York: Monthly Review Press.

Garegnani, P. 1970. "Heterogeneous Capital, The Production Function and the Theory of Distribution," *Review of Economic Studies*, 37:407–36.

Hahn, F. H. 1965. "On Two-Sector Growth Models," *Review of Economic Studies*, 32:339–46.

1968. "On Warranted Growth Paths," *Review of Economic Studies*, 35:175–84.

Harcourt, G. C. 1972. *Some Cambridge Controversies in the Theory of Capital*. Cambridge: Cambridge University Press.

Harris, D. J. 1972. "On Marx's Scheme of Reproduction and Accumulation," *Journal of Political Economy*, 80:505–22.

1973. "Capital, Distribution, and the Aggregate Production Function," *American Economic Review*, 63:100–113.

1978. *Capital Accumulation and Income Distribution*, Stanford: Stanford University Press.

Harrod, R. F. 1948. *Towards a Dynamic Economics*. London: Macmillan.

Hicks, J. R. 1936. "Distribution and Economic Progress, A Revised Version," *Review of Economic Studies*, 4:1–12.

1965. *Capital and Growth*. New York: Oxford University Press.

Hilton, R. et al. 1976. *The Transition from Feudalism to Capitalism*. London: New Left Books.

Inada, K. 1965. "On Neoclassical Models of Economic Growth," *Review of Economic Studies*, 32:151–60.

Kaldor, N. 1972. "The Irrelevance of Equilibrium Economics," *Economic Journal*, 82:1237–55.

Koopmans, T. 1965. "On the Concept of Optimal Growth." In Salriucci et al., *The Econometric Approach to Development Planning*. Chicago: Rand McNally.

Marx, K. 1967. *Capital*. Vols. I, II, III. New York: International Publishers.

1963. *Theories of Surplus Value*. Part I. Moscow: Progress Publishers.

Morishima, M. 1964. *Equilibrium Stability and Growth*. Oxford: Clarendon Press.

Nelson, R. R. 1956. "A Theory of the Low-Level Equilibrium Trap in Underdeveloped Economies," *American Economic Review*, 46:894–908.

Pasinetti, L. 1962. "Rate of Profit and Income Distribution in Relation to the Rate of Economic Growth," *Review of Economic Studies*, 29:267–79.

1969. "Switches of Technique and the 'Rate of Return' in Capital Theory," *Economic Journal*, 79:508–31.

Phelps, E. S. 1966. *Golden Rules of Economic Growth*. New York: W. W. Norton.

Robinson, J. 1959. "Accumulation and the Production Function," *Economic Journal*, 69:433–42.

1970. "Capital Theory Up to Date," *Canadian Journal of Economics*, 3:309–17.

Samuelson, P. A. 1962. "Parable and Realism in Capital Theory: The Surrogate Production Function," *Review of Economic Studies*, 29:193–206.

1966. "A Summing Up," *Quarterly Journal of Economics*, 80:568–83.

1973. *Economics*. 9th ed. New York: McGraw-Hill.

Schumpeter, J. A. 1954. *History of Economic Analysis*. New York: Oxford University Press.

Solow, R. M. 1956. "A Contribution to the Theory of Economic Growth," *Quarterly Journal of Economics*, 70:65–94.

1963. *Capital Theory and the Rate of Return*. Amsterdam: North Holland.

Sraffa, P. 1926. "The Laws of Returns Under Competitive Conditions," *Economic Journal*, 36:535–50.

1960. *Production of Commodities by Means of Commodities*. Cambridge: Cambridge University Press.

Sweezy, P. 1956. *The Theory of Capitalist Development*. New York: Monthly Review Press.

Terray, E. 1972. *Marxism and "Primitive" Societies*. New York: Monthly Review Press.

Young, A. 1928. "Increasing Returns and Economic Progress," *Economic Journal*, 38:527–42.

4

The end of orthodox capital theory

Scott Moss

In 1893, John Bates Clark (1893) described two complementary concepts of capital: a fund of capital and real capital. Both concepts were required for the analysis of capitalism. Capital as a fund was required in the study of interest and portfolio adjustment; capital as goods in the study of production.

The only one of these two concepts which was amenable to unambiguous measurement was the fund since it was comprised of money. Real capital could not be measured at all since it consisted of the heterogeneous machines and materials which were the embodiment of the fund. Clark reasoned that since, over long periods of time, investment goods are worn out or used up and replaced, changes in the fund of capital or in the capital fund–labor ratio could be effected through replacements of real capital goods. In effect, changes in the value of capital or the capital–labor ratio reflected changes in the stock of investment goods.

Clark offered this view as part of his explicit defense of capitalism (Clark, 1893, pp. 3, 4). Indeed, his concept of capital as a fund was essential to his demonstration of the necessary and sufficient conditions for capitalism to conform to utilitarian principles of natural law. There were two such conditions. First, Clark sought to demonstrate that under laissez-faire capitalism each individual who contributed to production received the value of what he produced. Second, Clark required that no individual receive a smaller income than he desired. The first point was satisfied by the marginalist theory of production. The wage rate is equal to the value of output which would be lost if any individual worker were to withdraw his services. If the return on each dollar of capital is equal to the marginal product of capital, then each capitalist gets the value of the product which would not be produced if he were to consume his wealth. Thus it is, said Clark, that each individual in the economy, be he worker or capitalist, receives the value of his contributions to production.

The second of Clark's points was demonstrated by the marginal utility theory of value. In all factor markets, individuals offer their productive services until the marginal disutility of the sacrifice exceeds the marginal utility of the income received. Thus, in the absence of government interference and frictions of one sort or another, each individual can receive as much income as he likes, the only limit being his own distaste for the sacrifice involved.

The juxtaposition of Marx and Clark is clear. It was Marx's well-known contention that all value is created by labor although capitalists are able to appropriate a share of that value because they own, and workers do not own, the means of production – machines and materials. Furthermore, the lower are wages the higher must be profits so that it is in the interest of capitalists to keep wages down to the level where workers are just able to keep themselves alive and to provide future generations of workers to replace them (Marx, 1967, Vol. I, Chs. X–XXV). By contrast, in the Clarkian world, there are entrepreneurs who bargain with capital and labor in the same way so that neither of the factors of production, so called, has a bargaining edge over the other. Against this, the Marxian world is characterized by a predominance of bargaining power on the side of capital as opposed to labor. It was the Marxian view of exploitation and minimal living standards for workers that Clark specifically, if not explicitly, sought to refute. The question examined here is whether Clark's approach is valid.

The problems with which we shall be concerned relate to the demand side of the factor markets. They are concerned with the relationships between the returns to capital and labor on the one hand and technology on the other. Technology may be specified as closely as desired by reference to the physically differentiable inputs and outputs of the economy and of each productive process therein. Within this framework, we may consider whether it is, in general, possible for the rate of profits to equal the marginal productivity of capital in equilibrium. If it is not possible, then Clark's social conclusions crumble with the collapse of the analytical apparatus of marginal productivity theory.

The formal analysis of the validity of marginal productivity theory recalls Joan Robinson's (1954) question: just how is capital measured? Its measure must be the sum of the quantity and price of each type of investment good. The marginalist dictum that the price of capital is determined by its marginal product is a special case of the more general statement that the rate of profits is determined by the value of capital employed in given technical conditions of production. In effect, the remuneration to capitalists is determined on two objective bases: technology and scarcity of capital relative to labor. If it were found that the value of capital itself could not be determined without a prior knowledge of the rate of profits, then it becomes difficult to see how the value of capital can determine the rate of profits. One can no longer claim that causation runs from technology and resource endowments, summarized by the aggregate production function, to factor remuneration.

The proposition that the value of capital depends on the rate of profits may be shown intuitively. The investment goods which make up the stock of real capital are themselves produced. In the production of any commodity, some expenditures usually will be made in advance of sales. Indeed, this is a necessary characteristic of investment in general. In addition, capitalists require profits on such advances. In an economy with barriers to entry or imperfect information flows, capitalists will invest their wealth in projects displaying the higher rate of profits. This is only to say that capitalists invest where the rate of profits is expected to be greatest. In a perfectly competitive economy, there will be a single equilibrium rate of profits, all costs incurred in the production of any commodity must be recouped with profits accrued at the competitive rate over the duration of time during which the capitalist is out-of-pocket.

It follows, that the price of any commodity cannot be determined independently of the technical conditions of production given by the time pattern of inputs and of the rate of profits. Furthermore, capitalists must anticipate that they will earn profits at the competitive rate on the cost of any capital goods they use in the production of new outputs. Thus it is that the market value of an economy's stock of real capital cannot be determined independently of that which it is supposed to determine – the rate of profits.

The principles of marginal productivity theory are not so easily vitiated a priori. There is much more to be said. But we shall see that the questions raised by admitting that the rate of profits is a determinant of the value of capital are damning for the theory as a whole.

The stationary state

In order to keep problems of aggregation separate from problems of conception, a very simple economy will be considered.

Suppose there is a machine which may be used to produce either more machines of the same kind or a single sort of consumption good. In each of its uses, one machine employs a given number of workers. A known and constant number of machines and workers are required for one time period in order to produce a machine; a different number of machines and workers are required over the same period to produce a unit of consumption good output. For the sake of extreme simplicity, we will assume that machines do not wear out, so we need not consider depreciation and replacement. Profits are accrued to the value of the stock of machines at the competitive rate over the time they are used in the production of any commodity and wages are paid at the end of the period. All workers, assumed to be equally efficient, receive the same wage. All values will be expressed relative to the consumption good.

In the stationary state there are no increments to the economy's stock of productive assets. In the assumed absence of any replacement of investment goods, therefore, the only output in the stationary state is of the single consumption good. There can be no difficulty in aggregating output in this case since aggregation is irrelevant by virtue of the assumptions made. In addition, there can be no ambiguity in the aggregation of inputs because there is only one type of produced input and labor is assumed homogeneous. Thus, any problems which arise must be conceptual since there is no aggregation whatever in the model. The cost of the resulting clarity is realism. But if the neoclassical analysis is inconsistent in the simplest of cases, more complex models can only obscure the nature of the logical errors, while the errors themselves continue to exist.

We shall use the following notations:

w The real wage per worker per time period
r The profit rate per unit of time

- p The price of the machine relative to the consumption good
- y The value of income per man (output per man)
- k The value of capital per man
- α The number of machines required per unit of consumption good output
- β The labor input per unit of consumption good output
- a The number of machines per unit of machine output
- b The labor input per machine output

Under capitalism, everything which is produced is owned so that, ignoring foreign trade and government activity, the value of each unit of each output is exhaustively divided between profits and wages. From the above assumptions, therefore, we may write the price equations for the consumption good and the machine as:

$$1 = \alpha pr + \beta w \qquad p = apr + bw \tag{1}$$

Solving for p and manipulating the resulting equality yields:

$$\frac{1 - \beta w}{\alpha r} = \frac{bw}{1 - ar}$$

This equality may be solved to yield the wage rate as a function of the rate of profits:

$$w = \frac{1 - ar}{(\alpha b - a\beta)r + \beta} \tag{2}$$

It was noted above that the value of capital in general is determined by the rate of profits. The exception to this rule is the case where the proportion of profits in total costs is the same in the production of all commodities. In a competitive regime such as that considered here, the sector employing the higher machine–labor ratio will distribute the larger proportion of its revenue as profits. The equilibrium price of that sector's output will be the more sensitive to differences in the rate of profits. In order to see just what is involved here, define

$$m = \frac{\alpha/\beta}{a/b} = \frac{\alpha b}{a\beta}$$

where m is the ratio of the consumption good sector machine–labor ratio to the machine sector machine–labor ratio. Thus, if m is greater than unity, the consumption good sector has the higher proportion of profits in total costs. If m is less than unity, it is the machine sector which has the higher proportion of profits in total costs. This definition may be used to reformulate the wage–profit function Equation (2) as

$$w = \frac{1 - ar}{a\beta(m - 1)r + \beta} \tag{2a}$$

This expression will be of considerable use to us in considering one important response to Joan Robinson's initial question. The response was by Paul Samuelson (1962), and the form it took was the surrogate production function. Samuelson sought to show that heterogeneity of investment goods did not invalidate the essential properties of the neoclassical production function. In so doing, as we shall see, he sidestepped important aspects of the question.

Samuelson made a special assumption that the machine–labor ratio is the same in each of the two sectors. That is, he set m = 1. In that case Equation (2a) becomes

$$w = 1/\beta - (a/\beta)r$$

This is the wage–profit function exhibited in Figure 4.1. In the stationary state there is no net investment so that there is no output of investment goods under the present assumptions. Hence, the entire output is composed of the consumption good and the value of income (or output) per man is $1/\beta$, the w-intercept of the wage–profit function.

The slope of the wage–profit function yields the value of capital per man. Since all income is exhaustively divided between profits and wages, we have the distribution identity

$$y = rk + w \tag{3}$$

which immediately may be rearranged to give the value of capital:

$$k = \frac{y - w}{r} \tag{4}$$

Now choose any point A on the wage–profit function of Figure 4.1. To any such point will correspond a wage rate w' and a profit rate r'.

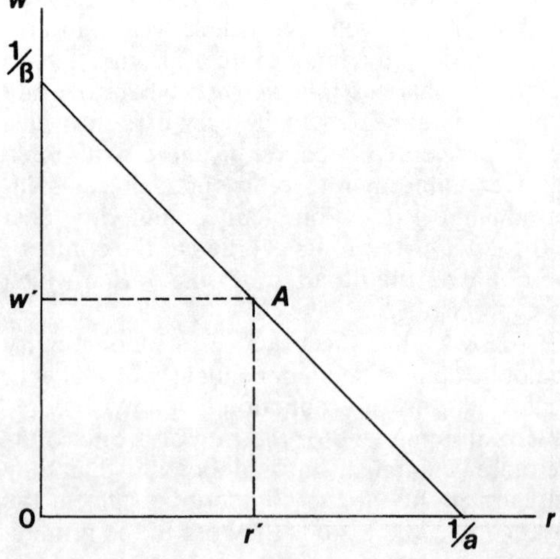

Figure 4.1

Since the function is linear, for any wage and associated profit rate we have

$$\frac{(1/\beta) - w'}{r'} = \frac{y - w'}{r'} = k$$

The last of the equalities follows from Equation (4). Since it makes no difference which wage and profit constellation is chosen, it follows that the value of capital per man is independent of the profit rate and, therefore, of the distribution of income.

What happens if there are two techniques of production, each with different machine–labor coefficients? This is the case represented in Figure 4.2. The wage–profit functions corresponding to each technique will intersect provided that the β coefficient is higher for technique I and the a-coefficient is higher for technique II. In the case of Figure 4.2, profit maximizing capitalists will choose technique I if the real wage is greater than w' and they will choose technique II if the real wage is less than w'. The point of intersection, where both techniques are efficient is called the *switch-point*. The profit rate r' is the *switching rate of profits*.

From the previous discussion, two points may be made immediately. First, if there are two techniques, that with the lower capital–labor ratio will be employed at higher rates of profits. Second, lower values of the capital–labor ratio are associated with lower values of output per man. It may be shown that lower values of capital per head also correspond to higher average products of capital.[1]

In the limiting case, there may be an infinite number of techniques, each of which is efficient at only one wage–profit configuration. The locus

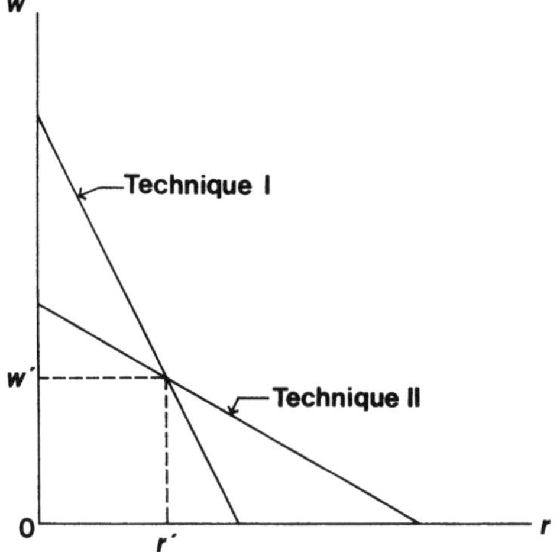

Figure 4.2

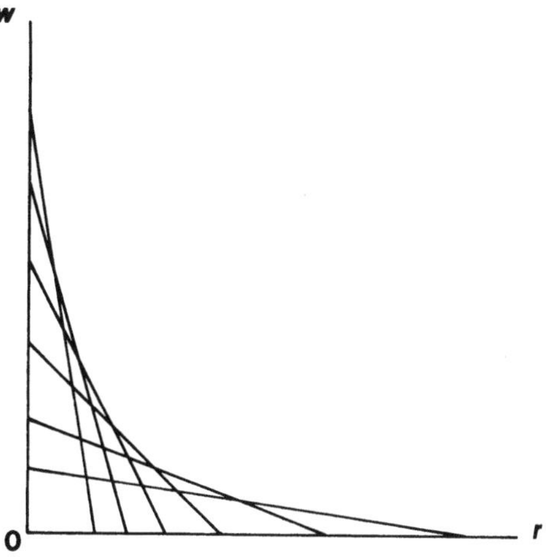

Figure 4.3

of such efficient wage–profit configurations (the grand wage–profit frontier) will be continuous and convex to the origin as in Figure 4.3. Successively higher rates of profit will correspond to lower capital–labor ratios, higher average products of capital and lower average products of labor.

These diminishing average productivities are essential to the neoclassical stories. However, they follow from the assumption that each successive dose of capital (with a constant labor force) yields less additional output than the preceding dose. That is, Clark and his neoclassical successors relied upon the principle of diminishing marginal productivity, from which diminishing average productivity follows. Since the rate of profits is inversely related to the capital–labor ratio under Samuelson's special assumption, diminishing marginal productivity of capital will be a necessary corollary of the equality between the rate of profits and capital's marginal product. We may see that this equality does hold – at least formally. The total differential of Equation (4) is

$$dk = (\partial k/\partial y)\, dy + (\partial k/\partial w)\, dw + (\partial k/\partial r)\, dr \qquad (5)$$

We already have shown that the value of capital is independent of the wage and profit rates in the Samuelson case. Thus, the last two terms on the right must vanish. The partial derivative in the first term is $1/r$. Substituting into Equation (5), eliminating the last two terms and rearranging, we have[2]

$$r = dy/dk \qquad (6)$$

Finally, we can show that for any given technique of production the capital–labor ratio determines the distribution of income. This time we take the total differential of the distribution identity Equation (3),

$$dy = rdk + kdr + dw \tag{7}$$

Dividing through by dy,

$$1 = r(dk/dy) + k(dr/dy) + (dw/dy)$$

From Equation (6) we know that the first term on the right is equal to unity so that

$$k(dr/dy) + (dw/dy) = 0$$

Solving[3] for k

$$k = -(dw/dr)$$

As Samuelson pointed out, the elasticity of his wage–profit function, defined positively, is

$$-(dw/dr)(r/w) = rk/w$$

the right side of the equality being the ratio of profits to wages, i.e., the functional distribution of income.

We must examine why Samuelson's special case yields these results. Returning to the price Equations (1), we may eliminate the wage rate w and solve for the machine price as a function of the profit rate. We have

$$\frac{1 - \alpha pr}{\beta} = \frac{p(1 - ar)}{b}$$

so that

$$p = \frac{b}{(\alpha b - a\beta)\, r + \beta} \tag{8}$$

or

$$p = \frac{b}{a\beta(m - 1)\, r + \beta} \tag{8a}$$

in the special case where $m = 1$, we have

$$p = b/\beta$$

That is, the machine and the consumption goods trade according to their relative labor values. In effect, the proportion of profits in total costs in each sector is the same so that the changes in money price due to changes in the profit–wage rate constellation must be in the same proportion in each case. What Samuelson did was to choose the one case in the stationary state where the relative prices are determined purely on the basis of the technical conditions of production and, hence, independently of the distribution of income. It is the same case that Marx used in the first two volumes of *Capital,* although Marx acknowledged that it was a special case and relaxed the assumptions in the third volume where he considered the transformation from values to prices (Marx, 1967, Vol. III, Part 2).

We now turn to the more general case where the machine–labor ratios may differ as between sectors. We continue to use the wage–profit diagram, although the function will not be linear.

The first derivative of the wage–profit function, Equation (2), is

$$\frac{dw}{dr} = \frac{-\alpha b}{|(\alpha b - a\beta)r + \beta|^2}$$

which, in the absence of negative input coefficients, must be negative. The form of the function may be derived most easily from Equation (2a). Solving for the value of m in that expression we have

$$m = \frac{1 - \beta w - ar + a\,\beta wr}{a\,\beta wr} \tag{9}$$

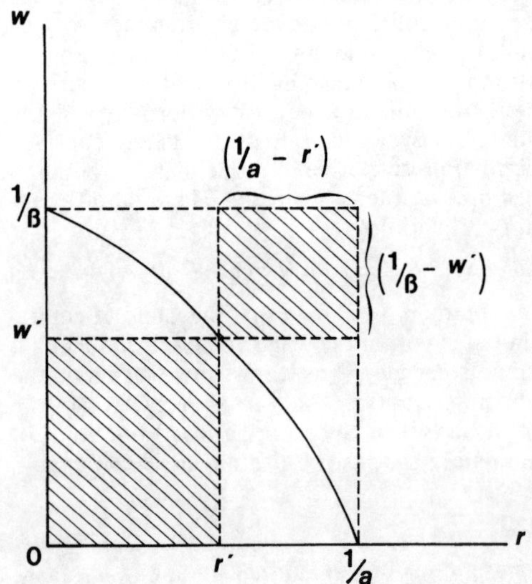

Figure 4.4a

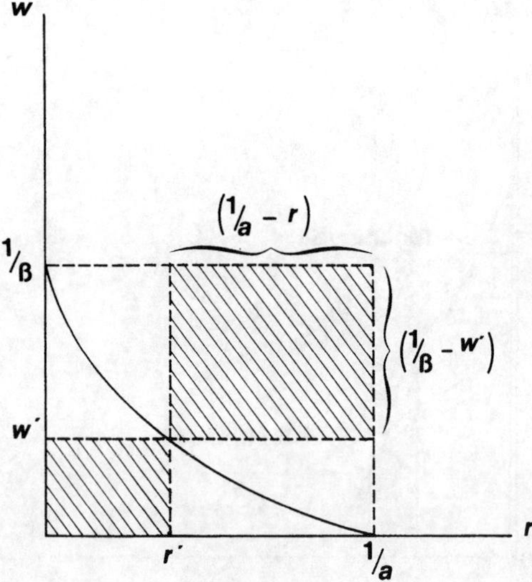

Figure 4.4b

Dividing the numerator and denominator on the right by $a\beta$,

$$m = \frac{(1/a\beta) - (1/a)w - (1/\beta)r + wr}{wr}$$

$$m = \frac{[(1/\beta) - w][(1/a) - r]}{wr} \tag{10}$$

Since m is a constant, the function relating w and r must be a rectangular hyperbola, such as in Figure 4.4a or Figure 4.4b. We know from the wage–profit function (Equation 2) that the maximum feasible wage rate is given by the w-intercept, $1/\beta$. The maximum feasible rate of profits is given by the r-intercept and is equal to $1/a$. The wage rate could exceed $1/\beta$ only if the profit rate were negative and the profit rate could be greater than $1/a$ only if the wage were negative. Neither of these eventualities could be consistent with long-period equilibrium.

In Figure 4.4, the shaded box to the northeast represents the value of the numerator in Equation (10) and the shaded box to the southwest gives the value of the denominator. This will be true for any wage–profit constellation (w', r') and for any technique of production. It should be clear immediately that for values of m less than unity, the wage–profit function is concave to the origin and, for values of m in excess of unity, the function is convex. This result is fraught with economic implication.[4]

We will consider the case of Figure 4.5, characterized by a concave wage–profit function. Since m is less than unity here, the machine–labor ratio is larger in the machine sector than in the consumption good sector.

It is an identity that the value of capital per man is equal to the value of profits per man divided by the profit rate, as given by Equation (4). Also, the value of income per man (= output per man) is the value of consumption goods output alone in the stationary state and on the assumptions made here. Thus, it is identically true that

$$k = \frac{(1/\beta) - w}{r}$$

irrespective of the curvature or linearity of the wage–profit function. In Figure 4.5, the algebraic value of the slope of the chords through the w-intercept and each successive value of the profit rate on the wage–profit function gives the value of capital per man. Evidently, when the wage–profit function is outward-bulging higher values of capital per man are associated with higher rates of profits. This result is called the *negative Price Wicksell effect.* When the wage–profit frontier is convex to the origin, lower values of capital per worker correspond to higher rates of profits (*i.e.*, chords through the w-intercept and points on the wage–profit frontier representing successively higher rates of profit have successively smaller, negative slopes). This inverse relation is the *positive Price Wicksell effect.* The watershed between these two effects is where both sectors are equally mechanized and the capital–labor ratio is independent of the rate of profits. That is the case of *neutral Price Wicksell effects.* Price Wicksell effects are the rubric given to the consequences of the phenomena noted at the beginning of this analysis: the value of capital requires for its determination a prior knowledge of the rate of profits. We now are in a position to see some of the wider effects of this truth.

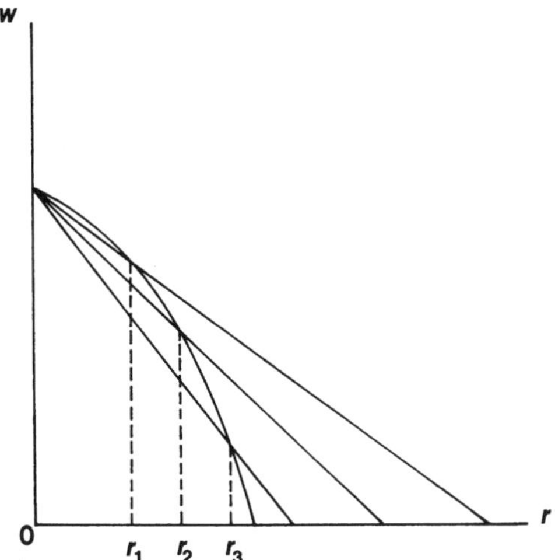

Figure 4.5

Clark assumed that each value of the fund of capital could represent only one stock of real capital for any given size of the labor force. The labor force equipped with that stock of real capital is assumed to produce a given output. Thus, on Clark's assumptions, given the fund of capital per worker, the production function determines output per worker and the output–capital ratio as a matter of technological necessity.

In conjunction with the assumption of a unique relationship between the stock of real capital for a given exployment of labor and the capital–labor ratio, the standard neoclassical assumption of diminishing marginal productivity should provide transitive ordering of production techniques. That is, if the rate of profits is equal to the marginal value product of capital, diminishing marginal productivity will result in the choice of less capital-intensive techniques at higher rates of profits. There really are three separate postulates which may be considered in order of increasing importance to marginal productivity theory. These are:

1. Techniques of production may be ordered transitively according to the rates of profits at which they will be used.
2. Less capital-intensive techniques will be employed at higher than at lower rates of profits.
3. The rate of profits is equal to the marginal product of capital.

The first two postulates may be considered in light of Figure 4.6. The wage–profit frontiers corresponding to two techniques of production are represented there. The machine–labor ratio in the consumption goods sector is larger than that of the machine producing sector in technique I, while the opposite is true of technique II. Also, output per worker (the w-intercept) is larger in technique I as is the output of machines per machine input (the r-intercept).

The first postulate may be seen immediately to be invalid. Technique I is efficient at rates of profit below r_1 and above r_2 (to R_I) while technique II is efficient at rates of profits between. This phenomenon is called *reswitching* since at r_1 there is a switch in techniques from technique I to technique II while at r_2 there is a switch back to technique I. The principal importance of reswitching is that it entails, by necessary implication, the vitiation of the second postulate. In any case where there are two switches between two techniques, one switch must involve a switch from a lower to a higher capital–labor ratio as the rate of profits is notionally increased.

Consider either switch-point in Figure 4.6. Both techniques yield the same wage–profit configuration at that point, so the technique entailing the higher output per worker (w-intercept) will have the higher capital–labor ratio. Thus, at each switch-point, in Figure 4.6, technique I will be more capital-intensive than technique II. The switch at r_2 from technique II to technique I is a switch from a lower to a higher value of capital per worker as the rate of profits is notionally increased. Moving from lower to higher rates of profits, switches from more to less capital-intensive techniques are *forward switches* or *positive Real Wicksell effects* while switches from less to more capital-intensive techniques are *backward switches* or negative *Real Wicksell effects*.[5]

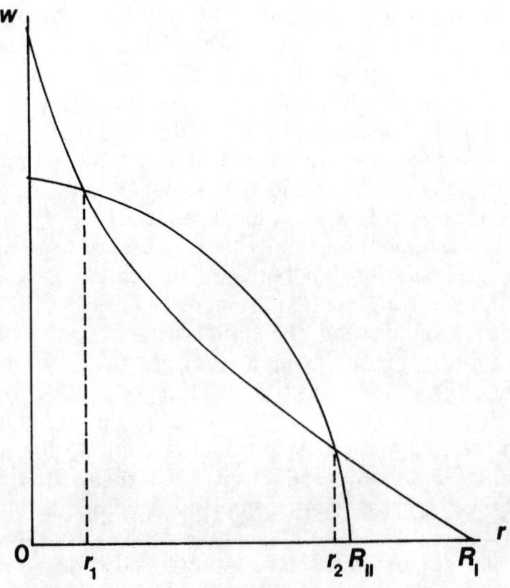

Figure 4.6

A bit of experimentation with the diagrams will convince the reader that the maximum number of backward switches among a total of n switches is $n - 1$. An example of this phenomenon is given in Figure 4.7 where the first switch, at r_1 is a forward switch while all of the remaining switches are backward. There is no inherent technological reason why there should be any one sequence of forward and backward switches and, in particular, a sequence of forward switches only. The second postulate, that less capital-intensive techniques will be employed at successively higher rates of profits, is not warranted either on intuitive or on technological grounds.

We are left to consider the third postulate: that the rate of profits is equal to the marginal product of capital.

There can be no higgling over this postulate. It is always true at switch-points. Consider any two techniques of production which are efficient at the same profit–wage configuration. If the output per worker and the capital–labor ratio are, respectively y_I and k_I for technique I and y_{II} and k_{II} for technique II, then from the accounting identity (3) dividing income exhaustively between profits and wages, we have

$$y_I = rk_I + w$$

$$y_{II} = rk_{II} + w$$

Eliminating w and solving for r,

$$r = (y_I - y_{II})/(k_I - k_{II})$$

That is, at any switch-point the rate of profits will measure the difference in outputs corresponding to the difference in capital between two efficient techniques of production. We already have seen that the technique with the higher value of output per worker will entail the higher value of capital per worker in the comparison with any other technique which is efficient at the same rate of profits. Thus, at a switch-point, the rate of profits is the additional output associated with additional capital and this, formally, is the marginal product of capital.

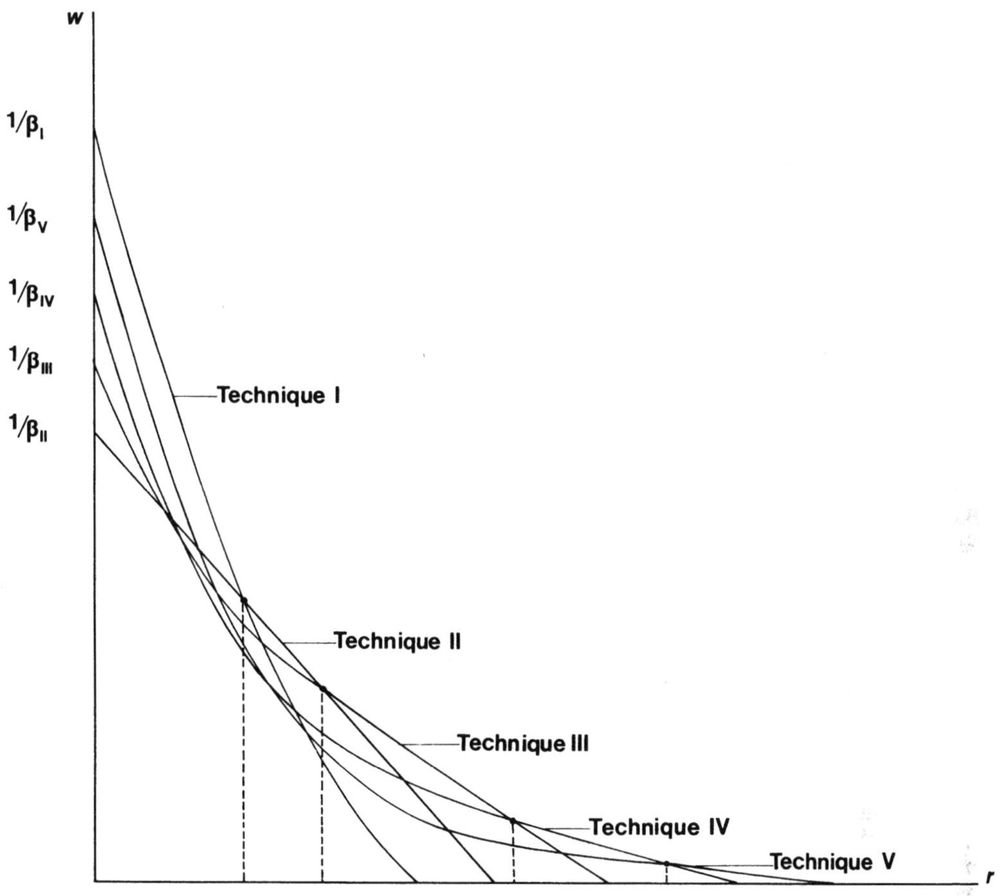

Figure 4.7

In order to see precisely what is involved in this result, we may expand upon our earlier consideration of Equations (4) and (5). These equations are reproduced here for convenience:

$$k = (y - w)/r \tag{4}$$

$$dk = (\partial k/\partial y)\, dy + (\partial k/\partial w)\, dw + (\partial k/\partial r)\, dr \tag{5}$$

We already have seen that whenever the last two terms on the right side of Equation (5) vanish, the rate of profits and the marginal product of capital are identical. There are two economically meaningful cases in which this occurs. The first is where the rate of profits and the wage rate have no role in the determination of the value of capital (i.e., $\partial k/\partial w = \partial k/\partial r = 0$). This result has been seen to follow from Samuelson's assumption of identical machine–labor ratios in both sectors. The second case is where differences in output and capital per worker may arise with no differences in the wage and profit rates (i.e., $dw = dr = 0$). This is the case at switch-points which were analyzed earlier.

By deriving formal expressions for Real and Price Wicksell effects from Equations (4) and (5), we will see that there is no difference between these cases (Bhaduri, 1966, pp. 284–88).

In the stationary state, alterations in net output per worker amount to changes in the coefficient β, hence changes in consumption goods output per worker. Thus, differences in the value of capital associated with differences in the value of output per head require switches in techniques. These are Real Wicksell effects and are given by the first term on the right side of Equation (5). Evaluating the partial derivatives by means of Equation (4), we may write

$$dk \text{ real} = (\partial k/\partial y)\, dy = (1/r)\, dy \tag{11}$$

Price Wicksell effects are differences in the value of capital associated with alternative rates of profits and wage rates but not with switches of technique. Therefore, they may be represented by the remaining terms on the right side of Equation (5) and

$$dk \text{ price} = (\partial k/\partial w)\, dw + (\partial k/\partial r)\, dr$$
$$= -(1/r)(kdr + dw) \quad (12)$$

In Samuelson's case, Price Wicksell effects have no role because relative prices are independent of the rate of profits and the wage rate. In Equation (8) or (8a) we showed the relationship between the relative price of the machine in terms of the consumption good and the rate of profit. Taking the first derivative of that expression we have

$$\frac{dp}{dr} = -\frac{b(\alpha b - a\beta)}{|(\alpha b - a\beta)r + \beta|^2} \quad (13)$$

or

$$\frac{dp}{dr} = -\frac{a\beta b(m-1)}{|a\beta(m-1)r + \beta|^2} \quad (13a)$$

That is, when the machine–labor ratio is higher in the consumption good than in the machine production process ($m > 1$) the machine price is inversely related to the rate of profits. When it is the machine production process which has the higher machine–labor ratio, the machine price is directly related to the profit rate. Since the number of machines in existence does not change in the stationary state, any increase in their price entails an increase in the capital–labor ratio of the same proportion. Thus the capital–labor ratio is directly related to the rate of profits when the machine production process is the more highly mechanised of the two and it is inversely related to the profit rate when the consumption goods production process is the more highly mechanized.

The reason is this: when the machine sector is the more highly mechanized the proportion of profits in total unit cost (and price) is higher in that sector than in the consumption goods sector. Thus, any increment in the rate of profits must increase total cost in greater proportion in the machine than in the consumption good sector. Since any increment in the rate of profits is associated with some decrement in the wage rate, and since wages constitute a larger proportion of total costs in the consumption good than in the machine sector, the price of the consumption good will tend to fall relative to the machine price. A higher degree of mechanisation in one sector increases the price of that output with increases in the rate of profit.

Samuelson's assumption of identical machine–labor ratios in both sectors, therefore, eliminated the possibility of Price Wicksell effects. More to the point, the assumption eliminated any possibility of more than one switch between any two techniques. In effect, the right side of Equations (12) and (12a) may be set equal to zero so that, for any one technique, $kdr + dw = 0$ or $k = -(dw/dr)$. Since relative prices are not affected in this case by the distribution of income, for any one technique the value of capital per worker must be constant and, once again, we see that the wage–profit frontier must be linear. At switch-points the rate of profits and marginal product of capital will be equal. Between switch-points, the marginal product of capital is not defined since both dy and dk are zero (nonzero values requiring at least two efficient techniques). Nonetheless, the rate of profit must lie between the marginal products of capital at the switching rates of profits above and below. As the number of techniques becomes great, the range of profit rates between switch-points becomes smaller until, in the limit, each technique is associated with only one rate of profits which is determined by marginal products which differ infinitesimally.

If Price Wicksell effects are allowed, then the marginal product of capital dy/dk is defined between switch-points but is nil ($dy = 0$, $dk \neq 0$). Once again, the rate of profits at which each of an infinitely dense set of techniques will be chosen, may be constrained to a point, in the limit, bounded by two marginal products of capital. The difficulty already has been seen: the value of capital itself, will not stand in any particular relation to the technology chosen or to the existing rate of profits. Nonetheless, the rate of profits will be bounded by marginal products of capital and we must consider whether this relation has any economic or social significance.

The neoclassical accounts of marginal productivity theory are couched in terms of economic processes. By virtue of the assumption of diminishing marginal products, profit maximization always entails increases in the capital–labor ratio, if the rate of profits falls short of the marginal product of capital and diminutions in the capital–labor ratio, should the rate of profits exceed capital's marginal product. In this context, a higher machine–labor ratio in the machine–producing sector than in the consumption good–producing sector implies a positive relationship between the rate of profits and the value of capital per worker between switch-points. Thus, in moving notionally from one switching rate of profits to the next highest, the value of capital per worker may increase. Since the rate of profits measures the marginal product of capital at each of these switch-points, a larger marginal product evidently is associated with a larger capital–labor ratio. That is, the law of diminishing marginal productivity turns out to be an unwarranted assumption.

While this result has unsettling effects for neoclassical accounts of stable economic processes, the trouble lies much deeper. In order to discuss profit maximization as a process, the economy must be able to vary the capital–labor ratio in response to changes in the rate of profits. In fact, we may not talk about *changes* in the rate of profits. We have seen earlier that the price of investment goods is determined by the anticipated rate of profits. Should the profit rate actually change, then the stock of machines will have been constructed and sold under one anticipated profit rate while another currently obtains. If the realized rate of return is changing willy-nilly over time, then there can be no unambiguous and confidently expected rate of profits on future outputs and, therefore, no unambiguous value of the investment goods used to produce those outputs. Furthermore, changes in production techniques are not, in general, costless. Thus, since the costs of transitions have not been considered explicitly here there is nothing in the analysis which can tell us anything about such transitions. We may do no more than to compare different rates of profits and different techniques of production.

Steady growth equilibrium

In the preceding section, we assumed that the economy was in the stationary state. We are now in a position to generalize this.

If the economy is expanding at a steady proportional rate, there must be some net output of machines. The larger the proportion of stock of machines employed to produce machines, the higher must be the rate of growth of the economy. In order to consider the composition of outputs we shall require the following notations:

- c The current output of the consumption good.
- x The current net output of machines.
- X The stock of machines in existence.
- N The size of the employed labor force.
- g The rate of growth of outputs, hence of plants and employment.

In addition to the price equations (1), we have a set of quantity equations giving the total employment of labor and machines. These quantity equations are:

$$\begin{aligned} N = 1 &= bx + \beta c \\ X &= ax + \alpha c \end{aligned} \tag{14}$$

By normalizing on labor, all outputs are expressed as units per worker. Together with the price equations, we have four equations in six unknowns: w, r, p, c, x, and X. We can reduce the excess of variables over equations by one by adding an equilibrium condition.

Suppose that there are capitalists who save and do not work and workers who do not save. Marx (1967, Vol. II, Ch. XX–XXI) showed that profits in the consumption goods sector are equal to the value of capitalist consumption plus the value of consumption by investment goods sector workers. If s_c is the capitalists' savings ratio, consumption goods sector profits must be

$$\alpha prc = wbx + (1 - s_c)rpX$$

Using the first entry of Equation 14, this may be rewritten,

$$\alpha prc = w(1 - \beta c) + (1 - s_c)rpX$$

or

$$c(\alpha pr + \beta w) = c = w + (1 - s_c)rpX$$

Rearranging,

$$s_c rpX = w + rpX - c$$

By definition, the value of capital per man is equal to the value per worker of the stock of investment goods. Hence,

$$pX = k$$

In addition, the value of output per man must be equal to the value of the investment goods produced (net of replacements) plus the value of the consumption good output. Since $x = gX$,

$$y = gpX + c = gk + c \tag{15}$$

As a result, the equilibrium condition just given can be written as

$$s_c rk = y - c$$

which says simply that savings is equal to investment. From Equation 15 this expression can be written

$$s_c rk = gk \quad \text{or} \quad s_c r = g \tag{16}$$

The last expression has been widely used by Kaldor, Pasinetti and other neo-Keynesians and is a special case of the classical savings function.[6] The preceding expression, of course, is the Keynesian savings–investment equilibrium condition. Thus, the Marxian, Keynesian and neo-Keynesian conditions of equilibrium are all in this respect logically equivalent, since any one may be derived from either of the others.

In each case, the model is left with one more unknown than equations. The model may be closed either with a theory of investment (growth) or a theory of distribution. The former approach has been taken by neo-Keynesians such as Kaldor and Joan Robinson while the latter was taken by Kalecki (1954). Whichever choice is made depends on one's view of the growth mechanism at work. In the remainder of this chapter we will ignore the question and concentrate on the structure of an economy in steady growth equilibrium.

It was asserted earlier that the growth rate is directly related to the proportion of machines used in the machine sector. This can be shown formally. First, we restate the quantity Equations (14), noting that $x = gX$.

$$\begin{aligned} 1 &= bgX + \beta c \\ X &= agX + \alpha c \end{aligned} \tag{14a}$$

The internal ratio (i.e. the fraction of the stock of machines used to produce machines) may be defined

$$\phi = agX/X = ag \tag{17}$$

or

$$g = (1/a)\phi \tag{17a}$$

As was stated in the preceding section, the stationary state exists when no machines are used to produce machines; i.e., when $\phi = 0$. The maximum growth rate is achieved when all machines in existence are used to produce machines; i.e. when $\phi = 1$. The growth rate in that case is $1/a$.

From the first of Equations (14a), it may be noted that a zero growth rate yields a value of consumption good output of $1/\beta$ which, from the output identity, Equation (15), is equal to the value of ouptut per head.

It can now be shown that the value of capital is affected not only by the price effects considered in the preceding section, but also by composition effects of different rates of growth. It is intuitively obvious that the average number of machines per man for the economy as a whole will be greater at higher rates of growth if the machine–labor ratio is higher in the machine sector than in the consumption good sector. For any given distribution of income (constant r) this will entail a higher value of aggregate capital per man. If the machine–labor ratio is lower in the machine sector than in the consumption goods sector, for any income distribution the value of capital per man will be lower at higher growth rates. It is apparent that *capital per man* cannot be determined independently of the rate of growth any more than it can be determined independently of the rate of profits.

These points can be made formally. From Equations (14a), eliminate the value of consumption good output per head. This leaves

$$\frac{1 - bgX}{\beta} = \frac{(1 - ag)X}{\alpha}$$

Solving for the stock of machines per worker,

$$X = \frac{\alpha}{(\alpha b - a\beta)g + \beta} \tag{18}$$

or

$$X = \frac{\alpha}{a\beta(m - 1)g + \alpha} \tag{18a}$$

The first derivative of each of these expressions is

$$\frac{dX}{dg} = \frac{-\alpha(\alpha b - a\beta)}{[(\alpha b - a\beta)g + \beta]^2} \tag{19}$$

or

$$\frac{dX}{dg} = \frac{-\alpha a\beta(m - 1)}{[a\beta(m - 1)g + \beta]^2} \tag{19a}$$

As expected, the stock of machines per man is inversely related to the growth rate when m is greater than unity (the consumption good sector is the more highly mechanized) and is directly related to the growth rate when m is less than unity (the machine sector is the more highly mechanized). In the case used by Samuelson and by Marx in the first volume of *Capital*, there are no composition effects.

The effects of different growth and profit rates on the value of capital and the value of output per man can be shown in a single diagram invented by Spaventa (1970) and based on the wage–profit diagram used by Sraffa (1960, p. 85) and by Samuelson. Eliminating X in Equations (14) and solving for consumption good output per man as a function of the growth rate, we have

$$c = \frac{1 - ag}{(\alpha b - a\beta)g + \beta} \tag{20}$$

or

$$c = \frac{1 - ag}{a\beta(m - 1) + \beta} \tag{20a}$$

It is immediately apparent that this equation has precisely the same form as the wage–profit function of Equation (2). What is more, both c and w are expressed in consumption good units per man and both r and g are pure numbers. For this reason, we are able to represent both functions by the single curve in Figure 4.8. We have taken the case where the machine sector is the more highly mechanized of the two.

Since the value of income is identically equal to the value of output, Equations (3) and (15) may be set equal:

$$y = rk + w = gk + c$$

Solving for the value of capital per man

$$k = (c - w)/(r - g) \tag{21}$$

This expression is easily seen to be a generalization of Equation 4 giving the stationary state value of capital. In the stationary state, $g = 0$ and $c = y$, so that the right side of Equation (21)

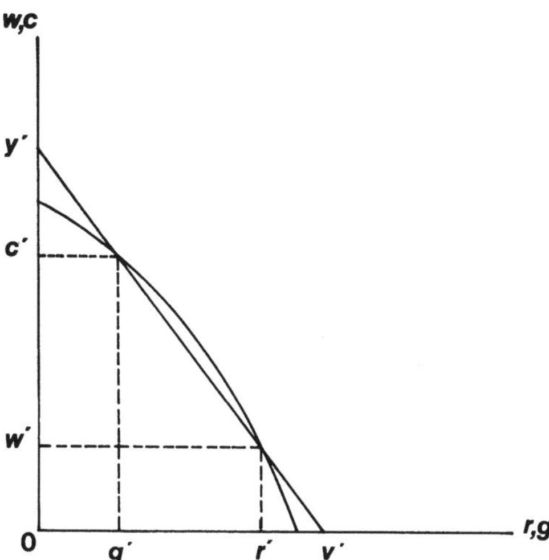

Figure 4.8

becomes $(y - w)/r$, which is also the right side of Equation (4).

In Figure 4.8, we have assumed that the growth rate is Og' and the profit rate Or'. Thus, the value of capital per man is, by Equation (21),

$$(Oc' - Ow')/(Or' - Og') = c'\,w'/r'\,g' \qquad (22)$$

which is the algebraic value of the chord $y'v'$ through the wage–profit (consumption–growth) function. The value of net income per man in the diagram is

$$Or' \cdot (c'\,w'/r'\,g') + Ow'$$

By similar triangles,

$$c'\,w'/r'\,g' = y'\,w'/Or'$$

Substituting into the income expression,

$$Or' \cdot \frac{y'\,w'}{Or'} + Ow' = Oy' \qquad (23)$$

Thus, the vertical intercept of the chord $y'v'$ gives the value of income per man.

The average value product of capital (y/k) can be represented in Figure 4.8 as well. Again by similar triangles, the value of capital per man is given by Oy'/Ov'. Thus, the average value product of capital may be written

$$Oy' \bigg/ \frac{Oy'}{Ov'} = Ov' \qquad (24)$$

The average product of capital in value terms, is given by the horizontal intercept of the chord $y'v'$

Now consider the value of output per man for different profit rates and for a growth rate in excess of zero. Clearly, the growth rate cannot exceed the rate of profits since, if it should, the wage rate would necessarily be greater than the consumption goods available. This result contradicts the assumption that workers do not save.

At higher profit rates for a given growth rate, the vertical intercept of the chord through the consumption–growth and wage–profit coordinates will be higher in Figure 4.8. That is, for a single technique, a higher profit rate yields a higher value of output per man, and therefore a higher value of capital per man. In addition, average product of capital is lower as capital intensity is greater due to the higher rate of profits. That greater capital intensity is associated with a higher average value product of labor and a lower average value product of capital is entirely consistent with neoclassical mythology. That it should occur with higher rates of profit and lower wage rates in equilibrium is indefensible on neoclassical grounds.

Now consider the case where the consumption goods sector is the more highly mechanized. Then for a given growth rate, the value of capital will be inversely related to the profit rate, although the average product of labor will be lower at greater capital intensities and the average value product of capital will be higher. Thus, the neoclassical relation between the value of capital and the profit rate will be broadly satisfied, although the neoclassical productivity relations will not be.

The results for a given rate of profits and different growth rates are entirely analogous.

There are two cases in which neoclassical results hold. The first is the uniform degree of mechanization case, which entails Marx's uniform organic composition of capital. There the wage–profit (consumption–growth) function is linear; the value of capital per man, the average value product of labor and the average value product of capital are all independent of the composition of output and the distribution of income. There is nothing notable in the growth version of this case which has not already been considered in the preceding section. The second case is where the rate of growth is equal to the rate of profits. Nell (1970) has shown that in such a case neoclassical results may be had at any switch-point, although not between.

In the first place, if $r = g$, the value of capital per man is given by the slope of the wage–profit (consumption–growth) function at that point since the chord $y'w'$ becomes a tangent. Formally, we may multiply Equation (8), which gives the machine price as a function of the profit rate, by Equation (18) which gives the number of machines per man as a function of the growth rate. Because the profit and growth rates are the same, we may write

$$pX = k = \frac{-\alpha b}{|(\alpha b - ab)r + \beta|^2} = -\frac{dw}{dr} \tag{25}$$

The last equality follows directly from the derivative of the wage-profit function.

At either switch-point in Figure 4.9, for $r = g$ the value of capital per man is lower at rates of profit just above the switch-point than just below it, presuming that the profit-maximizing technique is always chosen. Furthermore, the average product of labor is lower for the lesser capital intensities above the switch-point than for the greater intensities just below. The average product of capital is higher for the technique with the lower capital intensity at the switch-point than for the technique with the higher capital intensity. What is more, at the switch-point, with $dr = dw = 0$, there are only Real Wicksell effects so that the rate of profit is equal formally to the marginal product of capital. Finally, relative income shares are again given by the elasticity of the $w - r$ function at the relevant point.

Obviously, perverse results will be found in comparing different profit rates, even though the growth rate is equal to the profit rate at all points which are compared.

The neoclassicals had it that, at least in the stationary state, profit maximization results in the maximization of output value in conditions of scarcity. Consider Figure 4.10. If the wage rate in the economy there represented were w', profit maximizing entrepreneurs clearly would choose technique II which yields a profit rate r' greater than that which would be yielded by technique I. If, however, technique I were chosen, entrepreneurs would receive a lower rate of profit r'', but the output of consumption goods per man would be increased as would the value of capital per man. In effect, by maximizing the profit rate, capitalists give up absolute profits as well as consumption per man in the amount $c''' - c'$.

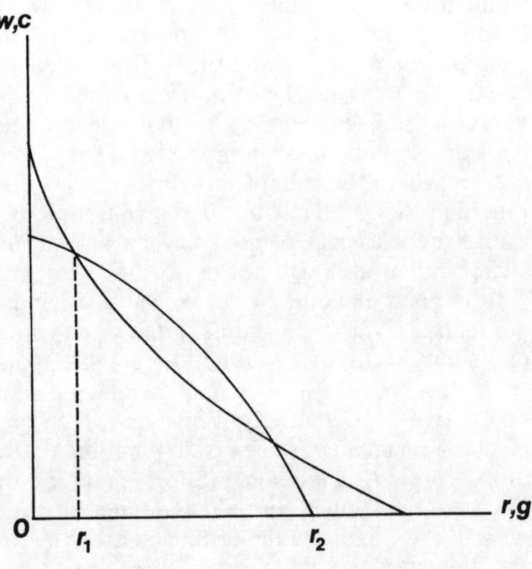

Figure 4.9

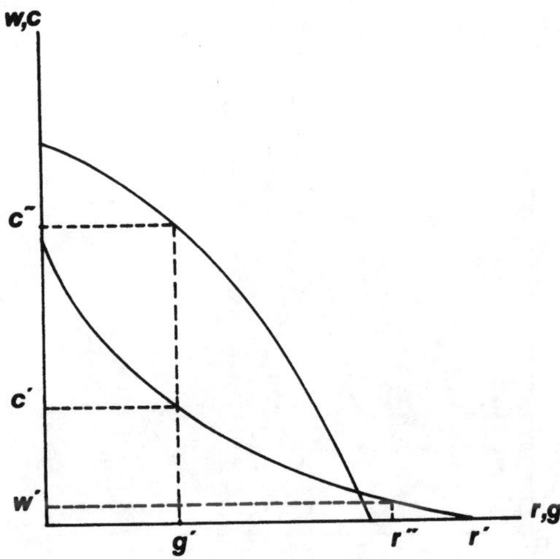

Figure 4.10

Basic and nonbasic commodities

The machine in the two-sector model is a basic commodity in the sense of Sraffa (1960, pp. 1–8, 28–33, 48–51). In the absence of multiple-product processes, a basic commodity is one which enters directly or indirectly into the production of all commodities. By implication, therefore, each basic commodity must enter directly or indirectly into its own production, from which it follows that basic commodities must be produced.

Basic commodities have played an important role in the capital theory controversies for two reasons. The first is that they provide a standard of value – or measure of price – which has certain remarkable and desirable properties in models more complicated than that considered so far. The second reason is that the chief economic implication of the distinction (between basics and nonbasics) is that basics have an essential part in the determination of the rate of profits while nonbasics have none (Sraffa, 1960, p. 54). The essence of the latter proposition is seen most easily in terms of the two-sector model.

On the face of it, the definition of basic commodities is entirely technological, depending on the flows of inputs required in the existing production processes. In several cases, however, a commodity may be represented as basic or nonbasic according to analytical convenience. The most important such commodity is labor power. Ignoring the most implausible cases, labor is a direct or indirect input to all production processes. However, if labor is not produced by any of these processes it must be nonbasic.

There is a widely known formulation in which labor is treated as a basic commodity. In the von Neumann growth model (von Neumann, 1945–46), it is assumed that there exists a basket of subsistence goods, which is consumed by each worker in the economy. So long as the basket of commodities per worker is constant, the employment of labor can be represented by the appropriate number of such baskets. There is then no explicit representation of labor. If these subsistence goods are produced, they will be basic since they enter directly into the production of all commodities which require labor power as an input. If labor is represented explicitly, then any commodities which serve only as wage goods do not enter into the production of any commodity which has a technologically defined production process. In that case, wage goods are themselves nonbasic.

It is apparent from these remarks just why the machine is a basic commodity in the two-sector model while the consumption goods and labor are nonbasic. The machine enters the production of all commodities which are produced while the consumption good does not enter the production of any commodity and labor is not produced.

In the foregoing exposition, all prices and quantities were normalized on nonbasics. In the price Equations (1), prices and the wage rate were expressed in terms of command over the consumption good while outputs and stocks per worker were used in the quantity Equations (14a). If instead, the price equations are normalized on the machine price and the quantity equations are normalized on the existing stock of machines, we have

$$\begin{aligned} \pi &= \alpha r + \beta w \\ 1 &= ar + bw \end{aligned} \tag{26}$$

and

$$\begin{aligned} N &= bg + \beta c \\ 1 &= ag + \alpha c \end{aligned} \tag{27}$$

From the second of Equations (26) and of (27), respectively,

$$r = (1/a)(1 - bw) \tag{28}$$

$$g = (1/a)(1 - \alpha c) \tag{29}$$

The symmetry of the relationship between the profit and wage rates on the one hand and the growth rate and consumption goods output on the other hand is maintained.

Excluding negative wages and consumption goods output, the maximum feasible growth rate and maximum feasible profit rate are $1/a$. This rate is Sraffa's standard ratio.

Consider the dimensions of the term bw. Having normalized price equations on p, the wage per man is in fact the number of machines (or the value-equivalent thereof) given each worker at the end of each period. Since b is the number of machine-producing workers per machine produced, bw is the proportion of net machine output paid as wages. Sraffa defined the wage rate used in his analysis (which we may denote w_s) as the proportion of standard net product paid as wages, where standard net product is composed entirely of basics. Since the machine is the only basic commodity in the model there is no replacement output (i.e., net and gross product are the same) and the product bw is the Sraffa wage rate w_s. Denoting the standard ratio by R, we may write the second of Equation (28) as

$$r = R(1 - w_s) \tag{30}$$

which is the distribution formula derived by Sraffa (1960).[7]

The dimensions of Equation (29) are even more straightforward. The fraction of the stock of machines employed in nonbasic production is αc. Thus, $1 - \alpha c$ is the *internal ratio,* the fraction of machines employed in machine production, which was considered above in connection with the quantity equations. The only differences between expressions (29) and (17a) are differences of notation.

The symmetry between Equations (28) and (29) is now clear. The rate of profits is the product of the standard ratio and the fraction of (the value of) machines left to machine sector capitalists after wages are paid. The rate of growth is the standard ratio times the fraction of machine outputs left to machine sector capitalists for further use in production. Whenever the distribution of income between capitalists and workers in the machine sector is the same as the distribution of outputs between production sectors, the growth and profit rates also are the same. The same function which relates profits and wages relates growth to consumption goods output. This time, however, it is clear that the rate of profits is diminished by payments for nonbasic inputs to basic commodity production while the rate of growth is diminished by the employment of basic commodities in the production of nonbasics.

If the economy is competitive, the profit rate,

determined by relative shares in the basic sector, is imposed upon the nonbasic sector. This must be the import of Sraffa's insistence that among all commodities basics alone are important in the determination of the profit rate. What is more, if the owners of machines determine to whom they sell the outputs, the basic commodity sector capitalists thereby determine the growth rate to which the rest of the economy must conform.

It is curious that Sraffa himself did not remark on this last point. Not only is it implicit in his value theory, it appears crucial to the determination of causal sequences in the analysis of capitalist accumulation.

An evaluation

What has been learned in the capital theory controversies is that the value of capital does not determine the rate of profits but is determined by it and that the relationship between the aggregate value of capital and technology is wholly without generality.

Little has been learned about accumulation. Perhaps we could sum up the controversy by saying that Clark made a mistake in supposing that the fund of capital could represent the important properties of the stocks of investment goods in theories of value and distribution. For slightly greater generality, we can note the errors of Bohm-Bawerk and Hayek in using time as their proxy for the stock of investment goods in an economy. But still we must ask if anything at all has been demonstrated except that a convenient simplification is erroneous?

Professor Samuelson answers in the negative. In reviewing the controversy he argues that none of its results affect "a general blueprint technology model of Joan Robinson and MIT type" (Samuelson, 1966, p. 245). Insofar as capital-reversal and reswitching are concerned, Samuelson is obviously right. No problems can arise regarding aggregate values of capital when no role is accorded to such values. But then the rate of profit cannot be determined by supply and demand for capital.

In fact, a number of issues lie hidden beneath the surface of the capital theory battlefield like unexploded mines. The most important of these issues, the nature of accumulation, could not be brought out with clarity in the context of these controversies. So far, there exists no model by which actual processes of capitalist accumulation can be analyzed or described in proper detail. But the concepts required for such an analytical framework already exist. They have been provided for us by the neo-Keynesian victors in the capital theory controversies and by the inventors of the classical tradition of political economy to which the neo-Keynesians are the modern heirs.

But here the reader must proceed with care. For the whole subject is fraught with passion and a remarkable inability to come to grips with the essential points at issue, as is amply demonstrated by the fact that thirteen years passed between Joan Robinson's initial salvo and Paul Samuelson's highly conditional surrender. The remaining essays in this book will try to develop at least part of the framework required for analysis of capitalist accumulation, but they will not be understood by those whose vision is circumscribed by the neoclassical horizon.

Notes

1 $Y/K = y/k$

$y = 1/\beta,\ k = (1/\beta)/(1/\alpha) = \alpha/\beta$

$\therefore y/k = 1/\alpha$, the r-intercept of the wage–profit frontier.

2 Product-exhaustion requires that the production function is linear homogeneous, i.e.,

$$\mu Y = F(\mu K, \mu N)$$

for any constant μ. Set $\mu = 1/N$

$$Y/N = y = F(K/N, 1) = f(k)$$
$$Y = N \cdot f(k)$$
$$\frac{\partial Y}{\partial K} = N\frac{df}{dk}\frac{dk}{dN} = N\frac{df}{dk}\frac{N}{N^2} = \frac{df}{dk} = \frac{dy}{dk}$$

3 The same relation may be derived directly from the aggregate production function

$$y = f(k)$$
$$r = df/dk;\ w = f(k) - (df/dk)k$$
$$dr/dk = d^2f/dk^2;$$
$$dw/dk = (df/dk) - (df/dk) - (d^2f/dk^2)k$$
$$\frac{dw/dk}{dr/dk} = dw/dr = -\mathrm{k}$$

4 This diagrammatical device is due entirely to E. J. Nell.

5 In most of the literature, "forward" and "positive" are applied to phenomena broadly consistent with neoclassical theory. "Perverse," "backward" and "negative" imply inconsistency with neoclassical theory.

6 The classical savings function was introduced into the analysis of long-period accumulation by Nicholas Kaldor (Kaldor, 1956, pp. 94–100). The role of these savings functions in neo-Keynesian theory is by now the subject of an extensive literature.

7 Of course, Sraffa developed his analysis in terms of a circulating capital model. In that case, substitute $1 + r$ for r in Equations (28) and (28a) so that $1 =$

$a(1 + r) + bw$ when $w = 0$, $R = (1 - a)/a$. In this case bw is the proportion of gross machine output paid as wages in the plant sector. The ratio of gross to net machine output is $1:1 - a$ since $1 - a = ar + bw$. Thus, the ratio of plant wages to net machine output is

$$bw/(1 - a) = w_s,$$

and we derive

$$1 = [ar/(1 - a)] + [bw/(1 - a)] = r/R = w_s$$
$$r = R(1 - w_s)$$

References

Bhaduri, A. 1966. "The Concept of Marginal Productivity and the Wicksell Effect," *Oxford Economic Papers*. 18:284–8.

Clark, J. B. 1893. *The Distribution of Wealth*. 1st ed. New York: Macmillan.

Kaldor, N. 1956. "Alternative Theories of Distribution," *Review of Economic Studies*, 23:83–100.

Kalecki, M. 1954. *The Theory of Economic Dynamics*. London: Unwin University Books.

Marx, K. 1967. *Capital*. Vols. I, II, III. New York: International Publishers.

Nell, E. 1970. "A Note on the Cambridge Controversies in Capital Theory," *Journal of Economic Literature*, 8:41–5.

von Neumann, J. 1945–46. "A Model of General Economic Equilibrium," *Review of Economic Studies*, 13:1–9.

Robinson, J. 1953–54. "The Production Function and the Theory of Capital," *Review of Economic Studies*, 21:81–106.

Samuelson, P. A. 1966. "A Summing Up," *Quarterly Journal of Economics*, 80:568–83.

1962. "Parable and Realism in Capital Theory: The Surrogate Production Function," *Review of Economic Studies*, 24:143–206.

Spaventa, L. 1970. "Rate of Profit, Rate of Growth and Capital Intensity in a Simple Production Model," *Oxford Economic Papers*, 22:124–47.

Sraffa, P. 1960. *Production of Commodities by Means of Commodities*. Cambridge: Cambridge University Press.

5

Laws of production and laws of algebra: Humbug II

Anwar Shaikh

The theoretical basis

Recent debates on capital theory have focused on the notion of capital as a factor of production, which along with labor, *can be used to explain the distribution of income in capitalist economy*. Though the intricate point and counterpoint of the controversy often obscure this simple fact, it has become increasingly clear that what is at stake in the current debate is in essence the same issue with which the classical economists, particularly Ricardo, grappled – that of the division of income between wages and profits. The argument thus rages around *descriptive* economic theory, whose aim it is to represent the workings of a competitive capitalist economy. In a sense this is a return to relevance, since much of modern mathematical economics has studiously concerned itself, not with descriptive, but instead with normative theory, such as the study of optimal and efficient growth paths, etc., (Lancaster, 1968, pp. 9–10).

In neoclassical theory, the model of pure exchange occupies a central position, for it illustrates simply and elegantly the fundamental truths of the paradigm, truths which any more complex representations may modify but certainly cannot undermine.[1] Thus, in the model of pure exchange, trading begins with selfish individuals each having an arbitrarily determined initial endowment of goods, and proceeds to a final state in which no one individual can improve his or her basket of commodities without making someone else worse off. Such a situation is known as a pareto-optimal allocation, and it implies a set of final exchange ratios between commodities – that is, a set of *equilibrium* relative prices. What is more, given the assumption of well-behaved neoclassical utility functions for each individual, the equilibrium prices of the model of pure exchange will be *scarcity prices:* the higher the relative availability of some commodity – other things being equal – the lower its relative price.

The next step in the analysis requires its extention to the case of production. Initial endowments are now assumed to contain not just consumer goods but also means of production, such as land, machines, raw materials, etc.; in addition, since the game cannot continue unless every individual has at least some wealth, it is generally assumed that each and every initial endowment includes potentially saleable labor services. By assumption, the ultimate objective of every individual is consumption; means of production and labor services, however, are not directly consumable. At this point, therefore, production is introduced as a roundabout way of consumption, a process in which inputs are transformed into outputs. In order to translate any given initial endowment into the production possibilities inherent in it, neoclassical economics commonly relies on the assumption of a well behaved neoclassical production function, one for each commodity produced.

Each individual then faces three basic methods of arriving at some preferred final allocation, methods which he or she is free to use in any combination permitted by the initial endowment and consistent with the utility function. First, he can trade any of the consumer goods or means of production in his possession for other goods he desires; second, he may rent out the *services* of the means of production he owns, and/or rent out his labor power; and third, if his

This chapter is an expanded, revised version of a paper entitled "Laws of Production and Laws of Algebra: The Humbug Production Function," which appeared as a note in *The Review of Economics and Statistics*, Vol. LVI, No. 1 (February, 1974), pp. 115–20, along with a comment by Robert Solow. The postscript to this chapter assesses Solow's comment.

initial endowment so permits, he may choose to become a producer, renting and/or buying means of production and labor-power and combining these with the elements of his initial endowment to turn out one or more commodities via a well-behaved neoclassical production function. Ruled only by his enlightened self-interest, which dictates that more is better, and constrained only by his native abilities and initial endowment, he is assumed to eventually arrive at some most "efficient" combination of the trader-rentier-producer modes, thereby attaining his personal optimum in the form of some final allocation.

Because preferences (utility functions) and initial endowments are *parameters* of the analysis, the whole structure of equilibrium is ruled by them, so that once again, the forces of consumer sovereignty lead us ineluctably to Pareto-optimality. Equilibrium relative prices are once again *scarcity* prices, a term which now covers the prices of consumption goods, the wage rate for labor services, and the rental and sale prices of means of production (Hershleifer, 1970).

Under carefully fashioned assumptions involving well-behaved utility and production functions, these sorts of models are determinate in the sense that one or more possible equilibria can be shown to exist. But the model, as outlined here, contains no reference to the uniform rate of profit which is supposed to characterize competitive capitalism. The explanation of this rate of profit is what (descriptive) neoclassical capital theory is all about. Moreover, given that the basic parables of the theory have already identified the equilibrium price of every good or service as a scarcity price, one that reflects its individual and social scarcity, the task that confronts the theory is clear: somehow, the rate of profit too must be explained as the scarcity price of some *thing* with both the price and quantity of this thing to be mutually determined in some market. This market, it turns out, is the capital market, in which demand is determined by individual's preferences for present versus future consumption – their "taste for investment" (Dewey, 1965) and supply is determined by the technological structure. The price that supposedly emerges from this interaction is the *rate of interest,* the scarcity index of the quantity of *capital,* and with the addition of a few more convenient assumptions, the rate of profit is made equal to this rate of interest. *If these conditions can be maintained,* then, it is argued, *the distribution of income in a capitalist society is a consequence of the efficient allocation of resources;* in fact, within this wondrous construct, capitalism itself represents the resolution of one of Nature's most problematical gifts – the "natural" selfishness of every individual!

Scarcity pricing parables and the aggregate production function

Traditionally, several models have been used to extend scarcity pricing to the theory of distribution. The simplest, and by far the most widely used in both the theoretical and empirical literature, is the aggregate production function model. Such a model, we are told, is an aggregated version of the general equilibrium model outlined above, constructed as an empirically useful approximation, *and strongly supported by the data.* Even the sophisticates, the so-called high-brows of neoclassical theory, at one time, took this and similar parables seriously:

> . . . In various places I have subjected to detailed analysis certain simplified models involving only a few factors of production . . . [These] simple models or parables do, I think, have considerable heuristic value in giving insights into the fundamentals of interest theory in all of its complexities. (Samuelson, 1962, p. 194)

> The originators of the "production function" theory of distribution (in the static sense, where I still think it should be taken fairly seriously) were Wicksteed, Edgeworth, and Pigou. (Hicks, 1965, p. 293, footnote 1)

Though aggregate or surrogate production function models occupy the bulk of the theoretical and empirical literature on the distribution of income in a capitalist society, the essential characteristic of this and all other parables of neoclassical theory concerns their attempt to explain the wage rate and the rate of profit as scarcity prices of labor and capital, respectively, determined in the final analysis by efficiency considerations. It was precisely this technocratic apologia for capitalism which became the target of the neo-Keynesian counterattack of the 1960s, during the so-called Cambridge capital controversies.

One of the most striking, and for neoclassical economics most devastating, results of the above capital controversies was the proof that *any* version of the neoclassical parable, in which the rate of profit varied inversely with the quantity of capital and the wage rate inversely with the quantity of labor (so that each at least behaved like a scarcity price) was valid in static conditions *if and only if prices in all possible* competitive equilibria were proportional to labor values.[2] These results, therefore, apply, *inter alia,* to that particular version of the parable known as the aggregate (or surrogate) production function, in which the wage rate and the rate of profit not only move inversely to the quantities of labor and capital, respectively, but are also equal to and determined by their respective marginal products. Considering that the neoclassical parables have their origins in a "conscious counterrevolution *against* the classical school, against Ricardo and Marx in particular" (Dobb, 1970, p. 1), and above all, against the labor theory of value in *any* form, it is gratifying to discover that in the end these parables themselves depend on the *simple* labor theory of value. The irony is inescapable.

These and other inimical results were not lost on the faithful. As awareness of the internal inconsistencies of neoclassical theory began to grow, many were led to abandon it. But for others, hope died hard; and hope, it seems, lay in the data. "As a neoclassical theorist, I can only reply that the relevant question is what is relevant: should we make our predictions on the basis of what Mrs. Robinson has called perverse technical behavior *or on the basis of relations that have been repeatedly observed*?" (Ferguson, 1971, p. 254, emphasis added)

What has been "repeatedly observed," it is argued, is the empirical efficacy of aggregate production functions. In spite of the very strongest theoretical requirements for their existence, the use of such functions flourishes – the current justification being that their empirical basis appears strong. In study after study, empirically derived functions appear to strongly support both the constancy of returns to scale *and* the equality of marginal products with "factor rewards"; in particular, for both time-series and cross-section studies (within any one country), the Cobb–Douglas function appears to dominate the field.

For the neoclassical faithful, these results represent their salvation; no matter what those critics from Cambridge say, the "real" world, it would seem, is neoclassical. Or is it? The answer is simple: no. *The so-called empirical strength of aggregate production is an illusion,* due not to some mystical laws of production, but instead, to some rather prosaic laws of algebra. To see why, however, we must first examine how production functions are estimated.

The empirical basis of aggregate production functions

The most popular methods of estimating aggregate production functions have been the single equation least squares method and the factor shares method (Walters, 1963). The former can be most generally described as fitting a function of the form[3] $Q(t) = F[K(t), L(t), t]$ to observed data while the latter consists of *assuming* that aggregate marginal products of capital and labor are equal to their respective unit earnings and then using this assumption to specify structural coefficients. In general, for both time series and cross-section data, the Cobb–Douglas function wins out; "the sum of coefficients usually approximate closely to unity" (thus implying constant returns to scale), with the additional bonus of a close "agreement between the labor exponent and the share of wages in the value of output" (thus supporting aggregate marginal productivity theory) (Walters, 1963, p. 27).

In a recent paper, Franklin Fisher concedes that the requirements "under which the production possibilities of a technically diverse economy can be represented by an aggregate production function are far too stringent to be believable" (Fisher, 1971, p. 306). He proposes therefore to investigate the puzzling uniformity of the empirical results by means of a simulation experiment: each of N industries in this simulated economy is assumed to be characterized by a microeconomic Cobb–Douglas production function relating its homogeneous output to its homogeneous labor input and its own *distinct* machine stock. The conditions for theoretical aggregation are studiously violated, and the question is, how well, and under what circumstances, does an aggregate Cobb–Douglas function represent the data generated? In such an economy, the aggregate wage share is often variable over time, so that in general an aggregate Cobb–Douglas would not be expected to give a good fit. What seems to surprise Fisher, however, is that when the wage share happens coincidentally to be roughly constant, a Cobb–Douglas production function will not only fit the data well but *also* provide a good explanation of wages, "*even though the true relationships are far from yielding an aggregate Cobb–Douglas,*" *suggesting that "the view that the constancy of labor's share is due to the presence of an aggregate Cobb–Douglas production function is mistaken. Causation runs the other way and the apparent success of aggregate Cobb–Douglas production functions is due to the relative constancy of labor's share.*" (Emphasis added.) (Fisher, 1971, p. 306).

It is obvious that so long as aggregate shares are roughly constant, the appropriate econometric test of aggregate neoclassical production and distribution theory requires a Cobb–Douglas function. Such a test would then apparently cast some light on the degree of returns to scale (through the sum of the coefficients), and the applicability of aggregate marginal productivity theory (through the comparison of the labor and capital exponents with the wage and profit shares, respectively). What is not obvious, however, is that so long as aggregate shares are constant, an aggregate Cobb–Douglas function having apparently "constant returns to scale" will always provide an exact fit, for any data whatsoever. *In addition, under fairly reasonable conditions, such a function will seem also to possess "marginal products equal to respective factor rewards," thus seeming to justify neoclassical aggregate distribution theory.* These propositions, it will be shown, are *mathematical* consequences of constant shares, and it will be argued that the puzzling uniformity of the empirical results is due in fact to this law of algebra and not to some mysterious law of production. In fact, in order to emphasize the independence of these results from any laws of production, an illustration is provided in the form of the rather implausible data of the Humbug economy, for even data such as this is perfectly consistent with a Cobb–Douglas function having "constant returns to scale," "neutral technical change," and satisfying "marginal productivity rules," so long as shares are constant.

Laws of algebra

Let us begin by separating the aggregate data in any time period into output data (Q, the value of output), distribution data (W, π, wages and profits, respectively), and input data (K, L, the index numbers for capital and labor, respectively). Then we can write the following aggregate identity for any time t:

$$Q(t) \equiv W(t) + \pi(t) \tag{1}$$

Given *any* index numbers $K(t)$, $L(t)$, we can always write:

$$q(t) \equiv w(t) + r(t)k(t) \tag{2}$$

where $q(t)$ and $k(t)$ are the output–labor and capital–labor ratios, respectively, and $w(t) \equiv W(t)/L(t)$, $r(t) \equiv \pi(t)/K(t)$ are the wage and profit rates, respectively. The above equation is therefore the fundamental identity relating output, distribution, and input data. Defining the share of profits in output as s, and the share of wages as $1 - s$, we can differentiate identity 2 to arrive at identity 3 (time derivatives are denoted by dots, and the time index, t, is dropped to simplify notation):

$$\dot{q} = \dot{w} + \dot{r}k + r\dot{k} \equiv w\left(\frac{\dot{w}}{w}\right) + rk\left(\frac{\dot{r}}{r}\right) + rk\left(\frac{\dot{k}}{k}\right)$$

Dividing through by q,

$$\frac{\dot{q}}{q} = \frac{w}{q}\left(\frac{\dot{w}}{w}\right) + \frac{rk}{q}\left(\frac{\dot{r}}{r}\right) + \frac{rk}{q}\left(\frac{\dot{k}}{k}\right)$$

By definition, the profit and wage shares, respectively, are

$$s \equiv \frac{rk}{q}, \; 1 - s \equiv \frac{w}{q}$$

so that we may write,

$$\frac{\dot{q}}{q} \equiv \frac{\dot{B}}{B} + s\frac{\dot{k}}{k} \quad \text{where} \quad \frac{\dot{B}}{B} = \left[(1 - s)\frac{\dot{w}}{w} + s\frac{\dot{r}}{r}\right] \tag{3}$$

It is important to note that all relations given so far are *always* true for *any* aggregate data at all, irrespective of production or distribution conditions.

Suppose now we are faced with particular data which for some unspecified reasons exhibit constant shares, so that $s = \beta$ (a constant). Remembering that the dotted variables are time derivatives ($\dot{q} = dq/dt$, etc.), we can immediately integrate the identity (3):

$$\int \frac{\dot{q}}{q}\,dt = \int \frac{\dot{B}}{B}\,dt = \int \beta\frac{\dot{k}}{k}\,dt$$

$$ln\, q = \int \frac{\dot{B}}{B}\,dt + \beta\, ln\, k + ln\, c_0$$

where for convenience the constant of integration is written as $\ln c_0$. Rewriting, we have,

$$q = \left[\exp\left(\int \frac{\dot{B}}{B}\,dt\right)\right] c_0k^{\beta} = [B]c_0k^{\beta} \tag{4}$$

where by definition

$$B = \exp\left(\int \frac{\dot{B}}{B}\,\mathrm{dt}\right)$$

Equation (4) is strikingly reminiscent of a constant returns to scale aggregate Cobb–Douglas production function with a shift parameter B. But in fact, it is not a *production* function at all, but merely an algebraic relationship which always holds for *any* output-input data Q, K, L, even data which could not conceivably come from any economy, so long as the distribution data exhibits a constant ratio. Furthermore, since the $\dot{B}/B$ term in identity (3) is a weighted average of the *rates of change* of w and r, respectively, it seems empirically reasonable to expect that measures of K, L would give a capital-labor ratio k which is weakly correlated with $\dot{B}/B$. With measures for which the above is true, *$\dot{B}/B$ may be considered to be primarily a function of time,* so that B will also be solely a function of time. Then we can write

$$q = B(t)\,[c_0k^{\beta}] \tag{5}$$

and since $q \equiv Q/L$ and $k \equiv K/L$, we get

$$Q = B(t)\,[c_0K^{\beta}L^{1-\beta}] \tag{5a}$$

The algebraic relationship just given has several interesting properties. First, it is homogeneous to the first degree in K and L. Second, since $\beta = s \equiv rk/q$, the partial derivatives $\partial Q/\partial K$, $\partial Q/\partial L$ are equal to r, w, respectively. And third, the effect of time is "neutral," as incorporated in the shift parameter $B(t)$. What we have, actually, is *mathematically* identical to a constant returns to scale Cobb–Douglas production function having neutral technical change and satisfying marginal productivity "rules." And yet, as we have seen, *any production data whatsoever can be presented as being "generated" by such a function,* so long as shares are constant and the measures of capital and labor such that k is uncorrelated with $\dot{B}/B$. Therefore, precisely because (5a) *is* a mathematical relationship, holding true for large classes of data associated with constant shares, it cannot be interpreted as a production function, or any production relation at all. If anything, it is a distributive relation, and sheds little or no light on the underlying production relationships.[4] In fact, since the constancy of shares has been taken as an empirical datum throughout, equation (5a) does not shed much light on any theory of distribution either.

I emphasized earlier that the theoretical basis of aggregate production function analysis was extremely weak. It would seem now that its apparent empirical strength is no strength at all, but merely a statistical reflection of an algebraic relationship. For the neoclassical old guard, the retreat to data is really a rout.

Applications

It is obvious that one can apply Equation (5a) in many ways. The section that follows will reexamine Solow's famous paper on measuring technical change. The "humbug production function" section will present a numerical example to illustrate the generality of Equation (5a). The section on Fisher's simulation experiments will extend the preceding analysis; and the final section will touch briefly on cross-section production function studies.

Technical change and the aggregate production function: Solow. In what is considered a "seminal paper" (Solow, 1957), Robert Solow introduced in 1957 a novel method for measuring the contribution of technical change to economic growth. Since that time several refinements of Solow's original calculations have been established, all aimed at providing better measures of labor and capital by taking account of education, vintages of machines, etc., but the basic approach has remained unchanged.[5]

Solow's approach is by now a familiar one. Equation (6) expresses the assumption of a constant returns to scale aggregate production function, with the parameter $A(t)$ expressing the assumption of neutral technical change.

$$q = A(t)f(k) \tag{6}$$

For such a function, the marginal product of capital is $dq/dk = A(t)\,[df/dk] = [q/f]\,[df/dk]$, since $A(t) = q/f$. By assumption, this marginal product is equal to the rate of profit r:

$$\frac{dq}{dk} = \frac{q}{f}\frac{df}{dk} = r$$

and by rewriting, we can express this in terms of the profit share s:

$$\frac{df}{dk}\frac{k}{f} = \frac{rk}{q} = s \quad \text{share of profit in output} \tag{7}$$

Solow's expressed purpose was to distinguish between shifts of the assumed production function (due to "technical change") and movements along it (due to changes in the capital–labor ratio, k).[6]

Figure 5.1 illustrates the geometric assumption implicit in Solow's paper. Points A_0 and B_1 are observed points, at times t_0 and t_1, respectively, while B_0 represents the "adjusted" point after "neutral technical change" has been removed. Thus points A_0 and B_0 lie on the "underlying production function."

Algebraically, in terms of Equation (6), the aim of his procedure is to partition output per worker q into A, the technical change shift parameter, and $f(k)$, the "underlying production function" to which I just referred. In order to do this, Solow first differentiates Equation (6):

$$\dot{q} = \dot{A}f(k) + A\frac{df(k)}{dt} = \dot{A}f(k) + A\frac{df(k)}{dk}\dot{k}$$

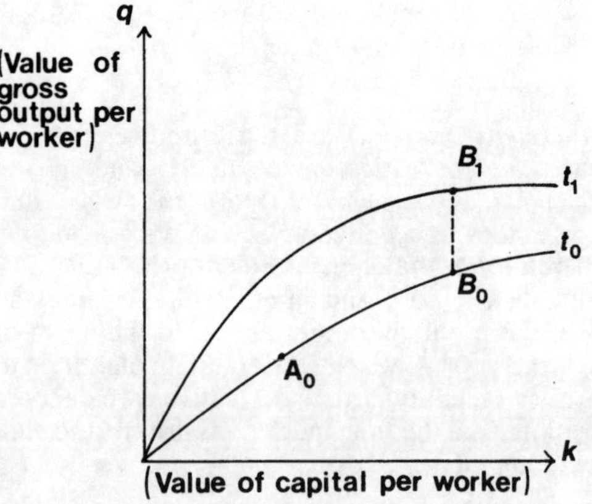

Figure 5.1

Rearranging,

$$\dot{q} = \frac{\dot{A}}{A} Af(k) + Af(k)\left[\frac{df(k)}{dk} \cdot \frac{k}{f(k)}\right]\frac{k'}{k}$$

Since from (6), $q = Af(k)$, and from (7),

$$\frac{df(k)}{dk}\frac{k}{f(k)} = \frac{rk}{q} = s$$

s being the share of profit in gross output, we can write

$$\frac{\dot{q}}{q} = \frac{\dot{A}}{A} + s\frac{\dot{k}}{k} \qquad (8)$$

Equation (8) is derived from the *assumptions* of a constant returns to scale aggregate production function, with distribution determined by marginal productivity rules. Equation (3), derived earlier from an *identity* and therefore always true for any production and distribution behavior, is mathematically identical to (8). It follows therefore that $\dot{A}/A = \dot{B}/B \equiv [(1 - s)\,\dot{w}/w + (s)\dot{r}/r]$; that is, Solow's measure of technical change is merely a weighted average of the growth rates of the wage rate, w and the rate of profit, r.

Solow's data provide him with a series for gross output per worker q, capital per worker k, and profit share s, for the United States from 1909–1949. From this data, he calculates the rates of change $\dot{q}/q$ and $\dot{k}/k$, and using these rates along with the data for the profit share s, he derives a series for $\dot{A}/A = \dot{q}/q - s\dot{k}/k$.

To Solow, the series for $\dot{A}/A$ represents the rate of change of technology; since a scatter diagram of $\dot{A}/A$ on k shows no apparent correlation, he concludes that technical change is essentially neutral. By setting $A(0) = 1$, he is able to translate the rate of technical change $\dot{A}/A$ into a series for $A(t)$, the shift parameter.[7] Finally, since by definition $q = A(t)\,f(k)$, he is able to combine his derived series for $A(t)$ with his given series on q to derive the underlying production function $f(k) = q/A(t)$.

Plotting $f(k)$ versus k, Solow gets a diagram with noticeable curvature, and notes with obvious satisfaction that the data "gives a distinct impression of diminishing returns" (Solow, 1957, p. 380). In fact, Solow finds this underlying production function to be extremely well represented by a Cobb–Douglas function:

$$\ln \hat{f}(k) = -.729 + .353 \ln k \quad (R^2 = .9992) \qquad (9)$$

Given our preceding analysis in the section on laws of algebra, it is not difficult to see why Solow's results turn out so nicely. We know for instance that his data exhibit roughly constant shares, and the residual term $\dot{B}/B = \dot{A}/A$ is uncorrelated with k. From purely algebraic considerations, therefore, one would expect the data to be well represented by the functional form in (5), $q = B(t)\ c_0k^{\beta}$, a form which is mathematically identical to a constant returns to scale Cobb–Douglas function, with neutral technical change and "marginal products equal to factor rewards." In fact, the *algebra* indicates that Solow's underlying production function should be of the form:

$$f(k) = c_0k^{\beta} \qquad (10)$$

$$\ln f(k) = \ln c_0 + \beta \ln k \qquad (10a)$$

β is of course the (roughly) constant share and c_0 is a constant of integration which depends only on the initial points q_0, k_0, of the data. Solow uses the years 1909–1942 in his regressions, and for these years the average profit share $s \cong \beta = .35$.[8] Moreover, since in any period t, $q_t = B(t)\ c_0k_t^{\beta}$ from Equation (6), in period $t = t_0$ we may write $q_0 = B(0)\ c_0k_0^{\beta}$, which gives us $\ln c_0 = \ln q_0 - \ln B(0) - \beta \ln k_0$. For Solow, this residual $B(t)$ represents the shift parameter $A(t)$ (compare Equations (3) derived from an identity, and Equation (8) derived from Solow's assumptions), so that $B(0) = A(0)$; as mentioned earlier, he takes $A(0) = 1$. From Table 1, p. 315 of his article, we get $q_0 = .623$, $k_0 = 2.06$, which when combined with $B(0) = A(0) = 1$, gives $\ln c_0 \cong -0.725$.

Thus, on purely algebraic considerations one would expect Solow's underlying production function to be characterized by

$$\ln f(k) = -.725 + .35 \ln k \qquad (11)$$

This, of course, is virtually identical to Solow's regression result, equation (9), as it should be, *for it is a law of algebra, not a law of production!*

The humbug production function. The analysis of the laws of algebra led to the conclusion that *any production data series q, k whatsoever, can be represented as being generated by a Cobb–Douglas production function* having neutral technical change and satisfying marginal productivity "rules," so long as shares are constant and the measures of capital and labor such that k is uncorrelated with $\dot{B}/B$. It is possible to illustrate the generality of the above result by means of a numerical example. Consider, for example, an economy with the output–input data illustrated in Figure 5.2 and having the same profit share as in Solow's data for the United States.

The Humbug data set gives us a series for q, k, and s, from which we can calculate rates of change $\dot{q}/q$ and $\dot{k}/k$. From these, in turn, we derive $\dot{B}/B = \dot{q}/q - s(\dot{k}/k)$. (The calculations appear in Figure 5.5.)

Plotting $\dot{B}/B$ on k gives us a scatter diagram

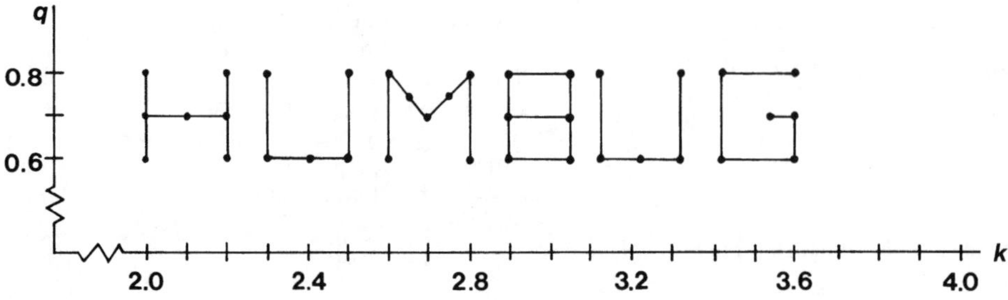

Figure 5.2

with no apparent correlations, so that we may safely assume that B is solely a function of time: $B = B(t)$

This above-mentioned result, combined with the approximate constancy of the profit share s, is sufficient for us to be able to state that even the humbug data can be thought of as having been generated by a Cobb–Douglas production function $q_t = B(t)\, c_0\, k_t^{\beta}$ having constant returns to scale, neutral technical "regress", and marginal products equal to factor rewards!

Let us, however, go on to derive the numerical values involved. To begin with, we follow Solow in setting $B(0) = 1$, and using that to translate the rates of change $\dot{B}/B$ into the series $B(t)$, which is represented in Figure 5.3.

Using the series just mentioned for $B(t)$, one may then derive the underlying production function $f(k) = q/B(t)$, which when plotted versus k in Figure 5.4 gives the same distinct impression of "diminishing returns" that Solow found in *his* data. As we saw in the section on Solow, this pattern is a necessary one, the algebraic consequence of a constant profit share s.

We have already seen that the numerical specification of $f(k)$ can always be anticipated from purely algebraic considerations. For instance, in the Humbug data we use the years 1909–47, and for these years, the average profit share is $\beta = .34$. Moreover, since $q_0 = .80$, $k_0 = 2.00$, and $B(0) = 1.0$ for Humbug data, we would expect the constant term to be $\ln c_0 = \ln q_0 - \ln B(0) - \beta \ln k_0 = -0.459$.[9] Algebraic considerations therefore tell us that the constant term will be $\ln c_0 = -0.459$ and the slope $\beta = .34$. The actual regression of $f(k)$ on k, presented below, gives virtually identical results.

$$\hat{f}(k) = -0.453 + .34 \ln k \quad (R^2 = .993) \tag{12}$$

The function $B(t)$ is of course much more troublesome. A simple glance at Figure 5.3 tells us that no linear or log-linear function will suffice for a numerical approximation. Nonetheless, even in this case a fair approximation is possible:[10]

$$\hat{B}(t) = a_0 + a_1 t + \sum_{i=1}^{2}\left[b_i \cos\left(\frac{c_i \pi t}{2}\right) + d_i \sin\left(\frac{e_i \pi t}{2}\right)\right] \tag{13}$$

$a_0 =$	.8565	$a_1 =$	-3.966×10^{-3}	$b_3 =$	.0206
$b_1 =$	$-.0325$	$b_2 =$	.0435	$c_3 =$	.5
$c_1 =$	.4	$c_2 =$	.6	$d_3 =$	$-.0295$
$d_1 =$	.035	$d_2 =$	$-.032$	$e_3 =$	.4
$e_1 =$	.5	$e_2 =$	.8		

($R^2 = .82$; corrected for degrees of freedom, $\bar{R}^2 = .68$.)[11]

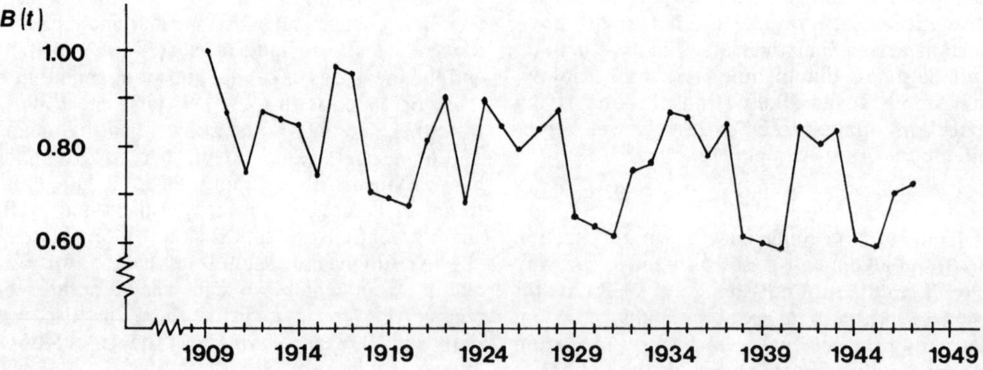

Figure 5.3

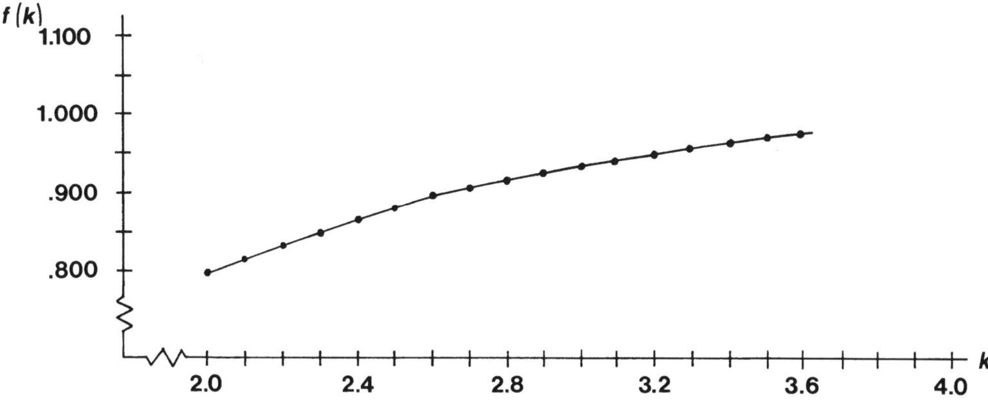

Figure 5.4

Combining these two fitted functions, one arrives at a numerical specification for even the Humbug data (Table 5.1)!

Fisher's simulation experiments. Earlier, I mentioned Franklin Fisher's extensive (and expensive) simulation experiments, in which he finds, to his surprise, that aggregate Cobb–Douglas functions seem to "work" for his simulated economy even when the theoretical conditions for such an aggregate function are carefully violated, so long as the particular simulation run happens to have roughly constant wage (and hence profit) shares (Fisher, 1971, p. 306).

It is worth noting at this point that what Fisher means by aggregate production functions working, is not simply that they give a good fit to gross output $Q(t)$ or gross output per worker $q(t)$, but also that the estimated marginal products of labor, and presumably of capital, closely approximate the actual wage and profit rates, respectively (Fisher, 1971).

I have already demonstrated in section on the laws of algebra why in general an aggregate Cobb–Douglas may be expected to work, in the sense explained earlier, for data which reflect constant wage shares. In this section, however, it will be shown that even Fisher's massive computer simulation is in reality only an application of the laws of algebra.

The structure of the simulation. Fisher's simulated economy consists of N industries, each producing the same type of output Q, using homogeneous labor L, but its own *distinct* type of machine stock K_i. Thus Q_i and Q_j are both quantities of the same good, produced by industries i and j, respectively, whereas K_i and K_j are stocks of different types of machines.

Each industry is assumed to be characterized by a microeconomic Cobb–Douglas production function:

$$Q_i(t) = A_i(t)\,[L_i(t)]^{\alpha}\,[K_i(t)]^{1-\alpha} \quad \text{where } i = 1, \ldots, N \tag{14}$$

(The α_i are constant over time, but in general $A_i(t)$, $L_i(t)$, and $K_i(t)$ are not.)

At any instant of time, the total stock of labor $L(t)$ in the economy is given. The basic procedure followed in the model is to allocate this given supply among the existing industries so as to equalize the industry marginal products of labor ($MPL_i = MPL_j = MPL$): this of course yields the maximum aggregate output $Q(t) \equiv \Sigma_{i=1}^{N} Q_i(t)$.

In general, the marginal product of a Cobb–Douglas function is $\text{MPL}_i = \alpha_i[Q_i(t)/L_i(t)]$.[12] Since these are all equalized for the various industries to a single level, we can denote this common level by $w(t)$ and write:

$$MPL_i = \alpha_i \frac{Q_i(t)}{L_i(t)} = w(t) \tag{15}$$

$w(t)$ represents the "imputed rental" (uniform wage rate) of a unit of labor, so that the wage bill in the ith industry is:

$$w(t)L_i(t) = \alpha_i Q_i(t) \tag{16}$$

Thus, the aggregate wage bill is:

$$w(t)L(t) = \sum_{i=1}^{N} w(t)L_i(t) = \sum_{i=1}^{N} \alpha_i Q_i(t)$$

so that the wage share in total output $Q(t) \equiv \Sigma_{L=1}^{N} Q_i(t)$ is:

$$\text{wage share} = \frac{w(t)L(t)}{Q(t)} = \sum_{i=1}^{N} \alpha_i \left[\frac{Q_i(t)}{Q(t)}\right] \tag{17}$$

Finally, since $Q_i(t)$ is the gross output of the ith industry, and $w(t)\,L_i(t) = \alpha_i\,Q_i(t)$ its wage bill, the difference between the two, the gross profit

Table 5.1. *Humbug data*

Year	Actual share of property income	"Humbug" output per worker	"Humbug" capital per worker					
	s	$q(t)$	$k(t)$	$\dot{q}/q$	$\dot{k}/k$	$\dot{B}/B$	$B(t)$	$j(k)$
1909	0.335	0.80	2.00	−0.125	0.000	−0.125	1.000	0.800
1910	0.330	0.70	2.00	−0.143	0.000	−0.143	0.875	0.800
1911	0.335	0.60	2.00	+0.167	0.000	+0.167	0.750	0.800
1912	0.330	0.70	2.00	0.000	+0.050	−0.017	0.875	0.800
1913	0.334	0.70	2.10	0.000	0.048	−0.016	0.860	0.814
1914	0.325	0.70	2.20	−0.143	0.000	−0.143	0.846	0.826
1915	0.344	0.60	2.20	+0.333	0.000	+0.333	0.725	0.828
1916	0.358	0.80	2.20	0.000	0.045	−0.016	0.965	0.830
1917	0.370	0.80	2.30	−0.250	0.000	−0.250	0.948	0.843
1918	0.342	0.60	2.30	0.000	0.044	−0.015	0.710	0.845
1919	0.354	0.60	2.40	0.000	0.042	−0.015	0.700	0.857
1920	0.319	0.60	2.50	+0.167	0.000	+0.167	0.690	0.870
1921	0.369	0.70	2.50	+0.143	0.000	+0.143	0.805	0.870
1922	0.339	0.80	2.50	−0.250	0.040	−0.264	0.921	0.869
1923	0.337	0.60	2.60	+0.333	0.000	+0.333	0.678	0.885
1924	0.330	0.80	2.60	−0.063	0.019	−0.069	0.902	0.887
1925	0.336	0.75	2.65	−0.067	0.019	−0.073	0.840	0.893
1926	0.327	0.70	2.70	+0.071	0.019	+0.065	0.780	0.897
1927	0.323	0.75	2.75	+0.067	0.018	+0.061	0.830	0.903
1928	0.338	0.80	2.80	−0.250	0.000	−0.250	0.880	0.908
1929	0.332	0.60	2.80	0.000	0.036	−0.012	0.660	0.908
1930	0.347	0.60	2.90	0.000	0.052	−0.018	0.652	0.920
1931	0.325	0.60	3.05	+0.167	0.000	+0.167	0.641	0.935
1932	0.397	0.70	3.05	0.000	−0.049	+0.019	0.748	0.935
1933	0.362	0.70	2.90	+0.143	0.000	+0.143	0.764	0.916
1934	0.355	0.80	2.90	0.000	0.052	−0.018	0.874	0.916
1935	0.351	0.80	3.05	−0.125	0.000	−0.125	0.860	0.930
1936	0.357	0.70	3.05	0.143	0.033	+0.132	0.752	0.930
1937	0.340	0.80	3.15	0.250	0.000	−0.250	0.852	0.940
1938	0.331	0.60	3.15	0.000	0.032	−0.011	0.638	0.940
1939	0.347	0.60	3.25	0.000	0.031	−0.011	0.633	0.948
1940	0.357	0.60	3.35	+0.333	0.000	+0.333	0.626	0.960
1941	0.377	0.80	3.35	0.000	0.070	−0.026	0.843	0.950
1942	0.356	0.80	3.60	0.000	−0.042	+0.015	0.820	0.975
1943	0.342	0.80	3.45	−0.250	0.000	−0.250	0.832	0.964
1944	0.332	0.60	3.45	0.000	0.044	−0.015	0.624	0.964
1945	0.314	0.60	3.60	+0.167	0.000	+0.167	0.614	0.978
1946	0.312	0.70	3.60	0.000	−0.014	+0.004	0.717	0.975
1947	0.327	0.70	3.55	—	—	—	0.721	0.970

in the ith industry, is treated as the "imputed rental" of its unique machine stock $K_i(t)$. Defining this gross profit (imputed machine rental) as $\pi_i(t)$, we have:

$$\pi_i(t) = (1 - \alpha_i)Q_i(t) = \text{gross profits in } i\text{th industry} \quad (18)$$

Since output $Q_i(t)$ and labor $L_i(t)$ are homogeneous across industries, their respective aggregates are derived by simple addition. But since each industry has a *unique* type of machine, an aggregate capital stock cannot be derived by adding machines together, each machine being a different type. An index of aggregate capital has therefore to be constructed, and it is known that in general any such index will violate the strict conditions under which the microeconomic Cobb–Douglas production functions can be theoretically aggregated into a macroeconomic Cobb–Douglas production function (Fisher, 1971, pp. 307–08). On the basis of aggregation theory, therefore, one would not expect the macroeconomic variables in this simulated economy to behave as if they were generated by a Cobb–Douglas function, even if aggregate shares happen to remain roughly constant over time. That, of course, is the reason for Fisher's surprise at his results.

Fisher chooses to construct an aggregate index in two steps. First, he runs the model economy over its 20-year period, from which he gets the gross profits $\pi_i(t)$ of any given industry, for each of 20 years. Similarly, over each of the 20 years he knows the machine stock $K_i(t)$ in the same industry: the ratio of the 20-year sums of these two is the average rate of return in the ith industry:

$$r_i = \left(\sum_{t=0}^{20} \pi_i(t) \Big/ \sum_{t=0}^{20} K_i(t)\right)$$
$$= \text{20-year average rate of return in } i^{th} \text{ industry} \quad (19)$$

The units of each average return r_i are output per machine type i. Thus Fisher can use these r_i in any one period t to aggregate the individual industry machine stocks into an aggregate index of capital $J(t)$:

$$J(t) = \sum_{i=1}^{N} J_i(t) = \sum_{i=1}^{N} r_i K_i(t) \quad (20)$$

It is useful to note that in the above expression the r_i are *not* functions of time, since they represent average rates of return over the whole 20-year period.

The constancy of wage shares. From Equation (19), the wage share is

$$\text{wage share} = \sum_{i=1}^{N} \alpha_i \left[\frac{Q_i(t)}{Q(t)}\right]$$

Now, as Fisher notes, since the parameters α_i are independent of time, the wage share will be roughly constant over time only if the relative outputs $Q_i(t)/Q(t)$ are roughly constant over time (Fisher, 1971, p. 321, footnote 21). Let us denote these roughly constant relative outputs by Pi, and the constant wage share by $(1 - s)$, the lack of time subscript denoting their constancy:

$$\frac{Q_i(t)}{Q(t)} \approx p_i \quad (21)$$

$$(1 - s) = \frac{w(t)L(t)}{Q(t)} \cong \sum_{i=1}^{N} \alpha_i p_i \quad (22)$$

In each industry, the wage bill, as derived in Equation (17), is $w(t)L_i(t) = \alpha_i Q_i(t)$. From (22), the aggregate wage bill is $w(t)L(t) = (1 - s)Q(t)$, and dividing one by the other, we get:

$$\frac{L_i(t)}{L(t)} = \frac{\alpha_i}{1 - s}\frac{Q_i(t)}{Q(t)} \cong \frac{\alpha_i p_i}{1 - s} \quad (23)$$

Finally, to prepare us for the last step, we need to note that the rough constancy of relative outputs $Q_i(t)/Q(t)$ and relative employment $L_i(t)/L(t)$ implies that each firm's output and employment grow at roughly the same rate. That is, dropping time subscripts and denoting time derivatives by dots:[13]

$$\frac{\dot{Q}_i}{Q_i} = \frac{\dot{Q}}{Q} \quad \text{and} \quad \frac{\dot{L}_i}{L_i} = \frac{\dot{L}}{L} = .03 \quad (24)$$

Algebraic considerations. It is the central result of this paper that *given constant shares,* any aggregate data Q, K, L whatsoever can be described by a function of the form $Q(t) = B(t)c_0K^{\beta}L^{1-\beta}$, providing the residual $\dot{B}/B$ is solely a function of time. What we must therefore do for Fisher's experiments, in order to see why aggregate Cobb–Douglas functions work for them, is to examine this residual $\dot{B}/B$.

By definition, from Equation (3)

$$\frac{\dot{B}}{B} = \frac{\dot{q}}{q} - s\frac{\dot{k}}{k} \quad (3)$$

Here, $q \equiv Q/L$, and $kK/L \equiv J/L$ since Fisher's index of capital is denoted by J. Thus $\dot{q}/q = \dot{Q}/Q - \dot{L}/L$, and $K/K = \dot{J}/J - \dot{L}/L$ and:

$$\frac{\dot{B}}{B} = \frac{\dot{Q}}{Q} - \frac{L}{L} - s\frac{\dot{J}}{J} + s\frac{\dot{L}}{L}$$

$$\frac{\dot{B}}{B} = \frac{\dot{Q}}{Q} - s\frac{\dot{J}}{J} - (1 - s)\frac{\dot{L}}{L} \quad (25)$$

Since s and $1 - s$ are (roughly) *constant* profit and wage shares, respectively, we need only examine the rates of change of $L(t)$, $J(t)$, and $Q(t)$.

The first is easy. In all of his simulations, Fisher specifies that "labor grows at an average rate of 3% trend" with small random deviations from the trend (Fisher, 1971, p. 309). Ignoring the small random deviations then,

$$\frac{\dot{L}}{L} \approx .03 \quad (26)$$

The growth rate of the aggregate capital index $J(t)$ is a bit more complicated. In Equation (20) we defined

$$J(t) = \sum_{i=1}^{N} J_i(t) = \sum_{i=1}^{N} r_i K_i(t)$$

where the r_i are constant over time. Differentiating this with respect to time,

$$\frac{dJ(t)}{dt} = \sum_{i=1}^{N} r_i \frac{dK_i(t)}{dt}$$
$$= \sum_{i=1}^{N} [r_i K_i(t)] \frac{dK_i(t)}{dt}\frac{1}{K_i(t)}$$
$$= \sum_{i=1}^{N} J_i(t)\frac{\dot{K}_i}{K_i}$$

Dividing through $J(t)$, we get:

$$\frac{\dot{J}}{J} \equiv \frac{dJ(t)}{dt}\frac{1}{J(t)} = \sum_{i=1}^{N}\left(\frac{\dot{K}_i}{K_i}\right)\left[\frac{J_i(t)}{J(t)}\right]$$

During all his simulations, Fisher assumes that each capital stock $K_i(t)$ grows at an essentially *constant* rate one which in general differs from industry to industry.[14] Thus,

$$\frac{\dot{K}_i}{K_i} \cong \beta_{i1} \tag{27}$$

and this in turn implies

$$\frac{\dot{J}}{J} \cong \sum_{i=1}^{N} \beta_{i1} \left[\frac{J_i(t)}{J(t)}\right] \tag{28}$$

Therefore $\dot{J}/J$ is a weighted average of the β_{i1}, with weights which sum to one, since $J(t) \equiv \Sigma_{i=1}^{N} J_i(t)$. (This type of weighted average is known as a convex combination, and implies that $\dot{J}/J$ will always be between the largest and smallest β_{i1}.)

Finally, we come to the growth rate of aggregate output $Q(t) \equiv \Sigma_{i=1}^{N} Q_i(t)$. From Equation (14), we know $Q_i(t)$, so

$$Q(t) = \sum_{i=1}^{N} Q_i(t) = \sum_{i=1}^{N} A_i(t)[L_i(t)]^{\alpha}[K_i(t)]^{1-\alpha}$$

From this, we can derive $\dot{Q}/Q$:[15]

$$\frac{\dot{Q}}{Q} = \left[\sum_{i=1}^{N} \frac{\dot{A}_i}{A_i} + \alpha_i \left(\frac{\dot{L}_i}{L_i}\right) + (1 - \alpha_i)\left(\frac{\dot{K}_i}{K_i}\right)\right] \frac{Q_i}{Q} \tag{29}$$

Of the terms in expression (29), we already know that $Q_i/Q \cong p_i$ from (21), $\dot{L}_i/L_i \cong \dot{L}/L \cong .03$ from (24), and $\dot{K}_i/K_i \cong \beta_{i1}$ from (27). To this, we need only add the fact that in general, ignoring small random deviations, Fisher assumes that the shift parameter A_i grows at an essentially constant rate, which differs from industry to industry.[16]

$$\frac{\dot{A}_i}{A_i} \cong \gamma_{i1} \tag{30}$$

All of this gives

$$\frac{\dot{Q}}{Q} \cong \sum_{i=1}^{N} \gamma_{i1}p_i + \sum_{i=1}^{N} .03\alpha_i p_i + \sum_{i=1}^{N} (1 - \alpha_i)\, \beta_{i1}p_i$$

But $\Sigma_{i=1}^{N} \alpha_i p_i = 1 - s =$ constant wage share, from (22). So

$$\frac{\dot{Q}}{Q} \cong \sum_{i=1}^{N} \gamma_i p_i + \sum_{i=1}^{N} (1 - \alpha_i)p_i\beta_{i1} + .03(1 - s) \tag{31}$$

Combining the expressions for $\dot{L}/L$, $\dot{J}/J$, and $\dot{Q}/Q$, we return to the all important residual $\dot{B}/B$ of equation (25);

$$\frac{\dot{B}}{B} \cong \frac{\dot{Q}}{Q} - s\frac{\dot{J}}{J} - (1 - s)\frac{\dot{L}}{L}$$

$$\frac{\dot{B}}{B} \cong \sum_{i=1}^{N} \gamma_{i1}p_i + \sum_{i=1}^{N} (1 - \alpha_i)p_i\beta_{i1} + .03(1 - s) - s\sum_{i=1}^{N} \beta_{i1}\left[\frac{J_i(t)}{J(t)}\right] - .03(1 - s)$$

$$\frac{\dot{B}}{B} = \sum_{i=1}^{N} \gamma_{i1}p_i + \sum_{i=1}^{N} \beta_{i1}\left[(1 - \alpha_i)p_i - s\frac{J_i(t)}{J(t)}\right]$$

$$\frac{\dot{B}}{B} = \sum_{i=1}^{N} \gamma_{i1}p_i + s\sum_{i=1}^{N} \beta_{i1}\left[\frac{(1 - \alpha_i)p_i}{s} - \frac{J_i(t)}{J(t)}\right]$$

Given that the constant wage share $1 - s = \Sigma_{i=1}^{N} \alpha_i p_i$ we can write the profit share $s = 1 - \Sigma_{i=1}^{N} \alpha_i p_i$. But by definition $p_i = Q_i/Q$, so that

$$\sum_{i=1}^{N} p_i = \sum_{i=1}^{N} Q_i/Q = 1$$

Thus,

$$s = \sum_{ip1}^{M} p_i - \sum_{i=1}^{N} \alpha_i p_i = \sum_{i=1}^{N} (1 - \alpha_i)p_i = \sum_{i=1}^{N} s_i,$$

where $s_i = (1 - \alpha_i)p_i$. From this, we at long last get

$$\frac{\dot{B}}{B} = \sum_{i=1}^{N} \gamma_{i1}p_i + s\sum_{i-1}^{N} \beta_{i1}\left[\frac{s_i}{s} - \frac{J_i(t)}{J(t)}\right] \tag{32}$$

in which it is important to note that the terms s_i/s and $J_i(t)/J(t)$, when summed over i, each sum to 1.

Laws of algebra and laws of simulation. In the expression (32) for $\dot{B}/B$ the basic structural parameters are β_{i_1} and γ_{i_1}. Of these, β_{i_1} represents the rate of growth of the ith machine stock over any given simulation run, whereas γ_{i_1} represents the rate of technical change in the ith industry. (Since the α_i are constant over any given run, changes in the shift parameter $A_i(t)$ represent the only possible technical change in any industry.)

Fisher partitions his simulations into two basic groups. In the first of these, which he calls "Hicks experiments," he sets all $\beta_{i_1} = 0$. Thus, in each of these experiments, there *is* technical change ($\gamma_{i_1} \neq 0$) but no growth in the size of the machine stock ($\beta_{i_1} = 0$). Under these conditions, $\dot{B}/B$ reduces to a constant over time.

$$\frac{\dot{B}}{B} \cong \sum_{i=1}^{N} \gamma_{i_1}p_i \cong b_1 \quad \text{(a constant over time)} \tag{33}$$

Thus, for Hicks experiments, one can expect from purely algebraic considerations that

$$\ln B(t) \cong a_0 + b_1 t \tag{34}$$

where a_0 is a constant of integration.

From the laws of algebra (Equation 5), we know that in general if $\dot{B}/B$ is solely a function of time, any data associated with constant shares $s \cong \beta$ can be represented by the functional form below (since Fisher uses J as an index of capital, what we previously called $k = K/L$ is now

$$j = (J/L){:}\ q = B(t)c_0 j^8 \tag{5}$$

Taking natural logs,

$$\ln q = \ln B(t) + \ln c_0 + \beta \ln j$$
$$= (a_0 + \ln c_0) + b_1 + \beta \ln j$$

and combining the constants into a single constant b_0, we get

$$\ln q = b_0 + b_1 t + \beta \ln j \tag{35}$$

What we have shown therefore is that for *Hicks experiments, purely algebraic* (as opposed to econometric) *considerations* lead us to the conclusion that whenever shares are (roughly) constant Fisher's aggregate data can be generated by what *appears* to be a Cobb–Douglas "production" function with a constant rate of technical change and a marginal product of labor equal to the actual wage.

This is precisely the result Fisher gets for his Hicks experiments: for this set of experiments, the functional form which repeatedly works the best (in the sense that the estimated marginal product of labor most closely approximates the actual wage) is one which assumes constant returns to scale and a constant rate of technical change.[17]

We now turn to the second set of experiments, what Fisher calls his "Capital experiments," in which all $\gamma_{i_1} = 0$. In this set of experiments, therefore, there is positive or negative growth of the ith machine stock ($\beta_{i_1} \neq 0$) but *no* technical change ($\alpha_{i_1} = 0$). Equation (32), the general expression for the residual, now becomes:

$$\frac{\dot{B}}{B} \approx s\left[\sum_{i=1}^{N} \beta_{i1}\frac{s_i}{s} - \sum_{i=1}^{N} \beta_{i1}\frac{J_i(t)}{J(t)}\right] \tag{36}$$

In Equation (36) each term in the brackets is a convex combination (a weighted average whose weights sum to one) of the β_{i1}, so that each term lies between the largest and the smallest β_{i_1}. One would therefore expect the *difference* of these terms to be close to zero; in addition, since the constant wage share $1 - s = \Sigma_{i=1}^{N} \alpha_i\beta_i$ is itself a convex combination of the parameters α_i, it itself will be within the range of *these* parameters;[18] since the unweighted average of the α_i is 0.75, the profit share s will be roughly around 0.25. Given that the term in the brackets is likely to be small, multiplying it by $s \cong .025$ will yield a number even closer to zero. In capital experiments algebraic considerations would therefore lead us to expect:

$$\frac{\dot{B}}{B} \cong 0 \tag{37}$$

so that

$$\ln B \cong a_0, \quad \text{where } a_0 \text{ is a constant} \tag{38}$$

In setting this result into the general functional form of Equation (5) $q = B(t)c_0 j^{\beta}$ and taking natural logs of both sides, $\ln q \cong \ln B(t) + \ln c_0 + \beta \ln j = (a_0 + \ln c_0) + \beta \ln j$ and combining the constant terms into a single constant b_0

$$\ln q \cong b_0 + \beta \ln j \tag{39}$$

For the capital experiments, therefore, purely algebraic considerations lead us to expect that Fisher's data can be represented by what *appears* to be a Cobb–Douglas production function with a constant level of technology and a marginal product of labor equal to the actual wage. *Once again this is precisely the result Fisher gets for his capital experiments.*[19]

It is important to note that Fisher himself never presents the exact regression results involved (an understandable omission considering that there were a total of 1010 runs of this simulated economy, each run covering a 20-year period). Instead, he tells us only that the best fits to the aggregate data were derived from an equation of the form $\ln q = b_0 + b_1 t + \beta \ln j$ for *Hicks experiments,* and one of the form $\ln q = b_0 + \beta \ln j$ for *capital experiments.* To Fisher this result comes as a surprise. But it should not, for as we have just seen, Fisher's complicated and expensive experiments have merely rediscovered the laws of algebra.

Cross-section aggregate production functions. The direct analogy to constant shares in time series is the case of uniform profit margins (profits per dollar sales) in cross-section data. Using the subscript i for the ith industry (or firm), and defining $\beta = s_i = r_i k_i / q_i$ as the uniform profit margin, we can rewrite Equation (3) as

$$\frac{dq_i}{q_i} = \left[(1-\beta)\frac{dw_i}{w_i} + \beta\frac{dr_i}{r_i}\right] + \beta\frac{dk_i}{k_i} \tag{40}$$

Then, so long as the term in brackets is uncorrelated with dk_i/k_i, the above equation is algebraically similar to a simple linear regression model $y_i = bx_i + u_i$, with the term in brackets playing the part of the disturbance term u_i. Obviously, for any data in which the bracketed term is small and uncorrelated with the dependent variable dk_i/k_i, the "best" fit will be a cross-section Cobb–Douglas production function with constant returns and factors paid their marginal products.

There are still other ways in which one may explain the apparent success of a Cobb–Douglas in cross-section studies, the best single reference being Phelps Brown's (1957) critique. In a subsequent note, Simon and Levy (1963) show that any data having uniform wage and profit rates across the cross section can be closely approximated by the ubiquitous Cobb–Douglas function having "correct" coefficients, even though the data reflect only mobility of labor and capital, not any specific production conditions.

Once again, it would seem that the apparent empirical success of the Cobb–Douglas function having "correct" coefficients is perfectly consistent with wide varieties of data, and cannot be interpreted as supporting aggregate neoclassical production and distribution theory.

Summary and conclusions

It is characteristic of theoretical parables that they illustrate the *fundamental truths* of a paradigm, truths which more developed theoretical structures may modify and elaborate, but cannot undermine. In the neoclassical progression of parables from simple exchange to capitalism as the final solution to Man's "natural" greed, one central theme which emerges right in the beginning is the conception of equilibrium prices as "scarcity prices:" relative prices which reflect the relative scarcity of commodities.

In their most developed form, neoclassical parables have sought to present the notion of scarcity pricing as an explanation of the distribution of income between workers and capitalists. Here, the task is to portray a capitalist economy in such a way that the wage and profit rates may be seen to be the scarcity prices of labor and capital, respectively. But for this to be even a logical *possibility,* it is at the very least necessary that the wage and profit rates behave *as if* they were scarcity prices – i.e., that the profit rate fall as the capital–labor ratio rises, and the wage rate fall as the labor–capital ratio rises. This correlation is minimally necessary for the internal consistency of the parable (though of course its existence would hardly justify the implied causation).

Alas, the grand neoclassical parables have fallen on hard times, and after repeated demonstrations of their logical inconsistencies, they have been abandoned by the high–brows of the theory; not without regret, though, for as Samuelson so insightfully notes, within the parable "the apologist for capital and for thrift has a less difficult case to argue" (Samuelson, 1966).

"If all this causes headaches for those nostalgic for the old time parables of neoclassical writing, we must remind ourselves that scholars are not born to live an easy existence. We must respect, and appraise, the facts of life" (Samuelson, 1966).

Not everyone was ready to give up the old time parables though, and those who chose to ignore the previously mentioned facts of life sought succor – where else? – in the "facts." The "real world," whose vulgar intrusions neoclassical theory had in the past so carefully avoided, became its last refuge. Facts, after all, are always better than facts–of–life.

And what are these facts? Simply, that again and again, aggregate Cobb–Douglas production functions work – that is, they not only give a good fit to aggregate output, but they also generally yield marginal products which closely approximate factor rewards. Since the aggregate production function is the simplest form of the grand neoclassical parable, its apparently strong empirical basis has often been taken as providing a good measure of support for the old time religion, regardless of what the theory says.

The main purpose of this chapter has been to show that these empirical results do not, in fact, have much to do with production conditions at all. Instead, it is demonstrated that when the *distribution* data (wages and profits) exhibit constant shares, there exist broad classes of *production* data (output, capital, and labor) that *can always be related to each other through a functional form which is mathematically identical to a Cobb–Douglas "production function" with constant "returns to scale," "neutral technical change," and "marginal products equal to factor rewards."*

Since this result is a mathematical consequence of any (unexplained) constancy of shares, it is true even for very implausible data. For instance, data points that spell out the word "HUMBUG" were used as an illustration, and it was shown that even the humbug economy can be represented by Cobb–Douglas production function having all the previously mentioned properties.

Similarly, we have examined Solow's famous paper on measuring technical change; and here too it is shown that the underlying production function which he isolates, by removing the effects of technical change, can be *algebraically* anticipated, even down to the fitted coefficients of his regression.

Next, Franklin Fisher's mammoth simulation experiments are examined and once again it becomes clear that the laws of algebra can anticipate the laws of simulation from the structure of the experiments alone.

Lastly, in the final part of this chapter, the analysis is extended to provide a simple explanation for cross-section aggregate production functions. The overall impact of these discussions, it is hoped, will be to demonstrate that the *reality* to which the neoclassical hangers-on clutch so desperately is as empty as their own abstractions.

Postscript

The point of this chapter is to demonstrate that as long as distributive shares are constant, it is an algebraic law that the Cobb–Douglas function "fits" almost any data. Hence, Solow's paper and the Humbug data stand on the same footing.

Solow has recently claimed that all along the intention of his 1957 paper was to "yield an exact Cobb–Douglas and tuck everything else into the shift factor" (Solow, 1974, p. 121). But his own printed words give quite a different impression; in the original paper, after he has derived the so-called shift factor $A(t)$, Solow expressly states his intention to "discuss the shape of $f(k, l)$ and reconstruct the (underlying) aggregate production function" (Solow, 1957, p. 317). To this end, he constructs a graph of $f(k)$ versus k, noting with obvious satisfaction that in spite of "the amount of a priori doctoring which the raw figures have undergone, the fit is remarkably tight" (Solow, 1957, p. 317), giving rise to "an inescapable impression of curvature, of persistent but not violent diminishing returns" (Solow, 1957, p. 318).

If, as Solow now claims, he knew all along that the underlying production function would be a Cobb–Douglas, then why bother "reconstructing" it? Why the surprise at the tightness of fit and the "inescapable impression of curvature"? Why does Solow need regression analysis to "confirm the visual impression of diminishing returns . . ." (Solow, 1957, p. 319). If Solow had indeed understood his own method, he should have known that regardless of the amount of a priori doctoring of the data, the laws of algebra dictate that the fit of $f(k)$ versus k would be very tight as well as being inescapably curved. But it is hardly necessary to rediscover these algebraic artifacts by means of graphs and regressions.[20]

Having just said that his method and his education lead him to conclude that even the Humbug economy is neoclassical, Solow next asserts the very opposite. With the help of Samuel L. Myers, he runs a regression of the form $\ln q = a_0 + a_1 t + b \ln k$ on the Humbug data, and finds to his obvious delight that this leads not only to a very poor fit but also gives rise to a negative coefficient for ln k. The moral seems clear: production functions do not "work" for the Humbug data, whereas they do for real data (Solow, 1974, p. 121).

But once again, his method and education betray him. The laws of algebra show that almost any production data associated with a constant profit share β could be cast in the form $Q = B(t)k^{\beta}$. The Humbug data was an illustration of this, and it was sufficient for my purpose in the original paper to show that even in this case the "underlying" function $f(k)$ was extremely well fitted by the Cobb–Douglas form $f(k) = k^{\beta}$ ($R^2 = .993$) and that the so-called shift factor B was solely a function of time. Hence, even Humbug data would be consistent with a neoclassical production function having "neutral technical change" and "marginal products equal to factor rewards".

Obviously, given that the underlying function f(k) was numerically specified by the laws of algebra (Equation (12) and note 9, in this chapter), all that would have been necessary for a complete *numerical* specification was a fitted function for $B(t)$. However, since such a fitted function was not necessary to the *logic* of my argument, I was content with merely graphing $B(t)$ versus time, as in Figure 5.3.

A glance at Figure 5.3 is sufficient to indicate that no simple linear or log-linear function will fit $B(t)$. *And yet this is precisely the form that Solow uses in his regression.*[21] He naturally gets a very poor fit. How clever.

In this version of the paper, for the sake of completeness, I do actually specify a fitted function for $B(t)$, with an $R^2 = .82$ (Equation 13). But the logic of the argument does not require this step; it only requires that the so-called shift factor be a function solely of time: *there is nothing in neoclassical theory, no law of production or of nature, which requires $B(t)$ to be linear or log-linear.* Struggling under the weight of their bag of tools, Solow and Myers seem to have forgotten that linearity is merely a convenient assumption whose applicability must at all times be *justified*, not merely assumed.

Notes

1 ". . . the core of the theory of a private ownership economy is provided by the theory of exchange" (Walsh, 1970, p. 159).
2 Garegnani in fact does not state it this way. He shows that the necessary and sufficient condition is that the wage–curves all be straight lines, and shows that this in turn is true when all industries have the same capital–labor ratios, i.e., when prices are proportional to labor values (Garegnani, 1970, p. 421).
3 $Q(t) \equiv$ value of output; $K(t) \equiv$ value of the utilized stock of capital; $L(t) \equiv$ employed stock of labor; $t \equiv$ time.
4 I thank Professor Luigi Pasinetti for having pointed this out in his comments on an earlier version of this paper.
5 R. R. Nelson gives a summary of subsequent refinements (Nelson, 1964).
6 "In order to isolate shifts of the aggregate production function from movements along it" (Solow, 1957, p. 314).
7 The discrete equivalent for $\dot{A}/A$ is $\Delta A/A$, where $\Delta A = A(t + 1) - A(t)$. Thus $A(t + 1) = A(t)[1 + \Delta A/A]$; in 1909, $t = 0$, and by setting $A(0) = 1$, Solow derives a series for $A(1)$, $A(2)$ . . . , from the data on $\dot{A}/A$.
8 Since Solow's calculations contained an arithmetical error, the points representing the years

1943–1949 clearly lay outside the range of any hypothesized curve. After expressing some hesitance, Solow leaves them out of his regressions (Solow, 1957, p. 318).

9 The deviation of the numerical value of the constant term is explained on pp. 20–21 of Solow's 1957 paper.

10 I wish to thank Larry Heinruth and especially Peter Brooks, for the time and effort expended in deriving this fitted function. Two steps were involved in the fitting. First, a two-year moving average $\bar{B}(t)$ was constructed from the data for $B(t)$, by means of the formula $\bar{B}(t) = [B(t) + B(t+1)]/2$ in which the year 1909 represents $t = 1$, 1910 by $t = 2$, etc. Second, the function $\hat{B}(t)$ of Equation (13) was fitted to this moving average $\bar{B}(t)$, with a $R^2 = .82$.

11 Since the fitted function has $K = 16$ parameters to it, and since there are $T = 38$ data points in the moving average $B(t)$, the R^2 corrected for degrees of freedom is (Goldberger, 1964):

$$\bar{R}^2 = R^2 \frac{K}{T - K - 1}(1 - R^2)$$
$$= .82 - \frac{16}{21}(.18) = .68$$

12 By the definition $MPL_i = \partial Q_i(t)/\partial L_i(t)$. Applying this to the expression for $Q_i(t)$ in Equation (14) yields $MPL_i = \alpha_i[Q_i(t)/L_i(t)]$.

13 From Equation (21), $Q_i(t) = p_i Q(t)$, where p_i is constant over time. Thus

$$\frac{dQ_i(t)}{dt} = p_i \frac{dQ(t)}{dt}$$

and

$$\frac{dQ_i(t)}{dt}\frac{1}{Q_i(t)} = p_i \frac{dQ_i(t)}{dt}\frac{1}{p_i Q_i(t)} = \frac{dQ(t)}{dt}\frac{1}{Q(t)}$$

Similarly for employment from (23).

14 Fisher assumes $\ln K_i(t) = \beta_{i0} + \beta_{i1}t$ + (small random deviations). Ignoring the small deviations, and differentiating gives (Fisher, 1971, p. 309)

$$\frac{dK_i(t)}{dt}\frac{1}{K_i(t)} \cong \beta_{i1}$$

15 $Q(t) = \sum_{i=1}^{N} A_i(t)[L_i(t)]^{\alpha}[K_i(t)]^{1-\alpha}$

Dropping the time subscript, and differentiating,

$$\dot{Q} = \sum_{i=1}^{N} [\dot{A}_i L_i^{\alpha} K_i^{1-\alpha} + A_i(\alpha_i \dot{L}_i)L_i^{\alpha-1}K_i^{1-\alpha} + A_i L_i^{\alpha}(1-\alpha_i)\dot{K}_i K_i^{1-\alpha-1}]$$

$$\dot{Q} = \sum_{i=1}^{N} \left[\left(\frac{\dot{A}_i}{A_i}\right) A_i L_i^{\alpha} K_i^{1-\alpha} + \left(\frac{\alpha_i \dot{L}_i}{L_i}\right) A_i L_i^{\alpha} K_i^{1-\alpha} + (1-\alpha_i)\left(\frac{\dot{K}_i}{K_i}\right) A_i L_i^{\alpha} K_i^{1-\alpha}\right]$$

$$\dot{Q} = \sum_{i=1}^{N} \left[\left(\frac{\dot{A}_i}{A_i}\right) Q_i + \left(\alpha_i \frac{\dot{L}_i}{L_i}\right) Q_i + (1-\alpha_i)\left(\frac{\dot{K}_i}{K_i}\right) Q_i\right]$$

so that

$$\frac{\dot{Q}}{Q} = \sum_{i=1}^{N} \left[\left(\frac{\dot{A}_i}{A_i}\right) + \left(\alpha_i \frac{\dot{L}_i}{L_i}\right) + (1-\alpha_i)\left(\frac{\dot{K}_i}{K_i}\right)\right]\frac{Q_i}{Q}$$

16 Fisher (1971, p. 309) assumes $ln\, A_i = \gamma_{i0} + \gamma_{i1}t$, so that $(dA_i/dt)(1/A_i) = \gamma_{i1}$.

17 The function form in Fisher's equation, (17), the best form for Hick's experiments, is $\log(Y^*/L) = a + b\log(J/L) + dt$ where his Y^*/L corresponds to our q and his J/L to our j. Fisher uses "log" for natural logarithms (Fisher, 1971, p. 313).

18 Fisher has two ranges of α_i: $.7 \le \alpha_i \le .8$, and $.6 \le \alpha_i \le .9$, in both the unweighted average = 0.75 (Fisher, 1971, p. 309).

19 The functional form Fisher finds best for Capital experiments is $\log(Y^*/L) = a + b\log(J/L)$ which, allowing for notation differences, is identical to equation 5.38 (Fisher, 1971, p. 313).

20 Yet confronted with the humbug data, Solow says: "If you ask any systematic method or any educated mind to interpret those data *using a production function and the marginal productivity relations,* the answer will be that they are exactly what would be produced by technical regress with a production function that must be very close to Cobb–Douglas" (Solow, 1957, p. 121). What kind of "systematic method" or "educated mind" is it that can interpret almost any data, even the humbug data, as arising from a neoclassical production function?

21 Solow uses the form $\ln q = a_0 + a_1 t + b \ln k$; since the general form under consideration is $q = A(t)f(k)$, so that $\ln q = \ln A(t) + \ln f(k)$, Solow has obviously specified $A(t)$ as log-linear: $\ln A(t) = a_0 + a_1 t$.

References

Brown, P. 1957. "The Meaning of Fitted Cobb–Douglas Functions", *Quarterly Journal of Economics,* 71:546–60.

Dobb, M. H. 1970. "Some Reflections on the Sraffa System and the Critique of the So-called Neo-Classical Theory of Value and Distribution," unpublished.

Dewey, D. 1965. *Modern Capital Theory.* New York: Columbia University Press.

Ferguson, C. E. 1969. *The Neo-Classical Theory of Production and Distribution.* Cambridge: Cambridge University Press.

1971. "Capital Theory Up to Date: A Comment on Mrs. Robinson's Article," *Canadian Journal of Economics,* Vol. IV, No. 2, 250–4.

Fisher, F. 1971. "Aggregate Production Functions and the Explanation of Wages: A Simulation Experiment," *Review of Economics and Statistics* 53:305–25.

Garegnani, P. 1970. "Heterogeneous Capital, the Production Function and the Theory of Distribution," *Review of Economic Studies,* 37, 407–36.

Goldberger, A. S. 1964. *Econometric Theory.* New York: John Wiley & Sons.

Hershleifer, J. 1970. *Investment, Interest, and Capital.* Englewood Cliffs, N. J.: Prentice-Hall.

Hicks, J. R. 1965. *Capital and Growth.* New York: Oxford University Press.

Lancaster, K. 1968. *Mathematical Economics.* New York: Macmillan.

Nelson, R. R. 1964. "Aggregate Production Functions and Medium-Range Growth Projections," *American Economic Review,* 54:575–605.

Samuelson, P. A. 1962. "Parable and Realism in Capital Theory: The Surrogate Production Function," *Review of Economic Studies,* 29:193–206.

1966. "A Summing Up," *Quarterly Journal of Economics,* LXXX, 4:568–83.

Shaikh, A. 1974. "Laws of Production and Laws of Algebra. The Humbug Production Function: A Comment," *Review of Economics and Statistics,* Vol. LVI, No. 1, 115–20.

Simon, H., and Levy, F. 1963. "A Note on the Cobb–Douglas Function," *Review of Economic Studies,* Vol. 30:93–4.

Solow, R. M. 1957. "Technical Change and the Aggregate Production Function," *Review of Economics and Statistics,* 39:312–20.

1974. "Law of Production and Laws of Algebra: The Humbug Production Function: A Comment." *Review of Economics and Statistics,* Vol. LVI, No. 1,121.

Walsh, V. C. 1970. *Introduction to Contemporary Microeconomics.* New York: McGraw-Hill.

Walters, A. A. 1963. "Production and Cost Functions: An Econometric Survey," *Econometrica,* No. 1–2, 1–66.

Part III

Microeconomics

6

Competition and price-taking behavior

Edward J. Nell

The nature of markets

Six months ago Babbitt had learned that one Archibald Purdy, a grocer in the indecisive residential district known as Linton, was talking of opening a butcher shop beside his grocery. Looking up the ownership of adjoining parcels of land, Babbitt found that Purdy owned his present shop but did not own the one available lot adjoining. He advised Conrad Lyte to purchase this lot, for eleven thousand dollars, though an appraisal on a basis of rents did not indicate its value as above nine thousand. The rents, declared Babbitt, were too low; and by waiting they could make Purdy come to their price.

Now, Purdy seemed ready to buy, and his delay was going to cost him ten thousand extra dollars – the reward paid by the community to Mr. Conrad Lyte for the virtue of employing a broker who had Vision . . .

Lyte came to the conference exultantly. He was fond of Babbitt this morning and called him "old hoss." Purdy, the grocer, a long-nosed man and solemn, seemed to care less for Babbitt and Vision, but Babbitt met him at the street door to the office and guided him toward the private room with affectionate little cries of "This way, Brother Purdy!" . . . then leaned back in his desk chair and looked plump and jolly. But he spoke to the weakling grocer with firmness.

"Well, Brother Purdy, we have been having some pretty tempting offers . . . for that lot next to your store, but I persuaded Brother Lyte that we ought to give you a shot at the property first. I said to Lyte, 'It'd be a rotten shame,' I said, 'if somebody went and opened a combination grocery and meat market right next door and ruined Purdy's nice little business.' Especially," Babbitt leaned forward and his voice was harsh, "it would be hard luck if one of these cash-and-carry chain-stores got in there . . ."

Purdy snatched his thin hands from his pockets, tilted in the heavy oak chair, and tried to look amused . . . "Yes, they're bad competition. But I guess you don't realize the Pulling Power that Personality has in a neighborhood business."

The Great Babbitt smiled. "That's so. Just as you feel, old man. We thought we'd give you first chance. All right then." "Now look here!" Purdy wailed, "I know for a fact that a piece of property 'bout the same size, right near, sold for less 'n eighty-five hundred, 'twa'n't two years ago, and here you fellows are asking me for twenty-four thousand dollars! . . . Why, good God, Mr. Babbitt, you're asking more 'n twice its value! And threatening to ruin me if I don't like it!"

"Purdy, I don't like your way of talking! I don't like it one little bit! . . . don't you suppose we know it's to our own selfish interest to have everybody in Zenith prosperous? But all this is beside the point. Tell you what we'll do; we'll come down to twenty-three thousand-five thousand down and the rest on mortgage. Heavens, man, we'd be glad to oblige you! We don't like these foreign grocery trusts any better 'n you do! But it isn't reasonable to expect us to sacrifice eleven thousand–five thousand down and the rest on mortgage. Heavens, man, we'd be glad to to come down?"

By warmly taking Purdy's part, Babbitt persuaded the benevolent Mr. Lyte to reduce his price to twenty-one thousand dollars. At the right moment Babbitt snatched from a drawer the agreement he had had Miss McGoun type out a week ago and thrust it into Purdy's hands. He genially shook his fountain pen to make certain that it was flowing, handed it to Purdy, and approvingly watched him sign.

The work of the world was being done. Lyte had made something over nine thousand dollars, Babbitt had made a four hundred and fifty dollar commission, Purdy had, by the sensitive mechanism of modern finance, been provided with a business-building, and soon the happy inhabitants . . . of Linton would have meat lavished upon them at prices only a little higher than those downtown.

What Babbitt knew. Anyone reading this passage will recognize what is happening; but there are some aspects which should interest economists especially. How was it that Lyte and Babbitt were able to get the lot so cheaply in the first place? Surely, because that was all it was worth, on the basis of the rents generated by its present use. However, Zenith City was growing, and Linton was a transitional district; Purdy was hoping to take advantage of this increased prosperity to expand his profitable neighborhood business. Instead Babbitt moves in to ensure that the capitalized value of the benefits of growth will go to Lyte, leaving Purdy just enough, after raising prices (and putting the people of Linton on the margin of a decision to go downtown after all) to make it worth his while, given the extra effort, to carry through the scheme.

The second question for the economist is, how did Babbitt know how much he could get? This has two parts, the first of which is easy. Babbitt, as well as Purdy could calculate the growth of Zenith, and estimate the effects of increased prosperity on shopping habits and acceptable prices in Linton, and with a little knowledge of the trade he could figure the minimum which would be necessary to keep Purdy's expanded business going. But how did he *know* that he could force Purdy to accept this minimum? For not only *did* he know, but he was so sure of himself that he had the agreement typed up a week in advance. This raises a serious problem, for Babbitt knew what no well-trained neoclassical economist could have known, namely the outcome of a confrontation in bilateral monopoly. For there were no competitors to Purdy, bidding for the lot – Babbitt's talk about "foreign grocery trusts" was bargaining talk, and plainly, just talk; he had neither looked for nor found another bidder. And there were no competitors to Babbitt, trying to sell another lot to Purdy. In neoclassical theory, the case of one buyer and one seller is indeterminate – yet Babbitt was certain of the result well in advance, so certain in fact that he advised Lyte to pay two thousand dollars more than the lot was currently worth in order to get it at once. Could Babbitt have possessed knowledge our best economists still lack?

Mechanism or battleground? Indeed, neoclassical theory taken strictly would have trouble providing answers to the simpler questions about the effects of prosperity on Purdy's market. For Zenith's growth is evidently a boom, not a steady-state expansion. In the latter, neoclassical theory tells us that the increased prosperity of Linton would have been foreseen at the outset with perfect certainty, and as a result the price of the lot would at all times have reflected the discounted value of its eventual earning power in Purdy's hands. There would have been no discontinuous jump in its price, and no opportunity for Babbitt and Lyte to make a killing. There is not much in such an approach to help in the analysis of a boom.

The reply will be that steady-state theory is a helpful measuring rod against which to set real-world disequilibrium growth. Just how it is helpful may not be clear, but let us allow the reply and turn to the more difficult question of how Babbitt could have known just how far he could push Purdy. In the neoclassical world there is no answer, for there is no theory in which economic power is exercised by one party against another. There is no theory of the optimal degree of coercion or pressure which one agent should apply to another in order to accomplish some objective to some desired extent. Insofar as modern theory treats of economic power, it does so in terms of "market power," power which is exercised not over opponents or other agents, but only over the abstract variable, price, and which depends on the competitiveness of the market. Even so, this power to set price is circumscribed by the fact that it cannot be exercised directly, but only through the medium of manipulating the quantity supplied to an extent not possible under truly competitive conditions. This power depends, moreover, on certain special circumstances, for example, where the suppliers are few in number (or organized into a cartel) and the demanders many. Or where customers, though numerous, are widely separated, immobile and out of touch with each other, leaving each local market, in effect, at the mercy of the local suppliers. In the general competitive case, power is so widely dispersed that no buyer or seller can exercise any; special cases where power (in the limited sense above) can be exercised are then derived from the competitive case by relaxing particular assumptions. But when all the competitive assumptions have been dropped on *both* sides of the market, the neoclassical theorist has nothing to go on. "It is commonplace in economic analysis that market price under bilateral monopoly is indeterminate, in the sense that there are no priori principles that enable us to judge precisely which price will be forthcoming . . . It will depend on compromise and strength, and on the bargaining wiles of the participants . . ." (Weintraub, 1964). There could hardly be a clearer admission that neoclassical theory is helpless when confronted with the task of analyzing economic strength and bargaining, in general, as opposed to treating economic strength as the result of some particular deviation from the competitive norm.

This should come as no surprise. Neoclassical theory begins from the social vision of the Invisible Hand. Out of the contending selfish drives of individuals will come not only harmony, but even progress.

"The natural effort of every individual to better his own condition, when suffered to exert itself with freedom and security, is so powerful a principle that it is alone and without any assistance not only capable of carrying on the society to wealth and prosperity, but of surmounting a hundred impertinent obstructions with which the folly of human laws too often incumbers its operations" (Smith, 1937, p. 508). Harmony and progress are brought about by the mechanisms of the marketplace. The image of the market as a smoothly functioning machine whose product is progress runs through the literature, and is even evident in the choice of words and phrases: the *price mechanism* with its occasional *inefficiencies due to friction,* reaches an *equilibrium* balancing the *forces of supply and demand* at a Pareto optimal point. The very terminology carries the suggestion that this mechanism will run automatically, allocating goods and services optimally including, as a by-product, a distribution of incomes in proportion to productive contributions. Insofar as there are attempts by individuals to exercise power in pursuit of their own interests, these will be counterbalanced by the efforts of other individuals, and so, incorporated in the general equilibrium, will end as pressures for the general good.

To articulate this image into a theory, neoclassical thinking has had to adopt certain conventions and assumptions. These are both well-known, and well known to be restrictive and unrealistic, though there is dispute about how much this last matters. Yet the point here is independent of that dispute. The importance of these assumptions is that they make it possible to conceive of the market as a smooth functioning machine – they sustain the image. They do this by eliminating economic warfare from the model. This involves severe measures. First, strategic weapons and strategic advantages have to be banned, for example, by ruling out collusion, inside information, technical immobility, etc. For these are all sources of economic power, or strategic advantage to someone. This first move is accomplished through the assumptions.

The next one works through the structure of the theory. The supply curve S is identified with the marginal cost curve, which in turn is derived from the production function. This has two important consequences: it conceals the *object* of economic power struggles, and, by assumption, it eliminates most of the costs of such warfare. The object of economic activity is concealed, because the supplier's returns, or profit, becomes defined as a certain kind of *cost,* interest or capital cost. (In practice, when a firm or its shares changes hands, or when a firm is set up by entrepreneurs who borrow their capital, returns are redefined as costs to individual agents. But although they are costs to the individuals, they are returns and not costs for the system as a whole.) That is to say, long-run normal profit becomes a cost by definition. In some versions of the theory it is the cost of capital, in others of *waiting* or *abstinence,* in still others it is the rental of capital goods, but it is the hallmark of neoclassical approach to distribute the value of the entire product as *returns to factors* through the interaction of supply and demand, costs and preferences.

This treatment of returns as a cost in the long run distinguishes the neoclassical theories from the Marxian and post-Keynesian, (and to some extent the classical) all of which regard the question of returns as the division of the surplus of total output over the needs of replacement and necessary subsistence among the social classes, defined according to their roles and rights in production.

The claim that the payment to capital is a cost for the system as a whole rests on the doctrine that the production of investment goods involves a sacrifice of present satisfaction. In this view, economic activity can be divided without serious ambiguity into consumption and investment, the sole purpose of the latter being to produce the former more easily or in larger amounts. Since the alternative to investment is always present consumption, investment means a sacrifice, for which there must be appropriate compensation – greater consumption later. Thus the productivity of a set of inputs can be seen as required for compensation for the consumption foregone in accumulating those inputs. But the claim rests on an illegitimate extension of the terms *consumption* and *investment*. Quite obviously there are many activities, enjoyable and fulfilling in themselves, which enhance society's productive powers – most scientific activity, for example and many exercises of specialized skills. Moreover, a large part of consumption is not especially "satisfying;" it is merely refueling to maintain life and the ability to work. Many other economic activities – advertising, finance, packaging, sales, sabotage, strikes – neither enhance productivity nor yield satisfaction, but enable one party to gain at the expense of others. So, the accumulation of productive inputs need not involve a "sacrifice," since investment activity may be an end as well as a means; consumption in turn, may be a means as well as an end; and much investment may be a means, not for producing output, but for obtaining income at the expense of others. It may, of course, be true that productive equipment, when owned privately can be withheld, providing neither employment nor products to the community, if a suitable return is not proferred. But that is a kind of extortion and should be sharply distinguished from genuine cost.

The second consequence of deriving supply curves from production functions bears even more directly on the issue of economic power. For it implies that all costs entering into supply decisions are costs of *production;* they are not, for example, costs of economic warfare. Yet, it should be evident even to casual observers of the business scene that a good deal of activity is concerned with imposing costs or threatening to impose costs on competitors, employers, employees, etc. And such activity absorbs resources that might have been used more productively, though quite probably less profitably.

Yet neoclassical theory has certain strengths that should not be ignored. Perhaps chief among them is that it is a theory in a very precise sense, for it indicates not only the general direction in which variables will move (assuming motivation, rationality, etc.) but it also determines *how far* the movement will go. In this it differs markedly from the theories which preceded the "marginal Revolution," and this gain in precision is certainly to be counted one of that revolution's main achievements.

Consider for a moment the really startling precision of standard microeconomics. It presents a very exact determination of how much to produce, what kinds of goods, how much they should sell for, what items, and how much of each should be included in a household budget, all under various circumstances – perfect or imperfect competition, monopoly, etc. In each case, for each agent, it claims to specify exactly, and usually uniquely, a rational course of action. There is nothing comparable in the whole corpus of classical and Marxian theory.

But this power and precision, though worthy of emulation has been bought at the price of error. I shall argue that this theory rests on a fundamental misconception of the idea of competition, a misconception revealed in the inability of neoclassicism to deal with a market consisting of a large number of individual transactions, and concealed by such devices as "the auctioneer" and "recontracting."

Uniform prices and market-clearing prices

Since the time of Walras, Wicksell and Marshall *the* display piece in the museum of conventional economics has been the mathematical theory of equilibrium in exchange. To be sure, the long-run version of the theory has never been free of difficulties, for neoclassical thinking has never been able to develop an adequate theory of profits and growth. But the *theory of temporary equilibrium* in competitive markets operating under *normal conditions,* as Marshall would put it, has long been regarded as the epitome of scientific investigation in economics. Yet, as generations of critics have observed, this theory rests on surprisingly sandy foundations. The implausibility of many of the assumptions, however, will not concern us here; but, one alleged consequence of them will – the doctrine that in purely competitive, and even in many imperfectly competitive markets, both buyers and sellers function as *price-takers* rather than as *price-makers.* (In more modern terminology, economic agents treat prices parametrically.) The market's presumed ability to function as an allocating mechanism, efficiently resolving otherwise insoluble social issues, flows from this characteristic, evidently absent in Zenith City; so, it is important to examine it closely.

Neoclassical market theory is based on individual preferences on the demand side and on technological possibilities on the supply side and on initial endowments, on both sides. From this information, given competitive, or certain other forms of market conditions, market-clearing prices can be derived, which the participants in the market must accept. These prices, among other things, distribute the gains from exchange among the traders. But in his early work, Wicksell drew attention to the peculiarity, first discovered by Edgeworth (and apparently missed by Walras) that the case of "bilateral monopoly," which he more appropriately termed "isolated exchange" was indeterminate, precisely because the division of the gains was not settled. How could the mere presence of large numbers of buyers and sellers convert indeterminate transactions into determinate ones?

The indeterminacy of isolated exchange

The reason for the indeterminacy can be seen very easily. Assume each of two parties has something to exchange, and that they meet in isolation. Each will trade until the ratios of the marginal utilities of the two goods are equal for both parties, for only then will trade stop; hence, if the goods are M and N, where m is an amount of M, and n of N, and the parties are 1 and 2, equilibrium requires:

$$\frac{\partial u_1/\partial m}{\partial u_1/\partial n} = \frac{\partial u_2/\partial m}{\partial u_2/\partial n}$$

where $u_1 = u_1(m, n)$ and $u_2 = u_2(m, n)$ are the respective utility functions of the two parties. But the price ratio depends on the whole amounts exchanged; that is, it will be the average ratio of exchange of those goods, and very different amounts will satisfy the above condition. Of course, trade will also cease if either party is about to make a loss. Hence limits exist to the possible sets of exchange ratios, where each party respectively obtains zero gain. Any price between those limits which satisfies the marginal utility condition will then be a possible equilibrium price. Each party can therefore set his price at the level which will return to him the gain he desires; but as there is no reason to suppose the prices so established will be compatible, the market is a stand-off. We have here a confrontation between two price-makers, and until the division of the potential gain between them is determined, the outcome will remain unsettled.

The same point can be made in the context of production. Consider a simple case, one among many possibilities. Let each of the two parties do specialized work to produce a good which he consumes himself and which the other uses in production. So each is dependent on the other's specialized work. Let the two goods be n and m. The producer of m works l_m days using n_m means of production to produce l units of m output. The producer of n works l_n days using m_n for his unit output. Taking the price of n as unity we have for exchange equations:

$$n_m + w_m p_m l_m = p_m \tag{1}$$

$$m_n p_m + w_n l_n = 1 \tag{2}$$

Where w_m is the wage of the m-producer and w_n the wage of the n-producer. (Even though both are paid in "real" terms, in the form of the respective producer's consumption good, both must be expressed in *value* since that good must be traded for means of production.)

Eliminating p_m yields w_m in terms of w_n:

$$w_m = \frac{n_m m_n + w_n l_n - 1}{l_n(w_n l_n - 1)} = \frac{1}{l_m}\left(1 + \frac{n_m m_n}{w_n l_n - 1}\right) \tag{3}$$

and, clearly, as this is a hyperbola,

$$\frac{dw_n}{dw_m} = \frac{-n_m m_n l_n l_m}{l_n(w_n l_n - 1)^2} < 0 \tag{4}$$

By substituting (3) into (1) we obtain p_m in terms of w_n:

$$p_m = \frac{1 - w_n l_n}{m_n} \quad \text{and} \quad \frac{dp_m}{dw_n} = -\frac{l_n}{m_n} \tag{5}$$

So we see that p_m varies continously and monotonically with the division of the gains between the parties. The real wage will be uniform for the two producers (even though paid in different commodities) when $w_n = w_m p_m$. In this case the original system reduces to two equations in two unknowns, the price and the uniform real wage. But in *general* the exchange ratio of the products, the price system, is indeterminate until the *division of gain* or *the relative worth of the two different lines of specialized work* has been settled.

No analogous problem arises in the pure exchange economy. It is not just a matter of relative pay scales; it is an issue of direct confrontation, for what one gains the other loses. The difficulty of reducing all labor to simple, abstract labor receiving a common wage, is now in plain view: different lines of work are not only different, they may also be interdependent, as a consequence of which *the gain of one party is the other's loss.*

There are really two points here. One, which we shall not pursue in any detail, is that this example suggests that labor is not a commodity like any other. On the contrary, the formation of a uniform wage for abstract or *pure* labor-time requires settling the issue of the distribution of gains between different kinds of work (Nell, unpublished). This is not a simple matter and its solution depends on institutional presuppositions which do not fit easily into the neoclassical framework. The other point is the same as that made above, in the context of the exchange model used by Edgeworth and Marshall, but now the problem has an added twist. For the two producers are *mutually dependent;* they *must* trade, for they need each other's products in order to produce their own consumption goods. But the rate of exchange cannot be settled until and unless agreement is reached about the relative worth of the two kinds of specialized work – that is, until the division of gain is settled.

Price and the gain from exchange. This point is obscured by the practice of calling some kinds of gain "cost." To bring it out clearly, we shall now examine two-party transactions more carefully, without drawing on utility theory or supposing any particular pattern of production or mutual dependence.

For convenience we will use a standard notation throughout. Let us designate the two parties by the random letters, GM and UAW, respectively. Then suppose UAW is offering a service or good to GM in return for a payment. Let a = payment received by UAW, b = value of service to GM, α = cost of payment to GM, β = cost to UAW of providing service. In the simplest case, α will equal a; that is, the cost to GM of paying for the service will be the same as the payment UAW receives. But in general, there will be costs of administration, or insurance that will cause α to be greater than a. Suppose the payment is an illegal bribe; then α will equal a plus an insurance premium, depending on the likelihood of discovery, to cover the costs of prosecution and fines. Suppose a represents wages; α will then equal a plus the costs of administering the wage fund, insurance schemes, workmen's compensation and the like. So in general it can be assumed that $\alpha = a + f(a)$, where $0 \leq f'(a) < 1$. By contrast, the cost to UAW of supplying the service will normally be less than the value of the service to GM. Were this not so, it would be impossible for GM to compensate UAW. On the other hand, the cost of providing the service will normally rise with the amount provided, but not by as much. Hence β will be some positive fractional function of b. For simplicity, let us assume that both these functions are linear. Let $\alpha = a + ka$, where $0 \leq k < 1$, and $\beta = xb$, where $0 < x < 1$.

Simple as this framework is, it allows us to say quite a lot. First, for there to be any reason for exchange at all, it will be necessary that $b \geq \alpha \geq a \geq \beta$, where, of course, $b > 0$. It follows at once that a gain from exchange will exist if and only if, $x < [1/(1 + k)]$. In turn, this raises the question, who will appropriate the gain? Let us consider some cases.

1. Suppose $a = \alpha$ and $b = \beta$. Then from the assumptions above, if there is to be any exchange at all, $a = b$, and $\alpha = \beta$. So the price paid is exactly equal to the value of the service, and the cost to the customer is equal to the cost of production. No one gains, because there is no gain. This is the neoclassical case, and it is achieved by including in costs the normal profit or interest in the branch of industry paying for the service. Suppose UAW provides labor services; then on the neoclassical accounting, the value to GM of this service will be the value of output minus the cost of materials, user cost (depreciation and depletion), and the "cost of capital," i.e. profit or interest, so the *gain* is subtracted as a cost. Similarly, suppose UAW sells a service or product; to the cost, β of supplying it will be added the cost of capital, or profit, bringing β up to the level of b. In each case the gain is eliminated by the simple expedient of redefining it as a cost. The existence of gain in the market is then explained by alleging that other purchasers would have paid more for the equilibrium amounts giving rise to consumer's surplus, while other suppliers would have supplied the equilibrium amount for less, so creating producer's surplus. Thus, while there is no gain to be obtained in the representative transaction, the market distributes benefits impartially to both sides.

2. Next suppose $a = b$. Then from the assumptions, $a - \alpha = b$. GM pays what the service is worth, and this is exactly what it costs GM to obtain the service. But this by no means implies that there is no gain from the transaction. For if $\beta < b$, there will be a gain, and it will go entirely to UAW, even though the exchange was perfectly fair and the payment exactly equals value received.

Both of these cases fit standard patterns of commodity exchange, the first representing competitive exchange, the second, exchange under monopoly conditions, where the seller makes a profit, over and above the normal rate. In fact all exchanges of final goods for money in productive economic systems organized along capitalist lines will actually be of this second kind, since some gains have simply been reclassified as costs.

3. Now consider the case where $a = \beta$. Provided $\beta \leq \alpha < b$, there will be a gain from exchange, which will go entirely to GM, even though the payment exactly covers the cost of production of the service. This is the basis of Marx's analysis of the buying and selling of labor; the wage covers the cost of production of labor, the cost of living plus any costs incidental to actual work. Hence, the worker receives the exchange value of his work, while the capitalist receives the use value – that is, he can use the worker's labor as he sees fit, and whatever is created by the worker's labor rightfully belongs to the capitalists. Hence since $a = \beta < b$, the capitalist receives the entire surplus created by the services of labor power.

Assuming that both the price and the amount of the service are variable, it is evident that the ratio a/b, representing the unit price, will be the crucial indicator. When a/b attains its maximum, $1/(1 + k)$, the entire potential gain goes to UAW; when a/b reaches its minimum, x, the entire potential gain goes to GM.[1]

More generally, UAW's gain is $a - \beta$ and GM's is $b - \alpha$. Hence the share of UAW in total gain is

$$U = \frac{a - \beta}{b - \alpha + a - \beta} = \frac{a - xb}{b(1 - x) - ak}$$
$$= \frac{a/b - x}{(1 - x) - (a/b)}$$

Since a/b is the unit price, let p = a/b. Then

$$\frac{dU}{dp} = \frac{d}{dp}\left(\frac{p - x}{1 - x - pk}\right)$$
$$= \frac{1 - x(1 + k)}{(1 - x - pk)^2} > 0 \quad \text{if} \quad 1 > x(1 + k)$$

and this will be positive, since the existence of any gain to be shared requires that $x < [1/(1 + k)]$. Hence the share of UAW in gain increases with price, as is surely intuitively obvious. Less obvious is the fact that it increases at an increasing rate; for

$$\frac{d^2U}{dp^2} = \frac{2k(1 - x)(1 + k)(1 - x\ pk)}{(1 - x - pk)^4} > 0$$

since every term in the numerator is positive. The curve of U against p then rises at an increasing rate, as in Figure 6.1. This provides a general demonstration that exchange is indeterminate until the division of the potential gain is settled.

Wicksell writes: "In the market, however, an element is added which causes the problem which we just now had to declare indeterminate, to appear relatively determinate . . . Under the influence of competition . . . only one price can rule on the market and in its neighborhood, so that all partial exchanges are carried out approximately in one and the same proportion of exchange" (Wicksell, 1934–35).

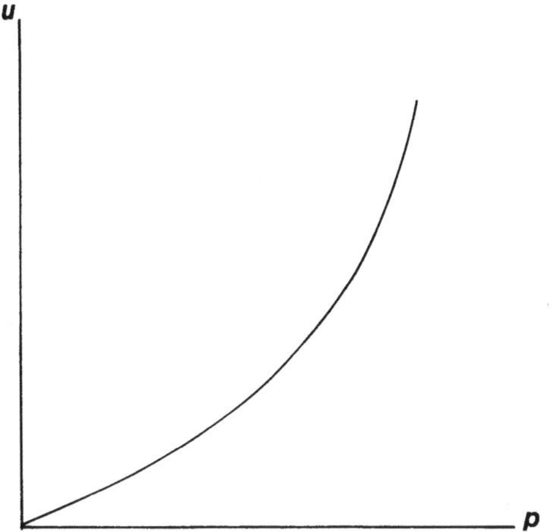

Figure 6.1

In the *market* (whether for labor or for goods), we are told, price will be determinate, even though the *very same transactions,* if they took place in isolation, would not be determinate as to price. This is a remarkable claim and it deserves a closer look, for it amounts to claiming that, under appropriate conditions, *aggregating price-making confrontations will lead to price-taking acquiescence in the dictates of the market.* How exactly does this happen? A market is simply made up of a large number of individual transactions; of course they influence one another, and obviously the possibility of a better bargain or sale elsewhere will exert pressure in any given exchange. But surely we must be given a precise account of how, exactly, those pressures and influences make themselves felt, and how the same determinate result is reached in a large number of transactions which individually would be indeterminate? Moreover, there might be different patterns of adjustment. For example, under some conditions a uniform price might be reached as a consequence of all parties being forced to adopt the result reached in some particular transaction. This would not eliminate price-making, however, or confrontation. It would simply establish price leadership. In other circumstances, the transactions might mutually condition one another, and again neither price-making nor confrontation need be absent – just more complex. In turn, such different characteristic patterns of adjustment might affect the working of the market in other respects.

Convergence to a uniform market-wide price. Strikingly, neoclassical theory has little to say to these questions. Indeed, little attention has been given to the way markets establish price-taking as the norm among transactions. The standard argument, in fact, is very simple, and is usually presented without much detailed analysis. Under competitive conditions, prices will be uniform in all transactions, for only one price can rule in the market. The question then becomes: what (uniform) price will clear the market, since that is the price which will have to be accepted by all buyers and all sellers.

Once price-taking is the norm, it is possible to show that offers of supply in response to the uniform market price will reflect costs of production and so will ultimately rest on technology and initial endowments, while quantities demanded in response to the uniform price will reflect preferences constrained by income. But if there is no uniform marketwide price, there cannot be offer curves or demand curves, either. Instead, offers and demands will be made by each transactor in response to immediate circumstances, rather than to marketwide conditions. Thus, offers and demands will be made by each market agent directly to specific others in one-to-one transactions. One would expect to find a demonstration that these will more or less rapidly converge on a uniform marketwide price which will eventually settle at the level which clears the markets.

Instead, most writers, following Marshall, as we shall see, assume that prices will be uniform in all transactions, and then proceed to the determination of the uniform price which will clear the market, wholly bypassing the prior question of how the uniformity of price will be established in the multitude of individual transactions. To his credit, Wicksell saw the problem and provided an argument, though, as we shall see, an invalid one:

> It would of course be possible, and indeed it occurs quite often, that one or the other party in a market attains in the first instance by an initial restraint a price higher than the one which later proves compatible with the general situation of the market; but then there is always the danger that some members . . . cleverly using this opportunity, might dispose of their whole stock at this artificially raised price, with the result that for the others the situation of the market would become so bad that in the end this procedure would bring them more loss than profit. It is just this latter circumstance that marks the principal difference between the market and the individual exchange. If one tries to avoid this danger by agreements . . . by cartels, etc., the conditions of individual exchange are more or less repeated (Wicksell, 1934–35).

The problem here is a subtle one, and has not been widely recognized. As a question of theoretical *consistency,* there is nothing wrong with the claim that in a fully competitive market, only one price can rule. But for *price-making behavior* to give way to *price-taking behavior,* more is needed; it must be shown that a sequence of *successive adjustments* will *converge* on a uniform price, and this is something that relatively few writers have attempted explicitly to demonstrate.

At first glance, Edgeworth, who first noted the indeterminacy of isolated exchange, seems an important exception. For he provided a systematic analysis of the convergence of exchange to competitive equilibrium, by showing that as the number of traders increased, the area of indeterminacy diminished. Moreover, his analysis is the foundation of the modern theory of the "core" of the economy and its relation to competitive equilibrium. But like the latter, Edgeworth's work relies on what has come to be called the parity theorem – that no allocation of goods among traders is final unless all parties are exchanging on the same terms. The proof is simple: if trades are taking place on different terms, it will always be to the advantage of one member of each exchange to opt out and recontract with an opposite number from another exchange at a price lying between the original trading prices. *But this is a consistency argument* – it is no more than a restatement of the point that nonuniform prices are inconsistent with equilibrium. This tells us nothing about how the market actually moves in response to the marketing strategies and behavior of particular buyers and sellers bargaining with one another. Wicksell clearly recognizes that the effect of competition in establishing a *uniform* price ruling in every transaction in a market must be demonstrated, not assumed. For, as he points out, there are many circumstances in which one or another parties to the same market will establish or attempt to establish quite different prices for the same goods at more or less the same time. His argument is quite straight forward: prices higher than the equilibrium will be marginally undercut, mopping up demand, leaving a poorer market for the rest.

Wicksteed, in an elaborate discussion of the problem (Wicksteed, 1933, pp. 219–29), begins essentially from the same position. That is, he sets out to show that beginning from a situation of higgling and price disparity, a competitive market will move in a pattern of successive transactions to the establishment of a uniform marketwide price, which all traders must accept, or withdraw from the market.[2]

But even on Wicksteed's own assumptions, there are difficulties. Buyers will move to the lowest price. As a result, a queue will form – and after a point, the price will start to rise. So some buyers may reasonably choose not to get in the queue and buy now at a higher price and get out of the market. As the queue forms, sellers in the other parts of the market will cut prices to attract demand back. So in some parts of the market, prices will be falling, in other parts prices will be rising, and there is no clear account of why these will not "overshoot" and pass one another, leading to a pattern of demand shifting back and forth, with some buyers and sellers choosing at various times to get out of the market, rather than continue the search for the best price.

Moreover, even if there is a convergence to a settled uniform price, Wicksteed (unlike both Knight and Wicksell) realizes that this does *not* bring the market to equilibrium (in the absence of complete recontracting) for the earlier purchases will have altered the wealth and utility positions of the traders.[3] "Anything . . . which increases the total resources of some members of the community and diminishes those of others, will *pro tanto* affect their estimates of the relative significance of different commodities . . . the equilibrating price of any article will be affected, even though the tastes of the community and the total amount of the commodity remain the same." (Wicksteed, 1933, p. 227)

Wicksteed's discussion is interesting for a number of reasons. For one he deals explicitly with marketing – buying and selling – quite apart from production. (Marshall's "very short run.") For another, he assumes that at the outset of a "marketing day," no one knows exactly what prices will rule; everyone comes to market expecting some disparity on each side among the initial quoted prices and offers and both buyers and sellers try to seek out the best deal or deals. Wicksteed's aim is to show that this situation will eventually settle down to a uniform price, but in fact, he admits that transactions will normally occur at quite various prices before a settled state is reached. Indeed, it is not clear that a settled state will ever be reached. In the end, he retreats to a consistency argument: "But although the consequences of mistakes may change the equilibrating price, there always exists such a price at any given moment, if it can but be discovered; that is to say, there is always a price such that, if it were now recognized and proclaimed, a single set of transactions at that price would produce equilibrium" (Wicksteed, 1933, p. 227).

This may be true, and it may further be true that such a price, once established, would require that all agents in the market acquiesce in it. The market would then consist entirely of price-takers. But this is quite different from demonstrating that sets of buying and selling agents confronting one another, beginning from quite diverse quotations, *would converge on this result.*

In fact, within the framework of competitive assumptions, reasonably and realistically interpreted, it should not be difficult to show that the market *need not* converge on a uniform price, but could establish a fluctuating pattern of disparate prices. The agents concluding transactions in these circumstances, then will not exhibit price-taking behavior but will continue to behave as price-makers engaged in confrontation.

Marketing strategies in competitive conditions. It is worth looking at this more closely. Sellers may be employees of producers or independent contracting agents who buy from producers to sell in the market. Buyers likewise may be employees of other firms, or household consumers. Let us suppose that the market consists of large numbers of buyers and sellers, that mobility among channels of trade is easy, and that there is a good network of communication so that information about transactions, offers and quoted prices is rapidly disseminated. Production takes a week, and outputs are available on Mondays, and must be sold by Friday, unless excess inventory is to be carried. Costs are generally known, as is the history of previous marketing. Let us suppose, for the sake of argument, that buyers currently on the market and those newly entering during the "day," in the aggregate would like to buy a certain quantity at a certain price, and that sellers also hope to sell that quantity at that same price. Thus, Wicksteed's equlibrium price which would exactly clear the market exists. But both buyers and sellers expect to find a wide variety of initial quotations, and to engage in a complicated and time-consuming process of seeking out and bargaining with the other side. Each side, sellers and buyers, will have to allocate time, effort and skill to *marketing*. Presumably, the more of these allocated, the better the results will be, but, of course, the higher the cost. One decision which will have to be made, then, is how much time and resources to devote to marketing. Another is what to do when these resources have run out, but the marketing goals have not been achieved. But perhaps the most important question is how to conduct the marketing itself. Output could be sold at once at the offers prevailing when it comes on the market, or all or some could be held back (Wicksell's initial restraint) in the hope of obtaining a better price. Similarly, buyers could buy at once or hold back all, or part, of demand. This is NOT the same as the question just posed which concerned the amount of resources to devote to marketing; this concerns strategy – how much of output or custom should be put on the market at once, and how much should be held back.

Let us try and set these problems out formally, in quite a simplified way:[4]

Sellers. First, let us examine a representative seller concerned to divide his sales most profitably between immediate (and safe) sales at the price he expects to prevail when he comes on the market, and more risky, speculative sales made later, hopefully at a higher price, but after time and effort have been expended in search and bargaining. Clearly, the objective will be to maximize the profit on sales, but this will be subject to the constraints of the total amount of product on hand, and the total time and resources available for marketing. Assuming that all the relations are linear in the relevant ranges, we have:

$$\begin{aligned} \max R &= p_1Q_1 + p_2Q_2 \\ \text{subject to} \quad & Q_1 + Q_2 \leq Q \\ & t_1Q_1 + t_2Q_2 \leq T \\ \text{where} \quad & Q_1, Q_2 > 0 \end{aligned}$$

This is a standard linear programming problem, but it requires careful interpretation, especially since its implications for the theory of competitive behavior are quite profound. It says that profit is the sum of immediate and speculative sales, and the object is to find the division of Q into Q_1 and Q_2, that will maximize profit. We can assume that the representative seller expects to find some distribution of offers to buy, and we can take p_1, as the mode of that distribution. The average expected time and resources necessary for the sale of a unit output, at price p_1, is t_1. This is quite a strong and objectionable assumption. Why should a sale of twice as much take twice as much time and resources? It is no more trouble to sell two packs of cigarettes than one. But the same is *not* true of automobiles or washing machines, or consumer durables generally where the most common sales will be of a single unit, and each unit requires the attention of sales personnel to inspect, and demonstrate the equipment and to persuade the customer. Even so, much of the selling cost will be charged to overhead, and so will be independent of the division into immediate and speculative sales. Such costs are not relevant here; think of door-to-door salespeople, selling hi-fi sets, vacuum cleaners or encyclopedias. Or, like Wicksteed, think of a market-place with stalls and customers milling about. Each of these images has a drawback, in that each presents *one* side as mobile, the other stationary, whereas in the competitive market of economic mythology, *both* sides are mobile. Some amalgam must be invented – motorized stalls in the market, perhaps. In any case, t_1 is the average expected unit cost of making an immediate sale at the most common price offered, and t_2 is the considerably higher expected unit cost of making a sale later on at the higher price p_2. $t_2 > t_1$ partly because of waiting, partly because it is expected to be necessary to seek out buyers, and partly because of the cost of special imaginative inducements to purchase (throwing in extras, taking clients to dinner, etc.). The expected values of p_1 and t_1 can be taken as given on the basis of past experience. But p_2 and t_2 are clearly functionally related, given the representative seller's expectations about the nature of the market. The greater the time and resources devoted to selling, at least up to a point, the higher the price

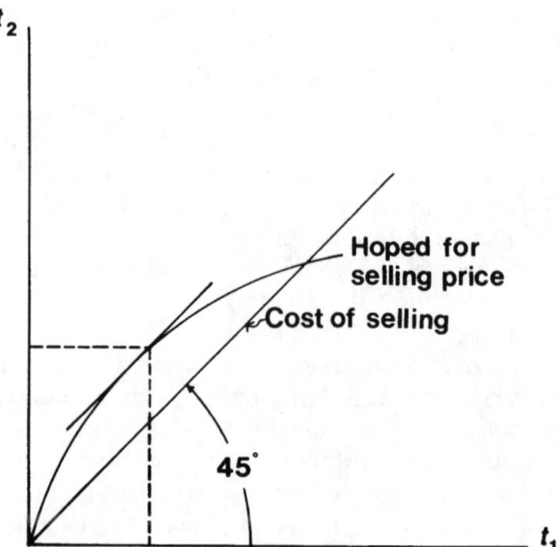

Figure 6.2

that can be obtained – p_2 is an increasing function of t_2. But additional investments of time and effort can be expected to yield progressively smaller increases in the obtainable price – p_2 as a function of t_2 shows diminishing returns. On these assumptions p_2 and t_2 will be determined together by a simple calculation, shown in Figure 6.2.[5] The cost function is simply the 45° line, and the point where the slope of the sales price curve is equal to 45° indicates the maximum difference between expected sales price and unit selling cost. These will then be the values of p_2 and t_2 which enter into the calculation of Q_1 and Q_2.

For the moment take Q and T as given. Then the program just mentioned has a straight forward solution, which can be shown graphically (Figure 6.3). Take the axes as Q_1 and Q_2 and

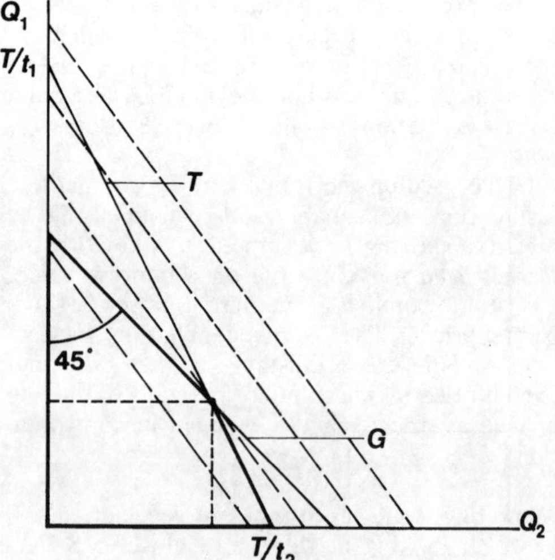

Figure 6.3

draw the constraints with solid lines, and the objective function with dotted ones. So long as $1 < (p_2/p_1) < (t_2/t_1)$ the solution will involve both immediate and speculative sales. However, if $(p_2/p_1) > (t_2/t_1)$ then all sales will be speculative, but not all output will be sold.

This program has a minimizing problem as its dual, which will provide the clue to the way Q and T are determined.

$$\begin{aligned} \min S &= W_1Q + W_2T \\ \text{subject to} \quad & W_1 + W_2t_1 \geq p_1 \\ & W_1 + W_2t_2 \geq p_2 \\ \text{where} \quad & W_1, W_2 > 0 \end{aligned}$$

The objective is to minimize the imputed cost of inventory and of sales, subject to the constraints of the expected unit profits. Again, the solution is easy to see graphically. (Figure 6.4) Measure W_1 and W_2 on the axes, and show the constraints with solid lines and the objective with dotted ones. So long as $t_1 < (T/Q) < t_2$, the solution will involve both variables.

From the basic duality theorem of linear programming, we know that the dual problem is automatically solved when the maximizing problem is solved. Hence, given the division of expected sales into Q_1 and Q_2, we know the imputed valuations of inventory and of sales time and resources, W_1 and W_2. From the duality theorem, then, $(\partial R/\partial Q) = W_1$ and $(\partial R/\partial T) = W_2$, that is, the marginal contribution to profit of additional inventory is W_1 and the marginal contribution to profit of additional sales time and resources is W_2. Thus, if, in accordance with conventional doctrine, marginal cost of production rises, output will be produced until marginal cost equals W_1, and on the same grounds, assuming that the marginal cost of providing sales effort rises, that will be provided up to the point at which its marginal cost equals W_2, the additional new revenue to be imputed to the sales effort. Thus, Q and T are determined by the conventional marginal cost/marginal revenue conditions.

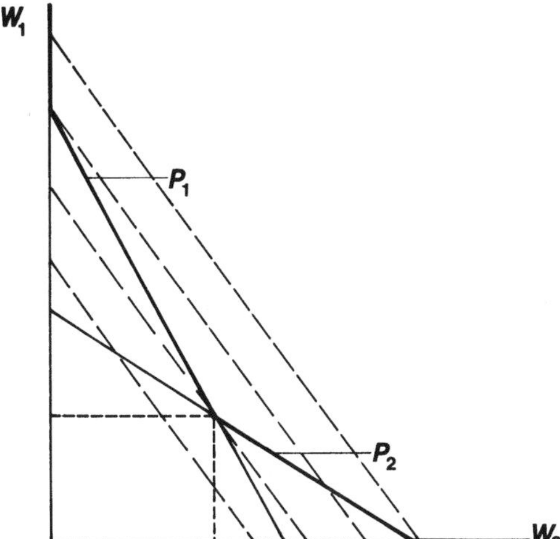

Figure 6.4

This shows that even in a competitive market with large numbers of mobile, well-informed buyers and sellers and one in which sellers' behavior is governed by the marginal cost/marginal revenue conditions, if sellers expect the prices they face to exhibit variation, and if they have resources to devote to marketing, it may well be in their interests to plan to sell parts of their output at different prices. This may be inconsistent with competitive equilibrium, but it is entirely rational behavior for the representative seller.

Buyers. To complete the picture, consider a representative buyer. The buyer's basic ambition is to buy as cheaply as possible. Like the seller he expects to face a certain distribution of prices on coming into the market. Let $\bar{p}_1$ be the modal price in this distribution, and t_1 denote the relatively small amount of time and effort and other resources needed to buy a unit amount at this price. As in the case of the seller, $\bar{p}_2$ will denote a more agreeable, because lower, price which can only be found after exerting a good deal of effort in search, persuasion and bargaining, where t_2 indicates the unit amounts of revenue devoted to this task. As in the case of the seller $\bar{p}_2$ is a function of t_2, exhibiting diminishing returns. A lower price can be found with effort, but additional effort diminishes the price less and less. The optimal condition is the same as before, and the program can be written out

$$\begin{aligned} \min z &= \bar{p}_1Q_1 + \bar{p}_2Q_2 \\ \text{subject to} \quad & Q_1 + Q_2 \geq Q \\ & t_1Q_1 + t_2Q_2 = T, \\ \text{where} \quad & Q_1, Q_2 > 0 \end{aligned}$$

(Here, since buyers' time and resources are limited, the second constraint binds strictly. Note that $\bar{p}_2 < \bar{p}_1$ and $t_2 > t_1$. The diagram in Figure 6.5 is much the same, except that it is a minimizing problem. The solution, however, is a corner solution – gamble everything! So buyers will not be in the market at all, initially, unless for some reason e.g. because they are risk-averters – they attach special weight to stocking-up early in part. (In that case, they will attach a special utility to $\bar{p}_1$, which will change the shape of the objective function, making possible strategy with both immediate and speculative purchases.)

As before, the dual follows directly, and gives the values to be imputed to the amount to be bought and to the time and resources to be spent

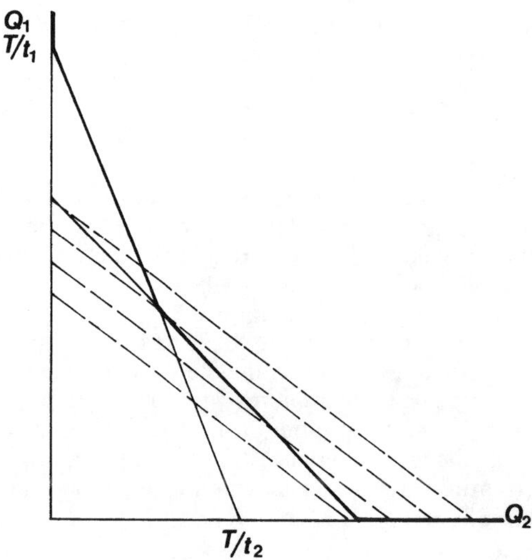

Figure 6.5

in the act of buying in the market. The dual of a minimizing problem is a maximizing one. Here buyers maximize the value they obtain by purchasing and spending time in the market, subject to the constraints given by the price they expect to have to pay.

$$\begin{aligned} \max S &= v_1 Q + v_2 T \\ \text{subject to} \quad v_1 + v_2 t_1 &= p_1 \\ v_1 + v_2 t_2 &= p_2, \\ \text{where} \quad v_1, v_2 &> 0 \end{aligned}$$

The solution to this gives the imputed value of Q and T, so that, as before, from the basic duality theorem, $(\partial z/\partial Q) = v_1$, and $(\partial z/\partial T) = v_2$ (Figure 6.6). Buyers, if they are final consumers,

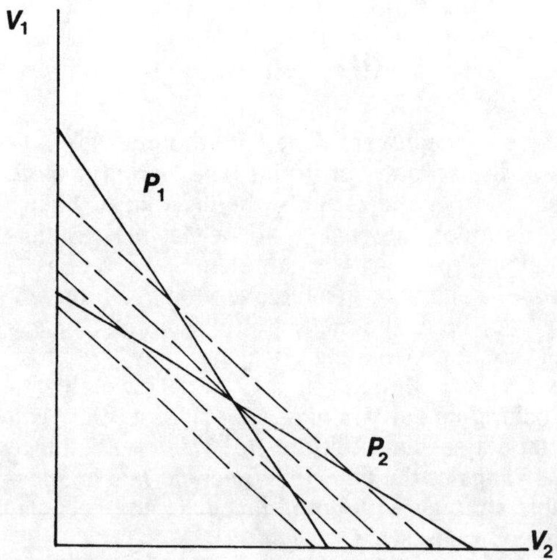

Figure 6.6

however, will have their own utility trade off between goods and time and effort. On conventional assumptions, we should expect that initially time and effort would be willingly expended to obtain more goods, but that progressively more goods would be required to compensate additional time and effort, finally rising very steeply, as the purchasing effort would have to draw attention away from other fixed commitments. At the point where the slope of this trade-off equals the ratio of the imputed valuations in the dual, we find the equilibrium ratio of Q and T. The absolute amounts then follow from the consumers maximizing his utility subject to his budget constraint, which is fixed by his income. According to our initial hypothesis the quantity in the buyer's problem, Q_B, is equal to the seller's quantity, Q_S.

Competitive price movements. As in the case of the seller, then, the buyer's behavior is guided by the conventional marginalist equilibrium conditions. For the buyer as for the seller, the market is competitive in the sense that there are many competing well informed and mobile agents on each side. But buyers can rationally choose to divide their offers into immediate and speculative and, as we have seen, the likely result is that they will "practice initial restraint," withholding their custom entirely. So not only do both sides plan strategies quite inconsistent with price-taking behavior, but they come to market with strategies inconsistent with each other. What then will happen? Will the market impose price–taking behavior on them? In a competitive market, prices must be flexible, responding quickly to any divergencies between supply and demand. Initially, buyers plan to buy nothing, but sellers plan to offer ΣQ_1, at the expected demand price of p_1. The market will, therefore, initially have an excess supply. Sellers will therefore begin cutting price. (Since customers are highly mobile, a small price cut relative to the going price should attract a large proportion of the available trade. So long as the expected gain from additional sales outweighs the loss on the previous volume due to the price cut, it will be worthwhile to cut.)[6] The initial price p_1 will begin falling as a result; but, sellers will *not* on that account begin withdrawing their Q_1. For, given the constraints, the solution is stable so long as $(p_2/p_1) \leq (t_2/t_1)$. Only when p_1 has fallen to a level reversing this inequality will sellers withdraw any goods, and they will withdraw everything. Of course, sellers do not all have exactly the same expectations about prices, or exactly the same patterns of costs. The same is true of buyers. Thus as price falls, some sellers will withdraw their immediate

supply first, just as some buyers will come on the market earlier than others. But the decline of price may put it in the range of the buyers' hoped-for speculative price. If price falls to the point where it equals or falls below the buyer's speculative price, $\bar{p}_2$, then *the buyer's strategic plan will shift*. Whereas before, the solution of the program called for only Q_2 in the amount of $(T_2/t_2) < Q$, now buyers will buy a mix of immediate and speculative purchases, $Q_1 + Q_2 = Q$.[7] So the total amount of the purchase plan will rise, and immediate demand will come on the market, at approximately the point at which suppliers are withdrawing immediate supply, and reducing their total planned offer from Q to $Q_2 = T_s/t_2$. So, having first fallen because of excess supply, price will now tend to rise because of excess demand. Just as a small cut below the prevailing price would attract demand, so a small rise in the bid above the prevailing price will attract supply. The bidder will gain custom, those sticking to the prevailing price will lose. Hence strategic considerations call for bidding, even in circumstances where the overall supply is insufficient and/or inelastic.[8]

It may help to think of things in terms of sections of a three-dimensional diagram. On one axis plot the planned prices for buyers and sellers, and on the other the various amounts the traders are respectively offering to buy or sell. (This is *not* like a conventional diagram, which shows the amounts that *would be* offered or demanded by the traders at different prices. Here prices and quantities have both been determined by the marketing program, and the diagram simply shows the aggregate amounts going at each price.) The third axis, then, is time. This makes it possible to examine how the price dispersion moves through time, and in particular, how the intersection of the buyers' and sellers' dispersions moves over time. (See Figure 6.7.) For this last shows the time pattern of the prices at which actual trades take place.

Initially, those sellers willing to sell part of their p output right away (a few, anticipating a high p_2, may opt entirely for later sales) are dispersed more or less normally around an expected normal price (which we may assume to be the equilibrium price.) Very few buyers will be in the market initially, however. There will only be those who, pessimistically, do not expect prices to decline significantly and those who attach special significance to buying quickly and getting out.

Assume that buyers and sellers are homogeneous in size, so the quantity axis also measures the number of transactions. Now integrate the curves to obtain cumulative frequency curves,

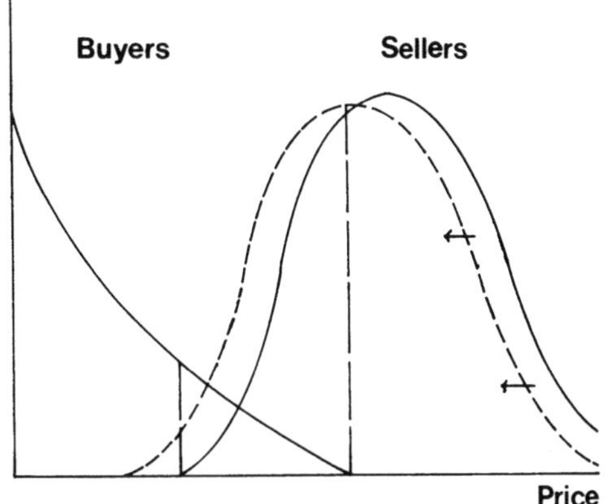

Figure 6.7

showing respectively all sellers willing to sell at a certain price or above and all buyers willing to buy at a given price or below.

Transactions will take place only in the area of overlap between the lowest seller's price and the highest buyer's price. Competitive pressures will shift the seller's cumulative frequency curve down, as all sellers lower their initial reserve prices. Buyers, however, can see that there are more sellers in the current market than buyers, so can confidently wait for prices to fall. Thus as the seller's curve shifts down, there will be traced out a sequence of frequency distributions of transactions at various prices (Figure 6.8).

When prices have fallen sufficiently, $p_2/p_1 > t_2/t_1$, so that sellers' plans will begin to switch, and sellers will begin withdrawing from the

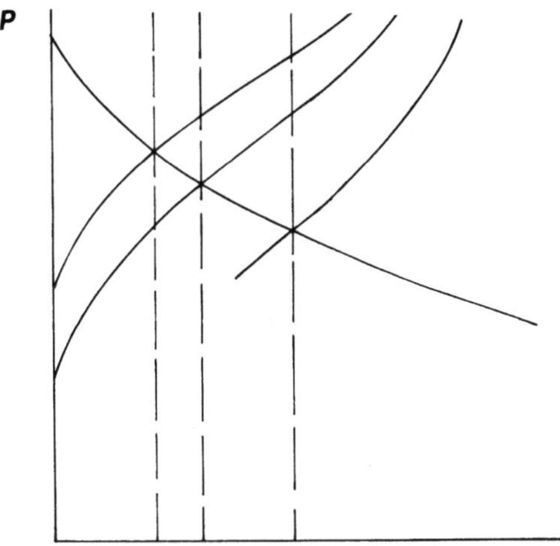

Figure 6.8

market. But as prices fall, p_1 comes near to the hoped-for level of p_2 for buyers, and buyers' plans begin to shift. The buyers' dispersion will take on the shape of a normal distribution around their expected speculative price, p_2, and the entire demand becomes effective. Since sellers are withdrawing (and were in any case only offering part of their supply) demand now comes to exceed supply, and price will be bid up. Sellers having gone through the trauma of initially low and falling prices, which forced them to recalculate their strategy, now see in the rising prices the justification of their wait. They will stick with their recalculated plan; the now rising prices represent the hoped for speculative prices, p_2.

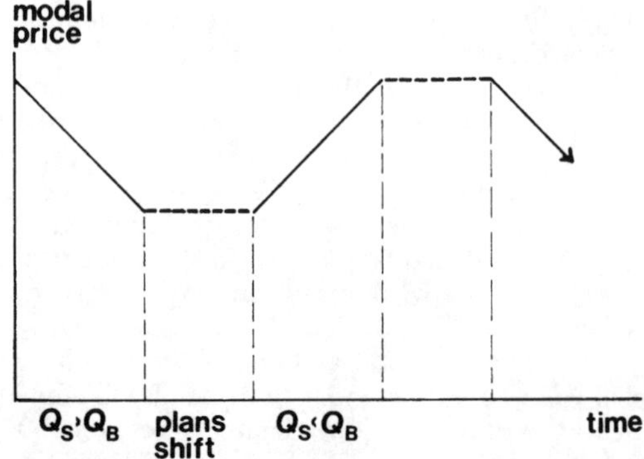

Figure 6.9

Buyers, on the other hand, find themselves desolated by the high prices. As the price rises and the period wears on, they find their hopes for a speculative low price evaporating; further time and effort will only result in a higher price than can be obtained now. With $p_2 > p_1$, the buyers solution becomes $Q_2 = 0$, $Q_1 = T_B/t_{B1}$, (where subscripts indicate both buyers and sellers respectively). Sellers are now each offering their $Q_2 = T_S/t_{S2}$. It is plausible to suppose that unit time and effort in marketing is not that different for buyers and sellers, so that $t_{B1} \cong t_{S1}$ and $t_{B2} \cong t_{S2}$. But, it is quite likely that the overall resources devoted to marketing will be greater for sellers than for buyers, $T_S > T_B$. If this is so, then we should expect to find buyers coming to the end of their planned marketing time and resources first, and having to pay whatever the prevailing price is. But as the marketing day draws to an end will $\Sigma Q_{B1} = \Sigma Q_{S2}$? That is, is $\Sigma(T_B/t_{B1})$ greater, equal to, or less than $\Sigma(T_S/t_{S2})$? If $\Sigma(T_B/t_{B1})$ is less than $\Sigma(T_S/t_{S2})$, if sellers have chosen to devote a great deal of resources to marketing, while finding the unit costs of speculative selling rather low, then as buyers buy up and leave the market, there will remain a residue of unsold supply still on offer, which will turn prices down again, at the very end. (See Figure 6.9.) But if $\Sigma(T_B/t_{B1}) > \Sigma(T_S/t_{S2})$, then prices will go on rising right to the end, leading sellers to dip into the inventory which they had not planned to market at all.

Thus the frequency distribution of prices in transactions will first decline, then rise, then perhaps decline again. There is no reason to suppose that the variance will be small; quite the reverse. Nor is there any reason to suppose it will be skewed in any particular way. The distribution of the prices at which transactions occur here confirms the expectations of buyers and sellers regarding price disparity. It also makes it reasonable for different buyers and sellers to hold differing views as to the prices they will initially face. Over time marketers will learn that excess supply will push initial prices down, while excess demand will push later prices up. For sellers, this confirms that $p_2 > p_1$. For buyers it also confirms that $\bar{p}_2 < \bar{p}_1$; but it also poses the problem for buyers of getting out of the market before prices begin rising again. In each case the history of the marketing period confirms the assumptions upon which the marketing plan was constructed. So there is no reason to suppose that over time there would be any tendency, through learning, for marketing strategies to adjust so as to narrow the variance of transaction prices, or to eliminate the fluctuations, let alone to converge upon the equilibrium.

Under the quite reasonable assumptions of this example, price will first decline, and then rise, never settling at any one level, nor becoming uniform. In spite of the fact that an equilibrium price exists in the abstract which buyers and sellers both would have found more satisfactory, the market need show no tendency to move towards that equilibrium. Quite the contrary: not only can price fluctuate continually throughout the market period, but there is no guarantee that all quantities (or demands) brought to market will be satisfied. Finally, and perhaps most important, this example shows that even though a small cut in price will attract most of the available demand, and a small rise above the going price will attract most of the supply – the standard prescription for a competitive market characterized by price-taking behavior – traders can rationally plan to behave as price-makers engaged in confrontations.

Of course, like any argument, this one depends on its special assumptions: in particular, it depends on buyers and sellers having both expectations of price disparity, and a belief that by devoting time and effort to marketing, they can improve the prices they obtain. These are surely not objectionable; the linearity assumptions are more problematic, but they have the advantage of simplicity. (Nor is it difficult to imagine a non-linear model which would yield very similar results.) The important point is that the assumption of competitive conditions is not in itself enough to convert price-making behavior into passive acquiescence in the dictates of the impersonal market. Nor does it lead to an orderly equilibrium. We are face to face with "the anarchy of the market place."[9]

The auctioneer

Walras provided the best answer of all (Walras, 1954, Lesson 5, et passim). He supplied the market with a device that positively guaranteed uniformity of price in all transactions – indeed he eliminated pure transactions altogether, by requiring that all exchanges be conducted through an auctioneer, who guarantees anonymity to every party and assures that all transactions will be carried out simultaneously at the common price. (As the Walrasian auctioneer calls out prices, bilateral trading parties would move along their offer curves until they reach the intersection.)

The special duties of the auctioneer. The substantive importance of this move can hardly be overstated. It is not merely a matter of convenience. It amounts in fact, to a reconstruction of the idea of competition. For competition, as conceived by Walras and his followers in the neoclassical tradition, is competition between those engaged in the same activity, each trying to outdo the other at what they both do. But in reality, in addition to this, there is the direct confrontation, between buyer and seller, employer and employee, borrower and lender. What the seller gains from setting a high price, the buyer who pays that price, loses; what the employer gains from setting a low wage, the employee, who must accept that wage, loses. This form of competition has not been stressed by neoclassical thinking, or rather it has been subsumed in the definitions of the supply and demand curves. (Demand curves implicitly treat yielding to pressure as just another form of doing what you want to do, and supply curves treat returns as a special form of cost.) As a consequence the advantages and disadvantages of applying pressure across the market have not been systematically studied. Yet the direct confrontation, which can be seen in its purest and most dramatic form in isolated exchange, is the basic form of market transaction. For every exchange, in the last analysis, is a direct confrontation, between one buyer and one seller. True, in the competitive cases each *might* have gone to another buyer or seller, and the possibility of such lateral displacement of trade will undoubtedly influence the terms on which the direct confrontation is settled.[10] But in the end every transaction is concluded between one buyer and one seller, and what the one gains from the terms of the transaction, the other loses. Regardless of how many buyers and sellers there are, unless it is mediated by an "auctioneer," the representative transaction is a confrontation between one buyer and one seller: the representative transaction has the form of an isolated exchange.[11] Before turning to the case of many buyers and/or sellers, surely theory should settle the one-to-one case first? Yet as we have already seen, neoclassical theory has no way of dealing with this case.

To the neoclassical eye, the indeterminacy of individual transactions is of no moment, for such transactions are lost in the general play of market forces. In Walras, markets are considered essentially as auctions. The auctioneer calls out a price, and matches up the supplies and demands at that price. If offers to sell exceed demands, he calls out a lower price; if offers fall short of demands, a higher, until he reaches a price at which the two just match up.

This picture is so simple and so familiar that we forget how special it really is. Most goods and services are not moved by auction, and for good reason, but that is not the end of it. The Walrasian auction is a very special kind of auction. In a normal auction, the goods are put up on the auction block (with at most a reservation price) and take their chances, in the hopes that the buyers competing against one another will bid the price up. But in the Walrasian auction, the goods are not even on offer yet. Conditional offers are made as the auctioneer calls out prices; sales are concluded only when the auctioneer announces that supply and demand balance.[12] Now it is perfectly true that no one takes what Edgeworth called Walras's "noisy and unconvincing dynamics" seriously as an account of the way markets, or even auctions, actually work. Yet the auction is more than a casual metaphor. For certain features peculiar to this image have been taken to be characteristic of markets in general. Moreover these are the very features which make it possible to claim that supply and demand settle the pattern of exchange and distribute the gains.

The principal such feature centers around the role of the auctioneer. For he assumes a number of important burdens and duties, from which he obtains no benefit since he has no economic motivation. For example, he absorbs transactions and marketing costs, by bringing buyers and sellers together; he eliminates most information costs; he guarantees the impartiality of the transactions process – no one is benefitted by the time or place of the sale; and finally, perhaps most important, the auctioneer provides anonymity to the buyers and sellers, making the market process impersonal. But in fact, even in markets approximating auctions, like the Stock Exchange, anonymity in many cases cannot be maintained. In most industries and for most goods, marketing is anything but anonymous; indeed, given the modern world of brand names and advertising, it is remarkable that economists have been willing to accept the assumption that buyers and sellers neither know nor deal directly with each other, or that nothing important follows from the fact that they do, i.e. that it is *as if* they did not know each other. But if this assumption is *not* accepted, the theory is in trouble. For if buyers and sellers are not anonymous, if transactions are not mediated by an auctioneer, then each transaction in the market will be a two-party exchange. Even when conditions are broadly competitive, buyers and sellers will plan strategies as price–makers, as we have seen, and there is no assurance that these strategies will prove compatible with market clearing. If, in addition, there are information costs, advertising or marketing activities, and/or transaction costs, which inhibit the parties from moving their custom about easily, the market will segment or divide into a number of separate confrontations. In these circumstances, the forces of supply and demand do not necessarily clear the market, or even establish that one and only one price will rule in the market for a given good.

Market – clearing and the auctioneer. But regardless of the degree of competition, without an auctioneer, or the equivalent, neoclassical theory faces a fundamental difficulty. For in the absence of some such device, there is a change in the direction of causality. The auctioneer collates the schedules of supply and demand for each possible *uniform* marketwide price finally settling on the one at which supply and demand balance. Thus the aggregate balance determines price. But when each buyer and each seller must search out their counterpart(s), *there is no way of performing the aggregate balancing,* hence no way of singling out the price at which demand and supply just balance. The individual transactions will or may be taking place simultaneously, under conditions in which no one can know either what the aggregate outcome will be – for no one knows the market-clearing price in advance, or even that a uniform price will finally be established. Individual agents may be influenced by their beliefs about what price would clear the market as a whole; they may be influenced similarly by what they believe they could obtain from other sellers or buyers. These beliefs may be correct or incorrect, and their influence may be great or small. But the price which results from the various individual transactions cannot, in *general,* be determined by the condition that supply shall equal demand, even when market conditions are competitive. For, as we argued earlier, individual transactions will be carried out in accordance with buyers' and sellers' marketing plans, modified in response to immediate market conditions. But these conditions will not reflect the aggregate balance of supply and demand *on the market;* at any given moment, the market reflects the balance of supply and demand generated by the *current market strategies* of particular buyers and sellers, confronting one another, quite a different matter. The effect of a current aggregate imbalance in supply and demand in a market, especially when repeated over several periods may show up not in pressure to raise or reduce prices, but rather as a change either in capacity, or in the development of specialized marketing services and techniques. An imbalance of overall supply and demand, in short, will be seen by firms as indicating either danger and overextension, or opportunity, and it will be reflected in changes in the constraints on the marketing strategy problem.

By contrast, the auctioneer, at no cost to the participants, finds that uniform price which equates supply and demand for the entire market, and arranges payments and deliveries, *in advance* of any binding contracts. The auction format for a market raises lateral competition, competition along the same side of the market, to its maximum pitch. For in an auction, all potential buyers and sellers are simultaneously present, and aware of each other's bids, yet deal with the opposite side of the market only through the impersonal agency of the auctioneer. There is no way of exerting pressure across the market; the parties there are unknown. But one's demands will come to naught, one's supplies go unsold, unless one out bids or undersells the others on one's own side of the market. Hence the tendency of the auction will be to push each side to its limit. The auction is thus a highly special market form, in which, because transactions are both mediated and incomplete until all are settled at once, the only competition is lateral. The dictates of the impersonal auctioneer rule absolutely.

For this very reason, auctions are relatively rare. Of course there are other reasons as well: it is difficult to assemble all potential buyers at one time; it is difficult to arrange for an impartial central information gathering institution – the auctioneer. For such an institution will be very influential and could itself fall prey to the powerful motive of self-interest. Moreover, it will be costly and will have to find some regular source of support. But it may well be that the basic reason so few markets are organized as auctions is that it is neither efficient nor in the interest of powerful parties that transactions be mediated and anonymous. It is not efficient because customers often require goods made to particular specifications, and so must deal directly with their suppliers. And it is not in the interests of the powerful precisely because they are in a position to exercise pressure across the market.

No doubt supply and demand in competitive conditions *can* yield stable outcomes; a model of the sort studied earlier *could* be arranged to generate convergence upon a uniform price which in time would adjust to an equilibrium level. But this would be a special case. There is no necessity for such convergence, and under quite plausible assumptions, it will not happen, even though conditions are broadly competitive and sellers and buyers are both governed by neoclassical marginal equilibrium conditions. Now we have seen that the other main line of orthodox thinking, the Walrasian approach to markets, is based on *a crucial and wholly implausible institutional assumption* – namely that markets are run as a very special kind of auction. This assumption could only be justified, if, as a matter of theoretical necessity, pure competitive conditions always resulted in the establishment of a single dominant price. But the argument given is that nothing else is consistent with equilibrium, which is true but irrelevant. The implications for the conventional, textbook theory of markets are considerable: if markets are not managed by Walrasian auctioneers; if there is no such thing as universal recontracting; and if competition permits price disparity and fluctuations,very little is left of the orthodox theory of markets. *For the main pillars of neoclassical market theory are the price-taking responses of households and firms to uniform marketwide prices.*

Firms are supposed to treat prices parametrically in competitive conditions, choosing output and employment levels in response to given, market-wide prices. But such prices are never given. What is actually present *ab initio* is a marketing situation, in which competitive behavior is supposed quickly to establish uniform market-wide prices. This, we have seen, need not happen. Firms, therefore, must plan their marketing strategies so as to obtain the best prices, in conditions of price disparity, both across the market at a given time and through time. We can expect that firms will schedule output and employment to fit in with their marketing strategy, and that eventually they will adapt and design their products to improve their marketing position. Moreover, we should expect to find them trying to alter the conditions of the market itself to their advantage, for example, by contracting alliances with other firms or entering into exclusive contracts with buyers. In other words, limiting competition.

The same applies to buyers. To get the best price a purchase plan will be needed. Therefore, consumption patterns should be adjusted. And exactly as for sellers, various kinds of coalitions, treaties, or alliances may prove advantageous. It is apparent that price disparity and the scramble for advantage impose costs on both sides of the market. Both buyers and sellers have to face uncertainty about what prices they will eventually get, and they must both invest time and energy in marketing. If these costs are large in relation to the potential gains, there will be an incentive to establish a fixed price, through some form of collusion or price leadership. In other words, to eliminate the anarchy of the marketplace there will have to be administered prices. The emergence of price administration from disorderly competition, and the principle on the basis of which administered prices are set, are thus proper subjects for the theory of markets. But they require a new approach.

Notes

1 Suppose, to take an intermediate case, that the potential gain were agreed to be divided equally between them, in proportion to their costs. We would have $(b - \alpha)/\alpha = (a - \beta)/\beta$ or, substituting, $[b - a(t + k)]/[a(1 + k)] = (a - xb)/xb$, which yields, $a/b = (x/(1 + k))^{1/2}$. If net gains were divided equally, in absolute amount, so that $b - \alpha = a - \beta$, the unit price will be $a/b = (1 + x)/(2 + k)$.

2 Many discussions of the contention that a single price will prevail in a competitive market overlook the fact that the adjustments which establish such uniformity must be sequential. Thus, Frank Knight states: "If exchanges be thought of as taking place at different prices the buyer at the higher price and seller at the lower will get together at an intermediate figure" (Knight, 1921, p. 82). More recently, Henderson and Quandt, for example, write: "Since the product is homogeneous and everybody possesses perfect information, a single price must prevail in a perfectly competitive market . . . (To prove, assume the contrary) . . . By hypothesis, consumers are aware . . . that 1) the commodity can be bought at two different prices, 2) one unit of the commodity is the same as any other. Since con-

sumers are utility maximizers, they will not buy the commodity at the higher price. Therefore a single price must prevail. (Henderson and Quant, 1958, p. 86.) If they mean the lower price, then they contradict Frank Knight. But the argument is specious, since it ignores the adjustment process. The consumers can't all buy it at once at the lower price. Some will have to wait for the higher price to come down. In the meantime the lower price will rise, and demand will be shifting back and forth, as described in the text.

3 Moreover, if, for example, someone started the market too low, others could gain, later, by going too high. By Wicksteed's own argument, any one mistaken price will make other nonequilibrium prices profitable (Wicksteed, 1933, pp. 224–25). But Hicks, following Marshall, argues that while false prices are very likely to occur they are also quite likely to prove unimportant, since they generate only income effects, which can be neglected if the amount spent on the good is small in comparison to the total spending on all goods of the traders in question. Therefore, trading at false prices will not shift the equilibrium very much. This argument wholly misses the point that since price disparity (the existence of trades at false prices) is likely, it will come to be anticipated, so that traders will form their trading plans on the basis of it. In that event, as shown above, price disparity will remain, and prices will fluctuate over the marketing period, exhibiting no necessary tendency to move towards uniformity, much less equilibrium (Hicks, 1946, pp. 120, 127–30).

4 Other more complex, perhaps more realistic ways, could be devised, but this will be sufficient to show that there is no necessary movement from price-making confrontations to price-taking behavior, even within broadly competitive conditions, even when an equilibrium uniform price exists. The example analyzed here concerns the product market, but it could easily be adapted to the labor market.

5 It might be objected that p_2 should also be a function of Q_2 (the amount the seller hopes to dispose of at a high but uncertain price), so that the greater Q_2 the greater the difficulty of obtaining such a price. This could be allowed for, but to keep matters simple it is assumed that each seller considers himself sufficiently small that if he can outwait the other side, he will then be able to dispose of whatever fraction of his output he has withheld.

6 Let the profits from sales at the going price be p. Next, since customers are highly mobile, a small price cut, relative to the going price, will attract a large volume of trade. Assume that the gain from such additional sales at the lower price outweighs the loss due to the price cut on the previous volume. Then the new level of revenue for the price cutter, will be $P > p$. The traders that do not cut will then make a loss, which will depend upon the amount of excess capacity the price-cutting firms were carrying. Assume that this loss is large enough at least to be noticeable, and designate it by $-i$. Finally, if all trade is cut, all profits not established as fixed costs will be eliminated. The strategic possibilities can be arrayed in a matrix, from

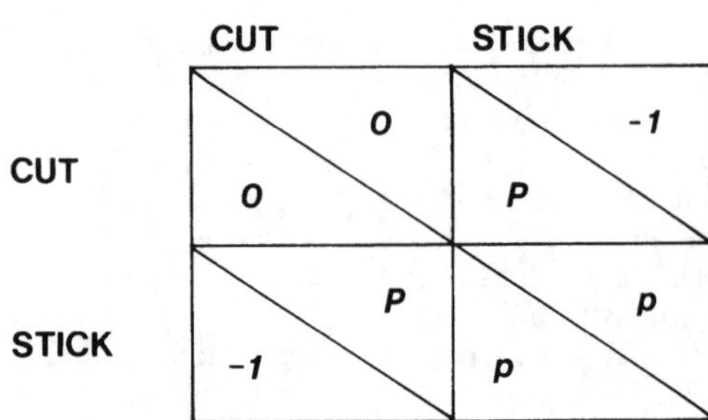

Figure 6.10

which it is clear that everyone's best strategy is to cut price, since $P > p$ and $C > -i$. As a result, all firms will be worse off, and across the counter power will be neutralized. (See Figure 6.10.)

7 If p_1 has fallen to the hoped-for level of $\bar{p}_2$ for buyers, there is no point in expending the extra per unit purchasing effort represented by t_2, so the entire demand will be effective at once.

8 Firms can switch customers, just as customers can switch firms. If there is a shortage, or fears of shortage, customers will bid against each other. Let us assume that even a small rise above the going bid will attract supply: the bidder will therefore gain, while those sticking with the going price will lose supply. There is no certainty of gain from bidding – the bidder has a larger supply at a higher price, rather than a smaller or minimal supply at a lower. If his marketing plan requires purchases of at least a certain amount, he will have to prefer the former. But even if he is merely indifferent, bidding will be advantageous. The strategic situation is illustrated very simply (Figure 6.11), using arbitrary numbers. If both stick at the established price, both obtain whatever initial advantage there was, call it 0,0. If both bid, both make a loss from the higher price, but since capacity is fixed in the short run, the bids call forth no additional supply. But if one bids and the other does not, the bidder gains the certainty of supply, while the sticker loses supply. Hence, there is a slight gain and a certain loss. Consequently, faced with shortage and the necessity of making purchases, everyone will bid rather than stick.

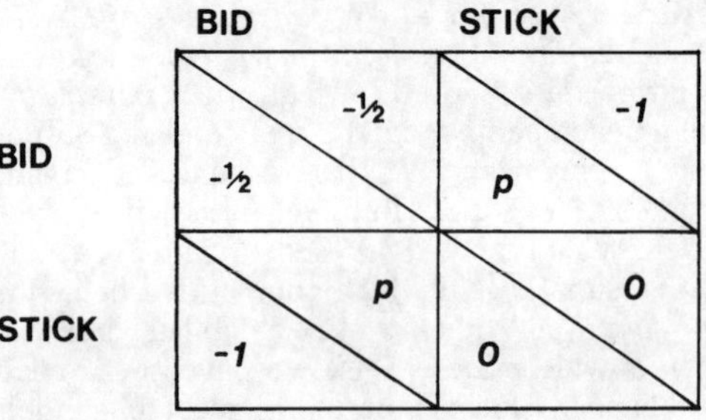

Figure 6.11

9 Wicksell, who raised the question with which we began, in fact finally evaded the issue: "We simply suppose here as a fact that on the market one price or a proportion of exchange between every two commodities establishes itself within a short time" (Wicksell, 1954, p. 70). And in his later work he conflates the two distinct notions of the uniform price (the same in all transactions) and the equilibrium price (that uniform price which clears the market): "If . . . we assume universal free competition, then so far as genuine market transactions are concerned, the relative prices of commodities will more or less rapidly approach a certain equilibrium position . . . To every price relationship, therefore, there corresponds for every individual a determinate combination of supply and demand" (Wicksell, 1934–35, p. 53).

Marshall never discusses the matter, and simply adopts the uniformity of prices as a postulate: ". . . this is the supposition on which we proceed; we assume that there is only one price in the market at one and the same time; it being understood that separate allowance is made when necessary for differences in the expense of delivering goods . . ." (Marshall, 1920, p. 284).

10 But the extent of such influence is commonly greatly exaggerated by neoclassical writers. John R. Commons terms this "the fallacy of inaccessible or nonconcomitant options" (Commons, 1924, pp. 65–6 et passim).

11 This is true even when there are "middlemen," for they, unlike the auctioneer, who has *no* economic motivation, are in business for profit.

12 The connection here with Edgeworth's idea of universal recontracting deserves mention. Like the auctioneer, unlimited recontracting is a way of eliminating the transactions from the market. It means in effect that all sales are made simultaneously at the last moment of the market period, thus assuming uniformity. No sale is final until all are final, which can only happen when all are made at the same price, for if any were recorded at a different price, one or another of the parties could gain by recontracting. To assume unlimited recontracting, then, amounts to assuming that no sales are final until a uniform price is established, which simply begs the question of how that price is reached. Why sales are not final is left unexplained. Why should buyers or sellers who have made a good bargain agree to recontract? Moreover, it must be assumed that all parties, both buyers and sellers, can equally afford to wait for sales to become final. Otherwise, some parties might find it advantageous to delay the process by engaging in false or spurious contracting.

References

Commons, J. R. 1924. *Legal Foundations of Capitalism.* New York: Macmillan.

Edgeworth, F. 1881. *Mathematical Psychics.* London: Kegan Paul.

Harcourt, G. C. 1968. "Investment-Decision Criteria, Investment Incentives, and Choice of Technique," *Economic Journal,* Vol. 78, pp. 77–95.

Henderson, J., and Quant, R. E. 1958. *Micro Economic Theory.* New York: McGraw-Hill.

Hicks, J. R. 1946. *Value and Capital.* New York: Oxford University Press.

Hollis, M., and Nell, E. J. 1975. *Rational Economic Man.* Cambridge: Cambridge University Press.

Knight, F. 1921. *Risk, Uncertainty and Profit.* New York: Houghton Mifflin.

Lewis, S. 1922. *Babbitt.* New York: Harcourt Brace.

Marshall, A. 1920. *Principles of Economics.* 8th ed. London: Macmillan.

Nell, E. J. "Abstract Labor and Uniform Wages," unpublished.

Smith, A. 1937. *The Wealth of Nations.* Modern Library ed. New York: Random House.

Veblen, T. 1963. *The Engineers and The Price System.* New York: Harcourt Brace.

Walras, L. 1954. *Elements of Pure Economics.* Homewood, Ill.: Irwin.

Weintraub, S. 1964. *Intermediate Price Theory.* Philadelphia: Chilton Books.

Wicksell, K. 1934–35. *Lectures on Economic Principles.* Vol. 1. London: Routledge.

1954. *Value Capital & Rent.* London: Allen and Unwin.

Wicksteed, P. H. 1933. *Common Sense of Political Economy.* Vol. 1. London: Routledge.

7

A general model of investment and pricing

Alfred S. Eichner

In the conventional theory of the firm as expounded in economics textbooks, someone called an ''entrepreneur'' sets up his production schedule so that the increment in total cost from producing one more unit of output is just equal to the increment in total revenue which can be expected from selling that last unit. As the theory correctly points out, if the firm were to produce and then sell either more or less than this quantity of goods, the entrepreneur would fail to maximize the net revenue being earned. Under certain conditions – when the firms in the industry are so numerous that no single one of them has a perceptible influence on the others – the output produced will simply be thrown on the market for whatever price it can command, this uncoordinated supply of goods being counterbalanced by the demand for the product in question to determine a unique market price. This is the competitive variant of the basic model. Under other conditions – when a single firm is in a position to influence the industry price directly through its own production and/or pricing decision – the output which equates marginal cost with marginal revenue may simply be thrown on the market for whatever price it can command. Alternately, a price may be set that, given the demand for that product, leads to the same quantity of output being supplied to customers. In either case, one has the monopolistic variant of the same basic model.

Both variants have been criticized so frequently and with such devastating effect that to flay them once more would seem to be beating a horse which, if not dead, is at least suffering from mortal wounds. But for those who must explain to the uninitiated in economic analysis how prices are actually set in a modern industrial economy, and want to do so with a certain degree of generality which goes beyond the mere commonsensical, even a mortally wounded horse seems better than no horse at all. And so, in the sections of this paper which follow, one more swipe will be taken at the conventional theory of the firm, less for the purpose of finally dispatching the poor beast than with the hope of persuading economists to transfer the weight of their analysis to a more serviceable animal. It is in fact the availability of another horse which is the principal message this paper has to convey.[1]

The relevant time horizon

The most serious shortcomings from which the conventional theory of the firm suffers is the relatively short time horizon which it implicitly assumes governs price determination. In the standard textbook treatment, the firm's goal is usually taken to be the maximization of net revenue from current sales. It's as though all of business enterprise reflected the habits acquired from selling souvenir programs at a Presidential inauguration, with firms oblivious to the morrow. One can question whether this limited time perspective is likely to characterize even the nineteenth-century type of proprietorship which Marshall had in mind when he wrote the *Principles* (Marshall, 1920) and which still survives in certain sectors of the economy. Hicks, in speaking to this point, has made a distinction between ''snatchers'' – firms out for a quick killing – and ''stickers'' (Hicks, 1954). When trying to explain the behavior of a twentieth-century large corporation – the type of firm which for linguistic convenience is perhaps best referred to as a megacorp – the positing of such a limited time horizon is no longer merely questionable. It is clearly absurd.

Two separate aspects of its objective circumstances demand that a megacorp take a long view. The first is the internal structure of such a firm – its bureaucratic organization and the resulting separation of management from ownership (Marris, chaps. 1-2, 1964). Because of this internal structure, it is somewhat misleading even to speak of entrepreneurs – except to the extent that a firm has not yet fully completed the transition from a managerially-owned proprietorship to a fully mature megacorp. Insofar as the locus of decision-making within the firm is concerned, one must speak instead of the self-perpetuating body of vice-presidents and inside directors who, collectively, form the executive group. It is a group whose overriding goal is likely to be the perpetuation and growth of the enterprise they direct (Gordon, 1961; Marris and Wood, 1971). Nothing of the snatcher mentality about them.

This attitude is reinforced by the strong market position which a megacorp, as the member of an oligopolistic industry, is likely to have. Indeed, the megacorp and oligopoly go together, the one being the representative firm within the other. As the member of an oligopolistic industry, a megacorp can reasonably expect, not just to survive but, more importantly, to grow as the industry (or industries) to which it belongs expands over time apace with the overall economy. To be sure, there is the danger that a rival megacorp within the same industry may succeed in cutting into its market share. There is even the danger that some outside firm may succeed in overcoming the barriers which make entry into the industry so difficult. Still, the danger is only a slight one, for megacorps have through the years developed a number of effective techniques for dealing with precisely these types of threat to their market position. The stability of market shares over time is, in fact, a striking feature of oligopolistic industries (Boyle and Sorensen, 1971; Gort, 1963; Jacoby, 1964). This means that the megacorp has a definite future, and must plan accordingly for it. Certainly the members of the executive group are aware of this imperative.

For the megacorp, then, the concern is with the net revenue that can be earned not just from current sales but rather over the foreseeable future. This shift in emphasis from short- to long-run maximization has a more radical implication for the theory of the firm than one might at first suspect.

For one thing, it makes irrelevant the standard Chamberlin – Robinson model of how prices are determined in industries which are not competitive.[2] The fact is that when it comes to the megacorp and oligopoly the behavioral rule for maximizing net revenue in the short run – the equating of marginal cost with marginal revenue – can no longer be applied. What sense does it make for a megacorp – or any other firm, for that matter – to push up its price in order to increase its net revenue in the current accounting period if the higher price will simply enable other firms to overcome the cost differential that prevents them from entering the industry or else will provoke the government into taking some type of retaliatory action? Indeed, the empirical irrelevance of the $MC = MR$ pricing rule can be quite easily demonstrated. One need only keep in mind three points: (1) with marginal costs greater than zero, marginal revenue must also be greater than zero – at least, if marginal costs and marginal revenue are to be equated; (2) for marginal revenue to be positive, the firm must be operating along the elastic portion of its revenue curve where $e > 1$; and (3) it is doubtful that any megacorp operates along the elastic portion of the revenue curve it confronts.

This last point requires perhaps greater elaboration. Another essential characteristic of oligopoly, beside the extended time horizon which characterizes those who make the decisions within its representative firm, is the recognized interdependence existing among the members of such an industry.[3] This means that no one firm within the industry can take any type of action, especially with regard to prices, without most if not all the other members being forced to respond in some manner. Given this condition, a demand curve for the individual firm's product in the conventional sense cannot, as Romney Robinson has pointed out be said to exist (Robinson, 1961). Still it is possible to derive a revenue curve, at least for the price leader, by assuming that every other firm in the industry will merely match whatever price the price leader announces. It happens that this assumption closely corresponds to actual behavior in oligopolistic industries.

This price-matching pattern, in turn, means that the price leader's revenue curve is the same as the marginal portion of the industry demand curve – at least they will both have the same price elasticities at corresponding price levels.[4] Thus, since the overwhelming evidence is that the products supplied by oligopolistic industries are price inelastic within actually experienced relative price ranges, one must conclude that the firms in an oligopolistic industry – and this is certainly true of the megacorp acting as price leader – are hardly likely to operate along the elastic portion of the revenue curve which pertains to them (Houthakker and Taylor, 1966; Stone, 1954; Hirsch, 1950–51). In other words, there is no way that they can equate marginal cost with marginal revenue, unless they are prepared to increase their price relative to other prices to a far greater degree than has ever been empirically observed. It is, of course, the likely consequences over the long run of so increasing their price which dissuades the price leader and the other megacorps within the industry from taking such a step, even though it would undoubtedly improve the current net revenue figures.

The shift from short- to long-run maximization has a second implication, besides the merely negative one of invalidating the Chamberlin–Robinson model. With such a change in perspective, one must take cognizance of the fact that not only are prices being determined but, even more important, investment decisions are being made. Indeed, with the firm presumed to have an extended time horizon going beyond the current accounting period, the pricing decision can no longer be separated from investment planning as is the practice in the conventional theory of the firm. This is especially true since the megacorp, unlike the nineteenth-century proprietorship, adds to its capital plant and equipment on a continuous basis.

Linking the pricing decision to investment planning is the key insight, one which permits the theory of the firm to become more than just a fairy tale of what life would be like in some never-to-be-realized Golden Age. It leads to a generalized model of price determination which not only encompasses all previously suggested models but also, for the first time, supplies a satisfactory explanation of how prices are determined under oligopoly itself. Moreover, by explicitly taking into account the investment decision, it provides a more suitable base for Keynesian and post-Keynesian macro-dynamic analysis than the conventional neoclassical microeconomic theory. Finally, the model is consistent with all that is known about a modern, technologically advanced economy – including the fact that it expands over time.

The pricing model

In the simplest case, the model deals with a megacorp that is a monopolist. The analysis begins with the recognition that the primary means which such a firm has for financing the investment it wishes to undertake is the net revenue earned from the sale of its product. In this model, then, the megacorp is viewed as using the price variable to alter its intertemporal revenue flows (Gaskins, 1971; Kamien and Schwartz, 1971; Phelps and Winter, 1970; Scherer, 1970, p. 213; Gutman, 1967). More specifically, because of its market power, the megacorp is presumed able to increase the margin above costs in order to obtain more internally generated funds, that is, a larger "cash flow," to finance its intended investment expenditures. For a number of reasons, it makes more sense to refer to this cash flow as a "corporate levy." But since the term "cash flow" is a more familiar one, this is a term that will be used throughout the rest of this article. Still, one should not think of the cash flow as simply a measure of the firm's current cash position. One must think of it instead as a measure of the discretionary funds, or savings, at the firm's disposal.

As a result of any price adjustment which the megacorp might make, the intertemporal revenue flows will be altered in two ways: (1) from the returns to the investment thereby being financed; and (2) from the decline in sales over time caused by the higher price. The first effect is encompassed by the firm's demand curve for additional investment funds; the second, by its supply curve for those same funds.

The firm's demand curve for additional investment funds is simply the familiar ex ante marginal efficiency of investment schedule, broadened in concept perhaps to include the returns from investment in advertising, research and development, and other means of enhancing an individual firm's market position (Asimakopulos, 1971). It indicates the rate of return, measured in terms of future additions to the firm's cash flow, which can be expected from increasing the current rate of investment. The firm's supply curve of additional investment funds, however, involves a radical departure from the usual way of thinking about the cost of internal financing. Rather than identifying the cost of internally generated funds with the rate of return from investment outside the firm – that is, rather than using an opportunity cost concept – this alternative approach focuses on the possible subsequent decline in net revenue from increasing the margin above costs in order to augment the current cash flow. The possible subsequent decline in net revenue may derive from any one of three sources: (a) the substitution effect; (b) the entry factor, and (c) meaningful government intervention. Each of these possible sources of future decline in revenue will serve as a constraint on the pricing power, or discretion, of the industry price leader.

The substitution effect reflects the fact that, as the relative price of a good rises, customers are more likely to switch to a substitute product. Its magnitude depends on the arc elasticity of demand associated with a given price change, both in the time period immediately following the change in price and over subsequent time periods. The entry factor reflects the fact that, as the margin above costs rises, new firms will find it easier to overcome the barriers that inhibit their entry into the industry; and that if a new firm of a certain size relative to total industry demand should gain entry, every established firm in the industry can expect its own sales to decline by that same percentage. The magnitude of this entry factor depends on the probability of new entry associated with a given price change, again both in the time period immediately following the change in price and over subsequent time periods.

Even taken together, the substitution effect and the entry factor are likely to be of negligible impact in the time period immediately following an increase in the margin above costs. This is because most megacorps, as already pointed out, are likely to find themselves operating along the inelastic portion of their short run revenue curve and because, furthermore, the entry of new firms into their industry has a long lead time. As the megacorp peers further into the future, however, the substitution effect and the entry factor are likely to seem more significant. At some point, they may even seem to presage a decline in the rate of cash flow below its current level, at which time the combined substitution effect and entry factor would, in fact, become positive. Even if this should seem unlikely to occur, the megacorp may nonetheless be apprehensive that the increase in the margin above costs will invite meaningful government intervention, whether in the form of antitrust prosecution or some similar measure that will thbreaten the firm's long term growth prospects.

The eventual decline in the rate of cash flow below its current level, due to the substitution effect and/or the entry factor, is analogous to the fixed sum of interest that would have to be paid if the same amount of investment funds were to be obtained instead by resort to external financing. It is only analogous, however, because while the interest payments on any externally derived funds would be due immediately, it will take a number of time periods for the cash flow to decline below its initial level. Moreover, while the interest payments on any external debt would be the same in every subsequent time period (assuming bond financing), the decline in the cash flow, due to the increasing strength of the substitution effect and/or the entry factor over time, will continue indefinitely into the future. For both these reasons, if the exact counterpart to the interest payment on external funds is to be derived, it is necessary to average out all the subsequent declines in the cash flow, once the cash flow falls below the initial level, and then apply a discount factor to this averaged sum so as to indicate its present value at the time interest payments on any externally derived funds would otherwise begin.

Against this eventual decline in the cash flow stands the additional investment funds which the megacorp will in the meantime have obtained as a result of the higher margin above costs. These additional investment funds are analogous to the lump sum obtained under an external borrowing arrangement. Again, however, they are only analogous, in this case because the investment funds are obtained, not all at once but rather, over a number of subsequent time periods. To derive the exact counterpart of the lump sum that could, alternatively, be obtained under some external borrowing arrangement, it is necessary to apply a discount factor to the additional cash flow obtained in each time period that there is an increment in revenue and then aggregate all of these separately discounted sums.

If the "interest" payment due to the substitution effect and/or the entry factor, properly discounted, is taken as a percentage of the additional investment funds generated in the meantime from the higher margin above costs, again properly discounted, the result is an implicit interest rate, R, on additional internally generated funds (Eichner, 1976, p. 302). This implicit interest rate is a function not only of time as just suggested, but also of the size of the margin above costs decided upon by the megacorp.

The latter, in trying to determine whether to increase the current margin above costs, is likely to confront a situation similar to that depicted in Figure 7.1. If it increases that margin (measured by the variable n along two of the four axes), it will increase the rate of cash flow over the current planning period, that is, the time interval required to bring new plant and equipment into operation. The higher the margin, the greater the increase in the rate of cash flow. This relationship is shown in quadrant II. If there were no substitution effect and no entry factor, the additional funds curve, $\Delta F/p$, would be a straight line emanating from the origin. Since, however, both the substitution effect and the entry factor are directly related to the size of the margin above costs, with there being a greater decline in sales over time as the margin above costs is increased, the additional funds curve falls downward from the origin at an increasing rate.

An increase in the margin above costs, n, will at the same time increase the implicit cost to the megacorp of obtaining additional investment funds from internal sources, R. This relationship is shown in quadrant IV. A small increase in the margin above costs, n, will give rise to an even smaller increase in the value of R. But as the size of n is increased, both the substitution effect and the entry factor can be expected to increase at

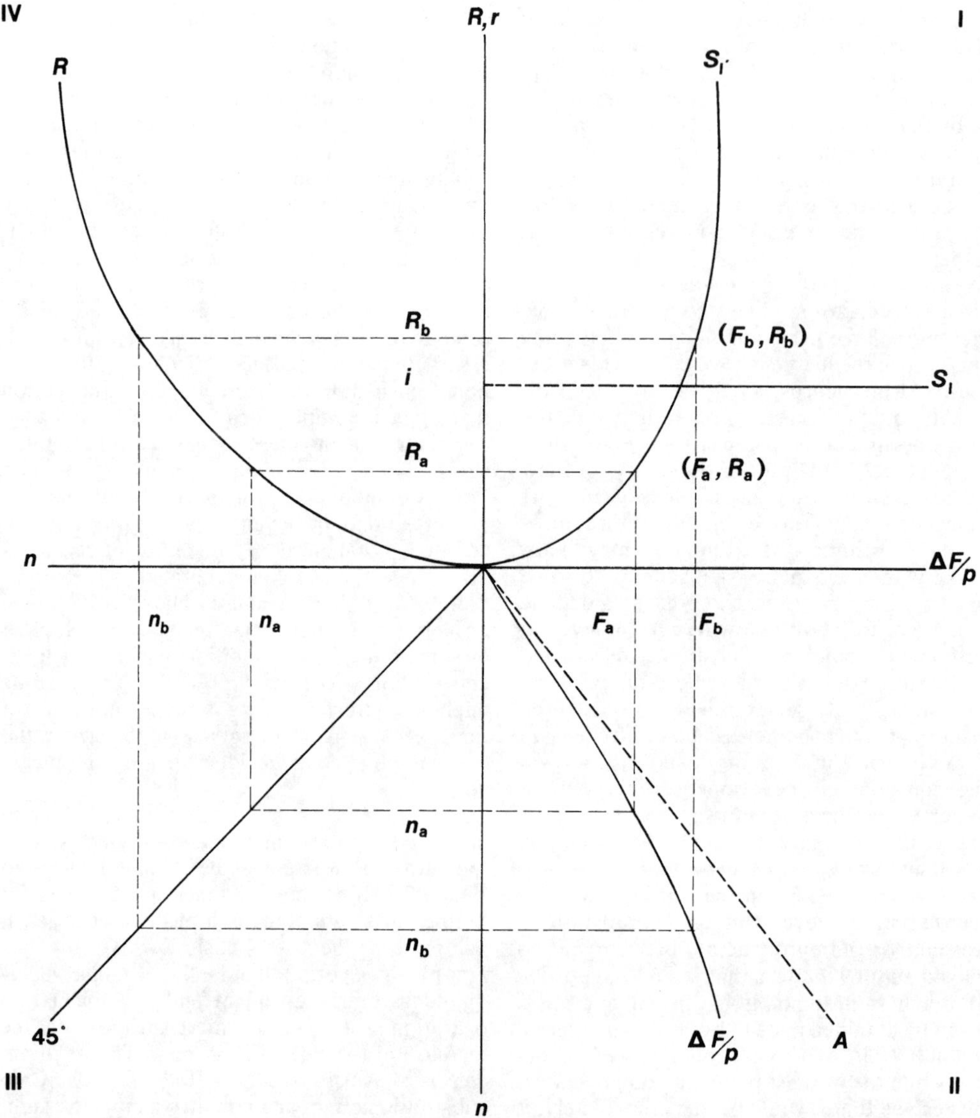

Figure 7.1

an increasing rate, with the result that the implicit interest rate function, R, will also rise at an increasing rate. At some point, the implicit interest rate on additional internal funds may even become infinite, as the probability either of new entry or of meaningful government intervention becomes greater than the price leader is willing to risk. Such a maximum acceptable risk of either new entry or meaningful government intervention will, in fact, place an upper limit on the amount of additional investment funds that can be obtained internally.

On the one hand, as shown in quadrant II, an increase in the margin above costs will lead to an increase in the amount of additional funds obtained internally. On the other hand, as shown in quadrant IV, the same increase in the margin will lead to an increase in the implicit interest rate on those additional funds. From these two relationships it is possible to derive a supply curve for additional internal funds, S_I', indicating how the implicit interest rate, R, on those funds varies as the amount of additional funds obtained per planning period, $\Delta(F/p)$, varies. This supply curve is shown in quadrant I. If it is assumed that the price leader, along with the other firms in the industry, can obtain all the additional investment funds it wishes from external sources at an interest rate, i, this supply curve for additional internal funds, S_I', can be transformed into a supply curve for all additional investment funds, S_I, whether the funds are obtained internally or externally.

Given this supply curve, S_I, the megacorp will then find itself in one of the three situations depicted in Figure 7.2.[5] In situation (a), the demand curve for additional investment funds, D_I, cuts the supply curve to the left and below the origin. Under these circumstances, since the rate of investment is to be reduced below the current level, the megacorp may decide to lower the margin above costs, n. Because, however, the gains from lowering the industry price are not exactly the opposite of the losses from raising the industry price – the probability of either new entry or meaningful government intervention cannot be negative – a reduction in the current level of investment will not necessarily be accompanied by a lower margin above costs (Eichner, 1969, pp. 97–9; R. Robinson, 1974). In situation (b), D_I cuts S_I to the right and above the origin but below i. Under these circumstances, the current rate of investment will be increased, with the margin above costs raised to n_1 and with all the additional investment funds, F_1, coming from the larger cash flow which will thereby be generated. Finally, in situation (c), D_I cuts S_I not only above the origin but also above i. Under these circumstances, the current rate of investment will again be increased but only part of the additional investment funds required, F_2, will be generated by increasing the margin above costs, in this case to n_2. The rest of the desired funds, F_3-F_2, will be obtained through external financing.

In all three cases, the change in the margin above costs is determined by the demand for additional investment funds relative to the supply cost of those funds, both internal and external.[6] That is, $\Delta CF = f(D_I, S_I)$ where ΔCF is the change in the rate of cash flow or margin above costs. What is thus being explained, of course, is not the absolute price level but rather the change in the margin above costs from one time period to the next.[7] Still, it is a relatively easy matter to convert the one into the other. Only two relationships need be kept in mind: (1) that the price in any given time period, P_1, is equal to the price in the previous time period, P_0, plus the change in price between the two periods, ΔP; and (2) that the price in the previous time period, P_0, is equal to the average variable costs at that time, AVC, plus the sum of the fixed costs, FC, and the desired rate of cash flow, CF, divided by the expected rate of output, Q^*. From these two relationships it then follows that $P_1 = P_0 + \Delta P = \text{AVC} + (FC + CF)/Q^* + \Delta CF/Q^*$.

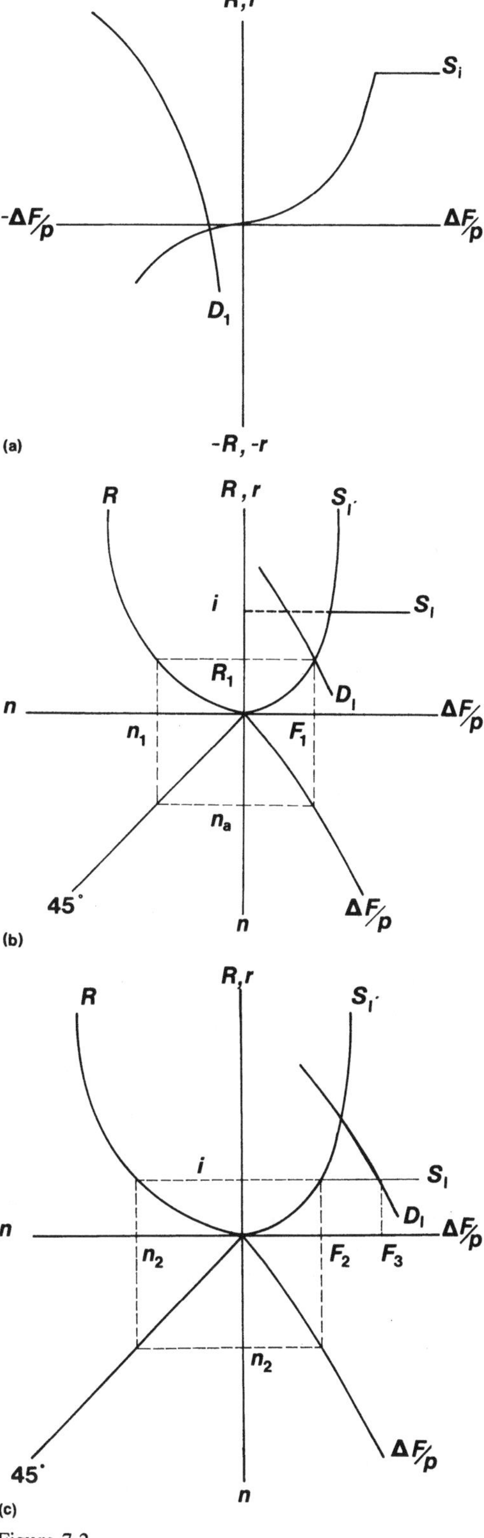

Figure 7.2

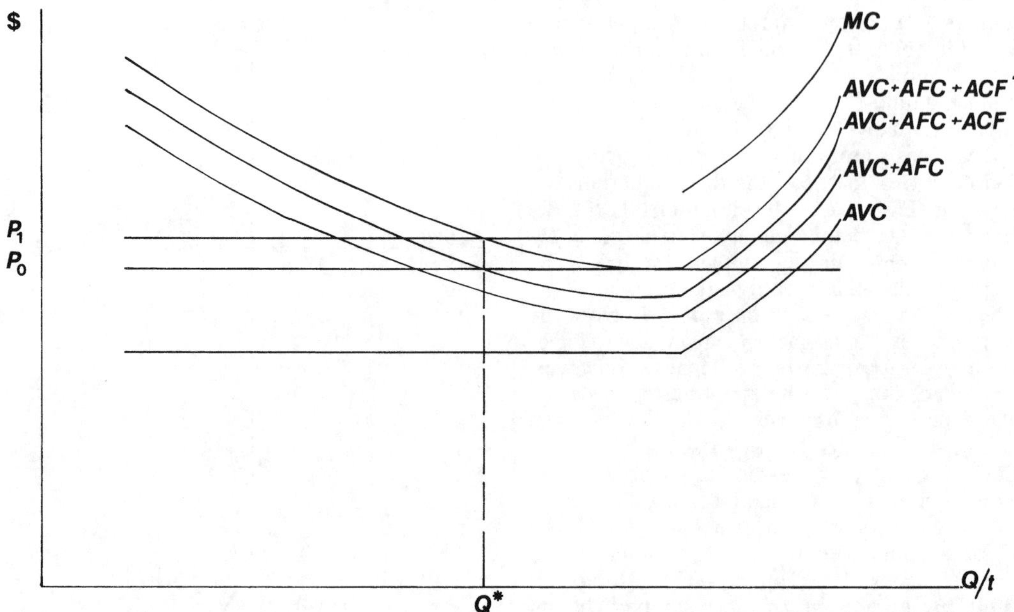

Figure 7.3

Figure 7.3 illustrates the point. The price at which the average revenue being obtained was, during the previous time period, equal to the average variable costs plus the average expected fixed costs and the average cash flow required to finance the level of investment determined to be optimal is P_0. It is this price which, during the previous time period, the megacorp will have announced and then tried to maintain. The price announced by the megacorp in the next period as a result of the change in the rate of planned investment and hence the rate of cash flow required is P_1. It should be noted that the constant average variable and marginal costs depicted in the diagram reflect yet another characteristic of the megacorp – the multiple plants which permit the megacorp to adjust the level of output by varying the number of plants being operated rather than the intensity with which any one plant is being utilized (Gort, 1962).

To complete the analysis of the pricing decision, it is necessary only to recognize that a change in price may come about, not just because of a change in investment financing needs but also, because of a change in certain required rates of remuneration. The rates which are of concern here include the wages paid workers and the prices paid for material inputs – a change in either one affecting the megacorp's average variable and fixed costs. Assuming that the price of material inputs reflects the wage rates in those industries, it then follows that any change in the megacorp's average variable or fixed costs will most probably derive from a change in the level of money wage rates in general. This would make the price level itself dependent on the general wage level. Figure 7.4 illustrates this possibility, with a change in money wage rates, as reflected by a change in average variable and fixed costs, leading to a new price, P_2. A change in price may, then, have either of two separate causes – the need to obtain a higher rate of cash flow and the need to cover a higher level of costs. Indeed, the two separate causes may both be present, leading to the dynamic sequence known as the wage–price spiral.

The pricing model just set forth can be modified in a number of ways to cover a variety of situations. For example, if the megacorp is regarded, not as the single firm comprising the industry but rather, as the price leader among several megacorps, the model becomes one for explaining oligopolistic pricing behavior. As already pointed out, with the other firms matching whatever price is announced by the price leader, each and every firm – including the price leader itself – has a revenue curve with the same elasticities as the industry demand curve. Indeed, monopoly is simply oligopoly without the problem of having to coordinate the pricing policies of several firms. Of course, if the megacorp faces a group of buyers which themselves are megacorps, the situation becomes one of bilateral monopoly, or oligopoly; and the pricing decision, as the work on bargaining theory makes clear, becomes indeterminate, at least

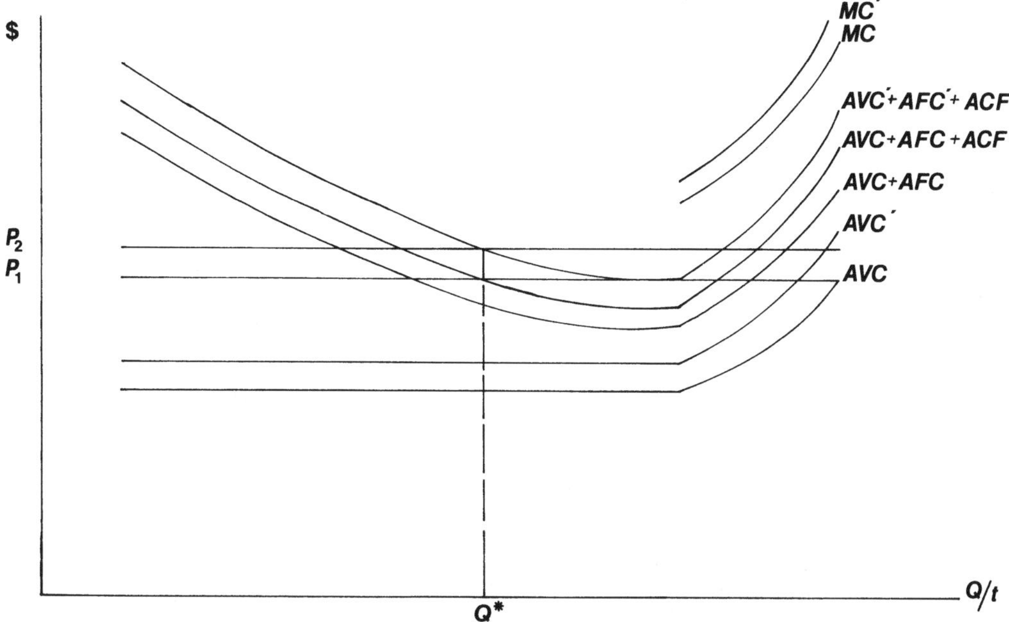

Figure 7.4

taking economic factors alone into account (Coddington, 1968; Galbraith, 1952).

Alternatively, if the megacorp is regarded, not as a member of just a single industry but rather, as a member of many industries, the model becomes one for explaining the pricing behavior of the diversified, or conglomerate, enterprise.[8] It is just that in this case, with there being different values for R and r in the several industries to which it belongs, the megacorp can be expected to use the price level to obtain funds from certain of the industries in order to finance investment in the rest, thereby maximizing the growth of the organization as a whole. Although either sales or assets are suitable proxies, the growth which the megacorp can be assumed to try to maximize within the context of a dynamic model is best measured by the rate at which the cash flow is being increased. There is not space in this chapter to do full justice to the topic of the conglomerate enterprise. Nonetheless, its principal analytical significance can at least be pointed out. To the extent that all megacorps are potential, if not actual, conglomerate enterprises, likely to diversify into the most rapidly growing areas of the economy, they constitute an alternative to the capital funds market as the means by which society's savings are shifted to where, within the business sector, they will bring the highest return. Indeed, the imperfections of the conglomerate megacorp as an allocator of investment funds are probably no greater in practice than those of the more generally esteemed capital funds market.

Finally, if the megacorp is subject to regulation such that it cannot raise its price in order to obtain a higher rate of internal cash flow for financing its investment needs, the model becomes one for explaining the predicament of public utilities in the United States.

Perhaps the most interesting modification of the general pricing model, however, is that which converts it into the standard textbook analysis of monopoly and competition. For this modification reveals the restrictive assumptions and unrealistic nature of the conventional theory of the firm.

Deriving the standard textbook models

The essential difference between the standard textbook analysis of competition and the pricing model set forth above is that in the former the rate of internal cash flow is limited to a depreciation charge alone. In other words, the conventional model of a competitive industry makes no allowance for growth financed from internal sources – except as a possible disequilibrium situation. This lack of internally financed growth is implicit in the argument that, over the long run, the price in a competitive industry will not exceed average total costs, with the latter including, of course, a market-regulated return on the externally derived funds invested in the industry. It is perhaps the most salient feature of the conventional model.

Actually, in the absence of technological change, it is not clear why any of the existing plants would need to be replaced, thereby necessitating new investment. With a well-planned program of preventive maintenance and the timely replacement of individually worn out parts – both properly regarded as fixed or overhead costs – plants can usually be kept in satisfactory working condition almost indefinitely. In any case, with a static technology, the only new investment within a given plant would be for replacement purposes, and this would be financed out of a depreciation allowance. Ignoring the effects of technological change, then, as the standard textbook treatment does, one can say that the conventional model of competition is simply a variant of the general pricing model set forth above with at least one important difference: the value of CF is equal to zero and, following from this, there is no internally financed growth. One might well ask whether such a model provides a useful starting point for analyzing a technologically sophisticated economy such as that of the United States, an economy which grows on the average by three percent a year and finances more than seventy-five percent of its investment from the cash flow generated within the business sector (Anderson, 1964, p. 25). Total internal finance is, in fact, even higher although in recent years, the "profit squeeze" has pushed it down somewhat (Nordhaus, 1974). It is more instructive, however, to inquire into the conditions necessary for reducing the value of CF to zero.

As already pointed out, the conventional model of a competitive industry – and of a monopolistic one, too – implies a much shorter time horizon on the part of those with the effective decision-making power within the firm than that assumed above. In view of the type of firm which predominated when the conventional model was being formulated, this presumption of a relatively short time horizon is perhaps understandable. With both management and ownership combined in the single person of its one or more entrepreneurial heads and with the enterprise itself subject any moment to the type of Darwinian fate described by Marshall, it was a firm radically different in its perspective from today's megacorp. The question is whether that one factor alone – the time frame within which pricing decisions are made – is sufficient to explain why, in the conventional model, the value of CF is zero.

The answer is that it is not – even if, at the extreme, one assumes that those with the effective decision-making power are concerned only with the net revenue flows within a single, relatively brief time period. The fact is that the shorter the time horizon, the less influence the substitution effect, the entry factor and the fear of meaningful government intervention will have on the pricing decision. It takes a while for customers to switch to competitive products, for new firms to execute their plans to enter an industry and even for the government to react. Indeed, within a single, relatively brief time period, the government is unlikely to act at all or interloping firms to make much progress in starting up a new plant. This leaves only the substitution effect to influence the pricing decision. Thus, with the assumption that pricing decisions are reached within the time frame of a single period, the general pricing model developed above reduces to the conventional Chamberlin–Robinson model of monopoly – but not to the conventional model of competition. The empirical irrelevance of this Chamberlin–Robinson model, at least for most of the manufacturing sector, has already been pointed out.

Another way in which the conventional models differ from the general pricing model developed above is by assuming – though not explicitly – that each firm consists of but a single plant. Again, this assumption is understandable in light of the type of firm which once predominated in the economy. Proprietorships owned and managed by one or two families are seldom capable of efficiently operating more than one plant (Beckman, 1970). Can this factor – single plant operation – account for the peculiar result deduced from the conventional theory of a competitive industry that the value of CF over the long run will be equal to zero?

No, such an assumption leads only to a positively sloped marginal cost curve. With a firm operating but a single plant, the level of output can be adjusted in response to changing demand conditions only by utilizing that one plant more or less intensively. If this means that some variable input, such as labor or materials, must be used in conjunction with the plant itself in a ratio that changes with the level of output, the firm will necessarily find itself confronted by the sort of U-shaped cost curves usually depicted in economics textbooks. This follows from the fact that only one ratio of variable to fixed inputs will be optimal – that is, will result in the lowest possible costs. If the firm should produce in excess of that optimal level of output, it is certain to incur higher average variable costs and even more rapidly rising marginal costs. Of course, if a firm consists of more than one plant, it can, as already suggested, adjust the level of output by varying the number of plants being operated rather than the intensity with which any one plant is being utilized. This will, in turn, lead to the constant average variable and marginal costs which, econometric studies indicate, actually confront firms that are megacorps (Koot and Walter, 1970; Zudak, 1970; Gold, 1966; Walters, 1963; Johnston, 1960).

Insofar as it determines the shape of the individual firm's supply curve and, following from that, the shape of the industry supply curve as well, the shape of the marginal cost curve is of considerable analytical significance. It has little to do, however, with whether any revenue in excess of costs will eventually be eliminated. Indeed, in the conventional Chamberlin–Robinson model of monopoly, as Figure 7.5 illustrates, the rising marginal costs usually assumed lead to a higher industry price, and thus to more revenue in excess of costs, than if marginal costs were constant. Even so, the shape of the industry supply curve needs to be taken into account. On this point, in fact, rests the efficacy of conventional antiinflation policy. For only if the industry supply curve is positively sloped can the curtailment of aggregate demand be expected to reverse any upward trend in the price level. This is not to argue that constant average variable, and hence constant marginal, costs will necessarily produce an industry supply curve which is itself horizontal – that is, perfectly elastic – over some relevant range. They do, however, make such an industry supply curve possible.

Neither the time frame within which decisions are made nor the number of plants operated can be expected – at least by themselves – to reduce the value of CF in the general pricing model to zero. The truth is that such a result can come

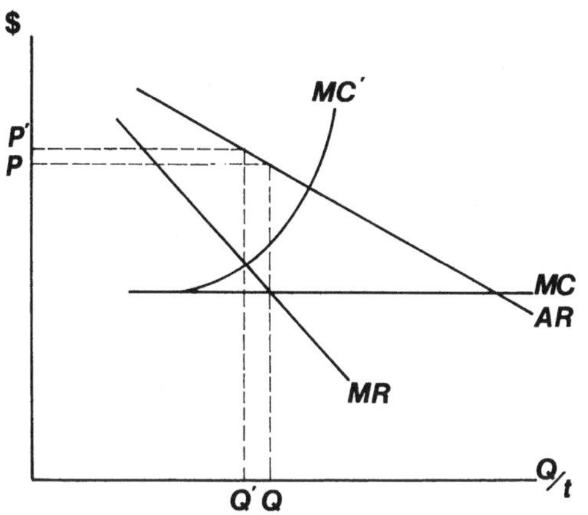

Figure 7.5

about only through some process of interfirm competition, one which leads to a bidding down of the price level below what any one firm alone would prefer. But what conditions must prevail for this process to operate? Certainly, it cannot be the mere existence of more than one firm. Two, three, even a dozen or so firms are likely to find that it is more to their advantage to work in concert than to undercut one another. From the time of Adam Smith on, economists have sensed the likelihood of this cooperative solution to the classic prisoners' dilemma (Cyert and DeGroot, 1971; Fellner, 1949). The cooperative solution has even emerged experimentally under controlled experimental conditions (Dolbear, Lave, et al., 1968; Harnett, 1967; Lave, 1962; Murphy, 1966). Only a snatcher – that is, a firm with a very short time horizon – is apt to behave in any other manner.

Of course, as the number of firms in an industry increases – assuming all those firms are of relatively equal size – the difficulty of coordinating their pricing activities will be compounded. And if a cyclical downturn of the economy or some even more delimited adverse condition should interrupt the normal secular growth of the industry, the individual members of that industry will be under strong pressure to cut their price. In this event, the price actually prevailing in the market may well be less than the price which the firms would like to charge and which, indeed, has been announced. If the decline in sales is especially severe, the actual price being charged may even be so low as to reduce the value of CF to zero.

Two points should be noted, however, about the possibility just described. The first is that the situation is quite different from that implied in the conventional model of a competitive industry. In the situation just described, the firms in the industry are manipulating the price variable in order to clear whatever unsold stocks of finished goods they may have accumulated. They are not, as in the conventional model of a competitive industry, simply throwing on the market the goods they have produced for whatever price those goods may fetch. Put another way, the firms are price setters – or administrators – rather than price takers (Wiles, 1956; Machlup, 1952). The point relates to the way in which the firms in the industry adjust to a disequilibrium condition in the market. In the one case, the manner of adjustment validates the excess demand hypothesis of Walras; in the other case, it validates the excess supply hypothesis of Marshall. But the traditional explanation of inflation depends on the validity of the Walrasian hypothesis (Hansen, 1970, Chs. 2, 10).

The conventional model of a competitive industry, it should be kept in mind, is a Walrasian one in which the individual firm, having no control over the industry price, faces a perfectly elastic average revenue curve. It is this model which is propounded in the economics textbooks and which econometricians, among others, usually have in mind when they invoke the assumption of perfect competition. The situation described above, however, is a Marshallian one in which the individual firm still has some ability to influence, on its own, the industry price – even if this implies no more than the possibility of its undercutting the price previously established at the industry level.

The second point to be noted is that the price in this Marshallian model is simply a departure from the price which the members of the industry would like to see prevail, one which will enable them to cover their full costs plus provide a certain amount of funds to finance further investment. One may be interested in explaining what factors are likely to cause the deviation of the actual price from the preferred price as Stigler attempts to do (Stigler, 1964), or in relating such a breakdown in the cooperative pattern within the industry either to cyclical conditions in general or to the life cycle of the industry (Abramowitz, 1938; Williamson, 1965). Still, the price actually prevailing at any given moment in time can be understood only by first analyzing and explaining the price initially announced. It is in this sense that the price level in the Marshallian model is determinate only as an extension of the general pricing model developed above. The conventional or Walrasian model of a competitive industry is, on the other hand, the Marshallian model carried one step further; and thus, it represents an extreme case.

What further condition must, then, prevail before the Marshallian situation in which the members of an industry still feel they have some control over the price they charge changes to a Walrasian one in which they feel they have absolutely no control. The answer is that the members of the industry must be so numerous and/or face such powerful buyers that no one firm feels that anything it does can possibly influence the industry price. This condition, it should be noted, is approximated in only two real-life situations. The first involves commodities traded in world markets and the second, material inputs sold to megacorps. In both cases, the firms in the industry are confronted by buyers with the resources and knowledge to speculate effectively – that is, hold goods in anticipation of a change in price. The lesser relative power of the buyers in the first instance is offset by the greater number of competing sellers in the second.

But even if the firms in an industry are in such a weak market position that they are unable, individually, to have any influence on the industry price level, the value of *CF* will not necessarily be reduced to zero. One can be assured that any excess of revenue over cost will be eliminated only if, over time, the growth of industry demand does not outpace the growth of production capacity. The conventional models, by ignoring the fact of economic growth, gloss over this limitation. In the real world, however, it is an important consideration. For should the growth of industry demand outpace the growth of production capacity, interfirm competition, no matter how vigorous, will not be sufficient by itself to eliminate any excess of revenue over costs. In the Marshallian situation, with demand rising, the firms in the industry will have little difficulty maintaining the price they would like to charge, since there will be more than enough sales for all. In the Walrasian situation, with demand rising, the unsatisfied demand will lead to a bidding up of the price level.

To assure, under these circumstances, that the value of CF will, over the long run, be reduced to zero, yet another condition must prevail. This further condition is that the probability of entry over the long run, following any rise in price above average variable and average fixed costs, be equal to 1. With firms limited to single-plant operation because of the typical proprietorship's managerial limitations, the entry of new firms into the industry is the only way in which, in the conventional model of a competitive industry, supply capacity can be expanded beyond whatever increase in the scale of optimal output technological improvements may permit. Yet unless the industry's supply capacity can be expanded at the same rate as industry demand, any excess of revenue over costs will not, over the long run, be eliminated. It is for this reason that, if the value of *CF* is to be zero, the probability of entry over the long run must be equal to 1.

Yet, with the probability of new entry equal to 1, it is unlikely that the individual members of an industry will be able to pursue a common pricing policy. What point is there in eschewing the short-run gains from cutting the price surreptitiously and thereby taking away sales from rivals if any margin above costs will soon be eliminated in any case through the entry of new firms? Why only to protect against a reduction in price below average total costs when industry sales are declining. However, any industry with sufficient internal cohesion to withstand the pressure to cut prices when demand is falling is an industry likely to be able to erect effective barriers against the entry of new firms.[9] Indeed, erecting barriers against newcomers is likely to prove easier than escaping from the prisoners' dilemma in which the members of the industry find themselves when, with demand falling, each firm attempts to pursue an independent pricing policy. For the individual firm, in jockeying for market position vis-à-vis its rivals through its expenditures on advertising, research and the like, is simultaneously making entry into the industry more difficult. In practice, of course, collusive behavior as a solution to the prisoners' dilemma and expenditures which have the effect of erecting considerable barriers to new entry are likely to be observed together. For this reason it can be assumed that, if the probability of new entry following a rise in price is equal to 1, the firms in the industry will be unable to work out or implement a common pricing policy.

Each firm will, in fact, follow the policy which maximizes its own short-run gain, and out of this dynamic it will appear that no individual firm has any control over the industry price level. The conventional model of competition found in the economics textbooks is therefore the general pricing model set forth above with the probability of new entry equal to 1 and, as a consequence of this, a time horizon limited to but a single, relatively brief period and a value for CF equal to zero. While the critical dependence of the Walrasian model on the existence of relatively unimpeded entry is hardly a novel point, it does suggest what is perhaps a better test of that model's empirical significance than simply the number of industries with a multitude of equally small firms. But even a probability of new entry over the long run equal to one is not sufficient by itself to assure that individual firms face a perfectly elastic demand curve – in some ways the most important implication of the conventional pricing model. In addition, the firms must face a network of buyers powerful enough to engage in effective speculation against them. Only under these circumstances will the firms have no choice but to throw the goods they produce on the market for whatever price those goods can command, thereby validating the excess demand hypothesis of Walras. With this listing of the final precondition, it should be perfectly clear how inappropriate is the conventional, Walrasian pricing model for most sectors of a modern, technologically sophisticated economy such as that of the United States. Fortunately, there is the general pricing model to fall back on – and even the Marshallian variant of that general model as a more relevant alternative.

Macrodynamic implications

In macrodynamic analysis, the choice of pricing model is critical because of what is thereby implied as to the ability of business firms to control the price variable, and thus alter the flow of savings into the business sector. In the general pricing model developed above, business firms have this ability undiminished. In the Marshallian variant of the general model, they have the ability only somewhat, the savings realized ex post being likely to fall short of the savings planned ex ante. Finally, in the conventional, or Walrasian, model, business firms have the ability to control the price variable not at all. To the extent that the general pricing model developed above has some relevance to the real world, and even to the extent that the Marshallian variant of the general model applies, the original Keynesian analysis must be broadened to encompass the effects of savings within the business sector. This, it can be suggested, will lead to a quite different process of adjustment between savings and investment than that implied in the conventional textbook treatment of the subject.

It will also lead to a quite different explanation of the inflationary process. The possibility that the supply curve in oligopolistic industries may be perfectly elastic, at least within certain ranges, has already called into question the conventional excess demand, or Walrasian, theory of inflation. Recognition that the firms in certain industries, especially those which are oligopolistic in structure, may have some control over the price variable lends support instead to the alternative cost and/or profit push explanation. One must not make the mistake, however, of assuming that inflation is simply the result of business firms exercising their power to control prices, just as one would not want to fall into the simplistic error of arguing that unemployment is merely the result of too little consumption.

As post-Keynesian macrodynamic theory points out, there can be no increase in the aggregate growth rate unless there is an increase in the relative proportion of national income that is saved (and simultaneously invested) (Eichner and Kregel, 1975; Kregel, 1971, 1973). When the aggregate growth rate increases, business firms may therefore have good reason to raise their prices, for the higher prices will enable the business sector to finance from its own increased cash flow the higher rate of investment which the higher growth rate necessitates. However, if trade unions are at the same time committed to using their power to prevent any change in the relative distribution of national income between wages and profits, the higher prices announced by business firms will touch off a wage–price spiral.

The point here is that higher prices increase the aggregate savings ratio while higher wages lower it. In the conventional pricing model, since the firm is viewed as having no control over the price variable, this point never emerges to inform the discussion of inflation. It is thus not surprising that the inability to suggest policies that can deal effectively with the type of inflation which the Western world has experienced since the end of World War II is one of the more conspicuous failures of the conventional economics (Eichner, 1976).

Appendix A

The formula for R is as follows:

$$R = \frac{(t - s + 1)^{-1}X}{(1 + r)^{s-1}} \div \frac{Y}{(1 + r)^{j}}$$

where

$$X = \sum_{j=s}^{t} [Q_0 \cdot MCL_0(|e_j| + k_j \cdot m)] - [P_0 \cdot Q_0(1 - n[|e_j| + k_j \cdot m])]$$

$$Y = \sum_{j=1}^{s-1} [P_0 \cdot Q_0(1 - n[|e_j| + k_j \cdot m])] - [Q_0 \cdot MCL_0(|e_j| + k_j \cdot m)].$$

where

Q_0 = level of sales before any change in price,
P_0 = price level before any change in price,
MCL_0 = marginal cash flow = the current price level, P_0, less average variable costs, which are assumed to be constant and equal to marginal costs,
e_j = arc elasticity of demand in time period j,
m = percentage of market represented by firm of minimal optimum size, that is, by firm large enough to achieve all production economies of scale,
k_j = probability of entry by a new firm of minimal optimum size, m, in time period j,
n = proportional change in price, $\Delta P/P_0$,
r = marginal efficiency of investment for the firm,
s = number of time periods required for the combined substitution effect and entry factor to become positive, and
t = number of time periods comprising the firm's long-run horizon.

The term $[Q_0 \cdot MCL_0(|e_j| + k_j \cdot m)]$ in both the numerator and denominator represents the net revenue loss to the firm in time period j from an increase in price, and is equal to the area of rectangle $B'GFE'$ in Figure 7.6. Of this amount, $[Q_0 \cdot MCL_0(|e_j|)]$ – rectangle $B'G'F'E'$ – represents the loss due to the substitution effect and $[Q_0 \cdot MCL_0(k_j \cdot m)]$ – rectangle $G'GFF'$ – the loss due to the entry factor on the assumption that a firm of minimal optimum size, m, is the type of firm most likely to enter the industry. (Rectangle $B'G'F'E'$ is equal to $MCL_0[=P_0 - AVC]$ times $\Delta Q'[=Q_0' - Q_1']$, with AR' and Q_0' the shift in the firm's average revenue curve and the level of sales respectively which the entry of a new firm into the industry would produce. But $\Delta Q' = n \cdot |e_j| \cdot Q_0' = n \cdot |e_j| \cdot Q_0$. A similar line of reasoning applies to rectangle $G'GFF'$, except that the expected change in sales due to the entry factor, $\Delta Q''[=Q_0 - Q_0']$ depends on $(k_j \cdot m)$ rather than on $|e_j|$. Since n can be factored out of both the numerator and denominator and thus can be cancelled, it does not appear as such in the equation.)

The term $n[P_0 \cdot Q_0(1 - n[|e_j| + k_j \cdot m])]$ in both the numerator and denominator represents the net revenue gain to the firm in time period j, and is equal to the area of rectangle $P_1A'B'P_0$. (This rectangle is equal to the change in price, ΔP, times the level of sales in time period j after the change in price, $_1'$. But $\Delta P = n \cdot P_0$ and $Q_1' = Q_0 - \Delta Q = Q_0(1 - n[|e_j| + k_j \cdot m])$ since $\Delta Q[=\Delta Q' + \Delta Q''] = (n \cdot k_j \cdot m \cdot Q_0)$.

The term $(1 + r)^j$ in the denominator is the means of determining the present value of the additional funds obtained in time periods 1 through s, in which the gains in net revenue from raising the industry price exceed the losses and the combined substitution effect and entry factor is not likely to be positive. The summation sign adds up the present values of the net revenue gains in each of these time periods to indicate the principal sum obtained through the price increase.

The term

$$\frac{1}{t - (s - 1)} \sum_{j=s}^{t}$$

in the numerator is the means of averaging out the net revenue losses in all subsequent time periods beginning with time period s.

The amount of additional investment funds obtained per planning period, $\Delta F/p$, is the denominator in the above equation multiplied by $n = p/(s - 1)$, with p being the ratio of the number of time periods in a planning period, p, to the number of time periods in which the com-

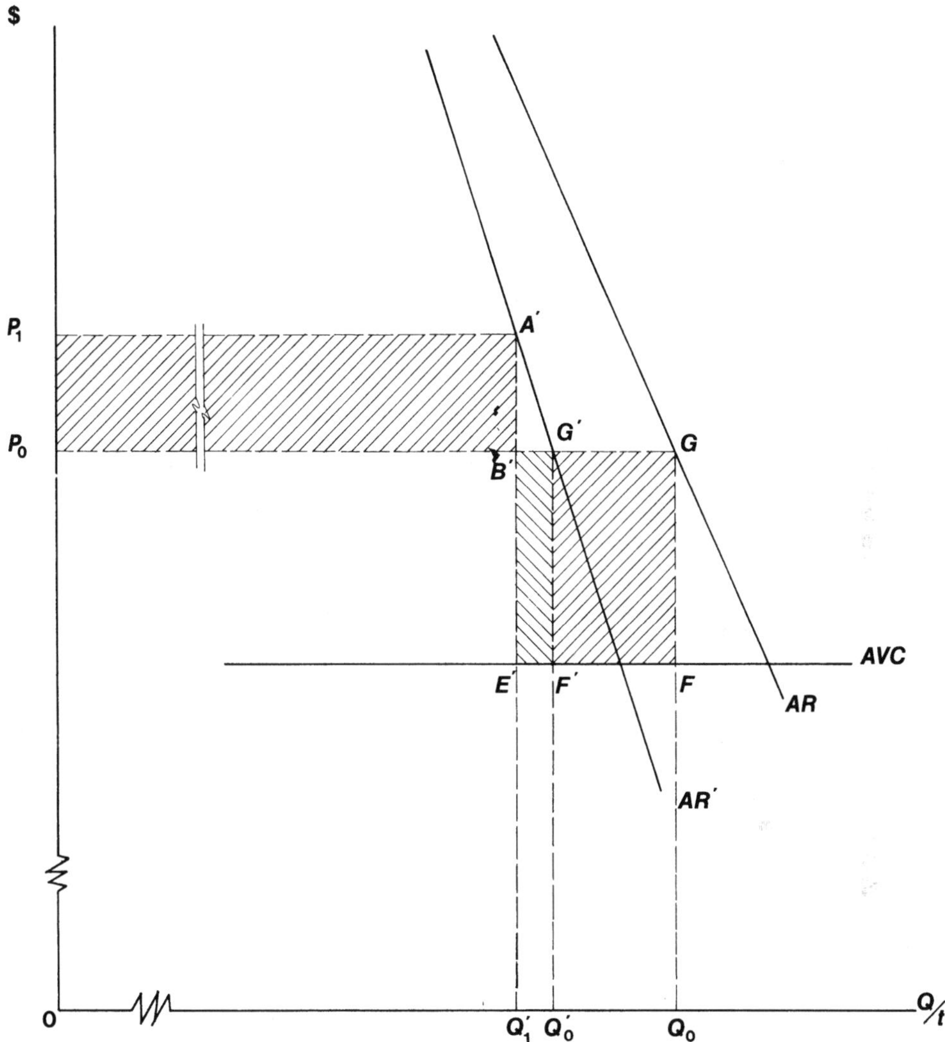

Figure 7.6

bined substitution effect and entry factor is not likely to become positive, $s - 1$.

Notes

1 For a further elaboration of the points covered in this paper, see Eichner, 1973, 1976.

2 It should be noted that Chamberlin was careful not to assert that in a "small group" oligopolistic situation the price is set so as to equate the marginal revenue implicit in a negatively sloped average revenue curve with marginal costs; and that Robinson, in the preface to the latest edition of her work, admits that she "had to make a number of limitations and simplifications which led the argument astray" (Robinson, 1969, Chs. 2, 3; Chamberlin, 1965, Ch. 3).

3 The industry consists of all firms supplying the good in question which keep watch on the same set of price quotations.

4 The slope of the price leader's average revenue curve will be greater than that of the industry demand curve by a factor equal to the inverse of the fraction representing its current market share. However, the quantity of output demanded from the price leader will be less than that demanded from the industry as a whole by the same factor. The price elasticity of demand being equal to the slope of the demand curve multiplied by the ratio of the initial quantity supplied, Q_0, to the initial price, P_0, the two factors cancel out one another. Thus, whatever the share of the market supplied by any firm, the elasticity of its average revenue curve will be the same as that of every other firm as well as the elasticity of the industry demand curve. This

means that relative market share will have no effect on the elasticity of a firm's average revenue curve seen as some portion of the total industry demand curve (Dewey, 1969, pp. 27–29; Triffin, 1940, pp. 28–29).

5 It can, of course, be argued that a firm, by increasing the margin above costs in order to obtain additional investment funds, will reduce that rate of growth of sales and hence the need for plant expansion. That there is thus a negative feedback effect of the higher price on the investment which the higher price is intended to help finance can hardly be denied, especially since the argument is based on the existence of a substitution effect which is operative over the long run. But whether this negative feedback effect is quantitatively significant is another matter. Even if it were, however, one would merely have to make the necessary adjustment for it in the marginal efficiency of investment schedule. Only if the higher price so reduced industry sales as to obviate the need for additional investment funds would the argument as a whole be invalidated, but this result seems implausible (Eichner, 1974; Hazeldine, 1974; R. Robinson, 1974).

6 Since at existing price levels the firm will already be generating a certain amount of cash flow, a change in the price level must be seen as causing a *change* in the amount of investment funds, or savings, being generated.

7 In other words, the current price level depends, in part, on past price levels and cannot be explained except in reference to those historical benchmarks.

8 Alfred Chandler has distinguished diversification from conglomerate expansion by restricting the first term to a situation in which a firm, although entering a new industry, nonetheless continues to exploit the same basic technology. Conglomerate expansion, according to Chandler, involves a shift to a different technological base.

9 One can observe, in the history of industrial consolidation in this country, how the solution to the problem of internal cohesion inevitably raised the question of how entry into the industry could be effectively impeded. The successful consolidations were those which solved this second problem as well as the first (Eichner, 1969, Ch. 8).

References

Abramowitz, M. 1938. "Monopolistic Selling in a Changing Economy," *Quarterly Journal of Economics*, 52:191–214.

Anderson, W. H. L. 1964. *Corporate Finance and Fixed Investments*. Cambridge: Harvard University Press.

Asimakopulos, A. 1971. "The Determinants of Investments in Keynes's Model," *Canadian Journal of Economics*, 4:382–8.

Beckman, M. J. 1970. "Some Aspects of Returns to Scale in Business Administration," *Quarterly Journal of Economics*, 74:464–71.

Boyle, S., and Sorensen, R. 1971. "Concentration and Mobility: Alternative Measures of Industrial Structure," *Journal of Industrial Economics*, 19:118–32.

Chamberlin, E. H. 1965. *The Theory of Monopolistic Competition*. Cambridge: Harvard University Press.

Coddington, A. 1968. *Theories of the Bargaining Process*. Chicago: Aldine.

Cyert, R., and DeGroot, M. 1971. "Interfirm Learning and the Kinked Demand Curve," *Journal of Economic Theory*, 3:272–87.

Dewey, D. 1969. *The Theory of Imperfect Competition: A Radical Reconstruction*. 2nd ed. New York: St. Martin's Press.

Dolbear, F. T., Lave, L. B., et al. 1968. "Collusion in Oligopoly: An Experiment on the Effect of Numbers and Information," *Quarterly Journal of Economics*, 82:240–59.

Eichner, A. 1969. *The Emergence of Oligopoly*. Baltimore, Md.: Johns Hopkins University Press.

1973. "A Theory of Determination of the Mark-up Under Oligopoly," *Economic Journal*, 83:1184–2000.

1974. "Determination of the Mark-up under Oligopoly A Reply," *Economic Journal*, 84:974–80.

1976. *The Megacorp and Oligopoly*. Cambridge: Cambridge University Press.

Eichner, A., and Kregel, J. A. 1975. "An Essay on Post-Keynesian Theory: A New Paradigm in Economics," *Journal of Economic Literature*, 13:1293–1314.

Fellner, W. 1949. *Competition Among the Few*. New York: Knopf.

Galbraith, K. 1952. *American Capitalism: The Concept of Countervailing Power*. Boston: Houghton Mifflin.

Gaskins, D. 1971. "Dynamic Limit Pricing: Optimal Pricing Under Threat of Entry," *Journal of Economic Theory*, 3:306–22.

Gold, B. 1966. "New Perspectives on Cost Theory and Empirical Findings," *Journal of Industrial Economics*, 14:164–89.

Gordon, R. 1961. *Business Leadership in the Large Corporation*. Berkeley, Calif.: University of California Press.

Gort, M. 1963. *Diversification and Integration in American Industry*. Princeton, N.J.: Princeton University Press.

1973. "Analysis of Stability and Change in Market Shares," *Journal of Political Economy*, 71:51–63.

Gutman, P. M. 1967. "Intertemporal Profit Maximization and The Firm," *Western Economic Journal*, 5:271–75.

Hansen, B. 1970. *A Survey of General Equilibrium Systems*. New York: McGraw-Hill.

Harnett, D. 1967. "Bargaining and Negotiation in a Mixed-Motive Game: Price Leadership Bilateral Monopoly," *Southern Economic Journal*, 33: 479–87.

Hazledine, T. 1974. "Determination of the Mark-up under Oligopoly: A Comment," *Economic Journal*, 84:967–70.

Hicks, J. 1954. "The Process of Imperfect Competition," *Oxford Economic Papers*, 6:41–54.

Hirsch, W. 1950–51. "A Survey of Price Elasticities," *Review of Economic Studies*, no. 1, 19:50–8.

Houthakker, H. S., and Tayler, L. D. 1966. *Consumer Demand in the United States, 1929–1970, Analyses and Projections*. Cambridge: Harvard University Press.

Jacoby, N. H. 1964. "The Relative Stability of Market Shares: A Theory and Evidence from Several Industries," *Journal of Industrial Economics*, 12:83–107.

Johnston, J. 1960. *Statistical Cost Analyses*. New York: McGraw-Hill.

Kamien, M. I., and Schwartz, N. L. 1971. "Limit Pricing, Potential Entry, and Barriers to Entry," *Econometrica*, 39:441–54.

Koot, R. S., and Walter, D. A. 1970. "Short-Run Cost Functions of a Multi-Product Firm," *Journal of Industrial Economics*, 18:118–28.

Kregel, J. A. 1971. *Rate of Profit, Distribution and Growth: Two Views*. Chicago: Aldine.

1973. *The Reconstruction of Political Economy: An Introduction to Post-Keynesian Economics*. New York: Halsted.

Lave, L. B. 1962. "An Empirical Approach to the Prisoners' Dilemma Game," *Quarterly Journal of Economics*, 76:424–36.

Machlup, F. 1952. *The Economics of Sellers' Competition*. Baltimore, Md.: Johns Hopkins University Press.

Marris, R. 1964. *The Economic Theory of "Managerial" Capitalism*. New York: Free Press.

Marris, R., and Wood, A., eds. 1971. *The Corporate Economy, Growth, Competition and Innovational Potential*. Cambridge: Harvard University Press.

Marshall, A. 1920. *Principles of Economics*. 8th ed. New York: Macmillan.

Murphy, J. L. 1966. "Effects of the Threat of Losses on Duopoly Bargaining," *Quarterly Journal of Economics*, 80:296–313.

Nordhaus, W. 1974. "The Falling Shares of Profits," *Brookings Papers on Economic Activity*, no. 1, 5:169–207.

Phelps, E. S., and Winter, S. G., 1970. "Optimal Price Policy under Atomistic Competition," in *Microeconomic Foundations of Employment and Inflation Theory*, E. S. Phelps, ed. New York: Norton.

Robinson, J. 1969. *The Economics of Imperfect Competition*. 2nd ed. New York: St. Martin's Press.

Robinson, R. 1961. "The Economics of Disequilibrium Price," *Quarterly Journal of Economics*, 75:191–233.

1974. "The Determination of the Mark-up under Oligopoly: A Comment," *Economic Journal*, 84:971–4.

Scherer, F. 1970. *Industrial Market Structure and Economic Performance*. Chicago: Rand McNally.

Stigler, G. J. 1964. "A Theory of Oligopoly," *Journal of Political Economy*, 72:44–61.

Stone, R. 1954. *The Measurement of Consumer Expenditures and Behavior in the United Kingdom, 1920–1938*. Cambridge: Cambridge University Press.

Triffin, R. 1940. *Monopolistic Competition and General Equilibrium Theory*. Cambridge: Harvard University Press.

Walters, A. A. 1963. "Production and Cost, An Econometric Survey," *Econometrica*, 31:1–66.

Wiles, P. J. D. 1956. *Price, Cost and Output*. Oxford: Blackwell.

Williamson, O. E. 1965. "A Dynamic Theory of Interfirm Behavior," *Quarterly Journal of Economics*, 79:579–607.

Zudac, L. S. 1970. "Productivity, Labor Demand and Cost in a Continuous Production Facility," *Journal of Industrial Economics*, 18:255–74.

1971. "Labor Demand, and Multi-Product Cost in Semi-Continuous and Multi-Process Facilities," *Journal of Industrial Economics*, 19:267–90.

Part IV

Macroeconomics

8

Keynes's paradigm: a theoretical framework for monetary analysis

Paul Davidson and J. A. Kregel

> The object of our analysis is, not to provide a machine, or method of blind manipulation, which will furnish an infallible answer, but to provide ourselves with an organized and orderly method of thinking out particular problems; and, after we have reached a provisional conclusion by isolating the complicating factors one by one, we then have to go back on ourselves and allow, as well as we can, for the probable interactions of factors amongst themselves. This is the nature of economic thinking. Any other way of applying our formal principles of thought . . . will lead us into error. (Keynes, 1936, p. 297)

Keynes started his revisions and extensions of his *Treatise on Money* in the belief that he was continuing his refinement of the theory of money. Instead, on his own admission, he finished by writing an entirely new and original theory of prices, employment, and output as a whole in which it was impossible to dichotomize the monetary and real relations of a modern production economy (Keynes, 1973, Vol. XIII, pp. 408–09).

> To me, the most extraordinary thing regarded historically, is the disappearance of the theory of demand and supply for output as a whole, i.e. the theory of employment, *after* it had been for a quarter of a century the most discussed thing in economics. One of the most important transitions for me, after my *Treatise on Money* had been published, was suddenly realizing this. (Keynes, 1973, Vol. XIV, p. 85)

It was in the enunciation of the principle of effective demand that Keynes showed that the monetary and real relations of a modern production economy were interdependent. Hence if we are to understand the analytical method that Keynes believed himself to be using, we must reject the "old-time ISLMic religion" of Hicks, Modigliani, and Samuelson which has as its basic tenets that equilibrium in the real sector is an independent function of equilibrium in the monetary sector, i.e., that the parameters of the IS function are independent of the LM function's parameters. Implicit in all this is that Walrasian microtheory (as well as the axiomatic value theory derived from Walras by Arrow, Debreu and Hahn) is inherently incompatible with Keynes's theory of output as a whole.[1]

Keynes, the monetary theorist, did not begin his analysis by studying the behavior of a world without money and then imagine why, in certain circumstances, "money" should of necessity be invented. Instead he took the view that what should be described from the very beginning was the operation of a "real world" monetary economy as he saw and lived in it. Keynes bypassed the impractical and irrelevant question of the behavior of a barter system when money is imposed upon it (Keynes, 1973, Vol. XIII, pp. 408–11).

Modern general equilibrium analysis of monetary relations simply presupposes the existence of a world of institutions and behavior identical to that found in a real world monetary economy except that initially only pairwise trades are possible. The technical problem of equilibrium exchange or prereconciliation of all trading plans before any economic activity is undertaken is then considered as an investigation of monetary relations (e.g., Howitt, 1973; Ostroy and Starr, 1974). General equilibrium (GE) analysis becomes a search for complete consistency of plans before any economic actions are undertaken so that in a GE world prereconciled ex ante decisions always equal ex post realizations. This ultimately requires unchanging expectations and continuous fulfillment of plans (at least in an actuarial sense) in a timeless setting.[2]

Keynes's approach, on the other hand, asserts that the exact opposite situation is the nature of the economic problem. Decisions are made in the face of an uncertain future. Seriatim forward contracting through time is the most important institution yet devised for dealing with an uncertain future in a market economy. These contracts permit time-consuming economic activities to be undertaken even though all economic agents recognize that errors and inconsistencies are human frailties that no market mechanism can completely abolish (Keynes, 1973, Vol. XIV, pp. 106–7).

How strange it must seem to the untutored reader of many "advanced" economic textbooks to find, in one part of the text, the GE world (where markets assure consistency of ex ante plans and ex post results) presented as the microfoundation of Keynes's macrotheory while, in the other part of the text, the mechanism for explaining changes in the level of income is the difference between ex ante and ex post, i.e., inconsistency in plans as they are reflected in nonreversible market actions. Only those with advanced degrees from our most learned universities are clever enough to ignore this basic incompatibility between the micro and macrocomponents as they profess the "neoclassical synthesis."

In contradistinction to the GE approach, Keynes's method is one where from the very beginning "money plays a part of its own and affects motives and decisions . . . so that the course of events cannot be predicted, either in the long period or in the short, without a knowledge of the behavior of money between the first state and the last" (Keynes, 1973, Vol. XIII, pp. 408–09). Keynes insisted that economic decision makers acted on the belief that their inexact expectations may be met, while recognizing that in all likelihood, they would not (Keynes, 1973, Vol. XIV, p. 107). Keynes took for granted that the economic system to be studied was a monetary–production economy in which the future is uncertain and in which there can be no market institutions that would permit the effective prereconciliation of all trading and production plans for all economic agents.[3]

Within the context of a production economy with an uncertain future, Keynes sought to shift the emphasis from actual to expected values of the economic variables (Keynes, 1973, Vol. XIII, p. 434). In essence Keynes was insisting that the economic paradigm should be "composed of thoughts about thoughts" (Shackle, 1972, p. 71). Thus, Keynes made the general state of expectations an explicit independent variable of all the functional relationships in the system (Keynes, 1973, Vol. XIII, pp. 441–42).

In order to develop his most fundamental contribution – the theory of effective demand – Keynes chose, in *The General Theory* (GT), to elaborate on a model where it was assumed that once the state of expectations is given, it would continue for a sufficient length of time for the effect on employment to have worked itself out (Keynes, 1936, p. 48). This static Keynes model permitted the specifications of simple, stable functional relationships that a dynamic or shifting expectational model would have rendered impossible.[4] The use of this simple static model was a pedagogical device to separate the effect of a given set of expectations in determining the equilibrium level of employment (which could be less than full employment) from the effect of disappointment and changes in expectations on shifting the level of employment; for it had already been understood that changing entrepreneurial errors of optimism and pessimism could result in a trade cycle. While recognizing the importance of expectations, Keynes thought that these parts of the economic nexus could be initially relegated to the background in order to give full scope to the role played by effective demand in producing an equilibrium level of employment which could be less than full employment.[5]

Keynes's two models

In Chapter 5 of the GT, Keynes explicitly introduces the notion of two possible approaches to economic analysis. The first is a static analysis where the state of entrepreneurial expectations is unchanged so that expected propensities can be uniquely specified, and where actually realized results have (by assumption) no effect on long term expectations. In this model even if small mistakes occur, such discrepancies may be eliminated by trial and error changes, while entrepreneurs are "not confused or interrupted by any further change in expectations" (Keynes, 1936, p. 49). The second approach is a dynamic model where expectational propensities shift over time, whether expectations are being fulfilled at any moment or not. In other words, this dynamic or shifting equilibrium approach is applicable whenever there is a change in the state of expectations due to either autonomous factors or induced by current realizations differing from past expectations.

For Keynes, the difference between a dynamic and a static model involved "not the economy under observation which is moving in the one case and stationary in the other, but our expectations of the future environment which are shifting in the one case and stationary in the other" (Keynes, 1973, Vol. XIV, p. 511).[6]

These two approaches to economic analysis

are given differing weights in the GT, and especially when Keynes is discussing policy. It is not always crystal clear whether his prescriptions are based on the fully developed static model of the GT, where expectations are unchanged and so *as a logical exercise (and not as a projection over time)* the position of equilibrium can be determined; or whether the prescription is based on the less explicit, dynamic approach of the GT where expectations are changing while the economy is moving through time.

The usual interpretation is that Keynes held the state of expectations constant while discussing functional relationships, hoping that with "the introduction of the concepts of user costs and of the marginal efficiency of capital" to give a role to expectations and bring static theory "back to reality, whilst reducing to a minimum the necessary degree of adaptation" (Keynes, 1936, p. 146). On occasion however, Keynes did appear to introduce the effects of disappointment into the static discussion of the stable spending propensities (e.g., Keynes, 1936, p. 51), thereby tending to weaken the link between disappointment and shifts in expectations.

After he completed the GT, Keynes recognized that his indiscriminate treatment of the relationship between disappointment and a given state of expectations in the GT could confuse the reader about the theory of effective demand. In his 1937 lectures, Keynes stated

> If I were writing the book again I should begin by setting forth my theory on the assumption that short period expectations were always fulfilled; and then have a subsequent chapter showing what differences it makes when short-period expectations are disappointed.
>
> For other economists, I find lay the whole emphasis, and find the whole explanation in the *differences* between effective demand and income; and they are so convinced that this is the right course that they do not notice that in my treatment this is not so . . .[7] The main point is to distinguish the forces determining the position of equilibrium from the technique of trial and error by means of which the entrepreneur discovers where the position is . . . *Ex ante* savings and *ex ante* investment *not* equal . . . *ex ante* decisions in their influence on effective demand relate solely to *entrepreneurs'* decisions . . . the disappointment of expectations influence the next *ex ante* decisions.
>
> [but even if we] suppose the identity of *ex post* and *ex ante*, my theory remains . . . I should have distinguished more sharply between a theory based on *ex ante* effective demand, however arrived at, and a psychological chapter indicating *how* the business world reaches its *ex ante* decisions. (Keynes, 1973, Vol. XIV, pp. 181–83)

Thus Keynes gives an insight into the intermingling of approaches that he used in the GT. On the one hand, there is the stark static model where, given expectations, the theory of effective demand is the prime determinant of the level of employment. In this model, where disappointment-induced shifts of expectations are removed, Keynes demonstrates that unemployment was not necessarily a short-run disequilibrium phenomena; that booms and slumps need not be the result of faulty entrepreneurial expectations, but that a monetary production system could settle, as a theoretical matter, in equilibrium at almost any level of employment.

To this stark model complicating factors of disappointment were added at some points in the GT, but not before the static model is completely laid out. Wholesale shifts in expectations were forcibly removed from the initial picture in order to permit the derivation of the stable functional relationships necessary for the elucidation of the theory of effective demand. When such large changes in expectations are discussed they are held separate from the static model of the GT, thus leading Friedman to catalog these discussions of Keynes as "many correct, interesting, and valuable ideas, although some wrong ones, and many shrewd observations on empirical matters . . . but all . . . strictly peripheral to the main contribution of *The General Theory*" (Friedman, et al., 1974, pp. 148–49).

In his 1937 lecture notes, Keynes has suggested that he might have better convinced his audience if he had more clearly separated the principle of effective demand under a given set of expectations from the effect of disappointment on effective demand changes.

Keynes and Hicks on expectations and economic analysis

Hicks's analysis of expectations in *Value and Capital* can be fruitfully used to clarify the distinctions between Keynes's static and dynamic approaches. Hicks suggests that there are three influences which affect expectations. The first two are due to either "noneconomic" or economic factors generated by forces other than those under discussion. These, Hicks suggests, cause autonomous changes in expectations, and although "we must never forget that . . . expectations are liable to be influenced by autonomous causes, . . . we must leave it at that"

(Hicks, 1946, p. 205). Hicks's third influence occurs when today's realized values differ from previous expectations about today's realized values, thereby inducing a change in expectations about future values of the relevant variables. Hicks's elasticity of expectations (E_e) measures the magnitude of this induced change in expectations. E_e is defined as the ratio of the proportionate change in the expected future values of X to the proportionate change in the current realized value of X vis-à-vis the previous expected value of the current X.[8]

Hence if there are no autonomous changes in expectations during the period of observation and if $E_e = 0$, then even though all variables are dated (Hicks's definition of dynamics), the analysis involves Keynes's static method.[9] If, on the other hand, either $E_e \neq 0$ and/or there are autonomous changes in expectations, then Keynes's dynamic analysis is applicable.

In sum, Keynes's static model where $E_e = 0$, permits stable aggregate demand and supply functions to be derived, and a point of effective demand to be developed which need not be full employment. Such a model need not have an unchanging equilibrium level of employment as long as existing expectations have correctly foreseen future changes (Keynes, 1936, p. 48 n. 1), but realizations cannot (by hypothesis) alter expectations. That this process was not one that Keynes expected to actually occur over time in the real world is emphasized by his calling the resulting equilibrium employment level a "long-period" position (Keynes, 1936, p. 49) and his direct method of severing the extent to which anything can alter existing expectations about the future (Keynes, 1936, p. 49).

Keynes's dynamic approach can provide models of shifting but stable equilibrium if $E_e \neq 0$ but it is not greater than unity, when, as Keynes assumed was the normal human condition, ex ante and ex post are unequal.[10] Nevertheless, in a dynamic economy there is no necessary constant relationship between realizations, E_e, and autonomous changes in expectations; nor need E_e even be constant over time. Only in the unlikely event that $E_e = 0$, will realizations of errors not alter the state of expectations. "The actual course of events is more complicated . . . for the state of expectations is liable to constant change" (Keynes, 1936, p. 50), thereby shifting the independent behavioral propensities. Thus, Keynes's model of shifting equilibrium will describe an actual path of an economy over time chasing an ever-changing equilibrium – it need not ever catch it.

This latter approach of shifting equilibrium is, however, conceptually distinct from the GE approach and/or the adaptive expectations approach used by most American economists. In Keynes's full view of the system it is the conjectural and often figmental state of human expectations which are the prime movers of a free enterprise economic system. Thus, in the Keynes paradigm, supply and demand functions exist at a point in time but they need not exist over historical time. As Shackle argues, this is just as much a part of Keynes's message as the static exposition of effective demand, for "stable curves and functions are *allergic* to the real human economic scheme of things" (Shackle, 1972, p. 517). It is in the shifting equilibrium analysis that the crucial role of historical time as well as the difficult methodological problems are most clearly seen.

Methodology and the time dimension

Time is a device which prevents everything from happening at once. Keynes recognized that the essence of real world economics is that calendar time normally elapses between the point where decisions are made and the ultimate outcome of these decisions. This is the blunt message of Chapter 5 of the GT.

Keynes believed that the time duration between the enacting of decisions based on ex ante expectations and the resulting ex post outcome was "incapable of being made precise" so that there could be no specification of a "definite relationship between aggregate effective demand [as expected by entrepreneurs] at one time and aggregate income [realizations] at some later time" (Keynes, 1973, p. 179–80). Thus, Keynes explicitly gave up on the ex ante – ex post approach to handling time.[11] "I used to speak of the period between expectations and results as 'funnels of process' but the fact that the funnels are all of different lengths and overlap one another meant that at any given time there was no aggregate realised result capable of being compared with some aggregate expectation at some earlier date" (Keynes, 1973, Vol. XIV, p. 185).

Instead of a Robertson period analysis or a Swedish ex ante – ex post approach, Keynes initially presented his static model which allowed, in a very arbitrary but exact way, the tracing through of the influence of a given state of expectations to the "long-period level of employment" associated with it. Keynes chose to associate "short run" with "the shortest interval after which a firm is free to revise its decisions as to how much employment to offer.[12] It is, so to speak, the minimum effective unit of time" (Keynes, 1936, p. 47, n. 1). Simultaneously he chose to blur the distinction between realized and expected sales proceeds by referring to a

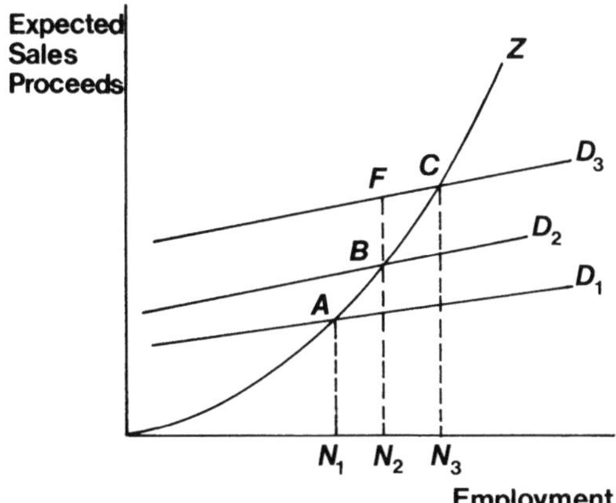

Figure 8.1

large overlap between them (Keynes, 1936, p. 51), so that the static model could operate under the assumption that a state of expectation will "continue for a sufficient length of time for the effect on employment to have worked itself out completely . . . the steady level of employment thus attained may be called the long-period employment corresponding to that state of expectation" (Keynes, 1936, p. 48).

For example, in Figure 8.1, the aggregate supply curve (Z) is derived on the basis of expected production techniques and factor prices, and each of the expected demand curves (D_1, D_2, D_3, etc.) represents a different state of expectations of possible sales in the minds of entrepreneurs.[13] Thus in Figure 8.1, there is a long-period level of employment associated with each possible expected point of effective demand, N_1 with point A, N_2 with B, etc.

Given a specific state of entrepreneurial expectations regarding the sales proceeds which can be expected to be spent by buyers for alternative levels of employment – as represented by D_2 in Figure 8.1 for example – entrepreneurs expected effective demand to be at point B. (Assume further, merely for expositional simplicity, that this point of effective demand is expected to prevail for a number of future production periods.) Acting on such expectations entrepreneurs hire N_2 workers in the current period. If D_2 is the realizable aggregate demand curve, the expectations will be fulfilled and N_2 will remain the equilibrium level of employment until there is a change in the state of expectations.

What if, however, the realizable demand function in the current period turned out to be D_3? Logically, the Keynes static model suggests that as long as entrepreneurs expect D_2 to prevail, i.e., as long as $E_e = 0$, employment will remain at N_2 even if realizations differ from expectations. "The actual realized result . . . will only be relevant to employment insofar as they cause a modification of subsequent expectations" (Keynes, 1936, p. 47), i.e., only if $E_e > 0$. That however would require dynamic, rather than static, analysis. Keynes's static model can apply to this situation only by stretching a verbal sleight of hand which Keynes used. If the actual aggregate demand curve is, say D_3, when they expected D_2, then entrepreneurs should be surprised by subsequent events when they find either an unexpected increase in spot market prices, and/or an unintended run-down of inventories, and/or an increased queue of buyers (as the realizable aggregate demand price associated with the actual hiring of N_2 workers is given by points F). The discrepancy between the expected and realizable aggregate demand functions (D_2 and D_3) should, it would seem, alter entrepreneurial expectations so long as $E_e \neq 0$. Keynes however blurred the difference between the state of entrepreneurial expectations underlying the initially expected aggregate demand curve (D_2 in Figure 8.1) and the expectations that would have brought forth the realizable demand curve (D_3) in the minds of entrepreneurs in order to maintain his static model assumptions by assuming

> in practice the process of revision of short-term expectation is a gradual and continuous one, carried on largely in the light of realised results; so that expected and realised results run into and overlap one another in their influence . . . Thus in practice there is a large overlap between the effects on employment of the realised sales-proceeds of recent output and those of the sales-proceeds expected from current input. (Keynes, 1936, p. 51)

In other words, despite the surprises that the point of effective demand was C rather than B, Keynes can be interpreted as assuming within a static framework that entrepreneurs can switch from the expectations underlying D_2 to those underlying D_3 *without a change in the state of expectations occurring*.[14] Thus, market signals will push entrepreneurs to increase their hiring towards N_3, the "long-period level of employment" (Keynes, 1936, p. 48).

Of course, Keynes realized that "the actual course of events is more complicated" since expectations "are liable to sudden revision" before any state of expectation "has fully worked itself out" (Keynes, 1936, pp. 50–51), i.e., the aggregate supply and/or demand curve could shift before point C (in Figure 8.1) is reached. Thus, Keynes envisioned his real world model as one of shifting equilibrium, a world in continuous movement without the necessity for the plans of the economic agents to ever be reconciled. It is unfortunate that only his pedagogical static model made any impact on the economics profession.

Equilibrium versus historical models. In economic methodology, there are two types of models – timeless, general equilibrium models and historical–humanistic models. The former are used by GE theorists, the latter by Keynes, and some of his followers.[15]

An equilibrium model builder proceeds by specifying a sufficient number of equations to determine all the unknowns in the system and then concentrates on the simultaneous solution of the equations. All the equilibrium theorist can tell you is if the equilibrium position exists, i.e., if all plans can be prereconciled. "A world where expectations are liable to be falsified cannot be described by the simple equations of the equilibrium path" (Robinson, 1963, p. 25). An equilibrium model is bound to a timeless system where all plans are prereconciled before any action takes place.

A historical model, on the other hand, specifies a particular set of values at a moment in calendar time. These particular values may or may not be in any sense in equilibrium.[16] The historical model can show (1) how entrepreneurial expectations lead to employment, output and pricing decisions, (e.g., Keynes's static model was supposed to explain "the process of transition to a long period [employment] position due to a change in expectations" (Keynes, 1936, pp. 48–49)); (2) whether entrepreneurial plans are consistent with buyer's realizable demands; and (3) for any given value of E_e, the possible effect of disappointment on future expectations. It should be obvious that a dynamic analysis of the real world, even more than the static analysis of the kind Keynes envisaged, can only be done in an historical model context. In the real world, the inevitable inconsistency of plans and unexpected changes in events must lead to shifts of economic relationships over time. This model of "shifting equilibrium" with its unpredictable shifts in propensities "is a far cry from smooth and quasi-stable curves or schedules, which Keynes paraded on the front of his stage to mask the horrid void of indeterminacy and nonrationality at its rear" (Shackle, 1972, p. 517).

Dynamics, time, and instability. If we are to utilize the dynamic Keynesian theory, where the state of expectations can and does change as the system moves irreversibly along the calendar time axis, it becomes essential to recognize that there is nothing in the logic of the dynamic theory which rules out violent instability. Nevertheless, Keynes noted the "outstanding characteristic of the economic system in which we live, whilst it is subject to severe fluctuations . . . it is not violently unstable" (Keynes, 1936, p. 249). Hence there must be certain conditions in the economic environment which promote relative stability in a dynamic world so that inevitable disappointment and surprise does not lead to violent alterations in the state of expectations, so that the $E_e < 1$.

As long as the future is uncertain the state of expectations may be liable to rapid unpredictable changes and hence the economic system is potentially very unstable. Recognizing the mercurial possibility of the economic system, man has, over time, devised certain institutions and rules of the game, which, as long as they are operational, avoid such catastrophes by providing a foundation for a conventional belief in the stability of the system and hence in the quasi-stability of the state of expectations. It is the existence of spot *and* forward markets, money, and concurrent seriatim time–length money (forward) contracts[17] and their enforceability, as well as the expectations that these institutions will continue to operate with continuity or "orderliness" for the foreseeable future, which limits the magnitude of E_e and keeps real world economic fluctuations in bounds (Hicks, 1946, pp. 264–67, 270–71, 297–98). If these institutions break down, as they did for example in Germany between 1921–23, a modern monetary economy may exhibit violent instability. For most developed interdependent production economies, however, where production requires considerable calendar time and therefore contractual commitments for the hiring of resources must occur a long time before everyone can possibly know how valuable the outcome will be, such instability will mean the breakdown of production flows. This occurrence is so costly to society that most members of the economy will cling to the hope that even a crippled monetary system can be resuscitated. This hope maintains some stability in states of expectations, i.e., $E_e < 1$, but if the situation deteriorates so that almost everyone is completely uncertain as to the meaning of contractual commitments then a catastrophic breach in the continuity of the system is inevitable.

Stability of economic functions

The well defined, *stable* functions of Walrasian (or even Marshallian) microeconomics do not exist over calendar time, and are of little use in the real world for they can be defined only for a given state of expectations. What Keynes insisted on was not the stability of demand and supply functions – they could shift every time the unpredictable state of expectations changed – but their momentary existence. This means we cannot predict what will happen over a period of calendar time, only what can happen for any given state of expectations.

Keynes spent considerable time discussing the formation of expectations in his *Treatise* and in the GT (e.g., Keynes, 1936, Ch. 12), but he remained adamant that there was no uniform relationship between a set of observable events and the subsequent state of expectations. In Keynes's paradigm, the "*indefinite* character of actual expectations" are the free autonomous variables which govern everything else, rather than being governed by everything else (Keynes, 1973, Vol. XIV, pp. 106–7). In the real world expectations may only be tenuously related to past economic facts as politics, acts of God, thoughts, and life-styles are also determinants – thus Keynes's and the post-Keynesians's emphasis on "animal spirits."

Keynes's independent psychological propensities (Keynes, 1936, p. 245) – consumption, investment, and liquidity preference – would be stable *but not independent* in any system (such as the GE model) where time and uncertainty are absent. Keynes's assumption of a given state of expectations about an uncertain future and the belief of economic agents that all production, consumption, investment and liquidity decisions do not have to be made simultaneously and for all time at the initial date (or at any other point of time) permitted Keynes to deal with these propensities as formally independent stable relations within his static framework. This static Keynes model, although unrealistic because of its undue formalistic approach did form the core of the Keynesian revolution. It liberated "men's thoughts from the concept of general equilibrium . . . [and] made possible the construction of effective theories of a *varying* level of output and employment" (Shackle, 1968, p. xxi).

Keynes's dynamic model is more applicable to a real world economic system which lurches from one historical position to another without even necessarily being in equilibrium. Unfortunately the dynamic model makes predictions about the future a very tricky and unsafe business. Unlike the GE system which is closed once tastes and endowments are given, Keynes's dynamic model is open with constantly changing unpredictable expectations driving the system onward through calendar time. Economists, unlike astronomers (but like weathermen?), are stuck with an open system. They cannot use the mechanistic approach of general equilibrium. They must instead provide a classificatory theory of economics using, when relevant, the E_e concept which puts situations into one box or another according to what can happen as a sequel under a given set of circumstances, not what will happen. This philosophy about the nature of economic models was summed up by Keynes in a letter to Harrod in which he said

> Economics is a branch of logic; a way of thinking . . . *Progress* in economics consists almost entirely in a progressive improvement in the choice of models . . . but it is of the essence of a model that one does *not* fill in real values for the variable functions . . . The object of statistical study is not so much to fill in missing variables with a view to prediction as to test the relevance and validity of the model.
>
> Economics is a science of thinking in terms of models joined to the art of choosing models which are relevant to the contemporary world. It is compelled to be this, because, unlike the typical natural science, the material to which it is applied is, in too many respects, not homogeneous through time . . . Economics is essentially a moral science and not a natural one. That is to say, it employs introspection and judgments of value. (Keynes, 1973, Vol. XIV, p. 296)

Real world stability and the current inflation

Keynes's dynamic model threatens the logical possibility of violent instability. Yet, except for rare historical episodes, capitalism has been relatively durable and homeostatic. Hence, it is important in these days of world-wide inflation and prophecies of economic cataclysm to delineate those characteristics of modern economic agents and institutions which have provided a homeostatic mechanism in an uncertain world.[18]

Contracts and price stability. Forward contracting is the most important economic institution yet devised for controlling the uncertain future course of markets. Since production takes time, entrepreneurs are always entering into forward contracts to assure the future costs of inputs, and in a nonintegrated production chain, into sales contracts to assure prices and revenues in the future. In fact, one may look upon the private institution of contracts as the way free enterprise markets attempt to assure wage and price controls.[19]

Since the money wage contract is the most ubiquitous forward contract in modern economies and since the duration of money wage contracts normally exceed the gestation period for the production of most goods, it is the institution of forward labor contracting which provides a basis for the conventional belief in the stickiness or stability in prices over time. Such a convention is necessary if entrepreneurs are going to take long-term positions in productive facilities.

In a capitalist economy, some people will employ hired labor on forward contracts for future profits; while some desire to save, i.e., not to exercise all of their currently earned claims on new goods produced by labor. Savers must hold resaleable assets that can last through time with a minimum of carrying costs and therefore serve as a store of value, unless they know what specific thing they will want to possess at a specific future date, for then they can buy a forward contract for the production of the item wanted and its delivery at the desired future date. But Keynes stressed: "an act of individual savings means . . . *not* . . . to consume any specified thing at any specified date" (Keynes, 1936, p. 210). Hence savings involves the possession of stores of value that are durable and liquid.

Durables possess liquidity or resaleability only if there is a well organized spot market in which they can be readily resold at any future date for a claim on resources available at that date. (As long as labor-hire contracts are made in terms of money wages, then money will be the primary claim on newly produced goods.) The current money value of any resaleable durable can increase or decrease *without limit* if expectations of future spot prices change. If, however, the durable has relatively high elasticities of production and substitution, a counterbalancing factor due to new production (or in the case of decrease in value – carrying costs and physical deterioration) comes into play, as over time the costs of production and new supplies limit the increase in future spot prices expected at future dates. Nevertheless for those assets which have negligible elasticities of production and substitution and well-organized spot markets – primarily financial assets – their conditions of supply (resource using reproducibility) do not, indeed cannot, act as a counterbalance to the effect of changing expectations of future spot prices on present (spot) market values.

Since all exchange values are relative and since the current values of all resaleable durables ultimately depend on their expected future spot prices, the only thing which will provide an anchor for the money price level over time is the belief in the stability or stickiness of money costs of production over time.[20] Hence as long as forward labor contracts are set in monetary terms for a period of calendar time which exceeds the gestation period of production, economic agents can expect stickiness in the price level of new goods and services. It is the money wage contract and the resulting stickiness of money wages which permitted Keynes to produce a stable but potentially shifting equilibrium model. As Hicks emphasized, Keynes

> assumes a unity elasticity of expectations only for [spot] prices expected to rule in the near future; for prices expected in the further future [where new production can come to market], he [Keynes] assumes that they move with money wages . . . Consequently the instability of the system is . . . in abeyance so long as money wages are kept constant (for then more distant prices have a zero elasticity of expectations and this acts as a stabilizer). (Hicks, 1946, p. 256)

Of course Keynes did not assume constant money wage rates, merely "sticky" ones so that E_e need not equal zero; E_e will be very inelastic as long as there are long term forward contracts for money wages.

The stability of the level of money prices over time therefore depends on habit and/or convention which makes the money price of something relatively sticky over time so that people can "expect" price stability. In the real world, in normal times, the efficiency money wage, i.e., money wages relative to productivity, is nearly enough constant so as to provide some basis for the convention of price stability to be incorporated into entrepreneurial expectations and therefore encourage them to undertake productive commitments.[21] The necessity of some conventional price stability is "a fundamental assumption essential to *any* dynamic economies" (Townshend, 1937, p. 163).[22]

The staunchest defenders of the "free enterprise system," however, advocate freely flexible money wages to relieve capitalist economies of the problems of unemployment and inflation. Sticky or controlled money wages (whether by private contract or social contract), in their view, inhibit a free enterprise economy from achieving a stable, full employment growth path over time – a state of bliss. Perfect flexibility of money wages could be possible if the labor market were a "bourse." Hence, if there was a well-organized spot market for slaves then wages could be perfectly flexible and continuous full employment of slaves could be attained. Rightly or wrongly, modern economies have made such slave markets illegal, and in capitalist countries almost all labor is hired on a forward contract basis with the duration of the contract equaling or exceeding the production period.

Recently, however, Friedman has publicly advocated reducing the duration of the labor contract to a time period less than the production period in order to fight inflation. Friedman's recommendation is to "index" all labor contracts and most other contracts to a current price index.

Wide-spread indexing of labor contracts would create wage flexibility and simultaneously destroy the conventionality of price stickiness which is necessary for capitalist entrepreneurs to undertake production commitments. In his classic study of *The Economics of Inflation*, Bresciani-Turroni showed that although Germany had suffered from double digit inflation since almost the beginning of World War I, the inflation really began to accelerate at the end of 1922 (Bresciani-Turroni, 1968, p. 442). The period from the end of 1922 to the end of 1923 was different in that it "was characterized by an enormous rise in nominal wage-rates" as the system of indexing wages became general throughout Germany (Bresciani-Turroni, 1968, pp. 308–10). The cost of living index which had been calculated monthly before 1922, was calculated twice a month in 1922, and weekly in 1923 as more wages were geared to the index. But even that was found to be insufficient as each increase in money wages pushed up domestic prices. By mid-1923 a daily index was substituted by most industries as wages were paid daily. But that only accelerated price increases, so that by the end of 1923 a daily index of forecasted prices was being used (Bresciani-Turroni, 1968, p. 310). The result was an accelerating inflation of over 400 percent per month.[23]

This historical episode of wide-spread indexing can be viewed as simply a form of incomes policy. Unfortunately it is the worst form of an anti-inflationary incomes policy since it will keep wages and prices stable only if they are already stable and there is nothing which alters expectations of their remaining stable.[24] Anything which touches off expectations of inflation can, under the indexing scheme of Friedman's, lead to unending inflation. In other words, under indexing, thinking can make it so!

This bootstrap theory of inflation under indexing can be readily analyzed via a Marshallian analysis of the interaction of market period (spot) prices and short-run flow supply (forward) prices (Davidson, 1974, 1972). In Figure 8.2, D represents the initial Marshallian demand schedule (including Wicksteedian reservation demand) for a durable good, while the vertical line S represents the stock of the good inherited from the past. If this good is not reproducible (e.g., old masters) then the resulting spot price p_s would allocate the stock without remainder among demanders. If the good is reproducible, the stock can be augmented by a flow of output if buyers are willing to promise to pay the flow-

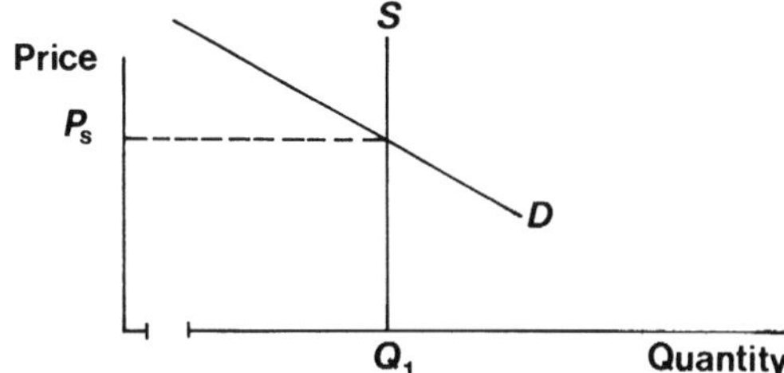

Figure 8.2

supply price and wait the gestation period for delivery. The curve s (Figure 8.3) represents the industry's Marshallian flow-supply schedule, i.e., it shows the alternative production offerings at alternative flow-supply prices. If producers are short-run profit maximizers, then p_m is the lowest point on the average variable cost schedule and represents the minimum flow-supply price.

The total market situation for a good can be obtained by laterally summing the stock and flow-supply schedules to obtain $S + s$ in Figure 8.4. Superimposing the demand schedule D onto this figure indicates that the spot price, p_s, exceeds the forward or flow-supply price, p_f, as some buyers are willing to pay a premium for immediate delivery rather than wait the gestation period for a new unit to be produced.[25] This situation (where $p_s > p_f$) is known as *backwardation* and production of $Q_2 - Q_1$ units will be forthcoming at the delivery date.

Assume all money wage contracts are geared to a price index which includes the spot price of many durables (e.g., housing, used cars, standardized commodities, tanker rates, etc.). Since the height of the s curve (Figure 8.3) depends on the money wage rate or wage unit at any point in time, the higher the price index the higher the wage unit and the higher s.[26]

At some initial date there will be a given "real" wage rate and hence a level of investment and aggregate output which is compatible with it; hence *any* attempt to change the rate of

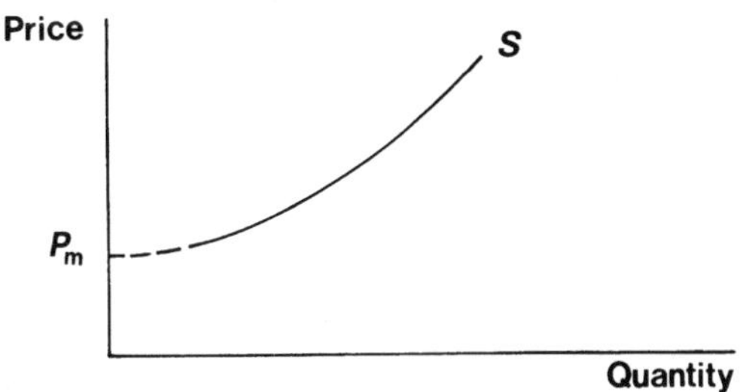

Figure 8.3

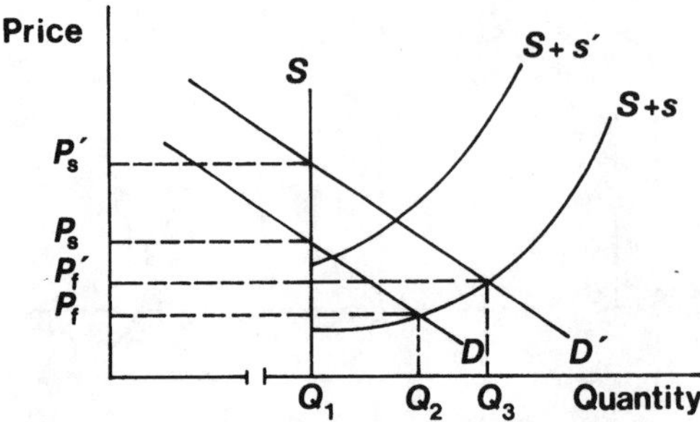

Figure 8.4

investment, the distribution of income, etc., will automatically upset the price index and induce shifts in the flow-supply curve as the indexing clause in wage contracts become operative. Let us analyze an extreme situation where the initiating force for change is an autonomous change in the state of expectations so that (given current production costs) buyers expect prices of all goods to rise more rapidly in the future than they did when the demand curve, D, was derived. This expectation of inflation will raise the marginal efficiency of all durables thereby shifting D outward to D' in Figure 8.4 immediately increasing the spot price to p_s' (Keynes, 1936, p. 142) and encouraging some buyers to order more goods for future delivery.

Forward prices would rise, *as long as money wage rates are unchanged,* from p_f to p_f', only if the elasticity of supply was not perfectly elastic. Moreover, even if the forward price rose because of short-run flow supply elasticity was less than ∞, if money wages were not indexed, the resulting increase in production flow would increase the existing stock over time (shifting S rightward) and returning the flow-supply price and the spot price to the initial p_f and p_s levels (assuming no further change in expectations). If, however, money wages are indexed, the immediate rise in spot prices (and those forward prices of goods whose flow-supply elasticity is less than perfect) will shift up the flow-supply function and therefore the total supply function (in Figure 8.4) to $S + s'$, thereby raising forward prices even more. This increase in actual forward prices could induce an additional increase in Marshallian demand curves as (1) money wage income increase and (2) the further increase in forward prices increase the marginal efficiency of durables even further as buyers recognize that indexing will assure that $E_e = 1$, indeed it will institutionalize this belief. Hence D' would shift out again (in Figure 8.4) and this will lead to money wage increases shifting up the supply curve $S + s'$ once again. Thus, indexing, by establishing a unitary E_e, will cause an initial disturbance due to any cause to spill over into an unending *incomes inflation* (Davidson, 1972, Ch. 14), which can feed back into a further spot price inflation, etc.

This institutionalization of an $E_e = 1$ via indexing must create an unstable economy, for as Hicks has noted "If all elasticities of expectations are unity, the stability of the system can only be maintained by the existence of rigid wage-rates; but if all elasticities of expectation are unity why should [money] wage rates be rigid?" (Hicks, 1946, p. 270). Hicks' response to this rhetorical question was money wages could remain fairly rigid if wage earners "have fairly *inelastic* price-expectations" (Hicks, 1946, p. 270) – the exact opposite of indexation. In fact, Hicks pointed out once workers's $E_e \rightarrow 1$, negotiators will have recourse to indexing and "the rigidity of money wages ceases altogether" (Hicks, 1946, p. 271). Stability requires, Hicks concludes, "A tendency to rigidity of certain prices, particularly wage-rates, but there must also be a tendency to rigidity of certain price expectations as well" (Hicks, 1946, p. 271). One must add, that these tendencies are to be found in the modern institutions of forward contracting in general and money-wage forward contracts for labor in particular.

Although in Figure 8.4, the destabilizing process was set off by an autonomous change in expectations creating an increase in demand, the process could have been initiated by a reduction in supply as well. Thus an act of God or man, such as either a drought, preventing replacements to the stock supply as a commodity is consumed, or an international cartel, deliberately withholding stock supplies from the market, will initially raise spot commodity prices and thereby, via indexing, start the process of a domestic incomes inflation which can only exacerbate the initial price increase problem.

Hence the unnerving conclusions that in a dynamic Keynesian model, where equilibrium may never have time to establish itself; or even if established may not long endure, it is only the stickiness and long duration of forward labor contracts which provide the conventional price stability required to avoid violently destabilizing processes. In the absence of the institution of seriatim forward contracting in money terms expectations of future price increases and/or spot market supply shortages could impinge on Marshallian supply and demand curves, shifting them up almost without limit as long as entrepreneurs can obtain working capital funds to finance their constantly escalating production commitments.[27]

In short, if conventional price stickiness is broken down by destroying the duration of private labor contracts fixed in money terms, then, since production takes time, a free enterprise system can become violently unstable. Furthermore, widespread indexing could destroy the liquidity of the existing monetary system, for no good produced in the system would have a sticky flow-supply schedule to limit its possible future price. In the absence of sticky flow-supply schedules the expected prices of all future goods are determined by the same expectations of the future prices of nonproducible durable goods.

Conclusion

In any perfectly indexed economy, any increase in the price index would start a process of continually shifting the flow supply curves of all goods upward, causing people to fly from currency (i.e., there is a dramatic fall in the liquidity of money) as people will prefer to hold liquid goods (whose future price is expected to be inflation proof). Thus without the "expectations of a relative stickiness of wages in terms of money"[28] one does not have the corollary proposition that the "excess of liquidity premium over carrying cost being greater for money than for any other asset" (Keynes, 1936, p. 238) and hence the way is open for system to become a "nonmonetary economy" where "there is no asset for which liquidity premium is always in excess of the carrying costs" (Keynes, 1936, p. 239). In such a world, time consuming production processes will grind to a halt for no one will undertake the required long-term production commitments. Hence a dynamic capitalist economy with wide-spread indexing would be precariously perched on a knife edge. Anything which set off spot price changes or even expectations of spot price changes (a condition which is quite a normal state of affairs in the real world) will cause the system to oscillate violently with prices racing to infinity (or to zero if indexed in both directions) (Keynes, 1936, pp. 269–70).

Under this conceptualization of the real world, the indexing of wage contracts is almost certain to bring about the destruction of any capitalist monetary system, especially if the index contains some spot price components whose basis is not anchored to the stickiness of production–flow prices. An upward movement (ephemeral or otherwise) in spot prices of producible goods will immediately set off a process of legalized and required upward wage and price recontracting which can continue as long as agents can finance their contractual commitments. Even if the money supply were not to increase endogenously as entrepreneurs required more working capital funds, expectations may encourage a flight from money sufficient to finance the ever increasing costs of production *and* inventory speculation for a long time.

Monetary stringency, if and when it comes, will occur when the debt structure of entrepreneurs becomes so precarious that they are unable to borrow additional sums to meet their forward contract production commitments. The inevitable chain of bankruptcies that will follow along the nonintegrated production system will ultimately mean the end of the system, as all contracts become meaningless. Such a catastrophe, by wiping out all existing contracts simultaneously, provides a foundation for developing a new monetary unit of account which is not indexed and can be utilized in denominating new input price contractual commitments with a reasonable expectation of these prices being sticky. Thus the system will attempt to restore flexibility of real wages at the same time as it stabilizes money wages. Without this property, the economy could not adapt to inevitable changes with any degree of stability.

Hence, economic society in the unconscious recesses of its being, knew what it was all about when men developed long-term forward contracts for labor and abolished spot markets for slaves. In so doing, society provided institutions which assured that an uncertain future does not mean an unstable future for any dynamic monetary economy where expectations govern decisions that drive the system through its environment of shifting equilibria.

This view was summed up by Townshend, one of the first to recognize the implications of Keynes's dynamic model:

> There can be no such thing as long period dynamic economic theory failing the . . . discovery of a plausible long-term convention of price stability. It is perhaps now being generally realised that such long-term dynamic theories as there are conceal unplausible ones. It is not unnatural that those who forecast the future in algebra or geometry should be chastened by hard fact more slowly than those who have to forecast it in arithmetic. Nor is the conclusion that the search for laws to enable us to predict economic events far ahead, like eclipses, must be given up, so surprising – not to say nihilistic – as it may seem (to some economists) at first sight. (Townshend, 1937, p. 166)

Notes

1 Keynes believed that Walras was "strictly in the classical tradition," a tradition which could not produce a general theory of employment, interest, and money (Keynes, 1936, p. 177).

2 In the most recent statements of GE not only does each economic agent have a complete set of punctiliously specified expectations for every conceivable state of the world for each future date, but all contracts for contingent commodities must be entered into at market clearing prices at the initial date *before* any production or exchange takes place and then no further contractual relations can be entered into for the rest of time. Moreover all future contracts must be paid for at the initial date so that financial constraints do not bind expenditure plans. Thus GE is a *timeless* system where *all* decisions and payments are made at an instant of time.

3 As Hicks recognized there is a device whereby coordination of expectations can occur in a private enterprise system, namely forward contracting. A complete "future economy" where all goods were always and only bought and sold forward should eliminate inconsistency in expectations, but the possibility of errors due "to *unexpected* changes in wants or resources would *not* be removed" (Hicks, 1946, p. 136, italics added). Hence even in such an economy, markets cannot prereconcile all trading plans *and* eliminate unwanted occurrences.

4 Keynes, of course, was aware of how precarious it was to balance his static model on the parameter of long term expectations. He noted that his analysis of spending propensities "shall not in any way be precluded from regarding the propensity itself as subject to change" (Keynes, 1973, Vol. XIII, p. 440). In an early draft of the GT, Keynes explicitly included in his propensity equations a variable, E, which represented the "state of long term expectations" (Keynes, 1973, Vol. XIII, 441–42). Hence if there is either an autonomous change in expectations or if current realizations differ from previous expectations and thereby induce a change in expectations about the future (i.e., if ex ante does not equal ex post and this causes a shift in the state of expectations), then there will be shifts in the functional relations of the system and Keynes's static model is inapplicable.

5 "Having, however, made clear the part played by *expectation* in the economic nexus and the reaction of realised results on future expectation, it will be safe for us in what follows often to disregard express reference to expectation. It is important to make the logical point clear and to define the terminology precisely so that it will apply without ambiguity in all cases. But when once this has been done, considerations of practical convenience may legitimately take charge . . ." (Keynes, 1973, Vol. XIII, p. 397).

6 This differs from Hicks's definitions where statics is "where we do not trouble about dating," while dynamics is where "every quantity must be dated" (Hicks, 1946, p. 115).

7 Keynes is referring primarily to D. H. Robertson's model where income is determined in a previous period while effective demand is determined in the current period and hence they may differ. But recently it has again become voguish to make differences between effective demand and income the basis of a Keynesian model (Tobin, 1975, p. 198). Nevertheless Keynes insisted that "the theory of effective demand is substantially the same if we assume that short-period expectations are always fulfilled . . . , subsequent discussion has shown that this seems to differentiate my treatment much more than I realized at [the] time, from those of other contemporary economists who have been thinking more or less about the same problem" (Keynes, 1973, Vol. XIV, p. 181).

Keynes believed that his approach would permit greater emphasis on why "the economic system may find itself in stable equilibrium with N at a level below full employment, namely at the level given by the intersection of the aggregate demand function with the aggregate supply function" (Keynes, 1936, p. 30).

8 Elasticity concepts are taxonomic and permit a classificatory methodology to be applied to economics. Shackle has called this approach *Keynesian Kaleidics* and argued that economic "theory ought explicitly to be a classificatory one, putting situations in this box or that according to what *can happen* as a sequel to it. Theories which tell us what *will* happen are claiming too much . . ." (Shackle, 1972, pp. 72–73).

9 Even in Hicks's dynamic model, if $E_e = 0$, static conditions apply (Hicks, 1946, p. 250). Recently Hahn recognizing the irrelevance of traditional GE methodology redefined the concept of equilibrium so that "an economy is an equilibrium when it generates messages which do not cause agents to change theories which they hold or policies they pursue" (Hahn, 1973, p. 25). This equilibrium concept, Hahn claims is "not at all clear," it is an "ill-specified hypothesis" but it does permit application to "rare instances" where realizations differ from expectations so long as these "rare" occasions do not induce agents to change their plans (Hahn, 1973, pp. 26–27). Contrary to Hahn's claim, however, this is the well-defined Keynes's static approach where $E_e = 0$. Thus after millions of man hours of economic research and progress in GE theory, the latest development is to work with a model which might be labeled as a "no learning by doing" system. For Keynes to start with such a pedigogical device 40 years ago in order to clarify the principle of effective demand to his "fellow economists" (Keynes, 1936, p. v) is, at least, understandable. For modern savants to present this ancient tool as the culmination of decades of research is lamentable.

10 A system where $E_e > 1$ "is definitely unstable" (Hicks, 1946, p. 255). Keynes recognized there was nothing in the logic of the analysis that required $E_e < 1$, nevertheless the real world was not violently unstable. Hence Keynes was continuously searching for conditions which are capable of causing the $E_e < 1$ (Keynes, 1936, p. 250).

11 As Keynes stressed in a letter to Harrod, ex ante is what entrepreneurs *plan* to do not what they *ought* to do to assure the equality of ex ante and ex post

(Keynes, 1973, Vol. XIV, pp. 322–27). In a dynamic (realistic) model of the real world, therefore, when entrepreneurs carry out plans which lead to a realized effective demand (actual rate of growth) which differs from that level of effective demand where plans are reconciled (warranted rate of growth), the result may be for economic agents to change their state of expectations (shifts in behavioral propensities) which may lead to a further divergence between actual and warranted paths.

12 Thus short-run decisions are not independent of contractual obligations.

13 The aggregate supply curve is derived essentially in the same conceptual manner as the Marshallian microsupply curve. Thus, for example, in the case of a profit-maximizing "price-taker" firm, the microsupply curve is obtained from the points of intersection between a family of alternative "expected" demand curves and the "expected" marginal cost curve (Samuelson, 1973, p. 454).

14 This verbal legerdemain was necessary if the simpler Keynesian static model was to make any impact on Keynes's "fellow economists." Keynes tried to dress his models with stable relationships even though he believed that psychological propensities were not because he required a forceful clear-cut exposition if he was going to make an impression on his peers. But in blurring the distinction between the static and dynamic models, Keynes created a schism between the growth model of Harrod and those of other English Keynesians such as Robinson and Kaldor (Davidson, 1972, Ch. 5).

In a similar analysis of Keynes's liquidity preference analysis, R. F. Kahn has demonstrated "the unsuitability of thinking of a schedule of liquidity preference as though it could be represented by a well-defined [*stable*] curve or by a functional relationship expressed in mathematical terms or subject to econometric processes. Keynes himself often gave way to the temptation to picture the state of liquidity preference as a fairly stable relationship, despite his institutional horror of undue formalism, but his treatment can be justified by the need at the time for a forceful and clear-cut exposition if it was to carry any weight at all" (Kahn, 1954, p. 250).

15 The Keynesian revolution involved a change in paradigm from equilibrium models to historical models.

16 The initial data contains values for tastes, endowments, and the state of expectations of the agents concerned.

17 In an economy where no contractual transactions are made for other than the current period, nothing will have much liquidity.

18 It follows from Hicks's analysis of expectations that this homeostatic mechanism requires the inelasticity of E_e and the absence of continuous large autonomous changes in expectations (Hicks, 1946, pp. 256–57). In what follows we show what institutions are needed to assure stable expectations.

19 Businessmen abhor what GE theorists love – namely recontracting.

20 The purchase of nonresaleable durables is like marriage "indissoluble except for death and other grave causes" (Keynes, 1936, p. 160). Such durables are illiquid and if all durables (including money) were illiquid we would be in a nonmonetary economy such as described by GE theory.

21 Keynes explained the historical relative stability of price level in terms of the balance between money wage ("wage-unit") increases and the increase in the efficiency of labor (Keynes, 1936, p. 308). Keynes predicted that "the long run stability or instability in prices will depend on the strength of the upward trend of the wage unit (or more precisely of the cost unit) compared with the rate of increase in the efficiency of the productive system" (Keynes, 1936, p. 309). In these days of rising raw material costs, the cost unit may be more relevant.

22 Hicks reminds us that if "all prices were equally flexible and all price expectations equally flexible," any change will lead to a "complete breakdown" of capitalism, and the only thing that prevents this instability is "price-rigidities" and "beyond price rigidity, . . . people's sense of normal [i.e., sticky] prices" (Hicks, 1946, pp. 297–98).

23 Real wages changed rapidly and drastically from month to month during this period, declining from a high in March 1923 (of 80 percent of 1913 real wages) to a low (of approximately 45 percent of 1913 real wages) in July and regaining the March level in August and October.

24 It also implies a fixed real wage or, given the rate of changes in labor productivity, it may incorporate a given rate of change in real wages. Hence indexing as an incomes policy is balanced on a Harrodian knife-edge.

25 If the good in question is not durable, then the stock supply schedule is coincidental with the ordinate axis and only a forward flow–supply market exists. If the good is not reproducible (i.e., its elasticity of production is zero), then only a spot market exists, or if forward markets are developed, the forward prices will, in a world of uncertainty, represent speculation as to future spot prices for goods where flow–supply consideration cannot affect the outcome.

26 If some basic raw material such as petroleum is also linked to the same index then we could adopt Keynes's "cost unit" as underlying the position of the short-run flow supply curve, s, in Figure 8.3.

27 If inputs did not require payments until after sales were completed the financial constraint would be on the buyers to meet their indexed forward contract commitments.

28 Keynes noted that in a flight from currency, e_w, the proportional change in money wages compared to the proportional change in effective demand becomes "large," i.e., wages are no longer sticky (Keynes, 1936, p. 306).

References

Bresciani-Turroni, C. 1968. *The Economics of Inflation*. London: Allen and Unwin.

Davidson, P. 1974. "Disequilibrium Market Adjustment: Marshall Revisited," *Economic Inquiry,* 12:146–58.

1972. *Money and the Real World.* London: Macmillan.

Friedman, M., et al., 1974. *Milton Friedman's Monetary Framework: A Debate with His Critics.* Chicago: University of Chicago Press.

Hahn, F. H. 1973. *On the Notion of Equilibrium in Economics.* Cambridge: Cambridge University Press.

Hicks, J. R. 1946. *Value and Capital.* 2nd ed. New York: Oxford University Press.

Howitt, P. W. 1973. "Walras and Monetary Theory," *Western Economic Journal,* 11:487–99.

Kahn, R. F. 1954. "Some Notes on Liquidity Preference," *The Manchester School,* pp. 229–57.

Keynes, J. M. 1973. *The Collected Works of John Maynard Keynes.* Vol. XIII. London: Macmillan.

1973. *The Collected Works of John Maynard Keynes.* Vol. XIV. London: Macmillan.

1936. *The General Theory of Employment, Interest and Money.* New York: Harcourt Brace.

Ostroy, J. M., and Starr, R. M. 1974. "Money and the Decentralization of Exchange," *Econometrica,* 42:1093–1113.

Robinson, J. 1963. *Essay in the Theory of Economic Growth.* London: Macmillan.

Samuelson, P. A. 1973. *Economics.* 9th ed. New York: McGraw-Hill.

Shackle, G. L. S. 1972. *Epistemics and Economics.* Cambridge: Cambridge University Press.

1973. "Keynes and Today's Establishment in Economic Theory," *Journal of Economic Literature,* 11:516–19.

1968. *Expectations, Investment and Income.* 2nd ed. New York: Oxford University Press.

Tobin, J. 1975. "The Legacy of Keynes," *American Economic Review Papers and Proceedings.* 65.

Townshend, H. 1937. "Liquidity-Premium and the Theory of Value," *Economic Journal,* 47:157–69.

9

A post-Keynesian development of the "Keynesian" model

G. C. Harcourt

Introduction

Outlined here is the "Keynesian" model that I have used, on and off, since 1967 for teaching third-year undergraduates at the University of Adelaide.[1] The weaknesses of the model are, first, that it follows, until the trade cycle expansions are considered in Appendix 2, the usual textbook treatment of the Keynesian investment demand function in terms of a downward sloping relationship between planned investment expenditure (I) and the rate of interest (r). Tom Asimakopulos (1971) has provided a cogent criticism of this approach, in particular, that it is an unholy mass of ex ante and ex post factors.[2] He also has provided a simple analysis which incorporates the two-sided relationship between investment and profits: the dependence of investment decisions on expected profits, on the one hand, and the dependence of actual (and expected) profits on the level of investment expenditure itself, on the other hand. It is true both to Keynes's own insights and to what actually happens. (I certainly agree with his approach and in a paper published in 1965 (Harcourt, 1965), I incorporated in a very crude way the rudiments of such an analysis.)

Second, the present models incorporate an *LM–IS* approach, though this is modified in order to take account of the contributions of the Radcliffe Committee (1959) and Gurley and Shaw (1960). The analysis is essentially comparative statics: first, the derivation of the *equilibrium* values of real income and the rate of interest from the underlying behavioural relationships and equilibrium conditions, and, second, comparisons of *differences*, that is, of new equilibrium values with either the old (preceding) ones or with what they would have been in the otherwise situation, when the values of exogenous variables and/or the forms of the relationships are changed. Nothing is said, formally, about the process of getting from one equilibrium position to another, or whether the economy actually will do so, and any statement about *changes* as opposed to *differences* requires an act of faith (which is common to all believers but is not always made explicit). That comparative statics results are so applied to process situations is not stressed enough in the textbooks. The model is therefore in part (but not ever in politics) a specie of the Bastard Keynesian genus (Davidson, 1972, Ch. 1).

The *LM–IS* approach has been justly (if not always fairly) criticized by Joan Robinson (1971, Ch. 6) and, of course, by Keynes himself, implicitly in the *General Theory* (Keynes, 1936) and explicitly in his letter to Hicks (1973, pp. 9–10). Hicks himself is not at all happy with it either.[3] The most succinct criticism in the *General Theory* is on page 173:

> We have now introduced money into our causal nexus for the first time, and we are able to catch a first glimpse of the way in which changes in the quantity of money work their way into the economic system. If, however, we are tempted to assert that money is the drink which stimulates the system to activity, we must remind ourselves that there may be several slips between the cup and the lip. For whilst an increase in the quantity of money may be expected, *cet.par.*, to reduce the rate of interest, this will not happen if the liquidity–preferences of the public are increasing more than the quantity of money; and whilst a decline in the rate of interest may

I am grateful to Denzo Kamiya for suggesting a considerable improvement in the form of the M_2 function, to Tatsuro Ichiishi for working out the implications of this for the analysis, and to Keith Frearson for helpful comments and suggestions. An earlier version of the paper was published in *Keio Economic Studies*, Vol. VI, (Harcourt, 1969).

be expected, *cet.par.*, to increase the volume of investment, this will not happen if the schedule of the marginal efficiency of capital is falling more rapidly than the rate of interest; and whilst an increase in the volume of investment may be expected, *cet.par.*, to increase employment, this may not happen if the propensity to consume is falling off. Finally, if employment increases, prices will rise in a degree partly governed by the shapes of the physical supply functions, and partly by the liability of the wage–unit to rise in terms of money. And when output has increased and prices have risen, the effect of this on liquidity–preference will be to increase the quantity of money necessary to maintain a given rate of interest. (Keynes, 1936, p. 173)

Anyone brought up on *LM–IS* analysis will see immediately that, given the *ceteris paribus* assumptions, this passage is easily interpreted in *LM–IS* terms. The passage also highlights, though, the enormous stress that is placed on the *ceteris paribus* assumption: the need to assume that, as we vary one parameter, so that there is, initially, a shift in one relation, the other relationships are themselves immune so that the new equilibrium position may be both identified and reached. Moreover, though Keynes talks about movement, logically his analysis is confined to comparisons only.

A feature of the model is that it can handle with very simple algebra the interrelations between the goods, money and labor markets, oligopolistic pricing behavior and the different consumption behavior of profit-receivers and wage-earners. Moreover, it illustrates a valid point of Leijonhufvud's (1968) that Keynes was analysing the implications for overall activity of the empirical observations that quantities respond more quickly to disturbances than do prices. The two key expressions are those for the short-run, equilibrium levels of real output and the rate of interest. The model is, if you like, "Ackley [1961] in Algebra," although the treatment of the price level and the production function differs from Ackley's. The preference for the use of algebra rather than geometry arises from the view that the "quadrant" approach can mislead students, who may settle for mechanical drill. The applicability of their results may seem uncertain and, moreover, geometry does not always bring out clearly the limitations of the methodology used. These dangers are less likely when algebra is used.

The analysis is short-period: the aim is to find the equilibrium values of output and the rate of interest in a period of calendar time of, say, three to six months. The capital stock is given and constant, and prices and money-wages are assumed to be decided and *held* for this period of time.

The argument is presented in a number of stages. First, only the goods and money markets are considered. The money market contains two assets – the stock of money (exogenously determined) and bonds. Using a one-commodity, closed two-sector model, and with all relationships assumed to be *linear* functions, the basic expressions for the short-run, equilibrium levels of real output and the rate of interest are obtained. Second, the equilibrium price level in a competitive setting is introduced. Third, a three-asset money market is included to allow a discussion of the Radcliffe Committee (1959), Gurley and Shaw (1960) model. The analysis is then extended by introducing the labor market and the short-run aggregate production (or utilization) function, price-making and the price level, and different consumption behaviour of wage-earners and profit-receivers. This allows a discussion of the impacts of different price levels and different distributions of real income on the equilibrium values.

The simplest case: goods and money markets

The equilibrium conditions. The equilibrium condition in the goods market is that plans and actuality coincide, i.e., that aggregate planned (and actual) spending match actual output (or, ex ante and ex post investment equal ex ante and ex post saving). The equilibrium condition in the money market is that the demand for money equal the supply of money, i.e., that the rate of interest settles at a level where people are content to hold the exogenously given stock of money.

The basic relationships

The goods market. The consumption function: This is the usual relationship in *real* terms.

$$C = \bar{A} + cY_p = \bar{A} + cY \quad (Y = Y_p) \qquad (1)$$

where C = consumption expenditure; $\bar{A}$ = autonomous item in the consumption function; c = aggregate mpc; and Y = real income (Y_p = real personal disposable income).

The investment function: Planned investment expenditure in real terms, following Keynes and taking as given the state of short-term and long-term expectations, is regarded as a simple, decreasing function of the rate of interest. For example,

$$I = \bar{I} - ar \qquad (2)$$

where I = planned investment expenditure per period; a = the slope of the line, i.e., the *abso-*

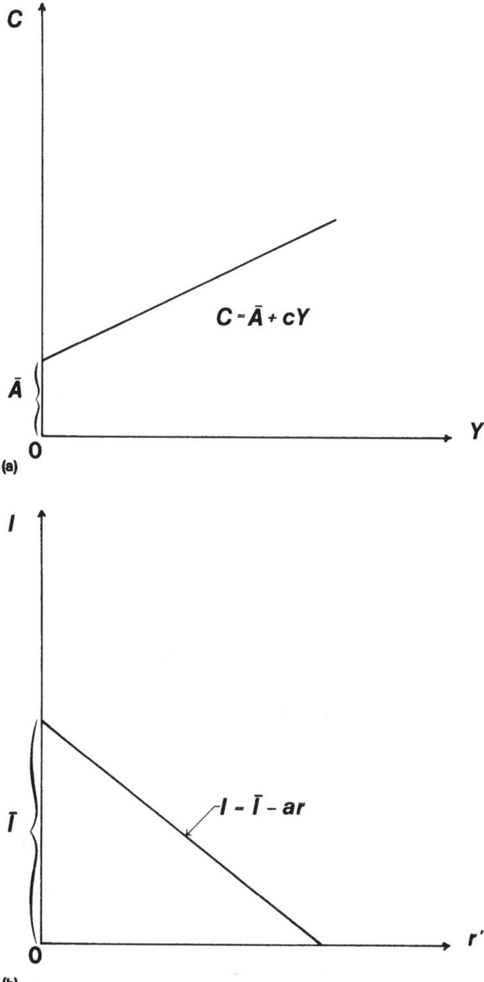

Figure 9.1

lute responsiveness of planned investment expenditure to changes in the rate of interest; r = rate of interest; and $\bar{I}$ = the level of investment expenditure when $r = 0$, which could, perhaps, be regarded as autonomous investment expenditure *in a very special sense*. The two functions are shown in Figure 9.1(a) and (b).

Because I is related to r, the aggregate demand schedule – the sum of planned consumption and investment spending – and the equilibrium level of output cannot be determined until the rate of interest is known. And, as will be shown below, the rate of interest cannot be determined until the level of output is known. The two key equilibrium values therefore have to be determined *simultaneously*, i.e., they are those values of the level of output and the rate of interest which, together, are consistent with (satisfy) the equilibrium conditions in both markets.

The money market. The demand for active balances: This relationship is the demand for money to satisfy the transactions motive. It is regarded as a simple proportional function of the level of activity (measured in real terms in this simple case, but generally in money terms).

$$M_1 = lY \qquad (3)$$

where M_1 = the demand for active balances; l = a constant reflecting the public's present spending habits and other transaction motives.

The demand for idle balances: This is the Keynesian liquidity preference function: the demand for money to satisfy the speculative motive. It is a function of the rate of interest and reflects people's uncertainty *now* about the *future* level of the rate of interest. It has two features: first, the function is downward sloping and interest-elastic. Second, it is perfectly elastic at a minimum positive rate of interest – the "liquidity trap" level.

The liquidity preference function may be drawn as a curve with a vertical stretch at the "liquidity trap" level of the rate of interest, r^* (see Figure 9.2).[4] This curve may be approximated by two straight lines (the dotted lines in Figure 9.2). They are, respectively, a vertical line at $r = r^*$, of which only the section *above A* has economic meaning, and the line BC, of which *only* the section AC has economic meaning. The equation of the line BC is:

$$M_2 = M^* - br \qquad (4)$$

where M_2 = the demand for idle balances; b = the slope of the line, i.e., the *absolute* responsiveness of the demand for idle balances to changes in the rate of interest; and M^* = ver-

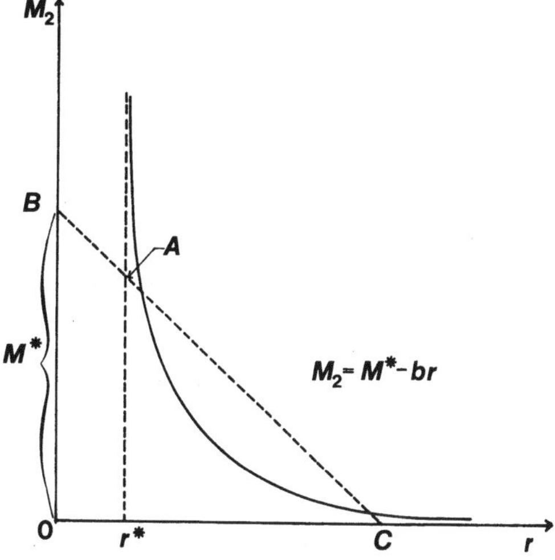

Figure 9.2

tical intercept on the M_2 axis (which has no economic meaning).

The supply of money:

$$M = \overline{M} \tag{5}$$

where $\overline{M}$ = the exogenously given stock of money.

The equilibrium values. The equilibrium values of Y and r may be obtained from the two equilibrium conditions.

The goods market condition. $Y = E(=C(Y) + I(r))$, i.e.,

$$Y = \bar{A} + cY + \bar{I} - ar = \frac{\bar{A} + \bar{I} - ar}{1 - c}, \tag{6}$$

where

E = aggregate demand.

(Expression (6), when written as: $r = (\bar{A} + \bar{I}/a) - [(1 - c/a)]\ Y$, is the Hicks–Hansen *IS* schedule.)

The money market condition. $\overline{M} = M_1(Y) + M_2(r)$ i.e.,

$$\overline{M} = lY + M^* - br \tag{7}$$

Expression (7) may be solved for r to give:

$$r = \frac{lY + M^* - \overline{M}}{b}\left(= \frac{M^* - \overline{M}}{b} + \frac{l}{b}Y\right) \tag{8}$$

(This is the Hicks–Hansen *LM* schedule.)[5]

Substituting (8) in (6), the expression for the equilibrium level of real income is obtained, viz.:

$$Y = \frac{\bar{A} + \bar{I} - (a/b)(M^* - \overline{M})}{1 - c + (a/b)l} \tag{9}$$

Finally, by substituting (9) in (8), and rearranging terms, the corresponding expression for the equilibrium value of the rate of interest is obtained:

$$r = \frac{l(\bar{A} + \bar{I}) + (M^* - \overline{M})(1 - c)}{b(1 - c + (a/b)l)} \tag{10}$$

(provided $r > r^*$)

The values implied by (9) and (10) correspond to the values of Y and r associated with the intersections of the *IS* (6) and *LM* (8) schedules (Figure 9.3).

It should be noticed that the value of r, so obtained, must be greater than r^*. If it is not, the "liquidity trap" level of the rate of interest prevails, idle balances will absorb whatever cash remains after the needs of active balances have been met, i.e., idle balances are purely residual, and the level of activity will be determined by the consumption function and the level of invest-

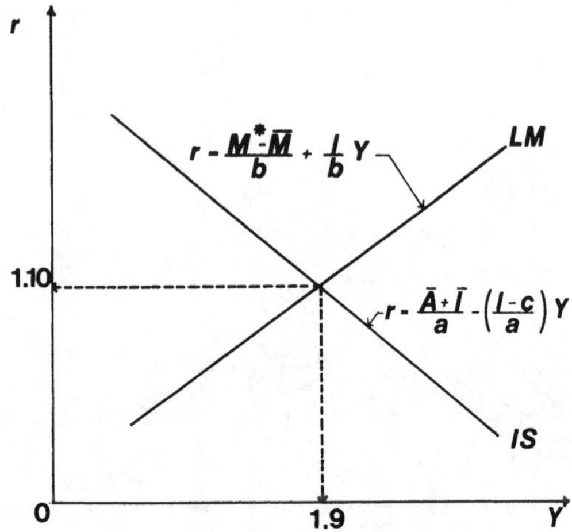

Figure 9.3

ment expenditure associated with the "liquidity trap" level of the rate of interest. The money market therefore has no impact (other than this) on the goods market, and the equilibrium level of real income is obtained from the goods market equilibrium condition, $Y = E$, alone.

Thus $Y = E = \bar{A} + cY + \bar{I} - ar^*$, that is,

$$Y = \frac{\bar{A} + \bar{I} - ar^*}{1 - c}$$

That $r = r^*$ is, of course, an important possibility which should not be lost sight of. For the remainder of this paper, though, it will be assumed that the value of r in Equation (10) exceeds r^* and that the value of Y in Equation (9) is greater than $(br^* + \overline{M} - M^*)/l$, the value of Y at which $r = r^*$ in (8), but is less than the full employment level of real output.[6]

Equation (9) contains elements which are familiar from the simple goods market model of income-determination, namely, the autonomous items of expenditure, $\bar{A}$ and $\bar{I}$, and $1/(1 - c)$, the expression for the simple multiplier: see Harcourt, Karmel, and Wallace (1967, Chs. 4, 10). That (9) reduces to $Y = (\bar{A} + \bar{I})/(1 - c)$ may be seen by supposing that the quantity of money is such that the equilibrium level of income is $(\bar{A} + \bar{I}/a) - [(1 - c/a)]Y$, is the Hicks–Hansen *IS* est, *if it could be established,* is zero. The required value of the stock of money may be found by solving for $\overline{M}$ in

$$\frac{\bar{A} + \bar{I} - (a/b)(M^* - \overline{M})}{1 - c + (a/b)l} = \frac{\bar{A} + \bar{I}}{1 - c}$$

i.e.,

$$\overline{M} = l\left(\frac{\bar{A} + \bar{I}}{1 - c}\right) + M^*$$

With this value of the stock of money, $Y = (\bar{A} + \bar{I})/(1 - c)$ and only a zero value of r is consistent with money market equilibrium. Thus $\bar{M} = M_1 + -M_2$; i.e.,

$$l\left(\frac{\bar{A} + \bar{I}}{1 - c}\right) + M^* = l\left(\frac{\bar{A} + \bar{I}}{1 - c}\right) + M^* - br$$

which is only true when $r = 0$.

So much for special cases. In the general case, the multiplier, which is now $1/[1 - c + (a/b)\,l]$, is seen to be reduced in value, relative to the simple case of $1/(1 - c)$, by elements which determine the absorption into active balances at higher levels of activity. These elements are, respectively, the (absolute) responsiveness of planned investment spending to changes in r (i.e., a), the (absolute) responsiveness of the demand for idle balances to changes in r (i.e., b), and the public's habits with regard to active balances (i.e., l). If a is small, so that planned investment expenditure is *little* affected by a given change in r, if b is large, so that the demand for idle balances is *greatly* affected by a given change in r, and if the public economizes greatly in the use of active balances, so that l is small, the monetary factors have little impact on the flow of induced spending and the value of the multiplier will be close to the simple value.

The multiplicand, $\bar{A} + \bar{I} - (a/b)(M^* - \bar{M})$, also has monetary factors in it. M^* may be regarded as the shift factor of the liquidity preference function – the greater is its value, the greater will be the cash demanded for idle balances at any *given* rate of interest and, *cet.par.*, the lower will be the level of economic activity associated with any given money stock. Given the value of M^*, the magnitude of its impact depends on the *relative* values of a and b. Similarly, the greater is the quantity of money, the higher will be the level of planned investment spending and therefore the greater will be the level of economic activity. The impact of a given quantity of money on the level of economic activity through the multiplicand also depends on the value of a/b.

The value of the equilibrium rate of interest will be greater, the larger are the values of $\bar{A}$, and $\bar{I}$ and M^*, and smaller, the larger is the value of $\bar{M}$. The impact of M^* perhaps needs explaining – the other results are clear intuitively. The larger is the value of M^*, the larger is the demand for idle balances at any *given* rate of interest. Therefore it is to be expected that the higher the value of M^*, the higher the equilibrium value of r and the lower the equilibrium value of Y will be.

The impact of different values of l, a and b on the equilibrium value of r is ambiguous (this is not always true of their impact on the equilibrium value of Y). The different values give rise to conflicting effects on the demand for money and the level of activity. For example, a lower value of l means that, *per unit of real output*, active balances are economised on and so the value of r would be lower. On the other hand, a lower value of r will be associated with a higher level of activity which will tend to offset the initial lower value of r. Which effect predominates depends on the values of other coefficients and autonomous items.[7]

The results to date can be summarized by setting out the impact of unit increases in $\bar{I}$, $\bar{A}$, M^* and $\bar{M}$ respectively, on the equilibrium levels of real income and the rate of interest (see Table 9.1). The signs of the resulting changes are also shown.

So far there has been no mention of the price level. If, for the moment, we may break our rules and use diagrams, there are two simple diagrams which allow the price level to be introduced explicitly. We assume profit-maximizing, price-taking behavior in the goods market so that the short-run equilibrium price equals the marginal cost of production (the money–wage rate divided by the short-run marginal product of labor). The *money*–wage rate is (for the moment) taken as given for the particular short period and there is diminishing marginal productivity of labor as the amount of employment associated with the given stock of capital goods increases.

Table 9.1.

Resulting change in the value of:	Unit change in: $\bar{I}$	$\bar{A}$	$\bar{M}^*$	$\bar{M}$
Y	$\frac{1}{1 - c + (a/b)l}$	as for $\bar{I}$	$-\frac{a/b}{1 - c + (a/b)l}$	$\frac{a/b}{1 - c + (a/b)l}$
r	$\frac{1}{b[1 - c + (a/b)l]}$	as for $\bar{I}$	$\frac{1 - c}{b[1 - c + (a/b)l]}$	$-\frac{1 - c}{b[1 - c + (a/b)l]}$

These assumptions are consistent with Joan Robinson's explanation, in her review of Leijonhufvud (1968), Robinson (1969), of why the British Keynesians "were saved from the misunderstandings rife in America," which Leijonhufvud's work has unravelled. Thus: "we started from the concept of the Marshallian short-period situation in which fixed plant, business organisation and the training of labour are all given and can be more or less fully utilised according to the level of effective demand. A short-period supply curve relating the level of *money* prices to the level of activity (at given money–wage rates) led straight from Marshall to the *General Theory*" (p. 582).

We may suppose also that the demand for money is a function of the money–price level, in the sense that the demand for money for active balances is related to money national income and that the demand for money for idle balances, given the level of r, is a demand for a given amount of money in *real* terms. It follows that, given the underlying demand for money functions and the supply of money, there will be as many *LM* curves as there are possible money–price levels. The lower is the money–price level, the further to the right will be the corresponding *LM* curve, i.e., given the value of r, the higher will be the level of real output that a given stock of money can support: see Figure 9.4(a) where the *LM* curves corresponding to money–price levels of p_1, p_e, and p_2 are shown ($p_1 > p_e > p_2$).

In Figure 9.4(b) we plot, first of all, the downward sloping relationship, $p_{LM,IS}$, between equilibrium real output and each price level which may be derived from the *LM*, *IS* intersections of Figure 9.4(a). It shows the combinations of prices and real incomes that are consistent with equilibrium in the goods and money markets. It ignores the short-run technical conditions of production and, therefore, the level of prices that would "justify" the production of given levels of output in the sense of these levels being profit-maximizing levels. The upward sloping line, p_{MC}, in Figure 9.4(b) shows the short-run marginal cost of producing each level of aggregate output, given the money–wage level and the underlying short-run production (or utilization) function. Each level of *MC* is also the profit-maximizing money price for the corresponding level of output. Where the two intersect, see Y_e, p_e, we have a level of output and a money price which are consistent both with profit-maximizing behavior and with equilibrium in the goods market.

Finally, we select in Figure 9.4(a) the *LM* curve corresponding to the money–price level, p_e, and, thus, the equilibrium rate of interest, r_e. This seems the simplest way of incorporating the money–price level in the "Keynesian" model in a manner which is consistent with the theory of prices that Keynes himself provided in the *General Theory*. (But then, of course, he never did take the twenty minutes necessary to understand the theory of value.) If the money–wage level is itself a function of the level of activity there still will be a unique p_{MC} relationship, but, corresponding to each level of real output, there will be a *different* money–wage level. Nevertheless, this does not ensure that the y_e, p_e intersection is the full employment one.

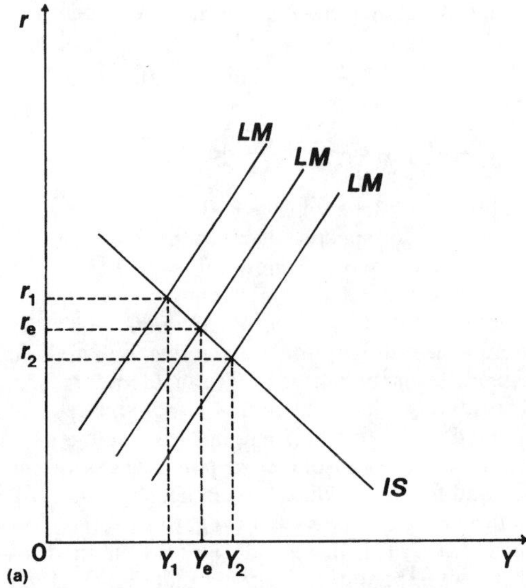

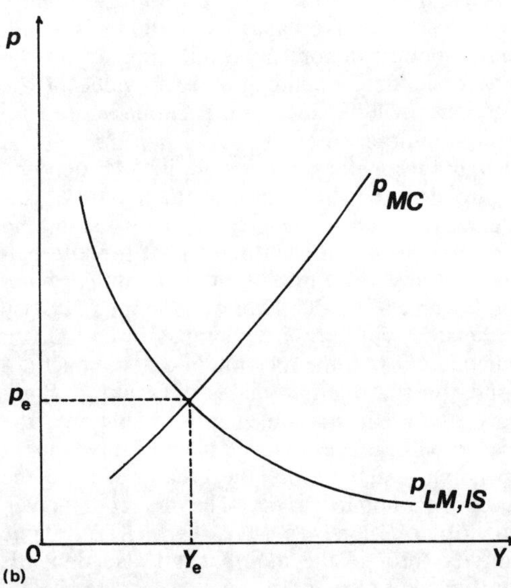

Figure 9.4

The Radcliffe Committee, Gurley and Shaw model

To this point, a strictly "Keynesian" analysis has been presented. In this section some post-"Keynesian" developments associated with the Radcliffe Committee and the works of Gurley and Shaw are introduced.[8] The essential point of these developments is that businessmen and consumers demand liquidity rather than money alone in order to satisfy the transactions and speculative motives. The money market must therefore be regarded as containing at least three assets – money; near-money and bonds; where near-money is short-term assets such as treasury bills and other assets which are traded on the short-term money market.

As a result of the existence of near-money, *shifts* in the functions of the demands for active and idle balances become important determinants of the levels of activity and the rate of interest in the short run. If planned spending rises, it is argued that economies will be made in the use of active balances, so that the demand for active balances will not rise *proportionately* with (money) income. Therefore l cannot be regarded as a constant. Moreover, the liquidity preference schedule may move to the left as well: people may prefer to hold near-money rather than bonds as activity rises because the capital loss is smaller and can be avoided altogether by holding the assets for only a short period of time (Ritter, 1966, p. 167).[9]

These effects are fitted easily into the model presented earlier by making l and M^* *variables* which are functions of the levels of autonomous planned expenditures, $\bar{A}$ and $\bar{I}$. ($\bar{A}$ and $\bar{I}$ are the parameters of the consumption and investment functions which determine their respective positions; changes in $\bar{A}$ and $\bar{I}$ cause the functions to shift.) Thus,

$$l = \bar{l} - j(\bar{A} + \bar{I}) \tag{11}$$

and

$$M^* = \overline{M}^* - k(\bar{A} + \bar{I}) \tag{12}$$

Writing Equations (11) and (12) in this form allows the demand for active balances to increase less than proportionately when income rises and produces the leftward shift in the liquidity preference schedule.

The expressions for the equilibrium values of Y and r now become:

$$Y = \frac{(\bar{A} + \bar{I})(a/b)(\overline{M}^* - k(\bar{A} + \bar{I}) - \overline{M})}{1 - c + (a/b)(\bar{l} - j(\bar{A} + \bar{I}))} \tag{13}$$

and

$$r = \frac{\{\bar{l} - j(\bar{A} + \bar{I})\}(\bar{A} + \bar{I}) + \{\overline{M}^* - k(\bar{I} + \bar{A}) - \overline{M}\}(1 - c)}{b\{1 - c + (a/b)[\bar{l} - j(\bar{A} + \bar{I})]\}} \tag{14}$$

It can be seen that Equations (13) and (14) reduce to Equations (9) and (10), respectively, if l and M^* are constants rather than variables. Now suppose that values of $\bar{l}$, $\overline{M}^*$, j and k, are chosen such that for *given* initial values of $\bar{A}$ and $\bar{I}$, the values of Y and r implied by Equations (13) and (14) are the *same* as those implied by (9) and (10) respectively. Then it is clear that a rise in $\bar{A}$ and/or $\bar{I}$ will have a greater impact on the equilibrium value of Y in the Radcliffe Committee, Gurley and Shaw model than in the "pure" "Keynesian" case. It can also be shown that while the value of r in the "Keynesian" case rises when $\bar{A}$ and/or $\bar{I}$ are increased, it may *fall* in the Radcliffe Committee, Gurley and Shaw case; and, even if it rises, it certainly will not rise by as much as in the "Keynesian" case.[10] It is results of this nature which have lead to suspicion of "pure" monetary policy and concentration, instead, on the importance of overall liquidity.

It should be added that this is as far as this particular form of analysis can go. $[M^* - k(\bar{A} + \bar{I})]$ and $[\bar{l} - j(\bar{A} + \bar{I})]$ are *not* reversible functions. The economies in the use of active (and idle) balances, once learnt, are not forgotten. This model therefore can be used only to make the point that the rise in activity is likely to be greater, following a rise in autonomous expenditure, and the change in the rate of interest is likely to be less than would be predicted by the simple "Keynesian" model with a two-asset money market.

The complex case – goods, money and labor markets, the distribution of income and the price level

In this section the labor market and the price level are considered as well as the goods and money markets: the short-run aggregate production (utilization) function and the different values of the mpc's of wage-earners and profit-receivers, respectively, are introduced. No (short-run) equilibrium condition is assumed in the labor market, i.e., it is assumed that equilibrium in both the money and the goods markets *in the short run* is consistent with the existence of involuntary unemployment. It is also assumed that the money–wage rate is given for the period of the analysis, i.e., that money–wage bargains are remade period by period – and are influenced by factors such as the current level of unemployment, and changes in prices and (national) productivity – but are held for the period concerned.

Similarly, prices are assumed to be constant for the period concerned but to change from period to period due to changes in capacity, labor productivity, expected sales, and the money–wage rate. A very simple form of oligopolistic pricing is assumed, namely, that firms mark up their average wage costs by a percentage markup,[11] the value of which is determined by existing capacity and expected sales. It could be argued that the greater is the existing level of capacity, the smaller will be the markup: and the greater is the existing level of expected sales, the higher will be the markup. Constant rather than diminishing returns to labor are assumed in the short run. These simple assumptions are more in accord with empirical findings concerning pricing and production behavior in manufacturing industry than the usual ones of flexible prices, perfect competition in the goods market, and diminishing marginal productivity of labor in the short run (Neild, 1964). All relevant quantities, unless the contrary is stated, are measured in terms of base period prices (indicated by the subscript b).

The labor market and money wages. The demand for labor may be written as:

$$N = \alpha Y \tag{15}$$

where N = employment per period, α = labor requirement per unit of output (the inverse of labor productivity), and Y = real output, i.e., the demand for labor is simply a derived demand from the goods market determined by expected sales and the short-run aggregate production function.

The money wage equation is:

$$w = \bar{w} \tag{16}$$

where w = money wage and $\bar{w}$ = *current* value.

The price level. The current price of a unit of aggregate real output (P_t) is:

$$P_t = (\bar{w}N/Y)(1 + \bar{v}) = \alpha\bar{w}(1 + \bar{v}) \tag{17}$$

where $\bar{v}$ = the percentage markup.

The price in base period (P_b) is:

$$P_b = \alpha_b\, \bar{w}_b(1 + \bar{v}_b) \equiv 1 \tag{17a}$$

as P_b is the numeraire. α_b is likely to be greater and $\bar{w}_b$ is likely to be less than its current counterpart, but $\bar{v}_b$ may be $\gtreqless \bar{v}_t$.

The goods market. The consumption function: To obtain an expression for the consumption function, it is necessary, first, to look at the national accounts of any period. GNI in terms of *current* prices is:

$$Y_m \equiv W + P \tag{18}$$

where W = total wages, P = total profits, and Y_m = money GNI. Now

$$Y_m \equiv \bar{w}N + \bar{v}\bar{w}N \equiv \bar{w}\alpha Y + \bar{v}\bar{w}\alpha Y \equiv \alpha\bar{w}Y(1 + \bar{v}) \tag{19}$$

It follows that output *in base period prices*, i.e., in real terms, is:

$$Y \equiv Y_m \frac{P_b}{P_t} \equiv \alpha\bar{w}Y(1 + \bar{v})\frac{P_b}{P_t} \tag{20}$$

It can be seen from Equations (19) and (20) that the higher is the money–wage rate, the greater is the money value of wages and profits associated with a given level of real output, but that their *real* values are unchanged because money wages, profits and prices all rise by the *same* proportion; i.e., if

$$\bar{w}_2 > \bar{w}_1,\ \alpha\bar{w}_2Y(1 + \bar{v}) > \alpha\bar{w}_1Y(1 + \bar{v}) \qquad \left(\text{by } \left\{\frac{\bar{w}_2}{\bar{w}_1} - 1\right\}\right)$$

but

$$\alpha\bar{w}_2Y(1 + \bar{v})\frac{P_b}{P_{t_2}} = \alpha\bar{w}_1Y(1 + \bar{v})\frac{P_b}{P_{t_1}}$$

On the other hand, the higher is the value of $\bar{v}$, the higher is the value of total money profits, total money wages remain unchanged, but total *real* wages are less (and total real profits are correspondingly greater). The rise in money profits is $(\bar{v}_2/\bar{v}_1) - 1$ and the rise in prices is $[(1 + \bar{v}_2)/(1 + \bar{v}_1)] - 1$, which is $< (\bar{v}_2/\bar{v}_1) - 1$. That is to say, there is a shift in the distribution of any given level of real income to profit-receivers.

The consumption function in terms of current prices may be written as:

$$\begin{aligned} C_m &= \bar{A}_{w,p}\,(P_t/P_b) + c_w\alpha\bar{w}Y + c_p\bar{v}\alpha\bar{w}Y \qquad (21)\\ &= \bar{A}_{w,p}\,(P_t/P_b) + (c_w + \bar{v}c_p)\alpha\bar{w}Y, \end{aligned}$$

where $\bar{A}_{w,p}$ = autonomous spending on consumption goods (assumed to be fixed in *real* terms) by wage-earners and profit-receivers combined, c_w = mpc of wage-earners, c_p = mpc of profit-receivers, and $c_p < c_w$. In real terms, i.e., Equation (19) is deflated by (P_b/P_t),

$$C = \bar{A}_{w,p} + (c_w + \bar{v}c_p)\alpha\bar{w}\,(P_b/P_t)\,Y \tag{22}$$

It should be noted that the higher is the value of $\bar{v}$ the greater is the share of real profits in any given level of real income; therefore because $c_p < c_w$, the *lower* is the level of planned consumption spending in real terms associated with this level of real income.[12]

The investment function: This is written as before as, for simplicity, planned investment demands are assumed not to be affected by the price level.

$$I = \bar{I} - ar \tag{23}$$

The money market. Demand for active balances: For obvious reasons, money held in *active* balances will be related to the *current* money value of any given level of real output. The M_1 function is therefore written:

$$M_1 = l(P_t/P_b)Y \tag{24}$$

Equation (24) should be compared with Equation (3).

Demand for idle balances: In Patinkin's view (Patinkin, 1965) Keynes would have argued that the demand for idle balances was unaffected by the price level, i.e., that people demand, at any given rate of interest, a certain amount of money for speculative purposes which is not, however, fixed in real terms. That is to say, a money illusion is present. If this view is adopted, the M_2 function may be written as before in Equation (4) i.e., as $M_2 = M^* - br$, for $r > r^*$.

However, if it is believed that people do not suffer from money illusion, i.e., that they demand, at a given rate of interest, a constant amount of money in *real* terms, this effect may be allowed for easily by writing the M_2 function (for $r > r^*$) as:

$$M_2 = (P_t/P_b)(M^* - br) \tag{25}$$

The higher is P_t, the greater is the demand for money to hold in idle balances at any given value of r. In what follows, Equation (25) is used rather than (4); but money illusion easily can be introduced by removing (P_t/P_b) from all money terms.

Supply of money: The supply of money equation is written as before (see Equation (5)):

$$M = \overline{M} \tag{26}$$

Equilibrium values of Y and r. Proceeding as before by imposing the equilibrium conditions in the money and goods markets, the following expressions may be obtained:

Equilibrium rate of interest (first step)

$$r = \frac{lY + M^* - (P_b/P_t)\overline{M}}{b} \tag{27}$$

Equilibrium level of real income

$$Y = \frac{\bar{A}_{w,p} + \bar{I} - (a/b)(M^* - (P_b/P_t)\overline{M})}{1 - \alpha\overline{w}(P_b/P_t)(c_w + \bar{v}c_p) + (a/b)l} \tag{28}$$

Equilibrium rate of interest (second step)

$$r = \frac{l(\bar{A}_{w,p} + \bar{I}) + (M^* - (P_b/P_t)\overline{M})(1 - \alpha\overline{w}(P_b/P_t)(c_w + \bar{v}c_p))}{b(1 - \alpha\overline{w}(P_b/P_t)(c_w + \bar{v}c_p) + (a/b)l)} \tag{29}$$

It should be noted immediately that Equations (27), (28), and (29) reduce to Equations (8), (9), and (10) respectively, if $(P_t/P_b) = 1$, or if the price level is ignored, $c_p = c_w = c$, and $\bar{A}_{w,p} = \bar{A}$. Whenever these conditions do not hold, the new expressions allow the impacts of the price level, different mpc's and the distribution of income on the level of activity and the rate of interest to be analysed. (The Radcliffe Committee, Gurley and Shaw modifications also could be introduced easily.)

With the new expressions it is possible to answer such limited questions as what will be the impact of a lower level of the money–wage on the *equilibrium* values of real output and the rate of interest? What will be the impact of a higher markup on the two equilibrium values? Notice again that these are not equivalent to asking: will a wage cut or a rise in the markup *in fact* raise (or lower) the level of economic activity (though the answer to the second rather than the first of these questions is more likely to be approximated to if the results of the equilibrium comparisons are used).

A lower money wage. The lower is the level of the money wage, the higher will be the equilibrium level of Y and the lower will be the equilibrium value of r. Examining, first Equation (28), it can be seen that the *positive* term, $(a/b)(P_b/P_t)\overline{M}$ in the numerator will be higher, the lower is the value of $\overline{w}$. This is the only term affected by a change in the value of $\overline{w}$, and it *raises* the value of Y. (At first sight, $\alpha\overline{w}(P_b/P_t)(c_w + \bar{v}c_p)$ appears to be affected as well; however, any change in $\overline{w}$ is exactly matched by one of the same amount in P_t, so that the expression as a whole is not affected. This is as it should be since, with the present assumptions, the distribution of income is not affected by a change in the value of $\overline{w}$.

Now examine Equation (29), and remember that conflicting factors are at work. On the one hand, the lower is the price level, the lower is the demand for money to satisfy the transactions demand per unit of *real output* and to satisfy the demand for idle balances at a given rate of interest. These two factors imply a lower rate of interest. On the other hand, the higher is the level of activity, the greater is the proportion of a given stock of money which will go into active balances, and, therefore, the higher will be the rate of interest. It appears, though, that the first two factors outweigh the third, for the only term affected, $-(P_b/P_t)\overline{M}(1 - \alpha\overline{w}(P_b/P_t)(c_w + \bar{v}c_p))$ in the numerator, is greater, the smaller is the value of $\overline{w}$, with the result that the equilibrium rate of interest is less, the smaller is the value of the money–wage rate.

A higher percentage markup. The higher the value of the markup, the lower the equilibrium

Table 9.2

Resulting change in value of:	Unit change in: $\bar{I}, \bar{A}_{w,p}$	M^*	$\bar{M}$
Y	$\frac{1}{1 - \alpha\bar{w}(P_b/P_t)(c_w + \bar{v}c_p) + (a/b)l}$	$-\frac{(a/b)}{1 - \alpha\bar{w}(P_b/P_t)(c_w + \bar{v}c_p) + (a/b)l}$	$\frac{(a/b)(P_b/P_t)}{1 - \alpha\bar{w}(P_b/P_t)(c_w + \bar{v}c_p) + (a/b)l}$
r	$\frac{1}{b[1 - \alpha\bar{w}(P_b/P_t)(c_w + \bar{v}c_p) + (a/b)l]}$	$\frac{1 - \alpha\bar{w}(P_b/P_t)(c_w + \bar{v}c_p)}{b[1 - \alpha\bar{w}(P_b/P_t)(c_w + \bar{v}c_p) + (a/b)l]}$	$-\frac{P_b/P_t[1 - \alpha\bar{w}(P_b/P_t)(c_w + \bar{v}c_p)]}{b[1 - \alpha\bar{w}(P_b/P_t)(c_w + \bar{v}c_p) + (a/b)l]}$

value of real output (beware of monopolists!). The equilibrium value of the rate of interest, however, can be either higher or lower, depending upon the actual values of the conflicting factors at work.

That the first result is so can be seen by examining Equation (28). The value of the positive term, $(a/b)(P_b/P_t)\overline{M}$, in the numerator is reduced and the value of the negative term $\alpha\bar{w}(P_b/P_t)(c_w + \bar{v}c_p)$, in the denominator is also reduced – both of which reduce the value of Y.

The lower equilibrium level of activity would, other things being equal, imply a fall in the equilibrium rate of interest. On the other hand, the higher price level raises the demand for active balances per unit of real output and the demand for idle balances at any given level of the rate of interest. These effects are all reflected in Equation (29) but the outcome is, in general, indeterminate. For completeness, the impacts of unit increases in $\bar{I}$, $\bar{A}_{w,p}$, M^* and $\overline{M}$ on the equilibrium values of Y and r are set out in Table 9.2.

Conclusions

The models presented here can be used to answer questions other than those explicitly mentioned. The questions can refer to short-period puzzles or period by period problems. In the latter case, the model in the section entitled, "the complex case," is especially suited to analysis of the period by period link between money wages, prices, and investment decisions.[13] It is also possible to bring in the rest of the world and government sectors, though, of course, this adds to the complexity of the results. Finally, the present approach makes a convenient link between the simple model of income-determination in the goods market and the capital–stock adjustment models of the trade cycle presented, for example, in Matthews' book on the trade cycle (Matthews, 1959) and Hudson's 1957 article (Hudson, 1957).

Appendix 1

In this appendix the following question is asked: in the simple goods market model, see Harcourt, Karmel, and Wallace (1967, Ch. 10), an increase in investment expenditure of $\Delta\bar{I}$ results in an increase in the equilibrium level of income of $\Delta Y = \Delta\bar{I}[1/(1-c)]$; what *simultaneous* increase in the quantity of money would be necessary in the present model in order that a *horizontal* shift in the investment demand schedule of $\Delta\bar{I}$ will result in an increase in the equilibrium level of Y of $\Delta\bar{I}[1/(1-c)]$? In answering this, it is also shown that the resulting change in the equilibrium level of interest is zero (as is intuitively obvious).

If there is no change in $\overline{M}$, a horizontal shift in the investment demand function of $\Delta\bar{I}$ will result in a rise in the equilibrium level of Y of $\Delta\bar{I}\{1/[1-c+(a/b)l]\}$. The corresponding change in the equilibrium level of r will be $(l/b)[1/[1-c+(a/b)l]]$ (Equation 10). However, the *desired* change in Y is $\Delta\bar{I}[1/(1-c)]$ and so the shortfall of equilibrium Y is:

$$\Delta\bar{I}\left[\frac{1}{1-c} - \frac{1}{1-c+(a/b)l}\right] = \frac{\Delta\bar{I}(a/b)l}{(1-c)[1-c+(a/b)l]} \quad \text{(A.1)}$$

A unit change in the stock of money has an impact on the equilibrium value of Y of $(a/b)/[1-c+(a/b)l]$ (see Equation 9). Therefore, the value of the desired increase in the money supply, $\Delta\overline{M}$, may be found by solving for $\Delta\overline{M}$ in:

$$\frac{\Delta\bar{I}(a/b)l}{(1-c)(1-c+(a/b)l)} = \frac{\Delta\overline{M}(a/b)}{1-c+(a/b)l}$$

i.e.,

$$\Delta\overline{M} = \frac{l\Delta\bar{I}}{1-c} \quad \text{(A.2)}$$

That a simultaneous shift in the investment demand schedule of $\Delta\bar{I}$ and a rise in $\overline{M}$ of $[l\Delta\bar{I}/(1-c)]$ does change the value of Y by $[\Delta\bar{I}/(1-c)]$ can be checked by putting these values in Equation 9 and finding the increase in Y relative to the original value. That $\Delta r = 0$ may be seen by examining Equation (10); the only changes which occur, as between the old and the new levels of Y and r, are:

$$\frac{l}{b}\left[\frac{\Delta\bar{I}}{1-c+(a/b)l}\right] - \frac{\Delta\overline{M}}{b}\left[\frac{1-c}{1-c+(a/b)l}\right] = \frac{l}{b}\left[\frac{\Delta\bar{I}}{1-c+(a/b)l}\right] - \left[\frac{(l\Delta\bar{I})}{b(1-c)}\right]\left[\frac{1-c}{1-c+(a/b)l}\right] = 0$$

Appendix 2: a linear version of the Hudson model of the trade cycle

This appendix shows how the "Keynesian" model can be easily extended to make a linear version of Hudson's model of the trade cycle. The extensions are two: investment is made a function of the level of real output and the capital stock as well as of the rate of interest; and the period to period changes in the capital stock are taken into account.

Goods market equilibrium. The equilibrium condition in the goods market in the short run is still that ex ante S = ex ante I. However, I is now a function of the level of real output and the existing capital stock K as well as of the rate of interest. For simplicity, S remains a function of income only (Hudson makes S a function of r as well, but this does not alter the analysis in any essential way). At low levels of Y (less than $\bar{Y}$), the marginal propensity to save, $(s = 1 - c)$, is assumed to be greater than the marginal propensity to invest (a_1). At high levels, the opposite result is assumed, i.e., $s < a_3$. $\bar{Y}$ might be interpreted, therefore, as the normal level of output for which the existing capital stock is designed. The response of investment to a change in Y therefore will differ as between $Y \leqslant \bar{Y}$ and $Y \geqslant \bar{Y}$, being sluggish and vigorous respectively. Thus

$$S = -\bar{A} + (1 - c)Y = -\bar{A} + sY \qquad \text{(A.3)}$$

and, for $Y \leq \bar{Y}$,

$$I = \bar{I} - ar + a_1 Y - a_2 K, \quad (a_1 < s), \qquad \text{(A.4a)}$$

For $Y \geq \bar{Y}$,

$$I = \bar{I} - ar + a_1 \bar{Y} + a_3(Y - \bar{Y}) - a_2 K, \quad (a_3 > s) \qquad \text{(A.4b)}$$

In any short period (as defined by a *given* value of K) and for all values of Y, there are, therefore, unique values of r which are consistent with equilibrium in the goods market. The IS schedule is obtained by imposing (i) for $Y \leq \bar{Y}$,

$$r = \frac{\bar{I} + \bar{A} - a_2 K}{a} - \left(\frac{s - a_1}{a}\right) Y \qquad \text{(A.5a)}$$

(ii) for $Y \geq \bar{Y}$,

$$r = \frac{\bar{I} + \bar{A} - (a_3 - a_1)\bar{Y} - a_2 K}{a} + \left(\frac{a_3 - s}{a}\right) Y \qquad \text{(A.5b)}$$

The IS schedule therefore contains two sections, one downward-sloping, the other, upward-sloping (see Figure 9.5).

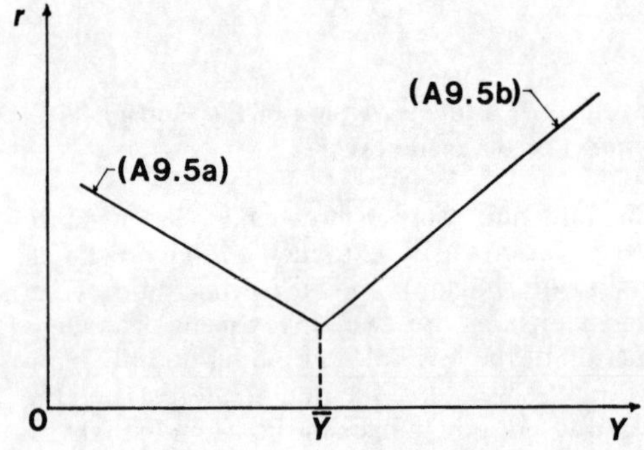

Figure 9.5

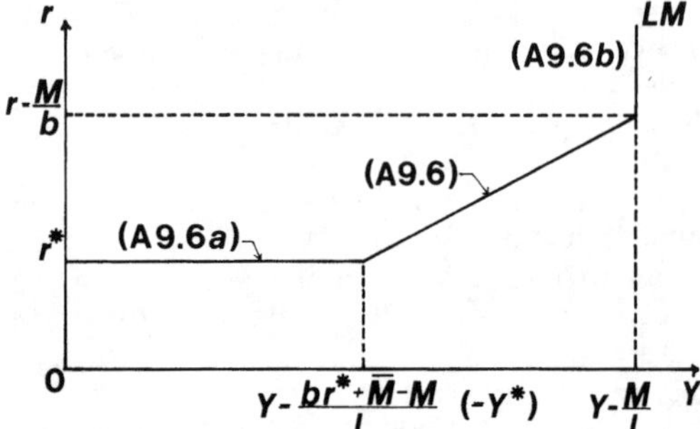

Figure 9.6

Money market equilibrium. A given money supply, $\bar{M}$, is assumed (but the analysis can be easily modified in order to include a flexible money supply, say $M = \bar{M} + b_1 \ (Y - Y^*)$ where $Y^* = (br^* + \bar{M} - M^*)/l$ and $b_1 < l$). The equilibrium condition implies that:

$$r = \frac{M^* - \bar{M}}{b} + (l/b)Y \qquad \text{(A.6)}$$

$$r \geq r^* \quad \text{and} \quad Y \geq \frac{br^* + \bar{M} - M^*}{l} (= Y^*)(> \bar{Y}).$$

For $Y \leq Y^*$,

$$r = r^* \qquad \text{(A.6a)}$$

$$\text{At } Y = \bar{M}/l,\ r = M^*/b \qquad \text{(A.6b)}$$

and Y cannot exceed $\bar{M}/l$, no matter how high is the value of r. The LM schedule therefore has three sections (Figure 9.6).

With a flexible money supply for $Y \leq Y^*$,

$$M = \bar{M} \quad \text{and} \quad r = r^* \qquad \text{(A.6c)}$$

For $Y \geq Y^*$

$$M = \bar{M} + b_1(Y - Y^*) \text{ and}$$

$$r = \frac{M^* - \bar{M} + b_1 Y^*}{b} + \left\{\frac{l - b_1}{b}\right\} Y \qquad \text{(A.6d)}$$

The LM schedule therefore has two sections only (see Figure 9.7) and the upward-sloping section has a flatter slope than its counterpart for a constant money supply. The value of Y^* depends on the value of $\bar{M}$. If the value of $\bar{M}$ with a flexible money supply differs from its value with a constant money supply, the LM schedule starts to rise at a lower (higher) level of Y, according to whether the value for the flexible supply is less than (greater than) the value for the constant supply. (The former case is shown in Figure 9.7.)

Full equilibrium in the short period. Next, the LM and IS schedules are put together. There are, in general, two possible stable equilibrium positions (A and C) and one unstable one (B)

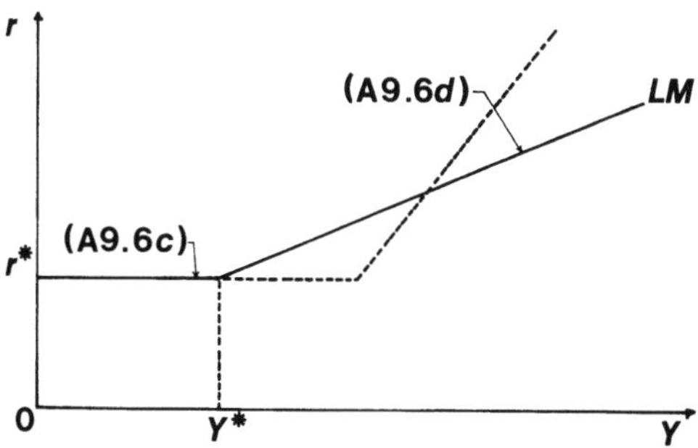

Figure 9.7

(Figure 9.8). At A, which is the intersection of Equation (A.5a) with Equation (A.6a),

$$Y = \frac{\bar{I} + \bar{A} - d_2 K - ar^*}{s - a_1}. \qquad \text{(A.7a)}$$

(Notice that Equation (A.7a) is the simple goods market solution, i.e., Equation (9) of the text, if a_1 and $a_2 K$ are ignored.)

At C (the intersection of Equations 5b and 6)

$$Y = \frac{\{[\bar{I} + \bar{A} - (a_3 - a_1)Y - a_2 K]/a\} - [(M^* - \bar{M})/b]}{(l/b) - [(a_3 - s)/a]} \qquad \text{(A.7b)}$$

IS is less steep than LM at C, which implies that $(l/b) > [(a_3 - s)/a]$ which implies in turn that the denominator of Equation (7b) is positive, for Y *must* be positive. Equation (7b) may also be written as:

$$Y = \frac{\bar{I} + \bar{A} - (a_3 - a_1)\bar{Y} - a_2 K - (a/b)(M^* - \bar{M})}{1 - c - a_3 + (a/b)l} \qquad \text{(A.7c)}$$

which becomes the goods and money market solution, i.e., Equation (9) of the text if a_1, a_3, $\bar{Y}$ and $a_2 K$ are ignored.

The corresponding condition with a flexible money supply is:

$$Y = \frac{\{[\bar{I} + \bar{A} - (a_3 - a_1)\bar{Y} - a_2 K]/a\} - (M^* - \bar{M} + b_1 Y^*)/b)}{[(l - b_1)/b] - [(a_3 - s)/a]} \qquad \text{(A.7d)}$$

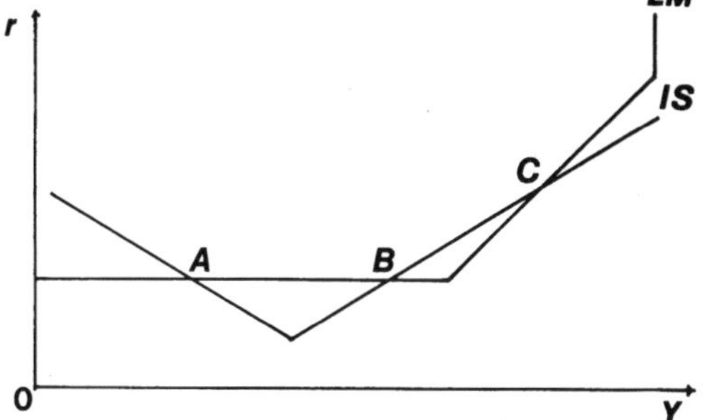

Figure 9.8

The cycle. Suppose the story is started in a slump, i.e., at A. Assume that realised investment per period (as given by Equations (A.7a) and (A.4a) is *less* than depreciation. K will fall from period to period and the IS curve will *rise* (because I is greater, *cet.par.*, the lower is the value of K) until A and B coincide. The economy will then expand to the boom position, C. At C, it may be supposed that gross capital formation is greater than depreciation; the IS curve therefore falls from period to period until C and B coincide, and the economy returns to A.

Hudson adds a number of refinements to this basic analysis which will not be discussed here. The main purpose of the appendix has been to show how this dynamic theory of economic fluctuations can be linked on simply to the comparative statics analysis of the "Keynesian" system.

Notes

1 "Keynesian" is, of necessity, in quotation marks following the publication of Axel Leijonhufvud's *On Keynesian Economics and the Economics of Keynes* (Leijonhufvud, 1968).

2 "Both *ex ante* and *ex post* factors are . . . involved, the expected returns which form the basis of the marginal efficiency of capital are clearly *ex ante* . . . , but the rising supply prices [of capital goods] are in part *ex post*, and the result is neither a relation such as a demand or supply function 'conceptually generated by individual experiments' [n] or a market equilibrium function 'conceptually generated by market experiments'" (Asimakopulos, 1971, pp. 383–84).

3 "May I conclude with some remarks on how the Keynes theory appears to me now, in our present much longer perspective? . . . The *General Theory* was his way of selling his policy to professional economists. It is tailored . . . skillfully . . . to their habit of mind . . . it provides a model on which academic economists can comfortably perform their accustomed tricks. With [*LM-IS*] I myself fell into the trap . . . , [A]t greater distance, we find (I believe) that the *General Theory* loses stature, while the *Treatise* . . . grows. The *General Theory* is a brilliant squeezing of dynamic economics into static habits of thought. The *Treatise* is more genuinely dynamic, and therefore more human" (Hicks, 1973, p. 11).

4 Usually the rate of interest is measured on the vertical axis and the demand for money is measured on the horizontal axis; this follows the Marshallian tradition of putting dependent and independent variables on their respectively "wrong" axes. By reversing this procedure in order to follow the usual mathematical convention I am trying to do for the liquidity preference function what Professor Knight failed to do for demand and supply curves.

5 It is assumed that $\bar{M} \geq lY = l[(A + \bar{I} - ar^*/(1 - c)]$.

6 At $Y \gtrless (br^* + \bar{M} - M^*)/l(= Y^*)$, the amount of money available for idle balances is $\lesseqgtr M^* - br^*$, the demand for money for idle balances at the intersection of Equation (4) with the vertical line at $r = r^*$. Thus when $Y > Y^*$, r must be greater than r^* so that cash is released from idle balances to finance the higher level of active balances.

7 If Equation (10) is partially differentiated with respect to l, whether $(\delta r/\delta l) \gtrless 0$ depends upon whether $(\bar{A} + \bar{I}) \gtrless (a/b)(M^* - \bar{M})$. It is not obvious which of these conditions is most likely to be met.

8 An excellent account of the implications of these developments for the "Keynesian" model is to be found in Ritter (1966). The analysis of this section is an algebraic presentation of Ritter's arguments.

9 Davidson (1972, Ch. 7) has a similar analysis of the Gurley and Shaw case on pp. 181–85 and of the implications of Keynes's finance motive: see, especially, pp. 160–88.

10 To show this, partially differentiate Equations (10) and (14) with respect to $(\bar{A} + \bar{I})$. For (10)

$$\frac{\partial r}{\partial(\bar{A} + \bar{I})} = \frac{l}{b\,(1 - c + (a/b)l)}$$

For (14) the expression for $\partial r/\partial(\bar{A} + \bar{I})$ can be written:

$$\frac{\bar{l} - 2j(\bar{A} + \bar{I}) - (1 - c)k}{b\{1 - c + (a/b)[\bar{l} - j(\bar{A} + \bar{I})]\}} + \frac{[(a/b)j]\{[\bar{l} - j(\bar{A} + \bar{I})][\bar{A} + \bar{I}] + (1 - c)[\bar{M}^* - k(\bar{A} + \bar{I}) - \bar{M}]\}}{b[1 - c + (a/b)(\bar{l} - j(\bar{A} + \bar{I}))]^2}$$

The first part of the expression is smaller than the *whole* of the expression for the partial differentiation of Equation (10) and, for some reasonable values of k, et al., may be <0; the second part of the expression, while almost certainly >0, is *small* in relation to the first part.

11 Strictly speaking, it is their average *direct* costs which *firms* markup. But, for the *economy* as a whole, raw material costs cancel out and it is *as if* overall average wage costs are marked up.

12 From Equations (17) and (22) we obtain:

$$C = \bar{A}_{w,p} + \frac{c_w + \bar{v}c_p}{1 + \bar{v}} P_b Y \qquad (22a)$$

$$\frac{c_w + \bar{v}c_p}{1 + \bar{v}} = \frac{1}{1 + \bar{v}} c_w + \frac{\bar{v}}{1 + \bar{v}} c_p,$$

where the "weights", $1/(1 + \bar{v})$ and $\bar{v}/(1 + \bar{v})$ are the respective shares of wages and profits in a unit of output, and $[(c_w + \bar{v}c_p/(1 + \bar{v})]P_b$ is the overall mpc. It is obvious that, when $\bar{v}$ rises, the first "weight" declines and the second rises; thus because $c_p < c_w$, the overall mpc declines.

13 The forms that these links might take have been discussed in the author's paper, Harcourt (1965).

References

Ackley, G. 1961. *Macroeconomic Theory*. New York: Macmillan.

Asimakopulos, A. 1971. "The Determination of Investment in Keynes's Model," *Canadian Journal of Economics*, Vol. 4: pp. 382–88.

Davidson, P. 1972. *Money and the Real World*. London: Macmillan.

Gurley, J. G., and Shaw, E. G. 1960. *Money in a Theory of Finance*. Washington, D.C.: The Brookings Institution.

Harcourt, G. C. 1965. "A Two-sector Model of the Distribution of Income and the Level of Employment in the Short Run," *Economic Record*, Vol. 41: pp. 103–17.

1969. "A Teaching Model of the 'Keynesian' System," *Keio Economic Studies*, Vol. 6: pp. 23–46.

Harcourt, G. C., Karmel, P. H., and Wallace, R. H. 1967. *Economic Activity*. Cambridge: Cambridge University Press.

Hicks, J. 1973. "Recollections and Documents," *Economica*, 40: pp. 2–11.

Hudson, H. R. 1957. "A Model of the Trade Cycle," *Economic Record*, 33: pp. 378–89.

Keynes, J. M. 1936. *The General Theory of Employment, Interest and Money*. London: Macmillan.

Leijonhufvud, A. 1968. *On Keynesian Economics and the Economics of Keynes*. New York: Oxford University Press.

Matthews, R. C. O. 1959. *The Trade Cycle*. Cambridge: Cambridge University Press.

Neild, R. R. 1964. *Pricing and Employment in the Trade Cycle*. Cambridge: Cambridge University Press.

Patinkin, D. 1965. *Money, Interest and Prices*. 2nd ed. New York: Harper & Row.

Report of the *Committee on the Working of the Monetary System*. 1959. London: Government Printer.

Ritter, L. S. 1966. "The Role of Money in the Keynesian System," in M. G. Mueller, ed. *Readings in Macroeconomics*. New York: Holt, Rinehart and Winston.

Robinson, J. 1969. "Review of Axel Leijonhufvud, *On Keynesian Economics and the Economics of Keynes*, 1968," *Economic Journal*, Vol. 79: pp. 581–83.

1971. *Economic Heresies: Some Old-fashioned Questions in Economic Theory*. New York: Basic Books.

10

A simple framework for the analysis of taxation, distribution, and effective demand

John Eatwell

Development of the theory of fiscal policy has been inhibited by the lack of a satisfactory theory of real fiscal incidence. By default, fiscal policies are proposed, analyzed and implemented using the naive assumption that the real incidence of fiscal measures is the same as their legal incidence.

The problem of the real incidence of the fiscal activity of the state has two dimensions:

1. The relationship between nominal tax rates (legal incidence) and the real distribution of income for any *given* level and composition of total output; and
2. The relationship between the mix of tax rates, the overall scale of fiscal activity, and the level and composition of effective demand.

The formidable complexity of the problem derives from the necessity of tackling both dimensions at the same time, and at the general (as opposed to the partial) level. This requires the integration of a theory of value and distribution with the theory of effective demand.

The objective here is to present a framework of analysis which is suited to this task. This framework is used to identify the crucial elements which must be incorporated into a full theory of fiscal incidence; it provides a setting within which such elements may be combined and manipulated, and represents, in itself, a check on the conditions which any theory of incidence must satisfy. The formal framework is constructed on a basis of strong simplifying assumptions, but is capable of extensive generalization. The incorporation of more complex relationships between the variables, or the extension of the framework to include functional specification of what are here expressed as constants, would make the analysis more complicated, but would not invalidate the general approach. Some suggestions for generalization are given in the notes.

In addition to presentation of the formal model, the argument stresses the importance of relating the analytical framework to the institutional environment in which the processes determining distribution operate, in particular those forces acting on the real wage.

The first part of this essay consists of an outline of the basic method adopted for the analysis of the relationship between value, distribution, and effective demand. The second and third parts contain the core of the argument: first, the distributional impact of taxes on wages and profits at any given level of output; and second the general analysis of the implications of fiscal activity for the distribution of income and the level of effective demand.

Distribution and effective demand

Analyses of taxation and fiscal incidence attempted within the framework of the neoclassical theory of value have proved unequal to the task (Mieszkowski, 1969). For within that framework prices, the composition of output and the scale of output are inextricably linked and must all be determined simultaneously. But the neoclassical theory of output (and hence all other parts of the theory too) is incompatible with the basic principles of the Keynesian theory of effective demand, and cannot, therefore, be a part of the necessary integration of the two dimensions of the problem identified above (Garegnani, 1978, 1979).

A quite different approach is that pioneered

I am grateful to Franco Donzelli, Geoff Meeks, Anwar Shaikh, Ian Steedman, and to the members of the editorial board seminar of the *Cambridge Journal of Economics* for aid and advice. I have also benefited from having seen unpublished work on this topic by Bob Rowthorn.

by Kalecki.[1] This involves an initial separation of the analysis of prices and distribution and the analysis of effective demand, and their subsequent combination to provide a general theory of the level and distribution of output. Kalecki's theory is the starting point for this essay, but first it must be rid of a significant weakness which is of particular importance in the analysis of fiscal incidence. Kalecki's theory of distribution, based on his concept of a normal markup determined by the degree of monopoly, is essentially *partial*. It is partial because it fails to take into account the fact that the markup in any one sector of the economy is a component of the costs of other sectors. The markup is, therefore, not only a reflection of the competitive conditions in particular markets, but also, more important, a reflection of the general rate of profit (and hence the general level of real wages) ruling in the economy as a whole. Only by examination of the determinants of distribution at this general, economy-wide, level, can the distributional ramifications of any particular change in circumstances, such as a change in fiscal policy, be properly analyzed. A partial analysis is incomplete and, inevitably, arbitrary.

The classical approach to the analysis of value and distribution provides a way out of the dilemma. In the classical formulation, in contrast to neoclassical theory, the determination of prices and distribution is treated separately from the determination of the scale and composition of output. In the analysis of value and distribution the scale and composition of output, the technique in use, and the real wage (all of which are, in principle, objectively measurable in physical terms) are taken as data; and, as is now well known, these data are sufficient for the determination of the rate of profit and all prices (hence sectoral markups, and the overall share of profit).[2] The problem of effective demand may then be expressed in terms of the conditions which ensure that there is sufficient demand to realize that scale and composition of output at those prices.

Suppose, for example, that the economy is characterized as consisting of a circulating capital technology defined by the $m \times m$ input–output matrix A (which is assumed to be indecomposable – all the produced commodities are basics), and the $m \times 1$ labor input vector a_0.[3] The price equations for this economy are then

$$Ap(1 + r) + a_0 w = p \qquad (1)$$

where p is the $m \times 1$ vector of prices, r and w, both scalars, are, respectively, the rate of profit and the wage rate.[4] In this section of the chapter, w will be set equal to one as numeraire, which means that all prices are expressed in terms of labor commanded.

The quantity system associated with this price system is

$$A'x + y = x \qquad (2)$$

where x and y are the $m \times 1$ vectors of gross and net output respectively; A' = transpose A. The value of net output in terms of the wage is $p'[I - A']x = p'y$, the value of total net profits $rp'A'x$, and the level of employment $a_0'x$.

As was shown by Kalecki, if it is assumed that workers do not save, and that the saving propensity of the capitalists is positive and less than, or equal to, one, then the relationship between investment and the overall level of activity may be expressed as a relationship between the value of net investment, the aggregate value of net profits and the shares of wages and profits in net output (which in turn depend on the rate of profits and the composition of output). If $p'y_I$ is the value of net investment, and there are no savings out of wages, then

$$rp'A'x = p'y_I k \qquad (3)$$

where $y_I = [I - A']x_I$ is the vector of goods comprising net investment, x_I the vector of goods comprising gross outputs in the investment sector, and $k = 1/s_p$, where s_p is the saving propensity of the capitalists.

Equation (3) may also be written as

$$rp'A'x = rp'A'x_I k + a_0'x_I k \qquad (4)$$

where the r.h.s. is the value-added in the production of investment goods multiplied by k. From this equation it is found that

$$rp'A'x_c = rp'A'x_I(k - 1) + a_0'x_I k \qquad (5)$$

where x_c is the vector of commodities required to maintain the net output of consumption goods $y_c = [I - A']x_c$. So from Equation (5) consumption sector profits are seen to be equal to the sum of the proportion of investment sector profits consumed $[k - 1 = (1 - s_p)k]$ and investment sector wages, multiplied by k.

The relationship between the distribution of income and the level of activity may be ascertained from (5). To simplify the analysis it is assumed that the economy operates under conditions of constant returns to scale,[5] and that the commodity compositions of x_c and x_I, and hence of y_c and y_I, do not vary with the scale of activity.

If two of the possible levels of the rate of profit between zero and the maximum are compared at the higher level all prices will be higher in terms of the wage – the real wage will be lower in terms of any commodity.

Suppose, first, that the volume of net investment is fixed as an amount of value, $p'y_I$ = a constant. Then, at the higher rate of profit y_I must be lower. Then x_I and x_c and the level of employment $a_0'[x_I + x_c]$ must be lower, since the r.h.s. of (5) is lower[6] while r and all p_i are higher (Schwartz, 1961, p. 34; Sraffa, 1960, pp. 38–40). This result is so straightforward because the composition of x_c and x_I are unchanged. If the composition of x_c and/or x_I were different as between the two situations, then the overall result would depend on the different commodity components of the weighted sums of profits and wages.[7]

If, on the other hand, the volume of investment is assumed to be fixed in real terms the analysis is a little more complicated. Suppose first that $k = 1$, $(s_p = 1)$. Then if r and p are higher x_c must be lower, and real investment being assumed constant, total output and employment must be lower. If $k > 1$, however, the result is no longer clear cut, but will depend on the proportion of profit in the value added of each commodity and the commodity composition of x_c and x_I. Should k be large, and the proportion of profit in the value added of the commodities comprising x_I be high relative to that of the commodities comprising x_c, then the increased spending on consumption by capitalists consequent upon an increase in the share of profits may outweigh the effect of the decline in the real wage. So, depending on these factors, x_c, x, and the level of employment may be higher or lower at higher r. Once again the result would be yet more complex if it were not assumed that the composition of all quantity vectors is unchanging.

Instead of considering the effect on output and employment of a change in distribution with net investment fixed in real or money terms, the relationship (5) may be viewed the other way around. Any increase in net investment, the rate of profit and the commodity composition of x_c being constant, will result in a higher level of activity.

But in whatever direction the problem is considered, the analysis still contains one degree of freedom. The model is incomplete without either a theory of the real wage or a theory of the rate of profit. This aspect of the model will be considered in the third part of the paper.

Taxation and the wage-profit line

This section is devoted to consideration of the impact of the introduction of taxes on wages and profits into the analysis of prices, the rate of profit, and the wage rate. Previous discussions of the subject (Metcalfe and Steedman, 1971) have concentrated solely on the effect of the imposition of taxes, including indirect taxes, on the form and location of the posttax profit–wage line and on prices, without attempting either to close the system or to relate taxation and distribution to the problem of effective demand. The two latter tasks will be discussed in the next section.

It is assumed that wages and profits are taxed at the proportional rates, t_w and t_p respectively.[8] The aftertax rate of profit, $r^* = (1 - t_p)r$ and the aftertax wage, $w^* = (1 - t_w)w$. Using these definitions the price Equation (1) may be rewritten

$$Ap\left(1 + \frac{r^*}{1 - t_p}\right) + a_0\frac{w^*}{1 - t_w} = p \qquad (6)$$

The pretax wage–profit line, $w = f(r)$, implicit in Equation (1) can now be compared with the posttax wage–profit line, $w^* = \phi(r^*)$, derived from Equation (6). If $t_p = 0$ and $1 > t_w > 0$, the posttax line is a contraction of the pretax line toward the profit axis. Similarly, if $t_w = 0$ and $1 > t_p > 0$, the posttax line is a contraction of the pretax line toward the wage axis. As t_w tends to one, or t_p tends to one, the posttax line tends to the profit axis, or to the wage axis, respectively.[9] In Figure 10.1 the pre- and posttax wage–profit lines are drawn for a given positive value of t_w with t_p equal to zero.

The relationship between the pre- and posttax distributions of income will depend on the phenomena embodied in the two wage–profit lines *and* on the underlying forces determining the

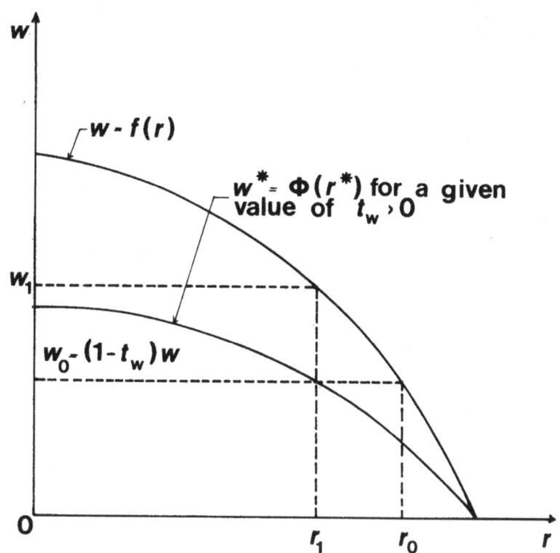

Figure 10.1

distribution of income in the economy. An hypothesis on the nature of these forces must be added to the model for a complete analysis.

Taxes, prices, and output

The analysis of the second section may now be integrated with an analysis of effective demand. To facilitate the discussion it will be assumed that all state expenditure is *exhaustive* expenditure, implying direct utilization of productive resources; all financial transfers, including interest payments on the debt, will be ignored. It will also be assumed, to begin with, that government expenditure and private investment are given in real terms. The economy is assumed to be closed.

The two last assumptions imply that variation in the overall level of activity can only derive from variation in the level of consumption. Thus, if the state wishes to maintain a particular level of activity its fiscal policy will be based on the necessity of ensuring the requisite volume of consumption expenditure.

The complete system consists of the price equations

$$Ap(1 + r) + a_0 w = p$$

and the effective demand relationship

$$s_p(1 - t_p)rp'Ax' + t_p rp'A'x + t_w wa_0'x = p'[y_G + y_I] \quad (7)$$

where y_G is the $m \times 1$ vector of commodities absorbed by government expenditure. Equation (7) expresses the familiar proposition that the sum of the values of net investment and government expenditure is equal to the sum of private net saving and taxation (s_w, it will be remembered, is assumed equal to zero).[10] The system consists of $m + 1$ equations which contain $2m + 3$ unknowns: $m - 1$ prices; the m components of x; r, w, t_p ad t_w. Since y_G and y_I are taken as given, and the composition of x_c is assumed fixed, the composition of x for any given scale of total activity is known from the condition $x = x_c + x_I + x_G$, hence only the overall scale of activity remains to be determined. So having eliminated $m - 1$ unknowns by this latter condition the three remaining degrees of freedom may be summarized as the distribution of income, the combination of tax rates, and the overall level of activity.[11]

With respect to the distribution of income it has already been noted above that the posttax distribution of income will depend on the posttax wage–profit line, *and* on the more fundamental forces acting on the distribution of income in a particular concrete situation. Frank Wilkinson has argued that in recent years the working class bargains for, and, in the absence of state intervention, successfully maintains, the real value of *posttax* wages. Wilkinson's study suggests that ". . . because the steady increase in wages in the market industrial countries has pushed a rising proportion of workers into the net of generally progressive tax systems, trends in *net* real wages – *i.e.* after allowing for direct tax and related deductions as well as for price changes – may be the more relevant parameter of reference [in the analysis of the labour market]." (Jackson, et al., 1972, p. 64.) In his 1972 paper Wilkinson argued that the struggle of workers to maintain the accustomed level and rate of increase in real posttax incomes ". . . was far from fully successful, for reasons partly intrinsic to the process and partly arising from the fiscal beliefs of governments. But it contributed very substantially (to say the least) to both industrial unrest and inflation." (Jackson, et al., 1972, p. 102.)

In a more recent paper, Coutts, Tarling, and Wilkinson have revised this conclusion and argued for a "real compensation" theory of wage inflation in the United Kingdom. They support their viewpoint with evidence that there exists an "underlying trend rate of growth" in real posttax wages, and that "periods of accelerating inflation are shown by [econometric analysis] to be only a catching-up process, returning real wages to their historical trend." (Cambridge Economic Policy Group, 1976, p. 27.)

If the workers do indeed succeed in maintaining posttax real income, then with the imposition of a given rate of tax on wages, the pretax real wage would have to be higher and in consequence the rate of profit would be lower than would be the case at a lower rate of taxation. This situation is illustrated in Figure 10.1, which is drawn taking a given real wage bundle as numeraire.[12] For the posttax real wage to remain constant at w_0 after the imposition of a wages tax, the pretax wage must be higher at w_1, and the rate of profit must be lower at r_1 instead of r_0.

The hypothesis of a successfully maintained posttax real wage will be used in most of the argument which follows, but two alternative hypotheses can be briefly considered.

Figure 10.2 is an illustration of the situation in which there are taxes on both wages and profits, and in which the capitalists succeed in maintaining a constant markup of pretax profit over pretax wages, $r = qw$.[13] In this case real and nominal incidence must coincide, for otherwise the imposition of taxes would lead to an alteration in the size of q, contrary to the hypothesis that q is a constant. Finally, if capitalists man-

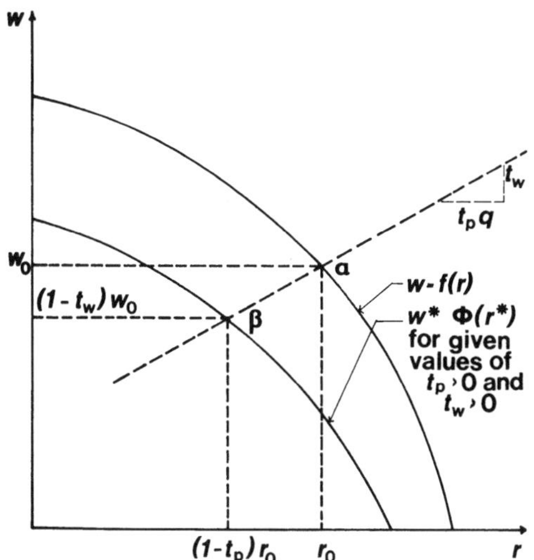

Figure 10.2

age to maintain the posttax rate of profit, then all taxes fall on wages.

The introduction of taxation into the wage–profit analysis implies the introduction of an additional institutional dimension, in the shape of the state, into the distribution process.[14] Since it is assumed here that the posttax wage is a constant, one degree of freedom in the system is eliminated. If it is further assumed that the state attempts to maintain a target level of activity $\bar{x}$, (and hence a target level of x_c) then the remaining degree of freedom rests in the set of combinations of the tax rates t_w and t_p which will result in the attainment of that objective.

To examine the implications of the argument in a simple setting Equations (1) and (7) may be rewritten for the case of a one-commodity world. One-commodity examples must be treated with some care, especially in cases such as this in which the problem of the distribution of income is involved. But while generalization to many commodities will affect the shape of some of the functions yet to be discussed, and, if the composition of output varies, introduce formidable complexity, the general structure of the analysis will not be altered. Assuming a unit of the single commodity to be the amount produced by one worker in one production period (so that $a_0 = 1$) the single commodity equations are

$$a(1 + r) + w = 1 \tag{1a}$$

$$s_p(1 - t_p)rax + t_p rax + t_w wx = y_G + y_I \tag{7a}$$

where a is the input coefficient of the single commodity into its own production. If the condition

$$(1 - t_w)w = w^* = \text{constant}$$

is added, and it is assumed that the state adjusts fiscal policy to achieve a target level of output $\bar{x}$, (which, because of the commodity unit chosen, is equal to the target level of employment) then (1a) and (7a) may be solved for the relationship between t_w and t_p (the algebra underlying the following discussion is presented in the appendix):

$$t_w = \frac{n + w^*z - bz}{n + w^* - bz} \tag{8}$$

where $b = 1 - a$, i.e. net output per worker; $n = (y_G + y_I)/\bar{x}$, i.e., the ratio of government expenditure and net investment to target gross output; and $z = s_p(1 - t_p) + t_p$, i.e., the proportion of profits not consumed. Since the posttax real wage is assumed constant, the target level of output can only be attained by manipulating the level of capitalists' consumption.[15] Real government expenditure, private investment and workers' consumption being given, all combinations of tax rates in (8) represent different means by which fiscal policy can result in the same posttax rate of profit, and hence, given s_p, the level of capitalists' consumption appropriate to attainment of the target level of output. The set of pairs of tax rates appropriate to the target level of output and the pretax distribution of income implied in the choice of tax rates is shown in Figure 10.3.

From Figure 10.3 it may be seen that with t_w relatively high and t_p relatively low, the requisite level of the posttax rate of profit is attained because the pretax wage rate is high and the pretax rate of profit consequentially low. If t_w is relatively low and t_p relatively high, then capitalist consumption is limited primarily by profits taxation.

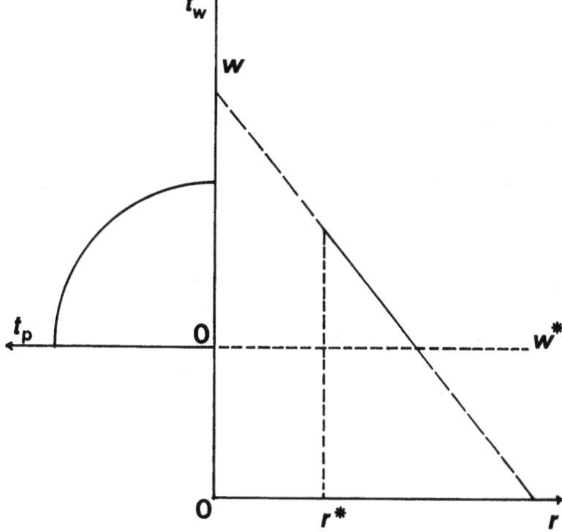

Figure 10.3

Although the outcome in terms of capitalists' consumption is the same in either circumstance, it is not obvious that the reaction of the capitalists will in both cases be the same. Should capitalists suffer from money illusion then they will prefer high pretax profits with high profits taxes. Should they suffer from tax phobia they will prefer the contrary.

Should they, however, demand a level of consumption higher than that implied by the value of r^* while still consuming the same proportion of profits, the system will be overdetermined.[16] The posttax wage target and the posttax profits target will both be sought in vain in a continuous inflationary spiral. The inflationary pressure will only be mitigated either by productivity increase in excess of the trend rate of increase of posttax real wages, or an upward revision of the target level of output, or by reduction in government expenditure and/or investment in favor of capitalists' consumption.

The simplification of the one-commodity world was introduced to illustrate the combinations of wage and profits taxes compatible with w^* and the target level of output. But the effects of different tax rates will be manifest through relative prices. Returning to the general system (1) and (7) we see that for given y_g, y_I and x_c, prices may be defined as functions of the distribution of income and of one of the tax rates. Of considerable importance for fiscal policy will be the price ratio between consumption goods, on the one hand, and investment goods on the other. This point may be particularly well illustrated by assuming consumption goods to be non-basics, and specifying the real-wage target in terms of consumption good prices. Supposing for the moment there to be one generic investment good and one generic consumption good, then the price ratio between these two goods may, for given w^*, be expressed as a function of t_w *alone*; i.e. as may be seen from Figure 10.3 given t_w, r and w (and t_p) are determined, and hence all prices are determined. Further elaborations are left to the reader.

Conclusions

The main objective here, apart from presentation of the formal analysis, is to emphasize the importance of social and political factors in the study of the economic outcome of fiscal activity. The formal model embodies many strong assumptions chosen to reduce the complexity of the argument; but, in general, the results would not be radically altered if some of these assumptions were relaxed.

If workers' saving is included in the analysis, for example, and workers achieve a given posttax real income (including posttax interest on savings) then capitalists' consumption remains the residual element in the determination of the level of activity. Should workers achieve only given posttax real wages, then workers' consumption out of nonwage receipts is also a part of the residual element.

Alternative distributional hypotheses may also be fitted into the same framework. As was noted earlier, adoption of the hypothesis of a fixed markup of pretax profits on pretax wages implies that nominal and real incidence coincide. The set of possible combinations of tax rates will then depend on the target level of activity. The total volume of taxation must be higher if taxes fall primarily on profits rather than on wages, to take account of the relatively high proportion of profits saved.

The most important assumption in the manipulation of the model was that the proportionate composition of the commodity vectors x_c, x_I, y_G were fixed. Relaxation of this assumption would complicate the analysis considerably. If the compositions of these vectors are unknowns then, even under the assumption of constant returns to scale, it is not possible to specify the location of the t_p, t_w line; a theory (or theories) of expenditure must be added to complete the model. However, for the purposes of empirical work it should be noted that while over a long period of time considerable changes in commodity compositions are inevitable, over the time span in which any given set of relationships is likely to have operational content, changes in composition are likely to be of lesser significance.

The intrusion of the state into the determination of the real distribution of income is an important facet of this analysis. For not only must the state step in to mitigate the consequences of contradictory real claims by workers and capitalists, but also by its manipulation of the level of activity it can attempt to reinforce or to frustrate particular claims. This manipulation will be complicated by balance of payments considerations in an open economy and by the fact that private real investment is probably not independent of tax rate changes, even if the same level of activity is maintained. Furthermore, the influence of fiscal policies alone is unlikely to be adequate for economic management, particularly in the case of contradictory claims on real output, and then the state must involve itself more directly in the process of the determination of posttax real incomes, as well as in the forces underlying the labor process, the level of investment, technical change, and other facets of the evolution of the system.

Appendix

The one-commodity system examined in the third section is based on two equations

$$a(1 + r) + w = 1 \tag{A.1}$$

the distribution equation, and

$$s_p(1 - t_p)rax + t_prax + t_wwx = y_G + y_I \tag{A.2}$$

the effective demand equation.

From the equation of the wage–profit line

$$r = [(1 - a)w]/a \tag{A.3}$$

Use the following definitions: $(1 - a)$ (net output per worker) $= b$; $s_p(1 - t_p) + t_p$ (nonconsumed proportion of profits) $= z$; $y_G + y_I/x$ (proportion of government expenditure and net investment in gross output) $= n$; and $(1 - t_w)w = w^*$. Equations (A.1) and (A.2) may be solved for the relationship between t_w and t_p, n and w^* being taken as constants:

$$t_w = \frac{n + w^*z - bz}{n + w^* - bz} \tag{A.4}$$

The characteristics of the relationship are

$$t_w\max(t_p = 0) = \frac{n + (w^* - b)\, s_p}{n + w^* - bs_p}$$

$$t_p\max(t_w = 0) = \frac{n + (w^* - b)\, s_p}{-(w^* - b)(1 - s_p)}$$

$$\frac{dt_w}{dt_p} = \frac{w^*(n + w^* - b)(1 - s_p)}{(n + w^* - bz)^2} < 0 \tag{A.5}$$

since b (net output per worker) $> n + w^*$ as long as consumption out of profits is greater than zero.

$$\frac{d^2t_w}{dt_p{}^2} = \frac{2w^*b(1 - s_p)^2(n + w^* - b)(n + w^* - bz)}{(n + w^* - bz)^4} \tag{A.6}$$

the sign of which depends on the sign of $(n + w^* - bz)$.

From (A.4) $1 - t_w = [w^*(1 - z)]/(n + w^* - bz)$, and hence $w = (n + w^* - bz)/(1 - z)$. Now since $1 - z \equiv (1 - s_p)(1 - t_p) \geq 0$ then $n + w^* - bz > 0$. So the second differential is negative and the t_p, t_w line is concave to the origin.

The negative sign of dt_w/dt_p may readily be demonstrated for the multicommodity case by means of the Frobenius theorem. The requisite level of activity implies target levels of w^* and r^*. Given w^* and r^* the inverse relation between t_w and t_p may be proved for Equation (6) in the same manner as the customary proof of the inverse relation between w and r (Schwartz, 1961, pp. 32–34).

Notes

1 Kalecki's first essay on effective demand was published in 1933, three years before Keynes's *General Theory*. (See Kalecki, 1971, Ch. 4.)

2 Since capitalists attempt to maximize the return on their financial wealth, there will always be a tendency toward a uniform rate of profit in a capitalist economy. This tendency will be frustrated by transitory events, such as new inventions or inaccurate estimation of demand, and by systematic phenomena, such as barriers to entry. Nonetheless the rate of profit remains a "center of gravity" of the system, and taking the rate of profit as uniform is the best starting point for a general analysis of distribution in a capitalist economy.

3 Although the notation of input–output coefficients is used there is no necessity to assume constant returns to scale. The analysis would go just as well if the coefficients of A and a_0 varied with changes in any or all of the activity levels.

4 If the rate of profit were not uniform, but systematically differentiated between sectors, Equation (1) would be written $HAp(1 + r) + a_0 = p$, where H is a diagonal matrix, the coefficients of which define the magnitude of differentiation between the profit rates of the various sectors, with, say, $h_{11} = 1$, $h_{22} = .8$, $h_{33} = 1.1$, and so on. H, therefore, encapsulates the systematic phenomena leading to differentiation of profit rates referred to in note 2.

5 The assumption of constant returns to scale is a simplifying assumption, it is not a necessary assumption; see note 3.

6 On the r.h.s. of (5) $rp'A'x_I + a_0'x_I = p'y_I$ = a constant by assumption, so the increase in $rp'A'x_I$ consequent upon an increase in r and p is matched by an equal and opposite diminution in $a_0'x_I$, (x_I must diminish since y_I is lower). Since the multiplier on profits is less than that on wages the r.h.s. of (5) is lower.

7 If the composition of x_c and x_I varies the outcome in terms of employment depends on the relative prices of the components of x_I, the relative shares of profit in the value added of the components of x_c and x_I, and the "labor intensity" of production given by the elements of a_0.

8 Tax rates may be negative, in which case they constitute subsidy rates; and greater than one in the case of t_p. It is assumed here, however, that the proportionate rates lie between zero and one inclusive.

9 Metcalfe and Steedman define their tax rates with respect to posttax incomes, rather than in the more usual manner with respect to pretax incomes as is done here (Metcalfe and Steedman, 1971, pp. 177–78).

10 If transfer payments by the state were included in the analysis the value of transfers should appear on the r.h.s. of (6) and taxation of transfers and saving out of transfers should appear on the l.h.s.

11 Fixing any three of the five variables r, w, t_p, t_w, x will determine the other two. However it seems most sensible to divide the degrees of freedom into the three groups listed in the text.

12 The wage is expressed in terms of a composite

wage good, G, consisting of s wage goods in the given quantities $g_1, g_2 \ldots g_s$. The real wage is defined as so many units of the composite good. Since the wage good is taken as numeraire, the value of one unit of G, $\Sigma g_i p_i = 1$ (Garegnani, 1970, p. 418).

13 Markups are expressed in terms of the share of profits in each sector rather than the rate of profit. But for a given composition of output there is a direct relation between mark-ups and the rate of profit which, in our example, may be embodied in the single coefficient q.

14 "The effect of the generally increased incidence of wage-taxation is to make the effective process of the determination of employee living standards . . . [a] highly . . . politicized one . . ." (Jackson, et al., 1972, p. 103).
"The view put forward here is that since political and social factors, though these are influenced by economic events, are so important, a good statistical explanation of real wages in terms of economic variables is unlikely to be found" (Cambridge Economic Policy Group, 1976, p. 27).

15 Given the assumptions of this section fiscal manipulation of the level of activity is not possible in the case in which $s_p = 1$, for in these circumstances variation in taxation cannot, with a given posttax real wage, lead to variation in consumption.

16 Capitalists will seek a particular level of r^* both to maintain their consumption, and to limit the long-run proportion of investment financed by borrowing of one form or another.

References

Cambridge Economic Policy Group. 1976. *Economic Policy Review*, No. 2. Cambridge: Cambridge University Department of Applied Economics.

Garegnani, P. 1970. "Heterogeneous Capital, the Production on Function and the Theory of Distribution," *Review of Economic Studies*, 37, pp. 407–36.

1978, 1979. "Notes on Consumption, Investment and Effective Demands," *Cambridge Journal of Economics*, 2, pp. 335–53, pp. 63–82.

Jackson, S., Turner, H. A., and Wilkinson, F. 1972. *Do Trade Unions Cause Inflation?* Cambridge: Cambridge University Press.

Kalecki, M. 1971. *Selected Essays on the Dynamics of the Capitalist Economy*. Cambridge: Cambridge University Press.

Metcalfe, J. S., and Steedman, I. 1971. "Some Effects of Taxation in a Linear Model of Production," *Manchester School*, 39, pp. 171–85.

Mieszkowski, P. 1969. "Tax Incidence Theory: The Effects of Taxes on Distribution of Income," *Journal of Economic Literature*, 7, pp. 1103–24.

Schwartz, J. 1961. *Lectures on the Mathematical Method in Analytical Economics*. New York: Gordon and Breach.

Sraffa, P. 1960. *Production of Commodities by Means of Commodities*. Cambridge: Cambridge University Press.

11

A classical model of business cycles

Alfredo Medio

Introduction

The foundations of the mathematical theory of business cycles were laid down in the 1930s in the same intellectual atmosphere in which Keynes published his *General Theory*. Indeed, most of the analyses of the cycle developed in those years and subsequently were interpreted as dynamic extensions of the Keynesian static theory of income.

In an attempt to rectify somewhat this bias in the literature on business cycles, we shall present a formal analysis of a competing approach to the problem of the cycle, which we have decided to call "classical," with many apologies to the historians of economic thought. This use of the term classical may be defended on two grounds. First, the appellative neatly contrasts our model with the demand-oriented models of Keynesian (or Kaleckian) inspiration. Second, the model contains some basic ideas that can be traced back to such classical writers as Adam Smith, Ricardo, and especially Marx (Steindl, 1952, pp. 237 ff.). Whichever terminology is used, the important thing is to clearly specify the concepts which are being employed.

The cornerstones of the classical approach, as we take it here, are the assumptions regarding the behaviour of capitalists and the role of the labor market. As concerns the former, it is assumed that, owing to the economic and social conditions within which they operate, capitalists tend to save and invest as much profit as they can, without regard to the overall effect of accumulation on the rate of profit. This means that a divergence between individual optimization and collective optimization may ensue, and that the outcome of the capitalists' collective behaviour may be quite different from that intended by the individual capitalists.

The second classical assumption concerns the mechanism through which accumulation affects profitability adversely. If we assume fixed production coefficients and constant returns to scale, there are two basic explanations of this problem. The first one is that, with a given level of real wages, over-accumulation will lead to a glut of commodities. Capitalists will therefore have to sell at a loss, or they might even be unable to sell at all. This argument may be found in the Marxist literature under the label "underconsumption theory of crises" (Sweezy, 1942, pp. 156–89). But it seems logically inconsistent with the hypothesis of blind accumulation. Tugan-Baranowsky was indeed right in maintaining that, so long as capitalists are prepared to invest whatever profit they get, only crises of disproportionality may occur and no *general* glut of commodities can be possible.[1]

The second, more convincing classical explanation of the adverse effect of accumulation on profits is as follows. Accumulation of capital increases the demand for labour and, unless technical progress and population growth neutralize this effect, the level of employment will rise with respect to population. This will strengthen the workers' bargaining power, higher real wages will be obtained and, sooner or later, profits will be squeezed. This idea, which can be found in the works of Adam Smith and Ricardo, was most forcefully argued by Marx by means of the concept of the "reserve army of labour." It is important to observe that none of these authors maintained that the labor market fixes the *absolute* level of real wages. They instead believed that demand and supply of labor determine the

This paper is drawn from a chapter of the author's Ph.D. dissertation, submitted to the University of Cambridge, July 1975. The author is indebted to Richard Goodwin for his helpful comments and criticisms. Edward Nell made a number of valuable suggestions which substantially improved the final version of the article.

fluctuations of real wages around their natural level, which depends on a number of historical and institutional factors.

Within the classical framework it is possible to produce a rigorous model of economic fluctuations in terms of the dynamics of profits, wages, and employment. This has been attempted by Goodwin in his recent article "A Growth Cycle" (Goodwin, 1967).[2] In Goodwin's model there are two dynamic forces at work, which we shall call employment effect and profit effect. The former is a positive relation between the level of the employment–population ratio and the rate of change of real wages. The profit effect is a positive relation between the profit share (or profit margin) and the rate of growth of output. With a given capital–output ratio, no saving out of wages and no consumption out of profits, the rate of growth will be equal to the rate of profit and a constant proportion of the profit margin. The equilibrium rate of growth will be equal to the "natural" rate of growth, namely to the population growth rate *plus* the rate of technical progress.[3] To this there will correspond certain equilibrium levels of the employment population ratio and of the profit margin, while, in equilibrium, real wages will be growing at the same rate as output per head.

The disequilibrium dynamics works as follows: when the actual employment ratio is higher than its equilibrium level, real wages will be pushed up, their rate of increase will soon exceed that of productivity and the profit margin will be squeezed. This will in turn curb the rate of income growth and, after a while, the employment ratio will decline. Real wages will eventually be reduced (or at least their rate of growth will be brought below that of output per head), profits and saving will soar, accumulation and employment will be stimulated and the cycle will start again.

The classical approach to the problem of business cycles, sketched briefly here, captures an important element of capitalist economies, and perhaps it looks less obsolete in the 1980s than it did in the 1930s. However, in its crudest form it is obviously open to criticism from a Keynesian–Kaleckian point of view. As a matter of fact, Steindl criticized the "No. 1 Marx theory of business cycles" for its taking the extreme classical views that saving entirely governs investment and that movements in money wages automatically result in corresponding changes in profits (Steindl, 1952). Surely, Steindl argues, if capitalists are able to carry out their investment (and consumption) plans in real terms, no increase in money wages can reduce profits at full employment, only prices will change. The argument is well grounded, although to deny money wages any effect on real wages, and to postulate that saving always and completely adjusts to planned investment is as extreme a view as the classical one. In real economies accumulation depends both on saving and on the state of demand, while changes in real wages are governed by the joint effect of changes in money wages and changes in prices brought about by imperfectly competitive firms. The relevance of the classical approach to business cycles would, therefore, be greatly increased if a generalized version of it could be constructed, in which effective demand has *some* effect on investment and changes in prices have *some* effect on real wages and profits.

Unfortunately, as we shall see in a moment, the Goodwin model, in its present form, does not lend itself to any extension whatsoever, since it does not possess structural stability. The exact meaning of this concept will be discussed later. Suffice it to say here, that any slight alteration that should be introduced into the structure of the model would destroy its essential qualitative feature, i.e. a self-sustaining cyclical motion of the relevant variables. This means that the Goodwin model can only be used as an idealization of the extreme classical view, which, as we have just seen, cannot be accepted.

The specific purpose here is to develop a classical model of cyclical growth which does not suffer from the limitations of the Goodwin one. The extensions we shall consider in the sequel are similar to those examined by Desai in his article on Goodwin's model (Desai, 1973). However, it is a distinctive feature of this chapter to study the conditions of permanent oscillations of the system, rather than the stability properties of its equilibrium. As will be apparent later, the mathematical structure of the model we shall use is similar to Rose's (1967), although it was developed independently and was stimulated by somewhat different economic problems.

The Goodwin model

The first step of the argument will be to substantiate the statement that the Goodwin model is structurally unstable, and to discuss its significance. The analysis will initially be conducted in formal terms, and then its economic meaning will be discussed.

Goodwin discusses his classical model in a rigorous, formal manner by making use of a system of differential equations studied by the Italian mathematician Vito Volterra (1931) and prior to him by the American mathematician Alfred Lotka (1925) in the context of a biological predator–prey problem. In what follows we shall refer to this model simply as the LVG (Lotka-Volterra-Goodwin) model, (Volterra, 1931).

The equations of the model are:[4]

$$\dot{x} = P(x, y) = (a - by)x \qquad (1)$$
$$\dot{y} = Q(x, y) = (-c + dx)y$$

where x indicates the employment–population ratio, y indicates the workers' share in the national income, so that $[1 - y]$ is of course the profit share, or profit margin, and a, b, c, d are positive constants, derived as follows.

First, let us introduce the auxiliary variables: m = rate of technical progress, neutral in the sense of Harrod; n = proportional rate of growth of population; u = proportional rate of change of the real wage rate when $x = 0$. The constants of system (1) will now be defined thus: $a = b - (m + n)$; b = output–capital ratio; $c = u + m$; d = coefficient of the employment effect on the rate of increase of real wages. Finally, dots indicate the operation (d/dt), t being time.

In his model Goodwin assumes that there exists a rate of growth of output, b, which is the maximum technologically achievable when workers live on air and capitalists invest all their lot. The corresponding maximum rate of increase of the employment ratio, a, is equal to $[b - (m + n)]$. Notice that, with constant population and no technical progress, the first equation of system (1) becomes

$$\dot{x}/x = b(1 - y) \qquad (2)$$

Remembering that, under Goodwin's assumptions, the rate of growth[5] is equal to the rate of profit, Equation (2) can be interpreted as a macrodynamic version of the Sraffian equation for the rate of profit, $r = R(1 - w)$ (Sraffa, 1960, p. 22).

When the rate of change of output per head is exogenously given, the rate of change of the workers' share is governed by that of real wages.[6] The latter is assumed to be a linear function of the employment ratio with a negative intercept on the wage axis. The system of Equation (1) admits only two singular (equilibrium) points. The first one is the origin of the axes, i.e., $x = 0$, $y = 0$.

The second singular point is defined by the coordinates $x = c/d$, $y = a/b$. If we designate national income by z and the wage rate by w, we have $\dot{z}/z = (\dot{x}/x) + (m + n)$, and $\dot{w}/w = (\dot{y}/y) + m$.

At the positive equilibrium point ($x = c/d$; $y = a/b$), we will therefore have $\dot{z}/z = m + n$, which is, of course, the Harrodian natural rate of growth, and $\dot{w}/w = m$, i.e., at the equilibrium point the wage rate will be growing *pari passu* with productivity.

System (1) is nonlinear and, generally speaking, its exact integration (i.e. the exact description of its dynamic behavior) presents difficulties. However, as is well known (see Appendix A), certain basic qualitative results concerning a system like (1) can be obtained by performing a linear approximation about its equilibrium points. We shall then have the modified linear system:

$$\dot{x} = \alpha x + \beta y \qquad \dot{y} = \gamma x + \delta y \qquad (3)$$

where

$$\alpha = \partial P/\partial x \qquad \gamma = \partial Q/\partial x$$
$$\beta = \partial P/\partial y \qquad \delta = \partial Q/\partial y$$

all the partial derivatives being taken at the equilibrium points. System (3) (or, more exactly the family of systems (3), one for each equilibrium point) is linear and can be promptly integrated. As indicated in Appendix A the dynamic behavior of the variables x and y, in a neighborhood of each equilibrium point, entirely depends on the roots of the *characteristic* (or *auxiliary*) *equation*.

$$\lambda^2 + \Theta\lambda + \Delta, \qquad (4)$$

where $\Theta = -(\alpha + \delta)$, $\Delta = (\alpha\delta - \beta\gamma)$. At the first equilibrium point, with coordinates ($x = 0$; $y = 0$) we have:

$$\alpha = a > 0 \qquad \gamma = 0$$
$$\beta = 0 \qquad \delta = -c < 0$$

The roots of Equation (4) are therefore real with opposite signs. As explained below, in this case the equilibrium point is called a *saddle point*, and it is unstable, except when, by a mere fluke, the initial conditions take special values.

At the second equilibrium point ($x = c/d$, $y = a/b$), we have:

$$\alpha = 0 \qquad \gamma = (ad/b) > 0$$
$$\beta = -(bc/d) < 0 \qquad \delta = 0$$

Therefore $\Theta = 0$, $\Delta = ac > 0$. In this case the roots of (4) are purely imaginary, and the equilibrium point is either a *center* or a special *focus* (see Appendix A). It is impossible to discriminate between these two possibilities on the basis of the linear approximation only. However, the equations of the LVG model can be integrated exactly, and it can be shown that the singular point in question is actually a *center* (Andronov, Vitt, Khaikin, 1966, pp. 142–45; hereafter referred to as AVK). For our present purpose it is sufficient to know that $\Theta = 0$ is a *necessary* condition for a *center* to appear.

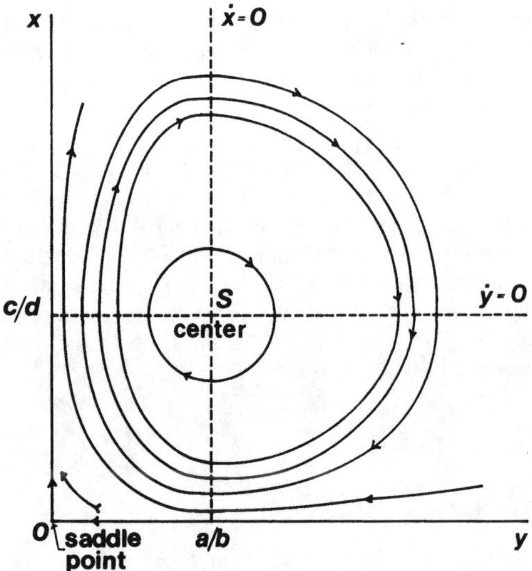

Figure 11.1

The *phase-plane* of (1) is depicted by Figure 11.1, which gives us a visual insight into the topological features of the LVG system. We can see that the origin of the axes, which corresponds to a zero level of employment and a zero level of the workers' share is unstable. All paths starting in the positive quadrant of the phase-plane, near the *saddle point* will move away from it as time goes by. After a sufficiently long period of time has elapsed, the motion will outstep the boundaries of the region in which the linear approximation is valid, and the system will enter the region controlled by the singular point S (a *center*). Here all the motions of the system are closed trajectories around the equilibrium point.

The system (1), therefore, describes a self-excited, orbitally stable, oscillatory motion of the employment ratio and of the workers' share. Whether the national income declines when the employment–population ratio falls depends on whether, during the depression

$$\left|\frac{\dot{x}}{x}\right| \gtreqless (m+n)$$

Whether real wages fall when the workers' share falls, depends on whether, during the depression,

$$\left|\frac{\dot{y}}{y}\right| \gtreqless m$$

It can easily be seen that the LVG model suffers from two major drawbacks. For one thing, it fails to pass the test of *structural stability*.

A rigorous definition of this concept will be provided in Appendix B.[7] Here we shall limit ourselves to certain intuitive considerations. Broadly speaking, a system is said to be structurally unstable when its dynamic behavior crucially depends on its parameters taking certain special values. As we can never have a complete and perfect knowledge of real systems, structurally unstable models cannot be accepted as correct idealizations of reality.

Now consider Goodwin's model and, in particular, consider the parameter b, which indicates the output–capital ratio. In general, we would expect that b should be affected by changes in the level of activity x and of the distribution of income y. (Similarly, c and d will not be totally insensitive to changes in x and y.)

However, if the influence of x and y on b, c, and d is small, and *if we can also postulate that this small influence does not alter the results of the analysis qualitatively,* it is reasonable to assume it away and to take b, c, and d as approximately constant.[8]

Unfortunately, the Goodwin model does not satisfy the latter condition. Consider in fact the modified system

$$\begin{aligned}\dot{x} &= P(x, y) + p(x, y)\\ \dot{y} &= Q(x, y) + q(x, y)\end{aligned} \tag{1a}$$

where the functions p and q reflect the weak relations existing between level of activity and distribution of income, on the one hand, and output–capital ratio and variations of real wages on the other hand.

The coefficients of the linearized version of system (1a) will be modified accordingly. In particular, around the slightly displaced equilibrium point S' we shall have

$$\begin{aligned}\alpha' &= \alpha + (\partial p/\partial x) = (\partial p/\partial x)\\ \delta' &= \delta + (\partial q/\partial y) = (\partial q/\partial y)\end{aligned}$$

as $\alpha = \delta = 0$. *However small the quantities* $(\partial p/\partial x)$ *and* $(\partial q/\partial y)$ *may be,* this implies that the coefficient $\Theta' = -(\alpha' + \delta')$ will cease to be equal to zero (unless, by a fluke, $(\partial p/\partial x) = -(\partial q/\partial y)$).

The equilibrium point S' will consequently cease to be a *center* and, if α' and δ' are small as we assume, it will become a focus, stable or unstable according to whether $\Theta' \gtrless 0$.

An immediate consequence of the Goodwin model being structurally unstable is that, if we try to generalize it by introducing further doses of realism (i.e., by adding certain functional relations which have been neglected in the first approximation), not only will its elegant simplicity be lost, but we cannot even be sure that the appellative growth cycle can be maintained. The fundamental feature of the system, i.e., that of describing *self-sustained* oscillations will be lost. The paths which describe the solution of the system will either wind onto the equilibrium, or spiral away from it without limit, eventually leading to the explosion of the system.

A second shortcoming of the LVG model, which is closely connected with the first one, as both depend on the relevant singularity being a *center*, is that the amplitude of the fluctuations entirely depends on the initial conditions. If, for example, we start far enough from the equilibrium point, we shall have wild oscillations that will not damp down as time elapses. We are prepared to admit that initial conditions may have *some* influence on the motion of the system, but there is no reason to expect that the entire motion should be so fundamentally altered by the choice of the starting point. A corollary of the propositions above is that the LVG model is not practically stable. That is, we cannot be sure that a motion starting in the practically acceptable region of the values of x and y will remain inside it.

The general model

It remains to be seen whether a dynamic model can be built along the lines suggested by Goodwin, possessing structural stability and providing a more comprehensive and satisfactory idealization of the capitalist growth cycle under classical conditions.

The first step in this direction is to introduce into the picture two dynamic elements which we have labeled *demand effect* and *markup effect*. In formal terms this amounts to admitting that some (or all) of the coefficients a, b, c, and d are functions of x and y rather than constant parameters. Given the level of abstraction of the analysis and the very limited knowledge of the parameters and functional relationships involved, we shall set up the relevant functions in a general (implicit) form rather than try to formulate them explicitly. Making use of the same notation as before, we shall then write the following system of differential equations:

$$\dot{x} = f_1(x, y)\, x \qquad \dot{y} = f_2(x, y)\, y \tag{5}$$

and shall introduce the following assumptions:

1. f_1 and f_2 are continuous and have continuous first derivatives for $x, y > 0$; also, f_1 and f_2 are polynomials without common factors. This does not imply any significant loss of generality, but does guarantee that f_1 and f_2 are analytic over the relevant domain and that they have only isolated intersections.
2. $(\partial f_1/\partial y) < 0$, that is, the higher the workers' share (the lower the profit share), the lower is the rate of growth of activity.[9] This seems justified on the ground that a reduction in the profit share, *ceteris paribus*, will reduce the finance for investment and, for any given capital–output ratio, it will reduce the rate of profit, therefore depressing the inducement to invest. (Assumption 2, of course, describes the profit effect.)
3. $(\partial f_1/\partial x) \gtreqless 0$ according to whether $x \lesseqgtr x_0$. If we take x as a proxy for the level of activity of the system, this means that the *rate of growth* of activity will be higher (up to a point) the higher the *level* of activity. This is because, if we start from a situation where excess capacity exists, a higher level of activity will lead to a higher degree of utilization and, for a given level of the profit margin, to a higher rate of profit. Consequently both finance for investment and inducement to invest will be increased. However, for unusually high levels of activity (beyond x_0) there will be increasing costs of production and increasing risk. To push the level of activity beyond x_0 will depress the rate of profit (and the rate of growth), unless the profit margin is increased too. Lacking any better expression, we shall call x_0 the normal capacity level of activity. (Assumption 3 describes the demand effect.)
4. $(\partial f_2/\partial x) > 0$, (the employment effect) i.e. the higher the level of the employment ratio, the greater will be the rate of growth of wages, and given the technical progress rate, the greater will be the rate of change of the workers' share. This functional relation between the level of employment and the rate of change of wages is very close to that analyzed by Phillips (1958).
5. $(\partial f_2/\partial y) < 0$, (the markup effect). This assumption, like assumption 3, depends crucially on the markets being imperfectly competitive. It is postulated that, when profit margins are threatened by increases in real wages greater than the increases in productivity, firms will react by raising prices. It is *not* assumed, however, that price changes offset changes in the workers' share fully and instantaneously.
6. $f_1(0, 0) > 0$, i.e. when the workers' share is very low (the profit margin is very high) the rate of increase of activity will be positive and greater than $(m + n)$. This seems justified when one analyzes a growing capitalist economy with fairly

high "animal spirits." In addition, even in a deep depression, there is always some investment which is undertaken independently of the current level of activity.

7. $f_1(x_1, 0) = 0$, i.e. there is a level of employment so high that no further increase is possible, no matter how low the workers' share may be. Obviously $x_1 < 1$.
8. Let us take any point s in the plane (x, y) and let us join it to the origin of the axes, O. Let us call S the segment Os. We postulate that, for any value of x, $(df_1/dS) < 0$ and, for any value of y, $(df_2/dS) > 0$. Broadly speaking, this means that, for any equiproportional increase of x and y, the employment effect on $(\dot{y}/y)$ will be stronger than the markup effect, and the "profit effect" on $(\dot{x}/x)$ will be stronger than the demand effect.[10] This assumption has been introduced to preserve the classical character of the model. This implies that (1) the fundamental obstacle to expansion is not lack of effective demand but lack of profits, and (2) changes in money wages, owing to high levels of employment, always lead to changes in real wages in the same direction.
9. $f_2(x_2, 0) = 0$, i.e. there is a level of employment low enough to prevent any increase in the workers' share, no matter how low it may be.

Equipped with assumptions 1–9 we are now in a position to draw the phase-diagram of system equation 11.5 and to study its motion. A possible graphic representation is given in Figure 11.2. The shape of the $(f_1 = 0)$, $(f_2 = 0)$ curves which appear in the diagram is suggested by the following considerations.

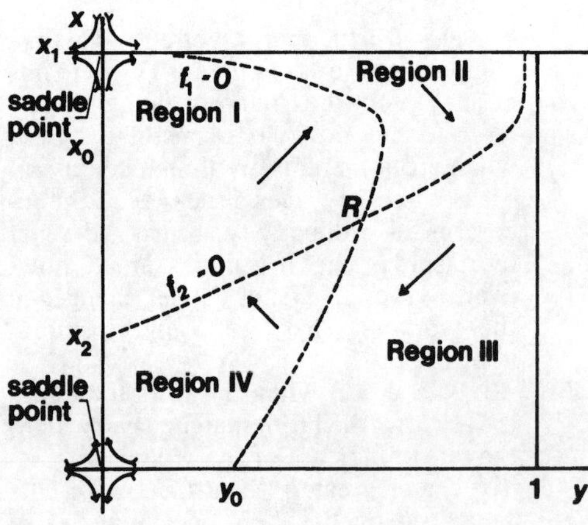

Figure 11.2

Assumption 6 tells us that the curve $(f_1 = 0)$ crosses the y axis on its positive side. Remembering assumptions 2 and 3, and considering that, along the $(f_1 = 0)$ curve, we have

$$\frac{dx}{dy} = -\left[\frac{\partial f_1}{\partial y} : \frac{\partial f_1}{\partial x}\right]$$

we may conclude that the $(f_1 = 0)$ curve will be positively sloped so long as $x < x_0$. As $x \to x_0$, $(\partial f_1/\partial x) \to 0$, and $(dx/dy) \to \infty$. For $x > x_0$, $(\partial f_1/\partial x) < 0$, and consequently (dx/dy) slopes backwards.[11]

As regards the curve $(f_2 = 0)$, from assumption 9 we know that it crosses the x axis on the positive side. Considering that, along $(f_2 = 0)$,

$$\frac{dx}{dy} = -\left[\frac{\partial f_2}{\partial y} : \frac{\partial f_2}{\partial x}\right]$$

and remembering assumptions 4 and 5, we also gather that the slope of $(f_2 = 0)$ is always positive. The curves $(f_1 = 0)$ and $(f_2 = 0)$ will intersect only once in the positive quadrant of the plane (x, y) and will divide the plane into four regions. The direction of the motion in the four regions is indicated by the arrows in Figure 11.2.

System (5) has three singular points: (i) the origin of the axes; (ii) the point $(x_1, 0)$; and (iii) the point R. The coefficients of the linearized system near the singularity (i) are

$$\alpha = f_1(0, 0) > 0 \qquad \gamma = 0$$
$$\beta = 0 \qquad \delta = f_2(0, 0) < 0$$

and those near the singularity (ii) are

$$\alpha = x_1 \frac{\partial f_1}{\partial x} < 0 \qquad \gamma = 0$$
$$\beta = x_1 \frac{\partial f_1}{\partial y} < 0 \qquad \delta = f_2(x_1, 0) > 0$$

(all derivatives being taken at the singular point). In both cases $\Delta = (\alpha\delta - \beta\gamma) < 0$. These singularities are therefore, saddle points, and consequently unstable.[12]

The only singular point of economic interest is the intersection R of the curves $(f_1 = f_2 = 0)$, whose coordinates we shall indicate by $\bar{x}$ and $\bar{y}$. The topological features of this singular point can be investigated by considering that, near R, we have

$$\alpha = \bar{x} \frac{\partial f_1}{\partial x} \gtreqless 0$$

according to whether $\bar{x} \lesseqgtr x_0$

$$\beta = \bar{x} \frac{\partial f_1}{\partial y} < 0$$

$$\gamma = \bar{y} \frac{\partial f_2}{\partial x} > 0$$

$$\delta = \bar{y} \frac{\partial f_2}{\partial y} < 0$$

In no case will R be a saddle point. In fact, assumption 8 implies that at the intersection of the curves $(f_1 = 0)$, $(f_2 = 0)$ it must be

$$\left.\frac{dx}{dy}\right|_{(f_1=0)} = -\left[\frac{\partial f_1}{\partial y} : \frac{\partial f_1}{\partial x}\right] \gtrless \left.\frac{dx}{dy}\right|_{(f_2=0)} = -\left[\frac{\partial f_2}{\partial y} : \frac{\partial f_2}{\partial x}\right]$$

according to whether

$$\frac{\partial f_1}{\partial x} \gtrless 0$$

These inequalities can also be written thus:

$$\frac{\beta}{\alpha} \lessgtr \frac{\delta}{\gamma}$$

according to whether $\alpha \gtrless 0$. In either case we have

$$\Delta = (\alpha\delta - \beta\gamma) > 0 \qquad \text{Q.E.D.}$$

The singular point R will, therefore, be either a node or a focus – stable or unstable.

Let us now consider the question of stability of the point R. There are two basic types of equilibria which we shall call E_1 and E_2. Equilibria of type E_1 occur when the curve $(f_2 = 0)$ cuts the curve $(f_1 = 0)$ in its negatively sloping section. Equilibria of type E_2 occur when the intersection points lie on the positively sloping part of $(f_1 = 0)$. (We neglect the special case in which $\bar{x} = x_0$). It is readily seen that the E_1's are stable equilibria. In fact the necessary and sufficient condition for a focus or a node to be stable is $\Theta > 0$ (Appendix A). This condition can be expressed thus:

$$\Theta = -(\alpha + \delta) = -\left[\bar{x}\frac{\partial f_1}{\partial x} + \bar{y}\frac{\partial f_2}{\partial y}\right] > 0$$

Therefore, since $(\partial f_2/\partial y) < 0$, $\Theta > 0$ if $(\partial f_1/\partial x) < 0$, Q.E.D.

It appears from Figure 11.2 that the steeper the $(f_2 = 0)$ curve and the flatter the $(f_1 = 0)$ curve, in its positively sloping section, the more likely it is that the equilibrium point will be located on the backward sloping part of $(f_1 = 0)$, and consequently be stable. In economic terms, the equilibria of type E_1 (characterized by a relatively high level of employment and a relatively low workers' share) are more likely to be obtained when workers are "understanding" (or poorly organized), and when capitalists have firm control of the product market, so that they may neutralize increases in money wages by raising prices. The same result may be obtained if, for any given employment effect and markup effect, entrepreneurs' reaction to changes in the profit margin is weak and their response to changes in the level of activity is strong. Notice that, for any given employment effect and for any given configuration of the $(f_1 = 0)$ curve, a pretty strong markup effect might be required in order for the curve $(f_2 = 0)$ to be steep enough to cut the curve $(f_1 = 0)$ in its backward sloping section. High and stable levels of employment and a low rate of inflation might well be incompatible.

When the demand effect $(\partial f_1/\partial x)$ is positive, an equilibrium of type E_2 prevails. In this case the condition for stability can be written thus:

$$\bar{x}\frac{\partial f_1}{\partial x} < -\bar{y}\frac{\partial f_2}{\partial y}$$

Roughly speaking, this condition can be expressed as follows. If, for small equiproportional displacements of x and y from their equilibrium values, the demand effect is smaller than the markup effect, then the equilibrium is stable. We therefore have a curious effect. Whereas the markup effect has a consistent stabilizing effect, the demand effect has a destabilizing effect, unless it is strong enough to lead to an equilibrium of type E_1 rather than E_2.[13]

The stability we have been discussing is, of course, local stability, whose conditions hold for small displacements from the equilibrium (how small they have to be is not known *a priori*). The interesting question is: what happens if the system is locally unstable, or if it is stable but the displacements from the equilibrium point are larger than is admissible?

To answer these questions we must study the problem which is known as "the limiting configurations of the paths" representing the solutions of the system (5).

The first step in the analysis is to establish that, in general, our system does qualify for structural stability.[14] The proof of this claim is given in the Appendix B, and it is taken for granted in what follows.

The study of Appendix B and the inspection of the related Figures 11.3 and 11.4 indicate that –

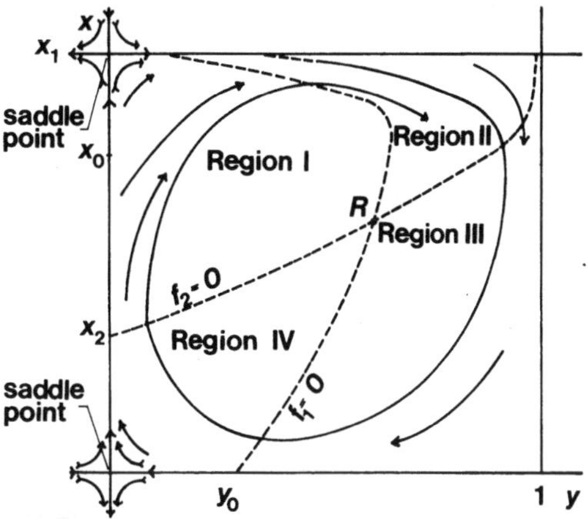

Figure 11.3

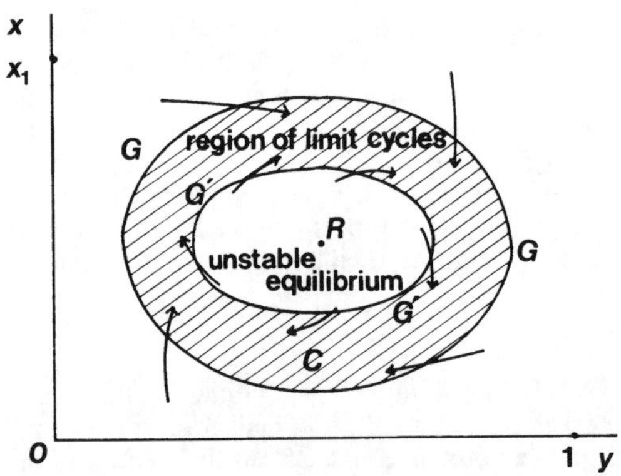

Figure 11.4

in the region of the space (x, y) for which ($0 < x < x_1$) and ($0 < y < 1$), i.e. for all the practically relevant values of level of activity and distribution of income – it is possible to define a ring G surrounding the nontrivial equilibrium point R, and such that every path originating on or outside the ring moves toward the equilibrium point itself.[15]

If the equilibrium point R is unstable, or if R is locally stable and we consider a motion originating outside the region of stability, it will be possible to define a second cycle without contact, G' (see Figure 11.4) such that all the paths originating on G' or inside it (with the exception of the equilibrium point R, and of the region of stability around it, if any) will move outwards. In this case the Poincaré–Bendixson theorem (Appendix C) warrants that in the region C contained between the two cycles G and G' there does exist at least one limit cycle, which defines a periodic motion of the system.[16]

This gives a precise answer to the question put forward at the beginning of this section: if the equilibrium point of system (5) is unstable (or if it is locally stable but it is subjected to disturbances larger than is admissible), the system will undergo *persistent* oscillations which will neither expire nor explode. The amplitude of the oscillations is determined (for each limit cycle) by the structure of the system.

Conclusion

Some interesting conclusions can now be drawn from our analysis. First, along the lines followed in this chapter, a dynamic model can be built which possesses structural, and practical, stability and is therefore eligible as an adequate, although simplified, idealization of certain real economies. Second, the solution of the model may be convergence toward equilibrium or cyclical behavior. If we exclude *global* stability,[17] we have two possible outcomes which we shall call soft generation oscillations and hard generation oscillations. The second kind of oscillations occurs when the system is locally stable and a cyclical behavior can only be brought about by displacements from the equilibrium greater than a certain threshold value. Soft generation oscillations only occur when the equilibrium point is unstable and *any* displacement from the equilibrium point brings about cycles around it.[18] The two cases can be easily visualized by observing Figures 11.5 and 11.6.

If only one limit-cycle exists (and consequently the equilibrium point is unstable) the amplitude of the oscillations entirely depends on the structure of the system and initial conditions play no role. If more than one limit-cycle exists, initial conditions determine which one will eventually be approached. If the equilibrium is locally stable, but there are cycles outside the dynamically stable area, initial conditions also determine *whether* there will be fluctuations.[19]

It is perhaps convenient to conclude the present investigation by briefly discussing the interesting case of a unique soft generation limit-cycle. Let us start by considering the properties of the equilibrium around which the system evolves. The equilibrium position will be indicated by the pair of coordinates ($\bar{x}$, $\bar{y}$), which denote a combination of employment ratio and distribution of income such that, if existing and not disturbed, it will perpetuate itself.

In order to have a constant employment ratio, the equilibrium rate of growth must be equal to the sum of population growth rate and technical progress. However, the equilibrium point need not correspond to the normal capacity level of activity, which we have located at $x = x_0$. In the

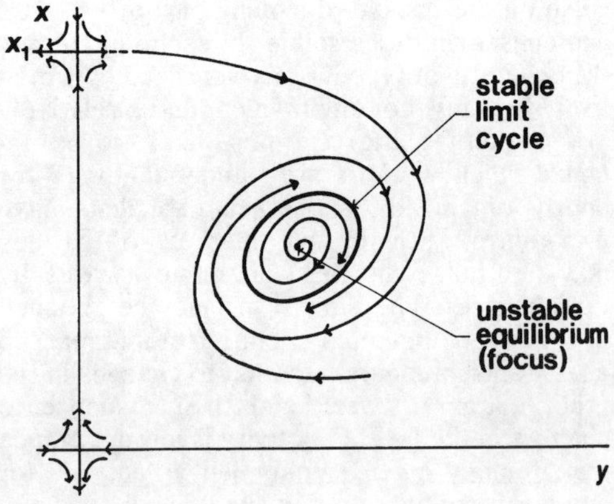

Figure 11.5

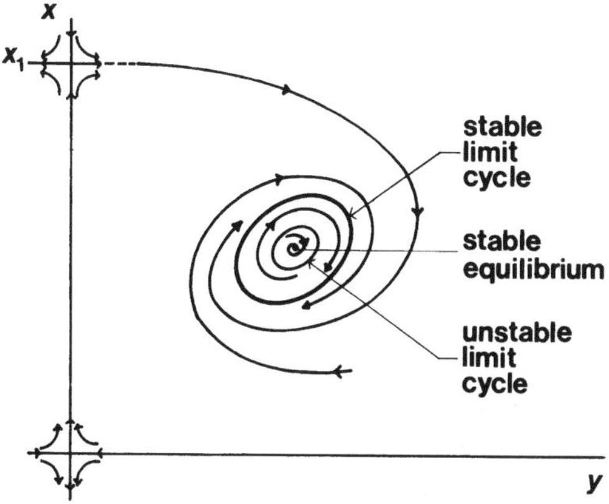

Figure 11.6

case under consideration, where $\bar{x} < x_0$, the equilibrium point will be characterized not only by a certain level of employment, but also by a certain degree of excess capacity.

In order to have a constant distribution of income, real wages must grow at the same rate as productivity. In general, however, this will be obtained by coupling an equilibrium rate of increase of *money* wages and an equilibrium rate of inflation.

Out of equilibrium, the cyclical movement can be described by commenting on Figure 11.7 as follows.

At x_{min} the employment ratio is at its lowest point. Income (output) has been growing, if at all, at a rate lower than $(m + n)$. Real wages have been growing less than productivity and they may have been declining. On the left of x_{min} the positive effect on production, owing to the high profit margin, more than offsets the negative influence of the low activity level. Income starts growing faster than population and technical progress combined, and the employment ratio increases. The workers' share continues to decline until y_{min} is reached. After that point the higher level of employment leads to real wages increasing faster than productivity, in spite of a higher rate of inflation. The workers' share starts increasing. Capitalists are getting less per unit of output but output is growing fast so that *total profits* increase, and so long as the increase in the output–capital ratio is proportionally greater than the decrease in the profit margin, the *rate* of profit must increase, too. But this situation cannot last. After $(x/y)_{max}$ the rate of increase of the workers' share becomes higher than the rate of increase of the level of activity, and the *rate* of profits must soon be squeezed.[20] Production is increasingly discouraged and, after x_{max}, the rate of growth of income becomes smaller than $(m + n)$, leading to a decline in the employment ratio. Money wages increase faster than productivity plus inflation, but at y_{max} the workers' share reaches its upper limit, and declines thereafter. After $(x/y)_{min}$ the workers' share declines faster than that of the employment ratio. This will soon lead to higher *rate* of profit, and production will therefore be stimulated. At x_{min} the rate of growth of income outruns its natural level and the cycle starts again.

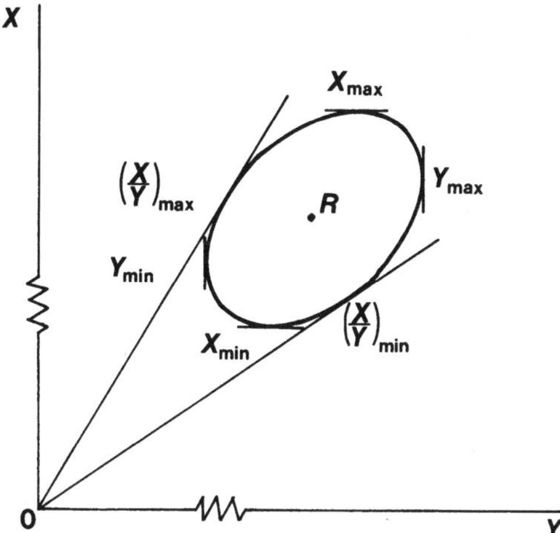

Figure 11.7

The present model lends itself to a number of extensions. Cost inflation, or government intervention designed to affect the rate of interest or the level of demand, could be easily introduced without radically altering the structure of the model, although the outcome would obviously be different. Perhaps the most promising development would be to introduce some hereditary elements into the system. In particular, technical progress should cease to be an exogenously given function of time, and should instead be treated as a function of the cumulate levels of income over a more or less distant past. A population function which might replace the constant n with a variable would also be most useful.

But these are matters for future investigation.

Appendix A. Integral curves, phase-plane, and singular points

In this chapter we have been concerned with differential equations of the form

$$\dot{x} = f_1(x, y) \qquad \dot{y} = f_2(x, y) \tag{A.1}$$

where dots indicate the operation (d/dt) (t being time), and the f's are regular functions of x and

y. The solution of the system – when available – can be given in terms of the parameter t, i.e.:

$$x = x(t) \qquad y = y(t) \tag{A.2}$$

Or, time may be omitted and the solution can be expressed in the form of a family of curves in the (x, y) plane obtained by integrating the function

$$\frac{dx}{dy} = \frac{f_1(x, y)}{f_2(x, y)} \tag{A.3}$$

These curves are called *integral curves* and the (x, y) plane is called *phase-plane*. On this plane it is possible to study the motion of the *representative point*, i.e., the point which defines the state of the system at any instant, t. Integral curves consist of *ordinary points* (which define a path along which the system moves in time) and *singular points*. The latter are those points at which the solution of equation A.3 does not exist – is discontinuous or not unique. The most common case occurs when a pair of values of x and y exists for which $f_1 = f_2 = 0$ (i.e., $\dot{x} = \dot{y} = 0$). Singular points can in this case be taken to represent the equilibrium positions of the system.

When equation A.1 is nonlinear its exact integration is, in general, an impossible task. However, by taking a linear approximation of the functions f_1 and f_2 about a singular point, it is possible to establish certain qualitative properties of the system in certain areas "controlled" by the singular point. The study of all the singular points (and the areas controlled by them) provides a global picture of the dynamic behavior of the system.

By taking the first approximation of f_1 and f_2 we obtain the simpler form

$$\dot{x} = \alpha x + \beta y \qquad \dot{y} = \gamma x + \delta y \tag{A.4}$$

where $\alpha = \partial f_1/\partial x$, $\beta = \partial f_1/\partial y$, $\gamma = \partial f_2/\partial x$, $\delta = \partial f_2/\partial y$, all the derivatives being taken at the relevant singular point.

The solutions of equation A.4 have the form

$$x(t) = c_1 e^{\lambda t} \qquad y(t) = c_2 e^{\lambda t} \tag{A.5}$$

where λ is a root of the equation

$$\lambda^2 + \Theta\lambda + \Delta = 0 \tag{A.6}$$

in which $\Theta = -(\alpha + \delta)$; $\Delta = (\alpha\delta - \beta\gamma)$ and which is called the characteristic equation of the system.

Four main cases are possible (excluding the special cases arising when $\Delta = 0$).

1. The two roots are real and of the same sign. The singular point is a *node*. It is stable if $\lambda_1, \lambda_2 < 0$, unstable if $\lambda_1, \lambda_2 > 0$. (Figure 11.8 illustrated a case of stable node. To obtain an unstable node it would be sufficient to suitably rotate the diagram and reverse the direction of the arrows.) In economic terms we may say that – if the larger root is sufficiently small – an unstable node may be taken as an idealisation of an economy asymptotically approaching a steady-state growth.
2. The two roots are real but of opposite signs. The singular point is called a *saddle point* and it is always unstable. In fact there are only two paths leading to the equilibrium point; any deviation from these paths will lead away from equilibrium as time goes by (see Figure 11.9).

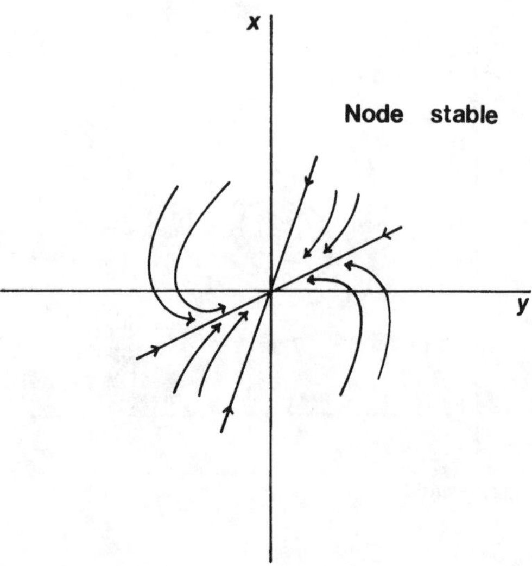

Figure 11.8

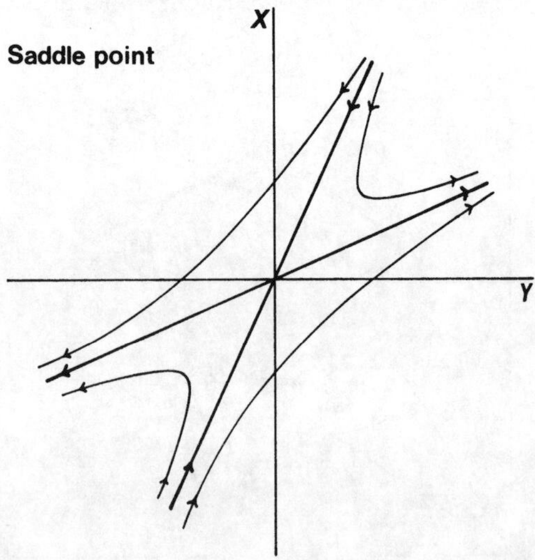

Figure 11.9

Cases of saddle point are often encountered in the theory of optimum growth, in which it is found that, if the initial conditions are not chosen appropriately, "optimal" programs of accumulation will become unfeasible or infinitely "inferior."

3. The two roots are conjugate complex. The singular point is a *focus* characterized by an oscillating behavior around the equilibrium point. A focus is stable or unstable according to whether the real part of the roots is $\lesseqgtr 0$. (Figure 11.10 illustrates the case of a stable focus. If we suitably rotate the diagram and invert the direction of the arrows we have an unstable focus.)
4. If the roots are complex and the real part is zero we have a special case whose topological features cannot be ascertained by means of the first approximation only. The singular point may be a weak focus (stable or unstable) or, under very special conditions, it may be a *center*, characterized by a continuum of closed paths around the equilibrium point (Figure 11.11). The various possibilities can be summarized as follows: (1) If $\Delta < 0$ the singular point is a saddle point; (2) If $\Delta > 0$ the singular point is a node or a focus according to whether $\Theta^2 \gtreqless 4\Delta$; (3) Nodes and foci are stable or unstable according to whether $\Theta \gtreqless 0$. The term Θ is, therefore, called the "damping factor." The saddle points are always unstable.

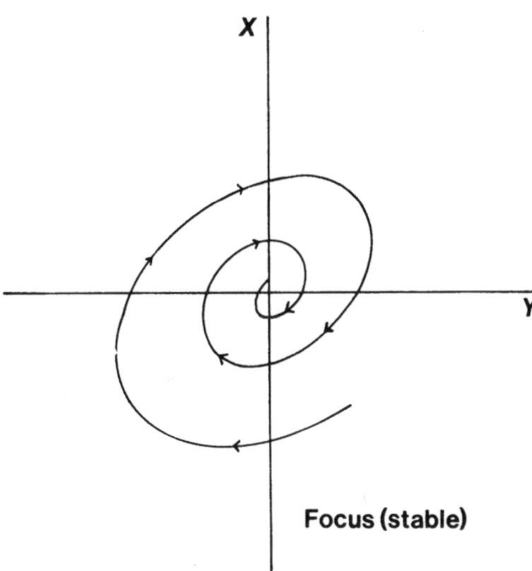

Figure 11.10

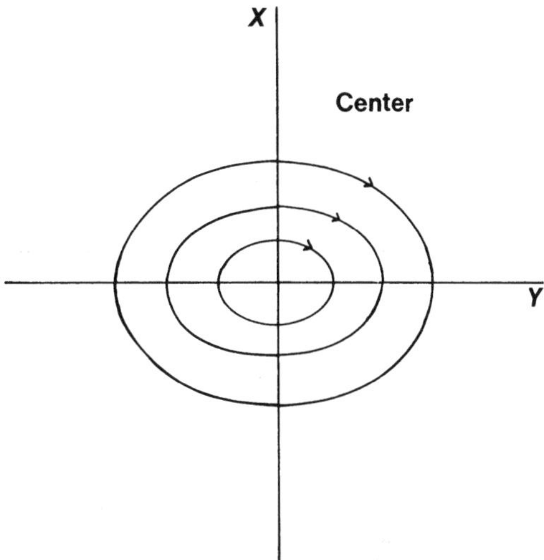

Figure 11.11

Appendix B. Structural stability

The term "stability," when used without qualification, usually refers to dynamic stability, i.e., the stability of system equilibrium position(s) with respect to changes in the variables (or their derivatives). However, there exists a different and equally important use of the term. In a system of differential equations arising out of practical problems, one never knows exactly what are the relevant functions and, therefore, only systems whose behavior is not qualitatively affected by very slight changes in those functions should be considered. Systems possessing this requisite, called "structural stability," may be rigorously defined as follows:

Consider the system of differential equations

$$\dot{x} = P(x, y) \qquad \dot{y} = Q(x, y) \tag{B.1}$$

Let D be the domain in which P and Q are analytic, and let S be a compact set, contained in D. Let the boundary G of the region S be a closed curve such that no vector (P, Q) is either zero or tangent to G at any point of G itself (such a curve is called a "cycle without contact"). The system (B.1) is structurally stable in S if there is a $\delta > 0$ such that, if the new functions $p(x, y)$ and $q(x, y)$ are analytic in S, and if

$$|p(x, y)| < \delta \quad |p'_x(x, y)| < \delta \quad |p'_y(x, y)| < \delta$$
$$|q(x, y)| < \delta \quad |q'_x(x, y)| < \delta \quad |q'_y(x, y)| < \delta$$

($p'_{x,y}$ and $q'_{x,y}$ being partial derivatives with respect to x, y), then the modified system

$$\begin{aligned} \dot{x} &= P(x, y) + p(x, y) \\ \dot{y} &= Q(x, y) + q(x, y) \end{aligned} \tag{B.1*}$$

has the same phase-portrait, qualitatively, as the original system (B.1).

Structural stability as defined above implies a number of far-reaching consequences, the most important of which can be described thus:

1. All the relevant topological elements of system (B.1) (paths, singular points, limit cycles, etc.) maintain their properties when (B.1) is transformed into (B.1)*. The points that correspond to each other in this transformation are found at a distance less than a predetermined standard $\epsilon(\delta) > 0$ (providing that the functions p and q have the aforementioned properties). An important corollary of this proposition is that for structurally stable nonlinear systems the behavior patterns of the solution curves (nodes, foci, saddle points, etc.) about the equilibrium point are the same as for the linear approximation.
2. The qualitative behavior of the system does not depend on mathematical peculiarities, which of course cannot be taken as correct idealizations of real problems.

In other words, structurally stable systems can be subjected to *some* alterations, concerning the form of the functions and the values of the parameters, within limits fixed by the quantity $\delta(\epsilon) > 0$, without the fundamental results of the analysis being destroyed.

Let us now turn to proving that the system of differential equations investigated earlier (See Equation (5).) is, in general, structurally stable. The necessary and sufficient conditions for a system of two first-order differential equations to be structurally stable can be formally stated as follows (AVK, 1966, pp. 374–96; DeBaggis, 1952, pp. 37–59).

The system (B.1), in a region S bounded by a cycle without contact G is structurally stable if it has:

1. only equilibrium points for which $\Delta \neq 0$ and, if $\Delta > 0$, $\Theta \neq 0$ (for the meaning of these symbols see Appendix A);
2. only limit cycles whose characteristic exponent is $\neq 0$;
3. no paths joining two saddle points, or returning to the saddle point they have left. Such paths are called "separatrices."

To prove that system (5) does possess these properties, let us first see whether it is possible to draw a cycle without contact in the positive quadrant of the plane (x, y). For this purpose, let us consider Figure 11.3.

From the saddle point $(x = x_1,\ y = 0)$ only one path leaves in the direction of the positive quadrant and it must enter region II. There exist two possibilities, namely: (1) the path, which we shall call ϕ, tends to the equilibrium point R, either approaching it from a definite direction or winding onto it, (according to whether R is a stable node or a stable focus); (2) ϕ does not tend to R. In this second case, ϕ cannot tend to either of the two saddle points of the system (i.e. the point $(x = y = 0)$, or the point $(x = x_1;\ y = 0)$). In fact, no path – with the exception of those located on the coordinate axes – approaches these equilibrium points. The path ϕ will instead enter regions III, IV, I, II in succession, crossing the curves $(f_2 = 0)$, $(f_1 = 0)$ twice.

After reaching region II for the second time, the path ϕ cannot cross itself, as only one path passes through an ordinary (nonsingular) point in the analytic domain – Cauchy's theorem (See AVK, 1966, p. 62, footnote 1). The only possibility left therefore, is for the path ϕ to wind inwards. The same is true for any path starting in the positive quadrant, and sufficiently far from the equilibrium point R.

Irrespective of whether the equilibrium point R is stable or not, it is then manifestly possible to define a compact (closed and bounded) region S belonging to the analytic domain D, in which $(0 < x < x_1)$ and $(0 < y < 1)$, such that no path originating in S leaves it or asymptotically tends to its boundary G, and such that all the paths along the boundary enter S. G is then a cycle without contact. (See Fig. 11.4.)

We can now verify that in general our system satisfies the three conditions just discussed. It has already been shown that there cannot be in the domain D separatrices joining two saddle points. Therefore we have to deal only with conditions (1) and (2). As regards the former, if we except very special cases in which the parameters of the system have certain particular values (such that $[(\partial f_1/\partial x)(\partial f_2/\partial y) = (\partial f_1/\partial y)(\partial f_2/\partial x)]$, or $[(\partial f_1/\partial x) = -(\partial f_2/\partial y)]$), there is no reason to expect that the quantities Δ or Θ should be identically zero. In any case we can always specify the functions f's so that these special cases may be avoided.

The same reasoning holds true regarding condition (2). Consider that, if a limit cycle exists, the related solution of the system will be a pair of functions $x(t)$, $y(t)$, which will be periodic with period, say, T. The stability of the cycle will be determined by the sign of its *characteristic exponent* $h = (1/T)\int_0^T [(\partial P/\partial x) + (\partial Q/\partial y)]\,dt$ where the derivatives are taken along the closed path from $(t = 0)$ to $(t = T)$ (Andronov et al., 1966, pp. 289–90). In particular the cycle will be stable or unstable according to whether $h \lessgtr 0$. It can be readily seen that the condition that $h \neq 0$ is the exact equivalent of the condition that $\Theta \neq 0$. The only difference being that the latter requires damping and explosive forces, which should not exactly compensate each other, *near the equilibrium point*, whereas the condition $h \neq 0$ requires that this exact balance should not exist near *the closed path*. Both occurrences only obtain for special values of the parameters and we can always specify the system in such a manner that these exceptional possibilities (never encountered in real systems) be ruled out.

The claim that system (5) is, in general, structurally stable seems therefore to be fully justified. Moreover, if we consider that the stable domain S contains practically all the relevant values of x and y, we may further say that our system is also practically stable.

Appendix C. Limit cycles and the Poincaré-Bendixson theorem

A structurally stable dynamic system consisting of two first-order differential equations is said to have *limit cycles* if there exist solutions to the system that are isolated closed paths, to which all neighboring paths tend as $t \to +\infty$ (stable limit cycle), or as $t \to -\infty$ (unstable limit cycle.)

There exist various criteria to establish the presence (or the absence) of limit cycles in such a system. In this chapter, the Poincaré-Bendixson theorem has been used. Its exact formulation is:[21]

Theorem. Let C be a closed anular region, that does not contain equilibrium states and is not left as t increases (as t decreases). Then inside such a region, C, there is bound to be one or more stable (unstable) limit cycles.

Notes

1 However, Tugan-Baranowsky was wrong in attributing this logical error to Rosa Luxemburg. As a matter of fact, Luxemburg's main point was precisely that no automatic reinvestment of saving exists in mature capitalist economies, and that effective demand constitutes a major problem in the process of accumulation of capital (Kalecki, 1971, pp. 146–55).

2 In spite of the title, in Goodwin's article the trend element is of rather secondary importance. For one thing, the growth factors (technical progress and population growth) are exogenously given in terms of functions of time, and therefore they remain essentially unexplained. Second, the cyclical properties of the model are the same, irrespective of whether a trend exists or not. (This is, of course, true of our own classical model, as well.)

3 In the following discussion, technical progress is assumed to be neutral in the sense of Harrod.

4 For the sake of consistency with the other parts of the chapter, notation has been conveniently changed.

5 With constant capital–output ratio and constant output per head, the rates of growth of output, capital, and employment are obviously the same.

6 Notice that here and generally throughout this chapter, the rate of change should be taken to mean the *proportional* rate of change.

7 A quick study of the appendix will show that all *centers* are structurally unstable, and so, therefore is Goodwin's system.

8 If b is constant, so is $a = [b - (m + n)]$, as m and n are constant by assumption.

9 With given and constant rates of population growth and technical progress, we can speak of the rate of growth of activity instead of employment ratio, if we measure the former from $(m + n)$ rather than from zero.

10 There is an exception to assumption 8. In the vicinity of $(y = 1)$, $(dx/dy)|_{f_2=0} \to +\infty$ as $y \to 1$. That is to say, y cannot be greater than 1, irrespective of the value of x. This implies that, near $(y = 1)$, $(df_2/dS) < 0$).

11 We assume that the $(f_1 = 0)$ curve slopes backwards before nearing the line $(y = 1)$.

12 It is also readily seen that the coordinate axes are solution paths to the dynamic system of Equation 5, i.e., if the initial position of the system is represented by a point on either of the coordinate axes (different from the origin or from the point $(x = x_1;\ y = 0)$), the subsequent evolution of the system will be represented by a movement along the coordinate itself. (For example, suppose that – at time $(t = 0)$ – we have $x(0) = \bar{x}$, $(0 < \bar{x} < x_1)$, and $y(0) = 0$. From (5) and the Assumptions 9 we can readily see that in this case we would $\dot{x}(0) = f_1(\bar{x}, 0) \cdot \bar{x} > 0$, and $\dot{y}(0) = f_2(\bar{x}, 0) \cdot 0 = 0$.)

13 It is interesting to observe that the classical assumption 8 is a necessary condition in order that equilibria of type E_2 may be stable. If the curves $(f_1 = 0)$, $(f_2 = 0)$ intersected at a point for which $(\partial f_1/\partial x) > 0$, and we also had

$$(dx/dy)|_{(f_1=0)} < (dx/dy)|_{(f_2=0)}$$

the equilibrium point would be a saddle point and therefore it would be unstable.

14 The phrase "in general" here means: "for those specifications of the functions $f(x, y)$'s which are not exceptional."

15 The mathematical term for such a ring is "cycle without contact."

16 The number of limit cycles is known to be finite, their actual number depending on the structure of the system and, in particular, on the degree of nonlinearity of the relevant equations, and on the values of the parameters. When there is more than one limit cycle, they will be alternatively stable and unstable.

17 More exactly if we exclude the case in which *every* motion asymptotically tends to the equilibrium point as $t \to +\infty$.

18 It may be observed that only "soft generation oscillations" occur in the LVG model.

19 In this respect also, the present model differs from the LVG model, where initial conditions always determine which cyclical pattern (out of an infinite number) will be actually followed.

20 In order to be more precise as to the conditions for the rate of profit to increase or decrease we should know the exact functional relation between the level of employment and the output–capital ratio.

21 To be precise, this theorem is a derivation of the Poincaré-Bendixson theorem, but in the economic literature the distrinction is not mentioned (AVK, 1966, p. 361).

References

Andronov, A. A., Vitt, A. A., Khaikin, S. E. (AVK). 1966. *Theory of Oscillators.* English translation of Russian 2nd ed. New York: Pergamon Press. Originally published in 1937.

DeBaggis, H. F. 1952. "Dynamical Systems with Stable Structures, in *Contributions to the Theory of Nonlinear Oscillations.* Lefschetz, L., ed. Princeton, N.J.: Princeton University Press.

Desai, M. 1973. "Growth Cycles and Inflation in a Model of the Class Struggle," *Journal of Economic Theory,* 6: pp. 527–45.

Goodwin, R. M. 1967. "A Growth Cycle," in *Socialism, Capitalism and Economic Growth.* C. H. Feinstein, ed. Cambridge: Cambridge University Press, pp. 54–58.

Kalecki, M. 1971. *Selected Essays on the Dynamics of the Capitalist Economy.* Cambridge: Cambridge University Press.

Lotka, A. J. 1925. *Elements of Physical Biology.* Baltimore: Williams, Wilkins.

Phillips, A. W. 1958. "The Relation Between Unemployment and the Rate of Change of Money Wages Rates in the United Kingdom, 1861–1957," *Economica,* 25: pp. 283–99.

Rose, H. 1967. "On the Non-Linear Theory of the Employment Cycle," *Review of Economic Studies,* 37: pp. 153–73.

Sraffa, P. 1960. *Production of Commodities by Means of Commodities.* Cambridge: Cambridge University Press.

Steindl, J. 1952. *Maturity and Stagnation in American Capitalism.* London: Blackwell.

Sweezy, P. A. 1942. *The Theory of Capitalist Development.* New York: Oxford University Press.

Volterra, V. 1931. *Leçons sur le théorie mathématique de la lutte pour la vie.* Paris: Gauthiers-Villars.

Part V

International trade

12

Internationalization of capital and international politics: a radical approach

Stephen Hymer

To be radical, or to be a scientist, is the same thing; it is a question of trying to go to the root of the matter. For Marx, this meant trying to uncover the "economic laws of motion of modern society," that is, first of all, seeing society as an organism in motion constantly changing and developing as it moves from its beginning to its end, and second, searching in the economy, i.e., in changing conditions of production and exchange, for the underlying basis of this motion.

In this chapter, I wish to follow Marx's approach by viewing the present conjuncture of international politics and economics in terms of the long-term growth and spread of capitalist social relations of production to a world level. More concretely, I want to try to relate the current crises in national and international politics to the world market created during the last twenty-five years by the American Empire, first by examining Keynes's 1933 warnings of the difficulties and dangers for the development of modern society posed by the world market, and second, by using Marx's analysis of the general law of capitalist accumulation, and, in particular, his theory of the reserve army to go deeper into the roots of our present difficulties.

The basic text for this analysis is a provocative statement Marx wrote to Engels in October 1858:

> We cannot deny that bourgeois society has experienced its sixteenth century a second time – a sixteenth century which will, I hope, sound the death-knell of bourgeois society just as the first one thrust it into existence. The specific task of bourgeois society is the establishment of a world market, at least in outline, and of production based upon this world market. As the world is round, this seems to have been completed by the colonization of California and Australia and the opening up of China and Japan. The difficult question for us is this: on the Continent the revolution is imminent and will immediately assume a socialist character. Is it not bound to be crushed in this little corner, considering that in a far greater territory the movement of bourgeois society is still in the ascendant? (Marx and Engels, 1965, p. 111)

The beginnings of industrial capitalism

Capitalism began as a world market system in the mercantilist age of the sixteenth and seventeenth centuries when the discovery of America and the rounding of the Cape led to an explosion of maritime commerce and the creation of the first international economy. The epoch-making significance of this great burst of international trade, however, did not lie in the world market itself, but in the transformation of the home market that it unwittingly brought about.

It has been said of Columbus, who died thinking he had discovered a new route to India, that he was a man who, when he set out, did not know where he was going, that when he got there did not know where he was, and that when he returned did not know where he had been. The same irony characterized the mercantilist system as a whole. The merchants, adventurers, financiers and sovereigns of this age set out on an international quest for gold, spices and new lands, but the really important discoveries were made at home. Specifically, the expansion of foreign trade and the growth of merchants and

Stephen Hymer was killed in an automobile accident on February 2, 1974. This paper is a blend of his well-known paper "The Internationalization of Capital" (1972) and a draft paper he prepared for a conference sponsored by the Brookings Institution. The blending is the sole responsibility of the editor, but follows the lines Steve suggested in discussion shortly before his death.

finance capital resulted, along with other factors, in the disintegration of the traditional nonmarket domestic economy and the setting free of labor from its precapitalist forms of production. This newly created wage–labor force, when harnessed by industrial capital first into manufacturing and then into modern industry, unleashed an explosion in productivity that provided society with an entirely new material basis for its existence and ushered in the modern world.

Once the force of this great discovery of the value of labor power had been demonstrated by the English industrial revolution, other nations were compelled either to adopt this new mode of production or to be subdued by those countries which did. The mercantilist era had been characterized by active state intervention and acute national rivalry. At first, the new world economy of the nineteenth century took on an internationalistic or a nationalistic guise as it seemed that this age of industrial capital would be dominated by market principles and a government that governed best by governing least.

This was certainly the trend in Britain where the newly triumphant capitalist class set about (1) to systematically dismantle the state apparatus used by feudalism and mercantilism to control production and trade, and (2) to enlarge the extent of the market internally and externally. To some extent this tendency was followed by other nations, but actually a double movement was involved. On the one hand, they too had to dismantle the system of precapitalist controls, but at the same time, they had to unify the nation and strengthen the state in order to industrialize.

The first focus of the new industrial state was primitive accumulation, i.e., a conscious political effort to establish the conditions of modern capitalist production by setting free a wage–labor force to work and fostering a national industrial class to organize it. Those countries which did not effect such a transformation of the domestic economy soon fell prey to one imperial power or another and became underdeveloped.

Once industrial capitalism got going, a second task emerged; namely, that of keeping it going by mediating the contradictions it inevitably produced. These contradictions stemmed from two basic interconnected conditions: (1) the anarchic relations between capitalists which produced great waste and resulted in periodic crises, (2) the concentration of people into factories and cities and their growing politicization. With the accumulation of capital, these contradictions intensified and a large and elaborate superstructure was formed to contain them.

Thus we find during the late nineteenth and early twentieth centuries that the growth and spread of industrial capitalism was accompanied by a strengthening, not a declining nation state, and an intensification of national rivalry rather than its withering away. Internally, the visible hand of the state operated continuously alongside the invisible hand of the market. Internationally, one by one, countries erected national barriers against trade and in the late nineteenth century a scramble began to divide the underdeveloped countries into exclusive spheres of interest and into a new colonial system. The end result of Laissez-Faire, Pax Brittanica and Free Trade was the "welfare state," the first World War, and the complete breakdown of the international economy during the depression.

The world market versus national welfare

It is at this point that our story begins. We find in 1930 a world economy in which:

1. The industrial revolution has more or less spread to Western Europe, America, Russia, and Japan, but is far from complete in the sense that to varying degrees large pockets of nonindustrial, noncapitalist sectors remain in each country. Although certain beginnings towards industrial capitalism have been made in isolated spots in Latin America, Asia, and Africa, the vast majority of the world's population lives outside these enclaves.
2. There is a strong disenchantment with capitalism and internationalism and a belief that the nation state and not the invisible hand will play the dominant role in economic development. (Even the fascists call themselves national socialists.) On the other hand, thinking still remains one-dimensionally capitalist as far as production is concerned since no alternative has emerged to the alienated work process of the capitalist factory. Marx had felt that the working class would organize itself in revolt against the dominance of capital and create a new system of production, but in the 1930s an international revolutionary working class to lead us beyond capitalism still had not emerged.

It is in this context that we turn to Keynes's analysis of the conflict between a world market and national welfare as presented in his 1933 article on "National Self-Sufficiency." In this article Keynes argues that a restoration of the world market would unnecessarily prolong capitalism with its inherent evils and interfere with our progress towards the good society.

Describing himself as a man "who in the last resort prefers anything on earth to what the financial reports are wont to call 'the best opinion of Wall Street,'" he argues that world peace, prosperity and freedom could best be achieved by emphasizing noncapitalist national self-sufficiency rather than international market capitalism (Keynes, 1933, p. 766). In stronger language than almost any other economist would dare use, he came to the following conclusion:

> I sympathize, therefore, with those who would minimize, rather than with those who would maximize, economic entanglement among nations. Ideas, knowledge, science, hospitality, travel – these are the things which should of their nature be international. But let goods be homespun whenever it is reasonably and conveniently possible, and above all, let finance be primarily national. (Keynes, 1933, p. 758)

He supports his case with three basic arguments. First, he notes that contrary to the belief of the nineteenth-century free traders, the world market created in the Golden Age of Pax Brittanica did not ensure peace but ended in war and a depression. In his words:

> To begin with the question of peace. We are pacifist today with so much strength of conviction that, if the economic internationalist could win this point, he would soon recapture our support. But it does not now seem obvious that a great concentration of national effort on the capture of foreign trade, that the penetration of a country's economic structure by the resources and the influence of foreign capitalists, and that a close dependence of our own economic life on the fluctuating economic policies of foreign countries are safeguards and assurances of international peace. It is easier, in the light of experience and foresight, to argue quite the contrary. The protection of a country's existing foreign interests, the capture of new markets, the progress of economic imperialism – these are a scarcely avoidable part of a scheme of things which aims at the maximum of international specialization and at the maximum geographical diffusion of capital wherever its seat of ownership (Keynes, 1933, p. 757)

Second, he deals with the question of economic efficiency. He argues that the spread of modern technology makes it easier to produce locally the basic needs of a community and makes the argument for international specialization and export-oriented growth less compelling.

Third, and I think this is the most important part of his case, he argues that the free trader's economic internationalism assumes the whole world was, or would be, organized on the basis of private competitive capitalism. In contrast, Keynes felt that we had to go beyond capitalism if the fruits of the industrial revolution were to be realized in a humane and rational way. But a world market would prevent experimentation in socioeconomic organization and thus inhibit the free and full development of our potential.

Expressing a view that is not very popular today except among socialists, Keynes argues:

> The decadent international but individualistic capitalism, in the hands of which we found ourselves after the war, is not a success. It is not intelligent, it is not beautiful, it is not just, it is not virtuous – and it doesn't deliver the goods. In short, we dislike it, and we are beginning to despise it. . . .
>
> We each have our own fancy. Not believing that we are saved already, we each should like to have a try at working out our own salvation. We do not wish, therefore, to be at the mercy of world forces working out, or trying to work out, some uniform equilibrium according to the ideal principles, if they can be called such, of laissez-faire capitalism . . . We wish – for the time at least and so long as the present transitional, experimental phase endures – to be our own masters, and to be as free as we can make ourselves from the interferences of the outside world. (Keynes, 1933, pp. 760–62)

The internationalization of capital

Keynes's view, as expressed in this article, had little effect on the policies which governed the post-second World War reconstruction and development plans for the world economy. Instead, the best opinion of Wall Street and the City prevailed.

"Let there be no mistake about it," wrote *The Economist* in 1942 in an article on "The American Challenge," "the policy put forward by the American administration is revolutionary. It is a genuinely new conception of world order" (*The Economist*, July 1942, p. 67). In this way *The Economist*, reflecting the policy discussions taking place in London during the war, welcomed the plan to create a postwar world economy based on international capitalism under American hegemony.

The goal of this plan was "a new frontier, a frontier of limitless expanse, the frontier of human welfare," and "the instrument will be industrial capitalism, operating, broadly speaking, under conditions of private enterprise" (*The Economist,* June 1942, p. 824). Or, as *The Economist* put it, "the idealism of an international New Deal will have to be implemented by the unrivalled technical achievements of American business. The New Frontier will then become a reality" (*The Economist,* June 1942, p. 825). Or as *Fortune* expressed it with regard to underdeveloped countries, "American imperialism can afford to complete the work the British started; instead of salesmen and planters, its representatives can be brains and bulldozers, technicians and machine tools" (*Fortune,* May 1942, p. 63).

As we now know, this plan was highly successful. The world experienced a twenty-five year long secular boom in which employment, capital and technology grew rapidly and even the Socialist countries began to be drawn away from autarky into the whirlpool of the international market.

Ironically, Keynes's theory of state policy, which he himself believed to be a tool for bringing about the end of capitalism, was used to preserve it. In the *General Theory,* Keynes argued that by restoring full employment through government intervention, we could in a reasonable time destroy capital's monopoly and free ourselves from its grip. He judged that "it might be comparatively easy to make capital goods so abundant that the marginal efficiency of capital is zero," and that this peaceful evolution might "be the most sensible way of gradually getting rid of many of the objectionable features of capitalism" (Keynes, 1964, p. 221). In his view technological change could rather quickly (one or two generations) reduce the rate of profit and thus bring about "the euthanasia of the rentier, and, consequently, the euthanasia of the cumulative oppressive power of the capitalists to exploit the scarcity-value of capital" (Keynes, 1964, p. 376). And at the same time we could save money on management through "a scheme of direct taxation which allows the intelligence and determination and executive skill of the financier, the entrepreneur *et hoc genus omne* (who are certainly so fond of their craft that their labour could be obtained much cheaper than at present), to be harnessed to the service of the community on reasonable terms of reward" (Keynes, 1964, p. 276–77).

Keynes was as far off the mark here as he was in his call for national selfsufficiency. One generation has already passed. The rate of profit has not fallen; instead, the state has been harnessed to shore it up and ensure the continued growth of private wealth nationally and internationally. [That is, it has not fallen for the reason Keynes thought it would, namely, because capital goods had ceased to become scarce. (Editor's note).] Neither have managers' salaries been reduced. Rather the technostructure has gained in status and income as it has become an even more crucial element in supporting the expansion of capital and preventing its euthanasia.

Thus, contrary to Marx and Keynes, the world market and the welfare state have not sounded the death-knell of capitalism. At least not yet. Instead capitalism revived from the interwar crisis and flourished in the quarter century following the war.

Now, however, there are signs of strain in the system and a wave of reexamination and reconsideration of its basic framework is taking place in the light of emerging contradictions and crises, national and international. The tightening of the web of interdependence, to use a now popular phrase, seems to be becoming increasingly uncomfortable as we progress into the 1970s. There is a certain unease in many quarters (dramatized by the oil crisis) that we may be too much at the "mercy of world forces" and too little "our own masters." And there are signs of an outbreak of the national rivalry that Keynes thought was scarcely avoidable if we placed too much emphasis on the world market.

However, due to the internationalization of capital, competition between national capitalists is becoming less and less a source of rivalry between nations. Using the instrument of direct investment, large corporations are able to penetrate foreign markets and detach their interests from their home markets. At the same time, capitalists from all nations, including underdeveloped countries, are able to diversify their portfolios internationally through the international capital market. Given these tendencies, an international capitalist class is emerging whose interests lie in the world economy as a whole and a system of international private property which allows free movement of capital between countries. The process is contradictory and may break down, but for the present there is a strong tendency for the most powerful segments of the capitalist class increasingly to see their future in the further growth of the world market rather than its curtailment.

"When labour cooperates systematically," Marx wrote, "it strips off the fetters of its individuality and develops the capability of its species." But in order for labor to cooperate, it must be brought together and linked through exchange. Under capitalism, the cooperation of laborers is entirely brought about by the capital that employs them. The history of social labor is the history of social capital since the number of laborers who can work together depends upon the degree to which capital is concentrated and centralized.

The two powerful levers for concentrating capital into larger and larger aggregates and then integrating these aggregates into a unified whole are *competition* and *credit*. Competition drives firms to continuously reinvest their profits and extend their markets as a means of self-preservation. The credit system unites individual capitals and stimulates further increases in their size. It acts as an immense social mechanism above that of the individual firm for the centralization of capital and the preservation of its collective interest. The market forces are now operating on a world scale and leading to the internationalization of corporations and capital.

The dynamics of corporate expansion

Business enterprises usually are built around some special discovery or advantage. Before their innovation becomes general, they can undersell their competitors and still sell at a price well above cost of production. But their position is constantly threatened by new entrants who may discover a new technology, a new product, a new form of organization, or a new supply of labor. The dialectic of the product cycle gives capitalism its forward motion. An innovation is introduced; if it succeeds, the product enjoys a high rate of growth as it displaces other products and more and more consumers come to use it. As the market becomes saturated, growth tapers off while profitability is squeezed. Simultaneously, other firms try to enter the market because the very success of the innovation provides tangible proof that the new product works and that a market exists. With the secret out, production costs begin to dominate. The competition of other firms using cheaper labor or accepting a lower rate of profit eats into the original innovator's profit.

There are two ways of coping with the competitive threat. First, a continuous effort can be made to develop new products; when the rate of growth slows, the firm can switch tracks and continue at a high rate of profit. Second, the product cycle can be prolonged by gaining control of marketing outlets, searching for and moving to places of cheaper labor, and secrecy. These two methods, of course, are intertwined, for the wider a firm's market, the more it can spread the costs of innovation, and the more it can afford to spend on research and development.

Both these methods require further investment. At a given point of time, a corporation may be earning a high rate of profit because it is onto a good thing, but competition and technological change threaten to wipe out its advantage. It must plough back its profits in order to improve production and expand its scale "merely as a means of self-preservation and under threat of ruin." Thus under capitalism change becomes normal and businessmen can never afford to look upon and treat the existing form of a process as final. The incessant revolutions in production and the depreciation of the existing capital this implies spur them on to new methods and new places.

The second great lever of capital concentration and centralization is the credit system. The formation of a world capital market has only begun, but if its development continues at the present rate, it soon will be a factor of great significance in the world economy.

The multinational corporation and the international capital market should be seen as parallel, symbiotic developments. The multinational corporation's need for short-term loans and investment arising from the continuous inflow and outflow of money from all nations, never quite in balance, has encouraged international banking and has helped integrate short-term money markets; its long-term financial requirements and excellent credit rating have broadened the demand for international bond and equity capital. This provides an impetus for free international capital mobility.

The Eurobond market, for example, attracts capital from all over the surface of the globe (a significant portion comes from underdeveloped countries, particularly the oil wealth of the Middle East and the war wealth of southeast Asia), concentrates it in an organized mass, and redirects it via multinational corporations and other intermediaries back to the country from which it came. It then bears the stamp of international capital and its privileges.

The development of the international capital market, in turn, gives multinational corporations increased access to the savings of many nations, enables larger undertakings to be formed, and fosters mergers and consolidations. Most important, it helps forge an identity of interests between competing national capitals, a vital ingredient for the survival of the multinational corporate system. We saw in the last section how international competition in the product market raised the horizons of corporations from the national to the international plane. Similarly, the international flow of private capital, through the multinational corporation or alongside it, gives individual wealthholders a stake in the international capitalist system as a whole, in proportion as their income comes less and less from their home country, and more and more from the world economy at large.

The overseas expansion of American firms, for example, has substantially diversified the investment portfolio of American shareholders internationally. In addition, Americans have purchased stock in non-American corporations, or invested in land or other assets abroad, and thus further transferred their interests from the United States to the world as a whole. Given the prospects for industrial growth outside the United States and the social and political problems within the United States, this diversification is likely to continue as a sort of capital flight. At the same time, capitalists from other countries have been buying corporate stock in the United States, lending money to multinationals in regional or local capital markets, and in this way shedding their national character and becoming part of international capital.

National corporations and national finance capital

An analogy might be made here to the development of the national corporation and national capitalism in the United States at the turn of the century. Prior to that time, the typical industrial enterprise was the closed family firm with only a few outside shareholders. With the merger movement and the development of a national capital market for industrial equity stock, the modern corporation began to emerge with many shareholders, none of whom owned a majority of stock.

Much has been written about how the dispersion of ownership and the lessening of direct control over management by owners has created an autonomous technostructure which operates independently of the specifically capitalist character of the production process. However, it seems to me to be more appropriate to look upon this process in exactly the opposite way. From the point of view of the large capitalists, that is, the 1 percent of the population that owns the vast majority of corporate stock, the modern corporation was an institutional device for maintaining their control and ensuring the continued accumulation of their wealth.

What happened, in effect, was that the wealthy exchanged shares among themselves, thus forging a common front. Far from relinquishing their interests, they generalized them. Instead of each family capital being locked into a specific firm, it became diversified over many firms and over other assets, such as government bonds and land. In this system, competition more or less assures the equalization of the rate of return; and each capital, if it is sufficiently diversified and prudently managed, will share in the general social surplus, according to its size. Rivalry remains as each capitalist strives to obtain an above-average rate of return, but a dominant general interest in the aggregate rate of profit emerges. At this higher level "capitalists form a veritable free mason society vis-à-vis the whole working class, while there is little love lost between them in competition amongst themselves" (Marx, 1967, Vol. 2).

The corporate structure and the development of a managerial class enabled capital to delegate the work of supervising labor to others and to rely on the market and the government to maintain the rate of profit and the rate of accumulation. In this connection Marx quotes Aristotle: "Whenever the masters are not compelled to plague themselves with supervision, the manager assumes *this honour* while the masters attend to affairs of state or study philosophy" (Marx, 1967, Vol. 3, p. 377). Or one might use Plato's system and say that owners of capital have been elevated to the position of guardians, while the technostructure performs the function of auxiliaries. The interests of the Rockefellers are no longer tied solely to Standard Oil, but their propensity to accumulate has not diminished now that they study economics and attend to the affairs of state as guardians in banking and government.

Multinational corporations and international capital

From this point of view, the national corporation abolished "private" property through collectivization and gave it a general social character as essentially the common capital of a class. The overriding interest of this class is not the war of each against each, but the common need of all to maintain the capitalist society, that is, the rights of property to income and the assurance of an adequate supply of labor to generate that income. Similarly, the multinational corporate system tends to abolish national capital and create a world system in which output is produced cooperatively to a greater degree than ever before, but control remains uneven; capitalists, as trustees of society, continue to pocket a good share of the proceeds.

Without the multinational corporate system, the growth of American capital, and European and Japanese capital, would be thwarted by the growth of new capitals or new socialisms based on the increasing productivity of world labor. With the multinational corporate system, the interests of the 1 percent can be better preserved as they absorb and co-opt some of their potential creditors while crowding out others.

The great pull of this system toward international class consciousness on the part of capital can be illustrated by the ambivalence of the successful industrial capitalist in underdeveloped countries. In the short run he may find it better to remain independent of international capital and continue his successful challenge, but his long-run interest often lies elsewhere. No matter how successful the family firm, it is faced with the problem of managerial succession and limited possibilities of obtaining capital for expansion as long as its shares are tightly held. In addition, there is the ever-present threat of nationalization. If this capitalist allows himself to be taken over by a multinational corporation, he can solve most of these problems. In return for a profitable but inflexible investment in a national firm, he obtains shares of a multinational corporation, traded on the world market, and guaranteed by all the forces that lie behind the international law of private property. He is no longer locked into his industry or his country; the viability of his concern is ensured by its connections to the multinational firm, and he can probably stay on and manage it. Furthermore, his need for Swiss bank accounts and other ways of escaping his own government is diminished because now his capital receives the special privileges of foreign capital. Although every state is absolutely sovereign with regard to national property within its borders, foreign capital is protected by the rule of no confiscation without reparation.

These considerations apply to every capitalist in the world seeking protection and future growth. In my view they help explain why Canadian and European capitalists preferred the positive response to American expansion (that is, becoming multinational themselves), rather than the negative response of blocking American penetration. I think Japanese capital might go the same way. Who knows – perhaps the Russian elite also see outward expansion as necessary for maintaining their internal power and, hence, are opening their arms toward multinationals in the name of science and technology.

In sum, the wealthy of the world have a strong interest in internationalism in order to preserve their position. Freedom to intermingle and compete in the world capital market allows them to diversify their holdings and escape supervision of national governments, that is, control by the majority. It thus protects them from the vagaries of specific markets and specific governments and gives them diversified, general interests in the maintenance of the capitalist system as a whole. This continued flow of aggregate profit is then divided among them more or less in proportion to their wealth, as equalization of world rates of profit is brought about by competition.

International division of labor

As we have just seen, market forces lead corporations and capitalists toward internationalization and a greater recognition of their mutual harmony of interests. At the same time, they divide labor, to whom increased cooperation appears as increased competition. The expansion of the market does not, for the most part, help labor diversify and expand, as it does capital; rather, in many cases it takes away their security and stability.

In order for the multinational corporate system to survive and expand, it must maintain the rate of profit. At its most fundamental level this depends on the state of the labor market and the gap between the productivity of labor and the share labor is allowed to control. Capital can be threatened within the system by labor's unwillingness to work efficiently at a "reasonable wage," and ultimately it is threatened by political revolution which would destroy private property as the basis of income and investment.

To maintain the separation between work and control, capital has erected elaborate corporate superstructures to unite labor in production, but divide it in power. On the political plane, it has used the state bureaucracy to maintain, by force or by education, the general structural conditions which cause laborers to come to work each day and to accept the authority of the capitalist and his right to higher income, either as managerial compensation or as interest and dividends.

Corporate structure as divide and rule

"An industrial army of workmen under the command of a capitalist," wrote Marx, "requires, like a real army, officers (managers), and sergeants (foremen, overseers) who, while the work is being done, command in the name of the capitalist" (Marx, 1967, Vol. 2, p. 322). Upon its various bases of national labor, the multinational corporation constructs local hierarchies to supervise and manage day-to-day operations, regional administrations to coordinate national branches, and, at the top, strategy apexes to give overall guidance and direction through the use of budgetary controls. At the bottom of this vertical hierarchy, labor is divided into many nationalities. As one proceeds up the pyramid, nationality becomes more homogeneous and increasingly north European.

The work of this hierarchy has a twofold character. In part, it fulfills functions of coordination and unification which are necessary wherever larger numbers cooperate; in part it fulfills functions that arise from the alienated nature of work in capitalist production. Under capitalism, the laborer does not think socially about his work, his machines, or his product. He regards his work as something he would rather not do, except that he needs the money. Because he does not participate voluntarily, each day is a constant struggle over labor time. The capitalist, or his representative, tries to get the laborer to do something he does not want to do. The laborer tries not to do it.

The twofold character of the technostructure is reflected in the twofold nature of division of labor, which partially is based on the greater productivity that results from specialization, and partially stems from the principle of divide and rule. The corporate hierarchy is essentially a structure to control the flow of information. It has strong vertical linkages so that information passes up and orders pass down easily, and it has strong lateral communication at the top in order to obtain concerted action. At the bottom, lateral communication is broken so that the majority cannot consolidate against the minority. This is done through a series of pyramids in which the president supervises *n* men, who in turn each supervise *n* men at the next lower level, and so on until everyone is integrated in a large pyramid that fans out from the center. Each supervisor controls the budget and promotion of the people below him.

In principle a person at any one level can only communicate with someone at the same level who is not in his group by going through his supervisor at the higher level. The higher up one goes, the more flexibility, opportunity, and discretion are permitted. At the bottom, people are rated on a daily or hourly basis, have little opportunity for advancement, and work within narrowly prescribed limits. At the management level, people have a career where promotion is the expected result of performance; the higher they rise, the more they move about, the greater the discretion (responsibility) given to them. People are rewarded doubly since the better the job, the higher the pay. People in the middle and at the top have positions rather than jobs, salaries rather than wages.

The vertical stratification of the corporation rests on a division of mental and manual labor. The higher-level intellectual functions concentrate at the top and vanish on the bottom. In the natural body, head and hand wait upon each other. In the corporation, they part company and become deadly foes. Although the multinational corporation spreads production over the world, it concentrates coordination and planning in key cities, and preserves power and income for the privileged.

The power of the bottom is thus weakened by the spatial division of labor. Each national or regional labor force performs a specialized function which is only meaningful to the integrated whole, yet it has no understanding of the whole. Its integration with other groups is not of its own doing, but is the act of capital (the head) that brings them together; it remains an isolated group whose connections to other groups are matters foreign and external to it. Even its national leaders – its government officials and local corporate executives – are only middlemen in a world system, and are themselves blocked from the information needed to obtain an overall picture. The national technostructures occupy an ambivalent position. On the one hand, they are in conflict with the top of the pyramid over their desire for better jobs or their nationalist identification with their country; on the other hand, they are subordinate and dependent because they lack the key ingredients of capitalist power – information and money.

The government may have apparent political sovereignty, but it too has limited real power and is forever looking to international corporations for technology and capital. It remains a weak state, subordinated to the dictates of the budget, the sternest taskmaster of all in a capitalist society. In this way, the corporate economy attempts to solve its dilemma: it requires an expanding state to solve its problems, but must prevent the state from coming under the actual control of the majority, who have formal control in a democratic state. As long as the state is barred from the process of production, it does not develop the capacity to generate capital and technology, which it always must seek from corporate headquarters, where it has been collected for redistribution. Yet the very process by which it obtains foreign aid ensures that the state will once again be dependent in the next round. The international division of labor keeps the head separate from the hand, and each hand separate from every other. It thus weakens the potential resistance to capital control.

The weakening of the state is a two-edged sword; it incapacitates the government from fulfilling social needs which require active participation, support, and understanding from the population as a whole. The demonstrative effect of capitalist growth creates rising expectations which it is unable to fulfill. In older established areas, resistance and unity grow, forcing capital to tap new untainted sources as a spatial industrial reserve army. Hence the contradictory nature of industrialization of the Third World.

The spread of technology potentially should

make everyone better off, but it appears to labor in advanced countries as a conflict for jobs. This is because their jobs and income are in fact threatened by international competition since under capitalism the burden of adjustment is placed on them. The cycle of depressed areas and depopulation which happened when textiles left the northern United States, for example, now might well be occurring on a world scale. As capital leaves one group of workers for another, in a process resembling slash and burn agriculture, the advanced group is forced to lie fallow in unemployment for use later when their resistance has been weakened.

In the next section, I would like to turn to the other side of the coin and examine the interests of labor in the world market. The main theme is that labor will tend to become more nationalistic and possibly more socialistic as the continued growth of the world market undermines its traditional strategy.

Labor and the world market stage of capitalism

"Accumulation of capital is, therefore, increase of the proletariat" (Marx, 1967, Vol. 1, p. 614). This is the key concept in Marx's analysis of the general law of motion of capitalist society. Capitalist competition leads, at one level, to the concentration and centralization of capital in large corporations tied together by a capital market and unified at the political level by the state. At another level, it draws an ever-increasing portion of the population into the wage laboring class, concentrates them into large factories and urban centers and develops in them a group cohesiveness which makes them a political force in opposition to capital. In this way, capitalism, which is based on the competitive wage labor system, creates within itself forms of social organization which are antithetical to competition and the market system and which, in Marx's view, serve as the embryo of a new society beyond capitalism.

The trend towards class consciousness is, however, a long-drawn-out process that proceeds dialectically out of the competition between workers. On the one hand, the continuous expansion of capital and extension of the market unifies wage workers into larger and larger groupings as they strive to eliminate competition between themselves; on the other hand, it also introduces new elements of competition which divide workers into antagonistic groups and inhibit their realizing the latent potential of their unity.

Marx identified two major forces in the development of capitalism (in addition to the ideological superstructure of the corporation and the state) which continually create competition between workers and allow capitalism to reproduce itself on an expanded scale and to survive even its worst crises. First, technological change substitutes machinery for labor: by throwing, or threatening to throw, the worker out of the factory and into the market, it breaks up the cohesiveness of labor organization and reduces workers to individuals or small groups competing with each other instead of cooperating. Secondly, capitalism continuously breaks down precapitalist areas – what Marx calls the latent surplus population – thus forming a fresh supply of nonclass-conscious workers to compete in the labor market.

These two dynamic forces create a stratified labor force which keeps the pretensions of the working class in check. Above the proletariat stands a vast officer class of managers, technicians and bureaucrats to organize it and to overcome its resistance by keeping it divided. Below it is a pool of unemployed, underemployed, and badly-paid strata continuously fed by technological change and the opening up of new hinterlands, which undercut its position and inhibit its development towards class consciousness. This reserve army drives the labor aristocracy to keep on working and keeps it loyal to the capitalist system from fear of falling from its superior position. By the nature of things, these different strata often come from different regions within a country, different racial or ethnic groups, and different age and sex classes. Thus, the competitive cleavages between workers often reflect lines of race, creed, color, age, sex, and national origin, which make working class consciousness more difficult.

The significance of the world market stage of capitalism into which we have now entered is that this competitive process, which both brings labor together and separates it, has not taken on an international dimension. The growth of world trade brings labor of different countries into closer contact and competition; the internationalization of production via the multinational corporate system was a reaction on the part of capital to this fact. American firms, for example, found that the recovery of Europe and the development of labor surplus economies in the Third World, made it possible to produce certain things more cheaply abroad than in the United States; and competitive pressure from emerging non-American capitalists forced them to invest abroad or enter into licensing and management contracts in order to preserve their position and maintain their growth. More generally, the emergence of a unified world commodity market, which in effect is the emergence of a unified world labor market, switched the domain of competition and its accompanying tendencies towards concentration and centralization from the national to the international plane. But this quest for profit, which led capital to shed its national character and escape the narrow confines of the nation state, has also intensified competitive pressure on labor and undermined its traditional organization and strategy. This, I suggest, is bound to bring about a new stage of development of labor organization, and it is here we must search for the root of the matter if we wish to understand our present predicament and the development track we are on.

In short, we must view present developments in terms of the long-term spread of commodity production, based on wage labor, from the local towns of the Middle Ages and the small enclaves of the transition period, to the national market and now the world market. The process of concentration and centralization of capital occurring within this framework led both to the steady growth and development of modern enterprise from the workshop to the factory to the national corporation to the multidivisional corporation and now to the multinational corporation, and to the parallel spread of the financial system from the local to the national and now to the international plane. At the same time, this growth has led to the continuous spread of labor organization in response to the opening up of new sources of competition and the emergence of new contradictions. This took place partly through the spread of the trade union movement to a broader and broader basis, and partly through the joint action of workers of different industries in the struggle over the working day, health, education, social security, unemployment, etc., at the political level. Workers' organization has so far taken place almost entirely within national boundaries through a struggle to obtain civil rights and national laws to protect labor from some of the necessitudes of the competitive labor process. Now internationalization of capital, combined with certain domestic contradictions of the welfare state, has brought the established structure of labor organization to a critical juncture, and it is to this problem that we must now turn.

The political role of labor

From a Marxist perspective, the main theoretical shortcoming of Keynes's analysis is that he paid no attention to the conditions of production and the political role of labor. He viewed the market system, based on greed and selfishness, with considerable disdain and wanted to go beyond the profit motive towards a society managed by a society-oriented elite, operating in a loose framework that combined state planning and large quasi-public operations. He did not believe that either the capitalists or the "boorish proletariat" could or would lead us to this higher form of organization, but felt that the process of capital accumulation and technological progress would achieve this end naturally despite the wrong-headed interferences by capital and labor. Thus, neither in his political nor his economic writings, did he pay attention to class struggle as a moving force in capitalist development.

Ironically, this limited perspective was also in one sense his genius, for in fact during the postwar period, the issue of class struggle was highly subdued and labor did not form a serious challenge to capitalism as a system, but instead cooperated within its framework. This was one of the reasons capitalism grew so rapidly and one of the reasons Keynes's theory of monetary and fiscal policy could work.

In the *General Theory,* Keynes shifted the focus of discussion away from the labor market to the capital market. Classical economists saw unemployment and stagnation as the result of too high a level of wages. (In Marxian terms, too low a rate of surplus value.) Keynes instead postulated an elastic supply of labor at the going wage and sought the breakdown of the system in the contradictions between savers and investors, i.e., the rentier class and the entrepreneurial/managerial class. Keynes's preferred way out of this dilemma seemed to be through an expansion of the state and public consumption at the expense of the rentier class, but the alternative preferred by the capitalist was an expansion of the state to promote the growth of private wealth through the stimulation of private investment and private consumption. It was this path that finally predominated.

This strategy was possible because of specific conditions emerging from the great depression and the war which restored the workings of the labor market. In Marxist theory, the functioning of the wage labor market, upon which capitalist expansion depends, is maintained in the first instance through the institutions of the reserve army.

> The industrial reserve army, during the periods of stagnation and average prosperity, weights down the active labour army; during the periods of overproduction and paroxysm, it holds its pretensions in check. Relative surplus-population is therefore the pivot upon which the law of demand and supply of labour works. It confines the field of this law within the limits absolutely convenient to the activity of exploitation and to the domination of capital (Marx, 1967, Vol. 1, p. 639).

In this sense, the long period of large scale unemployment of the 1930s served as a disciplinary action on labor to make it ready, willing and anxious to work again in the postwar period. But action at the political level was needed as well.

> As soon, therefore, as the labourers learn the secret, how it comes to pass that in the same measure as they work more, as they produce more wealth for others, and as the productive power of their labour increases, so in the same measure even their function as a means of the self-expansion of capital becomes more and more precarious for them; as soon as they discover that the degree of intensity of the competition among themselves depends wholly on the pressure of the relative surplus-population; as soon as, by trade unions, etc., they try to organize a regular cooperation between the employed and unemployed in order to destroy or to weaken the ruinous effects of this natural law of capitalistic production on their class, so soon capital and its sycophant, political economy, cry out at the infringement of the "eternal" and so to say "sacred" law of supply and demand. Every combination of employed and unemployed disturbs the "harmonious" actions of this law. But on the other hand, as soon as (in the colonies, e.g.) adverse circumstances prevent the creation of an industrial reserve army and, with it, the absolute dependence of the working class upon the capitalist class, capital, along with its commonplace Sancho Panza, rebels against the "sacred" law of supply and demand and tries to check its inconvenient action by forcible means and State interference. (Marx, 1967, Vol. 1, p. 640)

The New Deal, the World War and the Cold War made it possible in the United States to purge the labor movement of its radical elements and create a system of collective bargaining within the framework of the welfare state. This system left the basic capitalist institutions of private wealth and wage labor largely untouched and channeled labor protest into narrowly-defined trade unionism, which concentrated on selling labor at a more advantageous price without challenging the prerogatives of management and capital, either inside the plant or out of it. Trade unions confined their horizons to the interests of their own membership and instead of unifying all of labor in a class perspective, maintain cleavages within the best-paid aristocracy of the working class and between it and the reserve army. The law of supply and demand was thus altered by the growth of unions, but still kept working within conveniently confined limits. The history of the European movement was different in content but similar in effect, that is, the elimination of radical perspectives and the creation of a framework in which labor was willing to submit to the dictates of capital in order to obtain economic growth and capitalism's "New Frontier."

A major factor in making the system work was the existence of a latent surplus-population in the underdeveloped countries and backward sectors of advanced countries which could be broken down to form a constantly flowing surplus population to work at the bottom of the ladder. In the United States the replacement of southern sharecropping agriculture by modern capitalist methods created a flow of black labor to the northern cities, just as the "development" of Puerto Rico led to large-scale immigration into the eastern United States. Similarly, in Europe modernization of agriculture and the importation of labor from foreign countries played a major role in creating the labor supply needed for capitalist expansion. In addition, the advanced countries benefited from cheap prices for raw materials made possible by the creation of a labor surplus economy in the underdeveloped countries.

Thus, during this twenty-five year period, labor was able to enjoy prosperity and growth as it concentrated on working harder for steadily increasing standards of living and refrained from challenging the system politically. By and large the major source of rebellion and protest did not come from the established proletariat during the Fifties and Sixties, but from the new strata being incorporated into the wage labor force from their previous position in the latent surplus population. These groups were highly critical of the conditions of capitalist production, as they found themselves caught between the breakdown of the old system and the unfulfilled expectations of the new one. They were acutely aware of the coercive nature of the capitalist work relationship, since, unlike the traditional working class, they were "disadvantaged," i.e., they had not yet internalized the capitalist values of alienated work. And they were also extremely bitter at the inequality of their position and the discriminations they suffered.

These factors, which gave such great force to their reaction, also limited the scope of their challenge to capitalism. Because they were outside production and at odds with the privileged strata, they were relatively powerless to actually transform the capitalist system. Their programs often tended to be backward-looking, harking after a return to older forms of community production, and/or anarchistically radical, seeking to burn, destroy and sabotage the system which oppressed them, rather than to seize it for their own. They were caught in a dilemma. On the one hand, they were antagonistic to capitalism, but on the other hand, they also wanted to get into it and share its benefits and privileges. The result of this dualism was a tendency for their group to split as some entered the labor force and became part of the system, while others fell down into the stagnant part of the reserve army with extremely irregular employment, well below average conditions of life, and into the lowest sediments which dwell in the sphere of pauperism, thus forming an incredible pool of wasted human beings in the slums, ghettos and rural hinterlands of the capitalist economy.

Thus the uneven development of capitalism, accumulating wealth at one pole and misery at the other, was from the political point of view a stabilizing force because it divided the potential opposition to capitalism into conflicting groups. The question is, then, for how long can this go on? In the next section, I examine the pressures on the labor aristocracy which I believe are bringing this phase of capitalist expansion to an end and leading us to a period when class conflict between capital and labor will be a major force in the economy and polity, nationally and internationally.

The seeds of a new class conflict

The success of the "American Challenge" and the "New Frontier," we have argued, rested on a particular set of initial conditions arising out of the great depression and the World War. These wore down the resistance of labor, destroyed its radical wing and made organized labor into a willing participant in a strategy based on strong state action to promote growth and international expansionism. But the very success of the plan has tended to undermine these initial conditions and to lead us to a stage marked by crisis and reorientation of basic strategies.

In the first place, memories of the Thirties and Forties have faded in this period of affluence, while the "New Frontier" has turned out to be less rewarding than it promised. The growth of national income satisfied some of the pent-up needs of previous decades and created new needs which the market system cannot fulfill. The consumer durable revolution provided most families with a car, a television set, and a refrigerator, but also resulted in overcrowding, pollution, and an energy crisis. The middle class standard of living, towards which the working class aspired, is predicated in large part on only a few people having it. When everybody has a car, the result is not freedom to escape from overcrowded cities into the countryside, but a crowded countryside. Similarly, when everybody has access to higher education, its elite qualities and privileges are destroyed and a college degree no longer means a ticket to the top of the hierarchy, but an upgraded job at the lower level. Thus, many of the promises of capitalistic consumption tend to be illusory, while alienation and exploitation in the work process remain an ever-present reality. Therefore, job dissatisfaction and a decreased motivation to work has increased steadily over the last twenty-five years, and resulted in the productivity crisis causing so much discussion and concern in business circles.

In the second place, the latent surplus population has been steadily drying up, thus exhausting national pools of cheap labor and lessening the competitive pressure on the work force. Moreover, as more and more people from the nonwage sector are drawn into the wage labor force, the locus of their struggle against discrimination, alienation and exploitation shifts from outside to inside, thus infusing the labor movement with new dimensions of protest and militancy. At the same time, the demands for welfare and other support programs by those who are nonincorporated into the wage labor force eat up the surplus and limit the scope for expanding wages.

These two trends have seriously threatened the collective bargaining strategy which dominated the trade union movement over the last twenty-five years. Trade unions can obtain higher wages within capitalist expansion only to the extent that they are matched by increased productivity or passed on to lower strata of the labor force. However, the tightening of the labor market that accompanies capitalist expansion increases the pretensions of the working class, both with regard to wages and relief from work, at the same time that it diminishes the possibility of placing the burden on disadvantaged sectors. Hence, wage demands result in inflation and a crisis in labor organization. A recent article in *Business Week,* for example, focused on three crises in the union movement: dissatisfaction on the part of consumers concerning the inflationary consequences of wage demands; dissatisfaction on the part of businessmen over the ability of the unions to deliver the intensity of work contracted for; and dissatisfaction on the part of the rank and file over the responsiveness of union leadership to their needs (*Business Week,* 1972, pp. 66–76).

These tendencies in the labor market, which are occurring throughout the advanced capitalist world as capital expansions occur (usually called a shift in the Phillips curve by non-Marxist economists), have led to the widespread adoption of wage and price controls, thus signaling the de facto end, or at least the beginning of the end, of the era of collective bargaining. Trade unions can no longer confine their horizons to the struggle between their membership and its employers, but must bargain politically at the national level over the share of wages in national income. In Marxian terms, the material conditions of trade union consciousness are coming to an end in advanced capitalism since the trade unions can no longer confine themselves to wages, but must deal directly with the problem of the aggregate rate of surplus value which is a class phenomenon. At this point of development, they soon find out that there is very little that can be done about the rate of surplus value within a capitalist framework, since increases in the share of wages cut down on investment and result in unemployment and a slackening of growth. A socialist alternative, under which the working class seizes control of the investment process, could open new possibilities of organizing production and promoting the growth and development of the potential of social labor. Failing this radical break, the working class is a hostage to the capitalist class on whom they depend for capital accumulation and to whom they must provide incentives in the form of profit and accumulation of capital, that is, more work.

Thus, labor organizations must shift their horizons from the industrial to the national level, that is, they must shift from economic to political action. At the same time, the growth of the world market and the internationalization of capital implies they must also shift their horizons to the world level. Once again, they discover how limited their options are if they do not challenge the capitalist system. If, for example, they adopt a protectionist policy, they can lessen the competition from imports, but they cannot insure a high rate of national investment if capitalists can escape their national demands by investing abroad. If they try to control capital flight, they then discover that the size and complexity of multinational corporations and the international financial market provide capitalists with numerous escape valves and that unless they take over the whole system, they can only achieve partial control.

Another strategy is international trade unionism, which can alleviate competition in certain industries but is still partly limited on two accounts. First, organizing workers in developed countries for higher wages at the cost of reduced employment, though it obtains the support of some groups, increases the gap between the small local labor aristocracy and the vast reserve army and creates politically volatile conditions which have to be brutally suppressed. Second, international trade unionism can only struggle over industry wage and working conditions. But a great part of labor's historical gains have occurred at the political level and are embodied in national social infrastructure in the fields of health, education, welfare, social security, etc. Equalization of this infrastructure to remove competition involves far more political unification than a simple trade unionist strategy can provide.

Therefore, on both counts – the internal reserve army and the external reserve army – labor is in an objective crisis where its old institutions and policies no longer work, and, what amounts to the same thing, so is capitalism. This is what I believe to be the radical view of international economics and international politics at this juncture in history.

The next twenty-five years

Work in the Marxist framework is a political relationship. In the market, where workers sell their labor in exchange for wages, it seems to be only an economic phenomenon, but this is an illusion. What the workers sell is not labor but labor power, that is, their life activity. How this labor power will be used, its duration and intensity, is not settled by competition but by struggle and force. Hence there arises within the business enterprise a political superstructure whose function is in part to coordinate work and in part to overcome the resistance of workers arising out of the antagonistic social relations of production. Similarly, the struggle over work leads to the capitalist state whose function in the last instance is to insure the reproduction of the basic structural elements of the work relationship – capital and labor. The rise and spread of the market system is thus closely connected to a political struggle to create and maintain the wage labor force, divided by competition, upon which capitalism rests.

Politics – the getting, keeping, and using of power – is mainly a question of uniting your allies and dividing your enemies. Marx's analysis of the general laws of capitalist accumulation is an attempt to uncover the tendencies towards concentration and class consciousness that develop in the two main contending parties as capitalism progresses.

The peculiar feature of capitalism is that it obtained power and in some sense maintains it with an inherently limited degree of class consciousness. Capitalism is a system based on the mutual indifference of its participants, operating in a structure of competition and the pursuit of selfish interests. In economists' terms, it is a highly decentralized system based on private profit maximization and united through the invisible hand of the market, that is, the law of value. The great strength of this system, which differentiates it from all previous modes of production, is that the competition between capitalists and between capital and labor forces a continuous revolution in technology and an epoch-making expansion of material production. But this competitive market nexus is also its chief limit, for it prevents the development of a total view of society commensurate with the increasingly interdependent social division of labor that it is creating. The capitalist state attempts to provide some sort of total view, but is sharply limited by the divisions in capitalist society between capital and labor and between capitalists themselves. As capitalism progresses, this contradiction intensifies. The problems of "externalities," to use economists' language, and "socialization" and "legitimization" become more important as more and more problems arise which cannot be managed by the invisible hand of the market. The world market, created since World War II, has brought things to a critical point. Capital has expanded to global dimensions, but still maintains a consciousness based on narrow private calculation. The structure of the American empire, which kept some sort of order on this process in the past, is dissolving and a Hobbesian-like struggle of all against all seems to be emerging at the world level. As the anarchy of competition asserts itself, we find ourselves facing numerous crises, with even greater ones looming in the background.

Labor, in contrast to capital, though it too is divided by competition, steadily struggles to eliminate this competition at higher and higher levels until it reaches a world historic perspective far more total than capital and replaces capitalism by socialism. This unification, however, is a long-drawn-out process, requiring a high development of material forces, i.e., a long expansion of capitalist production.

> Competition separates individuals from one another, not only the bourgeois but still more the workers, in spite of the fact that it brings them together. Hence it is a long time before these individuals can unite, apart from the fact that for the purpose of this union – if it is not to be merely local – the necessary means, the great industrial cities and cheap and quick communications have first to be produced by big industry. Hence, every organized power standing over against these isolated individuals who live in relationships daily reproducing this isolation, can only be overcome after long struggles. To demand the opposite would be tantamount to demanding that competition should not exist in this definite epoch of history, or that the individuals should banish from their minds relationships over which in their isolation they have no control. (Marx, 1973, Vol. 1, p. 63)

In this chapter we have suggested that the world market, by expanding the edge of competition, has created a critical juncture in the labor movement which will force a change in its strategy and structure. During the last twenty-five years, capital has been able to expand and internationalize, first by strengthening and then by eroding the powers of the nation state. During the next twenty-five years we can expect a counter-response by labor and other groups to erode the power of capital. This response will take a political form, i.e., a struggle over state power around the central issue of capitalism and its continuance. Since states are territorial, the locus of the struggle will be largely national, or at least regional, even though the context is international. In the United States, it will probably tend to the formation of some sort of labor party. In Europe, it will probably lead to unification and a closer union between social democratic and communist parties. In the underdeveloped countries, it will lead to an increased role of labor in politics as the new proletariat emerges. And so on.

In this chapter we cannot even begin to examine the complexity of the struggle and the numerous paths it can take between the following two extremes:

1. A privileged part of the new working class in the advanced countries joins with capital in a new imperialistic alliance to get higher benefits in return for suppressing blacks, Third World people, foreign workers, women, the aged, etc. I personally think that this extreme is unlikely due to the large numbers and strength of the disadvantaged groups and the enormous brutality it would take to contain them.
2. At the other extreme, we can imagine a socialist consciousness which unites the disparate elements of labor to effect the transition from capitalism to socialism. Since socialism implies that communities obtain control over their own work and consumption, it would probably have to be based on national or regional self-sufficiency, as Keynes suggested; though with a great deal of international cooperation to permit the free flow of ideas, hospitality, etc.

Much research needs to be done on both labor and nonlabor political groups before we can sort out the possible sets of intermediate alliances that might emerge, and analyze their implications for the balance between capitalism and socialism, internationalism and nationalism. This chapter has attempted to point to the crucial role of the capital–labor struggle that we can expect in the future. We might end by noting that whatever the outcome – international fascism, socialism, or mixed free enterprise – a great deal of conflict and struggle domestically and internationally is in store for us, especially in the Third World, as the powerful forces unleashed by advanced capitalism come to a head. Our main problem as social scientists and human beings is not only to analyze what is happening, but also to decide which side we want to be on. That is why I spent so much time in this chapter on Keynes, who asked the right questions, even though he was sharply limited in his answers – because he tried to think history without Marx.

References

"Trouble Plagues the House of Labor," *Business Week*, October 28, 1972.
"The New Frontier," *The Economist* (June 13, 1942).
"The American Challenge," *The Economist*, July 18, 1942.
"An American Proposal," *Fortune*, May 1942.
Hymer, S. 1972. "The Internationalization of Capital," *Journal of Economic Issues*, Vol. 6, No. 1.
Keynes, J. M. 1964. *The General Theory of Employment, Interest and Money*. London: Macmillan.
1933. "National Self-Sufficiency," *The Yale Review*, Vol. 22.
Marx, K. 1967. *Capital*. 3 vols. New York: International Publishers.
Marx, K., and Engels, F. 1965. *Selected Correspondence*. Moscow: Progress Publishers.
1973. *Selected Works*. Moscow: Progress Publishers.

13

The laws of international exchange

Anwar Shaikh

Comparative costs

There is no proposition so central to orthodox theories of international trade as the so-called Law of Comparative Costs. From Ricardo to Hecksher-Ohlin to Samuelson, in one guise or another, the basic principle has remained unchanged. Even the relentless search of neoclassical economics for a state of perfect triviality has not emptied this particular principle of its content; from the time of its derivation by Ricardo to its current incarceration in an Edgeworth-Bowley Box, this law has continued to dominate the analysis of international trade. Even – and this is surely its greatest triumph to date – even its public exposure as having been all along the hidden law behind modern marriage has not (yet) led to its complete discreditation.[1]

It is not surprising that a principle capable of surviving "improvements" such as the above has managed to also withstand repeated attacks. Before we touch upon these attacks, however, it will be useful to briefly describe the law itself.

There are in fact two distinct propositions associated with this law, and the tendency to conflate the two has been a potent source of confusion in the literature.

Let us begin by considering a country in which cloth and wine are produced and sold at the price ratio $(p_c/p_w)_1$ in the domestic market. Across the channel is another country in which cloth and wine are also produced and sold locally, generally at a different price ratio $(p_c/p_w)_2$ than in the first country. Suppose the price ratios are different. Then, if the price of cloth relative to wine is lower in the first country than in the second, the price of wine relative to cloth must be lower in the second; that is, in each country one commodity will be *relatively* cheaper.[2]

The first proposition is a prescriptive one. It asserts that *if* each country were to export its relatively cheaper commodity and import the other, *and if* the terms of trade between cloth and wine were to settle between $(p_c/p_w)_1$ and $(p_c/p_w)_2$, then each country-as-a-whole would gain from trade. That is, by concentrating its production towards the relatively cheaper good and exporting part of that good in exchange for the other good, each country would end up better off, in the sense that through trade a given set of inputs could be translated into more outputs than before trade.

It is very important for our subsequent discussion to note that the above proposition in no way depends on the absolute costs of wine and cloth in the two countries. Thus, even if one of the two nations were absolutely more efficient in producing both commodities – so that both wine and cloth were absolutely cheaper in one country than in the other[3] – "trade can be beneficial if the country with the all-around inferior efficiency specializes in the lines of production where its inferiority is slightest, and the country with all-around superior efficiency specializes in the lines of its greatest superiority." (Yeager, 1966, p. 4) Therefore, this proposition argues that *if* under the right conditions (differences in pretrade relative prices, the "correct" pattern of exports, and an intercountry terms of trade in the "appropriate" range), each country, *no matter how backward its technology,* would benefit from trade. Absolute costs are of no moment; all that matters is relative costs. Hence the term "the principle of comparative advantage."

Taken by itself, the first principle says nothing at all about what actually happens in international trade. In fact, it would appear to be largely

I wish to express my thanks to Arthur Felberbaum, Robert Heilbroner, Edward Nell, Michael Zweig, John Weeks, and particularly to Adolph Lowe, for their comments, criticisms, and above all their support throughout this endeavor.

irrelevant to the real process. Exports and imports, after all, are undertaken by capitalists for the sake of profit, not gains to the "nation." Profits, moreover, depend crucially on absolute money costs: the lower-cost producer is always in a position to beat out its rivals. In trade between two advanced countries, each country might be expected to have some absolutely efficient producers, so that in this case absolute advantage and comparative advantage coincide: each country will then have one commodity for which it is the lowest-cost producer and hence the exporter. But how could a backward country in competition with an advanced one possibly hope to enjoy the "gains from trade" when both its producers are the higher-cost producers?

This is where the second proposition comes in. It is a descriptive proposition, for it asserts that in free trade the patterns of trade *will* in fact be regulated by the principle of comparative advantage – regardless of any absolute differences in levels of productive efficiency. The crucial element in this step, therefore, is the presence of some *automatic mechanism* that will cause free trade undertaken by profit-seeking capitalists to converge to this result.

The sum of the two propositions is what is generally called the "law of comparative costs": if permitted, free trade will end up being regulated by the principle of comparative (not absolute) advantage, and the resulting gains from trade will be shared among the trading partners.

In the original form given to it by David Ricardo, the crucial automatic mechanism was the relation between the quantity of money and the level of prices: the so-called *classical quantity theory of money*. In Ricardo's famous example, for instance, Portugal can produce both wine and cloth more cheaply than England. Trade between England and Portugal would therefore initially be all in one direction, with Portugal exporting both wine and cloth, which England would have to pay for directly in gold since its products were noncompetitive with Portugal's. But now the crucial equalizing mechanism comes into play: the outflow of gold from England is a decrease in its money supply and would therefore lower all money prices in England; similarly, the inflow of gold into Portugal would raise all money prices there. As long as the trade imbalance persisted, this mechanism would continue to make British wine and cloth progressively cheaper, and Portuguese wine and cloth progressively more expensive, until at some point England could undersell Portugal in *one* of the two commodities, leaving Portugal with the relative advantage in the other. The exact determination of the terms of trade was understandably not important to Ricardo, nor should it have been; the real point was that no nation need be afraid of free trade, for it humbles the mighty and raises the weak. Something like God, only quite a bit more reliable.

The more recent formulation of the law, the Hecksher-Ohlin-Samuelson *law of factor proportions,* leaves intact the basic principle set out by Ricardo. However, whereas Ricardo identified the real social cost of producing a commodity as the total labor-time that went directly or indirectly into production, the neoclassical formulation insists upon defining the social cost(s) of a commodity to the nation-as-a-whole as being the commodities it (the nation) must forego, at the margin, in order to produce an extra unit of the commodity in question. Since this concept of cost as opportunities foregone cannot be used if there are unemployed resources – for then any given commodity can be produced without the national individual (Uncle Sam) having to give up any others, that is, without any opportunity cost – neoclassical theory finds it necessary also to assume full employment. The assumption of full employment is therefore just the hidden dual of the concept of opportunity cost.

The second distinguishing characteristic of the neoclassical version is that, whereas Ricardo bases the patterns of international specialization on international differences in relative costs, whatever their origin, the Hecksher-Ohlin formulation attempts to tie the cost differences themselves to a single dominant factor: the national endowments of labor and capital. Thus, leaving absolute advantages aside, this approach would argue that, given any two countries, the capital-abundant country (the one having the higher national capital–labor ratio) would tend to be able to produce capital-intensive goods *relatively* more cheaply than the labor-abundant country. Conversely, the labor abundant country (the one having the lower national capital–labor ratio) would of course have the relative advantage in labor-intensive production. It follows therefore that capital-abundant countries (read industrialized capitalist countries) will and, for reasons of efficiency and the good of the world-as-a-whole, should, specialize in capital-intensive (secondary) products, exporting them in return for the labor-intensive (primary) products of the labor-abundant (underdeveloped capitalist) countries: In other words, the existing differences between developed and underdeveloped capitalist countries are *efficient* from the point of view of the world-as-a-whole. Poor Ricardo dared only to claim that free trade is better; neoclassical theory can boldly claim that international inequality is best. No wonder that Gary Becker found in this analysis so convenient an explanation for institutionalized sexism (Becker, 1973, 1974).

What is perhaps most striking about the neoclassical approach is that it completely assumes away any possibility of absolute advantage on the part of any one country: wine production in England and wine production in Portugal are assumed to be characterized by exactly the same production function; similarly, cloth too has its own universal production function. The central thrust of Ricardo's argument was of course that free trade leads to gains even for countries that are absolutely inefficient in comparison to their trading partners; in the Hecksher-Ohlin version all this is sacrificed to the need to prove that patterns of international specialization are consequences of the various national "factor endowments." It is interesting to note, however, that when Leontief's famous empirical test of the Hecksher-Ohlin model appeared to refute it, "Leontief rationalized this result by hypothesizing that American labor is three times as productive as foreign labor" (Johnson, 1968, p. 89)[4] – that is, he resorted to the argument that the U.S. pattern of trade could be explained by its *absolute advantage* over its trading partners! A fuller discussion of Leontief's study is at the end of the next section, "Orthodox critiques."

In general, modern presentations of the law of comparative costs make no reference to the actual mechanisms by which the law is to be brought about. The emphasis is almost entirely on the gains from trade that would be achieved if trade were to be based on comparative costs; nonetheless, because these discussions are also intended to be descriptive, "the implicit assumption is [made] that the adjustment of money wage and price levels or exchange rates required to preserve international monetary equilibrium do actually take place . . ." (Johnson, 1968, p. 84) As we shall see later, in the second major section, modern derivations of comparative costs rely on what are essentially variants of Ricardo's mechanism: in all cases, the very nature of the desired solution requires monetary variables (price levels and/or exchange rates) to adjust in such a way as to transform absolute advantage into a comparative one. In all versions, therefore, given England's absolutely lower efficiency and hence initially higher costs of production, its ensuing trade deficit must somehow result in a lowering of English prices while Portugal's trade surplus must lead to a raising of its prices – until at some point each country has a cost advantage in only one commodity.

The critique of comparative costs consequently requires us to contrast four basic theories of money: the Hume specie-flow version of the quantity theory (Ricardo), the cash balances version of the quantity theory, the Keynesian determination of prices through the level of money wages, and Marx's theory of money. In order to do this, we need a common ground of some sort.

Fortunately for us, most of the history of international trade, and hence most of its theory, has been dominated by precious metals as the standards of both domestic and international money.[5] Thus, in discussions of the theories of international trade, we always find a common theoretical ground – their operation under the so-called gold standard (The discussion of fixed versus flexible exchange rates and their relation to the gold standard is reserved for the second major section). By contrasting various theories on this basis, differences in the theories themselves may be separated from differences in institutional arrangements. And because neither the Ricardian nor the neoclassical versions of the law of comparative costs claim to be dependent on any specific monetary institutions, the gold standard is a valid common ground. So much so, in fact, that the neoclassical treatment of the adjustment mechanism under the gold standard is virtually identical to that of Ricardo: "The adjustment mechanism under the gold standard . . . was more or less automatic in the sense that central banks were expected to react to gold outflows and inflows by more restrictive and less restrictive monetary policies, respectively, which would in turn react upon price and wage levels, lowering them in the deficit countries and raising them in the surplus countries. These price changes, in turn, were expected to shift expenditure from surplus to deficit countries, thus reducing and eventually eliminating the disequilibrium . . . the theory is correct in its broad outline even if its practice has been somewhat oversimplified" (Mundell, 1968, pp. 8–9).

We find, therefore, that, in spite of their much discussed differences, the fundamental structure of both the Ricardian and neoclassical versions of the law of international exchange is the same: in both cases it is relative advantage and not absolute which determines the pattern of trade; in both cases trade is mutually beneficial (or, at worst, not harmful) to each country viewed as a single classless entity; and, above all, in both cases the mechanism which brings about the successful operation of the law is essentially the same.

Orthodox critiques

The law of comparative costs, whatever its form, has always been associated with the advocacy of free trade: Ricardo's own development of this principle was in fact part of his polemic against the corn laws (laws which prevented the free import of cheap corn into England), and from that time onward free traders of all kinds have based their own arguments on those of Ricardo. It is not surprising, therefore, to find that the primary thrust of critics has been to attack not so much that part of the law which argues that the pattern of trade will depend on comparative costs, as it has been to attack the proposition that free trade is efficient, mutually beneficial, and good for the world-as-a-whole.

Frank Graham, for instance, focuses on the assumption of constant cost, which he argues is essential to the operation of the law; thus, by working with combinations of increasing and decreasing costs, he is able to provide counterexamples in which free trade and specialization are harmful to every one of the countries involved (Emmanuel, 1972, p. XV).[6] In a similar vein, Keynesians often attack the assumption of full employment, which, as we have seen, is a necessary complement of the *neoclassical* versions of the law; here, it is possible to construct counterexamples in which hypothesized combinations of unemployment and inflation may under certain circumstances have a feedback effect on the operation of the law and thus counteract it.[7] Finally, there exists a whole series of modifications of the law, based on the analysis of international differences in taste, on the existence of tariffs and quotas, transportation costs, customs unions, and so on.

In spite of their apparent opposition to the law, all the above criticisms have this in common: *implicitly (and often explicitly), they accept the law as being theoretically valid on its own grounds*. Instead, they seek to modify one or more of these grounds so as to provide theoretical counterexamples. It is therefore not at all surprising that these criticisms are usually viewed not as refutations of comparative costs, but rather as its further development; typically, in neoclassical textbooks, the doctrine of comparative costs is presented as *the* fundamental principle underlying international trade, with the foregoing criticisms as extensions and concretizations of it.

Orthodox critics, however, have yet another recourse – attack by means of data. Here, the two examples most often cited are the results of Leontief's famous study (Leontief, 1953, 1956, 1958), now known as the "Leontief paradox," and those of the Arrow-Chenery-Minhas-Solow study, which gave rise to the so-called factor reversal issue (Arrow, et al., 1961). We will examine each in turn.

In the early 1950s, Leontief set out to empirically test the central proposition of the neoclassical version of the law of comparative costs. Beginning with the fact that the United States was by all accounts a capital-abundant country, Leontief reasoned that those goods which America exported should be more capital intensive than those which it replaced by imports. What he actually found, however, was just the opposite: "contrary to expectations United States exports are more labor-intensive . . . than United States imports" (Johnson, 1968, p. 88).

Neoclassical theory, it will be recalled, takes it for granted that, in accordance with Ricardo's law, each country will export the relatively cheaper commodity. What the Hecksher-Ohlin-Samuelson model seeks to do is to go one step further and argue that this relatively cheaper commodity will in fact be the one which uses proportionately more of the relatively abundant factor of production: hence the theoretical expectation that the capital-abundant country will export the capital-intensive commodity. In order to make the above links, however, it is necessary to assume away the possibility of absolute advantage. In neoclassical terms, this means that the production function for a given commodity, say wine, is assumed to be the same no matter whether wine is produced in England or in Portugal: thus wine *could* always be produced at the same cost everywhere. It is not surprising, therefore, that, when faced with the unexpected results of his study, Leontief was led to challenge precisely that assumption.

Leontief's challenge did not go unanswered for long. In 1961, Arrow, Chenery, Minhas, and Solow published a study in which they argued that cross-country comparisons of production functions did indeed indicate that American production was systematically more efficient than others: in other words, that the United States had an absolute advantage (Arrow, et al., 1961; see note 4 of this chapter). These results prompted an investigation of the properties of the Hecksher-Ohlin-Samuelson model when production functions differ across countries, which in turn led to the theoretical possibility that capital-abundant countries might export labor-intensive commodities (Minhas, 1962).

Distressing as these results are to the proponents of the Hecksher-Ohlin-Samuelson model, they have little bearing on the principle of comparative costs, for (as we have already noted) the model *begins* by assuming the Ricardian pattern of specialization according to comparative costs and then attempts to link this pattern to the "factor endowments" of the nations involved. At best, therefore, the above empirical and theoretical paradoxes merely sever the attempted link between national factor endowments and the pattern of trade. *They leave the Ricardian law untouched.*

Finally, we come to those critics who attack the law as being *no longer* valid, because one or more of its premises no longer hold in today's world. Here, we find that the empirical criticism of the law, and particularly of the efficacy of free trade, is based on modern developments such as the loss of wage and price flexibility, the demise of the gold standard, the death of competition, and systematic interference by governments.[8] For our purposes, it is sufficient to note that this historical school of orthodox criticism (which, as we shall see shortly, has its Marxist counterparts) implicitly accepts the law as valid where its premises – primarily those involving competitive capitalism – can be taken to hold. On its own grounds (which in this case involve a particular historical epoch), the law is accepted as valid.

In sum, we find that so far as orthodox criticism is concerned (whether it be theoretical, empirical, or historical), the basic principles of the doctrine of comparative costs emerge relatively unscathed.

Marxist critiques

Given Marx's exhaustive treatment of Ricardo's theory of value, it would seem that Marxists long ago have extended his analysis in one way or another to deal with the Ricardian law of comparative costs. Curiously enough, this is not so: instead, the issue is seldom mentioned (Mandel, 1968; Sweezy, 1942). Where it is discussed, Ricardo's attempt to determine the limits of international exchange is acknowledged only implicitly by accepting one of his central conclusions: whereas the law of value regulates exchanges within a competitive capitalist economy, it does *not* do so between such economies (Sweezy, 1942, p. 289).

Why this striking silence? In part, it arises from the fact that Marx himself never directly accepts or rejects Ricardo's principle of comparative costs. This appears to be a puzzle until we realize that, to Marx, Ricardo's chapter on foreign trade is essentially a special analysis of *merchant capital*: "The great economists, such as Smith, Ricardo, etc., are perplexed over mercantile capital. . . . [W]henever they make a special analysis of merchant's capital, as Ricardo does in dealing with foreign trade, they seek to demonstrate that it *creates* no value (and consequently no surplus-value). But whatever is true of foreign trade, is also true of home trade" (Marx, 1967, Vol. III, p. 324, emphasis added).

Historically, of course, merchant's capital precedes industrial capital. But in the capitalist mode of production it is industrial capital which is dominant; Marx's analysis therefore begins with the latter and only arrives at the former (merchant's capital) in Volume III of *Capital*. It is industrial capital which is involved in the production of commodities, and hence in the *creation* of value and surplus value. Merchant capital, on the other hand, is involved in the trading of commodities; it therefore accomplishes the *transfer* of value and of surplus value, nationally and internationally. It follows from this that in order to understand its role within capitalist (rather than precapitalist) modes of production, merchant capital can be introduced only after value and surplus-value have been properly developed. Moreover, because the essential circuit of merchant capital involves "buying cheap and selling dear," the question of the determination of prices is critical; and this in turn means that money – the connection between value and price, surplus-value and profit – must be adequately developed prior to the analysis of merchant capital. This last point bears repetition: a correct analysis of the role of money is absolutely crucial to an understanding of the laws of commodity trade. This applies whether the trading is done nationally or internationally.

It was of course Marx's original intention to extend the analysis presented in the three volumes of *Capital* to the treatment of international trade and the world market, each to be dealt with in separate volumes (Marx, 1973, p. 54). But this never happened; instead, at the time of Marx's death even Volume III of *Capital* existed only as a "first extremely incomplete draft" (Marx, 1967, Vol. III, p. 2). Nonetheless, as I shall attempt to prove in this chapter, the development of the law of value in *Capital* contains all the necessary elements for its extension to international exchange. As we shall see, Ricardo's law of comparative costs follows immediately from his law of value and his theory of money; and Marx has provided us not only with detailed criticisms of Ricardo on both value and money, but also with his own formulations of these subjects. The principal task of this paper is, therefore, to attempt an extension of the Marxian law of value to international exchange.

The paucity of references in Marx to international commodity trade is, however, only part of the explanation for Marxist ambivalence on the subject. Another, equally important, part lies in the fact that ever since the publication of Lenin's *Imperialism* (Lenin, 1939) it has become a Marxist commonplace to assert that capitalism has entered its monopoly stage. Now, in the case of monopoly, it is widely accepted by Marxists and non-Marxists alike that laws of price formation must be abandoned (Sweezy, 1942, pp. 270–1): "the most serious aspect of monopoly from an analytic point of view, is that the discrepancies between monopoly price and value are not subject to any general rules (Sweezy, 1942, p. 54). What remain therefore are the basic social relations of capitalist commodity productions, and it is to the various manifestations of these that the theory of monopoly capital turns.

Of course, once the laws of price formation in general are thrown out, the laws of international price formation necessarily follow. The focus shifts instead to the domestic and international rivalries of giant monopolies, to their political interaction with various capitalist states, and to the antagonisms and conflicts between these states themselves – in other words, to imperialism as an aspect of *monopoly* capitalism. The law of value, like competitive capitalism itself, fades into history.

It is beyond the scope of this chapter to attempt a proper construction of a Marxist concept of monopoly, so as to confront the views mentioned here. It must be noted, however, that even an acceptance of the aforementioned views in no way puts to rest the ambivalence among Marxists with regard to Ricardo's law, any more than it resolves the recurring conflicts on the transformation problem, the theory of wages, etc.; instead, it merely sidesteps them.[9] Like their orthodox counterparts, these Marxist criticisms leave the law of comparative costs still standing – in the case of competitive capitalism, at least.

Emmanuel and unequal exchange

In recent years, this whole issue has been once again brought sharply into focus by Arghiri Emmanuel's challenging new work entitled *Unequal Exchange: A Study of the Imperialism of Trade* (Emmanuel, 1972). In this book, Emmanuel sets out to overthrow the pernicious doctrine of comparative costs by attacking what he argues is its most fundamental assumption – the immobility of capital between different countries.[10] In Ricardo's original derivation of the law, Emmanuel notes, Portugal is by assumption absolutely more efficient than England in both wine and cloth; hence, if Portugal and England were mere regions of the same nation, capital invested in Portugal would be considerably more profitable, so that eventually the absolute advantage of the Portuguese region would lead to the cessation of both wine and cloth production in the English region. But, says Ricardo, Portugal and England are separate nations, and in general this erects significant barriers to the mobility of capital between them, barriers which he notes he would be "sorry to see weakened" (Ricardo, 1951, p. 136). In Ricardo, therefore, the analysis of flows between nations is essentially confined to *commodity* flows, and it is his contention that in this case Portugal's absolute advantage is of no lasting consequence; in the end, only relative advantage matters, so that each nation is assured of having at least one exportable commodity to specialize in.

Emmanuel accepts Ricardo's law on its own grounds (Emmanuel, 1972, pp. xxxii–iii). But, he argues, its fundamental structure results from the fact that Ricardo restricts his analysis to those situations in which only commodities flow between countries. The modern world, on the other hand, is characterized by massive international movements of *capital,* in addition to those of commodities (Emmanuel, 1972, p. xxxiv). To Emmanuel, therefore, the essential question is: how do the international movements of capital affect the previously valid Ricardian law of international exchange? In other words, what is the appropriate form of this law in the modern world?[11] The emphasis on international capital movements is of course not unique to Emmanuel. In Marxist analysis of imperialism, for instance, the internationalization of capital plays an absolutely central role; even modern day proponents of the law of comparative costs often go on to treat the issue of foreign investment and international capital mobility. In general, however, these existing analyses treat capital flows as a factor strictly separate from the laws of international commodity trade (Kenen, 1968); what Emmanuel proposes to do instead, is to integrate this movement into the law itself and, by so doing, separate the determination of the laws of international exchange from any apologetic for free trade. To Emmanuel, "modern free trade" is characterized by both capital *and* commodity flows between nations. It is his avowed intention, moreover, to demonstrate that it is precisely the laws of this modern free trade, which, when applied to the trade between developed capitalist countries and the so-called Third World,[12] give rise to a variety of phenomena normally associated with the term "imperialism": Imperialism is the highest stage of free competition.[13]

The first step in understanding Emmanuel's analysis is to pose the question: *why* does capital flow between countries? And the answer, of course, is because there exists a difference in profitability between the countries involved. So the question becomes, what are the intrinsic determinants of this difference?

Let us begin with the selling price. In general, international capital produces for the *world* market; if we ignore transportation costs (as being secondary factors in determining the pattern of trade), then, no matter where production is located, the selling price for a given type of product is more or less the same – it is the world market price. Moreover, because commodities do flow between countries, technology is also internationally mobile: aside from transportation costs, a given type of plant and equipment can be located for more or less the same cost in any country accessible to international capital.[14] But if the selling price is more or less independent of the international location of production, and the cost of a given plant and equipment is too, then what gives rise to international differences in profitability? The answer, it would seem, could only be: the abundance of natural resources and/or the cheapness of wage labor.

As long as the question is posed in terms of *any* two countries accessible to international capital, it is not possible to narrow down the list of factors any further. What Emmanuel has in mind, however, is not the relation between just any two countries but rather the relation between developed capitalist countries of the world and the so-called Third World, that is, the underdeveloped, capitalist-dominated countries. And in terms of *this* division of the capitalist world, the overwhelmingly significant difference arises from the relative cheapness of wage labor in the Third World. The United States is at least as rich in natural resources as India, but it is not uncommon to find Indian wages to be one-twentieth those in the United States. Emmanuel estimates that "the average wage in the developed countries is about thirty times the average in the backward countries" (Emmanuel, 1972, p. 48). According to Emmanuel, therefore, capital flows from the developed to the underdeveloped capitalist countries primarily to take advantage of the enormous difference in the cost of labor-power.

We come now to Emmanuel's analysis of the effects of these international capital movements. Wages, it will be remembered, are enormously lower in the Third World, so that, other things being equal, profit rates for local capitalists would be very high. If local capitalists tended to reinvest heavily, or if through government action these profits could be taxed away and reinvested, high profit rates would imply a high rate of growth of Third World countries – leading to rapid development, a narrowing gap between rich and poor countries, and, above all, domestic control of domestic resources. Whatever else was wrong, there would at least be no imperialism.[15]

But the actual pattern appears to be the exact opposite of the above; what we observe, Emmanuel notes, is stagnation, a widening gap between rich and poor countries, and widespread foreign domination of Third World countries (Emmanuel, 1972, pp. 262–3). The major cause of all this, he argues, is foreign investment: the very same low wage/high profitability combination which *could* make rapid development possible in the Third World is exactly the factor that also makes these countries so very attractive to foreign capital. Because foreign investment originates in countries in which the average rate of profit is much lower than it is in the Third World, foreign capitalists are generally willing to accept much lower rates of profit than local capitalists; they therefore invade local markets, driving out local capitalists, drawing down prices and thus lowering the average rate of profit in the Third World. In this way the surplus generated in the Third World is siphoned off by foreign capital, to the detriment of the Third World and to the benefit of the developed capitalist countries. As a consequence, in the developed capitalist world foreign investment leads to higher profit rates, higher prices, and higher growth: hence prosperity and full employment. In the Third World, on the other hand, the very same movement results in lowered prices, lowered profits, and lowered growth: hence stagnation, unemployment, and foreign domination (Emmanuel, 1972, p. 265).

It is Emmanuel's great merit to have revived the important issue of the laws of price formation in international exchange, and in particular to do so in a way that suggests that it is not necessary to abandon the laws of competition in order to be able to understand the intrinsic determinants of modern imperialism. But there are significant weaknesses in the manner in which Emmanuel himself deals with this issue. To begin with, though he uses Marxist categories such as value and surplus-value, the methodological basis on which his work rests, and from which he derives his *implications*, is fundamentally different from Marx's; hence his political conclusions, though radical, are as different from Marx's as were, for example, those of a radical contemporary of Marx – Pierre-Joseph Proudhon.[16] This, and the fact that his analysis of imperialism runs counter to that of Lenin, has led to a largely hostile reaction to his work among some Marxists (Bettelheim, in Emmanuel, 1972; Pilling, 1973).

Many of the criticisms of Emmanuel are quite telling. But the challenge implicit in his work remains unanswered by those Marxists who are content to merely locate the distance between Emmanuel and Lenin.[17] These little exercises, however illuminating, manage to neatly avoid two central questions. First of all, at the level of abstraction that Marx maintains in his three volumes of *Capital,* is it really true (as many Marxists appear to believe) that Ricardo's law of comparative costs is the international form of Marx's law of value? Second, is it true (as Emmanuel argues) that when the export of capital becomes significant the Marxian law of international value is transformed into Emmanuel's law of unequal exchange?

Posed in this way, these questions have exactly the same theoretical status as that of any other law developed by Marx in *Capital.* Marx lays bare the structure of capitalism on the basis of its "ideal" form, that of free competition, precisely because it is *this* form that gives the freest expression to the immanent laws of the system. It is on this basis that Marx derives exploitation, crises, concentration and centralization, and a host of other phenomena characteristic of capitalism. Is it not curious, then, that whereas free and equal exchange within a capitalist nation gives rise to all of these phenomena, it does not appear to do so when it takes place between capitalist nations? How is it that whereas Marx derives the unevenness of development *within* a capitalist nation on the basis of free competition, Marxists generally have to resort to monopoly to explain the unevenness of development *between* capitalist nations? These are the questions we turn to next.

Towards a Marxist law of international exchange

Over a period of many years, the phenomena of international uneven development have come to be extensively studied and well documented (Amin, 1974; Hayter, 1972; Jale, 1969; Magdoff, 1969; Payer, 1974). And, as we have seen, the existence of these phenomena has generally been attributed to the internationalization of capital – that is, direct investment by the rich capitalist countries in the Third World. According to standard Marxist analysis, this internationalization itself arises out of the monopoly stage of capitalism; for Emmanuel, on the other hand, it is merely a fuller development of the laws of competitive capitalism. In either case, the export of capital is the lynchpin of the theory of imperialism.

In addition to their common emphasis on international capital movements, both of the above theories of uneven development accept Ricardo's law of comparative costs as being valid on its own grounds. In fact, as we shall see, this law is in a sense the "hidden secret" of the above theories: the law insists that free trade between advanced and backward countries will be mutually beneficial and productive of even development. It is precisely because they are unable to refute this law that the above theories are forced to put the whole burden of uneven development on capital movements.

As long as Ricardo's law is left standing, the well-known phenomena of uneven development appear inexplicable without some additional factors: monopoly, foreign investment, political power, conspiracy, etc. Now it can hardly be denied that these factors exist and are important to any analysis of uneven development on a world scale. But the question is: are these factors in themselves the intrinsic causes, or does the cause lie elsewhere?

In this chapter it will be argued that the phenomena of international uneven development arise directly from the so-called free trade of commodities. That is, just as Marx derives the concentration and centralization of capitals (and hence their uneven development) from free and unrestricted commerce within a capitalist nation, so too is it possible to derive the phenomena of imperialism from free and unrestricted commerce between capitalist nations. Moreover, just as Marx's law of value is the basis for his analysis of uneven development within a capitalist nation, so too will the international form of this law be the basis of the analysis of uneven development among capitalist nations. What we will see, in effect, is that *Ricardo's law of comparative costs is false on its very own grounds.*

Once this great stumbling block has been overcome, the phenomena of imperialism will appear in an entirely new light. Free trade, rather than negating the inequalities between nations, will be seen to deepen them. The absolute advantages of the developed capitalist countries (such as Portugal in Ricardo's famous example) over the underdeveloped capitalist countries (England) will *not* be reduced to a comparative-advantage-for-all, as free traders have so long asserted. On the contrary, free trade itself will ensure that the advanced capitalist countries will dominate international exchange, and that the less developed nations will end up chronically in deficit and chronically in debt.

If in fact free trade *is* uneven development, then the question arises: what are we to make of the export of capital, which plays so prominent a part in most other theories of imperialism? Does it offset, or does it enhance, the inequalities arising from free trade?

The answer, it turns out, is that it does both. Foreign capital may improve an underdeveloped country's trading position (and hence offset its trade deficits) by modernizing and expanding its export capabilities; but this will be undertaken precisely under the control and domination of foreign capital, and only insofar as it is to its own benefit. This, as we shall see, will have important implications.

A note on the structure of this chapter

In order to undertake the criticism of the law of comparative costs, we must first see precisely how it is derived. The second major section therefore contains a brief exposition of Ricardo's theory of value, his theory of money, and then of their interaction in the infamous law.

The next step is to set up a similar path in Marx. In the third major section, first Marx's theory of value (and his criticism of Ricardo's) is outlined, and then his theory of money (with his criticism of Ricardo's).

The first part of the fourth major section unites the two theories in overthrowing the Ricardian law of comparative costs: that is, we see that when taken together they imply a determinate theory of international exchange which flatly contradicts Ricardo's law *on its very own grounds*. It is in this section that the intrinsic cause of international uneven development is seen to be free trade itself, quite independently of the traditional villains such as monopoly, foreign investment, political power, etc.

The second half of the fourth major section takes up the question of the export of capital. Here, it becomes possible to see how and why it is the very unevenness of development (as it is reproduced and deepened by commodity trade), which in turn posits foreign investment as both the salvation *and* at the same time the damnation of the underdeveloped capitalist countries. It is also possible at this point to see not only why Emmanuel's analysis of imperialism is incorrect, but also why his proposed solution would be useless.

At all times it is important to keep in mind that the very structure of the theory of international trade necessitates an introduction to theories of value and theories of money before we can even begin the analysis of trade. Obviously, to do justice to Ricardo or Marx on either of these scores could easily require volumes. And yet, we must cover both value and money, in both authors, if we are to proceed at all!

Within the confines of a chapter this task can be undertaken only if one sticks to the bare essentials. Consequently, in what follows, brevity has been attempted in the exposition of Ricardo's and Marx's theories. Particularly when dealing with Marx, it is a great temptation to not only present and document the relevant structure of his analysis but to also defend it against the misrepresentations which are so popular (and so convenient) with orthodox theorists, or at least to contrast his analysis with theirs. Nonetheless, I have tried to avoid doing this: the primary comparison which can properly be made here, and that only in a largely expository way, is the one between Ricardo and Marx. The rest must await another occasion. But let this much be clear: what follows is definitely not intended as a mere exercise in the history of economic thought. So-called modern economic theories of value and money are no more capable of withstanding Marx's criticism than were the classical theories. In a sense, the opposition between Marx and Ricardo explored in this paper is the historical prelude to the more modern confrontation.

Ricardo's derivation of the law of comparative costs:

The Ricardian law of price. Ricardo held that the principal problem facing political economy in his day was the determination of the laws which regulate the distribution of the product of (capitalist) society among the three great classes: that is, the laws which determine "the natural course of rent, profit, and wages" (Ricardo, 1951, p. 5).

But very soon in the course of his work Ricardo realized that his analysis could not proceed without a theory of price:

> Before my readers can understand the proof I mean to offer, they must understand the theory of currency and of price . . . If I could overcome the obstacles in the way of giving a clear insight into the origin and law of relative or exchangeable value I should have gained half the battle. (Ricardo, 1951, pp. xiv–v)

Ricardo's battle was never completely won; the question of the law of relative prices was to trouble him to the very end. But it is a measure of his greatness that the problems he posed have persisted in one form or another down to the present.

In order to appreciate the gains made by Ricardo we must carefully follow his line of reasoning. The problem he set himself was the determination of the *laws* which regulate relative prices. Now of course he was well aware that the immediate determinants of market prices were supply and demand; but over the course of time the ceaselessly fluctuating interplay of supply and demand was itself regulated by a more fundamental principle: equal profitability. Thus, if as a result of market conditions a particular sector's rate of profit rose above the average rate, then the flow of capital would tend to be biased towards that sector, causing it to grow more rapidly than demand, and driving down its market price to a level consistent with average profitability. Conversely, the sectors with low profitability would tend to grow less rapidly than demand, causing their prices and profitability to rise.

The classical economists were thus able to demonstrate that behind the continuously varying constellation of market prices there lay another set of more fundamental prices, acting as centers of gravity for market prices and embodying more or less equal rates of profit. The name given to these regulating prices in classical political economy was "natural prices," what Marx was to later call "prices of production."[18] Their discovery was the first great law of prices.

All this was well known long before Ricardo's time. What then was he searching for? Certainly not the means by which to calculate the prices of production. Ricardo exhibits many such calculations himself, in the process of investigating his greater problem; so it is clear that a system of calculation, no matter how elegantly set out in terms of matrices and vectors, would differ only in form from the arithmetic relations set out by Ricardo. *What Ricardo sought to do was something considerably more meaningful:* to get behind prices of production, to discover *their* "centers of gravity." That is, just as the market price of a commodity was shown to be regulated by its price of production, Ricardo sought to show that this regulating price was itself subject to a hidden governor – the total quantity of labor time required to produce the commodity, both in its direct production process and, indirectly, in the production of its means of production.

"In speaking . . . of the exchangeable value of commodities, or the power of purchasing possessed by any one commodity, I mean always that power which . . . is natural price" (Ricardo, 1951, p. 92).

"The great cause of the variation in the relative value of commodities is the increase or diminution in the quantity of labour required to produce them" (Ricardo, 1951, p. 36).

There we have it: the *great* cause of the variations in the price of production of a commodity is the variation in the total labor time that goes, directly or indirectly, into its production. The total quantity of labor time was the center of gravity of the commodity's price of production, just as this price was itself the center of gravity of its market price. This was Ricardo's attempt to formulate a second great law of prices.

Let me illustrate the logic behind this. Sraffa (1960) has shown that if one unit of some commodity *A* requires 1_a worker-hours for its direct production, $1_a^{(1)}$ for the production of its physical inputs (machines, raw materials), $1_a^{(2)}$ for the production of the inputs required to produce these inputs, and so on, then the total labor time λ_a required to produce one unit of commodity *A* is the sum of its direct labor requirement 1_a and its indirect labor requirements $1_a^{(1)}, 1_a^{(2)}, \ldots$ etc. (Sraffa, 1963, pp. 34–5).

$$\lambda_a = 1_a + (1_a^{(1)} + 1_a^{(2)} + \ldots) \tag{13.1}$$

On the other hand, Sraffa points out that if *w* is the uniform wage rate, and *r* the uniform rate of profit, the price of production of commodity *A* is given by (Sraffa, 1960, p. 35)

$$p_a = w(1_a + (1 + r)1_a^{(1)} + (1 + r)^{(2)}1_a^{(2)} + \ldots) \tag{13.2}$$

The preceding equations illustrate the importance of direct and indirect labor requirements: their simple sum is the total labor requirement λ_a, and their weighted sum is the price of production p_a.

We come now to the critical point in the Ricardian argument. In effect, what Ricardo argued was that even though both the labor requirements and their weights (the wage–profit combinations *w,r*) enter into the calculation of prices of production, they are *not* equally important in causing *changes* in these prices.

Let us first consider changes in the equilibrium price weights *w* and *r*. First, as Sraffa so elegantly demonstrates, a rise in the wage rate *w* is necessarily accompanied by a fall in the rate of profit *r* (Sraffa, 1960, pp. 39–40) so far as relative prices are concerned. Therefore, Ricardo argued that on the average the opposing movements of these two weights would tend to cancel each other out (Ricardo, 1951, p. 35–6). Furthermore, it was his belief that in any case the wage rate, being such a fundamental social parameter, is only susceptible to relatively small variations (Ricardo, 1951, p. 36): it is, as Keynes was later to say, "sticky." Last, Ricardo was careful to point out that the *net* effect of a rise in the wage rate and a corresponding fall in the rate of profit varied from commodity to commodity: whereas, it might raise some prices of production, it would lower others, and leave others still unchanged, so that it would have no determinate effect on the *direction* of change of any given commodity price (Ricardo, 1951, p. 46).

We turn next to the remaining factor – changes in labor requirements. Since any one commodity is only one of literally hundreds of thousands, an improvement in its conditions of production is not likely to have much of an effect on the general social parameters *w,r*. Any such improvement *will*, however, in general reduce its price by lowering its total labor requirement λ_a: either it will reduce direct labor costs by lowering direct labor requirements 1_a; or it will reduce costs of physical inputs used up by saving on their use, thus lowering indirect labor requirements $1_a^{(1)}$, $1_a^{(2)}$, . . . , etc.; or it will do both.

Of course, a lower price for commodity *A* might lower costs for other commodities, and hence their prices too. But it is intuitively plausible that these feedback effects will not in general be greater than the original, so that the *net* effect is a lowering of the commodity's price relative to the average: a reduction in the total labor requirement λ_a of a commodity would be associated with a reduction in its equilibrium price ρ_a.

> In estimating, then, the causes of the variations in the value of commodities, although it would be wrong wholly to omit consideration of the effect produced by a rise or a fall of real wages, it would be equally incorrect to attach much importance to it; and consequently, in the subsequent part of this work, although I shall occasionally refer to this cause of variation, I shall consider all the great variations which take place in the relative price of commodities to be produced by the greater or less quantity of labour which may be required from time to time to produce them. (Ricardo, 1951, p. 36)

Ricardo is true to his word. In the chapters that follow he ignores the secondary variations in prices by simply assuming that relative prices are more or less equal to relative labor-times. Both the analysis of money and that of foreign trade is conducted on this basis.

It should be very clear from the above, incidentally, that Ricardo's law of prices in no way depends on the "assumption of a single factor of production" (Johnson, 1968, p. 85), as is so often asserted. It is hard to believe that anyone who has ever read Ricardo can make this claim; even for a mind steeped in the marginalities of neoclassical thinking it must be difficult to confront Ricardo and come away with nonsense like that.[19]

The classical quantity theory of money. Having analyzed at great length the causes of the variations in relative prices, Ricardo then proceeds to the causes of variations in the *level* of (money) prices. For reasons outlined previously, we assume (as does Ricardo) that gold is the money commodity.

The money price of a commodity is of course its relative price expressed in terms of the money commodity; that is, its rate of exchange with gold. Thus, the price of steel is so many units of gold; normally, when gold is used as money, there arise special names for specific weights of it. In England around Ricardo's time, for instance, roughly a 1/4 ounce of gold was known as a pound (£). A quantity of steel exchanging for 1/2 of an ounce of gold would therefore be said to have a "price of £2."

By the Ricardian law of prices, all commodities exchange roughly in proportion to the total labor-times required for their production. It follows, Ricardo notes, that the *money* prices of commodities are determined by the quantities of the labor-times required for their production relative to the quantity of labor-time required for the production of gold. Of course, gold cannot have a money price in this sense, since it *is* money. But to Ricardo, the quantity of steel (or corn, or cloth, etc.) purchased by £1 (1/4 oz) of gold could be viewed as a "commodity price" of gold. He therefore often refers to the "value" of gold.

Suppose it takes 100 worker-hours to produce a ton of steel, and that in a given year 4,000 tons are produced. The steel will then require 400,000 worker-hours. If it takes 1/2 worker-hours to produce £1 (1/4 oz) of gold, then the money price of the year's steel output will be £800,000.

Steel, however, is only one of a whole range of commodities produced in a given year. During any one year, therefore, the same gold coin may change hands several times, being received by one person through the sale of a commodity and then being given over to someone else when it is used to buy another commodity. In this way the same gold coin can function as money more than once, in a given year. Let us say that on the average a coin changes hands five times a year; its velocity of circulation is then five.

Imagine now that the labor-time required for all the commodities produced in a given year is 40 million worker-hours. Since we stated previously that £1 (1/4 oz.) of gold requires 1/2 worker-hours, the money price of the society's yearly output will be £80 million. Moreover, if the velocity of circulation of £ coins is indeed five, this means that only 16 million gold coins, each weighing £1 (1/4 oz) will be required as money in that year.

Of course, the laws discussed so far apply only to prices of production. We know from the laws of market prices, however, that if a commodity's supply exceeds its demand, then the market price of the commodity will fall, that is, it will exchange for less of other commodities. If this law is also applied to money it leads straightaway to the proposition that when the quantity of gold coin exceeds the requirements of circulation (the demand for coin), the "price" of gold will fall. Now, since gold is money, it cannot have a money price; however, since it can be used to purchase any commodity on the market, it can be said to have literally thousands of "commodity prices," these being the quantities of the various commodities one can buy with £1 (1/4 oz) of gold. The quantity theory of money therefore asserts that when the quantity of gold coin exceeds the requirements of circulation, *all* the commodity prices of gold will fall; since this means that gold will purchase less of each commodity, it is equivalent to asserting that *all* money prices will rise.

If we consider England as a closed economy with gold produced within its borders, then the reduced price of gold – the higher prices of all other commodities – would, according to Ricardo's theory, result in reduced output from the goldmines. This reduction in the supply of gold would in turn eventually raise its price, so that once again gold would exchange against other commodities in proportion to their respective labor-times.

If instead, gold were produced in a foreign country like South Africa, then to say that the "price" of gold in England has been lowered is to say that its purchasing power over commodities has been reduced. Gold will therefore have different purchasing powers in different countries, and will flow out of England into countries where its "price" is higher; once again, the effect will be to lower the quantity of money in England, and hence raise the "price" of gold back towards its natural level. In this way the international flows of gold would lead to more or less the same purchasing power of (gold) money in all countries. This conclusion of the classical quantity theory of money is known as the doctrine of "purchasing power parity" (Johnson, 1968, p. 92).

The law of international exchange. The critical element in Ricardo's law of comparative cost is really the quantity theory of money, because it is through its operation that the law is derived. However, in order to follow Ricardo's analysis, we will also use his law of prices.

Let us begin by considering two commodities, cloth and wine, produced in England; cloth requires 100 worker-hours to produce, and wine 120 worker-hours. If, as in our previous examples, £1 (1/4 oz) of gold required 1/2 worker-hour to produce, then from Ricardo's law of prices the prices of production of cloth and wine would be more or less equal to their respective labor-times relative to that of gold. Cloth would sell at about £200, and wine at about £240, domestically.

Consider now the same two commodities in Portugal. The unit of money in Portugal we take to be an *escudo* (e.), roughly 1/6 of an ounce of gold; assuming the same labor-time for gold in

Table 13.1.

	England		Portugal		
Cloth:	100 hrs	50 oz gold	45 oz gold	90 hrs	:Cloth
Wine:	120 hrs	60 oz gold	40 oz gold	80 hrs	:Wine

all countries, one escudo (1/6 oz) of gold would then require 1/3 worker-hours to produce. If then in Portugal cloth took 90 worker-hours, and wine 80 worker-hours, their domestic prices of production would be roughly 270 e. and 240 e., respectively.

But note that both £'s and e.'s are merely different national money-names for quantities of gold. If England's payments to foreigners exceeded its receipts from them, that is, if it ran a balance of payments deficit, gold bullion would eventually have to be used to make up the difference.[20] Since both currency units are actually quantities of gold, and the international means of payment is in fact gold bullion, we can considerably simplify the exposition by expressing all prices directly in ounces of gold. Given that an ounce of gold requires two hours of labor-time, we have the following Ricardian tableau for England and Portugal (Table 13.1).

Clearly, in this initial situation Portugal's greater efficiency in production translates directly in an *absolute advantage* in trade. If transportation costs are not prohibitive, Portuguese capitalists will export both commodities. England will experience a continuing balance of trade deficit, which will have to be made up by shipping gold to Portugal.

According to Ricardo, it is at this point that the quantity theory of money becomes crucial. The outflow of gold from England is a decrease in its domestic supply of money, so that according to the quantity theory the gold prices of *all* English commodities will begin to fall. Conversely, the inflow of gold to Portugal will raise all prices there. As this happens, Portugal's competitive edge in international markets will gradually erode, even though it will of course have just as great an advantage in terms of efficiency as it did before. It is just that this greater efficiency will be increasingly offset by the rise in Portuguese prices relative to those in England.

Sooner or later in this process one of the two English commodities will become just competitive with its Portuguese counterpart. But which one? Well, in terms of efficiency, England always has an absolute disadvantage relative to Portugal in both commodities. But as all English prices fall and all Portuguese prices rise, the

English commodity with the *smallest* disadvantage will be the first to overtake its Portuguese rival. If we examine the Ricardian tableau, (Table 13.1) we find that English wine production is only 66 2/3 percent as efficient as its Portuguese rival (since Portuguese wine takes 80 hours and English wine takes 120 hours), whereas English cloth production is 90 percent as efficient as Portuguese. England's smallest disadvantage, its *relative* advantage, lies in cloth, and as English prices drop relative to Portuguese, it is English cloth which first becomes competitive. By the same token, it is clear that if England has an equal disadvantage in both sectors of production then both English commodities would become competitive at exactly the same point. Though trade could still take place under these circumstances, there would be no fixed basis for specialization. Only if England has different disadvantages in the two commodities, that is, only if it has a relative advantage in one, can Ricardian trade take place.[21]

Once England can compete in cloth, two-way trade will begin. This will improve England's trade picture, but it will probably not eliminate the deficit; price level movements will therefore continue to take place, strengthening England's international position and weakening Portugal's – *until finally at some point trade will more or less balance,* with each country exporting the one commodity in which it *now* has a relative advantage. If for some reason the adjustment process goes too far, to the point where even English wine undersells Portuguese, then the ensuing gold flows would reverse the price level movements until once again relative advantage reigned.

An important implication of the process of adjustment is that in the end each country's international terms of trade (the quantity of imports that can be bought with a unit of its exports) will necessarily be better than its domestic. In England, for example, the cloth on the market will be English cloth; but the wine available will generally be imported from Portugal. Those whose unbounded patriotism would require them to insist on English wine will have to pay a higher price for it than they would for the imported variety. Therefore, a unit of cloth, England's export commodity, will be worth more units of Portuguese wine than it will be of domestic wine simply because domestic wine costs more. Similarly, in Portugal, its export, wine, is worth more units of English cloth than it is of Portuguese cloth simply because the English cloth is cheaper.

The proposition just forwarded, on the terms of trade of each country has often been used as the basis of a proof that each nation-as-a-whole gains from trade. Thus it is said that England can get more wine for its cloth through trade than it can get domestically: trade is generally beneficial. Though Ricardo is careful to derive the laws of trade on the basis of its profitability to capitalists, when he turns to the analysis of the effects of trade he abandons the concept of classes and reverts to that of a nation-as-a-whole. Now, it is undeniable that the concept of a nation is both valid and necessary at some level of analysis; nations do exist and their interaction is a real process. But to assert that trade is beneficial to the nation-as-a-whole is simply to assert that "what's good for General Motors is good for the U.S." Trade is undertaken by capitalists because they can make more profits that way; it is they who always gain. Even if this gain for the capitalists happens to spill over to workers in either country, which is certainly not necessary from the above analysis, one can only say that in this instance trade also benefits a particular set of workers. It is not possible to reduce the fundamentally antagonistic relations of classes to the bland homogeneity of a nation-as-a-whole. Christians are not in a position to cheer for lions as long as they are both booked to play in the Coliseum.

Modern derivations of the law. It should be obvious from the preceding derivation how crucial the "right" sort of monetary theory is to the derivation of the law of comparative costs. Any monetary theory which translates the initial trade deficit of the backward country into falling price levels (falling relative to the price level in the advanced country) will do the trick. We need therefore to say a bit about the modern derivations of this law.

Let us begin with a modern version of the quantity theory, based on the cash balance approach. The classical quantity theory argued that an outflow of gold from a country would lead to a fall in the money supply and hence in the price level. Here, it is argued that the decrease in the money supply implies a decrease in the cash balances of individuals and firms; in order to "not let their cash balances shrink too far," people in the deficit country curtail their consumption and investment spending, and this drop in aggregate demand in turn leads to lower prices and wages (Yeager, 1966, p. 64). The opposite movement takes place in the surplus country, and eventually absolute advantage gives way to comparative.

An alternate path to this same result is made possible by tying the price level to the level of money wages. In this version, since the competition of cheap cloth and wine from abroad means a reduction in domestic wine and cloth production in the backward country, the resulting trade deficit will be associated with a rise in unemployment. Money wages in the backward country will consequently fall, and with them money prices; in the advanced country, the trade surplus is associated with expanded employment, a rise in money wages, and hence a rise in money prices. Even if money wages were relatively sticky downwards, the above result would hold since all that is required is a movement in *one* of the two price levels so as to arrive at the correct relative price levels. Once again, this leads to the eventual rule of comparative advantage (Amin, 1974, p. 47).

All discussions so far have been predicated in terms of the gold standard, in which the "ultimate" basis of international currency is a money commodity (which we call gold for convenience). In most theoretical discussions, the gold standard is treated as being equivalent to a regime of *fixed* exchange rates. The preceding modern derivations of comparative advantage are therefore also presented as holding true for the case of fixed exchange rates.

At the opposite theoretical extreme from fixed exchange rates, we are told, lies the notion of purely flexible exchange rates determined solely by the relative supplies and demands of the national currencies. Here it is possible that each nation will have a *fully independent monetary system* (Yeager, 1966, p. 104). In this case, the price levels in each country are "insulated" from external influences, and all adjustments are brought about through the exchange rate. In the backward country the trade deficit will imply a depreciation of the country's currency, which would make imports relatively more expensive to it and its exports relatively cheaper abroad. Since this process is assumed to have no limits, eventually the flexible exchange rate would settle at the level which made comparative advantage a reality.

We cannot consider the merits of these various derivations until we have examined Marx's theory of money. But it is useful to note even at this point that it is completely false to equate the notion of the gold standard with fixed exchange rates. As indicated at the end of this chapter, note 20, in actual fact the gold standard was a system of flexible exchange rates whose movements were *bounded* by limits determined by the costs of transporting gold. This meant that insofar as the "normal" variations of trade were concerned, the gold standard operated as if it were a system of purely flexible exchange rates. On the other hand, insofar as systematic imbalances were concerned, the exchange rate soon reached one of the two limits and it became cheaper to settle debts by shipping gold directly: in this mode, therefore, it operated like a system of fixed exchange rates. The theoretical notion of the two polar extremes of fixed versus flexible exchange rates thus have their origin in one-sided (and hence false) abstractions of the real process. We will return to this important point later on.

Marx's development of the laws of capitalist exchange

As the preceding discussion of Ricardo should have made clear, it is the interaction of the Ricardian theory of price with his theory of money which results in the law of comparative costs. Now, as we turn to Marx, we face the task of trying to present, in a few short pages, the essence of Marx's theories of price and money so that we may see what implications they in turn have for international exchange. Here, the overriding question is whether the international extension of Marx's law of value will indeed turn out to be the law of comparative costs (as has been generally assumed), or whether it will in fact turn out to be something quite different.

Marx's law of value has, of course, many points of comparison with Ricardo's analysis; often, through an emphasis on these common points, the impression is given that Marx was therefore a (major or minor) post-Ricardian classical economist. Such an impression is, however, completely misleading and can arise only through the *reduction* of Marx's analysis to only those points which overlap with Ricardo's. As long as one begins with Ricardo as the home base, all such comparisons are inevitably posed in Ricardian terms; Marx thus emerges as the cleverest Ricardian of them all.

Within the context of this brief exposition, it is hardly possible to do justice to even the notions of value and price in Marx, much less to the methodological break between Marx and the classical economists. Of necessity, many of the points we seek to cover are precisely points of comparison with Ricardo; nonetheless, the reader must be forewarned that the differences which do emerge are not merely variations on a Ricardian theme. On the contrary, it is exactly because Marx does *not* operate within a Ricardian framework that he is able to go beyond Ricardo's own analysis.[22]

Commodities. In the discussion of Ricardo's law of prices, the fundamental question seemed fairly well defined: what are the laws of the movements of prices of production?

What Ricardo perceives is that the "worth," the "exchangeable value," or commodities bears an intrinsic connection to labor-time (Marx, 1969, pp. 164–7). This, says Marx, is Ricardo's greatest scientific merit (Marx, 1969, p. 166). But at the same time, rather than developing the various intermediary links between labor-time and price, Ricardo attempts instead to fuse the two together in his law of prices. His failure to adequately distinguish between labor-time and price is, according to Marx, the first great source of error in his analysis (Marx, 1969, Ch. X; pp. 106, 164, 174–6).

In addition to that, however, there is another problem. How can Ricardo attempt to analyze the effects of a uniform rate of profit on prices, asks Marx, when he nowhere discusses what determines the *level* of this rate of profit? And this in turn leads to an even more basic question. A uniform rate of profit is simply a way of saying that profits on different capitals are proportional to the size of these capitals: that is, each capital gets a share of total profit in proportion to its own size. But Ricardo nowhere discusses what determines the total profit in the first place. How then can he attempt to isolate the factors which regulate the movements of prices of production when he is missing a crucial ingredient – profit?

It is apparent to Marx that before one can arrive at the laws which govern price, one must first answer two prior questions: first, what is meant by price and how does it arise? And second, what is meant by profit, and how does it arise?

Since the concept of price refers to the exchange of commodities, Marx begins by examining what a commodity is. In all societies, he notes, human beings produce useful objects. It is only in a particular type of society, however, that the useful products of human labor are intended not for some direct social use but for exchange. And precisely because exchange is a social process which quantitatively compares and equates different products, in societies which produce for exchange the products of human labor acquire the property of having quantitative worth. No longer are they merely useful; they are now also valuable: they are *commodities*. As Marx expresses it, a commodity is both a use-value and an exchange value.

But when we say that a commodity is worth something, just what is implied? Suppose I say that in barter, a bushel of corn is worth a ton of iron, and also a yard of silk, and an ounce of gold, and so on. At first glance, what I appear to be saying is that there are many different quantitative expressions for the worth of a bushel of corn, depending on which other commodity (iron, silk, or gold) I choose to *measure* it by.

But there is a deeper problem here. In order for me to measure the worth of corn in terms of gold, for instance, gold must also be worth something itself. Otherwise I cannot say how much gold is equivalent to a bushel of corn. It is just like my saying that a stone weighs 10 grams; what I mean is that on a scale it takes ten pieces of iron called gram-weights to equal the weight of the stone. But clearly, in order for me to carry out this operation, both stone and iron must already possess the property of being heavy, of having weight; the gram-weights don't make stones heavy, they only measure the already existing heaviness of stones.

Exactly the same conclusion applies to quantitative worth. The factors which cause commodities to have quantitative worth in the first place must be carefully distinguished from the measurement of this worth. Measuring the worth of corn in iron will give a different result from measuring it in gold; but neither measure causes corn to possess quantitative worth. Rather, each merely expresses the preexisting worth of corn in terms of some particular commodity.

The question of price is therefore really a two-fold one: first, what is the cause of quantitative worth; and second, how is this worth actually expressed, measured, in exchange?

Value. If we look at society as a regularly reproduced set of social relations, it becomes very clear that the production and reproduction of the masses of useful objects which correspond to various social needs requires a definite, quantitative distribution of social labor. Each different useful product requires a concretely different type of labor; reproduction of the material basis of the society consequently requires the existence and reproduction of the appropriate quantities of different concrete labors. That is to say, social labor from the point of view of its capacity to produce different use-values is what Marx calls social-labor in its role as *concrete* labor (Marx, 1967, Vol. I, p. 46).

We noted earlier, however, that in commodity-producing societies each product, in addition to being useful, acquires the further property of being valuable. Hence, labor which produces commodities (i.e., objects intended for exchange) itself acquires a new property: namely, the capacity to create value or quantitative worth. In this role, moreover, all commodity-producing labor is qualitatively alike, since different types of labor differ only in their resulting amounts of value. The very same social conditions which make varied useful objects quantitatively comparable by reducing them to a common denominator, also make the corresponding labors quantitatively comparable. In the case of the useful objects, their common denominator is quantitative worth; in the case of the labors, it is the capacity to result in quantitative worth. From the point of view of this latter property social labor is qualitatively alike and quantitatively comparable: it is what Marx calls social labor in its capacity as *abstract* labor. Abstract labor, that is, labor which is actually engaged in commodity production, is the cause of quantitative worth.[23] The total quantity of abstract labor required directly or indirectly for the production of a commodity Marx therefore calls the *intrinsic measure* of its quantitative worth, or its *value*.

The value of a commodity, the intrinsic measure of its exchange-value or worth, is the quantity of abstract labor-time necessary for the production of the commodity under average conditions. If looms, for instance, are made in one year by hand, and in a given year 100 looms are produced, 50 by efficient producers requiring 900 worker-hours per loom and 50 by inefficient producers requiring 1,100 worker-hours per loom, then the value of a loom in that year is 1,000 worker-hours. It is the average quantity of labor-time necessary, not as in Ricardo, the marginal, which counts here (Marx, 1967, Vol. I, p. 39).

Suppose the production of a bolt of cloth took 10 workers ten hours a day for one week (six days) to gather cotton seed, plant it, harvest the cotton, and with the aid of a loom, spin the cotton into cloth. Then the value of the cloth has two components: the living labor of the cloth worker, 600 worker-hours, which represents the value added in cloth production during one week; and that part of the value of the loom which is transferred to the cloth. But how is the latter to be determined? Well, if the loom was used up in one week then it is clear that all the value of the loom would be incorporated into the cloth, since from a social point of view the labor-time required to build the loom is the indirect social cost of producing cloth. If the loom lasted longer, say one year (50 weeks), then over one year it will be entirely used up and all of its value transferred to the 50 bolts of cloth produced in that period of time. On the average, therefore, the loom would transfer 1/50 of its value each year to a bolt of cloth. Because the second case is basically the same as the first, we will simplify the exposition from now on by assuming a uniform period of turnover of one week. Then the value of the cloth is 1,600 worker-hours: 1,000 of these *transferred* by the loom as it is used up, 600 *added* by living labor.

If we designate the total value of any output produced in a given week as W, the value transferred by its means of production as C, and the value added by living labor as L, then:

$$C + L = W \tag{13.3}$$

We turn now to the second aspect of price: how is quantitative worth actually expressed in exchange? To this Marx answers: in exchange, the quantitative worth of a commodity *must* necessarily take the form of money-price. Since exchange is the interchange of two commodities, at first glance it seems obvious that there are as many measures of a commodity's worth as there are other commodities to measure it by. And historically, where exchange is sporadic or irregular, this is in fact true. But as exchange spreads and develops, this variety of different possible measures increasingly becomes a barrier to the smooth functioning of the process; without a point of reference, the direct comparison of every commodity with every other becomes impossibly complex. Consequently it becomes increasingly necessary to settle on a given commodity out of all those available as the one commodity in which all other commodities express their worth; this special commodity therefore becomes the universal equivalent, the money-commodity. We will henceforth assume it is gold.

Notice that money does not by itself cause commodities to have worth, any more than gram-weights cause stones to have weight. On the contrary, it is only because both gold and the other commodities have quantitative worth (exchange-value) in the first place that we can express their worth in terms of gold. The money-price of a commodity is the "golden" reflection, the *external measure*, of its exchange-value. It is what Marx calls the *form* taken by value during exchange (Marx, 1967, Vol. I, pp. 47–8).

Price. We have already seen that value, the intrinsic measure of exchange-value or quantitative worth, and price, the external measure, are two very different things. Money-price is the manner in which the exchange process reflects value. This in itself implies that all the relations which intervene between the production of a commodity and its actual sale can give rise to further determinants of the precise form in which this reflection will take place. For instance, in general the market price of a commodity is an expression not only of the amount of abstract labor-time required for its production (its value) but also of the distribution of social labor – that is, of the correspondence between the amount of social labor devoted to the production of a given commodity and the amount necessary to supply the social need for this commodity. If at any moment this latter correspondence does not hold, it will show up in the process of exchange as a discrepancy between supply and demand; then even if on the average exchange is at value it will not be so in this case. Market price will deviate from natural price.

Marx himself points out this and other possible discrepancies between value and price (Marx, 1972, pp. 61–2). But he notes, the only way in which we can proceed to actually determine any quantitative differences between value and price is to first proceed on the assumption that price directly reflects value – that is, that supply and demand are balanced (so that market prices equal regulating prices, or natural prices) and that the money-price of a commodity is its value relative to the value of gold. In this way we can identify the structural determinants of the various steps in the movement from production to exchange, and hence of the transition from value to price. Only then can we show how these structural determinants can in turn give rise to more complex paths from value to price (Marx, 1967, Vol. I, p. 166, footnote 1).[24]

Surplus-value and profit. We come now to the second major criticism that Marx levels against Ricardo: his inadequate treatment of profit.

Let us begin by recalling that it takes 1,000 worker-hours of abstract labor-time to produce a loom by hand, and 600 additional worker-hours to use this loom in producing cloth: $C = 1{,}000$, $L = 600$, $W = 1{,}600$.

$$1000_C + 600_L = 1600_W = \text{value of cloth} \qquad (13.4)$$

But from the point of view of the capitalist, the matter looks very different. To him, the process starts with an investment of money M and ends with the sale of the loom for another sum of money M'. The difference between the two, $\Delta M = M' - M$, is that all important sum, profit. How does this have anything to do with labor-time, he asks?

Well, since exchange is in proportion to values, if the value of an ounce of gold is two worker-hours, then the money-price of the cloth must be 800 oz of gold. That gives us the end of the circuit of capital: $M' = 800$ oz of gold.

What about the beginning? From the point of view of the capitalists, the initial investment M goes to buy the inputs of the process. One part of M, which I will call M_C, goes therefore to buy a loom; since the value of a loom is 1,000 worker-hours, its price is 500 oz: $M_C = 500$ oz of gold.

The other input is, of course, labor. But what does it cost? Living labor, we have seen, transfers the value of the loom to the value of the product (cloth), and adds 600 worker-hours of value in the process. If exchange is at values, then the value-added by living labor is equivalent to 300 oz of gold-money. Clearly, if the labor input cost as much as 300 oz, then the capitalist's cost would be equal to his price: there would be no profit! For capitalist production to be profitable, workers must accept as wages the money equivalent of a value less than that which they themselves add to the product. But then, it would seem, exchange is no longer at values!

This paradox was in fact a major source of problems in classical political economy, and Marx considered the solution to it one of his great triumphs.[25] The way out, Marx shows, lies in the distinction between labor-time and labor-power. What workers sell in the market is their capacity-for-labor, not their labor time. The capitalist pays them a wage in return for the right to set them to work each day; but how long they work and how hard, how many hours of average labor-time the capitalist actually gets out of them, will depend on the struggle between capital and labor. Quite apart from the wage rate, the intensity of labor and the length of the working day have always been important battle grounds in the class struggle. The capacity-to-labor, what Marx calls labor-power, is therefore very different from labor-time: it is the sum of the mental and physical capabilities which a worker can put to use in production, and as such, its production and reproduction implies that workers must receive as wages enough money to buy their *means of subsistence:* food, shelter, education, and training – in short, whatever is necessary to reproduce themselves as workers. The value of labor-power, the social labor-time required for the reproduction of workers' capabilities, is therefore the value of their means of subsistence.

The paradox is now resolved. Workers enter production as inputs having a specific value; they leave production having added a quantity of value to the product through their labor-time. From the point of view of capitalist society, therefore, profit can only arise if the abstract labor-time socially necessary to sustain workers (the value of their labor-power) is less than the labor-time that they actually put in (the value they add to production); in other words, if workers produce *surplus-value.* Profit is the money equivalent, the money form of appearance of surplus-value. In the case of cloth production, the value added by 10 workers in a week is 600 worker-hours; if the value of their labor-power was 400 worker-hours, the surplus-value would be 200 worker-hours. Wages would be 200 oz of gold so that profit $\Delta M = M' - M = 800 - (500 + 200) = 100$ oz: profit is the money equivalent of surplus-value.

We can summarize all this diagramatically. Let V stand for the value of labor-power, and M_V for its money equivalent (the money-capital ex-

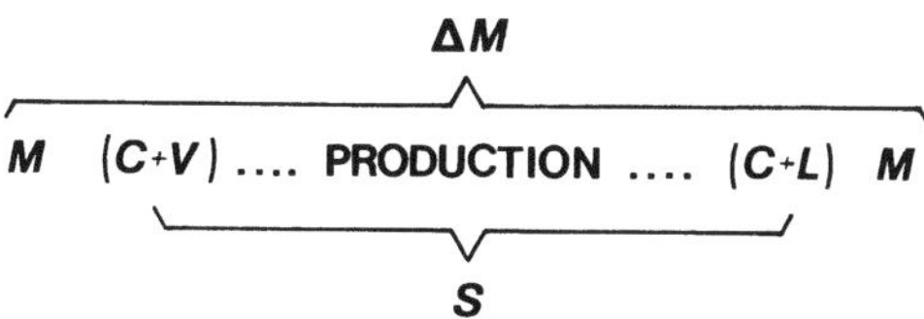

Figure 13.1

pended on wages). Since L is the value added by living labor, $L - V = S$ is the surplus-value produced by workers. In Figure 13.1, the circuit begins with a money investment $M = M_C + M_V$, with which the capitalist purchases means of production (a loom) having value C, and hires labor-power (10 workers) having value V; what emerges from the process of production is a product having value $C + L$, which then sells for its money-equivalent M'. The surplus-value S is thus reflected in its money-equivalent, the profit ΔM.

Prices of production. We have up to now assumed exchange in proportion to values, so that we may isolate the intrinsic determinants of price and profit. This is how Marx begins; but then he immediately goes on to point out that in general prices proportional to values would imply different rates of profit in different sectors.

Figure 13.1 illustrates the problem. If all money prices are proportional to values, then in every sector the money investment M will be proportional to the value cost $C + V$, and money profits M will be proportional to surplus-value S. It follows from this that the money rate of profit $(\Delta M/M)$ in each sector will be *equal* to the corresponding value rate of profit:

$$(\Delta M/M) = S/(C + V) = \frac{S/V}{C/V + 1} \qquad (13.5)$$

The expression for the value rate of profit obviously depends on the two ratios S/V and C/V. We therefore need to look at these a little more closely.

Recall that surplus-value S is the excess of the value added (L) by living labor over the value of its labor-power. Now, if the wage rate is the same for each worker (assuming that all labor is of the same skill level – the issue of skill differences is outside of the scope of this chapter), then the value of labor-power is the same for each; if in any given period each worker puts in the same amount of labor-time as any other, then each adds the same value to the product. Consequently, each worker produces the same amount of surplus-value. It follows therefore that in every sector the *proportions* of $L:S:V$ will be the same, though the respective size of each will vary with the number of workers employed.

This has two immediate consequences for the issue of profitability. First of all, the ratio S/V, the *rate of surplus-value*, will be the same in every sector. Second, since the proportion of $L:V$ is the same in every sector, the ratio C/V, the *organic composition of capital*, will in each sector be proportional to the ratio C/L. So whether or not C/V is, like S/V, the same in each sector will depend on whether or not C/L is the same.

The ratio C/L however, is in general not likely to be uniform across sectors. It is the ratio of the labor-time embodied in the means of production to the living labor-time required to transform these into the product; as such it reflects the technical conditions of production in each sector, and unless they are generally similar, it will vary from sector to sector. This in turn means that although the rate of surplus-value, S/V, is uniform across sectors, in general the organic composition, C/V, is not. From the expression for the rate of profit in equation 13.5 we can see that sectors with a high organic composition will have a low rate of profit, and vice versa. It is an inescapable implication therefore, that prices which are proportional to values will in general embody *un*equal rates of profit.

When prices are proportional to values, profit in any given sector is directly determined by the surplus-value produced in that sector alone; but then, as we have seen, rates of profit will differ from sector to sector. It follows therefore that if rates of profit are to be equalized, if high and low rates of profit are to be made equal to the social average, some sectors must get less profit, and others more, than that indicated by their respective surplus-values. This can only come about if prices of production deviate from direct prices in a systematic way so as to redistribute the total pool of surplus-value: in other words, in order that the equal rates of surplus-value in various sectors be realized in exchange as equal rates of money profit, the sale of products must actually take place at prices which differ systematically from direct prices.

Clearly, what is involved here is a change, a transformation, in the *form-of-value* (*money price*). But such a transformation can in no way alter the total sum of values or the total pool of surplus-value; the same products as before are circulated, only now at different prices which therefore entail a different sharing out of the pool of surplus-value.

Marx deals with the transformation in the form-of-value in a simple and powerful way. Basically, he points out that when exchange is ruled by direct prices, sectors with higher than average organic compositions C/V will have lower than average rates of profit, and vice versa (look at equation 13.5 to see why); from this Marx concludes that in order for each sector's profit rate to be equal to the social average, sectors with high organic compositions must therefore sell their products at prices above their respective direct prices, while sectors with low organic compositions must sell at prices below their respective direct prices. What takes place in the transformation from direct prices to prices of production is a kind of rotation of prices, with the average price as the (unchanged) center of rotation. The total sum of prices is unaltered, as is total profit; they remain directly proportional to the total sum of values and the total surplus-value respectively. Hence the average rate is simply equal to the value rate of profit, as in equation 13.5.

In his exposition, and in several other places, Marx notes the existence of what I call a feedback effect of the transformation just mentioned: since individual prices of production differ from direct prices, this also means that individual money investments, M, will in general differ from the corresponding value costs $C + V$ (Marx, 1967, Vol. III, pp. 161, 164–5). Such a feedback effect could make the relation between value magnitudes and their price forms more complex, Marx observes. But then he leaves this issue aside, clearly because he considers it to be of relatively minor importance in the process of deriving price from value and profit from surplus-value.

Marx's opponents immediately seized upon the incomplete nature of Marx's transformation, and, ever since then, this issue has been the focus of a long-running debate. Recently this debate has flared up once again, leading to some important new results which support the essential nature of Marx's derivations. It is entirely beyond the scope of this chapter to go into this matter in any depth; however, in a separate paper (Shaikh, 1977) I do treat this connection in detail. For our purposes here, three of its aspects are significant. First, that the procedure by which Marx transforms direct prices can be also viewed as the initial step in an iterative procedure for *calculating* the actual prices of production themselves. This helps establish a fruitful mathematical connection between Marx's procedure and further-developed prices of production. Second, it can be shown (in the case of three departments of production, at least) that for each sector both the actual and the regulating price of production deviate in the same direction from the sector's direct price, so too will be the actual price of production. (Seton, 1957, pp. 157–60) Last, it has been established that the transformed money rate of profit is directly related to the value rate of profit, though they need not be equal in magnitude.[26]

For most analyses, knowledge of the above connections is generally sufficient. In this chapter, therefore, I have used only direct prices and Marx's derivation of prices of production, on the implicit understanding of the connection between the latter and their further-developed form.

The theory of money. We began the analysis of price by noting that a commodity is a product of human labor which is not just useful but also valuable. This led us to examine the duality implicit in the notion of quantitative worth, which in turn led to the sharp distinction between value, the intrinsic cause of quantitative worth, and money-price, the measure or expression of this worth in terms of some universal equivalent (gold). In order for commodities to be equal in worth to some quantity of gold, that is, in order for them to have *money-prices,* they must already have worth: money does not cause worth, it only measures it.

It is a necessary consequence that the factors which determine how valuable a commodity will be in exchange, determine its money-price. And these factors, as we have seen, are the amount and distribution of social labor-time.

If the distribution of social labor is such that the commodities produced correspond to the various social needs, supply will equal demand, and the money-price of a commodity will equal its regulating price – direct prices if we assume exchange in proportion to values – prices of production at a higher level of analysis. In either case, it is the amounts of labor-time which determine these regulating prices.

If, on the other hand, the distribution of labor is not appropriate to various social needs, then the market price of a commodity will deviate from its regulating price, and a change will take place in the distribution of social labor so as to reduce the discrepancy between market and regulating prices. For the purposes of this analysis, therefore, we may leave out of consideration the constantly fluctuating market prices and focus directly on regulating prices.

In any given year, the sum of prices of all the commodities produced must equal the number of coins in circulation times the velocity of circulation. This, as Marx points out, is simply a *tautology*. In order to make it something more, we must embed it in a theoretical structure.

Let us begin by assuming that the regulating prices are direct prices. Then the price of any commodity is its value relative to that of gold, so that the sum of the prices of all the commodities produced in a given year is given by their total value relative to the value of gold. Let *TP* stand for the sum of prices, *TW* for the sum of values, and ω_g for the value of a *unit* (an ounce) of gold, we can write

$$TP = (TW/\omega_g) \tag{13.6}$$

In this equation, the sum of (regulating) prices is the direct expression of the sum of values of commodities. If the velocity of circulation is k, then the amount of gold, G (in the form of one-ounce coins), which is required as a medium of circulation is

$$G = TP/k = [(1/k)(TW/\omega_g)] \tag{13.7}$$

The causation in this is very clear: the sum of the values of the commodities produced in a given period determines the sum of their money-prices, and this in conjunction with the velocity of circulation,[27] determines the number of (1 oz) gold coins required for the circulation of the commodities (Marx, 1967, Vol. I, p. 123, et passim).

Though the preceding relations were derived on the basis of direct prices, they are not the least bit altered when we move on to prices of production, for, as we have seen, the regulating prices of production that Marx derives have the same sum of prices as do direct prices. This means that as far as the sum of the prices of all commodities is concerned, the determination is the same whether we assume direct prices or prices of production: the sum of prices equals the sum of values divided by the value of an ounce of gold. As a result, the quantity of gold required is the same in either case.

What happens then if there exist more gold coins than the required number? Well, the quantity G is the number of gold coins which circulate *because* they facilitate the circulation of commodities. Therefore any quantity of coin over and above this amount will be redundant in circulation: it will at first take the form of idle coin, excess coin (Marx, 1972, Ch. 2, Sec. 3a).[28]

But an excess supply of gold is a very different thing from an excess supply of any other commodity. All other commodities, in order to fulfill their function, must be sold, turned into gold through the alchemy of exchange; but gold itself does not have to be, in fact cannot be, sold. It *is* money,[29] the perfect and durable form of wealth which all other commodities seek to obtain. From the earliest stages of commodity production, therefore, gold circulating in the form of coin has existed side by side with noncirculating gold in the form of reserve coin, in the form of hoards, and in the form of luxury articles.

The very nature of commodity production, the unceasing fluctuations of market prices and quantities, requires that every commodity owner have on hand a reserve of money to accommodate day to day variations. Consequently, the first manifestation of a persistent excess of coin over the needs of circulation will be the buildup of these reserves above the requisite levels; but then this superfluous gold, being necessary neither for immediate circulation nor for its anticipated variations, will be withdrawn altogether from the vicinity of the sphere of exchange. It will either enter into hoards or it is transformed into articles of luxury:

> We have seen how, along with the continual fluctuations in the extent and rapidity of the circulation of commodities and in their prices, the quantity of money current unceasingly ebbs and flows. This mass must, therefore, be capable of expansion and contraction. At one time money must be attracted in order to act as circulating coin, at another, circulating coin must be repelled in order to act again as more or less stagnant money. In order that the mass of money, actually current, may constantly saturate the absorbing power of the circulation, it is necessary that the quantity of gold and silver in a country be greater than the quantity required to function as coin. This condition is fulfilled by money taking the form of hoards. (Marx, 1967, Vol. I, p. 134)

In countries where commodity production is still primitive, hoards take the form of private accumulations of gold scattered throughout the country. But as commodity production, and hence the banking system, develops and expands, hoards become concentrated in the reservoirs of banks (Marx, 1972, pp. 136–7). Under these circumstances, excesses or deficiencies of gold money relative to the needs of circulation manifest themselves as increases or decreases of bank reserves.[30]

Hoards in the form of bank reserves, however, are very different from private hoards: to the bank, an excess of bank reserves over the legally required minimum is a supply of idle bank-capital, money-capital which could be earning profit for the bank but is instead lying fallow. An increase in bank reserves is therefore generally accompanied by a decrease in the rate of interest as the banks strive to convert reserves into capital. Conversely, a drop in bank reserves below the legal minimum tends to lead to a rise in the rate of interest. Rather than raising the price level, the immediate effect of an excess of gold-money is to lower the rate of interest: "If this export [of capital] is made in the form of precious metal, it will exert a direct influence upon the money-market and with it upon the interest rate . . ." (Marx, 1967, Vol. III, p. 577).

But now it might be asked: surely the fact that the bank puts this extra money into circulation via a lowering of the rate of interest also implies that effective demand is thereby raised? And if so, won't this in turn imply that as a consequence of this higher effective demand prices will eventually rise – so that in the end the quantity theory is right after all? Marx's answer is unequivocal: no.

We begin by noting that an increased supply of gold can indeed lead to an increase in effective demand, either insofar as it is spent by its original owners, or indirectly because it will expand bank reserves and hence the supply of loanable money-capital, which will tend to drive down interest rates, which may in turn increase capitalist borrowing for investment.[31] However, even though this increase in effective demand may temporarily increase prices of some commodities, and hence raise profits in some sectors, it must eventually lead to an expansion of production to meet the new demand. And as production expands prices will fall until (all other things being equal) they regain their original levels. In this case the *sum* of prices of all commodities will have increased, not because the level of prices has increased, but because the mass of commodities thrown into production has itself increased. Thus, insofar as a pure increase in the supply of gold does generate an increase in effective demand (i.e., insofar as it does not simply expand bank reserves or go into the production of luxury articles) it will also generate an increased need for circulating gold coin.

It is important to note at this point that to Marx, the notion of a capitalism that tends to be more or less at full employment is a vulgar fantasy. First of all, Marx notes that it is an inherent tendency of capitalism to *create* and maintain a relative surplus population of workers – the reserve army of the unemployed (Marx, 1967, Vol. I, Ch. 25). Second, even with a given pattern of fixed capital (plant and equipment), expansion of production can easily be undertaken by extending and/or intensifying the working time in a given working day (Marx, 1967, Vol. II, p. 258). Last, it is an intrinsic requirement of capitalist commodity production, which is regulated only by the constant fluctuations of the circulation process, to maintain stocks of various commodities so that the exigencies of circulation may be met without disrupting the continuity of the production process. It is precisely because of these possibilities that the continuity of the production process is possible alongside constantly varying levels of production and sale. (Marx, 1973, pp. 582–6)

> It is extremely important to grasp this aspect of circulating and fixated capital as *specific characteristic forms* of capital generally, since a great many phenomena of the bourgeois economy – the period of the economic cycle, . . . the effect of new demand; even the effect of new gold-and-silver producing countries on general production – [would otherwise] be incomprehensible. It is futile to speak of the stimulus given by Australian gold or a newly discovered market . . . [if] it were not in the nature of capital to be never completely occupied . . . At the same time, [note] the senseless contradictions into which the economists stray – even Ricardo – when they presuppose that capital is always fully occupied . . . (Marx, 1973, p. 623)

Having located Marx's criticism of Ricardo's theory of money,[32] we can now turn to its implications for gold flows generated by changes in the balance of international trade. In the case of a surplus, for instance, there will be a net inflow of gold into the country and a consequent increase in the country's supply of gold. Insofar as this leads to an increase in effective demand, production will expand, and with it the needs of circulation. Part of the increased gold supply will therefore go to meet the expanded requirements of circulation, part will pile up in bank reserves, and part will be absorbed in the expanded production of luxury articles made of gold. In addition, once we take international trade into account, a part of the surplus gold may be re-exported in the form of foreign loans in search of interest rates, or as foreign investment in search of surplus-value. These last two possibilities, as we shall see shortly, become important in a Marxian analysis of international exchange.

In any case, Marx emphatically rejects the notion that a "pure" increase in the supply of gold will in general lead to an increase in prices:

> It is indeed an old humbug that changes in the existing quantity of gold in a particular country must raise or lower commodity-prices within this country by increasing or decreasing the quantity of the medium of circulation. If gold is exported, then, according to the Currency Theory, commodity-prices must rise in the country importing this gold, and decrease in the country exporting it . . . But, in fact, a decrease in the quantity of gold raises only the interest rate, whereas an increase in the quantity of gold lowers the interest rate; and if not for the fact that the fluctuations in the interest rate enter into the determination of cost-prices, or in the determination of demand and supply, commodity-prices would be wholly unaffected by them (Marx, *Capital*, 1967, Vol. III, Ch. XXXIV, p. 551)

It should be noted at this point that Marx's

theory of money implies not only a rejection of the Hume specie-flow mechanism on which Ricardo's results were based, but also rejection of the various modern versions (discussed in the fourth part of the second major section) which have replaced it.

The cash balance approach, for instance, relied on a fall in effective demand in the backward country to lead to a fall in money prices. But this connection between effective demand and the permanent level of prices is precisely what Marx denies. Similarly, the price level of commodities being determined by their value relative to that of gold, the money wage cannot permanently influence the price level: the Keynesian price theory therefore will not work either.

That brings us back once again to the possibility of purely flexible exchange rates. As noted in the fourth part of the second major section, the actual gold standard operated with a flexible exchange rate bounded by limits (gold-points) based on the costs of transporting gold. This meant that in its normal variations it was a system of flexible exchange rates, whereas in its "limited" mode it operated as a fixed exchange rate system.

It is out of this long experience that orthodox theory falsely abstracted fixed and flexible exchange rates as two separate regimes. In this context purely flexible exchange rates are presented as a mechanism whereby in theory a world capitalist system can be made up of fully "independent" national currencies (Yeager, 1966, p. 104). As a theoretical possibility this idea has always had an uneasy existence: the history of currency "floats" strongly suggests only a limited flexibility (Yeager, 1966, pp. 176–80), and the history of the international money system is very much a history of increasing monetary integration, not separation. In a sense, the notion of a purely flexible exchange rate determined solely by supply and demand considerations is one more manifestation of the general neoclassical method in which all "prices" are determined only by supply and demand. In opposition to this, Marx's method very much emphasizes the intrinsic limits to these apparent variations: in the case of prices, these arose from labor-times; in the case of exchange rates, from the existence of the money commodity (as in gold-points).

The law of value in international exchange

Perhaps the most fundamental result to emerge from Marx's criticism of Ricardo is the crucial distinction between value and price. Money price, to Marx, is the external measure of the value of a commodity. The very nature of commodity production requires not only that every commodity be assessed in terms of some universal equivalent (hence the necessity of money), but also that this assessment be contingent on a series of factors, ranging from the vagaries of supply and demand to the social limits imposed by reproduction (hence the ultimate regulation of market prices by value).

Marx's analysis of the exchange of commodities within a nation is thus characteristically distinct from Ricardo's. In what follows we shall see that it is these very same differences which necessarily imply an equally distinct Marxian analysis of international exchange.

Comparative costs reexamined. We begin once again with the familiar Ricardian tableau (Table 13.2). Portugal is absolutely more efficient in both branches of production, and given the value of gold[33] as two worker-hours per ounce, this greater efficiency translates directly into an absolute cost advantage. Portuguese capitalists will therefore export both cloth and wine, and England will have to counterbalance its ensuing trade deficit by shipping gold to Portugal.

According to Ricardo, the gold outflow from England would lower all prices there, since it would lower the domestic supply of money; conversely, the gold inflow into Portugal would raise the prices of all Portuguese commodities. As we have seen, this process implies that sooner or later English cloth would undersell its Portuguese counterpart, so that in the end two-way trade would always reign. No nation need fear trade, for it benefits all.

But the mechanism which leads us to this harmonious conclusion rests squarely upon the operation of the classical quantity theory of money. And this we know to be false. Let us therefore begin again.

Because of their absolute advantage, Portuguese capitalists in both branches are able to undersell their English competition. Portuguese cloth and wine invade English markets, and English gold begins to flow back to Portugal. In England, therefore, the supply of gold decreases, while in Portugal it increases.

It is at this point that Marx's theory of money becomes critical. In contrast to Ricardo, Marx

Table 13.2.

	England		Portugal		
Cloth:	100 hrs	50 oz gold	45 oz gold	90 hrs	:Cloth
Wine:	120 hrs	60 oz gold	40 oz gold	80 hrs	:Wine

expressly denies any link between pure changes in the supply of gold and the level or prices.

Instead, according to Marx's analysis, the primary effect of an outflow of gold from England will be to diminish the supply of loanable money-capital. On the other hand, as English cloth and wine production succumbs to foreign competition, the demand for money-capital will also decrease. Nonetheless, when these sectors have reached their minimal size (there will always be Englishmen who will *never* buy from foreigners), the continuing drain of gold will tend to raise the rate of interest; insofar as this curtails investment, production of other commodities will decline. In England therefore, the drain of bullion will lead to lower bank reserves, curtailed production, and a higher rate of interest.

In Portugal, the effects are just the opposite. As gold flows into Portugal, part of it will be absorbed by the expanded circulation requirements of cloth and wine production; part will be absorbed in the form of luxury articles; and the rest will be absorbed in the form of expanded bank reserves. This last effect will increase the supply of loanable money-capital, lowering interest rates and tending to expand production in general. Thus, in Portugal, the inflow of gold will raise bank reserves, expand production, and lower the rate of interest.

What we find therefore is that according to Marx's analysis England's absolute disadvantage will be manifested in a chronic trade deficit, *balanced* by a persistent outflow of gold. On the other hand, Portugal's greater efficiency in production will manifest itself in a chronic trade surplus, balanced by a persistent accumulation of gold.

Obviously such a situation cannot continue indefinitely.[34] If we stick to commodity flows alone, then as English bank reserves decline, so too will the credibility of the English £; eventually, the £ must collapse, and with it the trade between England and Portugal.

The end need not come in such a straightforward manner, however. We noted earlier that as English reserves shrink, the rate of interest in England will rise; conversely, as money-capital piles up in Portugal, the rate of interest there will fall. At some point, therefore, it will be to the advantage of Portuguese capitalists to lend their money-capital abroad, in England, rather than at home. When this happens, short-term financial capital will flow from Portugal to England;[35] England's rate of interest would then reverse itself and begin to fall, while Portugal's would rise, until at some level of short-term capital flows the two would be equal.

It may seem that at this point the situation would be balanced: England running a chronic trade deficit which it covers by means of short-term international borrowing, and Portugal running a trade surplus which enables its capitalists to engage in international lending. But of course this is not quite correct: capitalist loans are made in order to get profit (in the form of interest). Thus England would have to eventually pay back not only the original loan, but also the interest on it. The *net* effect must be an *outflow* of gold from England, albeit at a later date. All other things being equal,[36] the piper must be paid: in the end, beset by chronic trade deficits and mounting debts, England must eventually succumb.

The foregoing results take on an unpleasantly familiar ring when we express them in terms of developed and underdeveloped capitalist countries. Curiously enough, in Ricardo's example England corresponds to the *under*-developed capitalist country (UCC), its generally lower efficiency being the reflection of its lower level of development. Portugal, on the other hand, corresponds to the developed capitalist country (DCC).

Cast in these terms, we may say: *in free trade, the absolute disadvantage of the underdeveloped capitalist country will result in chronic trade deficits and mounting international borrowing. It will be chronically in deficit and chronically in debt.*

In our analysis so far, we have assumed only two commodities, so that an absolute advantage implies greater efficiency in producing both: otherwise it would obviously be a relative advantage. But when we consider the whole range of products possible in both countries, then it becomes evident that in spite of a *general* superiority in production, the DCC may nonetheless produce certain commodities at a greater cost than the UCC, and yet others not at all. Since we are still considering direct prices, the only possible exports of the underdeveloped country will conform precisely to these types: commodities it can produce at a lower value and/or those commodities peculiar to it only.[37] On the whole, these types of commodities will reflect some specific local advantages great enough to overcome the UCC's generally lower level of efficiency: a good climate, an abundance of particular natural resources, a propitious location, and so on; lower wages, however, will not matter here, since in the case of direct prices the level of wages affects profits but has no effect on prices. Under these circumstances, then, the underdeveloped country will be able to eke out a few exports; although, of course, its overall trade will still be in deficit, and its position still that of a debtor nation. Trade will serve not to eliminate inequality, but to perpetuate it.

This result is not substantially modified by the consideration of prices of production. Since within a given country the average price of production is equal to the average direct price, the overall advantage of the DCC remains unchanged. What may change, however, are the trading positions of individual sectors. Within each country, sectors with high organic compositions will have prices of production above their direct prices, and sectors with low compositions, prices of production below their direct prices; but this dispersion effect holds true in both countries, to differing degrees, so that it is quite possible that in either country some previously marginal sectors may enter international competition while others drop out.

What we are left with, therefore, is that in general the developed capitalist country will dominate trade because its greater efficiency will enable it to produce most commodities at absolutely lower values, and hence, to sell them on the average at absolutely lower prices of production.

Above all, it must be kept in mind that these results represent the automatic tendencies of free and *unhampered* trade among capitalist nations at different levels of development. It is not monopoly or conspiracy upon which uneven development rests, but free competition itself: free trade is as much a mechanism for the concentration and centralization of international capital as free exchange within a capitalist nation is for the concentration and centralization of domestic capital. We will return to this point after we consider the effects of direct investment.

Incidentally, it is worth remarking that trade between capitalist nations with more or less the same level of development will have a characteristically different pattern. Suppose we consider the example lying at the heart of the Heckscher-Ohlin-Samuelson model, in which both capitalist countries possess the same technology and level of productivity – so that absolute advantage is impossible. In this limiting case, factors such as climate, location, availability of resources, experience, inventions, and above all the competitive struggle among capitalists, become all important. We would expect a more or less balanced pattern of trade in this case, with a large variety of goods being produced in both countries, and with the advantage in particular commodities shifting back and forth in the short-run. This is quite different from the structural imbalance of DCC–UCC trade.

The effects of direct investment. It is traditional in the analysis of international trade to separate commodity flows from flows of capital (direct investment). The law of comparative costs is then used to justify the patterns of commodity trade, while direct investment is treated (separately) as a transfer of savings from the rich capitalist nations to their poor relatives.[38] The underdeveloped capitalist nations thus emerge as doubly blessed: the overwhelming productive superiority of the developed nations is manifested only in the cheapness of their exports, while their incomparably greater wealth manifests itself as a mass of capital eager and willing to go over there and help spread freedom, equality, property, and Coca-Cola.

The preceding section has demonstrated that the law of comparative costs is invalid *even on its own grounds*. The concentration and centralization which is inherent in capitalist production is as much a part of world capitalism as it is of any single national entity; no form of exchange, be it national or international, can do more than to give vent to the fundamental laws of capitalist production. Rather than negating the inequality of development, commodity trade affirms and reinforces it.

But then what are we to make of the existing analyses of the effects of direct investment?

On one hand, orthodox economic analysis argues that direct investment "redistributes world savings" (Kenen, 1968, p. 29) from the rich capitalist nations to the poor ones, which tends to eliminate international inequality by slowing down the growth of the investing countries and speeding up the growth of the recipient countries. As such, might it not offset the inequality-widening effects of commodity trade?

On the other hand, as I outlined earlier, both conventional Marxist analysis and that of Emmanuel rely heavily on the export of capital as being the critical factor in modern imperialism. But both analyses are based on an explicit acceptance of comparative (instead of absolute) advantage, a law which we now know to be incorrect. To what extent, therefore, does the overthrow of this law also modify either or both of the above theories of imperialism?

These issues lead us directly to the central question of this section: how does the consideration of direct investment modify the previously derived law of international exchange? In order to answer this, we begin by developing the determinants of foreign investment.

Let us recall the results of merchant capital (i.e., commodity) flows: on the average, the absolutely greater productive efficiency of the DCC translates into lower international prices for its products. If we consider products whose consumption is common to both,[39] the DCC will dominate trade, with the UCC managing to eke out exports only in those sectors where local advantages such as climate, availability of resources, etc. are so great as to offset their generally lower efficiency.

We must keep in mind the elements of this relationship. The DCC has the advantage precisely because it has a more developed structure of production, two aspects of which are of importance here: first, a superior technology; and second, a work-force more conditioned to capitalist production. The UCC, on the other hand, has an inferior technology and a work-force which is still new to wage-labor. The greater efficiency of production in the DCC is therefore due partly to the superior technology, and partly to the higher direct productivity of its work-force. The term, "direct productivity," refers to the fact that even when both work-forces use the same technology, the work-force of the DCC is likely to be able to produce more output, because of its greater conditioning to capitalist production, its greater familiarity with machines, etc.

On the basis of these differences, then, merchant-capital will facilitate trade between the two countries in those commodities which are of use in either country. But note that so long as the differences in development manifest themselves in the above-stated ways, the means of production of the two countries will not be among the traded commodities: each country's capitalists will use means of production consistent with its general level of development.

Merchant capital necessarily carries with it the possibility of modernization, however: the capitalists within the UCC may (and do) switch over to the superior technology of the DCC. But there are many factors which militate against this: the vastly greater cost and scale of advanced techniques, the complex interdependence required among different techniques for any one to be viable, and the greater socialization required of the work-force. For these reasons, modernization from the inside as an inherent tendency of trade relations is usually overwhelmed by another more powerful inherent tendency: modernization from the outside, or direct investment.[40]

Precisely those factors which work against modernization from the inside tend to work in favor of direct investment: capitalists from the DCC have much larger capitals available for investment, are familiar with modern techniques, have access to all the necessary skilled workers. But the most important factor which favors direct investment, as we shall see, is the low level of wages in the UCC.

During the analysis of commodity trade, wage differences did not appear to be an important factor. In the case of direct prices, price is determined immediately by value; wages affect only the rates of profit. In the case of prices of production, because the wage rate affects the average rate of profit, it can affect the extent to which individual prices of production deviate from direct prices; but the average price is still directly connected to value. Up to this point, therefore, it has been necessary to focus on differences in productive efficiency as the most important manifestations of uneven development, even though differences in wage rates between DCC and UCC are just as symptomatic of the disparity between their levels of development. Once we admit the possibility of international movements of industrial capital, however, wage disparities between capitalist nations become an important factor in their own right.

Consider the case of an individual capital in the DCC. If we ignore transportation costs, then the same price rules everywhere. Thus, it will take more or less the same amount of gold to build and supply a given type of plant anywhere in the world: the sole difference between countries will therefore arise from the differing costs of labor-power; that is, from the combined effects of the differences in direct productivity and the differences in wage rates.

In *Unequal Exchange . . .* , Arghiri Emmanuel points out that though the direct productivity of labor is generally lower in the UCC, the wage rate is much lower still: whereas the direct productivity "of the average worker in the underdeveloped areas is 50 to 60 percent of that of the average worker in the industrialized areas . . . the average wage in the developed countries is about 30 times the average wage in the backward countries" (Emmanuel, 1972, p. 48). This means that although it takes roughly twice as many workers in the UCC to produce the same output from a given plant than it would at home, each worker costs the developed country's capitalist only 1/30 of what workers cost at home; the net effect is that the average wage bill of a plant located in the UCC would be 1/15 of what it would be at home: cheap labor attracts foreign investment.

It must be emphasized at this point that cheap labor is not the only source of attraction for foreign investment. Other things being equal, cheap raw materials, a good climate, and a good location (if transportation costs are taken into account) are also important in making individual sectors of production attractive to foreign capital. But these factors are specific to certain branches only; cheap wage-labor, on the other hand, is a general social characteristic of underdeveloped capitalist countries, one whose implications extend to all areas of production, even those yet to be created.

One immediate consequence of considering

direct investment is that the export industries of the UCC emerge as the prime targets of foreign capital. As we have already seen, when we treat flows of merchant capital, the only sectors of the UCC capable of surviving are those whose products have no foreign counterparts, so that they face no competition from imports, and those which do face foreign competition but can overcome it due to local advantages such as plentiful raw materials, etc., which enable them to offset their generally inferior technology and lower labor productivity. The latter group of sectors, if they exist at all, become the export sectors of the UCC. And once the possibility of foreign investment is taken into account, these export sectors become leading candidates for foreign takeover: even if foreign capitalists had to ship over workers from their own country their superior technology would still enable them to take advantage of the cheap raw materials, etc., to make exceptional profits; in addition, since labor in the UCC is available at a lower net cost,[41] the export sectors begin to appear even more attractive to foreign investors.

The sectors confined solely to domestic production are not exempt from this process, however. Insofar as there exist within this group certain industries in which the superior technology of foreign capital and the lower net cost of domestic labor power enables the capitalists from the DCC to make higher profits there than they would at home, these industries too will be prey to the foreign invasion.

In all the sectors subject to this discipline, foreign capital enters because by selling at or even below the existing prices, it can enjoy a higher rate of profit than the rate which rules at home. The existing prices, however, are the prices of production of these sectors, embodying the average rate of profit in the UCC. At first glance therefore, it would seem that direct investment would only flow from the DCC to the UCC if the former's average rate of profit was higher than the latter's – because of the lower wage, for instance, in the UCC. *But this is not necessary at all.* By modernizing from the outside, foreign capital lowers the cost-price of a commodity and so raises its profitability. Thus even if the national rate of profit in the UCC were below that of the DCC, the sectors modernized by foreign capital could still yield for it a higher rate than either national average.[42]

Regardless of the actual differences in the average rates of profit of the two countries, therefore, foreign capital will seek to enter those particular industries in which it can enjoy a higher profit (at the going prices) than it would at home. As it does so, however, the competition among foreign capitals for these excess profits will lead to an increase in the supply of the commodities produced, driving down their prices and hence reducing the excess profits which attracted them in the first place. No matter where this process stops, it is clear that it will end up lowering the prices of the chosen industries until the foreign capital invested in them earns the same rate of profit as it would at home.

From the point of view of local capital the effects of foreign investment will generally be disastrous. The prices which existed before the modernization from the outside were prices of production embodying the average rate of profit in the UCC. When these prices are driven down by the influx of foreign capital, the domestic capitalists will be forced out – out of business, into yet unaffected areas or into new industries created in response to the needs of the foreign dominated sectors.

We have up to now confined ourselves to analyzing the effects of direct investment on industries already existing in the UCC. Given that only a few industries would survive the rigors of commodity trade, the question that arose was: will direct investment help offset the devastation of competition from foreign imports, or will it make matters worse?

From the point of view of local capital, the answer seems unambiguous: worse! Struggling to exploit their workers in peace, they find themselves beset by foreign devils: first their industries are ruined by cheap imports, and then those that survive are taken over by foreign capital! It is no wonder that protectionism becomes their religion.

The invasion and takeover of existing industries in the UCC does not, however, exhaust the possibilities inherent in direct investment. It must be remembered that all capitals compete against each other. This means that when capital from the DCC takes the form of foreign investment it competes not only with capital from the UCC but also with capital still at home. Where it can take advantage of the cheap labor in the UCC, new capital in the DCC can set itself up *in opposition to existing home industries,* by opening plants abroad and exporting the (cheaper) products.

We see, therefore, that attraction of cheap labor for foreign capital can be detrimental not only to local capitals in the UCC but also to certain capitals in the DCC. It is for this reason that the cry for protectionism resounds on *both* sides of the development gap. Where merchant capital dominates, or where foreign investment is still no threat to home capital, then only the plaintive wail of UCC capitalists is heard in favor of protectionism. But when foreign investment develops to the point of competing with home production itself, the protection quickly becomes the reality of the day. Only the free traders remain, tirelessly selling the patent medicine of comparative costs.

From a nationalist point of view, the effects of direct investment on the UCC seem mixed. We have seen that merchant trade will be dominated by the DCC; the UCC will emerge as perpetually in debt and perpetually in deficit.

Insofar as foreign capital invades the surviving industries, it adds insult to injury by increasing the dependence of the UCC on the developed capitalist world. Direct investment, it is true, does lower prices and modernize industry; but, as Emmanuel emphasizes, lowered prices of exports are actually a loss to the nation-as-a-whole, since they constitute a deterioration of the terms of trade and hence a worsening of the trade balance. Moreover, for Emmanuel the important point would be that both modernization and the lowered prices are in fact mechanisms by which the surplus-value produced by workers from the UCC is in fact transferred to the foreign capitalists. This, he argues, further widens the gap between developed and underdeveloped countries; by strengthening the rich and weakening the poor: "wealth begets wealth . . . Poverty begets poverty" (Emmanuel, 1972, p. 131).

What Emmanuel does not see, however, is that foreign investment may also transplant industries from the DCC to the UCC, because of the advantages of cheap labor. Insofar as this happens, the export capability of the UCC is strengthened (albeit under the aegis of foreign capital) by the addition of these new sectors. This side of foreign investment will tend to improve the underdeveloped nation's balance of trade, and create new avenues of employment for its labor.

The fundamental error in Emmanuel's analysis, however, is much more basic: because he accepts the law of comparative costs as being correct on its own grounds, he is forced to put the whole blame for international inequality on the effects of direct investment. Since he identifies the lower wages of the UCC as the basic factor leading to foreign investment, Emmanuel must argue that *the solution to the problem of uneven development is to equalize wages between countries*. By so doing, the flow of industrial capital from the DCC to the UCC would cease, and with it all the deleterious effects which arise from it.

But we know that in fact Ricardo's law of comparative costs is wrong: quite independently of direct investment, commodity trade by itself will result in the penury of the underdeveloped capitalist country. If anything, direct investment can be an "offset" of a sort, albeit one which eventually intensifies the unevenness of development: inflows of foreign capital, even though they may be eventually repaid many times over in outflows of profit, are nonetheless an important source of long-term borrowing to offset the chronic trade deficits, ones which are generally preferable to the volatile financial capital flows upon which short-term borrowing is based. Moreover, as noted above, direct investment can lead to the creation of new industries in the UCC, which can help reduce its trade deficit as well as increase employment within the country.

The basic point, which Emmanuel's proposed solution completely misses, is that you are damned if you do, and damned if you don't. What Emmanuel sees as an inequality between nations is in fact the international manifestation of the inequality between capitals which is inherent in the *necessarily* uneven development of capitalist relations of production. Concentration and centralization as inherent tendencies of capitalist development are just as valid internationally as they are nationally. In either case, the patterns of exchange are symptoms, not causes, of these fundamental laws. The international equalization of wage rates can no more solve the problem of uneven development in capitalism than can the suppression of a symptom cure the disease. The problem lies with capitalism, not its symptoms: to argue for the same wage everywhere is in reality to argue that the *exploitation* of workers should be equal in all countries[43] – without reference to race, color, creed, or national origin! Democratic, no doubt, but limited in its implications.

Summary and conclusions

The purpose of this chapter has been to work towards the treatment of the laws of international exchange from the Marxist perspective. This is a theoretical task, one which has its roots in the law of value as it is developed in the successive volumes of *Capital*. As such, this analysis is not a substitute for the concrete reality of international trade or of its historical development. No attempt is made, for instance, to explain the historical roots of uneven development; nor is primitive accumulation ever treated. Instead, the point is to uncover the sorts of forces which are inherent in the international interactions of capitalist nations precisely so that we may be better prepared to deal with their concrete existence.

Perhaps the most enduring proposition in the

analysis of international trade has been the so-called law of comparative costs, which, as we have seen, has generally been accepted by orthodox economists and Marxists alike as being valid on its own grounds. In all of its various disguises, this so-called law has asserted that when it came to international trade between capitalist nations, inherent inequalities will be negated. Thus even if one of two nations could only produce all commodities at a higher price than the other, it would nonetheless end up exporting some and importing others. No nation, however humble, need ever fear "free trade," for, like bourgeois justice, it is blind to differences in station. Or so the story goes, anyway.

But it turns out that aside from the multitude of proofs about the "optimality" of specialization according to comparative costs, the real heart of the matter lies in the assertion that the basic thrust of international trade is to *actually* bring about such specialization. And the automatic mechanism which supposedly accomplishes this, we found, was the operation of the various orthodox theories of money.

The second part of this chapter therefore presented the development of the principle of comparative costs in its original (and basically unaltered) form: that of David Ricardo. Only then were modern derivations of this law presented. It was important in this section to show that the so-called law was a logical outcome of the conjunction of Ricardo's theory of value with his theory of money; this enabled us to establish that the locus of a critique of the law lay in its antecedents – not in the law itself.

In his analysis of Ricardo, Marx provides us precisely with the necessary critiques of Ricardo's theories of value and money. Moreover, in his own work he treats these subjects under the developments of the law of value. The third section of this chapter presented Marx's critique of Ricardo as well as his own treatment of value, price and money. This has a double consequence: the critiques of these antecedents of the so-called law of comparative costs provides us with a basis for a critique of the law itself; and Marx's own development of the law of value provides us with the basis for an adequate treatment of the laws of international exchange. And when this is done the law of comparative costs is seen to be *impossible* precisely on its own grounds. Rather than finding, as Ricardo did, that Portugal and England will each end up specializing in one commodity – in spite of Portugal's absolute superiority in the production of both – we find that Portugal will necessarily export both. England, the *underdeveloped* capitalist country in this example, will end up with a persistent trade deficit balanced by gold outflows and/or short-term borrowing.

When this result is expressed in terms of its real content, we can say: free trade will ensure that the underdeveloped capitalist country will be chronically in deficit and chronically in debt. It is *absolute* advantage, not comparative, which rules trade.

This result represents the extension of Marx's law of value (which in Marx subsumes a theory of money) to the realm of the international exchange of commodities. But as Marx points out, these commodities are capitalistically produced commodities, the commodity-form of various national capitals. As such, the interchange of commodity-capitals among nations carries with it the seeds of other forms of international capital, such as financial capital (foreign borrowing/lending), and direct investment.

The question of direct investment is particularly important, since its analysis plays so important a role in various theories of trade. Orthodox theory, for instance, finds direct investment to be a means of closing the gap between rich and poor capitalist countries, on the grounds that it transfers savings from the developed countries to the underdeveloped ones. Marxist theories of imperialism, on the other hand, have traditionally derived the major phenomena of uneven development from direct investment; in this regard Emmanuel, too, makes the export of capital pivotal in his theory of imperialism.

But all these analyses of direct investment are based on an acceptance of Ricardo's law of comparative costs. Since the central result of this paper is the overthrow of this law, and the subsequent location of many of the phenomena of imperialism – previously attributed to the export of capital – in the workings of commodity trade alone, it became imperative at that point to extend the analysis to incorporate the effects of direct investment.[44]

In the second part of this chapter's final section, this question was taken up. There, it was found that though foreign capital can provide an offset to chronic balance of trade deficits, in part because of the capital inflow and in part through the modernization and expansion of the export sectors, it does so only at the expense of an eventual capital outflow (surplus-value transferred out in the form of repatriated profits), declining terms of trade, and increased foreign domination. Instead of negating international inequality, therefore, foreign investment tightens the grip of the strong over the weak – not merely through monopoly or state power, but through "free" competition itself.

There are many aspects of this analysis which need to be developed further in order to be theoretically capable of tackling the concrete history of trade among capitalist nations. Let me briefly cite two major areas to be investigated.

First, there is the question of a fuller development of Marx's theory of money to account for different forms of money and credit, so that we may trace their effects on the previously derived laws of money. This is a complex and controversial task, in which not only must the tangled history of monetary phenomena be theoretically absorbed, but also the various modern (Keynesian, monetarist) theories of money be confronted. In recent times there has been a rapid reawakening of interest in distinguishing a Marxist theory of money from its various orthodox counterparts, and a growing number of people are now focusing on this task (de Brunhoff, 1967; Foley, 1975).

Second, there is the question of distinguishing monopoly from concentration and centralization. It was Marx's concern to show that concentration and centralization are immanent tendencies of capitalist development, fostered precisely by what Marx calls the "competition of capitals;" it has been the intention here to demonstrate that precisely the same thing occurs internationally, for precisely the same reasons. To some Marxists, however, concentration and centralization imply monopoly; and monopoly being the *opposite* of free competition, it signals the end of the law of value and the beginning of the era of monopoly capital (Sweezy, 1942, p. 54). I would argue, however, that this notion of monopoly is inadequate; it stems largely from orthodox theory, whose analysis is located in the sphere of *circulation*, and refers to the ability of individual capitalists to control and influence the conditions of purchase and sale. As I outlined in the third section of this chapter, Marxian analysis is located primarily in production and reproduction; as such, it is not a question of the will of individual capitalists, but of the limits imposed upon them by those sets of relations which define the capitalist mode of production.[45] The analysis of the manner in which these limits manifest themselves is what the term law of value means in Marx; in this regard, the competition of capitals is not to be understood as the opposite of monopoly, and the era of monopoly capital need not be severed from the law of value:

> In practical life we find not only competition, monopoly and the antagonism between them, but also the synthesis of the two, which is not a formula but a movement. Monopoly produces competition, but competition produces monopoly. Monopolists are made from competition; competitors become monopolists . . . the more the mass of the proletariat grows as against the monopolists of one nation, the *more desperate competition becomes between monopolists of different nations*. The synthesis is of such a character that monopoly can only maintain itself by continually entering into the struggle of competition. (Marx, 1971, p. 152, emphasis added)

In any case, these are concerns to be followed up elsewhere. The central focus here has been the manner in which the inherent tendencies of capitalist development manifest themselves internationally. The law of uneven development, of the concentration and polarization of wealth which characterizes capitalism, can be seen to manifest itself in the form of a widening gap between poor and rich capitalist nations – not due to some external factor or political conspiracy, but precisely as the necessary form of development of free trade. This gap and its attendant consequences are symptoms, not causes: the cure must address itself to the disease.

Notes

1 Sexism is proved to be both rational and efficient: men and women enter the marriage market with various initial endowments consisting of home-capital and market-capital: men being in general relatively more endowed with market-capital, and women with home-capital, they specialize to their mutual advantage in market and home activities respectively (Becker, 1973, 1974). The potential of this fantastic analysis is, I feel, not even approached by Becker's use of it. What about blacks and whites? Nazis and Jews? Surely there is much more work still to be done.

2 $(p_c/p_w)_J \equiv$ relative price of cloth to wine in country J. Then if $(p_c/p_w)_1 < (p_c/p_w)_2$, $(p_w/p_c)_2 < (p_w/p_c)_1$.

3 One definition of absolute efficiency would be that if both countries had the same currency and the same level of money wages, the more efficient producers would have lower costs.

4 Similarly the scalar differences in production functions in different countries for the same good can also be interpreted as indexes of absolute advantage (Arrow, et al., 1961).

5 This is a period that by most accounts dominates the history of capitalism up to at least 1914, and by some accounts up to the 1960s. In any case, the period under consideration is one in which precious metals function as the ultimate international money; this by no means excludes the phenomena associated with token money and credit money. Though I do not develop the different forms of money here, the analysis outlined here can be extended to deal with token and credit money *based* on a commodity money (gold, silver, etc.).

6 Graham's examples, in a manner similar to Leontief's anomolous results, have come to be sanctified under the name of Graham's paradox.
7 Properly speaking, neo-Keynesian analysis seeks to trace the short-run consequences of changes in patterns of trade, rather than attempting to specify the actual determinants of trade. It is therefore often presented as a *complement* to the law of comparative costs.
8 Barrat-Brown surveys various arguments blaming "sectionalist monopoly and obstructionist principles," "postcolonial nationalism and self-imposed autarchy," "trade union action," and the inequality of "bargaining power" between developed and underdeveloped capitalist countries, for the historical inapplicability of free trade arguments (Barrat-Brown, 1974, pp. 32, 35, 38, 233).
9 It might be added that a satisfactory resolution of the problem of price formation in competitive capitalism (the so-called transformation problem) may well point the way to a better treatment of monopoly. An inadequate understanding of the former would almost surely hinder the development of a satisfactory understanding of the latter.
10 "The behavior of labor remains a matter of indifference for the application of the law of comparative advantage, the sole condition, both necessary and sufficient, for this proposition being the mobility of capital" (Emmanuel, 1972, pp. xxxi–ii).
11 Emmanuel does not abandon the law of comparative costs, even for the modern world. Rather, he sees the modern law to be the *sum* of two processes: first, the formation of international prices of production via international equalization of the rate of profit; and second, specialization according to comparative costs, where comparative cost ratios are determined precisely by the international prices of production. In Chapter 6 of *Unequal Exchange* . . . , he illustrates the effects of unequal exchange on the pattern of specialization, assuming throughout that this pattern is based ultimately on comparative costs.
12 The term Third World is used occasionally throughout this chapter in deference to its widespread popularity. It is, however, a very misleading term in that it suggests a separation between the poor *capitalist* countries and world capitalism.
13 Emmanuel particularly emphasizes stagnation, poverty, a widening "development gap," and declining terms of trade for Third World countries (Emmanuel, 1972).
14 It is clear from Emmanuel's analysis that capitalists are free to use the best technique of production available. On page 61 he refers to the example of page 63, which assume the same technology in both countries (Emmanuel, 1972).
15 Emmanuel's analysis tends to be posed in terms of nations as the primary units, not classes.
16 It is worth remembering that Proudhon's *philosophy of poverty* also depends on a notion of equal exchange.
17 It is interesting to note that Marx's reaction to Ricardo, for example, is critical, appreciative, and nonpolemic. This is different from Marxist critics of Emmanuel (who might rightly be called a neo-Ricardian).
18 The natural prices of Ricardo and the prices of production of Marx currently go by a variety of names, the most common being "long-run equilibrium" prices. We will stick to Marx's terminology here.
19 Adam Smith of course postulated a precapitalist law of prices in which relative prices equalled relative labor-times. In that sense, one could claim that Smith dealt with a case in which there were no *capitalists*. But this has nothing to do with ignoring means of production, which is what neoclassical assertions about Ricardo and Smith amount to.
20 In fact, the gold standard operated with exchange rates which could vary within certain limits. These limits, called gold-points, determined whether it was cheaper to change local currency into foreign currency via the exchange-rate, or to buy gold with the local currency and spend the gold abroad. The basic determinant of the gold-points was the cost of transporting gold-bullion from one country to another.
21 In neoclassical presentations, the comparison is between price ratios of cloth and wine in each country, rather than efficiency of production. But the conclusion is the same.
22 Althusser discusses the methodological break between Marx and the classical economists (Althusser, 1970).
23 The distinction between concrete labor and abstract labor is related to (though different from) the distinction between productive and unproductive labor. In both cases the properties of value (and surplus value) producing labor are at the heart of the distinction.
24 The case of rent is a good example of this method. Land is not a product of human labor and consequently has no value; yet land has a price. A clear contradiction in Marx's theory of value, it would seem. Not at all, Marx replies. One of the necessary steps in the theoretical transition from value to price is the formulation of the concept of rent. Once it is understood how value determines rent, and it is seen that the price of land is nothing but rent capitalized (percent-discounted) into a sum of money, then rather than contradicting the law of value the price of land affirms it!
25 Marx mentions his treatment of surplus-value independently of its fetishistic forms (interest, rent, profit) as one of the "three fundamentally new elements of" *Capital* (Marx to Engels, January 8, 1868).
26 See Morishima, 1973, Chs. 5, 6; and Shaikh, 1973, Ch. IV, Sec. 4. In both of these, it is established that there is a monotonic relationship between the money rate of profit r and the Marxian rate of surplus-value s/v, for given conditions of production. Of course, the Marxian value rate of profit $s/(c + v)$ is also a monotonic function of s/v, for given production conditions. Thus the money rate of profit is a monotonic function of the value rate.
27 The velocity of circulation of money is actually the rate at which commodities enter and drop out of circulation. But because money remains within circulation, and commodities enter to be sold and leave when consumed, it is the money which appears to cause, rather than measure, the movement of the commodity.

28 Marx distinguishes reserve funds of coins, which are really *within* the sphere of circulation from hoards, in which gold leaves circulation altogether. It is the reserve funds of coins which *first* manifest an excess of coin (Marx, 1972, p. 137).

29 Of course, gold bars may appear to be sold for an equal weight of gold in the form of coins; but this is only a change of form from bullion to coin. It is not a sale since there is no price involved: an ounce of gold is an ounce of gold regardless of its shape. The same conclusion applies to the sale of gold for paper money which is backed by gold. In this case the paper is a token of a quantity of gold equal to that which it buys. Marx discusses the illusions to which token money gives rise (Marx, 1972).

30 It is important to note that in Marx's analysis, hoarding arises out of *structural* reasons specific to commodity production and/or capitalist commodity production. In Keynesian analysis, hoarding is ultimately based on *psychological* propensities.

31 There is no automatic link in Marx's analysis between a fall in the rate of interest and an expansion in the level of investment. Investment depends ultimately on the possibility of making profits; a lower rate of interest raises the *net* profitability of investments financed out of borrowing. But this does not by itself imply an automatic expansion of investment.

32 Marx also notes that it is the empirical association of price rises with the discovery of new gold mines which leads to the idea that the increased supply of gold *causes* the higher prices. Yet, as he points out, the discovery of a new, more productive gold mine lowers the unit value (w_g) of an ounce of gold, and thus raises the price level. This by itself means that more gold would be needed for circulating even the same mass of commodities. This implies a rise in the sum of prices due to a rise in the price level, with a corresponding rise of gold in circulation. A portion of the new gold is thus absorbed by this increased need for circulating gold.

In addition, as outlined in the text, the remaining new gold will tend to raise effective demand and hence production. In this case the sum of prices rises because output rises, and this in turn requires more gold to be in circulation.

On the surface, therefore, what we will observe in such circumstances is a rise in price *accompanied* by a rise in the supply of precious metals extant in the world. To the quantity theorists this correlation becomes causation: the rise in price is *attributed* to the rise in the supply of gold (Marx, 1972, 160–65).

33 The value of any commodity is the *average* amount of labor-time required for its production. As such, gold produced in various countries will have a value representing the average of the differing amounts of labor-time required in the different countries (and mines). This distinction between individual labor-time required and the social average (value) plays an important role in Marx's analysis of rent and surplus-profit. Whether the individual labor-times refer to differing conditions of production of gold (different mines) within one country or between countries, does not matter as far as the value of gold is concerned.

34 We exclude the case where England is also a producer of gold (directly or through colonies), since that is obviously a special circumstance. If we treat gold production as taking place in a third country (South Africa), then the only way for England to *acquire* gold is through exports to South Africa. But given the conditions of this example, in which England is at a disadvantage in both (exportable) commodities, it is Portugal which will export to South Africa, not England.

35 Under the gold standard, in the event of a drain of gold, the central bank of a country would frequently make money scarce precisely in order to raise the interest rate and attract short-term foreign capital (Marx, 1967, Vol. III, Ch. 35, p. 575).

36 The crucial point of free trade arguments is precisely that, *all other things being equal,* trade will benefit all parties concerned.

37 Commodities whose production is peculiar to a single nation are really subsumed under the category of commodities which can be produced at a lower cost in that nation than elsewhere. Therefore, from now on we will refer only to the latter more general category.

38 This is the orthodox analysis of the *effects* of direct investment even though it is generally acknowledged that the factor–price equalization theorem (derived from the Hecksher-Ohlin-Samuelson model of commodity trade) eliminates any *reason* for international capital flows. According to this theorem, commodity trade alone will equalize wage and profit rates in all countries, so that there will be no advantage in foreign investment.

39 In this analysis we ignore the creation of consumption patterns, even though they represent an important aspect of the internationalization of capital.

40 This by no means implies that it is impossible for a particular underdeveloped capitalist country to modernize from the inside, any more than it is impossible for a particular small capitalist to make the leap into the big-time. I am only concerned to analyse the overwhelming tendencies of free trade and competition among capitalist nations within this chapter's scope.

41 Net cost here refers to the fact that the lower direct productivity of labor-power in the UCC is more than offset by even lower wage rates.

42 Suppose the average rate of profit in the UCC was 10 percent. Then if copper had a cost-price M = 100 oz of gold, its price of production (before direct investment) would be M^1 = 110 oz. Now, even if the average rate of profit in the DCC was 15 percent, foreign capital would attempt to enter copper production in the UCC if through modernization it could lower the cost-price of copper to say 80 oz – because then, at or even under the going price of copper of 110 oz, this foreign capital could receive a rate of profit above the 15 percent it would get at home.

43 This, too, is logically impossible. The standard of living (the real wage) of workers in any country must ultimately be limited by the level of development of its forces of production. By what magic will the Indian worker be able to achieve the same standard of living as the U.S. worker? The total social product per capita in India – by any conceiv-

able index – is lower than the real wage of the U.S. worker. Even if Indian workers were to consume their whole social product, real wage differences would not be wiped out – but of course Indian capital would be. Thus the incentive for foreign investment – wage differences – would remain, while the competition – the local capitalists – would be long gone!

44 As noted earlier, the location of uneven development in free trade itself implies that we must be more precise in distinguishing imperialism as a stage in capitalist development from uneven development as an immanent process in all stages. This task cannot be attempted here. I thank John Weeks for pointing this out to me.

45 "The will of the capitalist is certainly to take as much as possible. What we have to do is not to talk about his *will,* but to enquire into his *power,* the limits of that power, and the *character of those limits*" (Marx, 1970, p. 190).

References

Althusser, L., and Balibar, E. 1970. *Reading Capital.* Ben Brewster, trans. New York: Pantheon Books.

Amin, S. 1974. *Accumulation on a World Scale: A Critique of the Theory of Underdevelopment.* 2 vol. New York: Monthly Review Press.

Arrow, K., Chenery, H. B., Minhas, B., and Solow, R. W. 1961. "Capital Labor Substitution and Economic Efficiency," *Review of Economics and Statistics,* Vol. 43.

Barrat-Brown, M. 1974. *The Economics of Imperialism.* New York: Penguin Books.

Becker, G. 1973. "A Theory of Marriage: Part I," *Journal of Political Economy* Vol. 81, No. 4.

1974. "A Theory of Marriage: Part II," *Journal of Political Economy,* Vol. 82, No. 2.

Brunhoff, S. de 1967. *La Monnaie chez Marx.* Paris: Editions Sociale.

Emmanuel, A. 1972. *Unequal Exchange: A Study of the Imperialism of Trade.* New York: Monthly Review Press.

Foley, D. 1975. "Towards a Marxist Theory of Money," Technical Report No. 181, *Economic Series, Institute of Mathematical Studies in the Social Sciences.* Palo Alto, Calif.: Stanford University Press.

Hayter, T. 1972. *Aid as Imperialism.* New York: Penguin Books.

Jalee, P. 1969. *The Third World in World Economy.* New York: Monthly Review Press.

Johnson, H. 1968. "International Trade: Theory," *International Encyclopedia of the Social Sciences,* Vol. 8, David L. Sills, ed. New York: Macmillan.

Kenen, P. B. 1968. "International Monetary Economics: Private International Capital Movements," *International Encyclopedia of the Social Sciences,* Vol. 8. David L. Sills, ed. New York: Macmillan.

Lenin, V. I. 1939. *Imperialism, the Highest Stage of Capitalism.* New York: International Publishers.

Leontief, W. W. 1953. "Domestic Production and Foreign; the American Capital Position Reexamined," *Proceedings of the American Philosophical Society,* Vol. 97.

1956. "Factor Proportions and the Structure of American Trade: Further Theoretical and Empirical Analysis," *Review of Economics and Statistics,* Vol. XXXVIII.

1958. "Reply," *Review of Economics and Statistics* (Supplement) Vol. XL.

Magdoff, H. 1969. *The Age of Imperialism.* New York: Monthly Review Press.

Mandel, E. 1968. *Marxist Economic Theory.* Vols. I, II. Brian Pearce, trans. New York: Monthly Review Press.

Marx, K. 1967. *Capital.* Vol. I, II, III. Moscow: International Publishers.

1972. *A Contribution to the Critique of Political Economy.* New York: International Publishers.

1973. *Grundrisse.* New York: Penguin Books.

1971. *The Poverty of Philosophy.* New York: International Publishers.

1969. *Theories of Surplus Value,* Parts I–III. Moscow: Progress Publishers.

1970. "Wages, Prices, and Profits," in *Marx-Engels Selected Works in One Volume.* New York: International Publishers.

Minhas, B. S. 1962. "The Homophypallagic Production Function, Factor-Intensity Reversals and the Hecksher-Ohlin Theorem," *Journal of Political Economy,* Vol. LX.

Morishima, M. 1973. *Marx's Economics.* Cambridge: Cambridge University Press.

Mundell, R. A. 1968. "Balance of Payments," *International Encyclopedia of the Social Sciences.* Vol. 8. David L. Sills, ed. New York: Macmillan.

Payer, C. 1974. *The Debt Trap: The I.M.F. and the Third World.* New York: Monthly Review Press.

Pilling, G. 1973. "Imperialism, Trade, and Unequal Exchange: The Work of Arghiri Emmanuel," *Economy and Society.*

Ricardo, D. 1951. *The Principles of Political Economy and Taxation,* Vol. I of *Collected Works and Correspondence of David Ricardo.* P. Sraffa, ed. Cambridge: Cambridge University Press.

Seton, F. 1957. "The 'Transformation Problem'," *Review of Economic Studies,* Vol. 25. pp. 149–60.

Shaikh, A. 1973. "Theories of Value and Theories of Distribution." Columbia University; Ph.D. dissertation.

1977. "Marx's Theory of Value and the 'Transformation Problem'," in *The Subtle Anatomy of Capitalism.* Jesse Schwartz, ed. Santa Monica, Calif.: Goodyear Publishing, pp. 106–39.

Sraffa, P. 1960. *Production of Commodities by Means of Commodities.* Cambridge: Cambridge University Press.

Sweezy, P. 1942. *The Theory of Capitalist Development.* New York: Monthly Review Press.

Tooke, T., and Newmarch, W. 1838–57. *A History of Prices from 1792–1856.* Reprinted from the original published in six volumes, with an introduction by T. E. Gregory. New York: Adelphi.

Yeager, L. B. 1966. *International Monetary Relations: Theory, History and Policy.* New York: Harper & Row.

Part VI

Property and welfare

14

A radical critique of welfare economics

E. K. Hunt

Welfare economics is the heart of neoclassical economics. Together with the descriptive theory of self-adjusting markets, it provides the ideological foundation upon which the entire edifice of elaborate neoclassical apologetics for capitalism is constructed. Conventional economics has been criticized persistently for over a century for its grotesquely unrealistic assumptions about homogeneous, maximizing, *economic man* and the socially beneficial constraints imposed upon him by atomistic competition. Yet these assumptions have remained at the core of orthodox theorizing. They are the indispensible axioms of neoclassical welfare economics, and, as yet, no alternative ideology of capitalism has been able to provide an equally rigorous and elegant justification of the status quo.

The hedonistic foundations of welfare economics

Welfare economics rests squarely on hedonistic preconceptions. It contains both a psychological hedonism and an ethical hedonism. The psychological hedonism was, in the late nineteenth century, a rather crude theory of human behavior. *Utility* was conceived as a cardinally quantifiable relationship between a man and external consumable objects. This relationship was treated as though it were metaphysically given and fixed, and not a proper subject for further investigation. All human behavior was then reduced to attempts to maximize utility through the use or exchange of the commodities and productive resources with which the individual had been endowed (the source and propriety of the endowment, like the utility relationship was beyond the purview of analysis).

Psychological hedonism, however, had been thoroughly discredited by the late nineteenth century. The development and refinement of the behavioral assumptions of welfare economics over the last half-century represent attempts to obviate the objections against psychological hedonism while continuing to draw conclusions identical to those derivable from the discredited theory. *Indifference curves* permitted the substitution of ordinal quantification of utility for cardinal quantification. Further, the word utility was frequently dropped in favor of the word preference. Preferences were something, the bourgeois economist argued, that could be empirically observed, provided only that we assume that individual choices are *consistent.* The consistency, however, was merely the assumption that choices reflected a preexisting, metaphysically given preference ordering (empirical observation, of course, has continuously shown what common sense should have told these economists, that choices do not have this type of consistency). Cardinally quantifiable utility or ordinally quantifiable preferences have identical psychological and ethical import, and welfare economics remains a hedonistic theory of maximizing economic man behaving in a manner totally predetermined or programmed by two metaphysically given and, by implication, immutable entities: his preference ordering and his initial endowment of assets.

The ethical hedonism of welfare economics has been called "the pig principle" by Professor S. S. Alexander. The pig principle is simply "that if you like something, more is better" (Alexander, 1967, p. 107). Thus, the ultimate normative principle of welfare economics can be stated several ways: more pleasure is ethically better than less (Benthemite version); more utility is ethically better than less utility (late nineteenth-century neoclassical version); and a preferred position on one's preference ordering is ethically better than a less preferred position (contemporary neoclassical version). In each case, the isolated, atomistic individual is the sole judge qualified to assess the pleasure, utility or preferability of an object because these welfare magnitudes are presumed to depend only upon the relationship between the individual and the object of consumption. Individual desires, weighted by market purchasing power, are the ultimate criteria of social values. Externalities caused by interdependencies of preference orderings (that is, consumption considered as a social activity) can only be handled by treating them as isolated exceptions (of which more will be discussed later). Welfare economics ignores the fact that individual desires are themselves the products of a particular social process and the individual's place within that process. If they did not ignore this they would have to acknowledge the fact that normative evaluations can be made of totally different social and economic systems and their resultant patterns of individual desires. Welfare economics is the direct lineal descendent of the doctrines Marx labeled as "vulgar economy." A point of view which "confines itself to systematizing in a pedantic way, and proclaiming for everlasting truths, the trite ideas held by the self-complacent bourgeoisie with regard to their own world, to them the best of all possible worlds." (Marx, 1961, p. 81, footnote)

Pareto optimality

Upon this foundation of psychological and ethical hedonism is constructed the norm of Pareto optimality – the core concept of welfare economics. The usual exposition of this norm begins with a sharp dichotomy – the theory of the consumer and the theory of the firm. Each isolated, maximizing consumer is constrained by a fixed budget. Constrained utility maximization results in commodities being chosen in such proportions that the individual's marginal rate of psychological substitution between any pair will be equal to the ratio of their prices. This means that relative prices accurately reflect the psychic or utility evaluations (at the margin) for every commodity for every consumer – because in a competitive economy every consumer is faced with the same prices. And because prices reflect the relative evaluations of every consumer considered individually, they must, in a capitalist economy where the consumer is sovereign, perfectly reflect the relative *social values* of commodities.

Next, an individual business firm with a "continuous twice differentiable" production function is confronted by given prices in a competitive market. A mathematical or geometrical analysis of constrained profit maximization shows each firm choosing a point on its production function where (1) the price of any factor (including labor) is equal to the value of its marginal product, (2) the marginal rate of substitution between any pair of factors is equal to the ratio of their prices, and (3) the marginal rate of transformation between any two outputs is equal to the ratio of their respective prices.

The first of these conditions of profit maximization is equivalent to the neoclassical marginal productivity theory of distribution. It assures us that each factor of production (and, by implication, each human being) receives an income exactly equal to that which it contributes, an ideal which has long served as a bourgeois ideal of distributive justice. The third of these conditions of profit maximization assures us that the prices of commodities accurately reflect the marginal opportunity costs of society foregoing some of any commodity in order to get more of another commodity.

In the competitive world of the neoclassical apologist, every consumer and every firm faces the same set of prices as every other. This means that in equilibrium the mental evaluation of any pair of commodities by any consumer is a perfect reflection of the technologically determined opportunity cost of producing those commodities. No reallocation of resources through changes in consumption, exchange or production could *unambiguously* augment the value of the commodities being produced and exchanged. This is Pareto optimality – the fundamental norm of bourgeois economics.

The fundamental rule of Pareto optimality states that the economic situation is optimal when no change can improve the position of one individual (as judged by himself) without harming or worsening the position of another individual (again, as judged by himself). A Pareto improvement is a change that moves society from a nonoptimal position closer to an optimal position: "Any change which harms no one and which makes some people better off (in their own estimation) must be considered to be an improvement" (Baumol, 1965, p. 376).

Two points are significant in the Pareto rule: First, in the hands of many nineteenth-century reformers the notion of diminishing marginal utility had radical equalitarian implications. If all individuals have similar capacities for enjoyment, and if the marginal utility of income declines as one's income increases, then it follows that an equal distribution of income maximizes the total utility for all of society. Contemporary ideologists avoid this conclusion by insisting that interpersonal utility comparisons are impossible and that statements about the effects on the total social welfare of redistributions of wealth and income are thereby impossible. The insistence that an individual's welfare can only be judged by himself is the means by which these interpersonal utility comparisons are avoided.

The second significant point to note in the Pareto rule is its conservative consensual character. Defined away are all situations of conflict. In a world of class conflicts, imperialism, exploitation, alienation, racism, sexism, and scores of other human conflicts, where are the changes that might make some better off without making others worse off? *Improve the plight of the oppressed and you worsen the situation of the oppressor* (as perceived by himself, of course)! If there are any important social, political and economic situations where improving the lot of one person, group or class is not opposed by persons, groups or classes, who, by virtue of their roles in the economic, political and social spheres, are their natural antagonists, then such situations are indeed rare. The domain of this theory would, indeed, seem to be so restrictive that it would hardly warrant a serious social scientist's time to investigate it were it not for the fact that the theory is thought to be important not only by the overwhelming majority of bourgeois economists, but by many unwary Marxist economists as well (Hunt, 1975).

The neoclassical notion of market efficiency encountered in every branch of applied economics, as well as the bourgeois notion of rational prices encountered in so many discussions of the role of the market in a socialist society, have absolutely no meaning whatsoever other than the belief that a free competitive market will tend toward a Pareto optimal situation in which, *by definition*, resources are said to be efficiently allocated and prices are said to be rational. There is no further criterion or justification for using the words efficient and rational than the assertion that the particular resource allocation and price structure obtaining in a free competitive market will have some connection with that envisioned in the analysis of Pareto optimality.

The social values underlying welfare economics

Acceptance of the efficiency or rationality of the free market solution to the problem of the allocation of resources demands that one accept the social values underlying the analysis. Moreover, one must accept the general framework of empirical and behavioral assumptions as being tolerably good reflections of reality. The above discussion of hedonism alludes to some social values which form the basis of the analysis. Those values should be made explicit.

The only values which count in Pareto analysis are the preferences of each isolated individual weighted by the purchasing power of that individual. Both the individualism and the distributional assumption must be separately considered.

The axiom of individual preferences is extraordinarily constraining. Because in the neoclassical analysis we have no way of evaluating the relative merits of different persons' preferences, we likewise have no criterion for evaluating changes in a given individual's preferences. To be able to do the latter would be to be able ipso facto to do the former. At the level of abstraction on which this theory is constructed the only differences among individuals are different preference orderings. There is absolutely no difference in the theory between the change in a given individual's preference ordering and the complete withdrawal from society of one individual and his replacement by a new individual. For this reason the theory can consider neither the historical evolution of social and individual values nor their day to day fluctuations. To do so would be to admit the normative incomparability of any two events or situations which are temporally separated, i.e. to exclude all real life phenomena from the domain to which the theory is applicable. On the other hand, to permit such normative comparisons would be to return to the egalitarian conclusions of the philosophical radicalism of the early utilitarians and seriously weaken neoclassical economics as an intellectual support of the status quo.

It is therefore obvious that this theory is applicable only where individual preferences or tastes do not change over time. It is equally obvious that every person, including fanatics, lunatics, sadists, masochists, mentally incompetent persons, children, and even newborn babies must always be the best judge of their own welfare. (It might also be added that all decisions must be made individually and never simply by heads of families or other social groupings.) They must have perfect knowledge of all presently available alternatives and there must be no uncertainty about the future. Unless these conditions are realized then people will find that the utility they expect before an act will have no necessary relation to the utility realized after the act, and individual choices or preferences will have no demonstratable connection to an individual's welfare. This extreme individualism also breaks down when we admit the presence of envy and sympathy which make one individual's perception of his own welfare depend upon his perception of the welfare of others (this is, of course, a special case of the general problem of externalities, of which more will be discussed later).

The fact that any Pareto optimum can be defended as optimal only in relation to a specific distribution of wealth and income is, perhaps, the most decisive normative weakness of the theory. Although orthodox economists usually admit the incredibly restrictive relativity of any Pareto optimum, they tend to slur over it in passing and hurry on to safer topics before facing the embarrassing consequences of this condition. On the normative assumptions of Paretian analysis itself it can be shown that unless the existing distributions of wealth and income are socially optimal, then a situation which is Pareto optimal may be socially inferior to a large number of situations which are *not* Pareto optimal but which have distributions of wealth and income that are preferable to the one in question. Orthodox economists skirt this issue by inserting one standard sentence: "assume that the existing distributions of wealth and income are ideal *or that the government uses a system of taxes and subsidies to make them so.*"

After stating this standard caveat the bourgeois economist proceeds to his policy analysis using cost–benefit techniques which are based upon the assumption of the normative and empirical adequacy of standard Paretian analysis. Never is there hint of the fact that the government has *never* used its taxing and spending powers to attempt to obtain a just distribution of wealth and power.

The lack of such an admission is not surprising because it would force orthodox economists to come to grips with the nature of social, economic and political power – an analysis of vested economic interests and their relation to political power has always been taboo for orthodox economists (and political scientists as well). The reason that no serious effort has ever been made to achieve a more just distribution of wealth and income – and the reason seems painfully obvious – is that the ordinary social, legal and political means of making such a redistribution are themselves an integral part of the initial distribution of wealth. To possess wealth is to possess political power in a capitalist system. The orthodox economist's hope that political power will be used to redress economic inequities is perhaps his most glaring blind spot (Samuels, 1972).

In practice, economists merely accept the existing distribution of wealth without question. But only rarely do they have the candor to admit that accepting the existing distribution of wealth implies accepting the existing system of legal and moral rules (including the laws of private property). More generally, it implies the acceptance of the entire system of social power, all roles of superordination and subordination as well as the institutions and instruments of coercion through which power is assured and perpetuated. Thus most of the important issues with which radical economists are concerned are eliminated from the orthodox economists' analyses with the initial assumption of the Paretian approach.

The empirical and analytical assumptions

In addition to these assumptions of individualism and distributional justice, the theory requires many further empirical and analytical assumptions. These make up the familiar textbook recitation of the conditions necessary for equilibrium under pure competition (and no orthodox economist has ever argued for any alternative means of achieving Pareto optimality in a capitalist economy). These include the assumptions: (a) a large number of buyers and sellers, none powerful enough to appreciably affect the market; (b) ease of exit and entry; (c) homogeneous inputs and outputs each divisable into units of any desired size; (d) no uncertainty about the future; (e) perfect knowledge of all present alternatives in production and consumption; (f) production functions having the appropriate second-order optimality conditions (i.e., being of smooth curvature, not having increasing returns to scale, and having diminishing marginal rates of substitution along any isoquant curve); (g) similarly appropriate utility functions which are stable over time; (h) productivity being unaffected by the distribution of wealth income and power; (i) all external economies or diseconomies being correctable or nullified with taxes, subsidies, and/or the creation of new property rights; and (j) all markets being always and continuously in equilibrium, with all change represented as instantaneous, static shifts from one equilibrium vector to another.

These assumptions do more than merely limiting the domain of applicability of the neoclassical analyses of competitive equilibrium. They totally overwhelm the whole analysis. Assumptions (a) and (b) of large numbers and ease of entry are the foundations of the orthodox concept of competition. But in the real, concrete historical development of capitalism they are the first casualities of competition. Real capitalist competition, unlike the neoclassical textbook variety, is warfare – a deadly struggle to eliminate rivals and achieve a monopoly. Competitive neoclassical equilibrium is often called long-run equilibrium. Real capitalist development, however, moves inexorably in the opposite direction.

Assumption (j), concerning the static nature of the theory, is indicative of the general inability of neoclassical economics to deal with economic phenomena in their historical development. Despite a veritable mountain of articles and books on economic growth, the neoclassical economists are unable to consistently integrate welfare and growth analyses. Once economic growth is admitted the neoclassical analysis itself shows that instability is the inevitable result (Hahn and Mathews, 1966, pp. 1–124). When instability and unemployment are admitted the Pareto criterion seems unimportant even to most neoclassical economists. Moreover, not only is there nothing in the system to insure golden rule growth, the essential question of *what* maximizes welfare in a growing economy is not clear. Is it maximizing the rate of growth, maximizing profit, maximizing consumption, maximizing consumption per head? And with each of these questions comes the issue of the nature and significance of a social rate of time discount to appropriately weight the welfare of unborn generations which is being decisively affected by current consumption and investment decisions. The various criteria of welfare in a growing economy have no necessary consistency (Hahn and Mathews, 1966, pp. 99–113). The neoclassical Paretian criterion simply cannot handle such problems. It is, by its very nature, a static theory which cannot be extended to describe a growing or changing economy.

The remaining assumptions (c through i) all involve similar difficulties. Assumptions (d) and (e) about certainty and perfect knowledge abstract from two inevitable consequences of free-market capitalism which are of singular significance in understanding the human costs of the system's instability and misallocation of resources. Assumption (c) on homogeneity of inputs (particularly capital) and (f) about properly behaved production functions, have both been definitively shown to be untenable by the recent Cambridge capital controversy (see the contribution of Donald Harris in this volume). And finally assumption (i) about externalities is perhaps the most indefensible part of the entire analysis. We will examine it in greater detail later.

Welfare economics as a guide to policy making

Few neoclassical economists would argue that the assumptions underlying the theory of competitive equilibrium are realistic, but nearly all accept the social, moral and philosophical foundations of the Paretian welfare criterion. The lack of realism of the assumptions, however, does not prevent them from advocating the theoretical model as a basis upon which policy making by government officials should be based. The analysis should not, they argue, be considered as descriptive of reality, but as a normative model that can be used to guide government interventions into the market place whenever various of the above assumptions necessary for competitive equilibrium are not met (Hunt, 1968). Two comments should be made regarding this view of government interventionism in a capitalist economy.

First, this bourgeois view gives government a shadowy existence. As long as Pareto optimality exists it is nowhere. When an imperfection occurs (it is generally regarded as an isolated occurrence in an otherwise perfect world) the government becomes a *deus ex machina* which restores the system to a state of bliss. It is an aloof, neutral, impartial arbitrator that descends on the scene, enacts an excise tax or gives a subsidy, the only purpose of which is to restore Pareto optimality. If the neoclassical economist is asked about vested interests, about corruption (which is, after all, simply another aspect of the functioning of the market), about economic and political power, or about class control of government processes, he replies with disdain that these are the concern of sociologists and political scientists (although one searches in vain for such concerns in orthodox social science).

The second criticism of Pareto optimality as a norm for government policy is even more damaging. Perusing the several necessary assumptions and contemplating the hundreds of thousands of interdependent markets in the contemporary capitalist economy, one is impressed by the certainty that at any moment there are, in fact, innumerable departures from any potential state of Paretian optimality. But according to the theory of the second best, policies designed to remedy only some and not all of the defects (since simultaneously remedying all would obviously be impossible) will often result in effects diametrically opposed to those envisioned by the authors of these policies. In the words of William J. Baumol:

> In brief, this theory [of the second best] states, on the basis of a mathematical argument, that in a concrete situation characterized by *any* deviation from perfect optimality, partial policy measures which eliminate only some of the departures from the optimal arrangement may well result in a net decrease in social welfare. (Baumol, 1965; Lipsey and Lancaster, 1956–57)

Where then does this leave the normative theory of Pareto optimality upon which the neoclassical notions of market efficiency and rational prices (not to mention the whole classical liberal argument for laissez faire capitalism) are based? The answer is obvious: It is riddled by even more acute contradictions than the economic reality from which it springs and for which it attempts to provide an ideological defense.

Welfare economics and externalities

The Achilles heel of welfare economics is its treatment of externalities (if a theory so utterly indefensible in so many of its facets can be said to have an Achilles heel!) In the usual neoclassical approach, the processes of production and consumption are assumed to have direct effects on only one or a few persons who are doing the producing or consuming (Mishan, 1971). Externalities occur when the utility function of one consumer is affected by the consumption of another consumer, or the production function of one firm is affected by the production of another firm, or, most importantly, the utility of an individual is affected by a production process with which he has no direct connection. The traditional neoclassical approach is to assume that, except for a single externality, Pareto optimality exists everywhere. With all prices other than those in the market in question reflecting perfect market rationality, then through a supposed process of extrapolation and/or interpolation (commonly referred to as cost-benefit analysis) the welfare economists claim to be able to simulate what would be the correct, rational market price in the absence of this lone externality.

The cost–benefit analysis by means of which externalities are to be corrected is itself a mere extension of the Paretian theory of allocative efficiency. As E. J. Mishan has stated:

> A person who agrees to apply the principles of allocative efficiency needs no new assumption to extend his agreement to the application of existing cost–benefit analysis. In sum both the principles of economic efficiency and those of cost–benefit analysis derive their inspiration from the . . . Pareto criterion, and a person cannot with consistency accept the one and deny the other. (Mishan, 1973, p. 17)

The externality being analyzed is not really imagined to be the only actual deviation from Pareto optimality. Rather, it is asserted that this is only a tolerably close approximation to reality. Mishan, for example, asserts that

> although it is not expected that the economy at any moment in time, attains an optimum position, in its continuous adjustment to changes in the conditions of demand and supply, it may not be too far from an overall optimal position for any prolonged period. (Mishan, 1973, p. 80)

So when, in this set of circumstances, we find an externality, the beneficient, impartial *deus ex machina* is again called upon; this time to tax or subsidize in such quantities as to exactly nullify or neutralize the lone externality. Pareto optimality is restored. But the cost–benefit analysis that forms the foundation of the tax-subsidy approach to externalities is as unrealistic as a simple statement that there are no externalities at all, because it rests on the assumption of Pareto optimum prices in all markets except the one in question (Mishan, 1973, pp. 79–83).

Even more devastating criticism (if such is, indeed, needed) results when we realize that externalities are totally pervasive (d'Arge and Hunt, 1971). When reference is made to externalities, one usually takes as a typical example an upwind factory that emits large quantities of sulfur oxides and particulate matter inducing rising probabilities of emphysema, lung cancer, and other respiratory diseases to residents downwind, or a strip-mining operation that leaves an irreparable aesthetic scar on the countryside. The fact is, however, that most of the millions of acts of production and consumption in which we daily engage involve externalities. In a market economy any action of one individual or enterprise which induces pleasure or pain to any other individual or enterprise and is unpriced by a market constitutes an externality. Since the vast majority of productive and consumptive acts are social, i.e., to some degree they involve more than one person, it follows that they will involve externalities. Our table manners in a restaurant, the general appearance of our house, our yard or our person, our personal hygiene, the route we pick for a joy ride, the time of day we mow our lawn, or nearly any one of the thousands of ordinary daily acts, all affect, to some degree, the pleasures or happiness of others. Only the most extreme bourgeois individualism could have resulted in an economic theory that proceeded on the assumption of the existence of only a single externality.

With the recognition of the fact of pervasive externalities the tax-subsidy solution is seen clearly as the fantasy it is. This solution would require literally hundreds of millions of taxes and subsidies (in the United States alone)! Moreover, the imposition of any single tax or subsidy would undoubtedly create totally new externalities because a system of taxes and subsidies, as personalized as this system would have to be, would certainly create new patterns of envy and sympathy with each new tax or subsidy. This envy and sympathy would constitute new externalities for which there would have to be new taxes and subsidies. So the process would go on forever, with an infinitude of taxes and subsidies never getting us any closer to that most elusive of all bourgeois chimeras – Pareto optimality.

But the more reactionary element of orthodox theorists – the Austrian *cum* Chicago school – has never accepted the principle of discretionary government intervention into the market processes. Therefore, for many years they simply ignored externalities. In the late 1950s and early 1960s, however, Coase and his followers devised new formulations of their doctrines that permitted them to enter the debates on externalities that came into vogue in the late 1960s when even orthodox theorists could no longer ignore the environmental degradation of American capitalism.

The policy of the new reactionaries was to create new property rights to pollute the environment, and then to create new markets in which these rights to pollute could be freely bought and sold (Crocker and Rogers, 1971). Presumably such trade would continue to the point where the marginal utility to the polluter of another dollar's added pollution would just equal the marginal disutility to the sufferers of pollution of another dollar's added pollution. At this point it would be impossible to effect a Pareto improvement by either increasing or decreasing pollution, and a new, laissez faire, competitive, Pareto optimum with pollution is attained (one should never underestimate the ingenuity of apologists)!

One might ask the new reactionaries: to whom would the neutral, impartial government assign these rights to pollute? To the poor residents in the polluted slums? To people chosen randomly? Or to the giant monopolies and oligopolies who do the polluting? The answer to this question might have been anticipated from a knowledge of the Austrian *cum* Chicago school's answer to every policy question of the past one hundred years; *if* we assume perfect competition, and *if* we assume perfect knowledge on the part of all producers and all consumers, and *if* we assume there are *no transactions costs* (that is, *if* we assume, for example, that all of the isolated, powerless, low income sufferers who are the victims of a giant, monopolistic, corporate polluter, can *costlessly* organize themselves so they can bargain as one with the polluter), then, these apologists argue, it can be demonstrated that "the initial allocation of property rights has no effect on allocative efficiency." With these assumptions the inevitable conclusion is that within a laissez-faire capitalist market the "failure to reach mutual agreement . . . can be regarded as *prima facie* evidence that . . . a *net* potential Pareto improvement is not possible" (Mishan, 1973, p. 17). This is, however, too obviously apologetic for the more candid neoclassical economists. E. J. Mishan, for example, writes: "Rationalizing the *status quo* in this way brings the economist perilously close to defending it" (Mishan, 1973, p. 17). Perilously close indeed!

Reflecting the extremely individualistic orientation of the new reactionaries is their view of the nature of externalities. They simply take the externalities, for which property rights and markets are to be established, as somehow metaphysically given and fixed. In ignoring the relational aspects of social life their theory ignores the fact that individuals can create externalities almost at will. If we assume the maximizing economic man of bourgeois economics, and if we assume the government establishes property rights and markets for these rights whenever an external diseconomy is discovered, then each man will soon discover that through contrivance he can impose external diseconomies on other men, knowing that the bargaining within the new market that will be established will surely make him better off. The more significant the social cost imposed upon his neighbor, the greater will be his reward in the bargaining process. It follows from the orthodox assumption of maximizing man that each man will create a maximum of social costs which he can impose on others. In another paper I (and a co-author) labeled this process "the invisible foot" of the laissez-faire capitalist marketplace (Hunt and d'Arge, 1973). The "invisible foot" ensures us that in a free-market, capitalist economy each person pursuing only his own good will automatically, and most efficiently, do his part in maximizing the general public misery.

To see why this principle has some validity, note that a self-oriented individual will maximize the value, to him, of participating in organized markets and creating nonmarket transactions. Taking this production possibility set for creating external diseconomies, he will select only those with a higher return than he could earn by engaging in market transactions. But by so doing, he will maximize the cost to others in that his gain is someone else's loss. All individuals acting independently to maximize the cost imposed on others will yield a maximum of these costs or payments to society, that is, by selecting only highly productive external effects. The recipient of contrived or inadvertent external diseconomies will undertake defensive expenditures or pay bribes until the usual marginal conditions of efficiency are fulfilled. Thus, the recipient's cost will be minimized for each external diseconomy, and an efficient pattern of external diseconomies will emerge (Hunt and d'Arge, 1973, pp. 348–49).

But if external diseconomies, in terms of value to the generator, are maximized in the society and if they are efficiently contended with by recipients, then we have a mirror image of consumption theory and Pareto efficiency. That is, instead of allocation of a good to its highest value use with its production costs minimized, we have allocation of a bad (external diseconomy) to its most costly impact, with the impact being minimized in terms of recipient cost as well as production costs. The economy, of course, is efficient but efficient only in providing misery. To paraphrase a well-known precursor of this theory: *Every individual necessarily labors to render the annual external costs of the society as great as he can. He generally, indeed, neither intends to promote the public misery nor knows how much he is promoting it. He intends only his own gain, and he is in this, as in many other cases, led by an invisible foot to promote an end which was no part of his intention. Nor is it any better for society that it was no part of it. By pursuing his own interest he frequently promotes social misery more effectually than when he really intends to promote it.*

External economies also offer incentives for individual gain, but the incentive structure here is basically different than for external diseconomies. Without liability or nuisance rules that establish social responsibility, it is in the interest of both generator and recipient to negotiate on external diseconomies. However, with external economies the recipient gains more by attempting to be a free rider except, perhaps, at the margin. In consequence, the incentive for creating or producing external economies is less than that for external diseconomies, except perhaps for altruists. The policy prescriptions for resolving external diseconomies by assigning property rights or using governmental taxing and subsidy powers are doomed to failure because neoclassical economists fail to analyze the social forces underlying the incentive structure in the competitive system. It appears to be an impossible task to develop legal rights on every type of physical, biological, and social interdependence, or a rational taxation system that will eliminate external diseconomies. Rather, to move toward a better efficiency of the economic system the incentive system itself needs alteration. Needless to say, however, this is a task that goes far beyond the purview of orthodox neoclassical economics.

The theory's absolute inability to handle pervasive externalities should more than suffice to convince any reasonable person of its utter irrelevance, particularly in the light of the conclusion of the theory of the second best, viz., that attempts to partially achieve Pareto optimality may well have effects diametrically opposed to the intentions of the initiators of the attempts. But the theory is much worse than irrelevant. The more candid and honest orthodox economists are, themselves, admitting this. One of the most eminent recently wrote:

> The achievements of economic theory in the last two decades are both impressive and in many ways beautiful. But it cannot be denied that there is something scandalous in the spectacle of so many people refining the analysis of economic states which they give no reason to suppose will ever, or have ever, come about. It probably is also dangerous. Equilibrium economics, because of its well known welfare economics implication, is easily convertible into an apologia for existing economic arrangements and it is frequently so converted. On the other end of the scale, the recent, fairly elaborate analysis of the optimum plans for an economy which is always in equilibrium has, one suspects, misled people to believe that we actually know how an economy is to be controlled . . . It is an unsatisfactory and . . . dishonest state of affairs. (Hahn, 1970)

The normative critique of Paretian analysis

Many economists regret this state of affairs. "Too bad," they say, "that the theory is so irrelevant. It is so elegant and analytically sophisticated, and seems to have such universal normative appeal." This lament, it seems to me, is misplaced. The normative objections to the theory are more damaging than all of the practical, empirical and analytical objections raised to this point. Orthodox welfare economics accepts as the ultimate ethical criteria of social value the *existing* desires, generated by the institutions, values, and social processes of *existing* society, and weighted by the *existing* distributions of income, wealth and power. Accepting them as such the theory becomes by its very nature incapable of asking questions about the nature of an ethically good society and the ethically good man that would be the product of such a society. The plausibility of the normative criteria of the theory derives from the widely felt moral repugnance toward the notion of an omnipotent central government arbitrarily and capriciously dictating the choices and behavioral patterns of individuals. Moral rejection of this Orwellian spectre should not, however, be confused with the imagination that existing society reflects that spectre's antithesis. Orwell's *1984* was, after all, merely the extension of tendencies which he saw in the capitalist economies of his day. We are closer to *1984* than was Orwell.

Commenting on a lifetime of psychoanalyzing people afflicted by the system of desires generated by capitalist society, Erich Fromm has written:

> Man today is fascinated by the possibility of buying more, better and especially new things. He is consumption-hungry. The act of buying and consuming has become a compulsive, irrational aim, because it is an end in itself, with little relation to the use of or pleasure in the things bought and consumed. To buy the latest gadget, the latest model of anything that is on the market, is the dream of everybody in comparison to which the real pleasure in use is quite secondary. Modern man, if he dared to be articulate about his concept of heaven, would describe a vision which would look like the biggest department store in the world, showing new things and gadgets, and himself having plenty of money with which to buy them. He would wander around open-mouthed in his heaven of gadgets and commodities, provided only that there were ever more and newer things to buy, and perhaps that his neighbors were just a little less privileged than he. (Fromm, 1965, p. 123)

Human nature does not automatically produce the consumption-hungry capitalist man, so necessary for the smooth, profitable operation of our economic system. Capitalist man is created through an elaborate system of social control, manipulation, deception and general verbal pollution.

Deception is learned early through television advertising, magazine ads, sales pitches in department stores, pervasive cheating on income taxes, etc., etc. It soon becomes apparent that the entire system *runs* on corruption. In the late Professor Edwin H. Sutherland's survey of white collar crime in the nation's 70 largest nonfinancial corporations (Sutherland, 1961), he found 980 court decisions against these corporations (in a system in which law enforcement and the judiciary are certainly not noted for their vigorous enforcement of the laws typically broken by executives of giant corporations). One corporation had 50 decisions against it, and the average per corporation was 14. Sixty of the corporations had been found guilty of restraining trade; 53, of infringements; 44, of unfair labor practices; 28, of misrepresentation in advertising; 26, of giving illegal rebates; and 43, of a variety of other offenses. There were a total of 307 individual cases of illegal restraint of trade, 97 of illegal misrepresentation, 222 of infringement, 158 of unfair labor practices, 66 of illegal rebates, and 130 of other offenses (Lundberg, 1968, pp. 131–32). Not all those cases were explicit criminal cases. But 60 percent of the corporations had been found guilty of criminal offenses an average of four times each.

From May 10, 1950, to May 1, 1951, a United States Senate Special Committee to Investigate Crime in Interstate Commerce, under the chairmanship of Senator Estes Kefauver, probed the connections of business and organized crime. Senator Kefauver, Democratic vice-presidential candidate in 1956, later wrote a book based on those hearings. Although he emphasized the fact that there was no evidence to link most big corporations with organized crime, he was nevertheless greatly alarmed at the extent of such connections:

> I cannot overemphasize the danger than can lie in the muscling into legitimate fields by hoodlums . . . there was too much evidence before us of unreformed hoodlums gaining control of a legitimate business; then utilizing all his old mob tricks – strong-arm methods, bombs, even murder – to secure advantages over legitimate competition. All too often such competition either ruins legitimate businessmen or drives them into emulating or merging with the gangsters. The hoodlums are also clever at concealing ownership of their investments in legitimate fields – sometimes . . . through "trustees" and sometimes by bamboozling respectable businessmen into "fronting" for them. (Kefauver, 1951, pp. 139–40)

In 1960, Robert Kennedy, who later became Attorney General of the United States, published *The Enemy Within*. He gathered the material for this book while serving as chief counsel of the United States Senate Select Committee on Improper Activities in the Labor or Management Field. Kennedy, like Kefauver, stressed the fact that he was not condemning all, or even most, businessmen. He wrote that:

> we found that with the present-day emphasis on money and material goods many businessmen were willing to make corrupt "deals" with dishonest union officials in order to gain competitive advantage or to make a few extra dollars . . . We came across more than fifty companies and corporations that had acted improperly – and in many cases illegally – in dealings with labor unions . . . in the companies and corporations to which I am referring the improprieties and illegalities were occasioned solely by a desire for monetary gain. Furthermore we found that we could expect very little assistance from management groups. Disturbing as it may sound, more

> often the business people with whom we came in contact – and this includes some representatives of our largest corporations – were uncooperative. (Kennedy, 1960, p. 216)

Kennedy's list of the names of offending companies included many of the largest and most powerful corporations in the United States.

Ferdinand Lundberg has described the extent to which corporate leaders and management receive either very light punishment or no punishment at all when they become involved in improprieties or illegalities. Among the many cases he cites is

> the case of the bribe of $750,000 by four insurance companies that sent Boss Pendergast of Missouri to jail, later to be pardoned by President Truman . . . It was almost ten years before the insurance companies were convicted. Then they were only fined; no insurance executives went to jail. There was, too, the case of Federal Judge Martin Manton who was convicted of accepting a bribe of $250,000 from agents of the defendant when he presided over a case charging exorbitant salaries were improperly paid to officers of the American Tobacco Company. While the attorney for the company was disbarred from federal courts, the assistant to the company president (who made the arrangements) was soon thereafter promoted to vice president: a good boy. (Lundberg, 1968, p. 139)

In more recent times the escapades of I.T.&T. come to mind. Undercover, clandestine "deals" to "buy off" the antitrust division of the U.S. Department of Justice are matched in audacity only by an offer to the United States Government of one million dollars to help to subvert the duly elected government of Chile.

At the level of government the deception gets worse. The revelations of 3,500 secret bombing raids over Cambodia in the period preceding the President's speech in which he stated that the United States had not violated Cambodia's territorial sovereignty; the revelations of deliberate bombings of hospitals; the Watergate scandal in which it was learned that powerful Democrats and Republicans were fair game for the illegal spying and intimidations that the government had supposedly used only against socialists and radicals; all of these came on the heels of the publication of the *Pentagon Papers* which showed the pervasive long-term public deceptions aimed at hiding the motives and facts of American foreign policy from the voting public.

In this economic and political system based on corruption and deception, each lonely, isolated individual is pitted against all other individuals in merciless competition. Is it any wonder that the result is nearly universal disorientation, apathy, and despair? A pervasive sense of the emptiness and futility of life is the basic foundation upon which corporate advertising executives create the capitalist man. Such a man watches commercials in which bright, happy, vivacious people are buying new cars, houses, stereos. He then strives to overcome his own unhappiness and anxieties by purchasing. Purchase, purchase, purchase becomes his Moses and his prophets. But he gets no relief so he sets his sights on a bigger car, a more expensive house, etc., and he is aboard the Alice-in-Wonderland treadmill of consumerism.

Such are the desires of the isolated, egoistic, alienated, manipulated economic man created by the capitalist social system. These form the moral foundation upon which neoclassical welfare economics is constructed. Many bourgeois economists, when confronted with the arguments of this article (as well as many other criticisms which could be made) will admit that welfare economics cannot be defended on normative, empirical, or analytical grounds. Nevertheless, they continue to use concepts, which are only defensible on the assumption that the Paretian analysis is accepted, in most lines of applied economics. Paretian efficiency notions underlie the theory of comparative advantage in international trade theory, they underly most normative conclusions in the neoclassical theory of public finance, most cost–benefit analyses, and nearly every other area in which neoclassical economics culminates in policy recommendations. Even worse are the rarely defended, sanctimoniously stated cliches and shihboleths about rational prices and market efficiency in that most ideologically tainted of all neoclassical academic specializations, comparative economic systems or the analysis of socialist economies.

The pervasive use of subtle variations of the elements of Paretian analysis in most areas of applied economics is inherently conservative. Even when the economist using this analysis has the most progressive and humane intentions, the very foundational presuppositions of welfare economics have a significant tendency to thwart such intentions. Consider the presuppositions; a view of people as one dimensional, calculating maximizers, a basic moral postulate that exalts infinite greed, and an ahistorical view of isolated, alienated competitors that totally ignores their history, institutions, and power relationships, an acceptance of the existing distribution of wealth and income, the system of moral and legal rules, property rights, social power, all of which then enter into an assumed harmonious general equilibrium. Such an analysis can hardly be a useful vehicle for the study of class conflict, economic crises, alienation, racism, sexism, imperalism, militarism, and all of the other problems of contemporary capitalism. And if critical overkill is necessary, the theory can be shown to be riddled with empirical as well as logical shortcomings. For these reasons I believe the greatest barrier to constructive radical economic analysis for an individual trained in a bourgeois economics department to be the necessity of intellectually transcending the habits of thought inculcated through years of intensive study of neoclassical welfare economics in both its pure and applied forms.

References

Alexander, S. S. 1967. *Human Values and Economic Policy*. Sidney Hook, ed. New York: New York University Press.

Baumol, W. J. 1965. *Economic Theory and Operations Analysis*. 2nd ed. Englewood Cliffs, N.J.: Prentice-Hall.

1965. "Informed Judgment, Rigorous Theory and Public Policy," *Southern Economic Journal*, XXXII, pp. 137–145.

Crocker, T., and Rogers, A. J. 1971. *Environmental Economics*. New York: Holt, Rinehart and Winston.

d'Arge, R. C., and Hunt, E. K. 1971. "Environmental Pollution, Externalities and Conventional Economic Wisdom: A Critique," *Environmental Affairs*, 1: pp. 266–86.

Fromm, E. 1965. *The Sane Society*. New York: Fawcett World Library, Premier Books.

Hahn, F. H. 1970. "Some Adjustment Problems," *Econometrica*, 38: pp. 1–17.

Hahn, F. H., and Mathews, R. C. O. 1966. *Surveys of Economic Theory*. Vol. II. New York: Macmillan.

Hunt, E. K. 1975. "Orthodox and Marxist Economics in a Theory of Socialism," *Monthly Review*, 24: pp. 50–56.

1968. "Orthodox Economic Theory and Capitalist Ideology," *Monthly Review*, 19: pp. 50–55.

Hunt, E. K., and d'Arge, R. C. 1973. "On Lemmings and Other Acquisitive Animals: Propositions on Consumption," *Journal of Economic Issues*, 7: pp. 337–53.

Kefauver, E. 1951. *Crime in America*. New York: Doubleday.

Kennedy, R. 1960. *The Enemy Within*. New York: Harper & Row.

Lipsey, R. G., and Lancaster, K. 1956–57. "The General Theory of The Second Best," *The Review of Economic Studies*, 24: pp. 11–32.

Lundberg, F. 1968. *The Rich and The Super Rich*. New York: Bantam.

Marx, K. 1961. *Capital*. Vol. 1. Moscow: Foreign Language Publishing House.

Mishan, E. J. 1971. "The Postwar Literature on Externalities: An Interpretative Essay," *Journal of Economic Literature*, 9: pp. 1–22.

1973. *Economics for Social Decisions: Elements of Cost–Benefit Analysis*. New York: Praeger.

Samuels, W. J. 1972. *Perspectives on Property* (Wunderlich, G., ed.) Philadelphia: Pennsylvania State University Press.

Sutherland, E. H. 1961. *White Collar Crime*. New York: Holt, Rinehart and Winston.

15

Property theory and orthodox economics

David P. Ellerman

Introduction

Orthodox economics neglects property theory in favor of value theory. In place of an explicit theoretical description of capitalist property relations, orthodox economists have built into price theory an imaginative array of myths, metaphors, parables, emotive definitions, conventional misunderstandings, and fallacies – most of which are theoretical expressions of capitalist ideology. This ideological superstructure, which substitutes for an accurate description of property rights, is not simply grafted onto an otherwise sound value theory. Serious work in capitalist economics, such as the Arrow-Debreu model of a "private ownership economy," rests upon the assumed existence of certain "property rights" which turn out to be mythical.

We will be concerned with property myths and misunderstandings in capitalist economics; no broad and lengthy development of property theory will be attempted here. In the first section, we give a simple formalism for describing the creation and transfer of property. In the second section, we analyze the property structure of production and the distribution-of-the-product metaphor. Section three contains the main results of the chapter which concern the "ownership of the firm," the "ownership" of the future profits of production, and "management's prerogatives" – all in the context of a capitalist private property market economy. The section entitled "Capital theory" applies these results to capital theory and analyzes the attempts to beg property theoretic questions with loaded value theoretic definitions. The final section – on general equilibrium theory – gives an impossibility theorem for profitable capitalist competitive equilibria – which, in turn, implies the failure of the attempt by Arrow and Debreu, and others to model a competitive equilibrium in a capitalist economy with decreasing returns to scale and positive profits.

A formalism of property vectors

We must first develop a formal apparatus or model for giving an abstract description of either the factual (de facto) or legal (de jure) creation, transfer, and termination of property. In the factual interpretation of the model, the "creation, transfer, and termination" of a commodity will refer respectively to the production or creation of the commodity, the transfer in the exclusive factual possession and control of the commodity, and the destruction, consumption, or using up of the commodity. In the legal interpretation of the model, "creation, transfer, and termination" will refer respectively to the initiation or creation, the transfer, and the extinction or termination of the ownership title to the commodity. Unless otherwise specified, the abstract terms may be interpreted in either or both the factual or legal sense.

All commodities (i.e., goods and services) will be referred to as *assets*. In the case of durable property, both the entity itself or the services it yields for a certain time period may be referred to as assets. As usual, the *renting* of a durable entity for a time period may be equivalently described as the *purchase* of certain services yielded by the entity during the time period. For example, a capitalist economy permits the legal purchase of the labor services of a person which may be equivalently described as the renting of the person (even though it is customary in that instance to use other words like hiring or employing). We will define *liabilities* so that they will be the algebraic negative of assets. That is, the loss of $+x$ units of a certain type of asset (by termination or by transfer from a party) is equivalently described as the gain of $-x$ units of that type of liability (by creation or by transfer to the party).

A *property vector* is a list of real numbers $X = (x_1, \ldots, x_i, \ldots, x_n)$ where x_i represents the number of units of the ith commodity for $i = 1, \ldots, n$. If $0 \leq x_i$ (i.e., if x_i is greater than or equal to zero) then x_i is an asset, and if $x_i \leq 0$, then x_i is a liability. We write $X \leq Z = (z_1, \ldots, z_n)$ if $x_i \leq z_i$ for all $i = 1, \ldots, n$. Thus X is an *assets vector* if $(0, \ldots, 0) = 0 \leq X$, and X is a *liabilities vector* if $X \leq 0$. Otherwise X is simply a property vector which includes both assets and liabilities. Let us first restrict attention to transfers. If a party B transfers an assets vector $X = (x_1, \ldots, x_n)$ to party A, then, by the definition of liabilities, that transfer could be described as the A to B transfer of the liabilities vector $-X = (-x_1, \ldots, -x_n)$. If A transfers the assets vector $Z = (z_1, \ldots, z_n)$ to B and B transfers the assets vector $X = (x_1, \ldots, x_n)$ to A, then that bilateral transfer of assets could be described as the unilateral A to B (net) transfer of the property vector $Y = Z - X = (z_1 - x_1, \ldots, z_n - x_n)$ which would usually include both assets and liabilities.

Vectors are added by adding the corresponding components [e.g., $X + Z = (x_i + z_i)$, where we use the convention of specifying a vector by giving the typical i^{th} component]. A property vector Y can always be represented as a sum of a certain assets vector and a certain liabilities vector. Let $Y_+ = (y_1^+, \ldots, y_n^+)$ where $y_i^+ = \max[y_i, 0]$, i.e., the largest of the two numbers y_i and 0, and let $Y^- = (y_1^-, \ldots, y_n^-)$ where $y_i^- = \max[-y_i, 0]$ for $i = 1, \ldots, n$. Then Y^+ is an assets vector, $-Y^-$ is a liabilities vector, and $Y = (+Y^+) + (-Y^-) = Y^+ - Y^-$. In the example above, Y^+ is the net assets vector transferred from A to B, and Y^- is the net assets vector transferred from B to A (i.e., $-Y^-$ is the net liabilities vector transferred from A to B). Since $Y = Z - X = Y^+ - Y^-$, we have $Z - Y^+ = X - Y^- = (\min[z_i, x_i])$. Since the latter would be the round-trip assets vector of assets transferred from A to B and back to A, it would ordinarily be the zero vector.

The definition of liabilities is consistent with the evaluation of a property vector at a price vector $P = (p_1, \ldots, p_n)$. In the example just given, the market value of the property vector Y of assets and liabilities transferred from A to B is the scalar product $PY = p_1y_1 + p_2y_2 + \ldots + p_ny_n$. The exchange of Z for X is called an *exchange at the market prices P* or, simply, a *market exchange* if $PY = 0$ (i.e., if $PZ = PX$).

The property theoretic technical terms "assets" and "liabilities" are closely related to the corresponding terms in accounting. The property of a given party at a point in time is given by the party's accounting *balance sheet*. The left hand side (LHS) and right hand side (RHS) of a balance sheet are labeled assets and liabilities respectively. An asset can be acquired (by creation or by transfer to the party) in either or both the legal or factual sense. Accounting assets are assets which have been legally acquired. Thus accounting assets may fall into two general categories: (1) those assets which have been legally, but not factually acquired; and (2) those assets which have been both legally and factually acquired. The accounting assets of the first type are usually called accounts receivable or the like, and they arise from transfer contracts which have not yet been fulfilled by the factual transfer (delivery or payment) of the appropriate assets.

A liability is acquired when the corresponding asset is given up (by transfer from the party or by termination), and thus a liability can be acquired in either or both the legal or factual sense. When a liability has been legally but not factually acquired (i.e., when an asset has been legally but not factually given up), that is an account payable (or debt), and it is listed on the RHS of the balance sheet. When the liability is both legally and factually acquired (i.e., when the debt is paid by the factual delivery or payment of an appropriate asset), then that is usually *not* registered on the RHS of the balance sheet by changing the account payable to an account paid (although that might be done, on a temporary basis, within an accounting cycle). Instead, the account payable is deleted and the corresponding asset is deleted from the LHS of the balance sheet. Hence, the only accounting liabilities which *appear* on a balance sheet are the accounts payable or debts which are analogous to the first type of accounting assets called accounts receivable. Liabilities, which have been both legally and factually acquired, are just as important theoretically, but they do not appear as an explicit accounting category because they are registered by a LHS asset deletion (which reflects the property theoretic definition of a liability acquisition as an asset loss).

Assets are not only transferred; assets are created and terminated. The termination (respectively, creation) of an asset can be equivalently described as the creation (termination) of the corresponding liability. The transfers of an asset from party to party form a chain (or flow) which has an initial and a terminal point (a source and a sink). The same transfers can be equivalently described as the chain or flow of the corresponding liability in the *opposite* direction and *backwards* in time (if time is taken into account). The terminal transferee, terminal holder, or sink of an asset (respectively, a liability) is the initial holder, initial transferor, or source of the corresponding liability (asset) [where holder refers to the legal owner and/or factual possessor depending on the interpretation].

A party can be the terminal transferee and holder of an assets vector $X = (x_1, \ldots, x_n)$ as well as the initial holder and transferor of an assets vector $Z = (z_1, \ldots, z_n)$. As before, the two-way process involving only assets can be equivalently described as a one-way process involving both assets and liabilities. The party is the initial holder and initial transferor of the property vector of assets and liabilities $Y = Z - X$. The legal interpretation of creation (of Z) is the legal creation of the ownership title to the assets Z, and that is called the *legal appropriation* of the assets Z. The legal interpretation of termination (of X) is the legal extinction or termination of the ownership title to the assets X, and that is the original meaning of the phrase *legal expropriation* (Black, H. C., 1968). We will construe the term only in this sense of termination of title (so that it is the algebraic negative of appropriation), and not in its acquired sense of meaning the compulsory legal transfer of title to the government usually under the doctrine of eminent domain. However, the legal expropriation of an asset can be equivalently described as the legal appropriation of the corresponding liability. Hence the term expropriation can be avoided by simply considering the appropriation or initial ownership of property vectors of assets and liabilities, e.g., $Y = Z - X$.

The property structure of production

The factual interpretation of creation and termination are respectively the production or creation of an asset and the consumption or using up of an asset (where the use of durable property is construed as the using up of its services). The factual creation and termination of assets is involved in both production and consumption, but we will not consider consumption. The most important and controversial example of property appropriation in political economy is that which occurs in production. It lies at the heart of the so-called distribution problem.

In a given production process, the vector X of assets used up (during a given time period) is called the *input vector*. The vector Z of assets produced (during the given time period) is called the *output vector*. The property vector $Y = Z - X$ of assets and liabilities created in production is called the *input-output vector* (where we assume, for the sake of simplicity, that the vector $Z - Y^+ = X - Y^-$ of assets both used up and produced in the production process is the zero vector). We will call the output vector $Z = Y^+$ the *positive product*, and we will call the negative of the input vector $-X = -Y^-$ the *negative product*. Since the input–output vector $Y = Z - X = Y^+ - Y^-$ is the sum of the positive product and the negative product, we will also call Y the *whole product vector*.

An *income statement* lists (in value terms) the assets and liabilities acquired by a party over a given time period. The whole product or input–output vector Y lists (in quantity terms) the assets and liabilities created in a given production process during a given time period. Hence, the input–output vector Y together with the market price vector $P = (p_1, \ldots, p_n)$ define what might be called the *production income statement:*

Value of assets produced (= revenue)
y_1^+ units of 1st good @ p_1 $= p_1y_1^+$
.
.
.
y_n^+ units of nth good @ p_n $= \underline{p_ny_n^+}$
PY^+

Value of assets used up (= cost)
y_1^- units of 1st good @ p_1 $= p_1y_1^-$
.
.
.
y_n^- units of nth good @ p_n $= \underline{p_ny_n^-}$
PY^-
Total value of assets and
liabilities created (= profit) $= \underline{-PY^-}$
PY

One should carefully distinguish between the assets and liabilities (created and) acquired through production and those acquired by transfers from other parties (i.e., those acquired through exchange). The assets acquired through production are the output assets or positive product $Y^+ = Z$. A revenue vector R of assets is acquired in exchange at market prices for the output assets Y^+, where $PY^+ = PR$ (usually the outputs would be exchanged for PY^+ units of the numeraire asset but there is no need to be that specific). The assets given up in production are the input assets $Y^- = X$. A cost vector C of assets is given up in exchange at market prices for the input assets Y^-, where $PY^- = PC$. Since to give up an asset is to acquire the corresponding liability, the last two sentences may be paraphrased in terms of liabilities. The liabilities acquired in production are the input liabilities or negative product $-Y^- = -X$. A vector $-C$ of liabilities is acquired in exchange at market prices for the input liabilities $-Y^-$, where $-PY^- = -PC$. The total value of the assets and liabilities created and acquired in production is equal to the total value of the assets and liabilities acquired through exchange, i.e., the value of the whole product $= PY = P(Y^+ - Y^-) = PY^+ - PY^- = PR - PC =$ value of revenues minus value of costs $=$ net income $=$ profits of production.

In conventional economics, the analysis of production is formulated in terms of the paradigmatic conceptual framework which pictures the product as being distributed to the input suppliers. After they have received their distributive shares, some party is the claimant of the remaining residual. That is a complete misrepresentation of the property structure of production. It is at best only a metaphor. While the product-sharing metaphor may be convenient for certain purposes, a strictly accurate description of the property structure of production would better serve the scientific purposes of political economy than even the best of metaphors. One might bear in mind here the standard textbook refutation of the labor theory of value which asserts that one party cannot own all the product when there are several scarce inputs. The simple fact is that one party *does* own all the product, i.e., all the produced outputs or positive product $Y^+ = Z$. For example, the sales revenues listed at the top of a corporate income statement are not just the revenues from selling the capital owners' distributive share of the product. They are the revenues from selling 100 percent of the outputs.

One root of the product-distribution metaphor seems to lie in the mistaken preconception that the positive product Y^+ is the only product that might be legally held by the parties. That preconception overlooks the negative product, i.e., the input liabilities $-Y^-$ [which is one reason why we have emphasized the theoretical parity and symmetry of assets and liabilities]. The point is that the party which owns all the output assets Y^+ also holds all the input liabilities $-Y^-$. For example, the production income statement shows that the party which owns 100 percent of the outputs (and thus receives 100 percent of the revenues) also holds 100 percent of the input liabilities (and thus pays 100 percent of the costs). Instead of there being any distribution of the product, one party has the undivided ownership of the whole product vector, which is the sum of the positive product and the negative product.[1]

Furthermore, the assets and liabilities in the whole product vector Y are not transferred to that party from other parties. That party is the *initial owner* or *appropriator* of the assets and liabilities in the whole product vector $Y = Y^+ - Y^-$ (i.e., the appropriator of the output assets Y^+ and the expropriator of the input assets Y^-). The whole product appropriator is the initial party in the forward chain of legal transfers of the output assets Y^+ as well as the initial party in the backward chain of legal transfers of the input liabilities $- Y^-$ (or, to paraphrase in terms of assets, the terminal party in the forward chain of legal transfers of the input assets Y^-). These results may be summarized in the following proposition.

Production property relations theorem. One party appropriates the whole product of production – so there is no distribution of the product ownership.

It is often thought that the profits are not the price or value of anything. But we have seen that the profits are the market value of a certain complex piece of property which includes both assets and liabilities, namely the whole product or input – output vector. The element of truth in the mentioned view is that the profit receiver does not acquire the input – output vector by giving up certain property in a market exchange (the net market value gained in a market exchange is zero). The profit receiver is the initial owner or appropriator of the input – output vector which was created in production. Furthermore, when profits are zero (i.e., $PY = 0$), then one party still appropriates the input – output vector Y, which is quite different from acquiring the zero vector. A value equation (e.g., $PZ = PX$) should not be confused with (or metaphorically interpreted as) a property equation (such as $Z = X$). For example, in any market exchange, each involved party acquires a property vector of assets and liabilities with market value identically equal to zero (by definition of a market exchange), but utility would not be affected by acquiring the equal-valued zero vector.

Although the product-distribution metaphor is at least classical in origin (e.g., Ricardo), it reaches its highest expression as an imaginative interpretation of marginal productivity theory. Consider a competitive profit-maximizing firm with a production function $y = f(x_1, \ldots, x_n)$. Let $Y^0 = (y^0, -x_1^0, \ldots, -x_n^0)$ be the whole product or input – output vector which maximizes the profits PY, where $P = (p, p_1, \ldots, p_n)$ is the market price vector and $Y = (f(x_1, \ldots, x_n), -x_1, \ldots, -x_n)$. The first order conditions for profit maximization are $pf_i = p_i$, where $f_i = \partial f(x_1^0, \ldots, x_n^0)/\partial x_i$ for all $i = 1, \ldots, n$. Multiplying each side by x_i^0, we see that the *market value* $pf_ix_i^0$ of $f_ix_i^0$ units of output is equal to the *market value* $p_ix_i^0$ of x_i^0 units of the ith input, but the *ownership rights* to the two assets are quite distinct. What some input suppliers do own, namely x_i^0, is equal in market value to $f_i x_i^0$ units of output, but they do not also own, appropriate, or claim that share or any part of the outputs. The party which does appropriate all the outputs y^0 also appropriates the liability $-x_i^0$ and transfers it to the input suppliers by purchasing the asset x_i^0. Furthermore, the so-called residual claimant gets far more property than the residual (but not more value). The input – output vector Y^0 is equal in market value to $y^0 - \Sigma_{i=1}^n f_i x_i^0$ units of output, but the residual claimant claims not only that residual share of the outputs but *all* the output assets $(Y^0)^+ = (y^0, 0, \ldots, 0)$ as well as all the input liabilities $-(Y^0)^- = (0, -x_1^0, \ldots, -x_n^0)$. The residual claimant appropriates the whole product of production (even when the residual is zero). Some capitalist economists have made a very interesting attempt to use a metaphorical notion of imputation to account for an input supplier's share of the product. There is no need to consider that attempt here since an input supplier has no claim on a share of the product to account for in the first place.

So there is no distribution of the product (except, of course, metaphorically). One party appropriates the whole product of a production process, which means that the problem of distribution requires reformulation. The problem splits into a *value theoretic component,* concerned with the determination of the market price vector P (which gives the terms of the property transfers in the input and output markets), and a *property theoretic component,* concerned with the determination of which party has the initial ownership of the whole product or input – output vector of production Y, neglecting past appropriation of the input assets $+Y^-$ and the future appropriation of the output liabilities $-Y^+$.

Hence, the central question is: "which party is to appropriate the input – output vector of a production process i.e., "who is to be the whole product appropriator?" Since "whole product appropriator" is a lengthy expression, we will use the word *firm* as an abbreviation, i.e., firm $=_{df}$ whole product appropriator, in accord with customary theoretical usage, where firm denotes the legal party which chooses a particular input – output vector out of a production set. The definition allows the following canonical formulation: "Who is to be the firm?"

Theory of the firm

In order to analyze this question, we must first establish ground rules. We take a production set to be a technological concept which represents productive opportunities without presupposing which legal party will exploit those opportunities. When durables are used in production, the input variables will refer to their services which are used up in production and which are purchased by renting the durables.

It is customary to assume that all input variables refer to privately owned productive resources (since there are assumed to be markets for the inputs). We will further assume the converse – that all productive services which would be used up in production and which are privately owned are shown as input variables. There are no secret productive services, owned by some private party, hidden in the shape of the production set.

This "no birds in the bush" assumption is necessary so that this theoretical property question will not be begged by the mere specification of the productive opportunities. (There may be nonexclusive factors, such as unowned natural resources or publicly owned factors free for all to use, which are left implicit in the production set.) The "no birds in the bush" assumption does not imply constant returns to scale even if one believes (on metaphysical grounds) that the exposure of all factors and influences will guarantee constant returns. There is no necessary connection between what is exclusively owned by some party and whatever is assumed to limit production (e.g., the limiting conditions might arise from unowned natural parameters such as the gallons per hour flow rate of a river at a hydroelectric plant).

We also need to specify the type of economic system with which we are concerned. A *private* property system is one where the means of production and consumption may be privately owned. A private property *market* economy is a private property system where all privately owned nonhuman assets are legally alienable (i.e., marketable) both in the sense of being salable and rentable. There are three special types according to the legal alienability conditions on humans. The only existing one is a *capitalist economy,* which is defined as a private property market economy where humans may legally rent or hire themselves out but may not legally sell themselves. The hired labor contract is legally valid, but the voluntary self-sale contract is legally invalid. "Since slavery was abolished, human earning power is forbidden by law to be capitalized. A man is not even free to sell himself; he must *rent* himself at a wage" (Samuelson, 1973, p. 52; Samuelson's italics). For the sake of completeness, we will mention the two other positions. A *slavery economy* is a private property market economy where both the voluntary self-sale and self-rental contracts are legally valid. A private property market economy where *neither* voluntary self-sale *nor* hired labor contracts were legally valid might be called a *labor-managed, self-managed,* or *laborist economy*. In a laborist economy, the distinction between legal alienability (in the sense of salability or rentability) and inalienability would coincide with the distinction between things and persons. We will be concerned here with only a capitalist private property market economy, i.e., a capitalist economy.

The salient feature of a capitalist economy is that *all* privately owned productive services, human or nonhuman, are legally alienable, i.e., *all inputs are marketable*. To answer, "Who is to be the firm?" we ask "What are the legal characteristics necessary and sufficient to make a certain party the legal appropriator of the input-output vector $Y = Y^+ - Y^- = Z - X$?" It is clearly necessary that a party be the last legal buyer and owner of the input assets $Y^- = X$. Furthermore, that condition is sufficient since all the productive services which are someone's property are listed or exposed as inputs. Thus, *the firm is the party which is the terminal input buyer*, i.e., *the hiring party*.

The traditional concept of the entrepreneur splits into quite separate functional roles: (1) the contractual role of being the party in whose name the terminal input purchase contracts are made, i.e., the terminal input buyer role; and (2) the input supplier role of providing managerial labor services. Moreover, the functional roles are often separated in practice since the input contracts can be made by legal agents in the name of the hiring party (e.g., the separation of ownership and control in loosely held corporations). Of the second labor supplier role, Wicksell has said all that needs to be said here. "For the work and thought which the entrepreneur devotes to the management of production he must, of course, receive his wages like any other mental worker" (Wicksell, 1934, p. 126.) It should be carefully noted that "being the firm" (by virtue of being the last input buyer) is a *contractual role*. For example, the following quotation is correct (modulo the usual residual metaphor). "The particular contractual and financial arrangements of the firm determine who owns the residual – it might be the owner or financier of the capital equipment used (the capitalist) or the effective organizer and manager of the business (the 'entrepreneur'), who may have borrowed or rented all the capital used, or even the main labor supplier (small business, farms and professional activities)." (Lancaster, 1973, p. 338.) In short, the identity of the party that will be the firm is determined solely by *who hires what or whom*.

Since being the firm is a contractual role, we can immediately set aside one of the basic property myths of capitalist ideology. The usual answer to the basic question of who is to be the firm is "The owners of the firm!" But the concept of firm ownership is only a myth which dissolves, upon analysis, into the ownership of certain inputs, such as the capital services, plus the contractual role of being the terminal buyer of the remaining inputs. Another party could become the firm solely by virtue of a rearrangement (e.g., a reversal) of the input contracts so that the other party would be the terminal input buyer (i.e., the hiring party). There is no need whatever to additionally buy any alleged ownership of the firm. The ownership of all the inputs used up in production will give that terminal input buyer the legal claim on the produced outputs – and that is clearly sufficient.

These basic property theoretic results are summarized, for future reference, in the following theorems.

Nonownership theorem. There is no ownership of a firm.

Hiring party theorem. The hiring party (i.e., the terminal input buyer) is the firm, so the identity of the firm is determined by who hires what or whom and not by any ownership of the firm.

The stockholders' ownership of a corporation which plays the contractual role of being the hiring party is commonly misinterpreted as the stockholders' ownership of the firm. But there is no necessary identification between the *corporation* (the capital owning party formed by associated capital owners) and the *firm* (the legal party which undertakes production). For example, if the corporate capital (physical or financial) was hired out, instead of the workers being hired in, then the stockholders would still own the corporation but the hiring party would be the firm.[2]

The nonownership and hiring party theorems have a number of critical implications. As a production process is carried out over time, the terminal input buyer within each contractual time period will legally appropriate the input-output vector for the time period. By transferring those assets and liabilities to other parties at the market prices, the whole product appropriator receives its market value – namely, the profits of production for the time period. Hence the production profit recipient (i.e., the so-called residual claimant) is determined by who hires what or whom within each contractual time period. Let *ex ante* mean before (and let future mean after) the next set of input contracts. Then the contractual determination of the identity of the firm implies the absence of any *ex ante* ownership right to the stream of future production profits. It will all depend on who is the hiring party in the future contractual time periods. The future profits have a present value – but not a present owner. This is summarized in the following theorem.

Future profits theorem. There is no *ex ante* ownership of the stream of future production profits.

Here again, capitalist economic theory seems peculiarly prone to misinterpret the logic of the law in general and the logic of corporate law in particular. Of course, the stockholders have the (ultimate) legal right to the net income or profit *of the corporation*. Furthermore, the members of *any* legal party whatsoever have the legal right to the net income *of that party*. That is only a legal tautology (since otherwise it wouldn't be the income of *that* party). The problem is the determination of which party will have, as its net income, the net income from the production process, i.e., the production profits. If a corporation hired out its capital assets, then the income to the corporation would only be the interest or capital rentals, and the production profits would accrue to the hiring party which had purchased the services of capital.[3]

A primary motivation of capital theory is the need to explain the capitalization of future profits into the market value of corporate stock. The legal fact is that the stockholders have the legal right to the future net income of the *corporation*. The myth is that the stockholders have the legal right to the future net income stream of the *firm* (i.e., of the legal unit of production). While there is no such *ex ante* property right, the stockholders may well have the *expectation* that the corporation will maintain its contractual role of being the hiring party by exercising its bargaining power (so that then corporation = firm and corporate pure profits = production profits). The expectation might be fulfilled or frustrated, but it is only an expectation – not an enforceable legal right. The corporation is one resource owner among others, and it has no legal power to force other resource owners to sell to it (so that it can maintain its contractual role). Any market value of corporate stock above book value (replacement value) is based on these unenforceable expectations that the corporation will continue to receive the profits of production (as well as expectations about the magnitude of the production profits). Such expectations would be frustrated if the competition took the business away. The competition includes Labor (the association of people working in the production process) and one way of taking the business away is the reversal of the labor contract into a capital rental contract.

The hiring party also has the legal right of managerial control over the production process. That is, since the terminal input owner owns all the property services being used up in production, and since any party has the legal right to control its use of its property, that party holds the production management rights. The firm has the management rights and thus the identity of the production management is determined by the particular contractual arrangement (i.e., by who hires what or whom) – not by the ownership of capital. By managerial control right, we mean the right of discretionary decision-making control over an activity, not the decision-constraining veto control right which permits one to refrain from selling the services of one's property. All property owners have the veto control right over the use of their property.

Since the production management is determined by who hires what or whom, the capital owners have no *ex ante* or precontractual managerial prerogatives over a production process which will involve their capital.[4] The party capital acquires the legal right to direct the production workforce only by hiring them (i.e., by being the hiring party). The myth of capital's managerial prerogatives, like the myth of the present ownership of future production profits, is a submyth of the basic myth of the ownership of the firm.

Managerial prerogatives theorem. There are no *ex ante* (precontractual) managerial control rights over a production process (since the identity of the firm = production management is determined solely by who hires what or whom).

Once again, capitalist economics seems bent on implicitly identifying the corporation (the capital owning party) and the firm (the legal unit of production). Of course, the stockholders have the (ultimate) legal right to manage the activities *of the corporation* (which is delegated to the corporate managers). Indeed, any legal party whatsoever has the legal right to manage the activities of *that* party (within the usual constraints of the law). That is another legal tautology. But which party has *production* as *its activity* (from the legal viewpoint)? That depends solely upon who hires what or whom. In particular, if the corporation hires out the capital to Labor (instead of hiring in the laborers), then Labor will hold the production management rights. The stockholders would still have their legal right to manage (via their agents) the activities of the corporation (i.e., the capital union) – such as coupon clipping and perhaps bargaining over capital rental rates.[5]

In summary, *no* party has any *ex ante* or precontractual legal ownership of the production profits or the production management rights. Hence it might be said that *before the input contracts are made* (for a contractual time period); labor is as much the firm, the owner of the profits, and the management as capital.

Capital theory

We are concerned with the pure theory of capital in the sense of the Fisher tradition – not with theories of growth, capital accumulation, or the like. The focus is on specific *production projects* (also called capital projects or productive investment projects) which are intertemporal production opportunities. We will continue to use firm as the name of the party which legally appropriates the input–output vector (or stream of such vectors) of the production project (by virtue of being the terminal input buyer).

We have noted the conventional misunderstanding that the shareholders own the future *production* profit stream. In fact, the corporation receives the production profits only if and only so long as the corporation maintains its contractual position as the hiring party. While there is no *ex ante* ownership of future production profits legally attached to the shares of corporate capital, the stock market participants can, of course, speculatively buy and sell stock on the basis of their expectations. The apologetic purpose of capital theory is evidently to erect, as an abstract theoretical principle, this mistaken view that the future production profits are attached to capital.

The methodology is simple. Examples of hired out capital, such as annuities or bonds, play an important expository role in fixing the idea of a capital asset with a stream of future property revenues legally attached to the asset. Then capital theorists treat a quite different case as if it were the same. That is, they take the case where the party owning the capital assets used in a production project is *also* the hiring party (i.e., where capital is the hiring factor), and then they assume that the resulting net revenues to that party are similarly attached to the capital assets. But since the party then has the *two* roles of being the capital owner and being the hiring party, the net returns to that party will have two components: (1) the market return for the capital services used up in production (e.g., the capital rentals) which the party receives (implicitly) qua capital supplier; and (2) the production profits which the party receives qua hiring party. But the production profits are *not* legally attached to the capital assets. A party receives the production profits solely by virtue of being the hiring party – and the latter is not necessarily the capital owning party (i.e., when the capital is rented).

Capital theory attempts to attribute the profits to capital in two ways: the capitalized value approach; and the net productivity or marginal efficiency approach. These may be illustrated with a simple example. Suppose we have some capital assets (e.g., a machine, a plant, or even the productive assets of a corporation) with a market cost C which yield K units of capital services per year (with no maintenance required) for a fixed number of years n and then it has a scrap value S. If the market interest rate is i and the price per unit of capital services is the rental r (when paid at year's end), then arbitrage would enforce the equation: $C = \Sigma_{j=1}^{n}\ rK/(1 + i)^j + S/(1 + i)^n$. If we adopt the abbreviation $A(n) = \Sigma_{j=1}^{n}\ 1/(1 + i)^j$, then $C = rKA(n) + S(1 + i)^{-n}$. Now suppose that there is a production project which utilizes K units of capital services and L units of labor services in order to produce Q units of output each year for n years. Let w be the wage rate (when paid at year's end) and let p be the unit price of output (when sold at year's end) so that the price vector is $P = (p, w, r)$. The whole product or input–output vector for each year is $Y = (Q, -L, -K)$ and the annual production profits are $PY = pQ - \mathrm{wL} - \mathrm{rK}$. Hence the discounted present value of the production project's future profit stream is $V_0 = \Sigma_{j=1}^{n}\ (pQ - wL - rK)/(1 + i)^j = (PY)A(n)$.

By the future profits theorem, there is no present or *ex ante* ownership right to that future profit stream or its present value V_0 (even though we may take the *ex ante* or precontractual ownership of the capital and labor resources as given). The terminal buyer and owner of the input vector $Y^- = (O, L, K)$ for each year will have the legal claim on the annual output Q, and thus that party will receive the market value of the input–output vector, i.e., will receive the annual production profits, PY. Some capital theorists seem to assume that because those future production profits *will be* the income and property of some party in the future, the present value of those future profits must be the value of some *presently owned* property. "All potential income must be capitalized. That is to say, we start with institutional property rights. Each income account 'belongs' to some 'person.' " Samuelson, 1966, p. 169.) This is incorrect if the potential income is the return to a contractual role and the contracts are yet to be made. In more fundamental terms, it is incorrect if the potential income is the value of assets and liabilities to be created in the future and if it is yet to be determined which party will appropriate those assets and liabilities.

Let us now suppose that capital, the owner of the capital assets with replacement cost C, *also* plays the role of the hiring party. Since the capital owner already owns the stream of K units of capital services per year, that party only needs to purchase L units of labor services per year in order to be the terminal owner of each year's input vector $Y^- = (O, L, K)$. Then the net annual return to that party is $pQ - wL$ (plus the scrap value). Hence the discounted present value of the net returns to the capital owner and input buyer is $V = (pQ - wL)A(n) + S(1 + i)^{-n}$. Capital theorists call this present value V, the *capitalized value of the capital assets*. But, in fact, it is the present value of the market returns to the capital assets (i.e., the rental stream and the scrap value) *plus* the present value of the market returns to being the hiring party (i.e., the profit stream). Mathematically, $V = (pQ - wL)A(n) + S(1 + i)^{-n} = (pQ - wL - rK)A(n) + rKA(n) + S(1 + i)^{-n} = V_0 + C$. By including the present value $V_0 = V - C$ of the production profit stream in what is dubbed the "capitalized value of the capital assets," capital theorists evidently hope to semantically vouchsafe the profits to capital.[6]

Since the capital assets have one market value C, the attempt to describe $V = V_0 + C$ as the capitalized value of the self-same capital assets can lead to embarrassment when $V_0 = V - C$ is larger than zero. One might surmise that V is the present value of *more property* than C. And so it is, the additional property being the stream of input-output vectors $Y = (Q, -L, -K)$[which has the present value of $V_0 = V - C$]. Hence sophisticated capital theorists (e.g., the MIT school) are usually careful to cover up the property theoretic finesse involved in the capitalized value definition by assuming constant returns to scale and zero profits equilibrium. Then $V_0 = V - C = 0$, i.e., $C = V$, since the profits PY are zero. Thus they can prove the equivalence of the two methods (replacement costs and capitalized value) of evaluating capital assets (Samuelson, 1966, p. 309; Swan, 1956, pp. 352–53; Burmeister, 1974, p. 443). But this equivalence is only a value equality which hides the difference in the underlying property vectors. The owner of the capital assets owns the stream of property vectors $(0,0,K)$ plus the scrap, all of which has the present value C. The party which owns the capital assets, and which is *also* the hiring party, owns the same stream of property vectors $(0, 0, K)$ plus scrap and *additionally appropriates* the stream of input-output vectors $Y = (Q, -L, -K)$, all of which has the present value V. The value equation $C = V$ (when $PY = 0$) only veils the property inequation $(0, 0, K) \neq (0, 0, K) + (Q, -L, -K)$. It might be recalled that the party which appropriates the input–output vectors holds the management rights over the production project. Indeed, the equivalence proof hides the difference between being the firm and not being the firm.

A few words are also necessary on the net productivity of capital. The inverse to discounting or stepping back future to present value is the compounding or stepping up of present to future value. For example, since $V_0 = (PY)A(n)$ is the discounted value of the profit stream, one could imagine that income stream as being created by compounding V_0. Imagine that funds V_0 are put into an interest bearing savings account at time zero. At the end of one year, one could withdraw PY leaving $V_0(1 + i) - PY = (PY)A(n - 1)$ in the account. And one could similarly extract PY at the end of each year for n years. Hence, a value stream, that is equivalent to the profit stream, can be obtained by investing funds V_0 in an interest bearing account at time zero.[7]

By investing funds C in the interest bearing account, one could extract rK at the end of each year except the nth year when one could withdraw the remaining $rK + S$. Thus, by investing funds $V = V_0 + C$ in the interest bearing account, one could withdraw $rK + PY = pQ - wL$ at the end of each year except the last when one could withdraw the remaining $rK + PY + S$. Hence a value stream equivalent to the rental + profit stream is obtained by investing $V = V_0 + C$ at interest. Now suppose that one desires to obtain the same rental + profit stream but by investing only C (we assume that $V - C = V_0$ and PY are positive). Since only the rental stream (including scrap value) can be obtained by compounding C *at interest*, there is a higher annual rate r_a such that compounding C at that higher rate will allow one to obtain both the rental and profit streams. In terms of discounting, if such a rate r_a is substituted for i as the discount rate, then the rental + profit stream would be discounted back to C (whereas i discounted that combined stream back to $V = V_0 + C$).

In connection with the production project, that rate r_a may be called the *average rate of return over cost*, if return is understood to mean return to the capital owner and hiring party, and if cost is understood to exclude the implicit costs (evaluated at market rates) of the capital services yielded by the hiring party's capital assets. That rate r_a is, however, also called the marginal efficiency of capital (Keynes) or the "net productivity of capital" (Samuelson, 1973, p. 598) *as if both* the rental and the profits streams were the "yield" of simply the capital assets themselves.

The analytical wheat can, as usual, be separated from the semantic chaff by renting out the capital. For example, if labor (the owners of the stream of labor services L) rents the capital assets (i.e., buys the stream of capital services K), then the annual net return to that party will be $pQ - rK = wL + PY$. The discounted present value of these net returns is $W^* = (pQ - rK)A(n) = (PY + wL)A(n) = (PY)A(n) + wLA(n) = V_0 + W$, where $W = wLA(n)$ is the discounted value of the stream of (implicit) wages. The discounted value W^* is *not* the capitalized value of the labor. It is the discounted value W of the labor stream plus the discounted value V_0 of the stream of input–output vectors which are appropriated by the hiring party. Capital would receive the capital rental stream and the scrap value, all of which has the present value C, i.e., the market value of the capital assets. The capital owners would not receive V_0 even though V_0 is part of the so-called capitalized value of the capital as well as part of what would be generated from C by compounding with the so-called net productivity of capital.

These emotive definitions of capital theory are not a satisfactory substitute for property theoretic analysis. The point is that value theory fails (as the recourse to colored semantics emphasizes) to deal with the basic problem of who is to be the firm, i.e., of who is to appropriate the input–output vector of production and thus receive its market value, the profits of production. If capital theory is to "start with institutional property rights" (Samuelson, 1966, p. 169), then capital theory runs the risk of being built on a myth. There is *no ex ante* or present property right to the stream of future production profits to start with.

General equilibrium theory

In a capitalist economy, capital and labor are usually originally owned by different parties, i.e., by capital and by labor. Hence, in order for production to legally take place, *some* contract is necessary between these parties. The primary conflict between capital and labor is *not* over the *terms* of a given contract, i.e., is not over the prices analyzed in price theory. The primary conflict is over *which* contract will be made between capital and labor, i.e., whether it is a labor contract or a capital contract. We will call that basic problem of who hires what or whom, the *hiring conflict* (or the hiring problem). The outcome of the hiring conflict decides the property theoretic question of who will be the firm (i.e., who will receive the production profits and will hold the production management rights).

Orthodox value theory is based on a false dichotomy between value theory and property theory. That is, value theory starts with a given distribution of the ownership of resources and the ownership of firms. And that is the error. There is no ownership of firms to start with. The identity of firms (the parties legally undertaking production) is determined, not by any alleged ownership of firms, but by the particular contractual arrangements made in the input markets, i.e., by the outcome of the hiring conflict. That is, the determination of who hires what or whom is part of what is endogenously determined in the marketplace – not part of what is exogenously given in the property distribution. This additional degree of freedom – in the form of the game theoretically indeterminate hiring conflict – has been neglected in the orthodox theory of general equilibrium in a capitalist economy.

We are concerned with models of competitive general equilibrium for a capitalist economy which are not restricted to the special case of constant returns to scale in all firms. In particular, we are concerned with the well known models of Arrow and Debreu (1954), Debreu (1959), and Arrow and Hahn (1971), where the production sets (of possible input–output vectors) are convex sets (which only intersect the nonnegative orthant at the origin). Hence the production sets exhibit nonincreasing returns to scale. They are not assumed to be convex cones. The treatment in the expository text of Quirk and Saposnik (1968) can be taken as representative of these *Arrow-Debreu type models* which attempt to define a concept of capitalist competitive equilibrium under decreasing returns to scale (i.e., all production sets exhibit nonincreasing returns but not all have constant returns) and positive profits in some firms.

Given the jth production set $\bar{Y}_j$, these models define the *j^{th} firm* as the party which acquires the produced input–output vector $Y \in \bar{Y}_j$ in agreement with our definition of firms. The Arrow-Debreu type models of a private ownership economy unfortunately also assume that the ith consumer owns a share s_{ij} *of the jth firm* (Arrow and Debreu, 1954, p. 270; Debreu, 1959, p. 78; Arrow and Hahn, 1971, p. 77, Quirk and Saposnik, 1968, p. 79). There are no such property rights in a capitalist economy, but the origin of the misunderstanding is clear. The models present an abstract version of a corporation (proprietorships and partnerships are construed as corporations), and then they implicitly identify the owned corporations with the contractually determined firms. One can assume the existence of corporations (associations or unions of capital owners) where the ith consumer owns a share s_{ik} *of the* k^{th} *corporation*. But whether or not the kth corporation manages to be the party which acquires the input–output vector $Y \in \bar{Y}_j$ (i.e., manages to be the jth firm) is determined by the input contracts it makes and does not make – not by the given distribution of property.

The firm ownership myth is thus incarnated in the Arrow-Debreu type models by means of the assumed identification of a certain corporation, whose identity (in terms of voting and net income receiving membership) *is* determined by the ownership of shares, with a certain firm, whose identity is determined by who hires what or whom. The crucial theoretical role of the firm ownership myth in these models is to restrict access to production possibilities to only the corporations. But, in order to be the jth firm, i.e., to appropriate an input–output vector $Y \in \bar{Y}_j$, it is sufficient to be the terminal buyer of the input vector Y^-. Hence, the hiring party theorem reveals the possibility, in a capitalist economy, of what might be called *production arbitrage*[8] (or input–output arbitrage), i.e., buying the inputs and selling the outputs.[9]

The concept of production arbitrage could be viewed as the result of using the nonownership and hiring party theorems to strengthen the concept of free entry. The rather vague traditional notion of free entry has always been hobbled by the firm ownership myth. The assumption seems to be that, in order for a new party to be a firm in an industry, the party must construct new physical facilities and the like – which postpones the ultimate effect of the free entry assumption to the long-run. But the existent capital, like the existent workforce, is legally rentable at the beginning of each contractual time period. And the identity of the firms (which will utilize the existent capital and labor) is *only* determined by the outcome of the hiring conflict at the start of each contractual time period. Hence a production arbitrager can obtain *instant* free entry by joining and, of course, winning the battle over who hires what or whom.

In any real world capitalist economy, there are many restrictions to entry by production arbitragers due to transaction costs, imperfect credit and capital markets, uncertainty (about the outputs when given the inputs), and bargaining power – not to mention the role of capitalist ideology to insure that labor knows its place (e.g., the role of the firm ownership myth in forestalling contract reversals by labor). But all these market imperfections are assumed away in the idealized perfectly competitive models.

"Under perfect competition, either workers can hire capital goods or capitalists hire workers" (Samuelson, 1972, p. 237). For example, credit is no problem since the certain outputs of a profitable production opportunity are sufficient security for the purchase of the inputs. Indeed, the corporations in Arrow-Debreu type models have no equity and are supposed to buy all inputs in the market.

It is now clear that there can be no competitive equilibrium at any price vector which permits positive profits in any production opportunity in any economy where all privately owned input services are legally alienable, i.e., in a capitalist (or slavery) economy. The possibility of positive profits will initiate production arbitrage attempts (by labor or any other party) which will bid up input prices. Since competitive equilibrium is incompatible with profitable arbitrage opportunities, the following theorem is proven by the possibility of *production* arbitrage – and that possibility was, in turn, based on the nonownership and hiring party theorems.

Impossibility theorem (for profitable capitalist competitive equilibria). Competitive equilibrium is not possible at any price vector which allows positive production profits in a capitalist economy.[10]

This result does not imply any mathematical error in the Arrow-Debreu type existence proofs for competitive equilibrium under decreasing returns to scale and positive profits. Indeed, they are a mathematical tour de force. The impossibility theorem does, however, show that the Arrow-Debreu type models fail as models of an idealized perfectly competitive capitalist economy (which is with what the theorem deals and what they evidently intended to model). The modeling error is structural and basic; it is the property theoretic assumption that the identity of firms (the parties legally undertaking production) is determined by the given ownership of shares – instead of by who hires what or whom. This criticism should be differentiated from the usual criticism, familiar to all, that the real world capitalist economy is hardly a perfectly competitive system. The point is that the Arrow-Debreu type models fail even as a model or description of an *idealized* perfectly competitive capitalist economy (because the idealized system is precisely the sort of economy where labor or any other party would attempt production arbitrage, perhaps by contract reversals, whenever positive production profits are possible). In particular, when the legitimatizing myth of firm ownership breaks down, the capitalists need *noncompetitive* monopolistic power to keep the workers in their "place."

By the impossibility theorem, the modern attempt to extend the concept of a capitalist competitive equilibrium to the general case of nonincreasing returns to scale (convex production sets) breaks down, and the concept collapses back to the old special case of constant returns to scale. Furthermore, the theorem restores a theoretical symmetry (*mutatis mutandis*) between increasing and decreasing returns to scale. In short, a capitalist competitive equilibrium is not viable under increasing returns because *no one* will try to be the firm. Conversely, a capitalist competitive equilibrium is also not viable under decreasing returns because *everyone* will try to be the firm. A competitive equilibrium, in a capitalist economy, is *only possible* under constant returns to scale when there is universal indifference over who is to be the firm.

Samuelson, following Wicksell, has always emphasized the pecuniary indifference, under constant returns and zero profits, over the question of who is to be the firm. "Or as Wicksell so well put the matter, under constant returns to scale and statical conditions of certainty, it is immaterial which factor hires which" (Samuelson, 1972, p. 27). Furthermore, the constant returns models must (and always do) assume that workers are indifferent over whether a given quantity of a given type of labor is performed under the conditions of democratic self-management in a laborist firm (labor hires capital) *or* under the conditions of "the legal relationship normally called that of 'master and servant' or 'employer and employee' " (Coase, 1937, p. 403) in a capitalist firm (capital hires laborers). Thus the assumptions behind a competitive capitalist model with constant returns imply pecuniary and nonpecuniary indifference over who is to be the firm (so capital and labor might have to flip a coin in order to escape the fate of Buridan's ass). With the assumption that the hiring conflict is a matter of indifference, the constant returns models can avoid the property theoretic error of the Arrow-Debreu type models by altogether begging the question of who is to be the firm. As Samuelson has put the matter: "[P]erfect competition proceeds most smoothly when the extreme assumption of *constant returns to scale* is firmly adhered to. And yet it is precisely under strict constant returns to scale that the theory of the firm evaporates." (Samuelson, 1972, p. 27) And a capitalist competitive equilibrium is *only possible* in this extreme special case which manages to beg precisely the basic property theoretic question of who is to be the firm.

We will conclude by mentioning some related difficulties in capitalist economic theory. By the nonownership theorem, the identity of firms is not exogeneously given to price theory by the distribution of property. By the hiring party theorem, the question of who is to be the firm emerges as the market endogenous problem of who hires what or whom. This hiring problem adds a critical extra degree of freedom to price theory, and the solution to that problem is, in general, game theoretically indeterminate. But it is only the outcome of that indeterminate conflict which determines who is an input buyer and who is only an input supplier. Game theory strategies emerge which threaten the norms of orderly market behavior as well as the tools of market analysis. Why should any input owning party agree to supply any inputs at the quoted price, if by purchasing a complementary set of inputs, the party can net the value of the originally owned inputs plus the production profits? Hence, in a capitalist economy, the basic tools of market analysis, such as supply and demand curves, are threatened by the indeterminacy of the hiring conflict principally between capital and labor – a conflict which is part of what is usually called class struggle.

Notes

1 In the historical development of mathematics, formal innovations (such as negative or complex numbers) were not wholeheartedly accepted by mathematicians until a concrete interpretation was given. In particular, mathematicians would not accept negative numbers until Fibonacci, in the thirteenth century, interpreted them in terms of debts and losses, i.e., liabilities. Today, input–output vectors are the customary *formal* means of representing a production process. It seems somewhat ironic that seven centuries after the liabilities interpretation of negative numbers vouchsafed their acceptance into mathematics itself, mathematical economists refrain from giving that interpretation to the negative components of the input–output vectors, and they continue to informally use the conceptual paradigm which pictures the positive product or outputs as the only product of production. And if the outputs are the only product, then one must view them as being distributed or shared. But one must bear in mind that the product-sharing paradigm plays an important ideological role by representing a capitalist enterprise in terms of an as-if partnership where each factor supplier gets a certain share of the product.

2 It might be noted that the legal statement that "the stockholders own the corporation" is not particularly appropriate. If the corporation refers to the legal party, then it is odd to speak of owning a legal party. It would be more apt to say that the stockholders *are* the corporation in the sense that the

voting membership is the collectivity of stockholders. If the corporation refers to the corporate assets, then the phrase only expresses the tautoltively own the assets of that party. Apparently, the sole virtue of the legal phrase is that it engenders the misinterpretation (mentioned in the text) and thus it appears to put legal flesh on the firm ownership myth.

3 These points may be illustrated using the analogy of a two party game (which might be called the *hiring game*). The winner receives a prize with positive present value V_0 and the loser receives nothing. Before the game is played, neither side has an *ex ante* or present property right to the prize – even though the side which, in the future, succeeds in acquiring the role of winning party will own the prize. It should be carefully noted that while neither side has any *ex ante* ownership of the winner's prize, it is tautological that each side will own its *winnings* – whatever they might be (e.g., the prize or nothing). And each side *can* make a contract – before the game – to legally transfer to another party the future winnings of that side. These winnings rights of a side would be evaluated on the market according to the *expectations* that the side will win (and expectations about the prize value V_0 if that is not known with certainty). Let us further suppose that one side is itself owned by means of transferable ownership shares. A shareholder would own a certain portion of the book value C of the side and the same portion of the winnings of that side. The book value of a share and the winnings expectations would be prime determinants of the market value of a share. If the shareholders' side had always won the game every time it was played in the past, then the shareholders (and game promoters) might begin to *misinterpret* owning their side's winnings as owning the winner's prize. The hiring game, of course, symbolizes the conflict over who hires what or whom in each contractual time period. The two sides are capital (the associated capital owners) and labor (the associated workers), and the winner's prize is the production profits.

4 The contractual determination of management can be illustrated with a simple example. Let Mr. K be a car owner, let Mr. L be a car driver, and let the activity be Mr. L driving Mr. K's car. Of course, either party may veto the activity. But when both parties do consent, it will be to a rental contract, and the hiring party will be the management. Mr. L holds the management rights if he rents the car, and Mr. K holds those rights if he rents or hires Mr. L (e.g., as a chauffeur). In fact, a third party could hold the management rights by hiring both the car and Mr. L. Thus in spite of any bargaining bluffs, Mr. K's ownership of the car does not automatically give him the management rights over the activity of Mr. L driving Mr. K's car (only the veto rights). Mr. K acquires the legal right to direct Mr. L's driving *only* by hiring him. The car, of course, symbolizes the means of production, Mr. K symbolizes capital (the owners of the means of production), Mr. L stands for labor, and the driving activity stands for the production process. The logic is the same in the general case.

5 We focus on the *market* rental of corporate capital because we want to draw out the implications for economic theory of the reversability of the market hiring contract between capital and labor. A more practical method of labor hiring capital would be the legal reorganization of a stock corporation into a democratic institution by legally changing the stocks into bonds (debt capital) and by changing the voting membership from the stockholders to the people who work in the enterprise (Flynn and Dahl in Nader and Green, 1973).

6 There are several other colorful expressions which verbally attribute the present value $V_0 = V - C$ of the profit stream to the capital assets. "The difference between V and C we may call, . . . , the *'goodwill' of the equipment*" (italics added; Lutz and Lutz, 1951, p. 12). Another inspired expression is obtained by metaphorically extending the concept of rent. The annual market return to the capital assets is the rent rK. If the capital owner *also* plays the contractual role of being the hiring party, then the net annual return to that party is $pQ - wL = rK + PY$ which is metaphorically called the "quasi-rent earned by the machine" (Stonier and Hague, 1973, p. 328). Then apologists can say that the capitalized value of the capital is, after all, just the discounted value of the stream of "quasi-rents earned by the machine" (plus the discounted scrap value) – which is the bogus version of the genuine $C = rKA(n) + S(1 + i)^{-n}$.

7 It should be noted that the two streams are not remotely equivalent from the property theoretic viewpoint. The invested funds V_0 are owned assets at time zero, and they are simply exchanged at the market prices for a certain stream of future funds. However, the present value V_0 of the profit stream is only the result of an arithmetical calculation, and it does not represent the value of any assets owned at time zero (by the future profits theorem). It is the present value of the future input–output vectors which will be appropriated by whatever party is the hiring party in each future time period.

8 Arbitrage is usually considered to be an exchange operation but that is largely a matter of semantics. If the price of Chicago wheat exceeds the price of Kansas City wheat plus the required transportation costs, then the operation of buying the inputs (Kansas City wheat plus transportation services) and selling the outputs (Chicago wheat) would still be called arbitrage. If the price of a good one period hence exceeds the current price plus storage costs, then "a sure profit could always be made by the time arbitrage, so to speak, of buying the commodity currently – borrowing, if necessary – and reselling one period later" (Fama and Miller, 1972, p. 62). But in general equilibrium models, where commodities are differentiated by spatial and temporal location, transportation and storage would be examples of production. As more characteristics of the inputs, besides spatial and temporal location, are changed in the production process, there is no magic dividing line which suddenly prevents the production arbitrage of buying the inputs and selling the outputs. It is apparently only faith in the myth that production profits are legally attached to corporate stock which leads economists to believe

that arbitragers must switch operations to security markets instead of directly reaping the production profits by production arbitrage between the input and output markets.

9 It should be recalled that all privately owned productive services which would be used up in a production process are assumed to be exposed as inputs. There may be other nonexclusive factors, such as unowned natural resources (river water or air) or publicly owned property (free parking or driving on public roads), which could be left implicit in the shape of the production set without prejudicing the hiring question. These implicit but nonexclusive factors may prevent constant returns. If some economists "find it convenient" (Arrow and Hahn, 1971, p. 53) to leave certain privately owned productive services (e.g., managerial services or the services of fixed factors) implicit in the production set, then they are only contradicting the profit maximization assumption for certain price vectors. The possibility of production arbitrage is based on the fact that, in the capitalist system, all privately owned productive services (human or nonhuman) are legally alienable (which is quite independent of whether or not some economists use "birds in the bush" production sets in their formalisms). In particular, entrepreneurs and managers, being only human, are hirable, and it is not fixed as to who will lease a fixed factor. The mountain need not come to Mohammed in order for Mohammed to lease the mountain.

10 Some economists seem to be unaware that the Arrow-Debreu model claims to have shown the existence of a capitalist competitive equilibrium with positive (pure) profits. The following quotation from Arrow should clarify the matter: "The Arrow-Debreu model creates a category of pure profits which are distributed to the owners of the firm; it is not assumed that the owners are necessarily the entrepreneurs or managers . . . In the McKenzie model, on the other hand, the firm makes no pure profits (since it operates at constant returns); the equivalent of profits appears in the form of payments for the use of entrepreneurial resources, but there is no residual category of owners who receive profits without rendering either capital or entrepreneurial services" (Arrow, 1971, p. 70).

References

Arrow, K. J., and Debreu, G. 1954. "Existence of an Equilibrium for a Competitive Economy," *Econometrica*, Vol. 22, pp. 265–290.

Arrow, K. J. 1971. "The Firm in General Equilibrium Theory." R. Marris and A. Wood, eds. *The Corporate Economy*. Cambridge, Mass.: Harvard University Press.

Arrow, K. J., and Hahn, F. H. 1971. *General Competitive Analysis*. San Francisco, Calif.: Holden-Day.

Black, H. C. 1968. *Black's Law Dictionary*. St. Paul, Minn.: West Publishing Co.

Burmeister, E. 1974. "Neo-Austrian and Alternative Approaches to Capital Theory," *Journal of Economic Literature*, Vol. XII, pp. 413–456.

Coase, R. H. 1937. "The Nature of the Firm," *Economica*, Vol. IV, pp. 386–405.

Debreu, G. 1959. *Theory of Value*. New York: Wiley.

Fama, E. F., and Miller, M. H. 1972. *The Theory of Finance*. New York: Holt, Rinehart and Winston.

Lancaster, K. 1973. *Modern Economics; Principles and Policy*. New York: Rand McNally.

Lutz, F., and Lutz, V. 1951. *The Theory of Investment of the Firm*. Princeton, N.J.: Princeton University Press.

Nader, R., and Green, M., eds. 1973. *Corporate Power in America*. New York: Grossman.

Quirk, J., and Saposnik, R. 1968. *Introduction to General Equilibrium Theory and Welfare Economics*. New York: McGraw-Hill.

Samuelson, P. A. 1966. *The Collected Scientific Papers of Paul A. Samuelson*. Vol. I. J. E. Stiglitz, ed. Cambridge, Mass.: M.I.T. Press.

1972. *The Collected Scientific Papers of Paul A. Samuelson*. Vol. III. R. C. Merton, ed. Cambridge, Mass.: M.I.T. Press.

1973. *Economics*. 9th ed. New York: McGraw-Hill.

Stonier, A. W., and Hague, D. C. 1973. *A Textbook in Economic Theory*. 4th ed. New York: Wiley.

Swan, T. W. 1956. "Economic Growth and Capital Accumulation," *The Economic Record*, Vol. XXXII, pp. 334–361.

Wicksell, K. 1934. *Lectures on Political Economy*. Vol. I. E. Classen, trans. New York: Macmillan.

Part VII

Marxism and modern economics

16

Marx, Keynes, and social change: is post-Keynesian theory neo-Marxist?

J. A. Kregel

Introduction

The recent criticism of the neoclassical approach to economic analysis has come from a number of diversified areas. There has been a tendency to view these competing theories as a homogeneous group. This is correct in the sense that all present negative criticism of orthodox theory as represented either by Arrow-Debreu or the aggregate production function simplifications of the "neo-neoclassics." From this "negative" homogeneity it has been suggested that all can be grouped with the name of Marx or considered as neo-Marxist (Harcourt and Nell, 1970).[1]

Strict Marxists, however distinguish their own positions, first on the grounds of theoretical differences, but more importantly, on prescriptions for social change. Thus the anomaly that while all the non-neoclassical theories are said to be neo-Marxian, only "true" Marxist theory is supposed to possess the basic requirements necessary for valid political assessments of economic reality and to yield meaningful implications for social change. This chapter considers the post-Keynesian and Marxist approaches, and attempts to show that while the two lines have a surprisingly large number of theoretical similarities, they are only superficial. There is, however a strong common ground to be found between them and it is precisely in the implications of the two approaches for social change.

For some Keynesians this should not be surprising since Joan Robinson showed long ago that Keynes's theory could have what she jokingly called a distinctly "pinkish" hue. The implicit contention is that the affinity between Keynes and Marx, surprisingly, turns out to lie in the implications for social change rather than in the theoretical underpinning. This is not to say that Keynes himself might have found agreement with what follows, only that it is a possible logical deduction from the basic Keynesian framework. Keynes's own thinking, according to Professor Robinson, had a rather "blueish" hue (Robinson, 1953, pp. 19–23).

Marx and Keynes: some similarities

In his exposition of the possibility of involuntary unemployment, Keynes chose the assumptions that would give the existing theory the strongest possible case, i.e., flexible wages and prices responding to changes in supply and demand, but in a setting of actual historical time (Means, 1959; Keynes, 1936, p. 15).[2] Keynes was able to show that even when the classical assumptions were met, full employment equilibrium was not a necessary result. At this point there were two lines that could be followed, one negative and theoretical, the other positive and pragmatic. Keynes could have concentrated on why the classical price mechanism did not produce the intended results of full employment of all factors. But instead, being a practical man facing intolerable unemployment, Keynes completely recast economic theory, emphasizing the positive aspects of the new approach. The practical aspect of the theory was to show how to generate a level of expectations sufficient to produce the amount of investment that would generate a level of aggregate demand that would provide employment for all those willing and able to work at the going wage.

Uncertainty, expectations and investment replaced the operation of relative prices as the motive force in the determination of the macro-variables in the system. But Keynes, having relegated relative prices to a place of minor importance, nonetheless retained much of the supply and demand framework of Marshall as the micro basis of his theory; this even after he had implicitly proved that the price system in a realistic monetary economy (Keynes, 1936, Ch. 17; Keynes, 1963) did not operate as assumed in the nonmonetary classical world of Say's law and the quantity theory of money. The practical emphasis, in Keynes's view, was to be on uncertainty, expectations and effective demand, not on the operation of relative prices. The classical theory of relative price adjustment thus remained more or less intact despite the powerful but implicit critique; the niceties of criticism and the onerous reconstruction of the theory did not have the same urgency as ameliorating the conditions of the unemployed.

Marx was more direct in his criticism of the operation of the price system in producing full employment in a capitalistic economy. Speaking of the operation of the price system in response to a reduction in the supply of a primary product:

> On the contrary, when the product suddenly becomes dearer, on the one hand many workers are dismissed, and on the other hand the manufacturer seeks to recoup his loss by reducing wages below their normal level . . . Thus the normal demand on the part of the workers declines, intensifying the now general decline in demand, and worsening the effect this has on the market price of the product. (Marx, 1972, p. 223)

For Marx the general result of the price system's operation is not as the classical theory predicts and the disproof is generally the same for both Marx and Keynes. The movements of relative prices will not act to produce full-employment of all factors, the only condition under which scarcity or opportunity cost can be conceived of having any meaning at all. Thus both Marx and Keynes find a crucial weakness in the classical explanation of the operation of relative prices to naturally produce the only situation where the relative prices themselves can be meaningful. Unfortunately, this line of criticism is little noticed by those economists who wish to incorporate Keynes into the general equilibrium approach. For Keynes, price theory was not a crucial practical problem; for Marx the price system or, as it was then called, the theory of value, was all important.

While the failure of relative prices to produce full-employment was implicit in both theories, different lines of explanation were taken, although with certain similarities, by Marx and Keynes. For Keynes it was a problem covered by what he called the "state of long-period expectations," a euphemism for the information about the future profitability of present investment that the price system could not provide, and thus a major determinant of the decision to invest (in the guise of "animal spirits"). For Keynes it was the role of the State to make up for this deficiency in the function of the price system in passing information over time by undertaking the investment required to generate enough aggregate demand to generate proper expectations. Since each entrepreneur had to act individually, the ensemble of entrepreneurs could not know that their united efforts could produce the profitability to justify their investment. It was, therefore, rational for an entrepreneur not to go against the tide of expectations (which of course served to justify them), although the State could do this because it could comprehend the overall situation and was not limited by profitability.[3]

Marx predicted continuing crises in the same terms, but under the theory of class conciousness and the relations of production. By their very nature the capitalists could never grasp the nature of their role in class terms. They remained forever doomed because of their individualistic nature, each thinking solely of his own profit.[4] At the same time the increasing socialization of the production process becomes more and more contradictory in relation to the individual, private basis of the ownership and direction of the means of production, creating disproportions in the system of distribution and the realization of surplus value that can only be rectified by crisis and unemployment. As long as each capitalist thought only of individual profit (competing against labor and the other capitalists), the capitalist mode of production would produce ever deepening crises and rising unemployment which would produce class conciousness in the workers and the eventual socialization of ownership and control. Neither could economic theory approach this reality as long as it retained its individualistic interpretation of the system, i.e., as long as it remained within the realm of capitalist ideology (Bukharin, 1927). Thus in both Marx and Keynes there is the realization of the inability of the capitalists to grasp the overall import of their aggregate situation and what the future would bring. Neither even considered that the price mechanism should be capable of this function. The general problem for Keynes, was solely the problem of a sufficient level of investment, while for Marx, even if the capitalists were investing, the same result could occur. The difference in the two approaches is again in the underlying theory of value and price.

Keynes, unfortunately, did not have the time, nor apparently the inclination, to extend his propositions to their implications for the classical theory of value and price based on atomistic market relations. Instead, he moved directly to a remedy for the symptoms (unemployment) through the external action of a government sufficiently cognizant of its role as defender of the interests of the capitalist class to carry out the investment that they, as individuals, could not find the economic justification to do. It was with the appreciation of the implications of the theory of value and price for reality that Marx started; for Keynes, they hardly seemed necessary.

The post-Keynesian extension of Keynes's system

Since the comparisons regarding the social implications of Keynes's theory are to be made from its logical extensions, this section will outline (in a form most easily comparable with Marx) the post-Keynesian approach. Total output at a point in time in the system is divided into available (consumption) and nonavailable (investment) goods. The logic of the distribution mechanism is quite simple – the real wage of labor cannot exceed the amount of real consumption goods in the system. This is a limit – of course it may be less if, as is likely, the capitalists also consume some of the consumption output. This leaves the determination of profit. Kalecki simplified it like this:

Output	*Income*
gross investment	gross profits
+ capitalists' consumption	
+ workers' consumption	+ wages and salaries
= GNP	= GNP

If wages and salaries equal workers' consumption (i.e., workers spend all their income so the propensity to save out of wages, $s_w = 0$) then Gross Investment + Capitalists' Consumption = Gross Profits ($s_p < 1$) which is the other side of the wages limit. When $s_p = 1$, Gross Profits = Gross Investment. As a limit, then, real wages are equal to available output and profits are equal to net investment, making suitable depreciation adjustments.

Joan Robinson's main criticism of the neoclassical theory was that it had no explanation of what *determines* the rate of profit (which is assumed to be driven to equality in all sectors by overall capital mobility). It will be seen below that this is one of the points of difference between the post-Keynesians and Marx, whose fundamental question was rather different.

From the just mentioned limitational statements about distribution the determination of the rate of profit can be derived from Keynes's beliefs about the determination of investment. In Keynes's theory savings do not have any direct effect on, nor do they determine, investment (although through effects on the propensity to consume they can affect expectations negatively); but investment as an autonomous and independent factor creates the savings necessary to equate savings and investment.[5] Thus investment as an autonomous and independent variable subject to uncertainty and expectations determines the division of output between available and nonavailable goods.

With a given technology, a given level of the money wage, and a banking system which can create and lend money as needed to investors, the sum *total* of investment decisions will determine the amount of resources appropriated for investment purposes.[6] Thus expectations of future sales and the profits to be made on these sales (animal spirits) sets the overall ratio of investment to output (I/Y). If conditions are tranquil and expectations normally satisfied, the decision to invest will also determine I/K (or $\Delta K/K$), the rate of accumulation of the capital stock. The rate of profit earned on the capital stock employed can now be determined by calculating the price relations between the available and nonavailable sectors that allow expectations to be realized.

Since resources are given, the decision to invest also determines the quantity of available goods produced and the allocation of labor between the two sectors associated with the given technology. Thus the demand for available goods will be comprised of wages paid in the consumption and investment sectors combined. Assuming that capitalists do not spend and workers do not save, the price of consumption goods will settle at the level that just exhausts the workers' demand, or $pQ_c = wN_c + wN_i$, where Q_c is the quantity of consumption (available) goods determined by I/Y, w is the money wage rate and N_c, N_i, the employment in each sector. Equilibrium with realized expectations requires that p take a value that balances the relation. Total revenue for the consumption sector capitalists is thus pQ_c, while their prime costs of production equal the wage bill wN_c so profits $P = pQ_c - wN_c = wN_c + wN_i - wN_c = wN_i$. The sum of profit is equal to the wage bill in the investment sector.

It can now be seen that *if* investment had been *higher*, the equilibrium established would have involved a higher I/Y, a higher N_i/N_c and thus a higher price level and sum of profits. The smaller amount of consumption goods also directly implies a lower maximum consumption by workers and thus a lower real wage. Likewise, the rate of profit earned is a direct result of the decision to invest by the capitalists as a whole. As it has been assumed that all profits are saved, the higher investment is just balanced by higher profits so that the Keynesian equilibrium of $S = I$ is maintained in the form $P = I$, which ensures the equality of $P/K = I/K$, that is, the rate of profit is equal to the rate of growth. Thus, when capitalists invest more, they end up saving more and at the same time receiving more profits. The extra savings and the extra profits should not be confused so that it appears, as it may have to Marshall, that the capitalists in some sense deserve the higher profits because of the higher saving (or because they refrain from consuming the higher profits), forgetting that the other side of the higher saving and profits is a lower real consumption on the part of the workers.[7]

In fact it makes little difference to the capitalists' profits if they save or consume. If we add capitalists' consumption, the price equality must be rewritten as $pQ_c = wN_c + wN_i + cP$, where cP is consumption out of profits, and the profits equality becomes $P = pQ_c - wN_c = wN_c + wN_i + cP - wN_c = wN_i + cP$ and the savings-investment equality becomes $S = I = (1 - c)P$ which also implies a higher rate of profit for a given value of I/K so that the rate of profit is greater than the rate of accumulation. This situation corresponds exactly to Kalecki's presentation and can also be represented by the post-Keynesian formula $\pi = g/s_p$ where π departs from g in proportion to the consumption out of profits. Even if capitalists are less parsimonious, it does nothing to hurt their income from profits. Thus, although there is no way to explain the accrual of profits to saving (or abstinence), the mechanism of distribution appears to reward the capitalists for their saving.

This superficial appearance has led some democratic and liberal socialists to the belief that the poor are poor because they don't save, because they squander their chance to partake in the accrual of profits to saving. Welfare state schemes thus force contractual savings on workers and provide low cost social services in an effort to provide greater income equality. In this way, it is hoped, all can share in the fruits of laissez-faire capitalism. This is a chimera, as we will see presently; more importantly the welfare state has produced the contention that, in reality, the class of nonsavers is very small, so that the model with Kalecki's strict assumptions is hardly realistic in describing the claim to profits in modern-day welfare state capitalism.

The theory can be made more realistic to please liberal critics. Assume an economy comprized of households and firms. Also assume that each household owns an equivalent share in the existing firms as a claim on their profits. Household income is then made up of wages and dividends received from the firms. The households do not distinguish their income as to source and thus there is one savings ratio applied equally to combined household income. Total household income is then $Y_h = W + (1 - r)P = W + D$ where r is the proportion of profits the firms retain for internal funding of investment and D dividends received. Total income is $Y_f + Y_h = W + D + rP$ and the profits equality is $P = I + ((1 - s)D - sW)$ with the balancing relation $S = I = sW + s(1 - r)P + rP$.

The previous simple case with strict savings assumptions is marked by the fact that functional income classes correspond to social classes. In the present case there is only one social class and one overall relation of production. The formula for the rate of profit derived from these assumptions is modified from the simple $\pi = g/s_p$ and becomes the rather complicated (Kregel, 1971)

$$\pi = \frac{g - s(W/K)}{s(1 - r) + r} \quad \text{or} \quad \frac{g}{r + (1 - r)s + s(W/P)}$$

In terms of functional income categories the new formula resembles its more simple predecessor for inspection will show that $s(1 - r) + r$ is just another way of expressing the propensity to save out of total profits (distributed + undistributed). The second version of the formula takes account of market power relations (one might be tempted to say degree of corporate exploitation) in the appearance of W/P. The firms in this formulation subsume the capacity of the capitalists for the combination of their investment decisions and the funding of this investment (the value of r, or internal financing) determines the output of consumption commodities and the nominal value of household income (r effects D and thus Y_h) available to purchase them. If all households are in an equal position (equal W, s, D), they all have equivalently lower consumption when the firms as a whole carry out a higher rate of investment. Now saving is rewarded, not by profits, but by paper gains on the value of the corporations, which by definition can never be consumed by the households en masse, although they may feel better off.

But there is no reason to limit the analysis to a single household saving propensity and, therefore, received income. The limit is a different savings propensity for each level of income. But here exactly the same mechanism works. Those households with low incomes consume a higher proportion of their income, and therefore have a lower wealth position and a lower ability to save. In such conditions a higher rate of investment implies a proportionately greater rise in income for high income classes and a proportionately greater cut in real consumption for low income households. The $S = I$ balance is achieved by reducing the consumption of low incomes through rising prices that high income households can more easily absorb. It is not different amounts of saving or propensities to save but the ability to save that a given size income allows which determines who gives up consumption to allow the increased investment. On the tack of reality it should be noticed that this applies regardless of types of income received (as landlords in the nineteenth and rentiers in the twentieth century will testify).

Thus the implication that the brunt of economic growth and accumulation will be borne by low incomes irrespective of source. As long as real purchasing power is transferred from those who consume a higher proportion of their income to those who consume a lower proportion, no conceivable social scheme will bring equality in the burden of growth and investment. *A dynamic growing system that allocates output via the "price mechanism" will produce income inequality.*[8] This result holds whether or not prices are determined by the invisible hand or are set in relation to the investment requirements of firms.

To alleviate poverty and inequality then, one must reject the system itself – for if inequality is inherent in the capitalist mode of production, small changes in consumption and savings patterns or in the provision of social services will do nothing to change it. Here one is forced away from looking at wages and profits, or households and firms, or high and low incomes. To evade inequality it is necessary to do more than change the nomenclature of the problem. Along with Marx, one is eventually driven to reject *both* individual ownership of the means of production (or titles thereto) *and* the system of allocation and exchange based on the price mechanism (conceived merely as a market clearing mechanism, for nothing has been said about efficiency or optimality).

Following this line of thought, one arrives at a wholesale rejection of what Marx called the wages system; following Keynes, one would conclude only that the system is unfair, in the sense that it does not provide full-employment, a position he quite naturally took, since he stopped short of analyzing the price system. Thus, for Keynes, things only needed to be changed to the extent that would permit full-employment. A third position is that taken by the meritocratic socialists who bypass Keynes's problem and emphasize the creation of market equality, such that merit rather than wealth is rewarded. It is easy to see that this kind of position implies the same kind of inequality as a system based on property in physical wealth because it does not eliminate market exchange and private property. Further, it provides no convincing explanation as to why merit should deserve wealth any more than inherited property or even abstinence. It is precisely on this point that the theory of liberal democracy faltered in its quest for political equality (MacPherson, 1962).

Thus, the logic of the system that was used in preceding paragraphs implies that the social change required to eliminate poverty and inequality must be such as to change the mechanism of distribution itself. Small scale welfare state attempts can do very little. The price system not only fails to produce full-employment, but also produces income inequality as a natural result.

Marx

Marx's position, which he puts succinctly in *Wages, Price and Profit* while supporting the struggle by the working class for higher wages, is:

> At the same time, and quite apart from the general servitude involved in the wages system, the working class ought not to exaggerate to themselves the ultimate working of these everyday struggles. They ought not to forget that they are fighting with effects, but not with causes of those effects; that they are retarding the downward movement, but not changing its direction; that they are applying palliatives, not curing the malady. They ought, therefore, not to be exclusively absorbed in these unavoidable guerrilla fights incessantly springing up from the never ceasing encroachments of capital or changes of the market. They ought to understand that, with all the miseries it imposes upon them, the present system simultaneously engenders the *material conditions* and the *social forms* necessary for the economical reconstruction of society. Instead of the conservative motto "*A fair day's wage for a fair day's work!*" they ought to inscribe on their banner the *revolutionary* watchword, "*Abolition of the wages system!*" (Marx, 1947, p. 54)

The result is the same – what is the basic difference? While Joan Robinson's main question was "What determines the rate of profit?", Marx went deeper and asked "Why does profit exist in the first place and what determines how much profit will exist?" To answer this question Marx had to go beneath the phenomenal relations of commodity exchange at market prices and the prices of production. For Marx the story went something like this. In the specific mode of production and accompanying social relations identified as capitalism there is a division between owners of property in means of production and free labor. In this relation labor takes on all the aspects of a commodity – but a very special one, for its "*use value*" (to the capitalists who buy this commodity) is the production of goods whose *exchange-value* (measured in labor time) is greater than the *exchange-value* of the commodity labor itself, namely the cost of production of labor, or the goods needed to support and reproduce it. In other words, the cost of producing the wage in terms of labor time is less than the amount of time the laborer must exchange for the wage.

This difference in value, or surplus-value, is determined by general social relations between the class of free laborers and the class of owners of property in means of production: the proportion of paid to unpaid labor time (the amount of time it takes to produce the equivalent of the wage and the total working day) is what determines the rate of surplus value or the rate of exploitation. The total number of laborers productively employed times the general rate of surplus-value determines the total amount of surplus value produced. Thus Marx was interested to show that when labor-power, as well as all other commodities, exchanged at its value, surplus value still existed in terms of unpaid labor time. Much misunderstanding has been created because Marx was so anxious to show that profit was not "profit upon alienation," something in excess of the labor time contained in commodities, or a result of selling dear and buying cheap. Thus Marx took the case of equal exchange at values as an extreme case in Volume I.

> His profit – as far as the worker is concerned – arises not from his having sold the worker the commodity *above* its value, but from his having previously bought it from the worker, as a matter of fact in the production process, below its value. (Marx, 1972, p. 19)

> The excess of its value (that is, what the commodity itself costs) over and above the value of the capital expended (that is what it costs the capitalist) constitutes the profit which, therefore results not from selling the commodity above its value but from selling it above the value of the advances the capitalist made. (Marx, 1972, p. 81)

It is surplus-value determined in the production process that is the basis of profit and thus the explanation of distribution. In the post-Keynesian system it is in the relations of commodity exchange that profit arises and where it thus appears as if there is an excess, a surcharge on commodities sold to labor that must cover investment and capitalist consumption. This is a position most contrary to that of Marx. For the post-Keynes system, profit exists either because investment is taking place and/or the capitalists consume; for Marx it is because of the dual nature of labor, especially the role of labor power as a commodity utilized in the process of production, definitely not as a result of exploitation in commodity exchange.

Given Marx's emphasis on the existence of surplus value when all commodities exchange at their value (an assumption analagous to Keynes's of flexible wages and prices, i.e. an extreme case), it remains to clear up some problems related to the so-called transformation problem. In aggregate terms the relation is clear; the sum of surplus value produced is equal to the amount of profit. The assumption of uniform organic composition of capital allows the same result for individual sectors. But surplus-value is earned on the employment of variable capital, while under the capitalist mode of production, profit is allocated on the amount of total capital advanced; thus the production relations in terms of value depart from the exchange relations in terms of prices of production when the proportions of constant to variable capital depart from uniformity in all sectors. This way of viewing the system resulted because the capitalists dominated not only production relations but also the way economists viewed the system. It was not an arbitrary phenomenon, or an insoluble puzzle. Marx's most revealing statements on capitalist exchange relations come in *Theories of Surplus Value,* written before either the first or third volume of *Capital*. It also indicates why he found it necessary to concentrate Volume I on the assumption of price equal to value to show the underlying relations determining the existence of surplus value and therefore profit, unhindered by the superficial appearance of profit as an excess extracted by the capitalist in exchange and sale of commodities.

> *The cost to the capitalist consists in the capital he advances* – in the sum of values he expends on production – *not in the labour, which he does not perform,* and which only costs *him* what he pays for it. This is a very good reason for the capitalists to calculate and distribute the (social) surplus-value amongst themselves according to the size of their capital outlay and not according to the quantity of immediate labour which a given capital puts into motion, but it does not explain where the surplus value – which has to be distributed and is distributed in this way – comes from. (Marx, 1972, p. 74)

It is clear, therefore, that although the cost-prices of most commodities must differ from

> their values, and hence the 'cost of production' of these commodities must differ from the total quantity of labour contained in them, nevertheless, those costs of production and those cost-prices are not only determined by the values of the commodities and confirm the law of value instead of contradicting it, but, moreover, that the very existence of costs of production and cost-prices can be comprehended only on the basis of value and its laws, and becomes a meaningless absurdity without that premise. (Marx, 1972, pp. 82–83)

Marx not only understood the relation, found under capitalism, between prices and values, but also that this relation was necessary for the operation of capitalism. His main point, however, is that even when the transformation process is understood and explained, neither the process of transformation nor the prices that result from it are of any use in explaining the specific operation of the capitalist mode of production in producing profit. To answer his initial question Marx relied on his theory of value, under the simplified assumption of Volume I, more as an aid to strip the process to its bare essentials than to avoid an explanation of the far less important problem of transformation, which is merely the distribution of profit *among the capitalists*. Here, then, is the basic theoretical difference between Marx and the post-Keynesian theory. The latter is content to look only at relations of exchange, and only from the point of view of the capitalists. It is all the more striking, then, that the inequity of the wage distribution system shows through even from the perspective, so much so that it requires the assistence of ideology to accept such a system (Mandel, 1968, Ch. 15).

The main reason that post-Keynesian theory is so revealing, is that while refusing to analyze value, it nevertheless does emphasize production relations. In the Keynesian system the real wage is *not determined in exchange,* but only confirmed by it. Once the proportion of investment to output is fixed, as we have seen, a maximum to the real wage is given (this holds strictly in the $s_w = 0, s_p = 1$ version, other assumptions require modifications),[9] the price system only acts to confirm the distribution between wages (consumption goods) and profits (capital goods). To take an example: in the simple post-Keynesian model outlined above, assume that there is no investment. Then the real wage is equal to the output of each laborer, the rate of profit is zero (demand for goods is equal to the wage bill). It thus appears that only when investment is going on do profits exists and real wages fall below each worker's output. When investment exists, the consumption sector's workers must produce goods for themselves plus goods to feed the investment sector workers. These goods eventually form capitalist's profits in terms of capital goods produced in the investment sector. In this sense it is the workers who produce the capital goods that represent the capitalists' profit.[10] In fact, this scheme is not too different from the way Marx viewed the system: "If the surplus labour is equal to half a day, it is the same as if half the working class produces means of subsistence for the working class and the other half produces raw materials, machinery and finished products for the capitalists, partly as producers and partly as consumers." (Marx, 1972, p. 363)

Thus the I/Y relation in the Keynesian system corresponds broadly to Marx's concept of exploitation. It is therefore comprehensible that the two theories should lead to similar recommendations regarding the alleviation of inequality. The base of Marx's theory – the theory of value – is necessary to explain how this inequality arises, while the Keynesian theory pragmatically takes it as a matter of fact.

Conclusions

In sum, it could be said that the post-Keynesian theory is neo-Marxist, but only in the strict sense of the prescriptions for the change necessary to eradicate inequality. It must also be noted that this result, which can be logically derived from the basis of Keynes' theory, requires a rather great radicalization of that theory. The result also points up the fact that the inequality results not only from individual ownership of property in means of production, but also from the operation of exchange in terms of either prices or values to distribute the social product. It was in this realm of the dynamic function of prices that both Marx and Keynes heard discord in the neoclassical harmony, yet this realm still remains the most prized part of that theory in orthodox eyes. However, in respect of their own theories, one cannot find full accord between Marx and the post-Keynesians, although they analyze the same social phenomena in a similar way. Post-Keynesian theory takes capitalism as given, and therefore is forced to analyse the system from the point of view of the capitalists, i.e., from exchange and prices. It does provide an explanation of the determination of the rate of profit, and of distribution, but this explanation is based primarily in the sphere of exchange. The real relations, though little emphasized, lie in the simple production relations symbolized in the division of product between available and nonavailable goods. It does not explain or seek to explain why profit itself exists.

For Marx on the other hand, the theory of value was the crucial factor in explaining the real relations of capitalism, for he sought to go behind the illusory relations of exchange to the deeper relations of production. Understanding labor as a commodity, as a special commodity, the existence of surplus value could be explained even when all commodities exchanged at their values. Surplus-value then explained the existence of profits and distribution. The transformation problem, since it is only concerned with the distribution of profits among the capitalists, is of little importance to this question although it is arguably crucial in explaining the dynamic of capitalist crises.

Thus Marx would hardly accept the post-Keynesian approach as neo-Marxist, except possibly in the sense of his despairing disclaimer, "Je ne suis pas Marxiste."

Looking a bit deeper, the theoretical similarity that does exist can be traced back to the base of Ricardo and the concept of the economic surplus. The difference, of course, is that Marx went below the surface of Ricardo's analysis to try and rectify the theory of value. In this sense Marx considered his discovery of the dual nature of labor to be the basic point of difference between his theory and Ricardo's (and his missing it, naturally, the latter's greatest error). The post-Keynesian analysis has only so much of Ricardo as was ingeniously passed on through Marshall and Keynes, and has thus tended to reject the search for a measure of value as badly posed. Sraffa has now offered an alternate solution to Ricardo's problem of the measure of value, which has proved to be of great critical use to the post-Keynesians. It should also provide a basis to strengthen the revival of Ricardian thought in both the neo-Marxian and the post-Keynesian traditions.

Notes

1 It should be noted, however, that even the negative aspects are not exactly equivalent (Bukharin, 1927; Dobb, 1937; Sraffa, 1951, 1960; Garegnani, 1960; Robinson, 1953–54).

2 Keynes examined a given position at a given point of time with its associated expectations and uncertainty; he was not concerned with the solution price vector of a set of simultaneous equations. A further question is whether the money or the real wage should be taken as the price of labor. In Keynes's view the real wage could not be determined by supply and demand in the market for labor, but was a result of the macro relations of the system. The money wage could be so determined, but it was an observable fact and a desirable consequence for the preservation of a money economy that the money wage was inflexible downwards. In the *General Theory* (pp. 236–40) it is taken as a necessity to have flexible real wages with stable money wages if money as a store of value is to be preserved. To be realistic, one must recognize that in a capitalist economy, contracts are fixed for non-negligible periods of time in money (Keynes, 1936).

3 Here Keynes was calling for the State to provide the information function that the price system was incapable of providing in a dynamic sense (Keynes, 1936, pp. 213–17).

4 Yet some economists argue to the contrary and hold that capitalist class consciousness tends to preserve the capitalist system (Lukacs, 1971; Kalecki, 1971, p. 152; Leon, 1967).

5 This is, of course, a straightforward rejection of the operation of relative prices to yield sufficient information either at a point in time or over time.

6 The investors always have recourse to the banking system which issues command over resources in the form of money so that the funds required for desired investment are always available. For Keynes the problem was never an insufficient level of savings but the possibility of an insufficient supply of cash (Keynes, 1937, pp. 668–69).

7 The determination of the rate of profit and exchange with the investment sector is ignored for brevity (Robinson, 1956). Under the assumptions given here total profit is equal to the net addition to capital equipment in the period. It is usually assumed that competition equalizes the rate of profit earned in the two sectors. The system as outlined need not involve initial full-employment. When the system is at less than full employment the overall effect on distribution depends on whether I/Y rises or falls with a higher level of investment, i.e., on the change in N_i/N_c as total N grows. (See Kregel, 1973.)

8 Keynes expresses reserved satisfaction with the allocation of product by the price mechanism. His main complaint was that unemployment was inequitable (Keynes, 1936).

9 Under alternative formulations the concept of the real wage ceases to have clear meaning (Kregel, 1973, Chapter 11), where some of the problems between real and social categories that arise when $s_w \neq 0$ are discussed.

10 This example is somewhat misleading, since it ignores a basic problem in the Keynesian analysis. If employment in the investment sector is zero the system is not even replacing its capital stock; for the system to be in a stationary state some workers must be employed in the investment sector to provide replacements for machines that are wearing out. If this is the case net investment is still zero and thus the rate of profit is zero. But in such a case why would the capitalists continue to produce? One answer is consumption out of profits allowing $\pi > 0$; outside this case there is a gap in the continuum of the relation of the rate of profit to the rate of investment, when net investment approaches zero and is equal to zero. For Marx, however,

surplus value is being created, but is necessary to replace used up value in production. The capitalists must continue to produce to preserve their invested capital.

References

Bukharin, N. 1927. *Economic Theory of the Leisure Class*. London: Martin Lawrence.
Dobb, M. 1937. *Political Economy of Capitalism*. London: Routledge.
Garegnani, P. 1960. *Il Capitale Nelle Teorie della Distribuzione*. Milan: Giuffrè.
Harcourt, G. C., and Nell, E. 1970. "A Note on Cambridge Controversies in Capital Theory," *Journal of Economic Literature*, Vol. 8: pp. 41–45.
Kalecki, M. 1971. *Selected Essays on the Dynamic of Capitalist Economy*. Cambridge: Cambridge University Press.
Keynes, J. M. 1936. *The General Theory of Employment, Interest and Money*. London: Macmillan.
1937. "The Ex-Ante Theory of the Rate of Interest," *Economic Journal*, 47: pp. 663–69.
1963. "On the Theory of a Monetary Economy," *Nebraska Journal of Economics and Business*.
Kregel, J. A. 1971. *Rate of Profits, Distribution and Growth: Two Views*. London: Aldine.
1973. *The Reconstruction of Political Economy*, New York: Halsted Press.
Leon, P. 1967. *Structural Change and Growth in Capitalism*. Baltimore: Johns Hopkins Press.
Lukacs, G. 1971. *History and Class Consciousness*. London: Merlin Press Ltd.
MacPherson, C. B. 1962. *The Political Theory of Possessive Individualism*. Oxford: Oxford University Press.
Mandel, E. 1968. *Marxist Economic Theory*. London: Merlin Press.
Marx, K. 1972. *Theories of Surplus Value*. 3 vols. Moscow: Progress Publishers.
1947. *Wages, Price and Profit*. Moscow: Progress Publishers.
Means, G. 1959. "Administered Prices Reconsidered," *American Economic Review*, 49: pp. 451–61.
Robinson, J. 1956. *The Accumulation of Capital*. London: Macmillan.
1953. *On Re-reading Marx*. Cambridge: Students' Bookshops.
1953–54. "The Production Function and the Theory of Capital," *Review of Economic Studies, XXI:* pp. 81–106.
Sraffa, P. 1951 in "Introduction" to Ricardo's *Collected Works*. Cambridge: Cambridge University Press, pp. XII–LXII.
1960. *Production of Commodities by Means of Commodities*. Cambridge: Cambridge University Press.

17

Cambridge economics as commodity fetishism

Frank Roosevelt

> They fail generally from limiting themselves to a guerrilla war against the effects of the system instead of simultaneously trying to change it, instead of using their organized forces as a lever for the final emancipation of the working class, that is to say, [for] the ultimate abolition of the wages system.
>
> [Karl Marx, *Wages, Price and Profit*].

Introduction

The purpose here is to help students of radical political economics understand two of the main approaches available to them. On the one side, I present the basic concepts of Karl Marx and, on the other, I examine the recent work of the Cambridge school – a group of economists associated with the University of Cambridge, England (hereafter referred to as the Cantabrigians).[1] As the reader will see, my own preference is for the Marxian approach. Indeed, in the last section of the essay I argue that the approach of the Cantabrigians can be criticized in much the same way that Marx criticized the economics of his own time.

The task undertaken here is important for two reasons. Since the Cambridge school originally gained its fame by attacking some of the central concepts of neoclassical economics (Harcourt, 1969; Rowthorn, 1974), it has attracted the attention of many radicals. In addition, several writers have treated the new economics of Cambridge as if it were a continuation of the Marxian tradition: Maurice Dobb and Ronald Meek have praised one of the founders of the Cambridge school, Piero Sraffa, for having "rehabilitated" Marx (Dobb, 1973, pp. 248–66; Meek, 1967, pp. 161–78); Geoffrey Harcourt has asserted that Cantabrigians such as Amit Bhaduri, Joan Robinson, and Edward Nell "look to Marx's theory of exploitation" to explain the distribution of income (Harcourt, 1969, p. 394); Nell himself has used the word "neo-Marxian" as a label for the Cantabrigian approach (Nell, 1970, p. 43); and others have even talked about "the Sraffa-Marx model" (Hunt and Sherman, 1972, p. 35). If the interpretation of these writers is correct, it would seem that radicals have a lot to learn from the Cambridge school.

The position taken here is that it is fundamentally incorrect to link together the approaches of Marx and the Cantabrigians. In what follows it is argued that the two define their basic concepts in different ways, employ contrasting methods of analysis, orient themselves to different questions, paint conflicting pictures of the economy, and suggest alternative strategies for political action.

As broad as it is, this chapter confronts only one part of a larger task. In its fullest develop-

The ideas presented here were developed with the help of the following members of the faculty of the New School for Social Research: David Gordon, Robert Heilbroner, Edward Nell, Anwar Shaikh, and Thomas Vietorisz. I enjoyed invaluable assistance from the late Stephen Hymer, and I have had the benefit of constant criticism and support from Philip Harvey. As earlier drafts were circulated, I received helpful comments from Frances Foster, Richard Garrett, Makoto Itoh, Jinx Roosevelt, Lillian Salzman, Jesse Schwartz, Tom Seidl, Nina Shapiro, Paul Sweezy, and members of the editorial board of the *Review of Radical Political Economics*. I, of course, take responsibility for any remaining defects.

This chapter appeared originally in *The Review of Radical Political Economics*, Vol. 7, No. 4, Winter 1975, pp. 1–32. A more extended version of the argument of this essay is presented in my Ph.D. dissertation, "Towards a Marxist Critique of the Cambridge School," New School for Social Research, September 1976, available on microfilm.

ment, radical political economics should be able to help us answer two kinds of questions, one *static* and the other *dynamic:* (1) How can one type of society be *differentiated* from another? (2) How does one type of society become *transformed* into another? Here I consider the economics of Marx and the Cantabrigians only in relation to the first question; the whole problem of dynamic analysis is not dealt with here. Nevertheless, by pointing out how the Cantabrigians diverge from Marx in their method of differentiating societies it is possible to argue that they mystify the defining characteristics of capitalism and fail to grasp what the struggle for socialism is all about. This, in a nutshell, is the argument of the present chapter.

In the first section, I contrast the Marxian and the Cantabrigian approaches to the *general* problem of differentiating societies. This requires taking up the question of historical periodization, for we usually demarcate and identify historical periods according to the type of society that is dominant in each one. In the second part of the essay I explain how the application of the Marxian and Cantabrigian approaches to the *specific* case of capitalism results not only in two very different views of our own society but also in diverging images of what a socialist society of the future ought to look like.

In my examination of Cantabrigian economics I refer mainly to the writings of two people, Piero Sraffa and Joan Robinson. Sraffa (1960), is generally treated by Cantabrigians as the cornerstone of their theoretical edifice (Robinson, 1971b, p. 22; Nell, Chapter 1 of this book). Robinson is the most distinguished of the Cantabrigians and is widely regarded as their leader. She was the one who heralded their attack on orthodox economics in a 1953 article (Robinson, 1953), and in the years since then, she has advocated the Cambridge position all over the world. In the United States, for example, she recently published an article in *Monthly Review* urging the new generation of American radical economists to train themselves in Cantabrigian economics (Robinson, 1971b).

In 1973 Robinson joined with a Cambridge colleague, John Eatwell and published the first Cantabrigian textbook: *An Introduction to Modern Economics* (Robinson and Eatwell, 1973). Since this text explicitly presents the Cantabrigian approach, I refer to it frequently in this essay.

Methods of historical periodization

In the two parts of this section the Marxian and the Cantabrigian approaches to the problem of periodizing history are presented. In each approach the method of periodization is based on a particular way of looking at production in human societies; the way production is seen depends in turn on certain theoretical abstractions. Hence, in contrasting Marx and the Cantabrigians the connections between their basic abstractions, their views of production, and their perspectives on history are traced.

Marx's approach. Marx's approach to the problem of historical periodization was based on his concept of a *mode of production* (Balibar, 1970, pp. 199–308). The earliest discussion of this concept may be found in *The German Ideology* where it is defined as "the way in which men produce their means of subsistence" (Marx and Engels, 1970, p. 42). As straightforward as this definition is, the concept of a mode of production is not a simple one. Indeed, the only way one can grasp its full complexity is to take it apart, examine each of its components, and then see how its various parts are related to each other in the whole.

To take something apart in one's mind for the purpose of understanding it is to use the technique of *analysis,* and the intermediate results that one arrives at by using this technique are called *abstractions.* Thus the procedure employed here is essentially the one Marx referred to in the preface to the first edition of *Capital:* "In the analysis of economic forms . . . neither microscopes nor chemical reagents are of use. The force of abstraction must replace both" (Marx, 1967, Vol. I, p. 8). In what follows, we will see what it means to rely upon "the force of abstraction."

Marx's basic abstractions. Presented here is an exposition of the two notions that Marx often referred to as the "forces" and "relations" of production. However, for reasons which are elaborated in Balibar (1970, pp. 233 ff.), I prefer not to use these terms.

Marx's concept of a mode of production may best be understood as a combination of two basic abstractions. Marx himself must have arrived at these abstractions before 1846 as they appear in *The German Ideology* in a passage explaining the materialist approach to history: "This conception of history depends on our ability to expound the real process of production, starting out from *the material production of life itself,* and to comprehend *the form of intercourse* connected with this" (Marx and Engels, 1970, p. 58; italics added). Since the context indicates that what is meant by "the form of intercourse" in this sentence is identical with what Marx would later refer to as the social form of production, we can see in this passage the two basic abstractions that make up his concept of a mode of production: (1) The material aspect of production; (2) The social form of production. These two abstractions play a role in all of Marx's mature work for in his view the essence of any given society is the particular way that the material and social aspects of its production process are combined. But what is the nature of each of these abstractions, and how did Marx distinguish one from the other?

In *The German Ideology* Marx's basic abstractions are presented *as if* one of them refers to the *physical* aspect of production and the other to its *social* aspect. Near the beginning of this work, for example, the material aspect of production is described in the following way: "The first premise of all human history is, of course, the existence of living human individuals. Thus the first fact to be established is the physical organization of these individuals and their consequent relation to the rest of nature" (Marx and Engels, 1970, p. 42). On the same page, the social form of production is introduced in this fashion: "[A] mode of production must not be considered simply as being the production of the physical existence of the individuals. Rather it is a definite form of activity of these individuals, a definite form of expressing their life" (Marx and Engels, 1970, p. 42). After reading these two passages one might get the impression that Marx arrived at his basic abstractions simply by separating the social and the physical aspects of human production. This, however, is not the case. The basis for a correct interpretation of the above passages may be found a few pages later in *The German Ideology* where the discussion of the mode of production concept is summed up as follows: "The production of life, both of one's own in labour and of fresh life in procreation, now appears as *a double relationship:* on the one hand as a natural, on the other as a social relationship" (Marx and Engels, 1970, p. 50; italics added). The key phrase here is "a double relationship." These words capture the essence of Marx's concept of a mode of production. Their full significance will become evident as we examine the view of production that Marx developed in his later work.

Marx's view of production. In *Capital* Marx treated production as a process involving the interaction of four crucial elements. The three which he regarded as necessary to *all* human production were presented in the chapter on the labor-process: "The elementary factors of the labour-process are: (1) the personal activity of man, *i.e.*, work itself, (2) the subject of that work, and (3) its instruments" (Marx, 1967, Vol. I, p. 178). An additional element was introduced by Marx in his chapter on cooperation; it comes into play when production is carried on by a substantial number of people working together:

> All combined labour on a large scale requires, more or less, a directing authority, in order to secure the harmonious working of the individual activities, and to perform the general functions that have their origin in the action of the combined organism, as distinguished from the action of its separate organs. A single violin player is his own conductor; an orchestra requires a separate one. (Marx, 1967, Vol. I, pp. 330–31)

Relating these two passages, and modifying the terminology somewhat, we may say that Marx regarded all human production on a large scale as a process involving the following four elements: (1) a coordinating agency; (2) work itself (the activity of the direct producers); (3) instruments of production; (4) objects transformed in production. The interaction of these four elements may be seen with the help of a simple diagram:

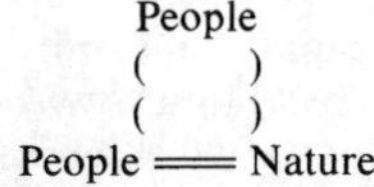

In this diagram, the "people" at the top are the "coordinating agency" while those on the lower level are the "direct producers" who do the "work itself." The symbol ══ represents "the instruments of production" and the word "nature" stands for "the objects transformed in production." Production, then, was seen by Marx as a process in which these four elements interact.

But in what sense did Marx think of production as a process which involves "a double relationship?" And how did he apply his two basic abstractions to the four elements listed above? To answer these questions we must consult the *Grundrisse,* the notebooks written by Marx in 1857 and 1858. At one point in these notebooks Marx temporarily treats the production process of a capitalist society as if it were "only a *material relation* . . . as distinct from its *formal relation* as capital" (Marx, 1973, p. 302; italics added). Then, using the word "capital" to refer to the specific character of production in a capitalist society, he proceeds as follows:

> Regarded from this side [i.e., regarded as a material relation], the process of capital coincides with the simple process of production as such . . . Thus the process of the production of capital does not appear as the process of the production of capital, but as the process of production in general . . . Its formal charac-

> ter is completely extinguished. (Marx, 1973, pp. 303–04)

In the same place Marx went on to define the *labor-process* as the aspect of production that one sees when "its formal character is completely extinguished." In his view, the labor-process is nothing more than the material aspect of production which, "owing to its abstractness, its pure materiality, is common to all forms of production" (Marx, 1973, p. 304). We will shortly be drawing out the implications of these quotations with regard to Marx's method of periodizing history. At this point, however, they are cited to indicate that *his basic abstractions are merely two different ways of looking at the interaction of the various elements in the production process*. In other words, when Marx used one or the other of his dual abstractions he simply pretended that the aspect of production not under consideration at the moment had ceased to exist.

Marx's two ways of looking at production may be distinguished in the following manner: (1) When the elements in the production process are regarded from the standpoint of their material interaction, the relations among them can be described in socially neutral terms. As we have noted, Marx himself used the metaphor of an orchestra and its conductor to express the quality of these relations in such a context. Using another kind of analogy, we might think of the material relations between the coordinating agency and the other elements as a set of information flows, the role of the coordinating agency being similar, let us say, to that of the main computer in an automated process of production. In any case, the hallmark of this way of looking at the production process is that each element in it is considered solely with regard to the material function it fulfills. (2) When one looks at production from the standpoint of its social form, on the other hand, both the elements and the relations among them appear in a different light. In this case, the elements themselves are either identified with or used by specific historical classes of people, and the relations among them are seen as antagonistic. (This statement applies of course only to societies in which there are class divisions; different wording would have to be used to discuss the social form of production in a classless society.)

The point, which needs to be stressed here, is that Marx conceived of his basic abstractions as but one-sided views of a total reality. Thus, even when he was focusing on one or the other aspect of the production process, *he always took into account the presence of all four of its constituent elements*. Referring to the social form of production in the first chapter of *Capital*, for example, he spoke of "the social relations within the sphere of material life, between man and man, and between man and Nature" (Marx, 1967, Vol. I, p. 79). Similarly, when he looked at the other aspect of the production process he continued to treat it as a relationship between four different elements. It is for this reason that his concept of a mode of production may be described as involving "a double relationship."

Marx on periodizing history. Marx's method of historical periodization was cogently summed up in a few sentences in Volume II of *Capital*. Here, the word "labourers" refers to the direct producers and the term "means of production" encompasses the two elements previously referred to as "the instruments of production" and "the objects transformed in production:"

> Whatever the social form of production, labourers and means of production always remain factors of it. But in a state of separation from each other either of these factors can be such only potentially. For production to go on at all they must unite. The specific manner in which this union is accomplished distinguishes the different economic epochs of the structure of society from one another. (Marx, 1967, Vol. II, p. 34)

In speaking here of "the specific manner in which this union is accomplished" Marx was clearly bringing to bear his concept of a mode of production. But how, exactly, do the two aspects of this concept enter into his method of periodizing history?

It is not difficult to see how Marx used the social form of production to differentiate one historical type of society from another. Consider, for example, the passage in *Capital* in which he drew a dividing line between the feudal and the capitalist epochs in history: "The starting-point of the development that gave rise to the wage-labourer, as well as to the capitalist, was the servitude of the labourer. The advance consisted in *a change of form* of this servitude, in the transformation of feudal exploitation into capitalist exploitation" (Marx, 1967, Vol. I, p. 715; italics added). From this we can see that Marx differentiated class-divided societies from one another on the basis of their form of exploitation. He could do this because, in his view, exploitation is the chief characteristic of the social form of production in such societies.

Marx's concept of exploitation was based on his distinction between "necessary" and "surplus" labor – the former being the amount of labor required to produce what the workers in any given society need to sustain and reproduce themselves, and the latter being the additional labor which a society's dominant class is able to induce its workers to perform (Marx, 1967, Vol. I, p. 216–17). Thus, it was no accident that he gave us a clear statement of his method of differentiating societies in the middle of a discussion of necessary and surplus labor:

> The essential difference between the various economic forms of society, between, for instance, a society based on slave-labour, and one based on wage-labour, lies only in *the mode in which this surplus-labour is in each case extracted from the actual producer,* the labourer. (Marx, 1967, Vol. I, p. 217; italics added)

In Marx's view, then, exploitation is the extraction of surplus labor from those who do the work in a given society, and the particular form of this exploitation is what differentiates one type of society from another.

So much for the social form of production as a tool for periodizing history. What about the other part of Marx's concept of a mode of production, the material aspect of the production process? Does it not also have a role to play?

A passage has already been quoted from the *Grundrisse* in which Marx defined the labor-process as a relation "common to all forms of production." This definition reappears in a more developed form in the chapter on the labor-process in *Capital:*

> The labour-process . . . is the necessary condition for effecting exchange of matter between man and Nature; it is the everlasting Nature-imposed condition of human existence, and therefore is independent of every social phase of that existence, or rather, is common to every such phase . . . As the taste of the porridge does not tell you who grew the oats, no more does this simple process tell you of itself what are the social conditions under which it is taking place, whether under the slaveowner's brutal lash, or the anxious eye of the capitalist. (Marx, 1967, Vol. I, pp. 183–84)

Such a passage could conceivably be interpreted to mean that Marx believed that the labor-process goes on in basically the same way throughout history. If this were in fact the case, he could hardly have referred to it in his method of historical periodization. As it happens, however, Marx did not think of the labor-process in this way.

Marx's comments on the labor-process may be understood if we recall that in his work this term refers only to the abstraction we have labelled "the material aspect of production." In the passage already quoted from the *Grundrisse* he defined this aspect of the production process as the side of it that one sees when "its formal character is completely extinguished." And, in the very same passage, he went on to issue the following qualification: "It will be seen that even within the production process itself this extinguishing of the formal character is merely a semblance" (Marx, 1973, p. 304). We may interpret this to mean that, in Marx's view, the labor-process itself takes on new forms as societies evolve. This interpretation is confirmed by a statement Marx himself made near the end of Volume III of *Capital:* "To the extent that the labour-process is solely a process between man and Nature, its simple elements remain common to all social forms of development. But each specific historical form of this process further develops its material foundations and social forms" (Marx, 1967, Vol. III, p. 883). Taking this passage as our guide, then, we may say that, for Marx, the presence of the various elements of production is a general requirement of all human societies, but the form they take and the way they are connected changes materially as well as socially from one historical epoch to the next. As a result, both the social form and the material aspect of production are taken into account in Marx's method of periodizing history.

We saw earlier that Marx's two basic abstractions may be thought of as alternate ways of looking at the "double relationship" connecting the various elements of the production process. We have now seen that both of these aspects of his concept of a mode of production are used in his method of historical periodization. All that remains to be discussed is the particular way in which Marx's basic abstractions are related *to each other* in his approach to history.

The way in which Marx thought of the relationship between his basic abstractions may be seen in a passage in *Capital* in which he stressed the importance of looking at one of the elements of production – namely, the instruments of production – when attempting to differentiate one type of society from another:

> Relics of bygone instruments of labour possess the same importance for the investigation of extinct economic forms of society as do fossil bones for the determination of extinct species of animals. It is not the articles made, but how they are made, and by what instruments, that enables us to distinguish different economic epochs. Instruments of labour not only supply a standard of the degree of development to which human labour has attained, but they are also indicators of the social conditions under which that labour is carried on. (Marx, 1967, Vol. I, pp. 179–80)

Since Marx was clearly treating the instruments of production here from the standpoint of the material aspect of production, we may interpret his "fossil bones" metaphor to mean that he regarded the connection between his two basic abstractions as an *organic* one: Though the material and social aspects of production may be distinguished from each other – just as the bones of an animal may be distinguished from its flesh – the organic relationship between them allows the form of the first to serve as an "indicator" of the form of the second.

Marx's method of periodizing history may be summed up as follows: His approach to history was based on his concept of a mode of production which, in turn, may be thought of as a combination of two basic abstractions, the social form and the material aspect of production. These abstractions are simply two different ways of looking at the interaction of four key elements in the production process; and, because they are but two perspectives on the same interaction, they are organically related to each other.

The Cantabrigian approach. The Cantabrigians are also interested in developing a method of periodizing history. At one point in *An Introduction to Modern Economics,* for example, Robinson and Eatwell make the following statement: "[We] cannot pretend to give an account of actual historical situations, but [our analysis] is intended to show the main principles underlying identifiable periods of economic evolution" (Robinson and Eatwell, 1973, p. 62). In developing their method of historical periodization, however, the Cantabrigians take an approach which differs from that of Marx at every step of the way.

The Cantabrigians' basic abstractions. Though they do not employ Marx's concept of a mode of production, Robinson and Eatwell begin their analysis by separating all economic relationships into two basic abstractions: "technical relations" and "social relations" (Robinson and Eatwell, 1973, p. 63). "Technical relations" are defined as those which occur "between mankind and the physical universe" (Robinson and Eatwell, 1973, p. 54). Whenever Robinson and Eatwell discuss such relations they isolate them from the surrounding social framework and focus only on the quantitative relationships between the inputs and outputs of the production process. (An example of such relations would be a situation in which additional increments of labor applied to a fixed quantity of land produce smaller and smaller increases in the output from the land.) When Robinson and Eatwell discuss "social relations," on the other hand, they abstract from the interaction between people and nature and focus exclusively on "relationships between people" (Robinson and Eatwell, 1973 p. 54). In contrast with Marx's view of production as "a double relationship," then, the Cantabrigians treat the productive interaction of people among themselves and with nature as if it consisted of *two separate relationships:*

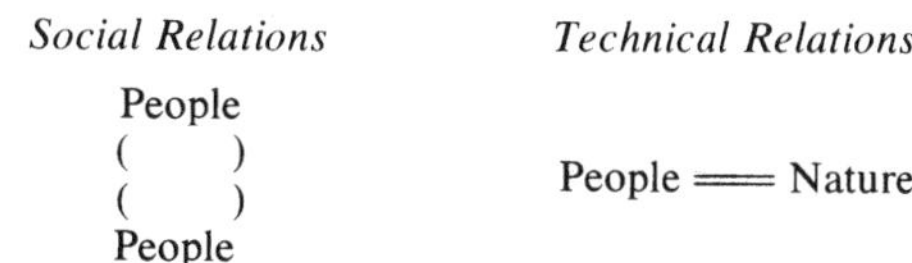

With the help of these diagrams (which employ the same symbols that were used to represent Marx's view of production) we can see that when the Cantabrigians use one or the other of their two basic abstractions *they alternately disregard the presence in the production process of one or more of its constituent elements.* For example, when Robinson and Eatwell define "technical relations" with reference only to "mankind" and "the physical universe" they collapse two of the elements of production, the coordinating agency and work itself, into one category. This procedure has the effect of obscuring an important aspect of the production process, namely, the interaction between the people who coordinate it and those who do the work itself. Similarly, when Robinson and Eatwell define "social relations" exclusively in terms of "relationships between people" they neglect the role of the two nonhuman elements in the production process (i.e., the instruments of production and the objects transformed in production). As we will see, the consequence of defining "social relations" in this manner is that the Cantabrigians find themselves able to think of such relations only as occurring outside of the production process itself.

The Cantabrigian view of production. In contrast with Marx (who employed both of his abstractions in his analysis of production), the Cantabrigians use only one of their basic abstractions to represent the production process: In their view, *production consists of those interactions between people and nature which can be portrayed as technical relations.*

The most important statement of the Cantabrigian view of production is Piero Sraffa's *Production of Commodities by Means of Commodities.* In this book production is represented by rows of mathematical symbols, each row showing the physical quantities of inputs that are required to produce a given amount of a certain type of output. Sraffa himself refers to the connections among these quantitative symbols as "relations" (Sraffa, 1960, p. 3) and, as we will see, they are one example of what Robinson and Eatwell have in mind when they speak of "technical relations." Sraffa's view of production has been summed up by Nell in Chapter 1 as follows: "The basic constituents of [the] theory are industries, sectors, processes, or activities, defined in technological terms." Thus people as human beings – and, more importantly, as historical social classes – are given no role in the process of production.[2]

The absence of social relations in the Cantabrigian view of production may also be observed in the Robinson and Eatwell textbook. In one of its chapters, for example, we are presented with a model of an economy consisting of only two activities, one producing corn and the other turning out machines. In this economy the following role is assigned to technical relations: "[The] technical relations of our model consist of one technique for producing corn and one for producing machines. These govern the relation of work to machines and to output in each sector" (Robinson and Eatwell, 1973, p. 90). Upon reading this passage, one wonders whether technical relations by themselves are sufficient to determine how much work gets done on each machine or how much output is produced in each sector. The authors themselves seem to be aware that something is missing since they do point out that the output per machine in each sector depends "first, on output per man hour of a team of men working [the] machines, and second, [on] the hours per day and days per year that the machines can be worked" (Robinson and Eatwell, 1973, p. 91). But, after noting that "the length of the working day for a team of men involves problems of great social and political significance," they immediately fall back to the following position: "These questions we leave on one side; we assume that there is a standard length [of the working day]" (Robinson and Eatwell, 1973). And nowhere do they explain how the direct producers in their economy are actually induced to perform the amount of work required on each machine by the model's technical relations.

It should be clear from what has been said that the Cantabrigians define and use their most fundamental concepts in a way that separates their approach from that of Marx. But how, we may ask, do they think of the relationship *between* their two basic abstractions? Again, the answer is to be found in Robinson and Eatwell.

The main part of *An Introduction to Modern Economics* is devoted to analysis, and near the beginning of this part the authors make the following statement: "Here, we shall first set up a model of very simple technological specifications and consider how it operates in various social settings" (Robinson and Eatwell, 1973, p. 61). They then proceed to posit the existence of a particular set of technical relations and to speculate on what would happen to output and distribution if these technical relations were associated first with a society of independent families, then with feudal social relations and, finally, with capitalist social relations (Robinson and Eatwell, 1973, pp. 64–77). Since this procedure is only valid if one assumes that there are no necessary connections between particular sets of technical relations and specific kinds of social relations, we may conclude that Robinson and Eatwell think of their two basic abstractions as fundamentally *independent* of each other. Recalling that Marx thought of his abstractions as organically connected, this is yet another instance of the divergence between Marx and the Cantabrigians.[3]

The crucial difference between the Marxian and the Cantabrigian views of production may now be pinpointed. By having both of his abstractions encompass all of the elements of production, Marx was able to develop an *integrated* view of the interaction of human beings with each other and with their physical environment: He saw production as a dual process, and took into account both its material and its social aspects. In contrast, the Cantabrigians begin their analysis by setting up abstractions which *separate* the two aspects of our economic life. As a result, they end up thinking of production not as a social affair but, rather, as a purely technical process involving only quantitative relationships among physical phenomena.

The reader might wish at this point to raise the objection that the Cantabrigians frequently do refer to social classes – and, certainly, no one familiar with their work would dispute such a statement. What needs to be pointed out, however, is that whenever they mention social classes the reference is always to phenomena *external to the process of production*. For example, many of the Cantabrigians refer to classes and class conflict when they discuss the distribution of income (Harcourt, 1969, p. 394; Nuti, 1971). In this case, however, classes are seen as fighting over the product *after* it has been produced, not as engaged with each other *in* the process of producing it. As Nell has aptly summed up the matter in Chapter 1, the Cantabrigian approach is one which involves "analysis of the system of production and of the social relations *surrounding* production." (Italics added.)

The Cantabrigian practice of dividing the economy into a physical process of production and a social process of distribution is not without precedent in the history of economic thought. John Stuart Mill set forth a century ago the view that although, on the one hand, "the laws and conditions of the production of wealth partake of the character of physical truths," distribution is, on the other, "a matter of human institution solely" (Mill, 1965, p. 199). To make the transition to our next section, we may note that it was precisely in reference to such a view that Marx spoke of "the ineptitude of those economists who portray production as an eternal truth while banishing history to the realm of distribution" (Marx, 1973, p. 97).

The Cantabrigians on periodizing history. When we turn our attention to their method of periodizing history, we see a further consequence of the way the Cantabrigians set up and use their basic abstractions: since they treat production as if it consists only of technical relations, they end up having to differentiate one type of society from another solely on the basis of what they call "social relations."

If production is treated merely as a set of technical relationships connecting various inputs and outputs, it cannot be thought of as assuming different forms in different historical epochs. For this reason the Cantabrigians inevitably regard the production process as occurring in essentially the same way throughout history. (A corollary of this is that their method of representing production may be applied without modification to any historical form of society.)[4] But then, if production is viewed as going on in essentially the same way in all societies, what characteristics can we use to differentiate one type of society from another? Here is how Robinson and Eatwell deal with the problem:

> [T]echnical relations . . . exist in every kind of society. But production is not merely a technical process, it involves social relations as well, in particular, legal rules and accepted conventions concerning claims to property . . . Social systems may be differentiated by the patterns of ownership they have adopted. (Robinson and Eatwell, 1973, p. 63)

Since it is stated here that "production is not merely a technical process, it involves social relations as well," one might infer that the term social relations refers to an aspect of the production process itself. As we can see, however, the authors immediately proceed to define this term with reference only to institutional phenomena *outside of* the actual process of production, namely, "patterns of ownership." Thus, for the Cantabrigians, "social relations" refers to property relations, and, in contrast with Marx (who focused on the complex way in which its various elements are connected with each other in production), societies are differentiated solely on the basis of juridical phenomena.

The differences between the Marxian and the Cantabrigian methods of historical periodization may now be summarized. First, the Cantabrigians depart from Marx both in the definitions they give to their basic abstractions and also in the way they conceive of the relationship between them. Then, separating technical relations from social relations – and treating each as if it were independent of the other – the Cantabrigians use the first to represent production and the second to periodize history. Whereas Marx regarded history as a succession of modes of production, the Cantabrigians see it as a succession of different types of property relations.

Perspectives on capitalism

Having outlined the differences between the approaches of Marx and the Cantabrigians to the general problem of periodizing history, we may now examine the way in which they apply their various analytical tools to the specific case of capitalism. As we proceed through this examination, the political implications of the differences between the two approaches will become evident.

Marx's view of capitalism. In the first part of this essay we saw that Marx distinguishes class-divided societies according to the *form of exploitation* characterizing their processes of production. Exploitation, in his view, is the extraction of surplus labor from those who do the work in a given society, and the particular form of this exploitation is what differentiates one type of class society from another. Accordingly, when Marx looked at capitalism as a distinct form of society he located its distinctiveness in the fact that, in the capitalist mode of production, surplus labor is extracted from the direct producers in the form of *surplus-value*.

In applying his concept of a mode of production to the study of capitalism Marx used his two basic abstractions in the following way: Looking at the capitalist process of production from the standpoint of its material aspect, he analyzed the interaction of its constituent elements as a *labor-process;* when focusing on the social form of this process, on the other hand, he treated it as a *process of creating surplus-value* (Marx, 1967, Vol. I, Ch. 7). To understand Marx's view of capitalism, then, we have to investigate what it means to say that *the labor-process takes the form of a process of creating surplus-value.*

In what follows we will see how Marx analyzed each one of the elements in the capitalist production process *both* with regard to its material interaction with the other elements *and* from the standpoint of the creation of surplus-value.

Moreover, we will see that the specific form taken by each of these elements is determined, in Marx's view, by the unique way in which all of them are related to each other in the capitalist mode of production.

Whenever he analyzed a society's production process, Marx always gave priority to examining the activity of the direct producers. We have already quoted him to the effect that the "essential difference" between a slave-owning society and capitalism is that, while the former is "based on slave-labour," the latter is "based on wage-labour" (Marx, 1967, Vol. I, p. 217). In presenting Marx's view of capitalism, therefore, it is appropriate to begin with his analysis of the form that work itself takes in the capitalist mode of production.

"Work itself" as commodity-producing labor. At the beginning of *Capital* Marx introduces us to the capitalist form of productive activity by discussing the case of "simple commodity production."[5] In the first chapter of this work he establishes the minimum conditions, or social relations, that must be present before one can say that *commodities* are being produced: "As a general rule, articles of utility become commodities only because they are products of the labour of *private individuals* or groups of individuals *who carry on their work independently of each other*" (Marx, 1967, Vol. I, pp. 72–73; italics added). While he does not refer to capitalists or wage-laborers at this point, Marx is already talking about one of the fundamental characteristics of the capitalist form of work, namely, that it is *not organized by the community as a whole;* as he put it in another part of the same chapter, "a community, the produce of which in general takes the form of commodities [is one in which] the useful forms of labour . . . are carried on independently by individual producers, each on their own account" (Marx, 1967, Vol. I, p. 42).

While Marx introduces us to the capitalist form of work by stressing its independent character, he does not of course ask us to think of society as a collection of Robinson Crusoes. The independent producers he has in mind are not self-sufficient; to meet their needs, they must exchange at least a portion of their products with the other producers in the society. Thus another part of Marx's definition of commodities is that they are "produced for the purpose of being exchanged" (Marx, 1967, Vol. I, p. 73).

Since commodities are generally exchanged, they necessarily possess both *use-value* and *exchange-value*. The first of these categories simply refers to the fact that a commodity must be useful in some way, otherwise no one will want to buy it. The exchange-value of a commodity, on the other hand, reflects the condition that it must be exchanged before it is consumed. Marx's conception of exchange-value is fairly complicated, but here we may think of it simply as a quantitative relationship between commodities.

For our present purposes, the use-value/exchange-value distinction is important because Marx employs it in his discussion of commodity-producing labor in the first chapter of *Capital*. After distinguishing between use-value and exchange-value in the first section of this chapter, he goes on in the second section to discuss "the two-fold character of the labour embodied in commodities" (Marx, 1967, Vol. I, p. 41). Since commodities have two aspects, he argues, commodity-producing labor must also have a dual character. Just as the use-value of a commodity may be thought of as the quality of it which enables it to satisfy a particular need, so also may the work that goes into it be regarded as a particular kind of work. Marx spoke of work in this sense as *concrete labor,* and he defined it as "productive activity of a definite kind and exercized with a definite aim" (Marx, 1967, Vol. I, p. 42). The other aspect of commodity-producing labor was referred to by Marx as *abstract labor.* For a clear presentation of the distinction between concrete and abstract labor, it is best to quote directly from *Capital:*

> As use-values, commodities are, above all, of different qualities; but as exchange-values they are merely different quantities . . .
>
> If then we leave out of consideration the use-value of commodities, they have only one common property left, that of being products of labour. But . . . [looking at] the product of labour itself . . . If we make abstraction from its use-value, we make abstraction at the same time from its material elements and shapes that make the product a use-value; we see in it no longer a table, a house, yarn, or any other useful thing. Its existence as a material thing is put out of sight. Neither can it any longer be regarded as the product of the labour of the joiner, the mason, the spinner, or of any other kind of productive labour. Along with the useful qualities of the products themselves, we put out of sight both the useful character of the various kinds of labour embodied in them, and the concrete forms of that labour; there is nothing left but what is common to them all; all are reduced to one and the same sort of human labour, human labour in the abstract. (Marx, 1967, Vol. I, pp. 37–38)

From this passage we can see that Marx arrives at his distinction between concrete and abstract labor by employing his two fundamental abstractions: Looking at the capitalist process of production from the standpoint of its material aspect he sees a labor-process in which concrete labor produces use-values; examining the same process from the standpoint of its social form, on the other hand, he is able to deduce the notion of abstract labor from the specifically social aspect of commodities, namely, their exchange-value.

The main significance of Marx's concept of abstract labor is that it reflects the particular social relations that exist in a commodity-producing society. We have already noted that, in such a society, the concrete labors of individuals are not coordinated on a society-wide basis: Individuals make their own decisions as to the specific kind of productive activity they will perform, and they do not think of their particular skills and energies as integral parts of the total productive capacity of the society. As a result, the various work activities of these individuals are coordinated only indirectly, through the exchange of their products, and their efforts have a social character only in the sense that each individual's work amounts to a quantity of abstract labor.

Because abstract labor reflects a particular set of social relations Marx refers to it as a "social substance" (Marx, 1967, Vol. I, p. 38). As such, he treats it as the substance of value (Marx, 1967, Vol. I, p. 537). "Value" itself, then, is what is created by abstract labor and, in Marx's work, it is something different from exchange-value. Whereas the latter is a quantitative relationship between commodities, "value" may be thought of as a quality possessed by a single commodity, in particular, that quality which it has as a result of the social conditions under which it was produced. Thus, for Marx, "value" refers to the very structure of a society in which individual producers relate to each other only through the exchange of their products: "The value-form of the product of labour . . . in bourgeois production . . . stamps that production as a particular species of social production, and thereby gives it its special historical character" (Marx, 1967, Vol. I, p. 81, footnote 2).

As is well known, the "law of value" is for Marx the mechanism through which *both* the exchange-ratios of commodities *and* the activities of their producers are regulated.[6] In a commodity-producing society – or what is nowadays called a market society – individuals have to shuttle around to different productive activities (or, in some cases, to no productive activity at all) as the exchange-ratios between commodities go up and down. In Marx's view, this type of social arrangement is defective in the sense that people living under such conditions lack control over the mechanism by which their individual productive activities are coordinated. As he put it in the *Economic and Philosophic Manuscripts* of 1844, this lack of control amounts to the alienation of people from the products of their labor:

> [T]he object produced by labour, its product, now stands opposed to it as an *alien being*, as a *power independent* of the producer. The product of labour is labour which has been embodied in an object and turned into a physical thing. . . . The *alienation* of the worker in his product means not only that his labour becomes an object . . . but that it exists independently . . . and that it stands opposed to him as an autonomous power. (Marx, 1964, pp. 122–23)

As Marx saw it, then, commodity-producing labor is alienated labor, and the market mechanism that we learn about in our textbooks is nothing more than the products of our own labor set against us as an autonomous power.

The last point that needs to be considered here in relation to commodity-producing labor is that, in Marx's view, it necessarily gives rise to certain *illusions* in the minds of those who perform it. Since the individuals in a commodity-producing society have no relationships with each other until they come to exchange their products, it appears to them as if the relationships between these products are the only ones that actually exist. Marx called this illusion *commodity fetishism* and he gave the following description of it in the first chapter of *Capital* just after he defined commodities as "products of the labour of private individuals . . . who carry on their work independently of each other":

> The sum total of the labour of all these private individuals forms the aggregate labour of society. Since the producers do not come into contact with each other until they exchange their products, the specific social character of each producer's labour does not show itself except in the act of exchange. In other words, the labour of the individual asserts itself as a part of the labour of society only by means of the relations which the act of exchange establishes directly between the products, and indirectly, through them, between the producers. To the latter, therefore, the relations connecting the labour of one individual with that of the rest appear, not as direct social relations between individuals at work, but as what they really are, material relations between persons and social relations between things. (Marx, 1967, Vol. I, p. 73)

(See also Geras, 1971.) Thus, as Marx had indicated in his earlier work, *A Contribution to the Critique of Political Economy:* "A social relation of production appears as something existing apart from individual human beings, and the distinctive relations into which they enter in the course of production in society appear as the specific properties of a thing" (Marx, 1970, p. 49).

Since the notion of commodity fetishism is of central importance in our later discussion of Cantabrigian economics, it should be noted here that Marx himself thought of the economics of his own time as an exalted form of such fetishism. His views on this topic were aptly summed up by Engels in a review of the book from which we have just quoted:

> Political economy begins with *commodities,* with the moment when products are exchanged . . . The product being exchanged is a commodity. But it is a commodity merely by virtue of the *thing,* the product, being linked with a *relation* between two persons . . . Here is at once an example of a peculiar fact which pervades the whole economy and has produced serious confusion in the minds of bourgeois economists – [In our view] economics is not concerned with things but with relations between persons, and in the final analysis between classes; these relations however are always *bound to things* and *appear as things.* (Marx, 1970, p. 226)

In Marx's system, the doctrine of commodity fetishism is simply the logical extension of his original injunction against separating relationships between things from relationships between people. Recondite as it may seem, this doctrine is the thread that runs through the critique of political economy contained in *Capital:*

> Political Economy has indeed analysed, however incompletely, value and its magnitude, and has discovered what lies beneath these forms. But it has never once asked the question *why labour is represented by the value of its product and labour-time by the magnitude of that value.* (Marx, 1967, Vol. I, p. 80; italics added)

Because bourgeois economists have a tendency to separate physical and social relationships, Marx argued, they end up confining themselves to the analysis of such superficial phenomena as the exchange-ratios between commodities. His own purpose, in contrast, was to explain the character and consequences of the social relations of capitalist production.

"Work itself" as wage-labor. Thus far we have presented Marx's analysis of capitalism with reference only to the point that, in his view, it is a system in which "work itself" takes the form of commodity-producing labor; on this basis we have been able to explain, at least in a preliminary fashion, the meaning he attached to such terms as value, abstract labor, alienation, and commodity fetishism. As noted at the outset, however, Marx thought of capitalism as a system "based on wage-labour." To penetrate to the heart of his analysis of it, therefore, we must go on to investigate why he referred specifically to wage-labor as the basis of the capitalist mode of production.

At this point it is necessary to point out that Marx made a distinction between (1) commodity production in general – or simple commodity production – and (2) commodity production in its specifically capitalist form. While he defined the former solely in terms of *horizontal* social relations (independent private producers exchanging their products), he thought of the latter as involving *vertical* as well as horizontal social relations (capitalists supervising workers in the production of commodities). Marx was well aware of the fact that simple commodity production has occurred in a variety of different societies throughout history; the point that interested him was that only with the development of capitalism does commodity production become not just a peripheral activity but the dominant form of social production: "Only when and where wage-labour is its basis does commodity production impose itself on society as a whole" (Marx, 1967, Vol. I, p. 587). What, then, is wage-labor?

In Marx's analysis the phenomenon of wage-labor is one of the results of the historical process that established the preconditions of capitalist production:

> The capitalist system presupposes the complete separation of the labourers from all property in the means by which they can realise their labour . . . The process, therefore, that clears the way for the capitalist system can be none other than the process which takes away from the labourer the possession of his means of production; a process that transforms, on the one hand, the social means of subsistence and of production into capital, on the other, the immediate producers into wage-labourers. (Marx, 1967, Vol. I, p. 714)

As is well known, this process is described in *Capital* as the process of "primitive accumulation" (Marx, 1967, Vol. I, Part VIII). Under this heading Marx recites the gory details of how, on the one hand, the direct producers were forcibly separated from the land (by such measures as the enclosures in England) and, on the other, the means of production became concentrated in the hands of capitalists. The upshot of this process, as we are concerned with it here, is that when people are deprived of direct access to "the means by which they can realize their labour'' they have no other choice but to sell their productive potential to those who control these means. Wage-labour, then, is that historical category of people who must sell their capacity to work and, hence, whose very life-sustaining activity is a commodity.

In order to analyze what happens when ''work itself'' takes the form of wage-labor Marx made a distinction between labor and labor-power. *Labor-power,* according to his definition, is a person's capacity to work; it is the commodity which the worker *sells* to the capitalist in return for wages. *Labor,* on the other hand, is not a commodity in Marx's system; rather, it is what the worker *does* under the control of the capitalist after the latter has purchased his labor-power. In terms of the definitions introduced earlier, labor was regarded by Marx as the use-value of the commodity labor-power; like other use-values, it is consumed by the buyer of the commodity, the capitalist.

With the help of his distinction between labor and labor-power Marx was able to explain why wage-labor is the essential ingredient of capitalism. In order for capitalist production to occur, he argued, capitalists must first be able to make contact with people who are willing to part with their productive potential: ''The whole system of capitalist production is based on the fact that the workman sells his labor-power as a commodity'' (Marx, 1967, Vol. I, p. 430). Once labor-power has been purchased by the capitalist, Marx went on to point out, it becomes labor. Thus the essence of capitalist production, as he saw it, is that it is a process in which labor-power gets transformed into labor. (To bring about this transformation is the task facing the capitalist in the realm of production.)

Labor is the basis of capitalist production in a sense both similar to and different from the sense in which it is the basis of simple commodity production. Just as it does in simple commodity production, labor also produces value when it is performed under the supervision of capitalists; likewise, when such labor is regarded from the standpoint of its value-creating aspect, it may be thought of as abstract labor. In Marx's system, however, the notion of abstract labor acquires a special significance in the context of capitalist production: Transcending its origins as a concept deduced from the mere fact that commodities are exchanged, it becomes a category that reflects the actual conditions of labor in a capitalist society. As Marx explained it in his introduction to the Grundrisse:

> This abstraction of labour is . . . by no means simply the conceptual resultant of a variety of concrete types of labour. The fact that the particular kind of labour employed is immaterial is appropriate to a form of society in which individuals easily pass from one type of labour to another, the particular type of labour being accidental to them and therefore irrelevant. (Marx, 1970, p. 210)

Clearly, the ''form of society'' Marx had in mind here is capitalist society, for only after masses of people have been separated from the means of production do ''individuals easily pass from one type of labour to another,'' and only when such individuals are put in the position of having to accept whatever jobs are offered in the market does ''the particular type of labour [become] accidental to them and therefore irrelevant.'' Under capitalist conditions, then, abstract labor refers to the historical phenomenon of wage-labor and, in this specific sense, it is regarded by Marx as the source of value.

The value created in the capitalist process of production is divided by Marx into two parts. One part of it corresponds to the value of the means of subsistence required by the workers and is actually paid to them in the form of wages. The other part of the total value produced is appropriated by the capitalists and, as we all know, is referred to by Marx as *surplus-value.*

The main significance of surplus-value in the Marxian system is that it reflects a division within the workers' labor-time itself. As we have already noted, Marx separated the total quantity of labor performed by the workers into necessary and surplus labor, the former being the amount needed to produce their own means of subsistence, and the latter being the additional labor extracted from them by the society's dominant class. The importance of surplus-value in Marx's analysis, then, is that it is the form in which surplus labor is extracted from wage-laborers and, as such, it refers to the form of exploitation characteristic of the capitalist mode of production.

The specific nature of capitalist exploitation was explained by Marx in terms of his distinction between labor and labor-power. Workers can be exploited by capitalists, he pointed out, because they are capable of performing more hours of labor than are required to produce the value of their labor-power. Thus, workers can be exploited in production even at the same time that they are paid the full value of the commodity which they sell to the capitalist. In Marx's view, it does no good to bewail the fact that the value of this commodity, like that of all other commodities, is determined by the quantity of labor-time needed to reproduce it: ''It is a very cheap sort of sentimentality which declares this method of determining the value of labour-power, a method prescribed by the very nature of the case, to be a brutal method . . ." (Marx, 1967, Vol. I, p. 173). Marx's point was not that workers are gypped in the market but, rather, that they are exploited in production.

As Marx analyzes it, the capitalist form of exploitation both generates and is reinforced by a peculiar form of commodity fetishism. When workers sell their labor-power to a capitalist, the deal is made in terms of a certain amount of money for so many hours of labor. Hence, to the workers it appears as if they are being paid for each and every hour of labor that they perform. In Marx's words: "The wage-form thus extinguishes every trace of the division of the working day into necessary labour and surplus-labour" (Marx, 1967, Vol. I, p. 539). In another part of *Capital* Marx pointed out that, as a consequence of this mystifying effect of wages, working people have a hard time seeing the true character of the relations that connect them with capitalists: "The Roman slave was held by fetters; the wage-labourer is bound to his owner by invisible threads" (Marx, 1967, Vol. I, p. 574). Just as in simple commodity production the relationships between the producers are seen by them as relations between their products, under capitalism the relationships between workers and capitalists are obscured by the fact that the former sell their labor-power to the latter as a commodity. Thus, in Marx's view, the fetishism that arises with commodity production per se becomes an element in the perpetuation of the specifically capitalist form of such production.

Finally, when "work itself" takes the form of wage-labor Marx identifies it as an advanced form of alienated labor. Since workers must give up control over their productive activity when they sell their labor-power to a capitalist, they become alienated not only from the products of their labor but from the process of production itself. Marx described this aspect of alienated labor in the *Economic and Philosophic Manuscripts* as follows:

> What constitutes the alienation of labour? First, that the work is *external* to the worker, that it is not part of his nature; and that, consequently, he does not fulfill himself in his work but denies himself, has a feeling of misery rather than well-being, does not develop freely his mental and physical energies but is physically exhausted and mentally debased. The worker, therefore, feels himself at home only during his leisure time, whereas at work he feels homeless. His work is not voluntary but imposed, *forced labour*. It is not the satisfaction of a need, but only a *means* for satisfying other needs. Its alien character is clearly shown by the fact that as soon as there is no physical or other compulsion it is avoided like the plague. (Marx, 1964, pp. 124–25).

In Marx's view, alienation is one of the defining characteristics of capitalism for, as he pointed out, the latter is a system that requires workers to alienate themselves from their own labor. Because the wage-transaction is the vehicle through which this alienation occurs he once referred to it as "the very transaction which characterises capital" (Marx, 1967, Vol. I, p. 533).

To conclude this discussion of wage-labor and to enable us to shift our attention to other elements in the capitalist process of production, let us examine a passage from *Capital* in which Marx translates his concept of alienated labor into a definition of capital itself:

> The labourer, on quitting the process [of production], is what he was on entering it, a source of wealth, but devoid of all means of making that wealth his own. Since, before entering on the process, his labour has already been alienated from himself by the sale of his labour-power . . . it must, during the process, be realised in a product that does not belong to him. Since the process of production is also the process by which the capitalist consumes labor-power, the product of the labourer is incessantly converted, not only into commodities, but into capital, [that is] into value that sucks up the value-creating power, into means of subsistence that buy the person of the labourer, into means of production that command the producers. The labourer constantly produces material, objective wealth, but in the form of capital, of an alien power that dominates and exploits him. (Marx, 1967, Vol. I, pp. 570–71)

As is evident from this passage, Marx used the word "capital" to refer to both the means of subsistence and the means of production concentrated in the hands of the capitalist. In the next section, the focus is on the means of production, looking in particular at the way Marx analyzed the specifically capitalist form of the *instruments of production* and the *objects transformed in production*.

The means of production as capital. In the introduction to the *Grundrisse* Marx noted that "All periods of production . . . have certain features in common: they have certain common categories . . . Production without them is inconceivable" (Marx, 1970, p. 190). In the same place, however, he pointed out that "it is necessary to distinguish those definitions which apply to production in general, in order not to overlook the essential differences [between the various historical periods]" (Marx, 1970). To illustrate his point Marx referred to the instruments of production and argued that, although they are a necessary element in all human production, they should not be routinely identified in all times and places as "capital:"

> For example, no production is possible without an instrument of production, even if this instrument is simply the hand. It is not possible without past, accumulated labour . . . Capital is among other things also an instrument of production, and also past, materialized labour. Consequently, capital is a universal and eternal relation given by nature – that is, *provided one omits precisely those specific factors which turn the "instrument of production or "accumulated labor" into capital.* (Marx, 1970; italics added)

Thus, in Marx's approach, "instruments of production" is one of "those definitions which apply to production in general" but "capital" is a specific historical category. Conversely, since "capital" is – "among other things" – the form which the instruments of production take in a capitalist society, it is one of the qualities which can help us to differentiate such a society from other historical types of societies.

But what exactly did Marx have in mind when he spoke of "those specific factors which turn the 'instruments of production' or 'accumulated labour' into capital"? One might say that what he had in mind when he wrote these words was at least the whole of the first volume of *Capital.* Consider, however, one passage from this volume in which we can see Marx using his two basic abstractions to analyze the form taken by the means of production in a capitalist society:

> If we consider the process of production from the point of view of the simple labour-process, the labourer stands in relation to the means of production, not in their quality as capital, but as the mere means and material of his own intelligent productive activity. In tanning, *e.g.*, he deals with the skins as his simple object of labour . . . But it is different as soon as we deal with the process of production from the point of view of the process of creation of surplus-value. The means of production are at once changed into means for the absorption of the labour of others. It is now no longer the labourer that employs the means of production, but the means of production that employ the labourer. Instead of being consumed by him as material elements of his productive activity, they consume him as the ferment necessary to their own life-process. (Marx, 1967, Vol. I, p. 310)

This of course is the kind of analysis which led Marx to refer (in the same volume) to capitalism as "a state of society in which the process of production has the mastery over man, instead of being controlled by him" (Marx, 1967, Vol. I, p. 81).

It is clear, from the passage just quoted, that Marx looked at the objects transformed in production in the same way that he treated the instruments of production: Together, they constitute the means of production and, in his approach, they both assume a specific form in a capitalist society.

On the basis of his analysis of the means of production, Marx criticized other economists for failing to see that they take the form of capital only in the context of a specific set of social relations. In his view, the bourgeois conception of capital was an expression of commodity fetishism in the sense that it referred only to *things* and was applied indiscriminately to objects facilitating production in any form of society. In the third volume of *Capital* he attacked this way of thinking and once more brought out the connection between capital and alienated labor:

> Capital . . . is not a thing, but rather a definite social production relation, belonging to a definite historical formation of society, which is manifested in a thing and lends this thing a specific social character. Capital is not the sum of the material and produced means of production. Capital is rather the means of production transformed into capital . . . It is the means of production monopolised by a certain section of society, confronting living labour-power as products and working conditions rendered independent of this very labour-power. (Marx, 1967, Vol. III, pp. 814–15)

We have now looked at three of the four elements that interact in the production process, explaining in each case how Marx treated them in the context of capitalist society. It is appropriate at this point, therefore, to focus our attention on the remaining element of production, the *coordinating agency,* and to examine the way that he analyzed it in its specifically capitalist form.

Coordination performed by capitalists. Marx discussed the specific form taken by the function of coordination in a capitalist society at the very point in *Capital* where he first mentioned the need for this function. Here, immediately after saying that all large scale production requires a "directing authority," he went on to make two points: (a) With the emergence of capitalism, "the work of directing, superintending, and adjusting becomes one of the functions of capital;" and (b) as a result of this, "it acquires special characteristics" (Marx, 1967, Vol. I, p. 331). In the next paragraph Marx explained what these "special characteristics" are, and here – once again – we can see how he used his two basic abstractions to analyze a particular element in the production process:

> The directing motive, the end and aim of capitalist production is to extract the greatest possible amount of surplus-value, and consequently to exploit labour-power to the greatest possible extent. As the number of the co-operating labourers increases, so too does their resistance to the domination of capital, and with it, the necessity for capital to overcome this resistance by counter-pressure. The control exercised by the capitalist is not only a special function, due to the nature of the social labour-process, and peculiar to that process, but it is, at the same time, a function of the exploitation of a social labour-process, and is consequently rooted in the unavoidable antagonism between the exploiter and the living and labouring raw material he exploits. (Marx, 1967, Vol. I, p. 331)

Because Marx saw production as a dual process – with both a material and a social aspect – he was able to analyze the role of the capitalist as one which involves not only the responsibility of coordinating production but also the power to exploit it for his own benefit.

It is interesting to note that in the passage just quoted, as in others throughout *Capital,* Marx refers to "capital" almost as if it were human: he attributes to it an impulse to dominate workers and to overcome their resistance by "counter-pressure." This may seem strange to readers who are used to thinking of capital merely as a collection of things, but it represents a deliberate effort on Marx's part to get us to think of things as elements within social relations and people as connected with each other through things. In his work, capital refers to *the whole structure of things and people* against which workers must struggle in order to put an end to their exploitation.

Just as Marx rejected the notion of capital conceived of as things, so also did he warn against thinking of *capitalists* simply as individuals: "I paint the capitalist . . . in no sense *couleur de rose*. But here individuals are dealt with only in so far as they are the personifications of economic categories, embodiments of particular class-relations and class-interests" (Marx, 1967, Vol. I, p. 10). Marx's usual procedure, when discussing the role of capitalists, was to refer to them as *personified capital.* He did this to indicate that they should be thought of not as individuals acting solely on the basis of their own free choices but as people caught up in, and molded by, a particular socioeconomic structure. Thus capitalists are treated by Marx as a specific historical class of people whose special relationship to the means of production puts them in the position of dominating and exploiting workers.

We have now presented Marx's analysis of how all four of the elements of production interact with each other in the capitalist mode of production. It is appropriate at this point, then, to quote a brief passage from *Capital* which seems to sum up his view of capitalism:

> Within the process of production . . . capital acquired the command over labour, i.e., over functioning labour-power or the labourer himself. Personified capital, the capitalist takes care that the labourer does his work regularly and with the proper degree of intensity.
>
> Capital further developed into a coercive relation which compels the working-class to do more work than the narrow round of its own life-wants prescribes. As a producer of the activity of others, as a pumper-out of surplus-labour and exploiter of labour-power, it surpasses in energy, disregard of bounds, recklessness and efficiency, all earlier systems of production based on directly compulsory labour. (Marx, 1967, Vol. I, pp. 309–10)

Thus, from Marx's standpoint, capitalism is a system in which work itself takes the form of labor performed under the direction of capitalists; capitalists are merely personified capital; and capital itself is defined as "a coercive social relation which compels the working-class to do more work than the narrow round of its own life-wants prescribes."

Before turning our attention to the Cambridge view of capitalism we should briefly consider two questions on which Marx's position contrasts sharply with that of the Cantabrigians: What is the relationship between production and distribution? In what way will socialism be different from capitalism?

Production and distribution. One of the distinguishing features of Marx's approach to economics is that he always treated the distribution of the products in any given society as a mechanism integral to that society's mode of production. His views on this topic were most clearly stated in the introduction to the *Grundrisse:*

> In the shallowest conception, distribution appears as the distribution of products, and hence as further removed from and quasi-independent of production. But before distribution can be the distribution of products, it is: (1) the distribution of the instruments of production; and (2), which is a further specification of the same relation, the distribution of the members of society among the different kinds of production. (Subsumption of the indi-

viduals under specific relations of production.) The distribution of products is evidently only a result of this distribution, which is comprised within the process of production itself and determines the structure of production. To examine production while disregarding this internal distribution within it is obviously an empty abstraction; while conversely, the distribution of products follows by itself from this distribution which forms an original moment of production. (Marx, 1973, p. 96)

The point of this passage is that, for Marx, distribution is not independent of production but, since particular class relations tend to perpetuate themselves, is actually determined by it. He believed, for example, that wages could not rise and profits fall beyond a certain point without bringing into question the very survival of the capitalist mode of production (Marx, 1967, Vol. I, p. 619). Marx also held that even the forms in which income is distributed are determined by the way in which the elements of production are connected with each other:

> The relations and modes of distribution thus appear merely as the obverse of the agents of production. An individual who participates in production in the form of wage-labour shares in the products . . . in the form of wages. The structure of distribution is completely determined by the structure of production. Distribution is itself a product of production . . . in that the specific kind of participation in production determines . . . the pattern of participation in distribution. (Marx, 1973, p. 95)

How socialism would be different. As is well known, Marx never offered a detailed blueprint for a postcapitalist society. In the *Communist Manifesto* he asserted that "the history of all hitherto existing society is the history of class struggles" (Marx and Engels, 1968, p. 35), and he clearly believed that such struggles would also shape the society of the future. In spite of his general aversion to utopian thinking, however, Marx's analysis of capitalism itself contains clear indications of what he thought would be different about a socialist society.

Having analyzed capitalism as a mode of production based on wage-labor, Marx clearly expected that socialism would be based on something else. As early as 1844 in the *Economic and Philosophic Manuscripts* he argued that wages are "only a necessary consequence of the alienation of labour" and, hence, higher wages would not really change the conditions of labor: "An enforced *increase in wages* . . . would be nothing more than a better *remuneration of slaves,* and would not restore either to the worker or to the work their human significance and worth" (Marx, 1964, p. 132). The point of view expressed here was not just a fancy of Marx's youth; throughout his work he consistently maintained that the point of socialism is to eliminate alienated labor. Consider, for example, the following passage from the first volume of *Capital* in which he noted that, even in a capitalist society, workers may at times receive an increase in wages:

> A larger part of their own surplus-product . . . comes back to them in the shape of means of payment, so that they can extend the circle of their enjoyments; can make some additions to their consumption-fund of clothes, furniture, &c., and can lay by small reserve-funds of money. *But just as little as better clothing, food, and treatment . . . do away with the exploitation of the slave, so little do they set aside that of the wage-worker.* A rise in the price of labour . . . only means, in fact, that the length and weight of the golden chain the wage-worker has already forged for himself, allow of a relaxation of the tension of it. In the controversies on this subject the chief fact has generally been overlooked, viz., the *differentia specifica* of capitalistic production. (Marx, 1967, Vol. I, p. 618; italics added)

Even at the end of his life Marx took issue with those who would try to improve the distribution of income without changing the fundamental relations of production. Thus, in one of the last things he wrote, he criticized the followers of Ferdinand Lasalle for giving priority to the goal of "a fair distribution of the proceeds of labour:"

> Quite apart from the analysis so far given, it was in general a mistake to make a fuss about so-called *distribution* and put the principal stress on it.
>
> Any distribution whatever of the means of consumption is only a consequence of the distribution of the conditions of production themselves. The latter distribution, however, is a feature of the mode of production itself. The capitalist mode of production, for example, rests on the fact that the material conditions of production are in the hands of non-workers in the form of property in capital and land, while the masses are only owners of the personal condition of production, of labour-power. If the elements of production are so distributed, then the present-day distribution of the means of consumption results automatically. If the material conditions of production are the co-operative property of the workers themselves, then there likewise results a distribution of the means of consumption different from the

> present one. Vulgar socialism . . . has taken over from the bourgeois economists the consideration and treatment of distribution as independent of the mode of production and hence the presentation of socialism as turning principally on distribution. After the real relation has long been made clear, why retrogress again? (Marx and Engels, 1968, p. 325)

As far as Marx was concerned, then, the "real relation" is that the distribution of the product is determined by the way it is produced; hence, we can achieve a "fair" distribution of products only by changing the mode of production itself. Although Marx was intentionally vague about what the new mode of production would look like, he did express himself clearly on one point. In the same essay from which we have just quoted, he described socialism with reference to the category that he had used to begin his analysis of capitalism:

> Within the co-operative society based on common ownership of the means of production, the producers do not exchange their products; just as little does the labour employed on the products appear here *as the value* of these products . . . since now, in contrast to capitalist society, individual labour no longer exists in an indirect fashion but directly as a component part of the total labour [of society]. (Marx and Engels, 1968, p. 323)

In his discussion of commodity fetishism in the first chapter of *Capital* Marx had made the following statement: "The life-process of society . . . does not strip off its mystical veil until it is treated as production by freely associated men, and is consciously regulated by them in accordance with a settled plan" (Marx, 1967, Vol. I, p. 80). Under socialism, he believed, people would not only be free from exploitation but would also be able to develop a clear view of the relations which bind them together in production.

Cambridge economics as commodity fetishism. Up to this point, we have presented the views of Marx and the Cantabrigians as if they were just alternative approaches in economics. As we proceed to examine the Cambridge view of capitalism, however, it becomes necessary to point out that the positions taken by the Cantabrigians are similar to the ones Marx criticized a hundred years ago. We will see in fact that the Cantabrigians' practice of separating the physical from the social aspects of production leads them to present the economic relationships of capitalism in precisely the way that Marx described as "commodity fetishism." In this section, therefore, I argue not only that the Cantabrigian view of capitalism differs from that of Marx but also that it mystifies the real nature of the system in a way that can only becloud our understanding and impede our practical efforts to work towards socialism.

Production of things by means of things. To establish a framework for thinking about Piero Sraffa's *Production of Commodities by Means of Commodities,* it is helpful to consider the following passage from Marx's discussion of commodity fetishism in the first chapter of *Capital:*

> A commodity is . . . a mysterious thing, simply because [1] in it the social character of men's labour appears to them as an objective character stamped upon the product of that labour; because [2] the relation of the producers to the sum total of their own labour is presented to them as a social relation, existing not between themselves, but between the products of their labour . . . [Thus] the value-relation between the products of labour which stamps them as commodities . . . is a definite social relation between men that assumes, in their eyes, the fantastic form of a relation between things. (Marx, 1967, Vol. I, p. 72)

Since Sraffa's book features the word "commodities" twice in its title, one might guess that it would contain an analysis of a particular social form of human production. As we have already noted, however, Sraffa defines production solely in terms of technical relations and makes no references to social relations within the production process. Can we not say, therefore, that production, as seen by the Cantabrigians, "is a definite social relation between men that assumes, in their eyes, the fantastic form of a relation between things"?

If one accepts Marx's concept of a commodity, Sraffa's book turns out not to be about commodity production at all. Since he insists upon separating relations between things from relations between people, Sraffa merely adds to that "serious confusion in the minds of bourgeois economists" which Marx called commodity fetishism. Instead of writing about the way in which commodities are actually used to produce commodities in a capitalist society, Sraffa has constructed an imaginary world in which things produce things (by means of magic). Had he been writing in the Marxian tradition, his book might better have carried the title *Production of Classes by Means of Classes* for, as Engels pointed out, the Marxist approach "is not concerned with things but with relations between persons, and in the final analysis between classes." (Marx, 1970, p. 226)[7]

Price theory without value theory. Since the Cantabrigians do not see capitalist production as something which involves specific social relations, they do not think of *value* in the way that Marx did. As we have seen, the latter founded his entire study of capitalism on an analysis of "the value-form of the product of labour" (Marx, 1967, p. 81, footnote). The Cantabrigians, on the other hand, "never once ask the question *why labour is represented by the value of its product and labour-time by the magnitude of that value*" (Marx, 1967, Vol. I, p. 80, italics added). The most that can be said of their work is that they shed light on certain issues that were discussed in Volume III of *Capital*. But, as Marx noted on the first page of that volume, to analyze such things as the effects of changes in distribution on relative prices is to deal with economic phenomena "in the form which they assume on the surface of society" (Marx, 1967, Vol. III, p. 25).[8] However ingenious the Cantabrigians are in analyzing price phenomena, they never connect such phenomena with social relations in the way that Marx did in *Capital* (Medio, 1972).

The gulf between the Cantabrigian and the Marxian conceptions of value may be demonstrated by quoting a passage from Joan Robinson's introduction to her first book, *The Economics of Imperfect Competition:*

> The main theme of this book is the analysis of value. It is not easy to explain what the analysis of value is, without making it appear extremely mysterious and extremely foolish. The point may be put like this: You see two men, one of whom is giving a banana to the other, and is taking a penny from him. You ask, How is it that a banana costs a penny rather than any other sum? (Robinson, 1933, p. 6)

While Robinson referred here to "the analysis of value" – what she actually had in mind was the analysis of *prices*. Indeed, in a later book she dismissed the whole notion of value as "one of the great metaphysical ideas in economics . . . [which] when you try to pin it down turns out to be just a word" (Robinson, 1963, p. 26). Her total lack of understanding of Marx's concept of value was displayed in her *Essay on Marxian Economics* wherein she stated that "under socialism the law of *value* will come into its own" (Robinson, 1966, p. xviii; italics in original).

Sraffa's book too, it should be noted, is oriented to the traditional economists' problem of analyzing prices. Since it is not specifically a study of commodity production, one could hardly expect it to deal with "value" in the Marxian sense. Though some have praised him for having "rehabilitated" Marx (Dobb, 1973; Meek, 1967), Sraffa does not in fact adopt Marx's approach to the analysis of value. Not only does he neglect to ask the question "why labour is represented by the value of its product," but, taking the existence of exchange-values for granted, he asserts that in an economy without a surplus "such values spring directly from the [technical] methods of production" (Sraffa, 1960, p. 33). Even after introducing a surplus, Sraffa continues to emphasize the role of a society's technical relations in determining its pattern of relative prices, for he sees prices only as relationships between things. Since he excludes social relations altogether from his view of production, it is not feasible for him to relate price phenomena to the social relations of capitalist production.

Distribution exogenous and independent of production. How do the Cantabrigians approach the question of distribution in a capitalist economy? In the Robinson and Eatwell textbook we are given the following clue: "Sraffa's analysis of the distribution of the product of industry between wages and profits in given technical conditions provides the indispensable framework for an understanding of the problem of distribution in a private-enterprise economy." Robinson and Eatwell, 1973, p. 187). However, another Cantabrigian, Krishna Bharadwaj, has written: "Distribution in Sraffa's system is not endogenously generated through production relations . . . No theory of distribution is offered in the book." (Bharadwaj, 1963, pp. 1450–54) Upon reading Sraffa himself, this statement by Bharadwaj proves to be entirely accurate. One can only conclude, then, that when Robinson and Eatwell talk about Sraffa's "indispensable framework" for understanding distribution in a capitalist economy, what they have in mind is Sraffa's practice of treating distribution as an independent variable, the determinants of which (in his view) lie "outside the system of production" (Sraffa, 1960, p. 33).

If distribution is treated as an independent variable, it is possible to think of it as being determined in some way by class struggle. Thus D. M. Nuti has credited Sraffa with opening the way for the reintroduction of political considerations into economics:

> The relation between the real wage rate and the profit rate uncovered by Sraffa . . . restates the conflict between capitalists and workers in the problem of income distribution, and provides scope for the concept of class struggle in the determination of relative shares. (Nuti, 1971, p. 32)

From this insight, some have jumped to the conclusion that the Cantabrigians are in fact reviving Marx's approach to distribution. Geoffrey Harcourt, for example, has commented on the work of certain Cantabrigians as follows:

> Some writers, for example, Bhaduri, Joan

Robinson, and Nell, look to Marx's theory of exploitation, brought up to date in the guise of relative bargaining strengths, to explain the distribution of the product, treated as a surplus, between profit-earners and wage-earners. (Harcourt, 1969, pp. 394–5)

Whether or not what Harcourt calls "Marx's theory of exploitation" actually resembles Marx's own theory of exploitation after the Cantabrigians have brought it "up to date" is a question we will deal with shortly. One thing which can be said immediately, however, is that it is inappropriate to link Marx's name with the Cantabrigian treatment of distribution.

The Cantabrigians generally follow Sraffa in treating distribution as an exogenously determined, independent variable. The reason Sraffa took this approach is that he wanted to construct a theory of how prices will change when distribution is altered and, in order to accomplish this task, it was convenient for him to *assume* that distribution is completely flexible and independent of production. Sraffa's followers, however, have translated this theoretical assumption into a way of thinking about distribution in the real world and, as a result, have neglected to tie distribution to the class relations of production.[9] Indeed, after reading the Cantabrigians one might form the impression that, once the means of production have been replaced, the output of the economy can be distributed in any proportions whatever between capitalists and workers without affecting the way production itself is carried on.

Marx, on the other hand, treated distribution as an endogenous variable, entirely interlocked with production. As we have seen, he believed that the distribution of the product in any given society is determined by the way in which people relate to each other in the process of producing it. In a capitalist society, for example, he argued that the product will be distributed in such a way that, after it has been distributed, capitalists and workers will again be ready and willing to perform their respective roles in the production process. He would have thought it ludicrous that someone might assume that distribution could vary in a capitalist society to the point where there were zero profits and wages absorbed all of the surplus product.

It is all well and good that certain Cantabrigians mention the class struggle when discussing distribution – but this hardly justifies placing them in the tradition of Marx. The distinguishing feature of Marx's approach was that he analyzed class conflict as a struggle rooted in the process of production. As we have noted, however, the Cantabrigians see only "technical relations" where production actually goes on. In a passage quoted earlier, Marx criticized such a view of production as "an empty abstraction" and argued that it can only lead to "the shallowest conception" of distribution. Would he not therefore have included the Cantabrigians among those to whom he referred when (in the same passage) he spoke of "the ineptitude of those economists who portray production as an eternal truth while banishing history to the realm of distribution" (Marx, 1973, Introduction, p. 97)?

We may now see that the Cantabrigian separation of production and distribution derives from the way they originally define their fundamental abstractions. Because they insist upon isolating the physical and the human elements of production – rigidly bifurcating them into "technical" and "social" relations – they end up blinding themselves not only to the complexity of the production process itself but also to the real connection between production and distribution.

Surplus rather than surplus-value. Perhaps the most obvious difference between the Cantabrigians and Marx is that they use the term surplus in place of the category of surplus-value. This is more than a semantic difference for, as we will see, the Cantabrigian practice of referring to the surplus is a reflection of the fundamental difference between their approach and that of Marx.

The Cantabrigian conception of the surplus is presented most clearly in Sraffa's book. Here, in the first sentence of the second chapter, we are simply told that "the economy produces more than the minimum necessary for replacement and there is a surplus to be distributed" (Sraffa, 1960, p. 6). This comes as something of a surprise because the entire first chapter of the book is concerned with "an extremely simple society which produces just enough to maintain itself" (Sraffa, 1960, p. 3), and nowhere does Sraffa tell us how the surplus suddenly arises. Since he does not see social relations in the production process, there is of course nothing in his discussion of the surplus comparable to Marx's concept of capital as "a coercive relation which compels the working-class to do more than the narrow round of its own life-wants prescribes."[10]

When Sraffa elaborates his view of the surplus, the differences between his approach and that of Marx become clear. Consider, for example, the following passage in which Sraffa defines his concept of the surplus using the "national income" terminology of modern economics:

The national income of a system in a self-replacing state consists of the set of commodities which are left over when from the gross national product we have removed item by item the articles which go to replace the means of production used up in all the industries. (Sraffa, 1960, p. 11)

In this definition we can detect three ways in which Sraffa's idea of a surplus is different from Marx's concept of surplus-value.

In the first place, Sraffa's surplus is a physical rather than a value phenomenon. It is the set of commodities (read: things) which are left after removing from the total output of the economy those articles which are needed, item by item, to replace the ones which have been used up in production. (Sraffa's decision to define the surplus in physical terms was a consequence, once again, of his initial choice of the problem to be solved. Since the task he set for himself was to explain the effects on prices of changes in the distribution of the surplus, it was necessary for him to define the surplus in such a way that its own measurement would not be affected by changes in prices.)

The second way in which Sraffa's conception of the surplus differs from Marx's notion of surplus-value is that both its existence and its precise magnitude appear to be technologically determined. In Sraffa's system, an economy's replacement needs are fixed by the technical relations that happen to exist in each of its industries – for these indicate the quantities of inputs that are required to produce given amounts of each kind of output. Hence, once we know the characteristics of a society's technology we can tell whether or not it will have a surplus and how large this surplus will be. The following argument has thus been put forward by Nell in Chapter 1 in defense of Sraffa's concept of the surplus: "The idea is important . . . for it anchors the concept of national income firmly in the sea of technology."

The third distinguishing feature of Sraffa's surplus is that, unlike Marx's concept of surplus-value, it includes the part of the economy's output that is consumed by workers. As can be seen in the definition quoted earlier, only those products are subtracted from the total output which are needed to replace used up means of production. All the rest of the economy's products are included in the surplus, and workers' consumption – as well as the capitalists' share of the total output – is provided for out of this surplus. (In Marxian value terms, Sraffa's surplus includes both V and S, whereas Marx's surplus-value only includes S.)

From a Marxian point of view, Sraffa's treatment of the surplus mystifies the actual relations of capitalist production in the following ways. First, his presentation of the surplus as something physical obscures the historical significance of the fact that all the products of a capitalist economy come into being as values. After reading Sraffa, one might think that there is really no difference between the surplus product of a capitalist society and that of any other type of society.

Second, Sraffa's preoccupation with the technical relations of production leaves the impression that the existence and magnitude of a surplus in any given society can be explained with reference only to such relations. Since he does not mention the social relations of capitalist production – or, for that matter, *any* social relations of production – we are not led to ask how it happens that a given amount of labor is performed in his system, neither more nor less, but just the amount that is required to produce the surplus. Although Sraffa does not actually say that the surplus is a gift of nature or that it results, as Marx once put it, "from some occult quality inherent in human labour," he certainly does nothing to combat such misconceptions (Marx, 1967, Vol. I, p. 515).

The most serious shortcoming of Sraffa's treatment of the surplus is that, since it includes workers' consumption as part of the surplus, it obscures Marx's distinction between necessary and surplus labor. The reason Marx did not include workers' consumption as a part of surplus-value is that he wanted to bring out the relationship between surplus-value and the value received by workers, on the one hand, and the two parts of the workers' labor-time, on the other. As we have seen, he treated the value received by workers as the product of necessary labor, and he related surplus-value to surplus labor.

Sraffa, on the other hand, never distinguishes between necessary and surplus labor. He does make a distinction between "basic" and "nonbasic" *industries*, but this has nothing to do with Marx's separation of the working day into two parts.[11] As far as Sraffa is concerned, there is no difference between the labor which produces the surplus and that which merely replaces the means of production that are used up; even if there were, such a difference would not correspond to Marx's way of dividing up the workers' labor-time. From Sraffa's point of view, then, every hour of labor seems to be just as necessary as every other hour.

Because Sraffa fails to distinguish surplus from necessary labor, on the one hand, and treats the surplus as a physical phenomenon, on the other, he leads us to believe that the surplus we produce is a surplus of *things* rather than of *labor*. To put it another way, the surplus in Sraffa's system is a relationship not between people but between two sets of products, one comprising the total output of the economy and the other consisting of what is needed to replace used up means of production. Sraffa's conception of the surplus may thus be seen as an example of commodity fetishism for, as Marx might have said, "the relation of the producers to the sum total of their own labour is presented to them as a social relation, existing not between themselves, but between the products of their labour" (Marx, 1967, Vol. I, p. 72).

The Cambridge view of capital. Since the Cantabrigians think of the surplus as a relationship between things, they fail to see that its very existence reflects an actual struggle between social classes in production. (As we have pointed out, they refer to class struggle only in connection with the distribution of the surplus after it has been produced.) This same blind spot prevents them from seeing, as Marx did, that the means of production take a particular form in the context of the specific class relations that define the capitalist mode of production.

When the Cantabrigians discuss capital they take the position that there are actually two meanings of the word. In order to avoid confusion, they say, we should distinguish between capital on the one hand, and capital goods on the other. The difference has been explained by Nell in Chapter 1 as follows: 'Capital' has two meanings. On the one hand, it is property in the means of production, enabling owners of equal amounts of claim in these means to receive equal returns . . . On the other hand, "capital" also means produced means of production – that is, specific materials, tools, instruments, machines, plant, and equipment, on which, with which, and by means of which labor works . . . *Capital goods are not the same thing as capital."* This way of dividing up the concept of capital follows more or less automatically from the Cantabrigians' basic tendency to separate physical and social phenomena. In contrast to Marx, who defined capital with reference to *both* the physical *and* the human elements of production, they treat capital as if it must be *either* a physical *or* a social phenomenon. Moreover, when the Cantabrigians divide capital into two separate categories they entirely overlook the aspect of it which was most crucial for Marx, namely, its quality as a specific social relation of production. Given the way they define capital, one can hardly imagine the Cantabrigians making the kind of statement that we have already quoted from *Capital:* "It is now no longer the labourer that employs the means of production, but the means of production that employ the labourer" (Marx, 1967, Vol. I, pp. 310, 423).

The Cantabrigians' divided view of capital reflects their separation of distribution from production. Consider, for example the statement that Nell makes in Chapter 1 immediately after saying that "capital goods are not the same thing as capital": 'Capital' is relevant to the analysis of the division of income among the members of society, but . . . has no bearing on production. 'Capital goods' are relevant to the study of production but have no bearing on the distribution of income." Here again we can see how the Cantabrigians' inability to comprehend the dual nature of production prevents them from grasping the way in which production (capital goods) and distribution (capital) are actually connected with each other.

The lacuna in the Cambridge conception of capital is also evident in the work of Joan Robinson. In a postscript to her 1953 article, for example, she criticizes the neoclassical economists for their "failure to distinguish between 'capital' in the sense of means of production with particular technical characteristics and 'capital' in the sense of a command over finance" (Robinson, 1971a, p. 63). Nowhere in Robinson's work do we find anything comparable to Marx's view that "within the process of production . . . capital acquired the command over labour, i.e., over functioning labour-power or the labourer himself" (Marx, 1967, Vol. I, pp. 309–10).

By some ironic twist, the way in which the Cantabrigians arrive at their non-Marxian conception of capital may be seen most clearly in an article by Amit Bhaduri the point of which is to place Cantabrigian economics in the Marxian tradition. Calling his article "On the Significance of Recent Controversies on Capital Theory: A Maxian View" (Bhaduri, 1969), Bhaduri first takes us through a brief review of Marx's basic abstractions. Having labelled these with their standard Marxian terms, the "forces" and "relations" of production, he immediately proceeds to *identify* these with the Cantabrigian abstractions we have come to know as technical and social relations. When Bhaduri discusses the "forces of production," for example, he makes no reference to the interaction between the human elements in the production process. When he presents Marx's concept of the "relations of production," on the other hand, he first translates it into "rules of the game" and later refers to it as "a social ownership relation." Bhaduri sums up his discussion of Marx's basic abstractions by distinguishing the "forces of production" from the "relations of production" in the following way: "The former concept relates to man's relation to nature and technology while the latter corresponds to man's relation to man in a social organization of production" (Bhaduri, 1969, p. 533). Marx, of course, did not begin with such a separation of the man–man and the man–nature interactions; his view was that people must always relate to each other *and* to nature and technology in a social organization of production.

Bhaduri's misinterpretation of Marx's basic abstractions leads him to make a truly astonishing error in his discussion of capital. Here, he presents the Cambridge definition of capital as if it were Marx's:

> Thus, "capital" as a Marxian "category" notion is: (a) an instrument of production – a pure physical object (belonging to the Marxian notion of "forces of production"); and (b) a social ownership relation giving rise to capitalists' income (belonging to the Marxian notion of "relations of production"). (Bhaduri, 1969, p. 534)

This is of course not the way Marx defined capital. In fact, it is precisely the kind of thinking he rejected. The following passage from Volume III of *Capital* must be quoted again at this point because in it Marx seems to be speaking directly to the Cantabrigians:

> Capital . . . is not a thing, but rather a definite social production relation, belonging to a definite historical formation of society, which is manifested in a thing and lends this thing a specific social character. Capital is not the sum of the material and produced means of production. Capital is rather the means of production transformed into capital . . . It is the means of production monopolised by a certain section of society, confronting living labour-power as products and working conditions rendered independent of this very labour-power. (Marx, 1967, Vol. III, pp. 814–15)

The point that needs to be emphasized here is that there is an enormous difference between treating capital as something "confronting living labour-power" in the realm of production (Marx) and thinking of it as "a social ownership relation giving rise to capitalists' income" (Bhaduri). The first view involves treating the means of production as an integral part of the social relations of capitalist production; the second leads inevitably to treating these same means of production not as capital but as "pure physical objects." Marx had this to say about the latter way of thinking in Volume II of *Capital:*

> This brings to completion the fetishism peculiar to bourgeois Political Economy, the fetishism which metamorphoses the social, economic character impressed on things in the process of social production into a natural character stemming from the material nature of those things. (Marx, 1967, Vol. II, p. 225)

In Marx's view, the consequence of this form of mystification is that it prevents people from seeing that the character of production itself is socially determined and therefore susceptible to change.

Work rather than alienated labor. At one point in their textbook Robinson and Eatwell make the following observation: "The fundamental element in production . . . is work" (Robinson and Eatwell, 1973, p. 61). As we have noted, however, they do not concern themselves with the conditions under which work is actually performed in the capitalist mode of production. To put it in Marxian terms, they do not treat work as alienated labor. As pointed out earlier, they merely assume that the amount of work specified in their technical relations will somehow be forthcoming. In this section, I argue that this kind of obliviousness to the actual character of work in capitalist production is widely shared by the Cantabrigians and that it stems from an inadequate treatment of the phenomenon of wage-labor.

One of the most surprising things about Sraffa's book, for example, is that it claims to be a study of commodity production but does not treat labor-power itself as a commodity. Although Sraffa frequently refers to the payment of wages, he never mentions the sale of labor-power. In his system, wages are the form in which income is received by workers, but this particular form of income does not have any implications regarding the nature of the work the workers must do in order to receive it. Like Robinson and Eatwell, Sraffa simply posits various quantities of labor-time among the inputs of his production activities.

A good example of the influence Sraffa has had on other Cantabrigians is the diagram Edward Nell uses (Chapter 1, Figure 1.2) to portray a capitalist economy. In this diagram Nell places workers on one side and industry on the other. Between them are two long arrows, one running from the workers to industry labeled "work," and one running from industry to the workers labeled "wages." In the diagram, however, there is no indication that the workers themselves ever enter the box where industry is located; and, even if we were to assume that they do, we would have no way of telling anything about their experiences there or of making a connection between these experiences and the arrows labeled "wages" and "work."

The shortcomings of Nell's diagram are also evident in the text of his chapter. Here, he first mocks the orthodox economists for treating distribution merely as an outcome of the process of exchanging commodities: "an exchange . . . means that *value equivalent is traded for value equivalent*. No exploitation there." So far so good. Marx took the same position. In order to explain exploitation, however, Nell goes on to deny that the wage-transaction is a proper exchange of value equivalents: "the payment of wages is not an exchange . . . or at any rate, not a fair one." Here, of course, Nell departs from Marx, for the latter explained how exploitation can go on even when workers are paid the value of their labor-power.

At the root of the difference between the Cantabrigian and the Marxian treatments of work is a difference regarding the nature of exploitation. For Marx, as we have seen, exploitation is the extraction of surplus labor in the process of production. For the Cantabrigians, on the other hand, exploitation has to do with the way a society's product is distributed. For example, Nell, again in Chapter 1, refers to exploitation in the following way: "the work of labor . . . has produced the entire product. Is labor not therefore exploited? Does it not deserve the whole product?" The implication here is that if workers could somehow receive the whole product they would no longer be exploited. While this is not actually wrong, it focuses on the symptom rather than on the disease itself. As Marx once said in reference to trade unions:

> They fail generally from limiting themselves to a guerrilla war against the *effects* of the system instead of simultaneously trying to change it, instead of using their organized forces as a lever for the final emancipation of the working class, that is to say [for] the ultimate abolition of the wages system. (Marx and Engels, 1968, p. 229; italics added)[12]

In Marx's view, it does no good just to raise ethical questions about the distribution of the product; capitalist exploitation will be with us as long as production itself continues to be based on wage-labor.

The Cantabrigians' tendency to focus exclusively on the distribution of the product may be seen as just another manifestation of their pervasive commodity fetishism. Instead of pointing to the need to eliminate wage-labor, it limits our attention to such things as increasing the bargaining power of workers. As we will see, this leads to emphasis on shifting the distribution of income in favor of workers rather than changing the mode of production itself.

Capitalists as workers. Since the Cantabrigians fail to bring out the fact that work is performed in the capitalist mode of production under oppressive social conditions, it is not surprising that they also mystify the role that capitalists play in the production process. In this section I argue that the Cantabrigians portray the functioning capitalist as if he were just a particular kind of worker and thus lead us to believe that the realm of production is a place of harmony rather than conflict.

Robinson and Eatwell describe their model of "a pure capitalist economy" as follows: "Production is controlled by *firms* which own machines, employ labour, and make profits. Consumption takes place in *households,* which receive income from the firms. There are two kinds of households, those of workers who receive wages, and those of rentiers, who have a claim on a share of profits" (Robinson and Eatwell, 1973, p. 92). At first glance, this seems to be a realistic view of capitalism, for it at least implies that workers participate in production. On second glance, however, one begins to wonder exactly *who* are these firms which control production, own machines, employ labor, and make profits. The answer given by Robinson and Eatwell is closely related to their view of *rentiers* as a specific group of households.

"The rentiers are identified with the households of the capitalists," say Robinson and Eatwell (Robinson and Eatwell, 1973, p. 92). Reading this statement, we might imagine that the capitalists are the people who exploit workers in the process of production, and the rentiers, those to whom surplus-value is distributed. Search as we might, however, we cannot find anywhere in the Robinson and Eatwell textbook a reference to capitalists as exploiters of workers in the process of production. What we find instead are references to people such as "*entrepreneurs,* who organize production" (Robinson and Eatwell, 1973, p. 77).[13]

The more one reads the Cantabrigians the more one realizes that they completely overlook the dual nature of the capitalists' role in production. Instead of recognizing that this role involves exploitation as well as coordination, they tend to see it only in terms of coordination. It would seem, therefore, that the Cantabrigians are subject to the same criticism that Marx addressed to his contemporaries:

> the political economist . . . when considering the capitalist mode of production . . . treats [1] the work of control made necessary by the co-operative character of the labour-process as identical with [2] the different work of control necessitated by the capitalist character of that process and the antagonism of interests between capitalist and labourer. (Marx, 1967, Vol. I, p. 332)

What happens when these two aspects of the capitalists' role are confused is that one tends to forget that capitalists as such have anything to do with production. Thus it turns out that when Robinson and Eatwell refer to capitalists, they actually have in mind only the people outside of the production process whom they classify as "rentiers."

At one point in their text Robinson and Eatwell do refer to entrepreneurs as members of the capitalist class: "With the spread of capitalism . . . the capitalist class became divided into *rentiers,* who receive income from property and *entrepreneurs,* who organize production" (Robinson and Eatwell, 1973, p. 77). Being part of the capitalist class, however, does not apparently mean that these "entrepreneurs" must come into conflict with workers. In the sentence immediately following the one just quoted, Robinson and Eatwell put their entrepreneurs on the same side of the social split as workers: "Thus, the division of the community into idle consumers and active producers becomes a division between rentiers of all kinds (including landowners), on the one hand, and managers and workers on the other" (Robinson and Eatwell, 1973, p. 77). This division of society into rentiers on one side and managers and workers on the other corresponds to what Robinson and Eatwell say in another place is one of "the most important differences" between their approach and that of the neoclassical economists, namely, "the distinction between income from work and income from property" (Robinson and Eatwell, 1973, p. 99). Both managers and workers receive "income from work," while only rentiers receive "income from property." From this one is led to believe that managers and entrepreneurs are really just particular varieties of workers and that their role in the production process is not in any way antagonistic to that of the rest of the workers.

By obscuring the role of capitalists in the production process itself and treating them merely as people who happen to *own* the means of production, the Cantabrigians engage in what Marx regarded as the most complete form of commodity fetishism: "The ossification of [the] relations [of production], their presentation as the relation of men to things having a definite social character is here likewise brought out in quite a different manner from that of the simple mystification of commodities . . . The transubstantiation, the fetishism, is complete" (Marx, 1971, p. 494). In the section of *Theories of Surplus-Value* from which this quote was taken, Marx criticizes as "vulgar political economy" the very thing that we have just associated with the Cantabrigians, namely, the tendency to displace from the realm of production the most essential feature of capitalism, the capital–labor relationship, and to project it as nothing more than a juridical relationship which gives certain people the right to an income from property. Thus, in the same passage Marx seems to be commenting directly on the writings of the Cantabrigians:

> Since the *alienated character* of capital, its opposition to labour, is displayed outside the exploitation process, that is, outside the sphere where the *real action of this alienation* takes place, all the contradictory features are eliminated from this process itself. Consequently, *real* exploitation, the sphere where these contradictory features are put into practice and where they manifest themselves in reality, appears as its exact opposite . . . The work of the exploiter is identified here with the labour which is exploited. (Marx, 1971, p. 495)

If one had the space – and if this chapter were not already too long – one could proceed directly from the above quotation to a critique of the way the Cantabrigians deal with the question of social change. In Marx's view, a proper understanding of social transformations can only be arrived at by examining the "contradictory features" of the production process itself (Footnote 3). Since space is limited, however, I will end with a brief look at how Robinson thinks our society *ought* to be changed.

A drastic remedy. In *Economics: An Awkward Corner,* Joan Robinson surveys the contemporary crisis of capitalism and makes certain suggestions for dealing with it (Robinson, 1967). In her last chapter the view is taken that what we have now is something called "managerial capitalism," the main defect of which is the existence of an anachronistic class of rentiers who receive "unearned income." To improve the distribution of income, eliminate "functionless wealth," and provide the state with more revenue for improving health and educational services, she proposes that we gradually eliminate rentiers and move toward a society in which there would be something that she calls "the nation as rentier" (Robinson, 1967, p. 59).

To institute "the nation as rentier," Robinson first suggests that a surplus in the government's budget be used to purchase corporate shares of stock. Then, after discussing the extreme inequality in the present distribution of income and wealth, she offers "a drastic remedy:"

> The concept of the nation as rentier points the way out of this situation. Concentrations of private property could be wiped out in a generation by confiscatory death duties (leaving a reasonable life interest to widows and orphans, and buttressed by equally heavy taxation on gifts). The titles to property could be handed over in the form in which it exists, to be held like any other endowment of a trust, and the income from it devoted to public pur-

poses. This would not only check the growth of rentier income . . . but take a large bite out of it. (Robinson, 1967, p. 61)

This proposal may seem somewhat naive – especially with regard to the benevolent character of the state – but it is remarkably consistent with the overall approach of the Cantabrigians. Have we not seen that they distinguish different forms of society according to "patterns of ownership" (Robinson and Eatwell, 1973, p. 63)? If the present social system is repugnant, then, what could be more logical than transferring the ownership of corporate shares from individuals to the state?

The question that must be asked, however, is how much of the present system would Robinson's proposal really change? If capitalism is the kind of system in which most people have to perform alienated labor under the direction of an autocratic elite, would it not still be capitalism even if the surplus-value produced were to be appropriated by the state rather than by a group of wealthy families? If our economic system were to continue to be based on wage-labor, would it not still be capitalism? And, if the state were to assume the functions that had previously been performed by private capitalists, would it not be fair to call the resulting system "state capitalism?"

Michael Lebowitz has argued that the Cantabrigian approach to economics should be understood as an expression of the interests of the *functioning capitalist* in opposition to those of the *money capitalist* (Lebowitz, 1973–74). This interpretation explains, among other things, why Robinson and Eatwell seem to be in such sympathy with their entrepreneurs and managers – picturing them as hard-working, talented, but not exploitative people.[14] It also explains why the Cantabrigians criticize only the ownership of the means of production by capitalists and the distribution of income to rentiers while neglecting the actual relations which characterize the capitalist process of production. For it makes little difference to the functioning capitalist whether the means of production are owned by private individuals or whether they are owned by the state. What counts is control, and this, as Robinson tells us, the Cantabrigians fully expect to be retained by the managers:

> In spite of its drawbacks, managers generally value the freedom that this peculiar system [managerial capitalism] gives them. For the most part, they dislike the idea of being nationalized or even of being financed by a public body which would have a right to supervise them. The great financial institutions such as insurance companies, which actually own a great deal of industry, lean backwards not to interfere. In principle, there is no reason why the state should not also enjoy ownership without control where management by private enterprise is considered preferable. (Robinson, 1967, p. 59)

The Cantabrigian dream, then, is a society in which the managers of its economic activities are free to run things as they please. This is not a very new kind of utopia; Thorstein Veblen had something similar in mind around the turn of the century. The only astonishing thing about it is that the Cantabrigians imagine that it has something to do with socialism.

Joan Robinson has long been a sympathetic observer of the transition to socialism in the People's Republic of China (Robinson, 1969), but her familiarity with China does not seem to have had much effect either on her understanding of socialism or on her attitude toward the struggle for it in the West:

> It is now clear that the revolutionary transition to socialism does not come in the advanced capitalist nations, but in the most backward . . . Current experience suggests that socialism is not a stage beyond capitalism but a substitute for it – a means by which the nations which did not share in the Industrial Revolution can imitate its technical achievements; a means to achieve rapid accumulation under a different set of rules of the game. (Robinson, 1960, p. 15)

The inadequacy of Robinson's view of socialism stems from her limited understanding of what is wrong with capitalism in the first place: "If the capitalists . . . invested the whole surplus there would be no need for socialism. It is the rentier aspect of profit, as a source of wealth . . . that makes the strongest case for socialism" (Robinson, 1960, pp. 10–11). While both of the above statements were made by Robinson in 1955, nothing in her later work indicates that she has altered her view of socialism. Since the Cantabrigians mystify the basic social relations of capitalism, one could hardly expect them to think of socialism as a radical alternative.

In closing, it is appropriate to recall Marx's argument that, in our analysis of contemporary society, we should be sure to distinguish those aspects of it which are historically specific from those which are common to all human societies (Marx, 1970, p. 190). His reasoning was that if we fail to distinguish the particular from the general – if we falsely attribute universality to something which is transient – we will have a harder time bringing about the transition from capitalism to socialism: ". . . on failure to perceive this fact depends the entire wisdom of [those] modern economists who prove the eternity and harmony of existing social relations."

Notes

1 In Webster's *New World Dictionary,* we find the following definition: "*Cantabrigian.* 1. a native or inhabitant of Cambridge, England. 2. a student or graduate of the University of Cambridge." In the same place the corresponding definitions for the adjective are also given (Webster's New World Dictionary, 1960).

2 See, for example, Nell's Sraffa-inspired drawing of a capitalist economy in which the realm of production is represented by a box containing factories but not people (Nell, Chapter 1 of this book).

3 This particular divergence between Marx and the Cantabrigians becomes extremely important when the problem of *dynamic analysis* is taken up: The organic relationship between Marx's basic abstractions allows him to focus on *contradictions* between the different aspects of the production process; the independence of the Cantabrigians' abstractions prevents them from engaging in the same kind of analysis.

4 The Sraffa approach has actually been applied to the analysis of feudal society (Nell, 1967).

5 While Marx never used this term, it has been frequently employed by commentators on his work (Sweezy, 1942, p. 23).

6 Marx first discusses the law of value without referring to it as such (Marx, 1967, Vol. I, p. 75).

7 The point I am trying to make here was stated explicitly by Marx: "Capitalist production . . . produces not only commodities, not only surplus-value, but it also produces and reproduces the capitalist relation; on the one side the capitalist, on the other the wage-labourer" (Marx, 1967, Vol. I, p. 578).

8 Marx devoted a chapter to the question that Sraffa deals with but at the end of it, he remarked: "This is but a very secondary question" (Marx, 1967, Vol. III, pp. 200–4).

9 An exception may be cited here: "Given the power structure of corporations, executives, at the top largely set their own pay; from these levels down the pay structure reflects relative position in the hierarchy" (Nell, 1972a, p. 445). This kind of consideration, however, is generally not taken into account by the Cantabrigians.

10 The contrast between Sraffa's and Marx's approaches may be highlighted here by quoting the following passage: "In the midst of our West European society . . . the idea easily takes root that it is an inherent quality of human labour to furnish a surplus-product. But consider, for example . . . the eastern islands of the Asiatic Archipelago, where sago grows wild in the forests. When the inhabitants have convinced themselves, by boring a hole in the tree, that the pith is ripe, the trunk is cut down and divided into several pieces, the pith is extracted, mixed with water and filtered; it is then quite fit for use as sago. One tree commonly yields 300 lbs., and occasionally 500 to 600 lbs. There, then, people go into the forests, and cut bread for themselves, just as they cut firewood. Suppose now such as eastern-bread-cutter requires 12 working-hours a week for the satisfaction of all his wants. Nature's direct gift to him is plenty of leisure time . . . before he spends it in surplus-labour for strangers, compulsion is necessary. If capitalist production were introduced, the honest fellow would perhaps have to work six days a week, in order to appropriate to himself the product of one working-day. The bounty of Nature does not explain why he would then have to work six days a week, or why he must furnish five days of surplus-labour. It explains only why his necessary labour-time would be limited to one day a week. But in no case would his surplus-product arise from some occult quality inherent in human labour" (Marx, 1967, Vol. I, p. 515).

11 If the reader has difficulty accepting this point, think about it with reference to an imaginary economy which consists only of "basic" industries (in Sraffa's sense) but which is characterized by the performance of surplus as well as necessary labour (in Marx's sense).

12 I am grateful to Bill Lazonick for bringing this passage to my attention.

13 The single exception to the statement in the preceeding sentence occurs where Robinson and Eatwell discuss Marx's approach to economics (Robinson and Eatwell, 1973, p. 92).

14 The sympathy which Robinson and Eatwell have for managers comes through, among other places, in the discussion of "socialist states" in their textbook (Robinson and Eatwell, 1973, Book Three, Ch. 2). Here, focusing on recent events in the U.S.S.R., they make the following statement: "The main obstacle to reforms . . . comes from the objections of the bureaucracy to giving up the power that it enjoys over industry and allocating more independence and initiative to managers, technicians, and engineers" (Robinson and Eatwell, 1973, p. 320). True as this may be, whatever happened to the idea of socialism as a system of workers' control?

References

Balibar, E. 1970. "The Basic Concepts of Historical Materialism," in *Reading Capital.* L. Althusser and E. Balibar. New York: Pantheon Books, pp. 199–308.

Bhaduri, A. 1969. "On the Significance of Recent Controversies on Capital Theory: A Marxian View," *Economic Journal,* 79, pp. 532–39.

Bharadwaj, K. 1963. "Value Through Exogenous Distribution," *Economic Weekly,* pp. 1450–54.

1971. "Value Through Exogenous Distribution," in *Capital and Growth.* G. C. Harcourt and N. F. Laing, eds. Harmondsworth: Penguin Books.

Dobb, M. 1973. *Theories of Value and Distribution since Adam Smith.* Cambridge: Cambridge University Press.

Geras, N. 1971. "Essence and Appearance: Aspects of Fetishism in Marx's *Capital*," *New Left Review*, No. 65, pp. 69–85.

Harcourt, G. C. 1969. "Some Cambridge Controversies in the Theory of Capital," *Journal of Economic Literature*, 7, No. 2, pp. 369–405.

Hunt, E. K., and Sherman, H. 1972. "Value, Alienation and Distribution," *Science and Society*, 37, No. 1. pp. 29–48.

Lebowitz, M. A. 1973–74. "The Current Crises of Economic Theory," *Science and Society*, 37, No. 4. pp. 385–403.

Marx, K. 1964. *Early Writings*. T. B. Bottomore, trans. and ed. New York: McGraw-Hill.

1967. *Capital*. 3 vols. New York: International Publishers.

1970. *A Contribution to the Critique of Political Economy*. New York: International Publishers.

1971. *Theories of Surplus-Value*, Part III. Moscow: Progress Publishers.

1973. *Grundrisse: Foundations of the Critique of Political Economy*, M. Nicolaus, trans. Harmondsworth: Penguin Books.

Marx, K., and Engels, F. 1968. *Selected Works*. New York: International Publishers.

1970. *The German Ideology*. New York: International Publishers.

Medio, A. 1972. "Profits and Surplus-Value: Appearance and Reality in Capitalist Production," in *A Critique of Economic Theory*, E. K. Hunt and J. Schwartz, eds. Harmondsworth: Penguin Books, pp. 312–46.

Meek, R. 1967. "Mr. Sraffa's Rehabilitation of Classical Economics," *Economics and Ideology and Other Essays*. London: Chapman and Hall, Ltd. pp. 161–78.

Mill, J. S. 1965. *Principles of Political Economy*. London: Routledge & Kegan Paul, for the University of Toronto Press.

Nell, E. J. 1967. "Economic Relationships in the Decline of Feudalism: An Examination of Economic Interdependence and Social Change," *History and Theory*, 6, No. 3. pp. 313–50.

1970. "A Note on Cambridge Controversies in Capital Theory," *Journal of Economic Literature*, 8, No. 1 (March), pp. 41–4.

1972a. "Two Books on the Theory of Income Distribution," *Journal of Economic Literature*, 10, No. 2 (June), pp. 442–53.

1972b. "Property and the Means of Production," *Review of Radical Political Economics*, 4, No. 2 (Summer), pp. 1–27.

Nuti, D. M. 1971. "'Vulgar Economy' in the Theory of Income Distribution," *Science and Society*, 35, No. 1, pp. 27–33.

Robinson, J. 1933. *The Economics of Imperfect Competition*. London: Macmillan.

1953. "The Production Function and the Theory of Capital," *Review of Economic Studies*, 11, No. 2, pp. 81–106.

1960. *Collected Economic Papers*. Vol. II. Oxford: Basil Blackwell.

1963. *Economic Philosophy*. Chicago: Aldine.

1966. *An Essay on Marxian Economics*. London: Macmillan.

1967. *Economics: An Awkward Corner*. New York: Pantheon Books.

1969. *The Cultural Revolution in China*. Harmondsworth: Penguin Books.

1971a. "The Production Function and the Theory of Capital; Postscript," in *Capital and Growth*. G. C. Harcourt and N. F. Laing, eds. Harmondsworth: Penguin Books.

1971b. "The Relevance of Economic Theory," *Monthly Review*, 22, No. 8. pp. 29–37.

Robinson, J., and Eatwell, J. 1973. *An Introduction to Modern Economics*. London: McGraw-Hill.

Rowthorn, R. 1974. "Neo-Classicism, Neo-Richardianism and Marxism," *New Left Review*, No. 86: pp. 63–87.

Sraffa, P. 1960. *Production of Commodities by Means of Commodities* (Cambridge: Cambridge University Press.

Sweezy, P. M. 1942. *The Theory of Capitalist Development*. New York: Monthly Review Press.

Epilogue: The hieroglyph of production

Thomas Vietorisz

> Value, rather, turns each product of labor into a social hieroglyph. Later on, people seek to decipher the sense of the hieroglyph, to get behind the secret of their own social product.
> Marx

Many of the preceding chapters analyzed the relations of dominance and subjection that organize the process of production. A recognition of these provides an indispensible framework for understanding the operation of markets. For these same dominance-subjection relations can be shown to translate into simultaneous deprivation and waste, and this, in turn, implies that the neoclassical notion of Pareto optimality contradicts the very essence of production in a class society.

Yet, in Marx's words, these essential social relations characteristically do not "carry written on their forehead" what they are. In Asiatic production systems, in the slave states of antiquity or in feudal societies, the dominance-subjection relations at the core of the production process are readily apparent; under capitalism, they sink beneath the surface. Production turns into a social hieroglyph; only the exchange relations observed in the market seem to organize social interaction. Yet once the essence of production becomes unfathomable, Pareto optimality – the principle that opportunities for social improvement cease at the point where you cannot give more to Peter without taking from Paul – offers itself convincingly as a reasonable scientific idealization of a well-working economic system.

The social relations at the core of capitalist production are hidden from mainstream economic theory by a triple veil. *First,* commodity production presents many of the immediate and important relations between people – such as cooperation in the production process of useful artifacts – in the guise of relations between things. Virtue is measured by productivity; relations between people are tied into a cash nexus; exchange value in the form of money, the *means* of facilitating useful transactions, becomes the end for which productive activity is organized. *Second*, these commodity relations are further transformed by the logic of domination and subjection that organizes the production process. Wealth embodied in the means of production is the key instrument for the maintenance of domination–subjection relations in a capitalist society, for with it goes the power to provide or withhold employment, and so income. Wealth controls production and in stabilizing this control, turns simple exchange values into the relatively fixed producer prices, based on a rate profit, which underlie the operation of markets. On the basis of these prices, property comes to be treated as a sum of money, mere riches, rather than as a form of domination. *Third,* this structure of wealth, prices, and profits itself is subject to both accidental and systematic fluctuations of prices and employment, reflecting short-term changes in supply and demand, which thus seem to govern the structure itself.

In order to decode the hieroglyph of production, economic theory would have to penetrate behind this triple veil. Yet mainstream economics today, far from investigating the social relations expressed in the observed productive structure, spends much of its effort on the generalization of the analysis of short-term supply and demand fluctuations. It aims to extend this analysis to structural phenomena that evidently originate in the production process, in order to arrive at the grand synthesis of general market equilibrium that is meant to represent most essential features of the economic functioning of society.

This raises the question: Why should such an effort be pursued with deliberate disregard for an intellectually appealing alternative that has been around for several generations? A crucial part of the answer pertains to the second veil referred to earlier – the transformation of cooperative productive activity by class forces into relations of dominance and exploitation. This transformation operates broadly; it hides class conflict from direct perception not only in the operation of markets but also in a number of other ways. It transforms the polarity of two classes, the dominators and the subjected, into a number of social hierarchies involving wealth, income, or labor market segmentation; it transforms authoritarian rule into political democracy, church authority into religious pluralism, colonial domination into free trade. Thus the logic that builds class conflict into the core of the capitalist production process at the same time hides that class conflict from the view of those who stand to benefit most from it; to an amazing extent, it even serves to hide the class nature of the conflict from the view of those who are most cruelly subjected to its force. This submersion of class conflict then becomes one of the most powerful mechanisms that serve to stabilize the existing social order.

The emergence of class conflict into social consciousness is thus not a matter of the ingenuity of particular individuals in constructing this or that kind of social theory. An elaborate set of interwoven psychological defense mechanisms protect the mental balance of an individual by preventing him from consciously recognizing his own hidden, conflict-laden motivations. Likewise, an elaborate web of interwoven social defense mechanisms evolves in a capitalist society and protects the status quo by preventing the society from recognizing, at the level of social consciousness embodied in mainstream scientific theory, its own hidden productive logic, laden with class conflict.

The ideas of the ruling class are in every epoch the ruling ideas; the class that is the ruling *material* force of society is at the same time its ruling *intellectual* force. These ideas in our capitalist society are remarkably progressive in that they put economic forces at the center of social causation. Yet, as shown by Lukacs, the consciousness of the ruling class, shaped by history, necessarily blocks out insight into the class forces upon which its hegemony rests. It is thus not coincidence or perversity that keeps the veil of market exchange from being pierced by mainstream economic theory. The veil is preserved by the very same logic that organizes the basic production processes of capitalist society, on which the institutional structure, including academia and other homes of formal social science, ultimately rests.